Nov. 5	Anglo-French assault on Port Said
Nov. 6	Eisenhower re-elected President of U.S.A.
Dec. 22	Last British troops leave Port Said

1957

Jan. 10   Eden resigns.
           Prime Minister: Macmillan
           Foreign Secretary: Lloyd
           Chancellor: Thorneycroft

Jan. 5   'Eisenhower Doctrine' promulgated

Mar. 6   Ghana becomes independent
           Railway, shipbuilding and
           engineering strikes settled

March 21–24   Bermuda Conference

March 25   Treaty of Rome signed

March 28   Makarios released from Seychelles
           Lord Salisbury resigns

April 4   Defence White Paper

April 9   Suez Canal reopens to shipping

May 15   First British H-bomb exploded

June 26   Commonwealth Conference opens in London

July 25   Independent Council on Prices Productivity and Incomes announced

Aug. 31   Federation of Malaya becomes independent

Sept. 19   Anti-inflation measures, including Bank Rate increase to 7%

Oct. 4   Sputnik I, first earth satellite, placed in orbit by U.S.S.R.

Oct. 23–25   Washington Conference. 'Declaration of Common Purpose.'

1958

Jan. 1   E.E.C. and Euratom treaties come into force

Jan. 3   Federation of the West Indies inaugurated

RIDING THE STORM

WINDS OF CHANGE
1914–1939

THE BLAST OF WAR
1939–1945

TIDES OF FORTUNE
1945–1955

RIDING THE STORM
1956–1959

Outside No. 11 Downing Street on returning from the Palace after appointment as Prime Minister, 10 January 1957

RIDING
THE STORM
1956–1959

HAROLD MACMILLAN

* * * *

LONDON

MACMILLAN

MELBOURNE · TORONTO

1971

First published 1971 *by*
MACMILLAN AND CO LTD
London and Basingstoke
Associated companies in New York Toronto
Dublin Melbourne Johannesburg and Madras

SBN (boards) 333 10310 6

Printed in Great Britain by
ROBERT MACLEHOSE AND CO LTD
The University Press, Glasgow

Contents

LIST OF ILLUSTRATIONS   vii

ACKNOWLEDGEMENTS   ix

1   Treasury Chambers   1

2   The Budget and After   20

3   Plan G   61

4   The Anglo-American Schism   89

5   The Change of Government   180

6   Aftermath of Suez   206

7   A New Strategy   240

8   Arabian Nights   269

9   Russia and the Bomb   288

10   Honeymoon at Washington   313

11   Money and Men   342

12   Commonwealth Tour   375

13   The Strange Case of the Bank Rate 'Leak'   415

14   The Wooing of Europe   431

15   The Two Worlds   460

16   More Arabian Nights   502

17   Chinese Puzzle   538

18   A Voyage of Discovery   557

19   The Cyprus Tangle   656

20   Boom or Slump?   702

21   The Last Lap   731

     Appendixes
       1. Plan G: 29 September 1956   753
       2. Members of the Cabinet: January 1957   755
       3. Declaration of Common Purpose   756
       4. Correspondence with Selwyn Lloyd: 24
          and 25 February 1958   760

     INDEX   763

List of Illustrations

Outside No. 11 Downing Street after appointment as Prime
    Minister   *frontispiece*

As Chancellor of the Exchequer   (*Central Press*)   *facing page* 150

With Lord Mackintosh   (*Fox Photos*)   150

Eden and Mollet during the Suez Crisis   (*Press Association*)   151

British paratroopers in Port Said   (*Paul Popper*)   151

Crowds in Downing Street, 10 January 1957   (*P.A.–Reuter*)   182

Returning from Buckingham Palace   (*Keystone*)   183

'The Middle Way'—Cartoon by Vicky   *page* 190

With Churchill   (*P.A.–Reuter*)   *facing page* 214

With Hailsham and Butler   (*Central Press*)   215

Leaving for Paris with Selwyn Lloyd   (*P.A.–Reuter*)   215

Bermuda Conference, March 1957   246

With Selwyn Lloyd in Paris   (*London Express News and Feature Services*)   246

On a visit to Germany for talks on the Common Market   247
    (*Radio Times Hulton Picture Library*)

With Eisenhower at the NATO Conference   (*Associated Press*)   247

Thorneycroft speaking at the Conservative Party Conference   374
    (*Press Association*)

Commonwealth Prime Ministers' Conference, 26 June 1957   375
    (*Fox Photos*)

Leaving for the Commonwealth Tour   (*Associated Press*)   406

With Nehru in New Delhi   406

Commonwealth Tour, Singapore   (*Singapore Information Services*)   407

Farewell to Australia   407

Replying to Khrushchev's speech of welcome at Moscow
    Airport   (*Associated Press*)   566

With Khrushchev   566
At the gala performance of *Romeo and Juliet*   (*P.A.–Reuter*)   567
Facing Khrushchev and Gromyko at the conference table   (*Life*)   598
Visit to a collective farm near Kiev   (*Associated Press*)   599
Signing the Joint Communiqué in Moscow   (*Associated Press*)   630
With John Morgan on Russian television   (*Keystone*)   630
With de Gaulle soon after his return to power   (*Central Press*)   631
Touring the North-East   (*Associated Press*)   662
Meeting the people   663

Acknowledgements

I AM indebted to the writers of a number of histories and auto-biographies which I have consulted, particularly those specified in the footnotes.

I should like to record my gratitude to Mr. David Dilks for his help in the tracing and collection of documents for both this and the preceding volume. I am also indebted to Miss Anne Glyn-Jones, who has continued to do the research into my own papers and other books and documents; and to Miss Anne Macpherson, Mrs. Christine Deman, Miss Christine Struthers and Mrs. Bunty Pilgrim for their careful and patient typing of the text.

July 1970   H.M.

CHAPTER I

Treasury Chambers

MY appointment as Chancellor of the Exchequer, with other changes in the Government, was announced on 21 December 1955. It was a great sorrow to me to leave the Foreign Office. I had thoroughly enjoyed my short time there. The problems, if often baffling, were fascinating. The officials with whom I lived were able advisers and delightful companions. The work involved a great deal of travel which I liked, and a certain isolation from the rough-and-tumble of the House of Commons. In addition I was brought again into direct contact with many old friends in Europe and America. Moreover, I was beginning at last to learn something of the work, and of the leading figures in many countries with whom I had to deal. The change was therefore, when it was first proposed, something of a shock. I had resisted for a few months, but was finally induced to fall in with the Prime Minister's wishes. Nevertheless, I did not exaggerate when, in opening my first—and only—Budget in April 1956, I observed reflectively that Churchill was said to have been quite surprised to find himself Chancellor of the Exchequer in November 1924, but not half so surprised as I was, thirty-one years later.

On 22 December, after making my farewells at the Foreign Office, I walked over to the Treasury. This great department was lodged in the uninspiring block known officially as the 'New Public Offices'—an Edwardian building without any great charm and singularly ill adapted to its, or any other, purpose. It was commonly known as the 'Mausoleum'. We occupied the long stretch of this vast edifice which looked out on to Great George Street and Parliament Square. The old Treasury offices with the Kent façade had been bombed in the war and were not yet reconstructed. They have now been restored; but when I was Prime Minister, partly realising that the Treasury could no longer be accommodated in so small a space, and partly coveting this most attractive Whitehall vineyard, I arranged for it to become the home of the Cabinet Office and Secretariat.

My two Ministerial colleagues were both, in their different ways, admirable. The Financial Secretary, Henry Brooke, was an experienced politician destined, as I could see, to reach high office. He had much local as well as national experience of administration, having been a member of the London County Council for many years. A good scholar, he was sound rather than brilliant, and was absolutely reliable and loyal. Sir Edward Boyle was the Economic Secretary. It was a high position for him to have reached so early in his political career, but he completely justified his selection. He combined an encyclopaedic knowledge, imperturbable good humour and great powers of debate with sterling integrity. These two came to see me with their different stories to tell, and explained their roles and functions.

The Permanent Secretary and Head of the Treasury was Sir Edward Bridges, whom I had known from school days and whom I greatly admired. He had been appointed in 1945 and was to preside over the Treasury for eleven years. He was responsible both for economic and financial policy on the one hand and the management of the Civil Service on the other. He was a typical product of all that was best in the tradition of the Civil Service, both in character and in intellectual gifts. A humanist and a scholar, he concealed under an almost boyish humour great strength and resolution. If he had no pretensions to being an authority on economics in the modern sense, he was a supremely sensible and wise man. Beneath him were the great row of Treasury knights—Bernard Gilbert, Thomas Padmore, Alexander Johnston, Herbert Brittain, Leslie Rowan—all admirable administrators and devoted to their task. In the last of these, in charge of overseas finance, I found an old friend, for he had been Churchill's Principal Private Secretary during the war.

During the course of the year Bridges retired from office. I persuaded the Prime Minister to allow me to appoint Sir Roger Makins in his place. This appointment of a member of the Foreign Service was a startling breach of tradition, but I felt justified from my experience of Sir Roger's outstanding qualities to risk the innovation. He had served me with singular skill and devotion in Algiers. He was now about to leave his post as British Ambassador in Washington. He had a profound knowledge of the American scene, equally important to us in the Treasury as in the Foreign Office, and a great power of organisation. So it was arranged.

At that time the economic side in its narrower sense had not been highly developed. There are now organs within and without the Treasury which provide a vast amount of information and guidance in the shape of statistics regarding past events and prognostications of future trends. Our professional economist, if one may use the term, was Sir Robert Hall, to whom I took an immediate liking. The fact that he was rather inarticulate was not altogether a disadvantage, for at any rate he was never dogmatic. For what was by now called 'public relations' I was glad to find an old friend in Clem Leslie, whom I had known in 1940 when he had worked for Herbert Morrison in the Ministry of Supply.

> As for the 'state of the nation', all seem agreed that it is precarious. Nobody agrees on the diagnosis or the treatment.[1]

Full employment, an expanding economy, stable prices and a strong pound; these were the balls which the Chancellor of the Exchequer, like a new Cinquevalli, was expected to keep in the air together. At this time, in spite of the protests of a few theorists who would have been ready to pursue growth and expansion without any regard to the value of sterling or the conservation of a reasonable price level, the pressure from all the pundits, in the Treasury, in the City and in the economic Press, was unhesitatingly for caution and, when necessary, for deflation. We were still in a period of cheap money. Even by January 1955, Bank Rate had stood at only 3 per cent. This was made possible by the massive fortifications by which the pound was still, at least nominally, defended, involving a vast entanglement of controls, as complicated as the moats and gabions of a medieval castle. But the defences were not unnaturally beginning to wear a bit thin, and many breaches could be made by

[1] 22 December 1955. Quotations from my private journals and other personal memoranda are indicated by the date of the entry.

expert operators. Fortunately for us, the rates for money in different parts of the world had not been raised to competitive levels.

Butler with great courage had reintroduced a flexible Bank Rate as one, if not the only, element in the attempt to control inflation.[1] Early in 1955 he had raised the Rate by two stages from 3 to 4½ per cent. Much argument at the time raged about the return to monetary methods. The sweet simplicity of the Dalton era had faded into the background, and there was general agreement that the Bank Rate should again be used in the traditional way. At the same time, Butler had introduced some degree of restriction on hire-purchase, and given what support was possible to sterling through the Exchange Equalisation Account. Nevertheless, he had felt justified in introducing what he called an 'incentive' Budget. Income tax was reduced by 6d., and various reductions were made in purchase tax, especially designed to help the Lancashire cotton industry. At the time of the Budget, Butler confidently announced that the general situation had been brought under control. The 1955 Budget certainly had its attractions from the electioneering point of view, although the Opposition, of course, denounced it as 'robbing the poor'.

Unhappily, during the months immediately following the 1955 Election there were many setbacks. A troublesome railway strike dragged on for several weeks; a dock strike in the summer caused a heavy loss to exports; and by the middle of July there was considerable anxiety, both on the industrial and financial fronts. Costs and wages were rising, but productivity was not keeping pace. By the end of the summer the Chancellor of the Exchequer had told his colleagues that he still hoped to cure this disease by orthodox means—credit squeezes, open market operations and the rest.

As the summer of 1955 progressed I had been invited by the Prime Minister to join in these discussions and was weak enough to yield to his wishes. I was myself attracted by a more dynamic policy. We could hardly go back to controls, high taxation and all the other nostrums. At Eden's request I wrote a paper giving my own proposals within the limitations of orthodoxy, of which I still

[1] Rt. Hon. R. A. Butler (later Lord Butler) had been Chancellor of the Exchequer from 1951 to 1955.

have the draft. It was called *Dizzy with Success*, and its theme, of course, was that we were trying to do too much with the resources available; this applied to the production both of capital and of consumption goods. There was full, even over-full, employment. We had travelled a long way from the terrible old days of massive unemployment, although in the years between the wars I had never dared hope to live to see such a transformation. But we could not disguise from ourselves the new problems which this situation of overload had produced, both materially and morally.

There are two ways of dealing with this situation. The first (as in war, siege or socialism) is to restore physical controls, especially on imports, and regulate all production by a Government plan. [We have] tried this, and, if we want it again, the Socialists had better do it. For they like it, since they really regard expansion and increase in wealth as rather immoral. Socialists are economic puritans.

I went on to describe the other approach which seemed to me more suitable for Conservatives; that is, a variety of remedial measures, which recognised that growth is healthy in itself and must be kept going, but at not quite so headlong a pace. Roughly, this plan amounted in the monetary field to continuing, or intensifying, the squeeze on credit with a higher Bank Rate; to reducing or abolishing government subsidies, including the high housing subsidies and the bread and milk subsidies, and retarding various capital development schemes; to substituting for the wasteful short-term national military service the traditional system of voluntary recruitment, to abandoning obsolete or unnecessary weapons; to encouraging production by a variety of means, including a reduction rather than a rise in direct taxation, especially devised to help the managerial and entrepreneur classes; to reducing or abolishing the tax on undistributed profits and increasing that on profits distributed; and to stimulating savings and adopting new methods for making savings more attractive.

There remained the question of the convertibility of sterling, which was accepted as a logical end to be pursued. In fact, now that we had freed commodity markets and decided to support transferable sterling, our currency was virtually convertible for those who knew how to do it. If the more orthodox methods succeeded, we could leave things to adjust themselves; but if we were faced with another devaluation, we must return to the arguments, which had been canvassed two or three years earlier, to let sterling float:

> Do *not* devalue to a *fixed* rate. Go on to a *floating rate*.
>
> The rate may fall violently at first. But, if so, a lot of people will get their fingers burned. In any case, in present conditions, it may be safer to take the strain this way than any other way. In the second half of the twentieth century sound government in our country is more likely to be endangered by either a collapse of the reserves or a million on the dole than by occasional fluctuations in the value of sterling in relation to the dollar. Of course, it reduces the use of sterling as a long-term store of value. But no currency in the world, except the dollar, can really be that today.

However, it was clearly right to use conventional weapons before embarking on so uncharted a course and Butler introduced an autumn Budget, which included increases in purchase tax and the tax on distributed profits; cuts in Government lending to local authorities; abolition of the Exchequer housing subsidy except for slum clearance; and increases in telephone charges and rentals.

The Budget and the other measures seemed slow in their operation. By the end of December, ten days after my appointment, I recorded: 'The position is much worse than I feared . . . and the reserves are steadily falling.'[1] It was clearly necessary for me, when I took command of the Treasury, to make a definite plan and to pursue it with determination. My own instincts were, as they have always remained, expansionist; but whatever might be the theoretical arguments in favour of expansion at all costs, without regard to inflation or to the inevitable devaluation that would follow, neither the political situation at the time nor the advice of the leading pundits pointed in this direction. On the other hand, if the policy was to be one of applying the brake from time to time, it was evident that there were greater dangers in delaying remedial action than

[1] 30 December 1955.

in acting too soon. The *Financial Times*, in an important article the day after my appointment was announced, stressed this argument:

> Had the Bank Rate been increased three months earlier the boom would scarcely have developed so much impetus. For this to be done depends on the creation of a much better system of statistics, and much more rapid response to each trend as it emerges.[1]

With both of these objectives I was in agreement. On the first, at any rate, I was able in due course to make some progress. The article continued:

> The Chancellor must not think of himself as the captain of a liner changing course only occasionally. He is rather in the position of a man driving a fast car on a greasy road. His speed of reaction is vital.[1]

Was this the origin of 'Stop–Go'? At any rate it seemed more sensible than using the brake and accelerator at the same time—a practice that later became fashionable.

Before Christmas there was little to be done except to make the acquaintance of the officials on whom I was to rely. Even in the first few days, apart from my official advisers, I did not lack suggestions from my friends. Unhappily, although all of them were helpful, they were often contradictory. Some of the Press, especially the *Economist*, were insistent that our troubles could never be overcome until Britain accepted an employment ratio of not more than 96 or 97 per cent, like America and Germany. Others, again, rode their particular hobby-horses with all the contempt of the intransigent for the adaptable. In the few days of the holiday I compiled a paper entitled *First Thoughts from a Treasury Window*. I felt strongly that if we accepted the need for action to restrict inflation we must work quickly and effectively. This was clear from the increasing pressure on the reserves. Unless we were to adopt an entirely revolutionary policy by a new devaluation or by instituting a floating rate, it was necessary to restore confidence at home and abroad as rapidly as

[1] *Financial Times*, 22 December 1955.

possible. Once this was done we could pass to methods of stimulating production and savings.

I circulated my paper within the Treasury on 2 January. I still have in my records all the admirable comments which were made upon it with commendable speed and devotion in the various departments. My proposals covered a wide field, no doubt in a somewhat perfunctory way. Many of them proved without value, although some became the basis of future policy. They fell into various groups. First, the need to mop up purchasing power with taxes and reduce private expenditure at source by a credit squeeze and increased Bank Rate. Secondly, the whole domain of public expenditure where reductions must be made even in fields hitherto regarded as sacrosanct. Thirdly, the use of controls; we ought not to shrink from building controls if necessary. Fourthly, how could we increase existing productivity? Perhaps with suitable stimulants to mechanisation and modernisation. If these measures did not result in a better balance of payments, we must face tariffs or import controls, together with discriminatory purchases. We had to be ready with a complete scheme for import controls. Finally, we must stimulate savings. Although savings would largely depend on other measures being taken which showed that we were at least halting the inflationary trend, perhaps something could be devised to attract a new class of investors. Here was the first germ of the idea that was to lead, with the splendid help of Lord Mackintosh, to various improvements over the whole range of National Savings, including the institution of Premium Bonds.

It is one of the melancholy occupations of retirement to browse among these faded documents and to read again the able and impressive, if sometimes discouraging, comments by my chief advisers, Ministerial and professional. The massive collection lingers among my records, a sad reminder of the enthusiasm with which recently appointed Ministers plunge into old problems, full of hope and daring. The streams of argument flow rapidly along, swollen by many rivulets and tributaries until, alas, like many great rivers, they are only too often dissipated in the sands and never reach the sea.

Before settling down to study all these large issues, I had my first call on 2 January from the Governor of the Bank of England, C. F. Cobbold, with whom I formed a firm friendship which lasted throughout my term of office as Chancellor of the Exchequer and during my Premiership. I am afraid he thought me dangerously unorthodox in my efforts to escape as soon as possible from these distasteful policies into a more expansionist field. However, I encouraged him to criticise the extravagant rate of Government spending so long as he would do his part on the monetary side. He made it clear that neither the credit squeeze begun in February 1955 and intensified in July nor the Budget measures in October had yet produced any real effect. The balance of trade showed a further deterioration, and, as the Governor kept reminding me, the reserves were only just above what was thought the danger-mark—$2,000 million. There were no reserves of labour—the unemployment figure for December was the lowest since the war. Even at this first meeting I was conscious that the old tradition of keeping the Governor and the Treasury officials rigidly separated was still in force. I was determined to bring about closer and more frequent contacts. I was anxious, in addition, to bring in other advisers, outside the sacred circle. Accordingly, I gave a dinner-party at No. 1 Carlton Gardens (we had not yet moved into No. 11 Downing Street) at which I entertained the Governor, Sir Oliver Franks the chairman of Lloyds, Tommy Brand the chairman of Lazards, together with Sir Percy Mills representing industry. I invited Sir Edward Bridges, Sir Edward Boyle and Sir Robert Hall to meet them.

I thus brought into being the committee of advisers which I wasn't allowed to have! It was an immense success. There was a most frank, informed, and helpful talk—and almost complete agreement about what ought to be done. (Fortunately, it hardly deviated from the plan.) Whether it would succeed seemed about even chances. Everyone agreed that if we were to drift on, we should go on the rocks.[1]

The next day we had a meeting with the Governor, Deputy Governor and Chief Cashier, together with Boyle, Bridges and

[1] 19 January 1956.

Brittain. I thus accomplished a formal meeting between the Treasury and Bank of England—which had never before been allowed—with minutes and records of decisions.

> In order to achieve this, I had (in addition) an informal meeting with Governor alone, for twenty minutes or so, *before* the other meeting. Thus honour is satisfied.[1]

This development was obviously necessary and had merely been prevented by old custom.

In order to prepare my colleagues for the worst, I had circulated on 6 January a report based on Hall's assessment of the actual situation. I made it clear that we were faced with the necessity of taking immediate action over a wide field and of a more drastic character than had hitherto seemed necessary. Time was running out. When we came to discuss it, my Ministerial colleagues 'were all impressed by the gravity of the position. Indeed, one or two were really shocked.'[2] This at any rate was a useful preliminary, for if my rescue plan proved to be less severe than I now thought, Ministers would be correspondingly relieved; if it had to include some very distasteful items, they would be in a better mood to acquiesce. There is nothing like softening up a Cabinet before an assault.

In taking over the Treasury at the beginning of the New Year a Chancellor of the Exchequer is greatly handicapped in one important respect. Estimates have been settled, or practically settled, for the following financial year. There is very little scope for manoeuvre or even for disagreement. There were a few outstanding matters to be settled. One arose in the Defence Estimates, and after a great struggle and the generous assistance of Walter Monckton, the new Minister of Defence, we got substantial savings in all the Service demands, including £15 million off Civil Defence. The chief battle was over increased Service pay. A plan had been proposed which would cost a very large sum, but if it succeeded it would increase recruitment and so lead to the reduction, and probably the abolition, of National Service. Since this would prove a good financial investment, whatever social advantages might be lost, I accepted, after

[1] 20 January 1956.   [2] 12 January 1956.

much bargaining, a figure of £70 to £75 million for the increase.

If we were to make cuts and restrictions, unpleasant as they were to me and contrary to all my natural inclinations, the sooner they were settled the better. The Bank Rate was not controlling demand as had been hoped, partly because so large a proportion of spending was, even then, generated by Government itself, and partly because, with such high tax rates and the growing inflation, it was often worth while to borrow money in order to buy something that would appreciate, or could be sold at a profit. Nor could we forget that high Bank Rate increased the cost of Government borrowing, much of it from abroad. Some of my younger colleagues were particularly insistent on this argument, and from it grew the method of controlling the volume of credit by Government regulation of the ratio between the Clearing Banks' holdings of cash and their total deposit. This led to the development of the 'special deposit' system.

All my advisers, official and unofficial, felt that if a new set of measures were to be introduced, the date should be the first week of February; January would seem panicky; March dilatory. My proposals were ready for the Cabinet to consider on 24 January, and were soon agreed in principle, if not in detail. But there was much division as to the timing. Some wanted everything put off to the Budget; but I felt that this was impossible for two reasons. Anything that had to be done, right or wrong, had better be done quickly for national reasons; and—an argument which was more difficult to question—since the Opposition were bound to ask for a debate as soon as the House met we must be ready with our own initiative. There followed the usual series of negotiations with particular Ministers. I was still anxious to cut the size of the Army and was exceedingly doubtful of the value of the R.A.F. Fighter Command in Britain, however valuable such squadrons might be overseas.

> Everyone really knows that there is *no* defence [against nuclear attack] yet we go on wasting immense [sums] on the design, development and production of 'fighters'—up to 1962 and further. This is a great burden on industry, as well as on the Exchequer.[1]

[1] 29 January 1956.

Several days were spent in parleys with my colleagues. It is un-happily the fate of every Chancellor of the Exchequer to quarrel—or seem to quarrel—with his old friends. But in this case the Ministers were co-operative and helpful. Unfortunately, at this critical moment the Prime Minister had left for an important meeting in America. Of all my plans he was chiefly critical of the proposed abolition of the subsidies on bread and milk. There were important wage-negotiations coming to a head, particularly in the engineering industry. Surely it would be better to withhold anything that might seem to increase the cost of living until after the claims had been settled. Why not leave it all at least to the Budget? With this point of view other leading Ministers agreed, but I was determined on immediate action.

To test industrial opinion I explained in detail to a meeting of the National Production Advisory Council on 3 February the gravity of our position. From 1946 to 1954 we had turned out 26 per cent more goods, and had paid ourselves 80 per cent more money for doing it. Our reserves had fallen by nearly a quarter in the last year. Action must be taken, however disagreeable, and everyone must bear part of the burden. This address was well received, and I was encouraged by the general attitude both of employers and trade unionists.

Meanwhile there was still much discussion inside the Treasury about import controls. Boyle and I were both attracted by this method; nevertheless there were powerful arguments against it, such as the possibility of retaliation by our customers. Broadly speaking, our need to sell was greater than theirs to buy. I finally agreed that a plan should be got ready for use in emergency, but we should rely on other measures before adopting it. This weapon therefore should be kept in reserve in our armoury, ready for use, but not to be deployed save in dire need.

It was now necessary to bring the matter to an issue and I pressed hard that a statement should be made on 15 February. By the time Eden returned, it was evident that the main point at issue was the abolition of the subsidies on bread and milk. Since the Cabinet were still hesitant, I thought it right to clinch the matter in a letter to the Prime Minister. After rehearsing all the arguments I sent it off on the 11 February. This was the significant passage:

So I feel I really must ask for your support at this critical moment. I am in something of a dilemma. I don't want to appear to threaten the Cabinet; I have never tried such tactics in all my service. But I would not like you to be under any misapprehension and afterwards perhaps blame me for not letting you know the depth of my feeling. I must tell you frankly that, if I cannot have your confidence and that of my colleagues in handling this problem which you have entrusted to me in the way that seems to me essential, I should not feel justified in proposing measures which seem insufficient for their purpose. Nor should I be any good to you and the Cabinet in such circumstances. One can compromise about minor points of policy that come up all the time in Cabinets, but I would not be any good if I were trying to defend policies in which I had no belief.[1]

On this particular point—the cost of living—the National Assistance Board were, whether by design or chance, of considerable help. So slight would be the impact of increased prices that they would not think it necessary to raise the rate of assistance benefits.

On Monday afternoon, 13 February, discussions with my colleagues—singly and jointly—continued. Meanwhile the Governor of the Bank of England had been to see me, much concerned about indications of a serious flight from the pound. There seemed no sign of a break in the crisis. I had made it clear that I would not be able to go on if I could not get general support. I must await the answer.

The discussions continued, behind the scenes, between Ministers chiefly concerned. I prepared my letter of resignation (of which I have the draft in my records) and waited for the crucial Cabinet which must decide my future. Wisely, the Prime Minister postponed the final decision and continued to depend on friendly negotiation. On 14 February,

Butler, Heathcoat Amory and Thorneycroft came to see me in my room to try to find a solution. They said P.M. was absolutely determined not to give in on Bread or Milk. In that case, I replied, he must get another Chancellor. The same

[1] 11 February 1956.

ministers came again (after dinner) with the idea of a compromise. Could a formula be devised, which would make a start? I said I would consider this, but did not much like compromises! The curious thing about this crisis is (*a*) that I have hardly had any talk with P.M. He has avoided this, and dealt through emissaries; (*b*) not a word of it has got into the papers. This is really remarkable and shows how friendly and sensible we all are! Actually, the quality and dignity of the discussions in the Cabinet have been remarkable.[1]

At last a plan was proposed which I was able to accept. We would take off 1*d*. from the 2½*d*. bread subsidy immediately, and the rest later; milk would be dealt with in July in accordance with my original proposal. On the evening of 15 February this was finally approved by the whole Cabinet.

In the calmer atmosphere of recollection, it is difficult to recall or portray the tenseness of a crisis of this kind, which, in comparison with greater and more dangerous episodes, seems almost trivial. Yet at the time it was exciting enough. I must pay tribute to the moderation and good sense of all concerned. The arguments were pressed strongly on both sides, but without bitterness or ill-feeling. On the day before the final settlement

> I had a talk late tonight with Bridges and with the Governor. I put them the problem fairly and squarely. Which would do most harm? My resignation or a compromise? Governor had no doubt. My resignation would cause a panic in the City.[1]

Accordingly, I felt encouraged to be content with four-fifths of my demands.

On 16 February, in view of the state of the market, the Bank Rate was raised from 4½ to 5½ per cent. On the next day, Friday the 17th, I made my statement to the House. I have never seen so many members present on a Friday morning, but this unusually large attendance was due to the fact that full notice had been given. The statement took about twenty minutes to deliver and was followed by a brisk interchange of questions for about ten minutes; the debate was to follow in the following week. The further

[1] 14 February 1956.

measures, supplementing the autumn Budget, which I announced were as follows: (1) hire-purchase: increase of deposits for consumer goods, and extension of control to hire-purchase of some capital goods; (2) food subsidies: cuts of £38 million which would increase the price of bread by 1*d*. on the 1¾ *lb*. loaf and milk by ½*d*. a pint; (3) private industrial expenditure: the investment allowance for capital expenditure was to be suspended and the former initial allowance restored; (4) public expenditure: the State industries programme for the year was to be cut by a further £50 million, capital expenditure by Government Departments reduced by over £20 million, and local authority projects restricted.

I regret my decision to suspend the investment allowance and revert to the old initial allowance. Even having regard to the general exception to cover contracts already placed, or work already started, and the special exception in favour of ships and scientific research, the withdrawal of this encouragement to capital investment seems to me now to have been misguided, in spite of the heavy investment boom. However, I hoped that it would not be permanent. Among the Government economies in public expenditure, both on capital and ordinary account, was a further cut of 10,000 to 15,000 in staff to Government Departments. In this exercise, although difficult and strongly resisted, we proved successful. As regards restriction of credit in the private sector, the Capital Issues Committee was still in being, and proved effective. On the question of the bread and milk subsidies there seemed to be no justification for these in a modern society. But the issue had acquired a disproportionate importance on both sides; some regarded their abolition as a brutal attack on the working classes; others felt that it was proof of our sincerity. Indeed, the need for strengthening confidence, at home and abroad, could not be disregarded. For, 'it is not Truth, but Opinion, that can travel the world without a passport'.

In announcing these decisions I insisted that our purpose was positive and constructive.

We want to fill the gap between our exports and our imports by successful trading, not by draining our gold and dollar reserves. We want to go further than that, and build up the strength and effectiveness of the whole sterling area by increasing our reserves. We want, in fact, to safeguard the striking gains in our standard of life that have been achieved since the end of the war.

Never before has the standard of living been so high or general well-being so widespread. Never before has every individual home had so great a stake in the continued prosperity and solvency of Britain. I believe, therefore, that although these measures will, naturally, result in some sacrifice or some disappointment, they will be accepted as wise and timely.[1]

When the debate took place on 20 February, my speech lasted an hour. After the first few minutes, it was listened to with attention. I could not help contrasting the new problems of today with those which had confronted us between the wars. Then the cost of living was at its lowest, but unemployment at its peak. Now we had full employment—some would say artificially full employment—but prices were all the time rising. I disclaimed altogether the idea that we were trying to produce unemployment. Nor was I even ready to accept the 3 per cent unemployment which Lord Beveridge had laid down as a fair average and which even Gaitskell had been prepared in certain circumstances to accept. It was in the interests of employment itself that these measures were taken, for if the rise in incomes continued to outpace production, it must in turn lead to greater increases in prices and so reduce the opportunities of selling our exports. This must in the long run lead to unemployment in many parts of the country, especially in those areas which had suffered most in the past. Everyone agreed (and for this I was able to find some useful quotations from Labour and Co-operative publications), that the mass of our people were far better off than ever before. Nevertheless,

> The trouble is that we are acting as if we are just a bit better off than we really are. Therefore, although I regard the situation as serious, and as one which easily might become dangerous if it were not dealt with firmly, I do not regard it as a situation which it is beyond our power to master if we but have the will.[2]

[1] *Hansard*, 17 February 1956.   [2] *Hansard*, 20 February 1956.

The Labour Party had not in fact disputed the diagnosis, nor in their amendment did they take the view, for which there was some support, that expansion should be pursued at all costs and the strain taken upon the value of the pound either by a devaluation to a fixed rate or by a floating rate. But if this were ruled out, there were two main lines of approach:

> There are those who say, 'Let us apply the direct methods of physical control, internally and externally. Let us reintroduce building controls. Let us revert to the control of imports by licensing. Let us by control, allocation, rationing and all the rest see that we do not use too much of the materials selected for control—including, of course, food.' Then, this argument would end, 'and, of course, let us not shrink from price control'. That is one line of treatment.[1]

We had had a great experience of controls during the war and in the period after the war. But once an inflation began, such controls did not really deal with the underlying reasons for the inflation but only tried to suppress the symptoms. Within the limits of the policies which both parties supported, I only asked myself a practical question: Would the controls suggested succeed? Would the measures which I had proposed be more likely to be effective without any lasting damage to the economy or to our way of life?

Harold Wilson answered me

> with a brilliant debating speech. He scored good party points ... But he did not say anything to stir up the trade unions.[2]

It was the trade unions' response which was of the greatest importance, and Wilson showed considerable restraint in this respect. Compared with my somewhat pedestrian approach, his speech was lively and sparkling. After these speeches, the debate petered out. The Press response was satisfactory:

> The Saturday and Sunday Press was unexpectedly good. Today's is better still. I am really very satisfied. The question remains—have we done enough?[3]

[1] *Hansard*, 20 February 1956.   [2] 20 February 1956.   [3] 21 February 1956.

I naturally felt a great sense of relief, but it had been a tiring ten days, with the Cabinet difficulties not the least exhausting part.

> I have now
> 1. Further measures to prepare, to protect reserves, if there are not enough.
> 2. Budget.
> 3. O.E.E.C. and a policy for Europe.
> 4. Economic General Staff – i.e. proper organisation of Government and Treasury.
> 5. Savings – especially in defence expenditure.[1]

As usual, every day was so filled with interviews, speeches, Parliamentary Questions, committees, Cabinet meetings, boxes of papers and the like that there was not enough time for reflection. One great and unexpected relief lay in the fact that no news of the Cabinet crisis had leaked out to the Press in any form. This was a splendid tribute to my colleagues and to all those who knew the tense arguments which had raged and the danger of a split at the end.

> It is a curious feeling for me. At one time Dorothy told the men to stop putting up our pictures, etc., in No. 11, because she thought we would be moving out again soon ![2]

Two nights after the division I dined alone with Churchill and found him in good form.

> He said, 'You were quite right to tackle bread and milk. If you don't do what's unpopular, they don't believe that you're in earnest' – a very shrewd comment.[2]

The Governor, in a charming personal letter, assured me, on the best opinion, that much as commercial and industrial circles disliked restriction in general, they approved our action and regarded our decision as fully measuring up to what the situation required. Even more comforting was the news that we were beginning to get some money in for the reserves.

I was sure that if we were to pursue the orthodox path, we were right to do so boldly and thus to give ourselves some breathing

---

[1] 22 February 1956.   [2] 23 February 1956.

space. I was not so clear as to what should be the next step. The Budget still lay before me, and within the next few days this had to be designed and perfected.

Although these first weeks at the Treasury were almost as hectic as any in my experience, there was still a difference between this Department and the Foreign Office. In both there was a multiplicity of problems and often the need for urgent action. But the pace was different. I have often compared the Foreign Secretary to the editor of a daily newspaper. Telegrams come in announcing some unexpected turn of events, or a first-class crisis occurs, often without him having any foreknowledge or anticipation. These heralds of disaster arrive from hour to hour and at all times of day and night. The Chancellor of the Exchequer is more like the editor of a monthly, or at worst weekly, newspaper. He has a little more time, and the stop-press news does not give him the same concern. Yet, in both cases, some attempt must be made to work out long-term policy under the pressure of immediate events. In this first struggle, whether right or wrong, I had at any rate succeeded. But in politics, as in other affairs of life, this often proves a doubtful satisfaction. Lord Melbourne is said to have observed, 'I wish I was as cocksure of anything as Tom Macaulay is of everything.' I had got my own way; but now I was by no means sure.

CHAPTER II

The Budget and After

Y wife and I had now moved from the Foreign Secretary's flat at Number 1 Carlton Gardens. This was a somewhat fake affair, constructed out of the main bedroom of the house, the first and ground floors of which were reserved for official entertaining. The dining-room had been panelled with dark oak, like a luxury liner; but there was little or no accommodation for servants. Nevertheless, it was comfortable and convenient, since it was within walking distance of the Foreign Office. Number 11 Downing Street, which we were to occupy for the rest of the year, was a sensible, plain house, outshone by its greater neighbour, but with some agreeable features. On the one side was the famous mansion which George II had offered to Walpole. With unusual forbearance, that great man had accepted it only as a temporary residence to be passed on to his successors. On the other side was Number 12, the top half of which had been burnt down in the middle of the nineteenth century and, with typical parsimony, had not been rebuilt. The lower section, which survived the fire, had originally been occupied by the Patronage section of the Treasury, and was now used as offices for the Government Whips. This block has lately been rebuilt, and a fine flat looking west has been built for the Chancellor of the Exchequer over the top of Number 12. But, in my time, Number 11 was a good, unpretentious house, used by many of my predecessors and regarded as desirable in the days when stairs presented no problem, either to masters or to servants. The front on Downing Street seemed narrow, but overlooking the garden on the ground floor, there were two good rooms, a sitting-room and a study, and these were the ones which we chiefly used. From the sitting-room the door opened out on to a stone terrace and the garden. Mr. Gladstone, when he was Chancellor of the Exchequer, had written a paper, said to have consisted of more than twenty paragraphs, with suitable divisions and sub-divisions and massive recapitulations of his argument, to show that the rights in the garden were shared equally between the tenants of Number 10 and Number 11. However, it was understood that, when he became Prime Minister, he prepared an even longer and more convincing paper to prove the opposite. At any rate my wife and I were scrupulously careful not to impinge upon the Edens. The most that we would venture during that summer would be a garden chair or two immediately outside our own windows, hugging the wall.

The study was a solid room, with a solid desk, solid furniture, and solid books of reference. Its chief ornament was, or had been, an impressive portrait by Millais of Mr. Gladstone. This, however, had been taken away before my time, and it was alleged, whether truthfully or not, that Dalton had demanded its removal. 'I could not bear' he is said to have declared, 'to sit, hour after hour and day after day, within the target of that flashing and reproachful eye.' I thought it in harmony with the task which had been set me to bring it back again.

Above the ground-floor rooms was a fine rectangular drawing-room or salon with two good chimney-pieces, and tolerably furnished. From a small adjoining recess one could pass, by a somewhat circuitous route, into Number 10. There was an easier communication on the ground floor between the two front halls. But the glory of Number 11 was the Soane dining-room, happily still preserved. It was not a large room; but it was, in a way, unique, with its curiously domed ceiling, ornamented with golden stars on a blue background.

The fault of the house was that it faced north and never saw the sun. The rooms with the southern aspect, which must have been delightful in the eighteenth and early nineteenth centuries, had been wrecked by that cliff of ponderous stone on the other side of the street—the Foreign Office block. The small dining-room which we organised on the second floor looked out this way. Occasionally, on a summer afternoon, there was an hour or so when the monstrous shadow of this vast edifice did not overwhelm us altogether; but these moments were rare. Some of my predecessors had not been able to face the gloom. Butler, for instance, had kept his own charming house in Smith Square and had only used Number 11 as an office. My wife, to whom a sunless London was almost intolerable, suffered acutely from this deprivation, and fled to Sussex whenever duty allowed. In her eyes the main – perhaps the only – benefit which she gained from our subsequent move to Number 10, was a drawing-room with a window facing west, gloriously flooded by the evening light.

A minor difficulty confronted us on moving into Number 11. Lord Cherwell, for whom I had a deep admiration and whose friendship I was privileged to enjoy both before and after the Second War, occupied, during Churchill's last Administration, a kind of bed-sitting-room and an office on the top floor. After the change of Government, since Butler had not used this part of the house, Lord Cherwell had continued to use these apartments in a desultory way. We naturally required them for our staff. When we came to examine them we found the walls adorned by shelf after shelf of paperback detective stories, as well as rows of tinned soup and vegetables. With the second of these the great man no doubt kept his frail body alive; by the first he refreshed his exhausted mind. I felt a little hesitant about what to do. Although we were particularly anxious to secure possession of the rooms, we were puzzled as to how to proceed without hurting the feelings of the tenant. However, this problem, like so many others, was resolved by the tactful intervention of the Cabinet Secretariat, without Dorothy or me admitting to our knowledge either of the Crime Club publications or the savoury products of Messrs. Heinz.

Although the Estimates for 1956–7 had in the main been settled before I became Chancellor, there was one formidable exception – a new horror, in the intricacies of which I had never allowed myself to become entangled, although I had vague memories of obscure and sometimes protracted Ministerial discussions of its hideous complications. It was known as the Farm Price Review. This annual debate was carried on with almost Byzantine deviousness, based upon a series of figures which few could understand and all challenged. In later years I was to become accustomed to the Alice in Wonderland method of calculation by which the final charge to the Exchequer at the end of the farming year bore little relation to the sum estimated.

Briefly, the Farm Price Review attempted to determine what the Exchequer should pay to the farmers to enable them to maintain a decent standard of living for themselves and a reasonable wage for farm workers while selling their produce in competition with food imported at lowest world prices (subject to certain special deals made with the great Dominions, primarily Australia and New Zealand). This gave us the benefit of cheap food, a large proportion of it imported; and it also preserved a thriving home agricultural industry, a vital asset in view of our experience in two world wars and the constant pressure on the balance of payments arising from huge imports of food.

In practice there were many disadvantages. 'Support prices' were based largely upon the needs of the small farmer, who might suffer from his own lack of efficiency, the size of his farm or his unfavourable geographical situation. The yearly bargaining was disagreeable and somewhat disreputable; and the mathematical assumptions on which it was founded were of doubtful validity. However, it can be urged in its favour that, during the period since the Second War, the agricultural industry has made greater progress than any other in capital development, mechanisation and general efficiency. During my premiership I accepted the Farm Price Review with all its difficulties, nor did I attempt to make any drastic or fundamental changes. This was because, in the concluding years, I hoped that it could be radically amended as a result of our entering into the Common Market.

The Price Review of 1956 ran its usual course. The farmers had asked for an additional sum of £41 million. We decided to offer £17 million, hoping to settle at something like £22½ million. The Minister of Agriculture, Derick Heathcoat Amory, and the Secretary of State for Scotland, James Stuart, were firm and sensible. They agreed that our policy should be

> to switch [the Farmers' Unions] off the immense increase which they ask for milk and try to get the extra money on feeding-stuffs (oats and barley) and cattle for beef.[1]

[1] 27 February 1956.

B

Under a convention which had grown up, there were two methods of settling the final figure. It could either be an 'agreed settlement' between the two parties (the Government and the Farmers' Unions), or it could be an 'imposed settlement' following an 'agreement to differ'. I felt that there was a good deal to be said in the present circumstances for the latter; I was accordingly pleased to be informed by the Ministers responsible, on 9 March, that this would be the outcome.

> I don't think [the Farmers] will launch a violent campaign against the Government, because [Sir James] Turner is too clever not to realise that, in the present economic climate, the public will think an extra £24 million a year is pretty generous. The example of an 'imposed' settlement will be very healthy.[1]

Although this had been settled, some of my colleagues began to have second thoughts and brought pressure on the Prime Minister to reopen the question. I had to accept certain minor adjustments which brought the additional cost to £25 million. When this was announced on 15 March it had a good press, especially from *The Times* and the *Manchester Guardian*. However, since the final outcome was altogether unpredictable, I could only comfort myself with the reflection that, if the actual figure at the end of the year involved a larger burden on the Exchequer in one direction because of the fall in world prices, there would be a corresponding relief to the balance of payments resulting from the lower cost of imported food.

After the Review had been finally settled, I pursued this matter with the Minister of Agriculture, Heathcoat Amory. I could not help feeling that by fixing the guaranteed prices at a level which enabled every farmer to remain in business, we were surely perpetuating inefficiency and the continued existence of too many small units in the industry. A further result was that we had to pay the guaranteed prices, over the whole of the output, to very many farmers who could get along quite well with a good deal less. It might also be that a disproportionate amount of imported feeding-stuffs was being used on the smaller farms. Our difficulties were, of

[1] 9 March 1956.

course, the security of tenure, recently made more rigid, and the undesirability – on humane as well as on political grounds – of reducing the support prices to an extent which would put the small man in a really exposed position, so that he would have to go out of business or allow his farm to be joined with a larger unit. But a variant of this might be positively to foster amalgamations, perhaps with financial assistance, and to provide improvement grants for holdings of an economic size. Another possibility might be to give special protection to small farmers (like the Highland crofters) where holdings could not always be grouped economically but there were strong social reasons for maintaining them. There might be other forms of action open to us. But first we needed to know how many of these people there were, to what extent they were concentrated or scattered, why their costs were so high, how much they produced, and so on. When we had the relevant information we could consider what steps to take.

This problem was to remain with me during subsequent years, and, with the help of successive Ministers and by a more positive management of the support system, as well as with the general tendency of agriculture to require larger units in order to justify heavy expenditure in plant and machinery, some progress has certainly been made.

Under the less sophisticated dispensation of the past, when our fathers, in their ignorance, built and developed a mighty Empire, the question which a Chancellor of the Exchequer had to decide was how to match the estimated national expenditure with an adequate revenue from taxation and other sources. But now *nous avons changé tout cela*. The centuries-old system by which the national accounts had been kept upon a cash basis had been, under Dalton, superseded by a more scientific system. The Budgets of the past dealt merely with the flow of 'cash in' and 'cash out'. It was in no sense a trading or profit-and-loss account, still less a balance-sheet. It took no account of stocks held by Departments at the beginning of the year, or their valuation at the end. The Dalton Budgets of 1946 and 1947 initiated a plan which has been followed ever since. Cash payments and cash revenue are accounted for 'above the line', including the interest—but not the capital repayments—of the National Debt. Capital investments are shown 'below the line', as well as any receipts on capital account. In days when we have left the austere era of nineteenth-century finance far behind us and modern governments approve heavy capital expenditure, not only on nationalised industries but over a wide field, this is undoubtedly a more comfortable arrangement. So long as the credit lasts, it can usefully be applied. But, like so many modern inventions, it has its own dangers and complications. For if a modern Chancellor of the Exchequer has to bear in mind more diverse and more uncertain aspects of the nation's financial and economic situation than his predecessors, his mistakes can have more devastating results.

Moreover, even this division of expenditure was not yet altogether scientific; large blocks which were really spent on capital account were still included as ordinary supply, either for traditional reasons or because of past legislation. But apart from these niceties, it was now necessary not merely to 'balance a Budget' as in the old ignorant days, but to decide as between 'deficit' or 'surplus' budgeting. In other words, I had now to determine, in the light of the inflationary pressure of the moment, whether the expected revenue would be sufficient, not merely to meet the expenditure 'above the line', but to make an appropriate contribution to the expenditure 'below the line'. Of course, in later years we got more experience and have recently managed everything much better—at least so we are told. But in this early period of the new financial revelation, there were many doubts and disputes. Some argued that there should be an overall Budget balance; that is to say that the revenue should be sufficient to cover the total expenditure, both 'above' and 'below' the line. Even this austerity took no account of the large capital investment of the local authorities, some of which borrowed on their own account and therefore did not come into the national figure, while others depended on loans from the central Exchequer. Moreover, some of the nationalised industries borrowed in the market on their own credit sustained by Government guarantee; and there were many other complications and qualifications— including the important consideration of private savings.

I soon found that the Governor of the Bank and the Treasury, while rejecting any fixed or pseudo-scientific formula, were anxious that, as a general aim, the total investments of the nation, whether private or public, should broadly be financed by the savings available—whether in the form of profits 'ploughed back', or revenue surplus or private savings. The sale of gilt-edged securities could broadly be identified with genuine savings.

Apart from the technicalities, if capital expenditure over the whole field, public, local and private, was broadly financed by savings—of all kinds—the danger of inflation would be correspondingly reduced.

A somewhat different and more scientific doctrine has been propounded in the famous White Paper, published in May 1963. The last paragraph is worth quoting:

> Although forecasts of the development of the economy and calculations of the effect of particular tax changes are inevitably imprecise, a judgement has still to be made to decide the general direction of the budget. This judgement will determine the government's net borrowing or 'financing' requirement, which then has to be considered in itself from the point of view of debt management and monetary policy.[1]

We had not, however, yet reached these exalted heights of prophetic power. For my part, while I rejected the crude concept of an 'overall budget balance' for the ensuing year, I felt that the main need was to increase the total savings of the nation. I knew from my experience in business that a great part of all industrial and commercial expansion is self-financed. This, in my view, could be encouraged by a wide range between the rates of tax on distributed and that on undistributed profits. (This was later held to be a heretical doctrine.) Unhappily, in recent years, the heavy cost of modern industrial plant, coupled with the reduced margin of profits available after taxation, has forced public companies to borrow more and more from the market, or to rely on heavy loans from the banks. Private companies, whose rate of taxation allows practically no margin, are increasingly forced either to merge with larger units or to sell out. But in 1956 the situation was different. In the industrial

[1] *Reform of the Exchequer Accounts*, Cmnd. 2014 (H.M.S.O., May 1963), para. 33.

and commercial world saving and investment could, by differential profits tax, be encouraged; in the field of public finance, by more attractive, and perhaps by novel, opportunities for personal thrift. I therefore felt that the main theme of the Budget should be Savings, whether corporate or individual.

At this time I naturally hoped to deploy a developing plan through three or four successive Budgets—at least to the end of the Parliament in 1959 or 1960. In the event, this was the only Budget which it fell to me to introduce, though naturally as Prime Minister I took a deep interest in those devised by successive Chancellors. Yet even a Prime Minister's concern is not the same as the feeling of intimate and almost loving care which every Chancellor bestows upon his yearly child. (Sometimes there have been two or even three such infants within the twelve months, but such philoprogenitiveness is generally regarded as unnatural and to be deplored.)

As early as 31 January, while awaiting the outcome of our rescue measures and the reaction upon the reserves, I sent a minute to Sir Edward Bridges, with a copy to my Ministerial colleagues. I was still working hard at economies in expenditure for the coming year. But these would, to some extent, have to be met by additional relief; for instance, as a counterpart to the abolition of the bread subsidies, there must be some increase in child allowances to help the poorer families. Any Budget, therefore, would be either a 'hard' Budget, to take still further from the public by increased taxation, or a 'standstill' Budget, in which reliefs in taxation must be balanced by new sources of revenue.

My minute included these paragraphs:

> It seems clear that a startling or revolutionary Budget is off. I must accept the Revenue's view that a Capital Gains Tax is out of the question this year. . . . But the Budget should have a theme. Lloyd George's 1909 Budget had as its theme 'Slosh the Land-lord'; Dalton's Budget was 'Slosh the Rentier'. Had we been able to make a Capital Gains Tax our theme could have been 'Slosh the Speculator'. . . . So I think it might be 'Savings and Incentives'.
>
> 1. Under Savings I would class:
> (a) All the schemes which Sir Edmund Compton has in

hand and any improvements now agreed which should be brought out at the same time as the Budget.

(*b*) Any inducements to the spread of property in as wide a form as possible, e.g. removal of Stamp Duty to owner occupiers.

In addition, anything we may do for the self-employed man following the [Millard Tucker] Report or any other benefit in that category comes in under Savings.

2. I want collected together all the things we might do for incentives; the remission of taxation to executives of £1,500 a year upwards and so forth.

Meanwhile the situation was improving in the sense that the position of the reserves was less alarming. In February we took in $60 million and there was a similar improvement in March. Nevertheless, they were $200 million lower than at the end of 1945, and $1,600 million less than the post-war peak in mid-1951. There were also grants and loans since the end of the war amounting to $8,000 million – a formidable volume of debt hanging over the future. On these, $200 million had to be paid back annually until the end of the century. Moreover, the deterioration of the reserves was due to the difficulties of the United Kingdom and did not result from the weakness of the sterling area as a whole.

Two questions, therefore, emerged: how to maintain stability and what additional taxations must be imposed, or – in default of taxation – what savings could be encouraged to support sterling. The first issue was dealt with in a White Paper, called *The Economic Implications of Full Employment*,[1] which I had not written, but for the publication of which I was nominally responsible. This was received with some derision by the Press, since they regarded it as containing too much exhortation and too little action. Yet action could only mean some form of compulsory wages freeze as opposed to the voluntary methods on which we were to rely. This question arose again in 1961, and, in recent years, it has become a main subject of contention. From my own contacts with the leaders of the Trades Union Council, which were always friendly and easy, I was persuaded any compulsory freezing would be deeply resented and

[1] Cmd. 9725 (H.M.S.O., 1956).

strenuously resisted. Moreover, even if successful temporarily, the subsequent thaw would be drastic, and 'perhaps disastrous. The union leaders were friendly enough: 'We want to help. But we do not want to be called "Tory stooges". You must help us.'

The time was now approaching when definite decisions had to be taken. The 'Savings' Budget was all very well, but it would start with a loss. More attractive terms on bonds and certificates would cost us at least £20 million. Against this,

> We will abolish the rest of the bread subsidy (£10 million this year saved and £20 million next year). We will tax tobacco still more (£27 million this year; £28 million next). The great question remains – what more to do and if any, by what means? This, in effect, boils down to getting £50 million odd through some new arrangements on Profits Tax, or (alternatively) a straight 6d. on Income Tax (undoing what Butler did last year). It's a difficult choice, but politically it's going to make a first-class row if I have to choose I.T.[1]

This certainly raised a very delicate question as regards my immediate predecessor, Butler, on which he was naturally sensitive. A reversal of his much criticised decision to take off 6d. last year would be thought a direct slur upon him. He might even have to resign. I discussed all this with him with complete openness. I told him that nothing could take away from the outstanding success of his four years at the Treasury; we really had to decide this on its merits. I was certainly unwilling to put on any indirect taxes which would only result in a demand for more wages, but there was still some room for manœuvre. My own advisers, both Ministerial and official, were divided. In the end I decided, partly on general, partly on political grounds, to leave Income Tax alone. I could not bring myself to believe that foreigners would be impressed by the stability and strength of a Government which reversed its own policy in so notorious a fashion. In place of an increase in the standard rate of Income Tax, the rate on distributed profits was to be raised from 27½ per cent to 30 per cent, and on undistributed profits from 2½ per cent to 3 per cent. (These increases would bring in some £30 million but would not accrue to the Exchequer until the year 1957–8).

[1] 28 March 1956.

To counter the abolition of the bread subsidy, Family Allowances were to be raised by 2s. a week for third and subsequent children, with a raising of the qualifying age for children at school or apprenticed. Among the encouragements to Savings was included a tax relief, following the Millard Tucker Report, on retirement pensions for the self-employed. At the same time, remembering my interest in Housing, I decided to make a substantial reduction in Stamp Duty on house purchases up to £5,000. As a result the Budget was negative in the sense that it gave away £20 million and took back £28 million, with the £30 million of Profits Tax for the following year.

An increase of 6d. in Income Tax would have produced £100 million. If I had decided to relinquish this impost on my fellow-countrymen, it remained a convenient instrument of pressure on my colleagues. I used my forbearance on one side of the national accounts to demand an equal contribution on the other—that is, a definite pledge to accept further cuts of £100 million in Government expenditure. Butler was an enthusiastic supporter of this solution.

Throughout my anxieties and uncertainties, I found the Prime Minister sympathetic and helpful. The plan for improving Family Allowances was immediately approved, and the Budget itself and the speech now began to take shape.

> Its theme now is at any rate simple. It can be summed up in one word—Saving. (1) There is the whole set of proposals for personal saving—new bonds, concession on Income Tax, etc. (2) There is the £100 million Government 'saving'. (3) There is the public or compulsory saving—the huge Government surplus, fully maintained and even increased by the tobacco tax and the Profits Tax.[1]

I was now living next door to the Prime Minister and saw him constantly. He was in good heart, and as charming and considerate as ever. Like many highly-strung men he was often more agitated by small worries than by serious difficulties. At moments of real crisis he was constant and determined. Although he was pre-occupied by foreign affairs, his judgement on domestic issues was

[1] 14 April 1956.

B2

always wise and based on imaginative understanding of the needs and ambitions of the mass of the people.

The days immediately before a Budget – especially a first Budget – are agitating for the protagonist. I was fortunate in having, in my Private Secretaries, Louis Petch and Evan Maude, splendid 'nannies' who looked after me with a mixture of affection and firmness. At the Budget Cabinet, Ministers seemed to like the whole plan

> and even accepted the idea of the £100 million cut – although when it comes to implementing the pledge there will be a lot of trouble.[1]

But the novelty which would hold attention, and even compete temporarily with the excitement caused by the visit of Bulganin and Khrushchev, was the proposal for Premium Bonds.

Within a few weeks of my installation at the Treasury, I asked for a re-examination of the possibility of encouraging private saving by the launching of a new certificate or bond to which an element of chance could be attached.

A lottery, in the full sense, must be ruled out, on grounds of orthodox finance as well as morality. But could not a system be devised, involving a modest distribution of prize money, which would not offend financial purists and be acceptable to the rank and file of the National Savings movement? It was vital to carry with us the members of this splendid organisation, which was responsible for the maintenance of the remarkable flow of individual savings. They were voluntary workers on whose untiring devotion we depended. Could they be induced to accept a plan by which, unlike ordinary gambling, the capital sums invested were not at risk, but prizes financed only from the interest accruing? Even if this involved some degree of 'backsliding', which would offend the more rigid moralists, could it be made acceptable to the general body of our members, especially to those on whom fell the responsibility of weekly canvassing and collection?

It was with these considerations in mind that the first plan for Premium Bonds was evolved. When I discussed it with Lord

[1] 16 April 1956.

Mackintosh, the head of the National Savings movement, on 23 January, I realised that he would need a little time to consider the question, both from the personal and the general aspect. His own upbringing and strong beliefs had made him instinctively suspicious of anything that could encourage gambling, with all its attendant evils. He fully recognised the distinction between our scheme and a lottery or ordinary betting. But apart from his own conscientious views, he must consider the matter objectively in order to advise me honestly as to the probable feelings of his members. Lord Mackintosh, Scottish by birth but Yorkshire by adoption—and accent—was one of the most sincere and honourable men whom I have ever known. He was also blessed with a sense of humour. The creator of a highly successful business, characteristically based on giving pleasure to great numbers of children—young and old—he had thrown himself wholeheartedly into the Savings movement. He was a man of the highest reputation, both in private and public life. As a leading nonconformist he was held in high regard by those very people who might be naturally suspicious of anything which appealed to the gambling instinct. It was quite true that a raffle, and even a lottery on a small scale, was a not uncommon method at fêtes, and other gatherings throughout the country, of raising money for religious and charitable purposes. Even Anglican dignitaries had been known to guess the weight of a cake or a pig, and were believed to be ready to turn an episcopal or archidiaconal blind eye to such goings-on. The Roman Catholic hierarchy were likely to be equally—if not more—tolerant. Yet it might be argued that there was a great difference between privately organised affairs on a limited scale and a national system which was expected to attract investments of many millions. Lotteries had been long abandoned as one of the more disreputable features of eighteenth-century finance. Although we owed the foundation of the British Museum to a lottery, yet the reverend and learned gentlemen who frequented the galleries and Reading Room had no doubt long forgotten this curious historical episode.

Apart, therefore, from the moral issue, it was argued that any such plan was financially unsound. If the State found it necessary, because of its falling credit, to attract money by lotteries or similar 'gimmicks', it would be taken as a proof that it had no confidence in itself, and was forced to use these adventitious means to command the support even of its own citizens. Moreover, would the new scheme draw in money from any untapped quarters? Surely not. It would merely mean that the same amount of savings would become available, but on terms slightly less favourable to the national Exchequer. As for the last argument, I felt confident that, if we made the price of each individual bond small—not more than £1, and if we distributed a large number of small prizes, rather than a small number of large prizes, so that people would become accustomed to prizes being won by their friends at home or by their comrades in the factory, we should begin to draw savings from many who had never before been willing to put money into this form of investment. We could not, of course, compete in attractions to tempt the inveterate punter, either on the races or the dogs; but we might easily tap new sources from those who would like a little element of chance but were not willing to risk their capital. Anyway, in this particular forecast it was anybody's guess, and only time would show whether my friends and I would prove right.

The first argument, however, was more impressive. If there was a general feeling in the public, among the Churches, and, above all, among the loyal men and women who served the National Savings movement that any form of saving certificate or bond which carried an element of gambling was morally wrong and contrary to the spirit and tradition of those who promoted thrift from the highest motives, then indeed we would be in danger. That there would be some pressure from Church and chapel was clear. I did not delude myself as to the likely attitude of some of the archbishops or bishops; but, with luck, their pronouncements would be obscure, and given more in sorrow than in anger. For the dignitaries, especially in the Established Church, must be aware how much the recent management of her affairs had added to her revenues from the exploitation of land values, and the judicious transfer of investments from gilt-edged to equities, with corresponding 'speculative' gains from the stock market. So far as the Government were concerned, our share of the football pools—a far more pernicious form of gambling since the unsuccessful 'investor' lost his capital stake—was considerable.

The Exchequer was, in effect, already a sleeping-partner through taxation to the extent of many millions. This revenue had been accepted as respectable even by so austere a Chancellor as Sir Stafford Cripps.

So the scheme began to take shape. On 26 March I heard from Lord Mackintosh that he was prepared to give his support. I wrote to him, therefore, as follows:

> I knew that I could rely on your judgement. If you are convinced yourself, you will quickly convince the National Savings movement. And I feel sure that on reflection you will be satisfied, as I am, that an investor in the Premium Bond is genuinely saving. The 'investor', so called, in a football pool or in a bet on a horse, is spending his stake. The Premium Bond investor is saving; for like the investor in an interest-bearing security, he is giving up, for the time being, the right to spend his money. Both types of investor get a reward for their restraint in spending. The difference is that the ordinary investor chooses the reward of interest on his money, while the Premium Bond investor chooses as his reward the chance of a prize.

I was now determined to announce the Bond at the time of the Budget. The important thing was that the Government should be firm, and not try to shelter itself behind a nominal 'free vote'. I was to announce the Bond as a concrete proposal, with definite terms and dates so that the public would know what they had to expect, and the Savings movement what they were being asked to support. In order to protect ourselves from any large encashment of existing savings, we decided on a small limit for individual holdings. £250 was the original suggestion, as announced in the Budget, but in the course of the debates on the Finance Bill, I raised it to £500. There were to be tax-free prizes for every £10,000 of subscription. There would be monthly drawings, with six months' holding as the necessary qualification. The prize fund was to consist of 4 per cent interest, free of tax on the Bonds, and each £10,000 of prize money would provide 237 tax-free prizes, ranging from one of £1,000 to 200 of £25. Minors could not subscribe, but parents would be entitled to buy Bonds on behalf of their children.

Lord Mackintosh, in spite of some criticism, carried out his undertaking with loyalty and even enthusiasm. He was responsible for the convincing slogan, 'If we cannot always save sinners, let us at least make sure that sinners save.' Sir John Erskine, the leader of the Savings movement in Scotland, was in full agreement. Within the Treasury the chief credit was due to Sir Edmund Compton who concealed behind a quiet – even retiring – exterior, a strong will. He was a keen promoter of our scheme, and I felt that his moral standards, like Lord Mackintosh's, were above reproach, for he sang in the Bach Choir.

The reception of the scheme followed expected lines. The Archbishop of Canterbury observed:

> that there are more important things to exercise one's moral judgement than the niceties of white and black gambling, and that the simplest rule a Christian can have for his gambling regulating is not to gamble at all.[1]

This judgement, although obscurely and even ungrammatically phrased, was discouraging. But the Roman Catholic Archbishop of Liverpool said a few days later that the principle of chance was bad only if carried to excess. Historic positions seemed thus to be reversed; the successor of Cranmer had allowed the principle of the *via media* to pass from Canterbury to Rome.

In the Budget Debate on 18 April, Harold Wilson perhaps not unnaturally, since it seemed a good enough wicket, plunged into a witty, although violent, attack. My speech was described as 'shambling, fumbling, largely irrelevant and, at one point, degrading'.[2] On Premium Bonds he let himself go:

> Now Britain's strength, freedom and solvency apparently depend on the proceeds of a squalid raffle. . . . They will be fighting the next Election on 'Honest Charlie always pays.'[2]

He was convinced that to use the power and prestige of the State for such a purpose would be deeply offensive on religious and moral grounds. In a speech in the country a few days later, he rose to even greater heights saying, among other things, that 'Horatio Bottomley

---

[1] *Hansard*, 18 June 1956.   [2] *Hansard*, 18 April 1956.

was Mr. Macmillan's inspiration.' Yet when we came to the Finance Bill itself the Opposition's tone was more muted. No doubt the Labour Party had found that the particular cock on which they were relying was not likely to put up a very vigorous fight. It was freely rumoured, and to this I made a reference in my reply, that the Opposition had taken their decision to oppose the clause at a meeting attended by only 55 members, of which scarcely more than half had favoured the decision to vote against Premium Bonds. Although Wilson insisted that these figures were incorrect, he seemed to concede that they were not far wrong.

In the Committee stage, on 18 June, I could not help ridiculing the exaggerated arguments about the downward plunge of the reckless gambler. According to Wilson's own calculations, for every pound risked or staked, only $9\frac{1}{2}d$. was at risk.

> I cannot see families broken up, children in rags, wives deserted, or the horrors of the 'Rake's Progress' falling upon a man's family for the sole reason that he has invested too deeply in Premium Savings Bonds. There will be no modern Hogarth who will draw a frightening series of cartoons called 'The Downfall of the Saver in Premium Bonds'.[1]

The debate was kept up with some impressive speeches by sincere but, I felt, misguided enthusiasts, including one or two from my own Party. But in the end the discussion fizzled out, and when the division came we carried our proposals with about our normal majority.

Investment in Premium Bonds began on 1 November. On 5 December I was able to write to Lord Mackintosh as follows:

> I have just been told that the first month of the Premium Bonds campaign has brought in a total of £45 million, and I hasten to write to you to congratulate you on this great success. You told me, as I remember, that your sights were a trifle higher than that for the first month. But I am sure that in present circumstances, in which the public eye has been focused on the Middle East, the result should be regarded as a very notable

[1] *Hansard*, 18 June 1956.

achievement indeed. It augurs well for the future; and I know that you and the whole Savings movement will feel encouraged by the result of the first month's campaign.

The Bonds proved popular with the public, and it was clear that many of the prizes were immediately reinvested. It is also not now disputed that they tapped sources which would not readily have found their way into the Exchequer by any of the more orthodox methods. The figures have continued to be encouraging; for instance, in the following seven years the average investment was £73·7 million.

The sequel is perhaps surprising. After the Election of 1964, the chief critic of this revolutionary venture of mine, both on financial and moral grounds, could find only one fault with 'the squalid raffle' – that the prizes were insufficient to attract the investor. The top prizes which I fixed at £1,000, and only reluctantly agreed to allow to rise to £5,000, were now to reach £25,000. One of the most sincere and dignified opponents of the whole scheme was Sir Cyril Black, Conservative member for Wimbledon, who spoke against it when it came out, and has continued in honourable opposition. In a debate ten years later, he was able to point out that thirteen members of the existing Labour Cabinet, including the Chancellor of the Exchequer, had voted against the Premium Bonds in 1956, as well as nine other Ministers in the Administration and many back-benchers. He described this as 'one of the most amazing cases of mass conversion since the 3,000 on the Day of Pentecost'.[1] But the chief, and perhaps the most important, convert was the Prime Minister of the day. It is only to petty minds that consistency is a necessary or even desirable attribute of statesmanship.

Apart from the Premium Bonds, the Budget was not of a character to attract much political conflict. At the same time, the delivery of a Budget speech – especially a first Budget speech – involves considerable mental and physical strain. It is difficult to hold an audience through the somewhat tedious account which custom requires of the performance of the economy during the past year and the prospects for the year ahead. For the audience, inside

[1] *Hansard*, 31 January 1966.

and outside Parliament, are more interested in changes in taxation than in an essay in practical or theoretical economics, however profound. Accordingly I began by observing that I had always thought of Budget Day as rather like a school speech day – a bit of a bore, but something which had to be endured.

The parents and the old boys like it. These occasions are very similar, for an unfortunate audience has to sit and listen to a long speech before it is told of the fortunate prize-winners. The analogy is not, of course, perfect, because on Budget day there are quite likely to be impositions as well as prizes for distribution. Sometimes there are nothing but impositions.[1]

In point of fact the increases and the remissions in taxation almost balanced; the purpose of the margin, to be added to the large surplus, was to meet the economic situation and impress our critics at home and abroad. Although it was necessary for this year to take steps to halt the process of growth which was proceeding at too rapid a rate, I was determined that an expansionist policy should be resumed as early as possible. I had to admit that the position of the reserves and of the balance of trade was not satisfactory; yet there was another side to this somewhat sombre picture. 1955 had been a year of great prosperity for ordinary men and women. Everyone had a job; consumption rose appreciably; investment also rose; industrial production was 5 per cent higher than the previous year. But, since productivity had only risen by 2 per cent, while wages and salaries went up by 8 per cent, prices had begun to rise. There were shortages of labour and material. Imports had increased; exports had been held back for the home markets, and the balance of payments had consequently suffered. The lesson was clear:

We cannot afford to run our economy flat out, with more jobs than men to fill them, more orders than industry can meet, easy profits at home and rising costs.[1]

This doctrine was then regarded as mere common sense, and not yet disputed even by 'progressive' economists. Indeed the main criticism of my measures was not that they were too fierce, but that

[1] *Hansard*, 17 April 1956.

they were too gentle. In the view of almost all experts I had not applied the brake too fiercely; on the contrary, I had been too lenient. Nor did anyone at that time controvert the general idea that the economy had to be managed with a certain amount of dexterity. The temperature could be forced up to excessive heat, or allowed to become unduly tepid. The object of economic statesmanship could only be obtained by manipulation in either direction. It was not until later that this principle was challenged and given the opprobrious name of 'Stop–Go', or the theory developed that growth could be pursued ruthlessly, and even recklessly, at the cost of every other consideration. It has now been possible to observe this new system in action, including the very drastic remedies that have to be applied – often too late – when less rigorous measures would have been sufficient had they been timely.

There was also in 1956 general agreement on the need to continue Butler's revival of monetary policy, and primarily Bank Rate, as an important instrument in the management of the economy. There was naturally much debate about its proper use. But two things had become plain:

> First, no one has yet found an easy way to restrict credit without high interest rates. I am told that if I appoint a committee, I may find out how to do it, but I am not altogether sanguine about this. Secondly, monetary policy cannot 'go it alone'. It can only operate effectively in conjunction with fiscal and other measures to check demand, taken by the Government of the day and supported by an informed public opinion.[1]

I next turned to the Public Debt:

> The total of the National Debt now stands at £27,040 million. It might interest the Committee to know that on 3rd September, 1939, it stood at about £8,400 million. On 4th August, 1914, it stood at about £645 million. These figures fill one with a certain awe.[1]

Yet there were few nations, victors or vanquished, in these forty years who had such an honourable record of trying to meet their

[1] *Hansard*, 17 April 1956.

obligations at home and abroad. If the dull, dragging funded Debt was a burden, the unfunded was a cause of constant and acute anxiety. But I insisted upon the lesson. We might suffer by trying to run too fast; if we stood still we should be lost. Inflation must be curbed, because runaway inflation ended by being itself restrictionist. But deflation, in the sense of seeking stability by methods which would increase the debt burden in relation to the national income, or result in a return to unemployment, was out of the question: 'We must all be expansionists, but expansionists of real wealth.'[1]

I then recalled to the House a famous passage from one of Macaulay's essays, describing the seemingly overwhelming increases in the National Debt as the result of the wars of the eighteenth century. But the burden had been carried, not by its absolute but by its relative reduction; not by repayment of debt, but by a vast increase of wealth. 'On what principle', the essayist had asked, 'is it that, when we see nothing but improvement behind us we can expect nothing but deterioration before us?' This was very appropriate to our present circumstances, and if we made use, as our ancestors had done, of prudence and daring in the right proportion, we should again succeed.

One passage, upon the difficulty of accurately estimating future prospects, attracted considerable attention:

> Here, alas, there is no true science which can give us certainty in this uncertain field. Some people feel that what passes for such is more like astrology than astronomy. Lyndoe or Old Moore may turn out just as reliable as Professor What's His Name or Dr. So and So. I do not share this extreme view. Nevertheless, I think that we should all agree that if there is such a science, it is not an exact one. There are too many unknowns and too many variables. Then I am told that some of our statistics are too late to be as useful as they ought to be. We are always, as it were, looking up a train in last year's Bradshaw.[1]

The phrase, 'last year's Bradshaw', stuck.

Some immediate steps we could take, which I announced to the

[1] *Hansard*, 17 April 1956.

House in August. Others have followed. In spite of the inconvenience and work involved, we asked for much more detailed information from manufacturers and commercial firms. We began the improvement and development of the Economic Section of the Treasury and of the Central Statistical Office. Now other organisations, both within and outside the Civil Service, have added greatly to the accuracy by which economic weather can be predicted. There will be unexpected squalls and storms, so sensitive is our island position to changing conditions in any part of the world. Nevertheless we did improve the equipment for the economic forecaster.

Before the reintroduction of monetary methods, the chief instrument of restoring and maintaining stability had been what had been called public saving – that is, a large Budget surplus: public saving was, in effect, the excess extracted from citizens, singly or corporately, beyond what was necessary to carry on the work of government. It was this instrument that Cripps had relied on, and had wielded with such relish. Although I too was budgeting for a surplus of £460 million in all 'above the line', including an additional £15 million as the result of the tax changes, I rejected the pressure to increase this to a still higher figure. I pledged myself to find another £100 million reduction in Government expenditure. But in general, it seemed better to look to all the forms of private saving as more healthy and desirable in a free society. After all, this public saving, which really meant compulsory saving, was not attractive in normal times. It was a product of war and the aftermath of war.

> Does anyone read Dickens nowadays – except, of course, the Russians? If so, they will remember Mrs. Pardiggle in *Bleak House*. 'My family,' boasted this philanthropic lady, 'are not frivolous. They spend the whole amount of their allowance in subscriptions, under my direction . . . they enrol their contributions, according to their ages, and their little means.' Just so – first pay out far more money to the people than it is good for them to have. Then take it all off them again by taxation. It is as simple as shelling peas.[1]

Therefore, although the main theme of the Budget was to be devoted to Saving, the new emphasis would be on voluntary effort. Industry

[1] *Hansard*, 17 April 1956.

would be encouraged to save by ploughing back profits into development. There would be new inducements to the self-employed to
save for their own retirement. Individual savings would be stimulated by improvements in the well-known methods, by 'putting a
new cutting edge on the old tools'. The financial critics had
declared that I must reduce bank deposits and the Floating Debt to
reduce the money supply.

> Very well. Let us see bank deposits turned into National
> Savings. As the National Savings rise the Treasury bills will fall.
> In this way, the National Savings movement will carry out a
> funding operation of the most effective and beneficial kind, and
> will prove itself a powerful ally in the battle against inflation.[1]

The slogans should, therefore, be 'Save to Fund', 'Save for Solvency',
'Save for Security'. But we must also save capital resources in order
to develop other countries as well as our own, and thus to take our
part in the struggle for the soul of the neutral world. We must, in a
word, 'Save to be Free, Save to be Great'.

In accordance with tradition, the debate continued on 18 and 19
April, and was concluded on 23 April.

My final speech ended in a more reflective mood. After reviewing
our problems, I declared that they were not, in my view, insoluble,
although precisely the right techniques for modern conditions were
difficult to devise and apply. I was opposed to the over-regulation
which comes with Socialism. I was equally convinced that, in the
second half of the twentieth century, we could not revert to the
laissez-faire of a hundred years ago. What certainly was never Tory
doctrine, I did not believe today was even Liberal doctrine. In any
case, we had better let sleeping dogmas lie. We had to find a proper
balance between excessive freedom and excessive regulation. We
could only discover, by trial and error, the right amount of guidance
and management to be exercised by a central Government. Nevertheless, in broad terms, I felt

> that the Government must be like the commander-in-chief in a
> campaign. He must plan the broad strategy . . . but if he tries to

[1] *Hansard*, 17 April 1956.

take control of the divisions, brigades and battalions, then he is lost. It is the search for that course and that policy, in which both sides must act together, and certainly on this side . . . that we are determined to pursue.[1]

That search continues.

It seemed as if, at least from the Parliamentary point of view, I should have no more trouble during the rest of the session. But in the course of June one of those strange storms which arise in the clearest sky suddenly blew up. It is this uncertainty which gives Parliamentary life its excitement and zest. At the same time, these unexpected squalls can be distracting and even dangerous. This one arose from an offer by the Texas Oil Company to purchase all the assets and rights of the Trinidad Oil Company. The bid was a very high one, the price offered being £63 million—about twice the value of the shares as recently quoted on the market. The immediate reaction on both sides of the House was hostile; the Conservative 1922 Committee met immediately and urged the Government to use its powers to disallow the transaction.

Now *I* have to decide whether to allow the deal to go through, or whether to stop it under the Exchange Control Act. Since the deal is obviously beneficial from the economic and financial point of view, this would seem rather a doubtful course. But of course there is a howl of excitement and fury in the Press and the Party.[2]

During the next few days it became possible to sort out some of the details and to assess the advantages and disadvantages. Everything to do with investment and trade in oil seems always full of complications; this was certainly no exception.

In relation to the total production of crude oil, the Company's annual output of one million tons was negligible. Another three million tons were sent to Trinidad for refinement—most of this being supplied by an American company in Venezuela. The Trinidad Oil Company held a small concession in Canada not in any way comparable to the large investments which British Petroleum and Shell—the only alternative purchasers of the Trinidad

[1] *Hansard*, 23 April 1956.   [2] 7 June 1956.

shares—had already obtained in that country on their own account and to which they could easily add as opportunity occurred. The proposed sale did not include the exploration rights, mostly submarine, vested in a company called Trinidad Northern Areas, in which Shell and B.P. each held and would retain one-third of the equity.

The main attraction to the prospective purchasers lay in the opportunity of acquiring half the shares in the Regent Oil Company —the other moiety was held by Caltex—which was rapidly developing retail outlets in the United Kingdom. But since Shell and B.P. were already the main suppliers in this market it would be embarrassing, not advantageous, for them to find themselves partners in a rival company, apart from any question of a monopoly being created.

The gain to the economy of Trinidad was clear. The present company had not sufficient resources to develop its assets effectively. A strong American company would be able and willing to do so as rapidly as possible. On the other hand it was distasteful, some thought disastrous, to allow this British investment to pass into American control.

We had to consider all these points of view. I was naturally sorry to lose this property on sentimental, if on no other, grounds. But it could not be said to be of any strategic importance. Nevertheless, it would be convenient, at least politically, if B.P. or Shell would step into the breach, although I could readily see that there was little attraction, and some serious objections, from their point of view. Accordingly I asked Lord Godber of Shell and Basil Jackson of B.P. to come and see me separately. As I expected, they were both strongly in favour of allowing the sale. Their reasons seemed pretty convincing. The half share in the distributing business in the United Kingdom was of no use to them. They had their own organisation, and if they had to enter into such a partnership it would be an impossible situation. As regards Canada, they had nothing to gain from obtaining the very small concession which the Trinidad company enjoyed. Shell and B.P. were already, singly and jointly, involved in far more impressive developments in Canada. Nor would there be any difficulty in providing the necessary currency if they wished to extend their operations. After consultation with the Trinidad Government, whose present and future interests it was our primary duty to protect, I became convinced that neither from the point of view of the United Kingdom, nor from that of the colony, would we be justified in using our authority under the Exchange Control system to veto this transaction. Nevertheless, since these arguments did not meet the strong objections made on wider grounds, the political hazards looked formidable.

The Trinidad affair is developing into a major political crisis. Lord Beaverbrook's *Daily Express*, the *Daily Herald* (Labour) and the *Daily Worker* (Communist) are linked in a somewhat strange alliance—but all against the Government. I am accused of 'selling out the Empire' to the Yankees. It is not yet announced what the Government decision will be. But I intend to recommend to the Cabinet . . . that, subject to certain conditions, some to protect U.K. and sterling area interests and some to protect the local inhabitants, permission . . . be given.[1]

The conditions were indeed of the greatest importance and had to be effective. First, to protect sterling, we required that the marketing operations within the sterling area be carried on under arrangements satisfactory to the British Government. The production and refining operations within Trinidad must be carried on by a company registered in Trinidad. We also specified that both we and the Government of Trinidad must receive satisfactory undertakings that the refinery would be operated to full economic capacity, exploration intensified and existing oil resources in Trinidad exploited on the basis of sound operating practice at the maximum economic rate. Further assurances were required concerning industrial relations, the fair treatment of existing employees, and increased opportunities for local men to train for high positions in the company. Finally, there was to be no racial discrimination in company plants or camps.

I arranged for Bridges and Rowan to see Simon Vos, chairman of the Trinidad Oil Company, to obtain a clear agreement on the vital terms.

I was naturally anxious to find out whether these conditions (especially that about the sterling–dollar payments for oil sold

[1] 12 June 1956.

in the sterling area in future, and that for the Company being registered in Trinidad) were likely to be accepted by the Texas Company. At the same time, I was anxious to avoid any negotiation with Texas. Nevertheless, the worst political position of all would be to incur all the odium of granting permission, only to find that the deal fell through in the end because of one or other of the conditions.[1]

The Treasury representatives were given oral assurances, both by Mr. Vos and by the Texas Oil Company, that these conditions were acceptable. They would of course have to be translated into formal agreements, and the matter was still subject to the approval of the Cabinet. After a full discussion this was forthcoming, and I made the necessary announcement in the House the same afternoon.[2] I had fully expected that the Opposition would demand an adjournment under the appropriate rule. This would involve a debate at 7 p.m. with a division at 10 p.m. But since I purposely made my statement long and obscure, and undertook to publish a White Paper on the whole issue, the Opposition preferred to wait. This suited me well enough, for I felt that public opinion would begin to change when the details became more understood with all their implications. I was therefore very ready to postpone the debate but not the decision.

I refused to postpone action till after the debate. I would send my formal approval at once—after my announcement. If the House wish to censure me, they must do so. Gaitskell tried to bluster a bit, but it was clear to everybody that the thing was beginning to 'fizzle' out.[1]

By the time the debate came, a week later, the atmosphere had become less tense. Many of the Labour members, especially those with a genuine interest in the welfare of the colonial populations, were beginning to have second thoughts. Some, no doubt, of the Conservatives had been impressed by the weight of argument deployed in the White Paper and by the changing attitude of the Press. The first group stayed away; the second went to Ascot.

As so often happens in a much advertised Parliamentary situation, when the time came the crisis turned into a flop. Indeed, the

[1] 14 June 1956.   [2] *Hansard*, 14 June 1956.

only redeeming aspect of the affair was the brilliant attack delivered by Wilson. I had listened to many of his speeches before and was destined to hear many in the years ahead. But I never heard him give such a display of virtuosity. Epigram followed epigram, and the continual flashes of wit were from time to time relieved by more serious arguments. He had of course little difficulty in chaffing the Tories who seemed to have abandoned their traditional creed. One point Wilson repeated with considerable effect. He attacked the enormous and unearned capital profit which would accrue to the existing shareholders if the deal went through. This gave him an opportunity of returning to the theme of what he called the 'Windfall State', with fortuitous and undeserved gains making no contribution to the Revenue. (Fortunately he did not know how urgently I had tried to press my advisers to devise a tax on these lines.) The scene was admirably summed up by a writer in the *Annual Register*.

> This debate . . . presented the somewhat ludicrous spectacle of an anti-imperialist party desperately upholding the Union Jack in a remote island (against the interests of the, in other contexts, downtrodden islanders) but suffering parliamentary defeat at the hands of a Government which had apparently no difficulty in bringing its . . . imperialists to heel. . . . Still, Mr. Wilson got in a witty allusion to 'drooping primroses', so perhaps it was all worth while.[1]

I contented myself in opening the discussion with giving a full explanation of the circumstances, rehearsing once more all the arguments pro and con. There was one point which I thought it right to deploy in spite of its possible unpopularity. Most of the Press, as well as the public, facing the facts dispassionately, had become daily more sympathetic to the Government's difficulty. But there had been some notable exceptions.

> By a strange conjunction the three newspapers which have specially opposed this have been the *Daily Worker*, the *Daily Herald* and the *Daily Express*.
>
> It would be indelicate for me to inquire into the spiritual affinity that ties this group together. . . .[2]

---

[1] *Annual Register, 1956* (London, 1957), p. 30.   [2] *Hansard*, 20 June 1956.

There was one passage, however, from the *Daily Express*, under the sub-heading 'Shameful, sordid', to which I thought it right to call attention. It ran as follows:

> Resources like oil and water power are a vital portion of a nation's patrimony. To keep them out of foreign control is an elementary act of self-preservation. Failure to give that measure of defence is irresponsible.[1]

I commented as follows:

> I could hardly imagine a doctrine so dangerous to us. The people of this island, 50 million of them, live in a country with very few resources of raw materials. What would be our position if this doctrine were rigidly enforced by all the countries of the world? What would be our position in the field of oil? . . . no nation had a greater interest than our nation in opposing the narrow, exclusionist point of view. We have learned that from bitter experience, and I should have thought that we had enough trouble with Mossadeqs abroad not to wish to encourage them at home.[1]

This kind of isolationism or economic nationalism, amounting to xenophobia, seized all nations, great and small, from time to time. However damaging such policies might prove for others, for us they must be fatal. We of all people had to resist these tendencies, for we had so much to lose and so much to protect.

The day ended with a noble speech from the Colonial Secretary, Alan Lennox-Boyd, which deeply impressed the House. When the division came we had a majority of 68, well above our normal figure. I was glad when this affair, which had so agitated my colleagues both in and out of the Government for over a fortnight, was finally out of the way. It had, however, one pleasing sequel. Wilson's sarcasms about unearned capital gains, the result of City 'speculation', had stuck in my mind. So had the Archbishop of Canterbury's somewhat patronising criticisms of my Premium Bonds. I learned that the Church authorities, under the able management of their financial advisers, had netted a capital profit from the Trinidad take-over running not into tens of thousands but

[1] *Daily Express*, 15 June 1956.

into hundreds of thousands of pounds. Later in the year I attended a dinner of one of the great City companies at which the Archbishop was present. I made some gentle allusion to his animadversions on my Premium Bonds, under which I had been content to suffer in silence. But perhaps His Grace would take a more generous view now that he could look back with satisfaction on his successful little flutter in Trinidad Oil!

In introducing the Budget I had undertaken an important commitment, the execution of which was to prove tedious and often embarrassing. Partly in order to salve my own conscience and partly because I believed that major economies could still be made, I had agreed with the Prime Minister in April that if I abandoned the proposal to raise Income Tax I could expect the co-operation of Ministers in obtaining an additional reduction of £100 million in Government expenditure. Eden had accepted this, and throughout many weary weeks of argument supported me loyally. Although during the Budget debates a good deal of scepticism was shown as to the prospects of success, the Treasury immediately began to bring pressure upon the various Ministries. It was in Defence that I looked for at least half the economies to be secured. In early May I sent a detailed minute to the Minister, Walter Monckton, an old and intimate friend on whose co-operation I could rely. In this document I set out a detailed list of reductions which I thought might well be made in each of the three fighting Services, as well as in various expenditures undertaken by the Ministry of Defence on their behalf. Unfortunately, under the organisation of Defence as it then was, the powers of the Minister were limited. Although the nominal head of the three Service Ministers and their spokesman in the Cabinet, his authority, like that of some medieval king or emperor, was openly and successfully challenged by his powerful feudatories. It was not until the end of my premiership, when we completely reorganised the whole structure of Defence, that this defect was remedied.

During this exercise Ministers, like the public, were more enthusiastic about the principle than the practice of public economy. If they often proved active and ingenious in proposing savings in one another's departments, they were sceptical and resistant as regards their own. By the middle of June I was able to inform the Cabinet that I had succeeded in obtaining cuts to the order of £76 million of which £36½ million came from defence, and £12½ million from the bread and milk subsidies already agreed.

It seemed wise, therefore, to give the figures to Parliament. In doing so, I insisted that this was an interim statement, the result of eight weeks' work. (Of course I knew in my heart that the last quarter would be the hardest to obtain.)

The House seemed rather uncertain how to take it. The Opposition had a disappointment, for they expected a wide 'attack on the social services' and there was nothing (except the 1d. on school meals which follows precedent). Our side was quiet, but on the whole satisfied.[1]

On 3 July a Vote of Censure was moved by the Opposition, on no particular topic but on familiar lines.

Harold Wilson opened the debate with a very clever, but rather too 'party-political' a speech. This allowed me to make, in contrast, a speech on very high, national, non-party lines. (Anyway, it was prepared on these lines; for I had a shrewd idea what Wilson would do.)[2]

This approach was certainly wise, for I noticed quite a number of Labour Members nodding agreement with large parts of my speech. In the course of it I was at any rate able to claim that the gold and dollar reserves had risen by nearly £100 million—not as large a figure as we might have wished, but still a start.

By the end of the year I was able to announce a further £17¼ million cut. This sum was almost equally divided between defence and civil expenditure. This was not a bad result, leaving us only £7 million short of our target.

Of course this search for further economies after the estimates for the following year had been agreed and published was a crude and unusual procedure. It was only permissible for a Chancellor of the Exchequer who had taken up his post after this process had been completed. Moreover such an administrative contrivance could not

[1] 26 June 1956.   [2] 3 July 1956.

supersede the normal and continuous process of scrutinising Government expenditure in respect both of immediate details and of underlying policies involved. Nevertheless, the continual pressure upon my colleagues, with frequent reports to the Cabinet of the success or ill-success of our endeavours, was a healthy exercise. Apart from the actual economies which we secured, undoubtedly this operation resulted in a tighter control of each department by its Minister and his staff, and a greater determination to avoid those supplementary estimates which can so often wreck the whole structure of a Budget.

Apart from these distractions, our main efforts during this year continued to be concentrated on the restoration of external and internal stability. Accordingly all the instruments of monetary policy and other measures to restrict undue expansion, including the credit squeeze and hire-purchase restrictions, had to be maintained. The Capital Issues Committee was still in being and operated as a further check. The effort to meet the Government's requirements, not merely by the issue of Treasury Bills but by some genuine funding, was pressed forward successfully with the issue towards the end of April of a long-dated loan amounting to £250 million.

It was necessary during this time to keep up pressure upon the Clearing Banks and other finance houses, and towards the close of the summer I proposed to invite them to a meeting at the Treasury. The Governor did not altogether like this, since he regarded himself as the right person to deal with the heads of these institutions. So we compromised. He would see them first, and I would see them later. This gathering duly took place on 24 July and proved a great success. After all, even bankers are human, and a short and flattering speech, with a modicum of sherry, can still do wonders. I do not know whether my successors followed this precedent, but at any rate I do not regret having made it.

By the end of the year we could see some results. Both the balance of trade and the balance of payments were improving, and international confidence was returning. Although I had to tell the bankers at the usual Mansion House dinner that there could be no question of relaxation, I felt that the tide had turned. I reminded them of the

Duke of Wellington's famous remark at Waterloo: 'Hard pounding this, gentlemen; let's see who will pound longest.' The fight against inflation would be hard pounding in every sense of the words, but the battle, if not yet won, was going well.

The most difficult task of a Chancellor of the Exchequer in such a period is to maintain a sufficiently optimistic attitude to impress the outside world and yet be realistic, even pessimistic, enough at home to encourage all classes to show moderation and restraint. He must be an external 'bull' and an internal 'bear'.

At a luncheon of the Foreign Press Association in May I made a bullish declaration. There were two important items regularly left out of the assessment of our economy by many foreign observers; but they were vital. The first was defence; the second overseas investment. According to the last available figures, Britain was devoting 9 per cent of her gross national product to defence. The figure for all the other countries of the Organisation for European Economic Co-operation was 5 per cent. In other words, for every rifle that our comrades in Europe carried we were carrying two. If we were to follow the European example, we would save £700 million a year. If only half of these resources were shifted into exports the picture of our foreign balances would be transformed. If the other half were available for investment, there would be less critical comment about our low rate of investment compared to many other countries. Nor should it be forgotten that our military expenditure overseas was running at the rate of £160 million. This was equal to the exports of the whole of our tractor industry, of our agricultural machinery industry, of all our aircraft, to which could be added the total exports of whisky and cocoa preparations—'all gone down the drain, as it were, to pay for our military expenditure abroad'. At the same time, our net investment overseas was running at between £150 and £175 million a year—'far and away ahead of that of any other nation, when compared with national income, including even the United States'. I thought it right to say these things—which seemed rather to surprise my audience—in order to protect our reputation and our good name and in justice to our own efforts.

At the same time the ever-present problem of German 'support' costs was becoming acute. This was to be the beginning of a long and unrewarding dispute carried on over all the succeeding years of my political life. A few days before my appointment as Chancellor was announced, I had been in Paris at the North Atlantic Treaty Organisation meeting and had been alarmed by the heavy price which Britain would have to pay for having rescued Europe from the confusion of its own rearmament plans and thus ensured the effective organisation of our common defence.[1]

The biggest headache which we have (U.K.) is the cost of our troops in Germany in the future, both in *money* and in *balance of payments*. Not only are the Germans refusing any contribution to 'support costs' this year, but they are not making any contribution to the joint effort of defence parallel to our own.
I had long discussions late last night at the Embassy and Edward Boyle and Selwyn Lloyd are to try their best with Herr [Fritz] Schäffer and Herr [Theodor] Blank. My own feeling is that our only hope lies with the Chancellor (Dr. Adenauer). No one will take any generous (or indeed any) decision but he.[2]

By the end of June the Germans were still dragging their feet. Our total costs in German currency for maintaining British troops was running at £64 million. We had asked for a contribution of £50 million. The German Government had begun by saying that they would do nothing. They were with difficulty induced to offer £34 million, to which they attached with characteristic bluntness a declaration that they would never pay anything again. This was made all the more irritating because Dr. Ludwig Erhard—the Finance Minister—thought fit to state publicly that sterling should and would be devalued. I agreed to the Treasury issuing firm denials, but reluctantly, for I remembered the famous apophthegm: 'No story is worth believing until it has been officially denied.' Dr. Erhard, with whom I was to become closely acquainted, was not without charm. He looked like an actor cast for the role of Henry VIII. But he was a brilliant executive in his own field, although as Chancellor of the Reich, after Adenauer's resignation, he proved less successful.

[1] See *Tides of Fortune*, pp. 569–70.   [2] 16 December 1955.

Although these and other questions occupied a good deal of time and caused a flood of minutes and telegrams, the main problem, then as later, was the question of wages and prices. The situation was one which has since become only too familiar. It soon became clear that a voluntary plan of wage-restraint—still less a freeze—was not to be expected if prices continued to rise. But since the last round of wage-increases had not yet been fully reflected in retail prices, there was bound to be some increase in the next few months. We looked, therefore, like being once again the victims of the inevitable spiral. Ministers responsible for the nationalised industries could bring pressure on their respective chairmen to prevent them from capitulating to new wage-claims on the railways or in the mines. But what would be the general attitude of industrialists when industry was still booming and the demand for labour strong? How would the trade unions respond? With these thoughts in mind, I decided upon making an appeal which could perhaps influence the uncertain but not unfriendly mood of both sides of industry. Remembering my long association with the North-East Coast, and believing that the memories of past troubles would make the people of that area especially sensitive to any weaknesses in the national economy which might threaten their continued prosperity, I selected for my platform the City of Newcastle, where I spoke to the Northern Conservative Club on 25 May.

After reviewing the general situation and giving an account of the Government's action to date, I came straight to the point—the vital question of prices:

What makes prices rise? Oh, I know what you will say—the Government. I wish it were as simple as that.

Of course, some people argue that the Government ought to fix all prices. They could do this—it is said—either by controls or subsidies. Well, if we do it by controls, it's obvious that we must also fix wages, salaries and profits.

It's a possible system—but it isn't really consistent with freedom and democracy. It's the end of the trade unionist as well as of the capitalist.

I then turned to the suggestion that prices could perhaps be kept down by subsidies:

c

We tried that with food—and when the subsidies got to nearly £500 million a year even a Socialist Chancellor of the Exchequer had to call a halt.

I have thought it right to bring these subsidies to an end. For it's obvious that—whether it be food, or coal, or transport, or gas, or electricity—if we allow wages and salaries to rise (without a corresponding increase in production), and then try to clamp down on the natural results of such rises by subsidising certain basic prices out of taxation, we are very far from reducing the excess of home demand which threatens our exports. On the contrary, we are increasing it.

It was clear that if this additional money was pumped into the system it must go somewhere. If the prices of certain goods and services were kept artificially low by subsidy, the demand for other goods and services would correspondingly increase. In any event, even after the removal of the remaining food subsidies and taking account of the last round of wage-increases in the nationalised industries, prices would not rise by more than two or three points during the current year. Nor did I believe that there would be any substantial effect on the cost of living, either as the result of fluctuations in the cost of food because of weather, or from any unfavourable turn of the terms of trade.

To sum up: it seemed that neither internal costs nor action by the Government, nor action by the nationalised industries were likely to cause any significant rise in prices. The only factor that could lead to a major increase in prices and costs would be that which lay within the power of the organised forces of industry. The foreigner could not injure us, the Government could not help. The issue lay with the employers and the trade unions—the management and the men in industry and commerce. We were already on a plateau of price stability. We could stay there if we chose.

I do not say that there should be no flexibility or minor adjustments. As production rises and techniques improve, of course such changes are right and proper. But another general round of increases, such as we have had, cannot be repeated without disaster. It won't bring any benefit to anyone. It would only benefit men in a particular industry if they were the only ones to get it. But they won't be. If one starts, others will follow. No one will gain anything, except more and more paper money, which will buy less and less.

It was for this reason, I concluded, that the Prime Minister and I, in co-operation with the employers and the trade unions, wished to devise a policy which could bring us, if we could implement it, lasting benefits.

The first reaction from the trade union leaders was by no means hostile.

All the unions are about to have conferences, and all will recommend increases in wages, with varying degrees of urgency and insistence. But I hope that the Government lead will bring the employers to the point of resisting these demands. If they do, nobody will be more pleased than the moderate trade union 'leaders'.[1]

But I soon realised that, whatever was said in public, the test would not be what new wage-claims were presented. The test would be how far they were pressed.

At the end of the month I repeated the theme of the Newcastle speech to a large meeting of British Chambers of Commerce, where it was well received.

As usual, there were irritating mistakes and apparent contradictions. For instance, an increase in the price of coal, long agreed upon, was not properly explained, and appeared as the beginning, instead of the end-result, of a series of wage-claims which had been under negotiation for many months. Nor were tempers in the House of Commons improved by a troublesome dispute in the motor industry which arose primarily in the British Motor Corporation factories about the dismissal of a number of men. Since this appeared to be concerned with the method, or rather lack of method, of negotiation, rather than with the actual decisions of the managers, there seemed a good hope of settlement. But the dispute was not well handled, and a strike began on Monday 23 July. It was confined to the B.M.C. factories and did not spread throughout the industry. Moreover, many of the men stayed at work. The Minister

[1] 28 May 1956.

of Labour assured me that he did not intend to interfere, basing himself on the private advice of the trade union leaders.

From the broader point of view, what was needed was a proper method of arranging for the mobility of labour. This was all the more necessary because the extreme inflation was beginning to be reduced. In other words, the prescribed medicine was working. I learnt with pleasure that five-sixths of the displaced men had found work elsewhere; and when the dispute was finally brought to an end on 10 August, we had certainly gained rather than lost from the economic point of view. It was clear, however, that this question of redundancy must be faced. In speaking to the National Production Advisory Council at the end of July, I laid great stress on the fact that the State could not guarantee individual jobs or prevent redundancy without getting very near to direction of labour. Surely we must devise means of alleviating the hardship and improving the conditions under which men could change their jobs or be trained in new techniques. This was the beginning of a system which has now been considerably extended.

Our efforts continued till the end of the year with, on the whole, gratifying success. On 29 August I held a Press conference at the Treasury, making a further plea for wage and price stability.

We had worked very hard at the text—and I think it was a good effort. Clem Leslie did most of it; I altered it in detail and tone; and the Treasury boys got the facts right. I sent a copy to [Sir Vincent] Tewson (Secretary of T.U.C.) who was rather alarmed at such a clear appeal to the Congress (which is just about to meet). I made some alterations to help his point of view. Tewson is a good fellow. . . .[1]

Although when the Congress met they formally rejected my appeal,

both . . . by the [terms of their] motion and in their speeches, they have really admitted my case. They have not reverted at all to profits and dividends. They have not really attacked the employers. They have attacked the Government for abandoning 'planning'. This is really rather a battle of words, because (except for the building control) we operate a pretty stringent system of

[1] 29 August 1956.

general and even particular planning controls. Capital Issues Committee (which means that you can't borrow £10,000 without permission); Hire-Purchase; Import Licensing; the Credit Squeeze and all the rest. It's really a fake attack, and is only used as a smoke-screen to cover the trade union leaders.[1]

It was difficult not to feel that this chatter about planning was a mere evasion. I therefore took the opportunity to take up this theme where the trade unions left off. This I did on 19 September in a speech to my constituents. It was really humbug to say that anyone wanted a 'fully planned economy'. No one had pointed out more clearly than Gaitskell that a fully planned economy must involve

> 'a national wages policy, and a control of labour'. 'There is no difficulty,' he wrote, 'in preventing a wage–price spiral where free collective bargaining does not exist and trade unions are simply the instruments of State policy.'

Gaitskell had gone on, in a very pregnant passage, as follows:

> Whereas in a free economy this [the free system] could easily lead to a balance of payments crisis, in a fully planned economy no such consequence follows. . . . The only effect would be longer queues, a growth of the black market and a rise in prices. And the ensuing discontent which in a democracy could bring down a Government can be ignored in a totalitarian dictatorship.

We might disagree, I declared, about the precise methods of control or guidance, but the differences between us were in reality very narrow margins. It had almost come down to the question as to whether there was to be a new building control, and to whether we were to restore and strengthen import controls.

> These are important issues. But they are not, in my view, articles of faith. They are not dogmatic truths for which men should face the stake; above all, they are not matters on which labour and capital should knock each other about and bring the whole country to ruin.

This again was well reported and supported by leading articles.

[1] 3 September 1956.

The *Daily Herald* really had nothing to say in reply—only that it was 'feeble'. Of course they know that it is not possible to refute the arguments.[1]

During the rest of the year I maintained steady pressure of propaganda and pleading on the same lines. While my policies did not receive the public approbation of trade union leaders (which I could not expect), in fact the so-called 'plateau', greeted with much derisory criticism, was successfully maintained for a period of many months, giving a corresponding relief to the pressure upon the economic system.

[1] 20 September 1956.

CHAPTER III

Plan G

IN order that the reader may understand the state of the various movements for European integration when I became Chancellor of the Exchequer at the end of 1955, it is necessary briefly to recapitulate the developments in previous years.

In the period immediately following the Second World War the statesmen of the world were faced with a distracted and divided Europe. Yet out of this slough of despair there rose, through the European movement, a new feeling of hope. In the spring of 1948, under the high authority of Churchill, a triumphant conference was held at The Hague, attended by leading politicians and other notabilities from all the countries of Western Europe. As a result, after much discussion and some opposition from the British Government, an organ of European unity came into being at Strasbourg in 1949 under the title of the Council of Europe.[1] This consisted of two bodies, one composed of Ministers and the other of delegates from the various European Parliaments. It is not difficult to see what were the main causes for the wave of enthusiasm which swept through Continental Europe. If the movement did not yet command any popular support in Britain, this was no doubt because our island had been spared the cruel experience of actual invasion.

There was a widespread determination throughout Western Europe that the terrible conflicts in which France and Germany had been locked in three destructive wars—1870, 1914 and 1939—must never be repeated. These struggles, involving in the two world wars almost every European country, had brought untold loss, human and material, to their populations and now at last threatened their traditional pre-eminence in the world. The first motive, therefore,

[1] See *Tides of Fortune*, chaps 7 and 8.

and perhaps the strongest, which influenced the enthusiasts was the hope of a final end of the age-long rivalry between Teuton and Gaul. However bitter their memories, over three generations, a great part of the French nation, especially young people, were determined 'to shake off the past—to rescue the world from the reign of the dead'. Nevertheless, there was a not unnatural suspicion and even fear which caused many French anxieties, especially among older people, and threatened any French Government which moved too rapidly towards this goal. Many hesitated long between the present fear of an aggressive Russia and the future danger of a renascent Germany.

An equally powerful motive for European unity was a realisation that in comparison with the population and potential resources of the giants of East and West—Russia and the United States—the nations of Europe could scarcely hope to preserve their independence, and certainly could not expect to exert their old influence in a changing world unless they could form themselves into a sufficiently coherent and powerful unit, operating as a whole—politically, economically and militarily.

In the early years the movement towards European unity, or integration, or whatever the phrase might be, seemed to be moving surely, if slowly, towards the realisation of its ambitions. The position of Great Britain was generally recognised by the statesmen of Europe to be unique owing to the prior claims of her Imperial commitments and the mutual obligations between the Old Country and the nations of the Commonwealth. But it was confidently hoped to find a method by which these obligations could be safeguarded and Britain could be fully associated with the unfolding life of Europe.

Meanwhile there was a broad division in the movement between the extremists and the moderates. There were the Federalists—those who looked forward to a United States of Europe, similar to the United States of America, comprising all the non-Communist countries in a federal and democratic system, electing federal organs in which the constituent nations would be reduced to the position of dependent states within the federal union. The more prudent supporters of the movement realised that in the independent development and separate histories of the European countries, with different languages and traditions, some with republican, others with monarchical institutions, there was no real analogy with the situation in which the English-speaking colonies, revolting from Britain, were able to form themselves into the federation of the United States of America. These accordingly maintained that Europe should be brought into a 'confederation'—not a federation—in which there would develop some organs to which over-riding powers could be granted, for specific purposes in the general interest. If these were to become supra-national bodies in particular spheres, economic or military, or even political, they would result from an agreed transfer of sovereignty to a central organ to meet each particular need. This was all the more necessary if Europe was to include all the countries of Western Europe and not to suffer a further subdivision; for some of the European countries, like Sweden, were determined to follow a policy of neutrality so far as defence was concerned. The pattern of the new Europe, if it was to be comprehensive, must therefore be flexible; above all, it must be pragmatic not theoretical.

While these constitutional discussions were going on at Strasbourg and in the capitals of Europe, urgent needs had to be met and immediate dangers to be faced. Here, in both the economic and military sphere, a Europe stricken and destroyed by war could not rely upon its own efforts. The economy of Europe was to be restored through the Marshall Plan. It may now be convenient for some critics to forget this historical fact; but it can never be anything except an act of deep ingratitude to minimise the massive aid which the Government and the people of America gave to their stricken comrades, ex-enemy as well as allies. In order to operate this majestic concept effectively, some machinery was required. Hence the creation of the Organisation for European Economic Co-operation (O.E.E.C.).[1] Similarly, in order to withstand what appeared to be dangerous Soviet aggression, the North Atlantic Treaty Organisation (NATO) was hastily devised, to which not merely European countries but the United States and Canada made generous contributions. Indeed, from an objective view, it was the American

[1] See *Tides of Fortune*, p. 117.

military strength and resources which alone gave reality to the Atlantic Alliance.

There thus appeared at an early point a dualism of approach, if not an actual conflict. As regards economic co-operation, the Schuman Plan for the European Coal and Steel Community was launched in May 1950, covering a vital part of industrial production. Owing to the unwillingness of Britain to join, the Community became in effect an effort limited to six countries in the centre of the West European continent, excluding the nations on the periphery. The same Governments attempted to set up a European defence system on an analogous plan. But since this involved the rearmament of Western Germany progress was less rapid. Indeed nearly three years were spent in a long and often acrimonious dispute as to the principles on which the 'European Army' was to be formed. Ultimately, the European Defence Community, to which the six European Governments had adhered, was rejected by the French Assembly. The problem of the rearmament and participation of a separate German force in NATO was only resolved at the end of 1954 by the efforts of Eden's diplomacy.[1] It is ironic to recall that through all these years fear of German recovery and suspicion of German motives made the French Parliament and people unwilling to admit the Germans as armed allies. It was only because Britain undertook heavy military responsibilities in Europe that the French finally agreed. Only by the British promise to keep troops in Europe for fifty years was France persuaded to accept final reconciliation with Germany.

Thus, when I was appointed Foreign Secretary in the spring of 1955, there seemed not one straight and simple road towards the objective of unity in Europe but several paths, sometimes parallel, sometimes crossing each other. Was the unit of co-operation to be extended into the concept of a North Atlantic Treaty Alliance? Was this to replace the European ideal? At the other extreme, was Europe, already partitioned between East and West, Communist and Free, to be again divided between the three great countries of the Western continent—France, Germany and Italy—with Holland, Belgium and Luxembourg at their side, and the rest, led by Britain?

[1] See *Tides of Fortune*, chap. 14.

Was the economic future of Europe to lie in the O.E.E.C., more comprehensive in its membership than even the Council of Europe, or was it to be based upon the Schuman concept, now to be extended into a customs union and to be entitled 'The European Economic Community', but limited to half of half of Europe? In defence, were we to rest on Western European Union, which had been the instrument for persuading the French to accept German participation, or should we concentrate upon NATO with the Americans and Canadians and other countries outside the seven who were members of W.E.U.? These were wide and baffling problems indeed.

Churchill, though careful to avoid entangling himself in detail, had always claimed that Britain's position entitled her to special consideration. She was closely allied by language, law, tradition and co-operation in two wars with the United States. She was the head of an association of free peoples then forming the British Commonwealth, based upon the old dominions of British descent—Canada, Australia, New Zealand and South Africa—and now enlarged by India, Pakistan and Ceylon. With all these she had long understandings in trade and commerce as well as in general policies. She was a European country and a part of Europe; and throughout the whole of modern history had—sometimes reluctantly, but always decisively—played her full role as a European power. But none of us had ever worked out in any detail how these different conceptions were to be reconciled. Indeed British opinion, both in the major political parties and in the nation itself, was hesitant about any new participation in Europe which might prove irreconcilable with other ties. In Churchill's last administration I had done my best to urge my colleagues to press forward and to take the lead in the integration of Europe.[1] But in spite of support from some of my friends—notably David Maxwell Fyfe, Peter Thorneycroft and Duncan Sandys—Churchill had been unwilling to press the issue against the hostility of the Foreign Office and the indifference of the Treasury. Moreover it was too late for us to reverse the Labour Government's decision not to enter into the European Coal and Steel Community. In the last years of Churchill's administration the whole European scene was dominated by the problem of defence. Until this could be

[1] *Tides of Fortune*, chaps 7, 8 and 14.

resolved and the French Government and people had reached a final decision, no progress could be made. Indeed, it is vital to an understanding of this period to realise how deep was the French distrust of Germany—especially of the Germany that might follow Adenauer, already an old man, and above all of the revival of German military power.

At a meeting in London in April 1955, the French Foreign Minister made no attempt to disguise his apprehensions. Antoine Pinay was a man of considerable quality. He was conservative on home affairs, but he was broad-minded and generous in large issues. I found him in every way an admirable colleague. He talked frankly and without reservation, and I always felt him fair and trustworthy. Moreover, we had this in common: we were both *bourgeois* and both partners in family businesses of moderate size. In the course of his visit, after reviewing many of the immediate questions arising out of the formation of Western European Union, and more especially the problem of the Saar, we discussed European affairs in general. Pinay expressed the view that E.D.C. had failed in France because its supra-national elements were unacceptable. Nevertheless, he regarded it as important that the Western powers should give evidence of their desire to continue with the integration of Europe and, in particular, to co-operate with Germany. In welcoming this I emphasised the importance of maintaining the European impetus which alone offered us the hope of keeping Germany in the European family. But too great a multiplicity of European organisations, overlapping with each other, ought to be avoided. We both agreed that the first task of W.E.U.—apart from its wider role in the field of defence—was to preside over the final Saar settlement as a symbol of Franco-German reconciliation. Nevertheless it should develop into a genuine and lively organisation through which political, as well as military, problems could be jointly discussed and settled. But we also agreed that it was important to work in close co-operation with NATO and O.E.E.C. Somehow or other the fact that a country like Switzerland was in O.E.E.C. but not in NATO, and Sweden in the Council of Europe but not in NATO, must be overcome. Europe must be comprehensive, not exclusive.

It was clear from these conversations, and those which I held

with Pinay at other times, that France relied on British support to
keep the balance of Europe in face of a reviving Germany. Some
of the smaller powers were not slow to express similar anxieties.
Although we had always made clear our reservations, we supported
the idea of 'Confederation' as a framework into which a sovereign
Germany could be fitted with advantage to Europe and indeed to
the whole world. German policies were sound at the moment; but
we had to look to the future. It would be good to know that Germany
was in full association with the other members of our European
club before any change of policy or leadership. On 9 June, therefore, I made it known throughout the Foreign Office, what was the
general attitude which I wished my fellow Ministers and the Office
to follow:

> What we must do . . . is to study how we are to clothe the
> bones of the Council of Europe and the Western European
> Union with more flesh; or perhaps really how all these various
> European organisations are to fit into one another and work
> successfully together. This raises difficult issues, but our purpose
> should definitely be, in my view, the strengthening of everything
> that leads to the unity of Europe on a basis which is acceptable to
> the British Government, that is what we used to call a confedera-
> tion as opposed to the federal concept.

The House of Commons had agreed earlier in 1955 to our accepting an association with the European Coal and Steel Community,
which was finally established in the middle of November after the
ratification of the six countries concerned. But a new and more far-
reaching—almost revolutionary—project was about to be launched.

On 10 June a conference between the six powers who were
principals of the European Coal and Steel Community was held at
Messina. At this historic meeting the pace was set by the Benelux
Governments under the leadership of Paul-Henri Spaak. Both the
French and German Governments were initially hesitant; but the
Foreign Ministers of the six countries finally agreed, although
somewhat reluctantly, to the objective of 'a general common market'
between them, and asked that an intense study should be undertaken of the steps by which it could be brought into being. From
this small seed was to grow a great and powerful tree.

Although the resolution adopted at Messina was destined to develop into the creation of the European Economic Community based on the six members of the Schuman organisation, the likelihood of a treaty being adopted in the form that it was ultimately agreed seemed at least doubtful. The actual Messina resolutions laid down four objectives. The first three were to promote the joint development of communication by road, rail and air; joint production and exchange of power resources; a common programme for development of atomic energy, taking into consideration the special arrangements already made by certain Governments with third countries. It was the fourth which was to become the vital issue. It was defined as follows: 'a common European market, free from all tariff barriers and free from all quantitative restrictions, *to be realised in stages*'.[1]

The Netherlands Foreign Minister, Dr. Johan Beyen, came to London to explain the purpose and results of the conference at a series of meetings which were presided over by Butler, then Chancellor of the Exchequer. There followed a formal invitation for Britain to take part in the work of the preparatory committee. This was fully discussed in the Cabinet, and it fell to me, as Foreign Secretary, to write the formal answer accepting this invitation. In doing so I made it clear that we did not wish to see the work of O.E.E.C. unnecessarily duplicated, or the views of other interested countries overlooked. On this understanding, we were glad to appoint a representative to take part in the studies. My letter continued as follows:

There are, as you are no doubt aware, special difficulties for this country in any proposal for 'a European common market'. They [H.M.G.] will be happy to examine, without prior commitment and on their merits, the many problems which are likely to emerge from the studies and in doing so will be guided by the hope of reaching solutions which are in the best interests of all parties concerned.[2]

[1] *Monthly Survey of Foreign Affairs* (Conservative Research Department, July 1955), no. 76, p. 7.
[2] Quoted by Miriam Camps, *Britain and the European Community 1955–63* (London, 1964), p. 30.

We used the word 'representative' in order to make clear that the Under-Secretary from the Board of Trade, who was to attend on our behalf, was not a mere observer. It was our wish to take an active part in the work of the committee but, of course, without prior commitment to the resolution which was shared by the other countries. Our choice fell on R. F. Bretherton, of the Board of Trade, a man of exceptional ability who was in full sympathy with the 'European' views of his political chief, Peter Thorneycroft.

At this time Ministers in every country were becoming concerned about the relations between the various European organisations which were now developing. On 10 June, I had a long discussion with Guy Mollet, the French Prime Minister, who was on a visit to London,

> about the plans for Strasbourg. This time there will, in addition, be the meeting of the assembly of Western European Union. It is very important that there should be no friction between this new organisation and the Council of Europe.[1]

It was on this theme that I spoke at Strasbourg on 3 July, welcoming the committee which had been set up following the Messina Conference as one, but not an exclusive, method of developing the larger European unit to which all the countries of Europe were aspiring. As to the prospect of a common market being agreed upon the basis of the Benelux memorandum, which envisaged a tightly organised community with a supra-national structure in command, there seemed at this period, and in the first months of 1956, considerable scepticism. The French coolness towards the plan was well-known. German commercial and industrial interests, represented by Dr. Erhard, were definitely hostile. Although Adenauer was known to be attracted on political grounds, his economic advisers were more than doubtful. In view of the German hesitation, and the Parliamentary weakness of the French Government, it was difficult, with so many other anxieties, for the British Cabinet to bring any concentrated attention to the question. Yet no doubt we should have been more alert to the dangers. For the Messina Committee was meeting under the strong and powerful direction of Paul-Henri Spaak, and it was more than likely that he would obtain,

[1] 10 June 1955.

by one means or another, a report in line with his own ideas. Moreover we had been warned that the French attitude might well change
after the French elections. At present it was hesitating or hostile;
but when the elections were safely over French politicians would
become more favourable to the concept of the Common Market.

Towards the end of the year the result of the Saar plebiscite
became known.[1] Two-thirds of the voters were opposed to the so-
called 'Statute', which would, in effect, have severed the Saar from
Germany. Although this was a severe blow to the French Government, they

> have taken the rebuff with surprising calm and dignity. Although
> the juridical situation reverts to the *status quo ante* the Adenauer–
> Mendès-France agreement, they are going to agree to (*a*) the
> resignation of Hoffmann, (*b*) the formation of a *gouvernement
> d'affaires*, (*c*) free elections in December. So many of our fears (I
> hope) will not be realised.[2]

This moderate and statesmanlike attitude was a great relief. But
perhaps it should have indicated to us that the Franco-German
reconciliation was deeper than had previously appeared. At the
same time, those of my colleagues who had been the strongest
'Europeans' were conscious of the weakness of their support, both
in the Party and throughout the country. In the Cabinet itself there
were many, including Eden himself, who had genuine doubts in
view of our other obligations. I knew also that Butler and many of
his advisers at the Treasury shared these anxieties. I had even heard
towards the end of October that there was some talk of disengaging
ourselves, or withdrawing our representative from the work of the
committee set up at Messina. One of my oldest friends, Harry
Crookshank, who was himself strongly against commitment to
Europe, told me that he had expressed his views to Butler. Accordingly I wrote to Butler on 23 September:

> The Lord Privy Seal [Harry Crookshank] has sent me a copy
> of his letter to you of October 21 about the danger of our being
> drawn into a European Customs Union.

[1] See *Tides of Fortune*, pp. 563–6.
[2] 24 October 1955. Johannes Hoffmann was Prime Minister of the Saar.

Let me say straight away that I fully understand his pre-occupations over the potential embarrassment in our relations with the Commonwealth of becoming too closely involved in European integration. At the same time, we should have to look most carefully at the effects on our foreign policy in Europe of any attempt at disengaging ourselves from the current discussions during the next few weeks. I am sure that you would wish that all the necessary consultation should take place before any such steps were taken.

Meanwhile, I am glad to note that there is no suggestion of our withdrawing our delegate as yet. What is more, our recent information suggests that it is most unlikely that we shall have to face any decisions until the French elections have taken place next year. This should give us plenty of time to consider the report which the present [committee] is preparing.

Happily the President of the Board of Trade, Thorneycroft, was giving loyal support and encouragement to his representative. But I was anxious, if prepared to wait.

At the end of December Lady Rhys Williams, the Cassandra of our movement, wrote me a letter of warning in prophetic terms.

In my view, there is nothing for it but to take over the leadership of Europe, and to do this we cannot sit on the fence much longer about a customs union. New factories—e.g. atomic power—must be built on some intelligible plan, and people must know what is the size of the market they are building for, and what capacity plant they ought to order. If there are to be only small national markets, it is often not sense to scrap old plant, as modern American machines aren't economic unless sales are huge. Larger markets involve reducing tariffs and letting some existing industries suffer, unless they can go over to the new ideas and develop *complementary activities*. . . . But it seems to me that the 'protected by the Channel' mentality is so out of date that the risks of *not* going in with Europe are much greater than those of going in . . . a 6-Power Customs union *with Britain out*, such as America is still pushing . . . may go through unexpectedly soon if we don't take a hand to prevent it by coming in too while the door is still open.

Almost my last duty as Foreign Secretary was to defend the Government's attitude at a meeting of W.E.U. in Paris on 14 December:

> Beyen (Netherlands) and Spaak (Belgium) opened rather a sharp attack on U.K. policy regarding the 'Messina' or '6-Power' plans for a common market. . . .[1]

It seemed significant that neither the Germans nor the French spoke up at all. I could only reply that our representative was taking his full part in the discussion of the Messina Plan. We still felt that our co-operation depended upon a proper relation being established between any new structure, whether for six nations or more, with the rest of the European nations who were operating through the O.E.E.C. The situation, therefore, when I left the Foreign Office to go to the Treasury at the end of 1955, although still fluid, was one of doubt and uncertainty. It was clear to me that the weight of British opinion in the Government, in the Conservative Party, in the Opposition and in the Press was against our joining as a full partner in the Common Market, more especially if it seemed to be organised on an inward- rather than an outward-looking basis. Nevertheless, I was haunted by the fear that we might fall between two stools. From the purely economic point of view, the importance of the Commonwealth preference system must decline. What would be our position if we found ourselves excluded from the benefits of the large European market which seemed likely to develop? Moreover, although the French Government had accepted, with apparent calm, their setback over the Saar, almost in the last days of my term as Foreign Secretary they were making a strong protest about the reviving German army.

> A row is beginning to develop about the German 'Force Level'. The French are going to behave in a foolish way, I fear. . . . The more forces the Germans have, the better; especially as the French army is useless and has (anyway) gone to Morocco.[2]

This incident seemed to show that France's suspicion and fear of a reviving Germany were by no means allayed.

[1] 14 December 1955.   [2] 28 November 1955.

I was now Chancellor of the Exchequer, and since I felt that we ought to be ready with some constructive proposals, instead of waiting on events, I sent a minute on 23 January to Sir Leslie Rowan, who was in charge of overseas finance and similar questions, in the following terms:

Messina

1. We spoke about this.
2. I feel that our approach is too negative.
3. I would like to propose a joint Treasury/F.O. study by officials of possible alternatives.
4. These might be based
   (*a*) on O.E.E.C.
   (*b*) on N.A.T.O.
5. How do I arrange this?

I was worried about the perilous situation in which we might soon find ourselves. Yet it was difficult to know how to proceed. On 1 February I summarised my apprehensions in a note which I sent to the Head of the Treasury, Sir Edward Bridges. In this I referred to my talks with Rowan and the anxiety which he shared that we were getting into a negative position. The official view seemed to be a confident expectation that nothing would come out of Messina. In the statement which we had circulated to all the capitals at the end of 1955 we had made it clear that we were uncommitted. Although we were willing to join in the search for a solution, we had grave doubts as to the formation of a limited Common Market on an exclusive rather than an inclusive basis. This communication had been very ill-received by my colleagues in the Western European Union (I was then Foreign Secretary) and I could defend it only on the ground that Britain had so often been accused of waiting too long before making her position clear that this time we wished to risk no misunderstanding from the very start. Although there were powerful forces in France and Germany which might well prevent the Messina plan being adopted, yet there were other pressures which might operate contrary to the general expectation in Whitehall. For instance, the United States would certainly be working hard to promote the plan, on the general ground that if a United States of

America was an almost divine plan for 'God's Own Country' a similar constitution might revive a decadent Europe. The accession to power of M. Mollet in France, leaning largely on the Mouvement Républicain Populaire, would reinforce support in the Assembly for European integration. What then were we to do? Were we just to sit back and hope for the best? If we did so, it might be very dangerous to us. For perhaps Messina would come off after all; and that might mean Western Europe dominated in fact by Germany and used as an instrument for the revival of German power through economic means. It would be really giving them on a plate what we fought two wars to prevent. Of course, the great increase in Russian and American power made the danger of a revived Germany far less formidable than before and this would affect French opinion. Nevertheless I did not like the prospect of a world divided into the Russian sphere, the American sphere and a united Europe of which we were not a member.

The problem of course was easy to pose, although difficult to resolve. It was how to reconcile our position as head of the sterling area and of the Commonwealth with our place in Europe. I felt we ought to try to work out a plan however sketchy of which we should be the promoters. After all, there were many other European countries beside the Six, and these, especially the Scandinavian countries, would welcome a lead. I proposed therefore that we should set up our own team, with representatives of the Foreign Office, the Board of Trade and the Treasury, and I asked for advice as to the most practicable and acceptable method of proceeding, having regard to the divergent views in various Government departments, to get this matter going. Bridges responded nobly to my appeal, and a powerful team of officials set to work without delay.

When Eden and Selwyn Lloyd, the new Foreign Secretary, returned from their visit to the United States in February 1956, they reported to us that opinion in Washington was as enthusiastic for the Messina project as it had been for the European Defence Community. We knew the sad story of defence. The Americans were equally ignorant of all the difficulties in the new plan; they were either unaware of or hostile to the conception and strength of the Commonwealth. This was particularly true of Dulles, whose vanity more than equalled his talents. At the same time, American influence would be persistent and embarrassing. The Canadian Government had shown themselves much more alive to the risks of the creation of a high-tariff group in Europe, inward-looking and self-sufficient. It was therefore important that we should not seem merely to be fighting a rearguard action. We must make our own proposals for something which would be recognised as an advance. Yet even those must be properly timed.

The O.E.E.C. was about to meet, and we had to devise a policy which would somehow reconcile the various plans. The Prime Minister told me a few days later, on 25 February, that Spaak had written to him enquiring as to the probable British attitude. What reply should we make? I advised him

> that there were great disadvantages in a detailed and reasoned reply on this subject at this moment. We ourselves need time to examine whether there are some counter-proposals we can make which will be not less attractive to Europe but less damaging to us than those made by M. Spaak. On his side also, they are really very far from knowing precisely what it is they want to do or can do.

It would therefore be wise to write only briefly and allow me to discuss the broad situation with Spaak at the meeting in Paris at the end of the month.

It had been reported to the Council of O.E.E.C. that the French were acting in various respects contrary to their undertakings. As chairman it was a somewhat embarrassing duty for me to enter a protest. Accordingly, I went to call on Paul Ramadier, the French Minister of Finance.

> He is a dear old boy, shrewd and very tenacious. My object was to protest at the flagrant way in which the French disregard their obligations under O.E.E.C. They pay export subsidies and special import taxes, against the rules and openly flouting their commitments. I got very smooth words from him, but I doubt if we shall get much action.[1]

On 28 February, Spaak, an old and valued friend, came to see me before the meeting. Spaak was one of the founders of the European

[1] 27 February 1956.

Movement and the first President of the Assembly of the Council of Europe. Although an enthusiast for the principles of a united Europe, he was always moderate and reasonable in their application. He was a good friend of Britain, and looked back with pleasure and gratitude to the kindness which he had received during the war when the Belgian Government was in exile in London. Spaak

> was most friendly, but took a very depressing view of Europe. France was no good; Italy hovering on the verge of Communism; Germany becomes more and more aggressive. Could not U.K. take the lead? The Six-Power movement would fail, in spite of all his efforts, for France would never really enter a 'common market'. It would be the story of E.D.C. all over again.[1]

Spaak insisted, as often before, that coming from a small country he tried to see matters in an objective light. I am certain that he was frank and honest in his prognostications. I made a full report of this talk, which I sent to Eden and Lloyd. Spaak's most urgent plea was for Britain to seize the initiative. Without Britain there was no future for Europe except further division. Even if the Common Market came into being, which he doubted, it would be an unhappy relationship.

> Even in O.E.E.C. [the French] did not keep the rules regarding export subsidies and import taxes and he did not believe that the French economy or political system would allow them to enter into a common market.

At the same time he thought this was the last possible opportunity for uniting Europe. For his part he did not care about rules and regulations.

> When he suggested the Common Market, he had not believed it possible that the French would accept, and he knew in his heart that they had only accepted with reservations. They would never implement it. Therefore, he would appeal to you and me and any other British people to take the lead in the creation of a united Europe before it was too late.[1]

Since Belgium was outside the conflicts of the great powers, I

[1] 28 February 1956.

regarded his advice as particularly valuable; and it is worth now recalling, in the light of subsequent events, his scepticism about the future of the European Economic Community.

Peter Thorneycroft, President of the Board of Trade, was one of the keenest to find some workable solution. He had long pressed his views upon his colleagues. Until I became Chancellor of the Exchequer the Treasury did not seem inclined to join in any practical examination of a solution. Now Thorneycroft could look to the Treasury for active and sympathetic help.

Throughout the following months our interdepartmental committee—now extended in range—was hard at work. The report of the committee of the Messina powers, which had been meeting in Brussels under Spaak's chairmanship, was published in April. By the end of May it had been officially considered by the six Foreign Ministers and accepted as the basis for the drafting of two agreements, one on atomic co-operation and one on the Common Market. This work proceeded throughout the summer and autumn.

It was thus becoming urgent that we too should agree a definite plan. This was all the more necessary because the Commonwealth Prime Ministers' Conference was to open at the end of June. I kept Eden closely informed on the various solutions which were being proposed. Altogether there were nine variations on this novel and inspiring theme. As so often happens, that ultimately adopted, generally known as Plan G, was in effect that worked out the year before by Thorneycroft himself. This, however, could not be put into shape for the Government to consider until the end of July. At the Commonwealth Conference, therefore, we could only inform the Prime Ministers of the situation which was developing. Since we were not able to present any specific proposals they were naturally contented to issue warnings in general terms. These were sometimes, perhaps not unnaturally, rather one-sided. For instance, the Australians wanted

to abolish (or whittle away to nothing) U.K. preferences in Australia, but keep—and improve—their favoured position in our market. We had two hours or more of very tough negotiations—and got nowhere at all. I thought Bob Menzies seemed rather ashamed, but McEwen (Country Party) was ruthless and unsmiling.[1]

Most of the delegates became more sympathetic as the discussion proceeded. Others enlarged their knowledge without abating their prejudices.

There were other anxieties. It was important, for instance, that we should not commit ourselves to any long-term assurances to British agriculture which would leave us too little room for manœuvre. We should now have to deal with three problems at the same time—agriculture in Europe, the interests of Australia and New Zealand and the legitimate needs of British farming. This was my first introduction to the maze of difficulty through which we were to seek to thread our way a few years later.

At the O.E.E.C. meeting on 17–19 July there were two problems closely allied. The first was that of Euratom and how far it would be possible to obtain co-operation between the Six and the rest of the European countries on atomic development. As a result of the discussions it was clear that a clash between the two groups could be avoided and complementary plans developed if there was the real will to work out an agreement. But the main question was that of trade liberalisation. Prior to the meeting the low tariff countries—Benelux, Norway, Sweden, Switzerland—had circulated a project for the automatic reduction of tariffs on those goods which figure largely in inter-European trade. But they made it clear that, before further reducing quantitative restrictions or agreeing to the 90 per cent liberalisation which was the declared purpose of all the constituent countries, they required some definite decision to be taken by the European countries as a whole. It was not easy to reconcile this position with the restricted Messina system.

As chairman of the Council it was my duty to give a dinner to the delegates, and I thought it right to refer to our special troubles:

Since I took over my present job, just six months ago, I have had plenty of advice. Advice is about the only thing of which the price has not risen in recent years. It has never been rationed. It's free—and in good supply. Indeed, there's always a surplus. I have

[1] 13 July 1956. John McEwen was the Australian Minister for Trade.

been strongly pressed to deal with our present difficulties at home by turning our back on liberalisation, and by limiting imports through a rigid system of import controls. This is the constant theme—day after day—and debate after debate, of all my critics. It is the demand of all the Opposition leaders, and of some of my own political friends. It is urged by much of what is called 'progressive opinion' and by many economists or self-styled economists. It sounds very easy. If you are importing too much, just slap on controls. The temptation to yield has indeed been great. But I have resisted. On the contrary, we have decided to make a move in the opposite direction—and meet our obligations to O.E.E.C. by accepting 90 per cent liberalisation.

This announcement was received with enthusiasm. When, therefore, the Secretary-General proposed that a special group should be set up to study all possible forms of co-operation between the Messina group and the European countries outside the Six, this was readily accepted.

On returning to London, I was able to announce in Parliament on 20 July that, as chairman of the O.E.E.C., I had tried to guide our work into useful collaboration between the two sets of countries —those inside and those outside the Messina plan. The British Government welcomed these studies by O.E.E.C. because it was only in the light of them that we could find a method—all methods being, in principle, open—by which we could most usefully co-operate. This at least held the position pending a decision by my colleagues as to what plan, if any, we should put forward as our contribution. By the end of July, Thorneycroft and I were able to circulate an agreed paper resulting from the work of the officials of the Foreign Office, the Treasury, the Board of Trade, the Ministry of Agriculture, the Commonwealth Relations Office, the Colonial Office, Customs and Excise, and the Bank of England. It was a long and complicated document, but we were anxious that it should be available for study in order that we could reach a definite conclusion in September as to whether we should put it forward to the O.E.E.C. working party as the British contribution. The plan in its final form was based on the assumption that the Six would succeed in forming a common market or customs union. It was, therefore, proposed

that there should be a Free Trade Area consisting of the Six—
regarded as a single unit—the United Kingdom and such other
O.E.E.C. countries as we hoped would agree to join. These would
almost certainly include Norway, Sweden, Denmark, Switzerland
and Austria in the first instance.

Foodstuffs were to be excluded. There was, of course, considerable difficulty in forming a precise definition. But this could be a
matter for negotiation. It certainly seemed at the time that the
difficulty of fully freeing trade in agricultural products, even among
the Six, was so great that there seemed little likelihood of reconciling
the divergent interests between France, Italy and Germany, quite
apart from the special needs of Holland and the fruit and horti-
cultural producers. This made us hope that all European countries,
even the Messina group, would be content to leave agriculture as a
matter for long-term discussion. On all other goods we proposed
that tariffs should be progressively eliminated over a period, perhaps
of ten years. Quotas would equally be abandoned, except for an
escape clause to deal with any balance of payments crisis. Even this
relaxation must be operated under strict conditions and protective
quotas would not be allowed. We and other participating countries
would retain our existing freedom of action as to tariffs and imports
from the rest of the world, subject to commitments under the
General Agreement on Tariffs and Trade (GATT). We should remain
free to give free entry to Commonwealth goods. The preferences
given by our tariff against imports from foreign countries outside
Europe would not be affected.

The supporters of this scheme—the British plan—had no hesitation in arguing that the Free Trade Area thus to be created would
be to the final advantage of British industry. Of course we recognised that there were difficulties in the way of excluding foodstuffs
in the first instance; we might have to help some of our European
friends, especially in pigs, bacon and perhaps fruit. This, however,
would be a matter for discussions outside the main plan.

At the same time as the document was distributed to the Cabinet,
the President of the Board of Trade and I circulated a memorandum
urging our colleagues to accept these proposals. The Commonwealth system of preferences, we argued, was becoming eroded and

less valuable for British industry. A European Free Trade Area would create a market comparable in size and resources to the United States of America. The scheme would give us an opportunity of re-establishing the commercial leadership of Europe. We believed that if we could act quickly we had a good chance of getting general agreement. Of course there would be difficulties and disappoint-ments on the agricultural side, but it was common knowledge that the Six would have great problems to overcome amongst themselves. We were not without hope that the countries of Europe as a whole would see a great gain in the additional strength given to Europe by the Free Trade Area. We might have to make some concessions here and there, but we believed that our scheme could be made to hold the field. There would, of course, be criticism of our proposal to exclude foodstuffs from the Free Trade Area. Apart from the inherent difficulties, we did not disguise our wish to preserve the interests of Commonwealth countries, and to preserve what re-mained of the preferential system. But given the confused state of Europe, with Germany ambivalent and Russia menacing, we hoped that our European friends would realise that the strength of the Commonwealth added to the security of the Free World as a whole.

On 4 September Spaak came to London to see me.

We then had a long talk (with a host of officials) about O.E.E.C., the Messina plan and the possibility of British association (what we call Plan G). It was a most useful discussion, but of course the great problem remains for H.M.G. to settle 'will we, won't we?' The arguments have been admirably deployed in a number of papers by our officials, but the great decision remains with us Ministers to take.[1]

It seems strange, looking back over the years, that Ministers were so doubtful about the proposal which now seems so clearly to our advantage, had we been able to obtain the consent of the other European countries. But all of us were naturally looking to the traditions and struggles of the past. We could hardly foresee the rapidity of change over the next decade. The Commonwealth and Empire constituted a powerful force, politically and militarily,

[1] 4 September 1956.

as well as economically. Most of the European countries were more anxious about Germany even than about Russia. It still seemed unlikely that the Messina group would be able to agree upon a treaty to implement the Common Market. The French Government was weak, with continual changes of personnel and a certain hold upon the Assembly and the nation. The European concept made little appeal to the imagination of our people at home. Up to now, the movement had commanded no mass support. British industry was divided; but we were still living in a period in which protection, in one form or another, either through exchange or other methods of control, was still a comfort to the less competitive and the less efficient. It was not easy, therefore, to persuade our colleagues to take the plunge.

On 5 September we had a three-hour meeting of the Economic Policy Committee of the Cabinet, at which we decided to discuss Plan G before it finally came to the Cabinet. To my surprise nearly all the Ministers present were enthusiastic for this venture.

It was an excellent discussion, first on the merits and demerits of the policy; second, on the chances of being able to sell it to the Commonwealth and to the British people. I was much impressed by the combination of knowledge and enthusiasm of these younger Ministers. . . . But I cannot disguise from myself that it will in fact be very difficult to persuade the whole Cabinet and very hard to sell to the Party and the people. What we are all agreed is that we cannot paddle in these dangerous waters. We must either stay on the bank or plunge boldly into the flood and strike for the opposite shore.[1]

The Commonwealth Finance Ministers' meeting was to take place at Washington on 26 September. It was, therefore, necessary to reach some conclusions before that date. In spite of other preoccupations now beginning to press upon Ministers, and in spite of the vast documentation which had begun to appear, the discussions were informed and fair. The younger Ministers seemed definitely favourable; some of the older ones doubtful or hostile. Without reaching a definite decision it was agreed that I should

[1] 5 September 1956.

discuss our proposals in general terms with our colleagues from the Commonwealth.

This meeting took place at the British Embassy in Washington in the last days of September. A document had been prepared setting out as shortly as possible the plan which the British Cabinet had now under serious discussion.[1]

As agreed, Peter Thorneycroft *explained* the plan, as objectively as possible. Then I followed with some account of the political background. Then we distributed a memorandum and had a short adjournment for them to study it. (Each Finance Minister had, of course, received a letter from me giving some account of it, before this meeting.)[2]

We then were able to add some details. The United Kingdom would enter a Free Trade Area together with the Messina Six acting as a single unit, and all other O.E.E.C. countries that wished to join, which we believed would gradually include almost all European countries. We should not expect the area to include dependent territories of any of the principals, as opposed to independent dominions, but this would remain uncertain until we had reactions to the main proposals. We had informed the Common Market countries that we were already consulting our own Commonwealth friends. The Free Trade Area would cover all commodities without exception—except foodstuffs, which we now broadly defined to include feeding stuffs, drink and tobacco. Within the area tariffs—except revenue tariffs in the strict sense—protective quotas, and all other protective devices, including export taxes and controls and export subsidies, would be reduced and ultimately abolished by stages over a period of about ten years. The members of the Free Trade Area would retain their existing freedom of action as regards tariffs for the rest of the world, subject of course to commitments under GATT. Indeed this was the essential difference between a free trade area and a customs union. This provision would completely protect the interests of the Commonwealth countries. There would be no discrimination by the Messina Six in each other's favour against the other principals of the Free

[1] See Appendix One.   [2] 29 September 1956.

Trade Area. In other words the tariff reduction timetable would apply all through. We would retain certain rights to protect sterling in emergencies. The new Free Trade Area would work under the present GATT and O.E.E.C. rules and be bound by them. This plan would not be contrary, but indeed complementary, to freer world trade and international payments and should lead, in due course, to general convertibility. It should be regarded as a step forward to the world reduction of trade barriers. The very size of the Free Trade Area, and the extent of its interests outside Europe, would ensure that it did not develop into an inward-looking regional bloc.

The document was not a long one, and after an adjournment we had a period for an hour or more when each of the Ministers asked questions. I then concluded the discussion.

I thought the Ministers and their advisers took the plan very well. But, of course, there will be trouble when the inevitable Press leakages begin.[1]

There was no question, at that time, of Britain becoming one of the Six, even if the Messina powers, which were still hesitating, reached the point of signing a definite treaty. It was then universally believed that our obligations to the Commonwealth and our outside interests made it impossible for us to adhere to a tightly drawn plan for a Common Market, with all its supra-national apparatus. The controversy and the doubts were confined to whether we should make a determined effort to promote the creation of a European Free Trade Area of as many nations in Europe as could be persuaded to join, of which the Common Market group was to be one. Even this was thought by many of our Cabinet colleagues to be entering doubtful and dangerous ground. Nor could its promoters claim any general approval in the political parties or the nation at large.

The news of Plan G and reports of the Washington talks naturally appeared immediately in the Press:

The Sunday papers carried it as a headline story, and the Monday and Tuesday papers have a great deal about the European plan. On the whole, this is to the good, although I fear that

[1] 29 September 1956.

many of the papers have got the plan wrong in many important details. No. 10 and the Treasury people have done their best to put this right, and also (which is most important) to make clear that our discussions in Washington were only tentative and that we have reached—as a Government—no final decision.[1]

I got back to London on 2 October and saw the Prime Minister on the same day. Naturally there were many other preoccupations,

> chiefly Suez and United Nations, Jordan and Arab states gener-
> ally, the dangers of another Nasser coup, and the possibility of a
> Russian intervention.[1]

Eden was personally sympathetic to our plan, which he approved; but he warned me that there would be troubles in the Cabinet and within the Party. Many of the older members were doubtful, or even opposed. However, now that the plan had 'leaked', it was important that it should be properly understood. Therefore

> I persuaded P.M. to let me have a [Press] conference (with
> Peter Thorneycroft) in order to put the whole European plan on
> a right footing. He readily agreed—but I could see that Butler
> didn't like it. But (right or wrong as the plan may be) it's as well
> to have it put before the public, here and overseas, correctly and
> accurately.[1]

The next morning, 3 October, it was soon clear that the great majority of my colleagues were in favour of our putting forward our plan—some were enthusiastic, others resigned. In any case, I felt that we had now passed the point of no return. The Press conference was duly held and went off pretty well. My next step was to write to Spaak, in whose wisdom and discretion I had every confidence, to try to keep the situation among the Six as fluid as possible. I told him of the outcome of my talks at Washington with the Commonwealth Ministers and the development of opinion at home. Although the Cabinet would not take any final decision until we got some further reaction from the Commonwealth Prime Ministers, I was hopeful of the result. My letter continued:

> I am writing to you now to let you know the exact position.
> These are difficult and complicated questions, and we shall need

[1] 2 October 1956.

a little time to complete our consideration of them. On the other hand, bearing in mind our conversation when you were last in London, I would earnestly hope that at your meeting with the Foreign Ministers next week, you will be able to keep things as fluid as possible, so as to permit us and other countries to associate with the Customs Union in a wider free trade area if we find we can do so. Binding decisions at this stage might make this difficult.

In view of our long association in the European movement, I feel sure you will wish to help me at this time.

The Conservative Party Conference that year was held at Llandudno; a charming resort, with agreeable restaurants on the land and a fascinating type of jellyfish basking in the sea. The weather was perfect—a real St. Luke's summer. Naturally the crisis in the Middle East caused by Nasser's actions and menaces occupied the main attention of the delegates. But there was considerable interest also in the European question. It seemed proper to give, in general terms, an account of our new initiatives, and to warn the conference of the dangers, both of action and inaction, at this stage. In my speech on 12 October I said:

I must emphasise that the Government has not reached final decisions. But we have entered upon discussions with the Commonwealth on the plan. We shall discuss it with representatives of industry, employers and employed. We must soon decide whether to enter on discussions with our friends in Europe.

I do not conceal from the Conference that there are great risks in this policy; but there are also great prizes. Our industry will have to meet competition. But it must be competitive, or it will lose its export markets in any case, whether inside or outside Europe. Modern factory production requires large markets and big economic units. This is the secret of American success.

I concluded by appealing to the long tradition of the Party, which had always been resilient and even pragmatic in its philosophy:

our party has never been afraid of new ideas, from Benjamin Disraeli to Joseph Chamberlain. While our opponents still cling, with all the fervour of bigoted devotees, to the obsolete dogmas of an outworn socialist creed, we must reach out into new and dramatic fields of endeavour.

We must live, not *in* the past, but *for* the future.

The Foreign Ministers of the Six were now due to meet on 20 October. Early reports had suggested that something very near a breakdown in the negotiations had occurred. Later versions, however, stated that compromises had been reached on a number of points, although no final agreement had been made. The Germans were thought to be very unwilling to accept the French proposals for the harmonisation of wages, particularly as regards the length of the working week and overtime. They also objected to the proposed monopoly provisions of Euratom. In other words, they were torn between the political appeal of six-power integration and their practical objections to French preponderance. The French, on the other hand, the closer they came to the point of decision, became increasingly concerned to secure all possible safeguards to make their entry into the Customs Union a relatively painless operation.

The British Government had now to reach a definite conclusion before the debate on European policy which must take place when Parliament met. A growing body of opinion in the country now favoured the plan. Commonwealth Governments were, on the whole, not strongly opposed, though naturally not enthusiastic. Accordingly, Thorneycroft and I requested, and obtained, the approval of our colleagues to go ahead.

In informing the House of our intention to open negotiations with O.E.E.C., I set out as clearly as I could the triple duties which lay upon Britain:

We in this island are founder-members of the great community with which we all feel the strongest of ties, and that community is of great importance to all of us in our daily lives. No small part of our own economic and financial strength and that of our partners depends upon our association with the various countries, independent and dependent, within the British Commonwealth. And, even stronger than these most material interests, are, of course, deep emotional bonds.[1]

[1] *Hansard*, 26 November 1956.

D

Secondly,

> we are European geographically and culturally, and we cannot, even if we would, dissociate ourselves from Europe. We are moved by the continued efforts in the post-war world to strengthen the unity and the cohesion of the old world.[1]

Finally, we must bear in mind that

> we are members of a great alliance which itself links across the Atlantic the old world and the new, and we can never be unmindful of any of these three forces at work upon us.[1]

We had therefore to search for a course of action which, while serving the vital domestic interests of our island people, would enable us to play our role in strengthening Europe as an integral part of the whole free world. At the same time, we must not neglect to strengthen our Commonwealth links.

Wilson replied with a careful and objective speech, and the whole debate was carried on at a high level. It had a special interest for me, as my son Maurice made his maiden speech on this occasion. He pleased the House by referring to me as 'my right hon. Friend the Chancellor, whom I am only moderately happy to see in his place'.[1]

It was clear from the general mood that in spite of many misgivings on both sides of the House there would be general support for the Government in proceeding with the plan which had been outlined. Nevertheless, since the House of Commons finds it difficult to deal with more than one great issue at a time, there was a certain unreality about the discussions, for we had now reached and even passed the climax of the Middle Eastern crisis in which we had been gripped for five months or more.

[1] *Hansard*, 26 November 1956.

CHAPTER IV

The Anglo-American Schism

URING my short tenure of the Foreign Office from April to December 1955 the situation in the Middle East was a cause for anxiety and often alarm. It had not yet developed into crisis. During 1955 we carried out our obligations in strict conformity with our undertakings. We took the first steps towards the total evacuation of the Canal Zone by the military, leaving only civilian engineers in charge. The last stage was not completed until June 1956; but our military presence had already faded to almost nothing. We made way for an independent Government in the Sudan without any irreparable dispute with the Egyptian Government, although with their reluctant consent. We made generous arrangements for the release of sterling to Egypt, and we agreed to provide arms on a limited scale. There remained the problem of the blockade against Israel and the dangers of an attack by Gamal Abdel Nasser upon Israeli territory. In May 1955, Moshe Sharett, the Israeli Prime Minister, asked the United States for a positive guarantee; but Dulles took the line that it was impossible to guarantee frontiers which had not been agreed between Israel and her neighbours. Although this may have been a logical decision, it was not altogether helpful. If a general agreement could be reached between Israel and the Arab states concerned, a guarantee would become almost superfluous. Meanwhile, we gave full support to the elaborate plan which Dulles had contributed for a settlement of the Arab–Israeli dispute.[1] When this failed it was difficult to resist the Israeli argument that if a guarantee had to await a final settlement this was in effect giving Nasser a power of veto.

Throughout the summer of 1955, Nasser's propaganda and subversive intrigues in almost every Arab state were beginning to

[1] See *Tides of Fortune*, p. 631.

bring about an increasing sense of insecurity. The sudden incursion of Russian diplomacy into a sphere from which they had, up to now, kept aloof was a new factor. The large supply of arms, nominally from Czechoslovakia, was a grave departure from previous Russian policy and caused the Western powers corresponding anxiety. If we armed Israel in return, we should lose all hold upon the Arabs; if we refused, Israel might be tempted into a preventive war. Nevertheless, rightly or wrongly, and in spite of the small response which Nasser was making to all our approaches, Eden and I agreed with Dulles to help Egypt in the ambitious scheme to improve the irrigation of the Nile Valley and to develop hydro-electric power by building a new dam across the Nile some miles south of the existing dam at Aswan. British, French and German firms had already joined in a consortium to carry out this project. The Governments of all three countries were willing to give substantial financial aid. The United States Government agreed to assist, and in view of the large sums involved the World Bank was brought in to play a leading part. By the end of 1955, after prolonged negotiations, an understanding with the Egyptians had been virtually reached. Naturally, since the World Bank was dealing with the money entrusted to it, certain guarantees were required, but they were not unreasonable or unusual. The dam must be given priority over other projects; contracts must be awarded on a competitive basis, and the usual degree of supervision that was inherent in the World Bank procedure must be applied. At the end of 1955 I was hopeful that, although the arguments might be long and tedious, an agreement was in sight.

In 1956, the year opened badly with rioting in Jordan, clearly fomented by Egypt. Nevertheless, it appeared that the game was not altogether lost.

> The young King of Jordan is keeping his head and playing up very well. The old feud with the Saudis (now reinforced by . . . oil money and Egyptian ambition) has taken a new form. With this vast revenue . . . they are trying to buy every leading man and newspaper throughout the Middle East. They have also spent large sums in organising sedition in Jordan and elsewhere. After some anxious days, the Arab Legion (under Glubb Pasha) seem to have restored order in Amman and else-

where. We have sent some reinforcements to Amman from other stations, and we have sent a parachute brigade to Cyprus to be ready to go to Jordan if necessary.[1]

I told Eden that, in my view, we ought to try, with the help of the Iraqi Government, to encourage Syria to resist the pressure from Egypt to which she was being subjected. For it was now evident that Nasser would not work with the Western powers, or co-operate in the task of securing peace. He was clearly aiming at the leadership of the Arab world, and did not want any settlement of the dispute with Israel. On the contrary, his activities, by radio and bribery, were intended to eliminate Israel completely as a separate nation.

At the beginning of February, Eden and Selwyn Lloyd paid a visit to Washington. One of the most troublesome of Dulles's experiments in vicarious brinkmanship was his attitude over the Baghdad Pact. He had used every possible pressure upon us to become full members and to give it our active support; but he continued, throughout 1955, to refuse on what seemed somewhat legalistic grounds to commit the United States to membership.[2] This decision placed the whole burden upon Britain. The Americans were anxious that we should persuade Jordan to join in order to relieve the isolation of Iraq, at present the only Arab member inside the Pact. If only they had taken the plunge themselves a great sense of confidence would have been created. I was, therefore, particularly anxious to hear what Eden had to say on this issue. It seemed that Dulles was still hesitant, and evasive.

> On Baghdad Pact, U.S. have moved a long way and will give us all support, moral and material, 'Short of membership' (anyway, till after the Election). They will give various sorts of aid to member states—Persia, Pakistan, Iraq and Turkey. They will buy more Centurion tanks from us to give to Iraq.[3]

Eden seemed on the whole satisfied with his talks which had covered a very wide field.[4] He told me

> that he had found the President very well, and—as usual—very friendly also. Both [he and Dulles] sent many messages to me.[3]

[1] 12 January 1956.   [2] See *Tides of Fortune*, pp. 631–55 passim.
[3] 9 February 1956.
[4] The Earl of Avon, *The Eden Memoirs: Full Circle* (London, 1960), pp. 328 ff.

Yet like so many of these conversations there was little tangible result.

A serious blow came on 1 March. Acting partly under influence from Nasser, partly perhaps under that of his uncle and with Saudi support, King Hussein took a headstrong and self-willed step. Although Jordan largely depended on British financial assistance, the people were always liable to erupt against the King, who then, and since, was only able to keep control by a remarkable combination of agility and determination. Sometimes he was forced to bow to the storm. The dismissal of Glubb Pasha, without warning and without justification, was a disturbing step, taken at the very moment that Selwyn Lloyd was on a visit to Nasser, who naturally flaunted this trump card in his face. Sir John Glubb, the British creator of the Jordanian army, was a legendary figure, and the blow to British prestige was serious. The King sent private assurances that this *coup* was not intended to disrupt relations between Great Britain and Jordan. He professed himself much disturbed at the prospect of any lasting breach. But the dismissal of British officers which followed Glubb's departure involved a disruption and perhaps a reorientation of the Arab Legion. Yet there was no practical riposte that we could make, and I supported Eden in his refusal to take any drastic action. It was clear to us all that if we were to withdraw our subsidies from Jordan, the Russians would be quite likely to step in. Indeed a few months later, just before Nasser's seizure of the Canal, the Soviet Government made an offer of arms to Jordan without payment. Sir Alec Kirkbride, who had long experience of the Middle East and had been our Ambassador in Jordan, told me at the time that he

> felt sure that if we abandoned Jordan it would fall into Saudi and/or Egyptian control, and that this might easily lead to the collapse of the Hashemite regime in Iraq.[1]

Meanwhile the Israelis remained confident of survival, and even of victory if forced to a preventive war. Nor were the governments of Iraq and Jordan anxious to initiate any attack in spite of their vulnerability to internal and external pressures. I gathered from

[1] 8 March 1956.

occasional conversations with the Prime Minister that he was more worried at the continued wavering in Washington. No clear policy or promise of support seemed to be forthcoming. At this time of growing anxiety many friends, including Randolph Churchill, suggested to me that we should make a definite treaty with Israel, thus guaranteeing the communications with Jordan and Iraq which our departure from the Canal Zone had endangered. There was reason to believe that such a proposal would be acceptable in Tel Aviv; yet at this stage it seemed doubtful whether we could get American support, and without it other larger issues would be imperilled. Meanwhile, news from Cairo became steadily worse.

Some rather alarming news is reaching us about Nasser. He seems to be aiming at a sort of League of Arab Republics (the monarchies are to go) to include Libya, Tunisia, Algeria, Morocco, as well as the Arab States in Asia Minor, etc. Egypt would have a sort of hegemony in this League, which would be a strong and immensely rich affair, especially if the oil revenues were pooled. To start it off, and gain prestige, Egypt will attack Israel in June (after the last British soldiers have left Egypt under the Treaty). They will seize a part of Israel's territory (Beersheba area) and when called on to stop by United Nations, they will do so. But they will not retreat and [will] hold on to their gain, and establish tremendous popularity, etc., with all Arabs.[1]

In view of subsequent events, this plan, knowledge of which had come to us from reliable sources and sounded plausible, is worth recalling.

Negotiations about the Aswan Dam were still proceeding slowly, but I was becoming sceptical. The Russians were clearly beginning to dabble more and more. Libya now asked for a power station, with the usual implied threat:

If we don't build them a power station, the Russians will. It is going to be Jordan all over again—large subsidies and no results.[2]

I was now, of course, Chancellor of the Exchequer and therefore took a rather more jaundiced view of these large outgoings than

[1] 16 March 1956. [2] 21 March 1956.

when I was Foreign Secretary. Yet, apart from such considerations, I began to wonder whether this portended a Russian intervention in the larger question of the Dam.

Our relations with Washington continued somewhat ambivalent. From what I could hear, Dulles was in one of his most indecisive moods. We continued to press for strong action to counter the growing hostility of Egypt. This would clearly involve increased support for the Baghdad Pact and an attempt to draw Iraq and Jordan more closely together and even, perhaps, with American influence to detach Saudi Arabia from Egypt. There was already suspicion and resentment among the rulers of Saudi Arabia caused by Nasser's flirtation with Communism. Such an Anglo-American policy would also involve seeking a more friendly Syrian Government and greater support for Libya, together with a real effort by all available means to counter Egyptian subversion in the Persian Gulf and the Sudan. Apart from any pressure that we might put on Egypt, visible Anglo-American co-operation such as we had together operated during the war, and were to resume in 1957, might well have brought decisive results. Our Government put up many suggestions, both through formal diplomatic means and in private conversation. But the American response, although friendly, was hesitating. It reflected the strange uncertainty of Dulles's own character and the light rein with which the President chose to ride him. Between the obscurity of the State Department and the shy reticence of the White House no firm policy evolved. Our proposals were not rejected; they were lost in a vast ocean of prolonged but unfruitful discussions. Eden, baffled by Dulles, was induced to address personal appeals to President Eisenhower. But this tactic, as Churchill found, was in present conditions neither welcome nor successful. Even with Churchill during his last Administration, it had become clear that the President acquiesced in this procedure only out of respect for the great war leader. With Eden, either by calculation or mischance, a new method seemed now to have been adopted.

Apparently the President has made a real gaffe. He told the Press Conference that he had not received a letter from the P.M. (The White House had, it appears, mislaid it!) Then he told them the exact opposite of what Foster Dulles wanted him to say about American intervention in the Egypt–Israel dispute. . . . He holds these conferences (which are much worse than Parliamentary Questions–for there is no notice given of the questions which will be asked), makes great pronouncements (often confused), and then leaves for a holiday. Unkind American commentators are calculating that his golfing holidays amount to 150 days or so out of the year![1]

At this juncture there took place the long-awaited visit of Khrushchev and Bulganin. The invitation had been extended at the Geneva Conference in 1955, when it was clear that the Russian leaders looked forward with pleasure to this new experience. It is true that Khrushchev's recent speeches, violently attacking 'the colonial powers', had not made a very happy prelude. But Eden rightly determined that these more or less formal insults were part of conventional Communist oratory. Eden has given a full but restrained account of this episode in his own memoirs.[2]

In principle, at any rate, the Russians agreed with us to call upon the states concerned to prevent the increase of tension in the Gaza strip and promised to support United Nations action to secure a peaceful settlement of the Arab–Israel dispute. But these were mere words. Sir Ivone Kirkpatrick allows himself a more racy comment:

They [Bulganin and Khrushchev] arrived in a mood of blatant confidence and told us very frankly that whilst in every other part of the world there would be no conflict they would make as much trouble for us in the Middle East as they possibly could. They were as good as their word.[3]

Naturally, since my new department was scarcely concerned except in the discussions on Anglo-Russian trade, I took very little part in this visit beyond attending formal functions. The Russian leaders arrived on 18 April and stayed a week. There was a good deal of anxiety before they actually came.

We have had rather an agitating week [in preparing for] the Bulganin and Khrushchev visit. First, the F.O. published . . .

[1] Diary–10 April 1956.   [2] The Earl of Avon, *Full Circle*, p. 354.
[3] Ivone Kirkpatrick, *The Inner Circle* (London, 1959), p. 262.

the full details of each day, hour by hour. This is a gift to the would-be assassin ! Secondly, the public are getting rather upset, especially about their visit to the Queen. Thirdly, some of the Cabinet don't like it. . . . P.M. has been very calm and sensible.[1]

The day after the Budget:

Bulganin and Khrushchev have arrived—and this, with the marriage of Grace Kelly to the Prince of Monaco, has over- shadowed the Budget. There was a luncheon at the Russian Embassy—with glaring lights (for British T.V. and Russian colour film); there was caviare; and vodka; and those terrible Russian wines. But the unexpected thing was an impromptu (and very interesting) speech by K. The P.M. thinks that he may be able to do some business with them—not about Europe or Germany (which is hopeless) but about the Middle East.[2]

Certainly Eden was frank. The Russians were told explicitly that the Middle East oil was a vital British interest. If necessary, we should fight for our rights. Whether this was wise or not, it seems to have made a deep impression upon our visitors. Eden is certainly right in claiming that when the troubles came in the autumn, the opening Russian moves were prudent, even restrained. It was only when British and American policy fell hopelessly apart that the Russians joined in the hunt. Those who were present at the talks told me that they were particularly struck by Khrushchev's open contempt for the non-nuclear powers; while America and Britain stood firmly together they took notice.

One ludicrous incident took place which excited great public interest:

They had a row with the Labour leaders at a dinner given for them at the House of Commons by the Labour executive. Our Labour friends asked about the fate of the Social Democrats, now in prison in Russia and the satellite states, and got a very dusty answer.[3]

I am bound to say that my sympathies were with the Labour protesters. In any case, it was perhaps good for them to get a more realistic picture of the Communist point of view than they were

[1] 14 April 1956.   [2] 19 April 1956.   [3] 25 April 1956.

sometimes apt to draw for themselves. Meanwhile, the British public

> behaved with admirable reticence and discretion. Their sight-seeing visits are being curtailed, in order to give more time to serious talks with our Ministers. The British are certainly an odd people. It is said of one of K.'s speeches that when he talked of Capitalism and Socialism and so forth, he held the attention of an audience. But he lost them when he began to talk about rockets with H-bomb heads. Then ... they were bored![1]

Towards the end of the tour, 'B. and K. have gone to Scotland with James Stuart [Secretary of State for Scotland]—a curious party.'[2]

The last contingent of British troops left the Suez Canal base on 14 June in accordance with the agreement of 1954. Newspaper comment and speeches in Egypt connected with the British evacuation were on the whole conciliatory. Nasser even paid tribute to the honourable fulfilment by Britain of her obligations. All through June and July the tedious haggling continued over the conditions on which Egypt would accept aid for the Aswan Dam. Nasser was determined that no financial commitment, even in support of the dam, should obstruct his own ambitious programme. Nor was he willing to agree to any control of armaments in the Middle East. Nevertheless, when Eden asked for my view I had no doubt as to what our attitude should be:

> I feel that we should neither abandon the project [of the dam] in a pet, nor be manœuvred out of it. We and the Americans should have a *position*, and state it frankly and publicly.[3]

During these months evidence poured in from every part of the Middle East of the activity of Egyptian agents and the subversive efforts of Egyptian propaganda. The Cairo 'Voice of the Arabs' blared forth day by day hostility to the West at the same time as the Egyptians continued to press for Western financial aid.

Both we and the Americans were becoming increasingly dubious as the summer progressed as to the possibility—or even desirability—of concluding an agreement on the dam project. Nevertheless it

[1] 25 April 1956.   [2] 26 April 1956.   [3] 5 July 1956.

came as a shock to us when we heard that, on 19 July, Dulles
had bluntly told the Egyptian Ambassador, Ahmed Hussein, that
the United States had decided to withdraw their support from the
scheme. It is said that the scene was strangely undiplomatic. In the
course of a long interview the Ambassador nervously blurted out,
'Don't please say that you are going to withdraw the offer, because
we have the Russian offer to finance the dam right here in my
pocket!' Dulles is reported to have been stung into the reply,
'Well, as you have the money already, you don't need any from us!
My offer is withdrawn!'[1] Whether this is an accurate account or
not of the final scene in this tortuous drama, the Americans were
clearly becoming more and more disillusioned by Egyptian dupli-
city and arrogance. A whole series of events had antagonised Dulles
and his colleagues. In April, Nasser gave an interview to a New
York newspaper, declaring that he already had a Soviet offer of help
in financing the dam, and would certainly consider it if there were
any breakdown in the negotiations. In May a barter agreement was
arranged between China and Egypt by which 45,000 tons of
Egyptian cotton was to be exchanged for 60,000 tons of Chinese
steel. This involved the recognition of Communist China, accorded
on 16 May, with all that this implied for American susceptibilities.
D. T. Shepilov, the Soviet Foreign Minister, paid a visit to Cairo in
the middle of June, and it was freely rumoured that the Soviet Union
had offered to loan the total cost of the dam, with very low interest
and a very long period of repayment. Shepilov actually joined Nasser
at Port Said to see the last British soldier leave the Suez base.
Nasser's triumphant election as President, by a 99 per cent vote
(reminiscent of the system of elections in Russia and other dictator
countries), was wildly acclaimed. Russian weapons were paraded
through the streets, and Russian aeroplanes gave a display. Token
military forces were present from Jordan, Lebanon, Yemen, Libya,
Sudan, Saudi Arabia and Syria.[2] All these events caused equal disquiet in London and Washington. Congress was becoming increasingly reluctant to finance the loan, and George Humphrey, the
Secretary of the Treasury, was taking a critical line. He doubted
whether the loan would be repaid either to the United States or to

[1] Herman Finer, *Dulles over Suez* (London, 1964), p. 48.   [2] Finer, p. 44.

the World Bank. Humphrey played an important, sometimes decisive, role in affairs, having almost equal weight with the President as Dulles himself.

In Britain we too were having our doubts. Was it right that we should make so great a sacrifice out of our slender resources to help a government becoming daily more unfriendly, and passing more and more under Russian influence? Would it not be better to confine ourselves to the support of our many friends? As Eden has recorded, we were being slowly driven to the conclusion that it would be difficult to go on with the project. Nevertheless, we were extremely reluctant to force the issue. Although we were prepared to leave the final decision to the Americans and the Bank, we made it clear that we did not wish them to act precipitately. We wanted to 'play it long'. When we heard that the Egyptian Ambassador was on his way to Washington to obtain the loan, presumably on terms still to be agreed, we were all the more anxious that nothing should be done to produce a sudden or violent change of position. The French shared our view and were indeed even more concerned as to the possible reaction to a sudden break. Here, as so often, they showed their traditional wisdom on how to play a diplomatic hand. After our strong plea to the Americans that we should 'play it long' it was a considerable shock to find that the opposite tactics had been adopted. We were informed, not consulted. Eden states this with his usual moderation:

> We were sorry that the matter was carried through so abruptly, because it gave our two countries no chance to concert either timing or methods, though these were quite as important as the substance. At this moment Colonel Nasser was in Brioni at a meeting with Marshal Tito and Mr. Nehru, and the news was wounding to his pride.[1]

Nasser was subsequently to claim that the failure of the negotiation of the Aswan Dam was his main reason for the seizure of the Canal. This is manifestly false. The discussions were drawn out by the Egyptians over many months; they could easily have been clinched before the end of 1955 or, at the latest, early in 1956.

[1] The Earl of Avon, p. 422.

During that time neither the British nor the Americans would have had any hesitation in accepting the burden; nor were the conditions of the World Bank onerous or unusual. Dulles's abrupt conclusion of the affair was a diplomatic error, but it was the occasion not the cause of Nasser's illegal action. During the spring and early summer he had fallen more and more to the wiles of Soviet diplomacy. Thus his ambitious and dangerous dreams of Arab imperialism began to inflame his imagination to a degree of fanaticism. Dulles's clumsy handling of the final stages played into Nasser's hands; but it is clear from all the actions which he was taking, as well as the wild propaganda which he was spreading throughout the Middle East, that he was preparing for a *coup* which would strike the imagination of the Egyptian people and of all the Arab world. Fortified by Russian arms and finance, he would strike a blow at the prestige of Britain and her American ally. If one traces his tactics, they bear a considerable likeness to those adopted by Mussolini, whom in many respects he resembled. In dealing with others, every display of timidity or weakness was seized upon and exploited; no action, however generous or fair-minded, could reap any reward. He had received from the British Government nothing but honourable, even generous, dealing. He repaid every benefit with a new injury, and answered every act of generosity by a fresh demand. While, therefore, Dulles can be, and has been, strongly criticised for the handling of the last phase of the Aswan Dam negotiation, it is wrong and contrary to the facts to regard the ending of the negotiations as the real reason for Nasser's violent reply.

On 20 July, the day after the decision communicated by Dulles to the Egyptian Ambassador, the British Government followed suit. Since the three parts of the scheme were interdependent, the World Bank formally withdrew on the same day. On 26 July, in a bitter speech filled with scorn and abuse of the Western powers, Nasser announced the nationalisation of the Canal, and the transfer of the Suez Canal Company, with all its assets and commitments, to the Egyptian State. Egyptian military and police forces immediately took possession of the Company's offices and installations in Cairo and on the Canal. The die was now cast.

Eden has vividly described the scene when the news reached him on the night of 26 July, when the King of Iraq with the Prince Regent and Nuri es-Said, who were on a formal visit to London, were dining in Downing Street. I did not hear of these grave events until the next morning.

Nasser has declared his intention to 'nationalise'—that is, seize, the Suez Canal Company. He offers 'compensation at market price for the shares'. He will 'pay for the Aswan Dam from the profits of the Canal'. The speech is very truculent—an Asiatic Mussolini, full of insult and abuse of U.S. and U.K. P.M. rang me early and we met just before 11 a.m. to agree a short factual statement to be made (it's a Friday) immediately after Prayers. This was all arranged; Gaitskell made polite noises, and there was no great trouble.[1]

The unanimous view of my colleagues was in favour of strong and resolute action. Our reasons were simple but compelling. They were given by Eden to Parliament with admirable clarity in the discussion of 2 August. We had to consider our own material interests and those of the Western world. At that time, before the birth of the giant oil tankers, the Canal was the essential and indeed the only means by which Western Europe could be supplied. Seventy million tons a year passed through the Canal, representing at least half the oil supplies of Western Europe. Moreover, the normal route to Australia, India, Ceylon and South-East Asia used the Canal, and most ordinary trade went backwards and forwards by this means. The international position of the Canal had been recognised by the original agreement reached at the Convention of 1888. Nor could Nasser argue that this was one of those commitments which a successor Government could plausibly repudiate. In the Anglo-Egyptian Treaty of 1954 the position of the Company and of the rights of the parties to the Convention was specifically recognised. Still more was at stake. Arbitrary action without consultation or notice, in breach of solemn undertakings, many of them recently given, revealed the true character of the regime.

Eden showed the greatest moderation and prudence, for there were many considerations which influenced him and his colleagues. Britain, ever since the conclusion of the First World War, had

[1] 27 July 1956.

enjoyed a long and friendly association with the Arab countries. We had taken the leading part in their liberation from the old Ottoman Empire. We had given them aid, financial and technical, on a generous scale. Our military installations, including the important Air Force contingents, were to the mutual benefit of these countries and ourselves, and helped to support the peace of the Middle East. Since the Second War, with the new threats of Communist aggression in Europe and in Asia this connection was of even greater importance. We had worked amicably with the rulers of these countries and helped them to develop their resources and sustain their economic growth. We had carried out the mandate in Palestine for nearly thirty years to the best of our ability and even when we had abandoned it in despair we had worked loyally for moderation and conciliation.[1]

In this position of uneasy balance it was clear that Nasser was determined to throw his weight in favour of revolution and Arab expansion with the help of Communist intrigue and supported by Communist money and arms. With a jealous eye on the oil-bearing countries, he was determined to pursue an aggressive policy on lines of which we had only too recent and too painful experience. As Gaitskell was to put it, 'It is all very familiar. It is exactly the same that we encountered from Mussolini and Hitler in those years before the war.'[2] Indeed, Gaitskell's speech was a severe indictment couched in less diplomatic language than the Prime Minister thought fit to use. He denounced Nasser's action on four main grounds—first, the breach of the rights and interests of all maritime nations; secondly, the manner in which it had been taken without negotiation, without discussion and with the excuse that the revenues of the Canal were to be used to finance the Aswan Dam, completely contrary to international undertakings. Thirdly, we could not forget Nasser's boasts of his intention to create an Arab Empire from the Atlantic to the Persian Gulf. Finally, there was the danger to the Arab States, especially Iraq, Jordan and Saudi Arabia. It was noticed at the time how firm and even belligerent in tone was the Leader of the Opposition's first reaction. The mood was soon to change.

[1] See *Tides of Fortune*, p. 147.   [2] *Hansard*, 2 August 1956.

But if Eden had been restrained in public, he had been firm in his private declarations. From this moment and throughout the crisis we stood firmly with our French friends, and discussions and consultations with Mollet, the Socialist Premier of France, and Christian Pineau, the Foreign Minister, were close and continuous. But even more important would be the attitude of the United States. Eden's vital message to Eisenhower at the end of July left no room for uncertainty or equivocation. After rehearsing the position which had been reached—the danger to oil supplies, the worsening outlook if Nasser succeeded in his aims—he made it clear that, while we would use all our efforts in conjunction with other countries to apply economic sanctions and political pressure, we could not be content with anything but success:

> My colleagues and I are convinced that we must be ready, in the last resort, to use force to bring Nasser to his senses. For our part we are prepared to do so. I have this morning instructed our Chiefs of Staff to prepare a military plan accordingly.[1]

When Eden showed me a copy of this telegram, I was happy to see not only the clarity of his exposition but the firmness of his declaration.

Through the long and tangled discussions and negotiations and the various schemes which Dulles put forward for some international solution by peaceful means, neither he nor Eisenhower could ever have been under any misapprehension. Britain and France in the long run would not shrink from force. This was not merely because of our commercial and strategic interests in the free use of the Canal in peace and war. It was also because of our fear that so flagrant a breach of an international convention, so recently reaffirmed, would be the beginning of a decline in international good faith such as had led to the disasters of two world wars. We had, moreover, a more immediate anxiety—that Nasser would not hesitate to subvert the regimes of his neighbours, and having acquired by menaces and intrigue the leadership of all the Arab peoples, he would turn to the final destruction of the state of Israel.

At this time we could not believe that the American Administration especially under the President, who was so friendly, who

[1] The Earl of Avon, p. 428.

had commanded our great armies and had shown such generous appreciation of British qualities of tenacity and courage, would allow our rights and our interests to disappear in a fog of argument or sentiment or misunderstand our fixity of purpose. Therefore I was quite happy to concur in the protracted series of plans and expedients which the maritime nations of the world under Dulles's inspiration were to devise during the next few weeks. I was confident that if and when the moment for action arrived we should have, if not the overt, at least the covert sympathy and support of the Government and people of the United States.

I was soon to have an opportunity to add my own warnings. My old friend and colleague from Algiers days, Robert Murphy, who was still serving in the State Department, was sent immediately to London. Since the Ambassador, Winthrop Aldrich, was at this moment on leave, this visit was of the greatest possible importance. Eisenhower had notified Eden that Murphy was being sent as his personal representative. He arrived without instructions, to reconnoitre and report. Here was my opportunity and, with the Prime Minister's full acquiescence, I was determined to make full use of it.

Accordingly I invited him to dinner at No. 11 Downing Street on 30 July. The only other guests were Andrew Foster, the American chargé d'affaires, and Field-Marshal Lord Alexander. Murphy has given in his memoirs a very objective account of our talks. So practised a diplomatist clearly understood its purpose.

> Through many months of working closely with Macmillan and Alexander, I had developed great admiration for both of them. Both had successfully borne heavy responsibilities and great honours, and both had successfully retained their sense of realism and sense of humour. Our conversation that night was easy and relaxed but it was not reminiscent of past associations. Our thoughts were on Suez. . . .[1]

I made it quite clear that we and France must accept the challenge, or sink into the rank of second-class nations. Murphy continues:

> I was left in no doubt that the British Government believed that Suez was a test which could be met only by the use of force,

[1] Robert Murphy, *Diplomat Among Warriors* (London, 1964), p. 463.

and I was not surprised at this reaction because it seemed not unjustified. I was told that the French saw eye to eye with the British on the necessity of making a stand, and that they were prepared to participate in a military operation. Although Alexander was retired, the distinguished soldier obviously was in close touch with the campaign plans and approved them.[1]

Earlier in the day I had attended a luncheon at Number 10 at which Murphy had been present as well as Pineau. The French had stood absolutely solid and, at a subsequent meeting, Murphy observed:

Nobody can be more ruthless in playing power politics or more intellectually insolent than French Socialists, once they believe their ox has been gored. Pineau did not conceal his contempt for what he called American naïveté.[2]

Murphy had little to tell us of American feeling. He was frank in admitting that he had no formal instructions. Eisenhower had merely said to him, 'Just go over and hold the fort.' This was perhaps necessary because Dulles was absent in Peru. We certainly did our best to frighten him, or at least to leave him in no doubt of our determination.

It seems that we have succeeded in thoroughly alarming Murphy. He must have reported in the sense which we wanted, and Foster Dulles is now coming over post-haste. This is a very good development.[3]

Meanwhile, there had been plenty to do in my own sphere. There was the immediate problem of the payment of the shipping dues. I proposed that we should tell our shipowners—and seek to get other maritime countries to give similar instructions—to continue to pay the dues to the old Company in the same manner as hitherto (this would mean that British shipowners would pay in London, French in Paris, and others, including the American, in Egypt) and, entering the Canal, to say that the dues were paid. If this were challenged, we should have then to consider what action to take. A more difficult question arose over Egyptian sterling. We

[1] Murphy, p. 463.   [2] Murphy, p. 465.   [3] 31 July 1956.

wished to control it, so far as possible, but in a way calculated not to damage confidence in holders of sterling throughout the world. We were able to achieve this by making an order putting Egypt out of the transferable sterling account, and making all transactions on Egyptian controlled accounts subject to specific approval. We also took steps to protect the Company's securities in gold. All this was agreed before the end of July, and the French took similar action. My advisers at the Treasury gave me, as usual, the most devoted and skilful support in long and sometimes hectic discussions. Although I, of course, had no official part in the negotiations, when Foster Dulles arrived he came to see me in view of the close friendship during the period when I was Foreign Secretary. He brought with him Bob Murphy and the American Ambassador, now returned to his post.

> We had an hour's talk. I told Foster, as plainly as I could, that we just could not afford to lose this game. It was a question not of honour only but survival. . . . There was no other choice for us. I think he was quite alarmed; for he had hoped to find me less extreme, I think. We *must* keep the Americans really frightened. They must not be allowed any illusion. Then they will help us to get what we want, without the necessity for force.[1]

In addition to my share in these months as Chancellor of the Exchequer, I took my full part during the negotiations in the weeks and months that followed in the deliberations in the Committee of Ministers especially appointed to deal with the crisis. A detailed account of the various moves has been set out by Eden, and by many other historians. I shall confine myself to those parts of the story which affected me particularly. But the Prime Minister kept me in close touch with all his plans during these anxious times, from the day of the seizure of the Canal to the cease-fire. I share to the fullest extent the responsibility of all the decisions, not merely from the normal responsibility of a Cabinet Minister, but because I was one of the circle of colleagues whom Eden consulted. Naturally, as I was fully employed with my own problems from the financial point of view, I could have only a general knowledge of the intricate but,

[1] 1 August 1956.

alas, ineffective attempts to reach a peaceful solution in accordance with the claims of justice and equity.

On 2 August the United States, French and British Foreign Ministers issued an invitation to the eight original signatories of the Convention of 1888, which guaranteed the international character of the Canal, and to the sixteen principal users, selected by tonnage and trade, to meet at the earliest opportunity in London. 'On the whole, this seems a good result. The Americans have certainly moved a long way.'[1] The invitation included condemnation of Nasser's action and support for the principle of international control.

There was now a short delay, in the course of which I was drawn into a somewhat ludicrous conflict with one of the banks, whose representative came to see me.

They were in doubt as to whether they could pay out to the Suez Canal Company (the legitimate one) moneys in their account. I asked 'Why not?' Because, they said, it was possible that a court would hold that Nasser's action was justified and that the money now belonged to the new nationalised authority. I was so angry with them that I turned in fury on them and called them harsh names. They went away saddened; but they promised to do what seemed obviously right and take a chance.[2]

Both the British and the French Governments stood firm on all these financial sanctions, and European countries began to show a real willingness to assist. On 12 August, Egypt announced her refusal to attend the Conference. Nevertheless, twenty-two out of the twenty-four invited nations accepted; the only other absentee besides Egypt being Greece.

Although Dulles wished for a later date, a compromise was reached, and the Conference met on 16 August. It ended on the 23rd. At this stage it seemed to me that Dulles was determined to take a strong line. He had even put himself into the forefront of the dispute. Both he and Eisenhower fully understood that an acceptable solution must be found. But if every peaceful means had first been used, and force then used, Dulles believed that the world would understand. He had even committed himself in conversation with the Foreign Secretary to the statement that Nasser must be made to

[1] 2 August 1956.   [2] 3 August 1956.

'disgorge what he was attempting to swallow'. It should be possible, thought Dulles, 'to create a world opinion so adverse to Nasser that he would be isolated. Then if a military operation had to be undertaken it would be more apt to succeed and have less grave repercussions than if it had been undertaken precipitately.'[1] Dulles proposed an international Suez Canal Board to manage the Canal. To this eighteen nations agreed. India, supported by Russia, preferred a plan of an Egyptian-run Canal with an international Advisory Board. But the Americans agreed with us that this would soon prove a mere farce. The next step was to appoint a committee led by Robert Menzies, Prime Minister of Australia, and comprising representatives of Persia, Ethiopia, Sweden and the United States, to make a direct approach to the Egyptian Government. Before the Conference ended Dulles had made a further call upon me, and I was able to report that he seemed in a very determined mood. He was certainly most friendly, frankly discussing his own future after the election if Eisenhower should be returned.

For myself, I was anxious about the procedure.

The weaker brethren want a 'negotiation'. This would be very bad. The declaration should be presented to Nasser, with a request to know whether he will negotiate a treaty in conformity or consonant with its terms. A small committee (*not* including U.K. or France) might be formed to give any explanations and elucidations which he might ask, but *not* to negotiate. There is an absurd and dangerous idea being put about that this Committee should go to Cairo to negotiate. This is very alarming. It's too much like Canossa![2]

However, the plan was generally accepted and I felt that 'the fact that Dulles has played such a prominent part certainly helps to commit the prestige of the U.S.'[3] Before he left I told him that

we had no alternative, if we could not get our way by diplomatic pressure, but to resort to force. The French were equally determined. . . . Dulles had not seemed shocked.[4]

Although Dulles was not prepared to go himself to Cairo as we had hoped, the United States was admirably represented on the

---

[1] The Earl of Avon, p. 437.   [2] 21 August 1956.
[3] 22 August 1956.   [4] 24 August 1956.

Committee by Loy Henderson, and we could rely with an absolute confidence on the strength of character, pertinacity and integrity of the chairman, Menzies. There was nothing now to be done but to await events.

During this interval, as a result of a comprehensive survey under Treasury leadership by all the Ministries concerned, I was able to give my colleagues some estimate of the likely effect of the crisis on the British economy. The direct budgetary cost of the precautionary military measures during August and September was not likely to be great—not above £12 million. If the emergency continued, the rate of expenditure would be about £2 million a month. Compared with a total defence expenditure of £1,600 million this was not in itself disturbing. Nor would the removal of 26,000 reservists from the labour market cause much difficulty in view of the recent increase in unemployment of nearly 60,000. As regards the balance of payments, the direct effect in terms of foreign exchange was small. Perhaps the most important expense would result from leasing ships. Realising that to requisition liners at the height of the tourist season would be sadly wasteful, I had persuaded the Admiralty to bring into use every possible reserve vessel—bulk carriers, cruisers, etc.—on which they could lay their hands. Nor would there be any serious effect upon the immediate cost of ordinary commodities which we imported, other than oil.

In a word, the direct cost of our precautionary measures would be insignificant. The indirect repercussions were more difficult to foresee. The American refusal to give the same instructions to their shipowners as we had given was disturbing, partly because it reduced the pressure on Nasser, who would receive about 35 per cent of the normal dues, and partly because when this became known it would have a harmful effect on confidence. We had done our best to organise the blockage of Egypt's sterling balances so as not to alarm other holders of sterling. But there was bound to be a sense of anxiety. Yet so long as America was firmly on our side on the main issue there would be no 'flight from the pound'.

We also tried to estimate the actual cost of military operations if they became necessary. Unless these were short and localised they would certainly prove expensive. Meanwhile we did not think it necessary to allow for more than £100 million above the estimates for the year.

Far more serious would be the interruption of oil supplies, either as the result of military operations or through some further action by Nasser if he were successful in mobilising the Arab world against us. But assuming that the supplies from the Persian Gulf and Saudi Arabia remained open and the Americans co-operated to the full, it should be possible to meet the full needs of Europe, after two or three months of tolerable shortages. If both the Canal and the pipelines were cut, the situation would be serious, even with American support. If the Canal remained permanently closed and a new pattern of trade were established there would be an additional cost to the whole of Europe amounting to several hundred million dollars. Prices would rise, and Europe would be paying in dollars.

For the immediate future, stocks of oil in Britain at this time were fortunately at their maximum; and they could to some extent be supplemented by drawing on strategic and Admiralty stocks. Yet there would later be dislocation and loss even if motor spirit were cut by a quarter—a course which could certainly be followed without serious damage to the economy. We also did our best to foresee the picture as regards shipping and commodities. There would be some rise in freight rates and possibly in commodity prices as happened at the time of the Korean war.

Our general conclusion was that if action had to be taken it must be short and successful. For immediate needs we could no doubt expect American aid. On the other hand, Britain and all Western Europe depended in the long run on the free use of oil from Asia. If we allowed Nasser to pursue his aggression without interference, we could easily be subject to a total stranglehold. We must try to balance the risks of a short struggle against an extended period when Western Europe could be in fee to the holders of power in the Middle East.

One of our difficulties at this time was how to present the full case for 'making Nasser disgorge' without endangering confidence in sterling, all the more so because the Americans were blocking neither private Egyptian accounts nor fresh dollar accruals to the Egyptian Government. They had only put in escrow the money which was standing to the Egyptian account when the crisis began. This decision was neither logical nor helpful. If the Americans had agreed to block new accruals in dollars, we would have had little difficulty in persuading the Germans and other European countries who were hesitating to do the same. Until this could be effected it was hard to persuade others to follow. Even on this basis, exchange controls were often evaded. For instance, the Chinese owed the Egyptians money and they were now buying Swiss francs with promises of payment in sterling. By the beginning of September the loss on the reserves would have to be announced, and this could not be less than $120 million. On the whole, it seemed to me wise to do nothing in our propaganda to undermine confidence in sterling balances. There were too many sterling balances which could easily be withdrawn. Yet the inhibitions from which we suffered for these practical reasons made it difficult to deploy our full case to the public at home and overseas.

Although the matter was outside my sphere, I ventured to express my views about the character of any military operation and what should be its target. It seemed to me that merely to reoccupy the Canal would place us back in the position in which we had been in past years, with all the troubles and all the disadvantages of a hostile Egyptian Government in command. In other words, we should be back in a position which we had already found untenable—and with rather smaller forces than before. If force was ever to be used, its purpose must be to contain or nullify the threat to the whole peace of the Middle East. We knew well—for we had all lived through those terrible years—that had we taken action against Mussolini in 1935 at the time of his attack on Abyssinia, or against Hitler in 1936, when he remilitarised the Rhineland, the world might have been spared the horrors of the Second War. Moreover, there was the virtual certainty that Israel would take advantage of the present situation to free herself from constant menaces. All history had shown that statesmen of character would seize such a chance; the Israelis were bold and determined. Above all, we must stop them from attacking Jordan. In view of our alliance with that country this would put us in a hopeless dilemma. If Israel were to move, we could at least interpose Anglo-French forces to hold the field and bring about a settlement, not merely of the Canal question which, although vital, was of relatively less importance than the whole problem of pacification of the Middle East. These ideas were accepted by the Prime Minister and the Chiefs of Staff. I was encouraged to intervene by a talk which I had with Churchill when I dined with him at Chartwell on 5 August. Naturally, we hoped that the Americans would assist us to bring about a solution by the strength of world pressure, led by the United States; but, if that failed, we must take whatever opportunity might present itself or we should be unworthy of our responsibilities to Britain and the free world.

I also circulated some thoughts on what should be our political aims. Surely we should try to achieve the rapid emergence of a friendly Egyptian Government. With such a Government we could soon agree a generous plan for the Canal, giving the world the protection of international control and Egypt the prospect of substantial financial advantages. We should pursue an active and constructive policy throughout the Middle East. Our purpose should be to organise a common policy among the oil-producing countries, the oil transit countries and perhaps the countries that were without oil resources. We could paint a picture of the vast potential capacity of the whole area, if harmony and co-operation could be restored and a firm basis created for an increased European and American investment. In a word, we should appear not as reactionary powers returning to the old days of 'colonialism' but as a progressive force trying to bring about permanent and constructive settlements. Thus we should not resemble Louis XVIII returning in 1815 to a dull restoration, but rather Napoleon breaking through the Alps towards the reunification of Italy. These ambitions were far-reaching, but I still believe that if the Western alliance had held, they might have been achieved.

During these weeks the temper of the country remained constantly firm. Eden made an admirable broadcast and television statement on 8 August which had an excellent effect. At the beginning of the crisis *The Times* had set a good note and still continued helpful. Before the first debate in Parliament on 2 August they used these words:

When the Commons take up Suez tomorrow there is one thing they can be sure of. It must be their guiding thought. If Nasser is allowed to get away with his *coup* all the British and other western interests in the Middle East will crumble. The modern world has suffered many acts, like Hitler's march into the Rhineland or the Stalinist overthrow of freedom in Czecho-slovakia, which were claimed to be assertions of domestic sovereignty. They were, in fact, hinges of history. Nasser's seizure of the canal company is another such turning point. Quibbling over whether or not he was 'legally entitled' to make the grab will delight the finicky and comfort the fainthearted, but entirely misses the real issues.[1]

Alas, even in Printing House Square such fair dawns are often strangely overcast. The 'popular' Press was equally robust—at least to begin with. The 'intellectual' papers were already wavering; but I was not surprised at this phenomenon.

One further action the British Government took in the hope of consolidating opinion among the Western and Atlantic powers. At Eden's suggestion, a meeting of the Council of NATO was held in Paris, over which Selwyn Lloyd presided. Dulles was not enthusiastic about this and was not himself present, although the Americans were represented. All the other Foreign Ministers came, and took a remarkably sturdy line. Dr. Joseph Luns, the Netherlands Foreign Minister,

> urged that the North Atlantic powers should refuse to recognize the seizure of the canal, withhold dues from the new authority and join in a reference to the Security Council. The Canadian Foreign Minister, Mr. Lester Pearson, endorsed these views. Though he was averse to military sanctions, he did not exclude them in the last resort.[1]

Spaak was even more emphatic. He believed that if the Western powers, especially the European powers, quailed at this crisis they would have to tread a long and ignoble path of retreat for the next generation. Like so many other Europeans who had been through the period of Hitler's rise, he was deeply imbued with the need to take action at an early stage.

[1] The Earl of Avon, p. 458.

Menzies was now in Cairo, and awaited Nasser's answer. Menzies has published a detailed account of his mission. It throws, for the first time, a clear and dramatic light upon a historic meeting. Menzies is scrupulously fair to Nasser, by whose character and bearing he was favourably affected.

> Nasser was a man of imposing physique and presence; obviously the master of his Government, of much intelligence, but with some marks of immaturity and inevitable lack of experience. But he was impressive and clearly courageous.[1]

Owing to the fact that the Prime Minister of Australia happened to be in England in the month of July for some trade discussions, he somewhat reluctantly agreed to accept this task. His chief anxiety was naturally to get home as soon as possible; but great pressure was brought upon him to stay in England, and we were indeed fortunate that he yielded to the demands of patriotic duty. His opponents naturally accused him of seeking the limelight. I had already known Menzies for a great number of years and came to know him intimately during my period as Prime Minister. I never found him seeking the limelight. However, he always cast a substantial shadow in which it was possible for others to obtain coolness and repose.

Menzies was, in fact, 'drafted'. Nevertheless, since the interests of Australia were so deeply involved, it was perhaps not unnatural that he should have yielded to Eden's urgent request. He and his colleagues were under no illusions. After a purely formal meeting on 3 September, an *aide-mémoire* was presented on the following day giving the credentials of the Committee which represented eighteen nations, the major users of the Canal, together with a memorandum setting out the chief points in courteous and non-provocative language. The *aide-mémoire* stated their conviction that, if the Canal was to be maintained and developed, it should be detached from politics, and the management should be placed on such a basis as to secure the maximum of international confidence and co-operation. At the same time, they wished to make it clear that those whom they represented had not approached the problem

[1] Sir Robert Menzies, *Afternoon Light* (London, 1967), p. 164.

in any spirit of hostility. On the contrary, they had all enjoyed a long friendship with Egypt; they welcomed her recent achievement of self-government and independence. This spirit had been clearly manifested at the London Conference. The Committee added:

It is our deep conviction that the negotiation of a convention along the lines suggested in our proposals would be for the benefit of Egypt and of all nations and individuals using the Canal and would certainly help to restore the kind of peaceful international atmosphere which the world at present so desperately needs.[1]

They went on to state that they did not feel the sovereign rights of Egypt had been affected by the Convention of 1888, nor would they suffer from any new agreement, voluntarily and amicably reached. The Committee sought by discussion and conference with the Government of Egypt to secure a peaceful settlement on a basis of justice to both sides. Menzies presented the full case on behalf of the Committee by a speech which was at once moderate and persuasive. The text of the actual proposals was formally presented.

Nevertheless, neither he nor his Committee felt very hopeful of a favourable response. Menzies therefore took upon himself a considerable responsibility. He decided, although such an action was outside his strict terms of reference, to ask Nasser for a private interview. This was agreed. Menzies hoped, in the atmosphere of private and unofficial discussion, to impress Nasser with the gravity of the position. He was encouraged to do this because he had noticed in the local Press the day before the meeting that Nasser, in addressing his military leaders, had assured them that the Franco-British mobilisation and military preparation were all bluff and could safely be disregarded. If this was really Nasser's opinion, it was of vital importance that he should be disillusioned. In the course of this talk, while making it clear that what he had to say must not be regarded as a threat, and was spoken without authority, Menzies felt it right to treat Nasser with complete honesty and candour. Accordingly he used these words:

I notice that yesterday you described certain British and French military mobilizations as 'all bluff'. Now, I have just come from

[1] Menzies, p. 163.

London, and I know something of the state of opinion there. I know something of the French state of mind. There seems to be a general assumption in the Egyptian press that the London Conference decided against force. This is not so.[1]

He continued as follows:

The London Conference did not discuss that matter at all; it devoted itself to securing a peaceful settlement by working out fair and constructive proposals. It would, in my opinion, which I offer in the friendliest way and in no sense as an agent, be a mistake for you to exclude the possible use of force from your reckoning. I repeat: the members of my Committee and I are not talking force, or contemplating that it should become either necessary or adopted. But I don't want you to be misled about the state of opinion in London or Paris.[1]

This firm but moderate approach seemed to make some impression on Nasser, and Menzies even thought that the chances of reaching an agreement had materially improved. Nevertheless, to use Menzies's own words, 'next morning, when I read the newspapers, I knew that it was all over. President Eisenhower had spoken.'[2]

The eighteen powers had met for long conferences in London. They had appointed a powerful committee with one of the most determined statesmen in the world to lead it. They had been: they had seen: but they had not conquered. They had been—unwittingly and, no doubt, quite unconsciously—torpedoed by the President of the United States, whose Secretary of State had taken the main lead in organising the maritime nations, and drafting the resolutions to which they had agreed. How was the fatal blow struck? On the morning of 5 September, the day after Menzies's private warning, the French and English newspapers in Cairo carried flaring headlines, not of the Nasser–Menzies meeting, but of a statement of President Eisenhower to the American Press:

For ourselves, we are determined to exhaust every possible, every feasible method of peaceful settlement . . . and we believe it can be done, and I am not going to comment on what other people are doing. I am very hopeful that this particular proposal

[1] Menzies, p. 164.   [2] Menzies, p. 165.

will be accepted but, in any event, not to give up, even if we do run into other obstacles.

We are committed to a peaceful settlement of this dispute, *nothing else.*[1]

Although, read carefully, the last phrase could be interpreted to refer only to present undertakings, these words clinched the matter. If force was excluded, all Nasser had to do was to sit tight and wait until the convention of angry powers dissipated into an ineffective rabble. As Menzies sadly reflected, American statesmen are often fond of answering an awkward question by the phrase 'no comment'. Had President Eisenhower only used this valuable cliché, he would not have destroyed the success of a project to which his country, as well as all the other nations, had trusted so much. Nasser was now clear on two things. First, the use of force could be disregarded; for he could not believe that there was any question of force being used against the will of the United States. Secondly, he could reject these immediate proposals without anxiety, confident that America would soon be coming along with new and more favourable offers. Such are the difficulties of international negotiation under democratic conditions, with the free Press, the free radio, free television, which the marvels of science have provided, ensuring that there shall never be a moment of silence on any political issue during the whole twenty-four hours of the earth's daily revolution. Yet, in private life, the President was generally reputed to play a good game of poker.

Before leaving for Cairo, Menzies had shown his co-operation by a helpful measure to support our financial position. I had asked him towards the end of August whether he would be willing to arrange for the sale of £20 million worth of Australian gold to the Bank of England in order to improve the position of the central reserves. After consultation with his colleagues, he agreed and the matter was accordingly arranged. As I wrote in my letter of thanks, this was indeed a 'timely and encouraging gesture of support and solidarity'.

The news of Nasser's complete intransigence led to a re-examination of a question which had been much discussed by the Cabinet

[1] Quoted by Menzies, p. 165.

ever since the seizure of the Canal. Should we appeal, without further ado, to the United Nations through the Security Council? Gaitskell had raised this as early as 2 August, in the concluding sentences of his speech violently attacking Nasser. So far, we had decided to wait, at least until the outcome of diplomatic measures. I had been particularly impressed by a talk with Winthrop Aldrich and Lord Salisbury at Hatfield on 19 August. The Ambassador had insisted that Dulles was strongly opposed to this course, whether because he doubted the legal and juridical strength of our claim, or whether, as I suspected, because the whole idea of international control of waterways was a sensitive matter for the Americans, in view of the Panama Canal. A more powerful objection was the probability of a complete stalemate through the use of the veto. We could not forget that the only time that the United Nations had been able to mobilise to defend justice as well as to secure peace had been over Korea. But this had been possible because at that time the Russians were boycotting the United Nations altogether. They were not likely to repeat this error.

Nevertheless, the question which Gaitskell had raised was now being freely canvassed. While we had been ready to await the results of the first London Conference Nasser's rebuff to the Menzies Committee made it necessary to reconsider our position. Of course, there was the danger of protracted and ultimately ineffective debates at New York. Nevertheless, public opinion both in Britain and in the world would require that we should at least make an attempt to obtain justice through the United Nations before embarking on any more drastic remedy.

Towards the end of August, Ministers were inclined to favour going to the Security Council in view of the state of public opinion. We assumed that we should obtain full American support in the Security Council. Indeed, in late August, Dulles had 'expressed the view that quite a good resolution, in favour of the declaration, could be "rail-roaded" through the United Nations'.[1]

A few days later, he reverted to his earlier view. He described the Security Council as a quicksand. Once in it, we would not know how deep it would prove, or whether we would ever get out. In

[1] 24 August 1956.

spite of the earlier messages which Eden had received from the President, maintaining that reference to the United Nations must precede any question of force, Dulles would not pledge himself to give us full support in the Security Council. On 30 August we sent a draft resolution to Washington about which he found every possible objection to almost every clause. Indeed, if we had not had confidence in the good faith of our American allies, we must have concluded that the State Department was merely trying to waste time. At this time I certainly never doubted that in the long run or in a real crisis we could rely on the at least tacit assistance of our American friends. Perhaps I ought to have taken warning at the new attitude of the State Department, and rather sinister references to the undesirability of seeming to 'gang up with Britain and France'. It was not till it was too late that the strange blindness of the American leaders to the true tactical and strategic significance of the struggle for power in the Middle East was removed. The Eisenhower Doctrine of 1957 would have saved us all in 1956.

If I, with my American background and the experience of the American machine in the Mediterranean campaign, was baffled by this fog of contradictions, Selwyn Lloyd, who, both now and until the end of the crisis, showed admirable skill and sang-froid, was even more handicapped. Nevertheless, he remained calm, efficient and confident throughout. The strain upon him during these months was almost as great as that upon Eden; but I never saw him show fatigue or irritation.

In view of the need soon to recall Parliament and the growing feeling throughout the country that we should now appeal to the United Nations, we had virtually taken the decision, when there was a new turn of the wheel. Dulles had devised a new plan. Even before the result of the Menzies mission was known, he had thought out an ingenious contrivance—to be called the 'Suez Canal Users' Association'—commonly known as SCUA. On the face of it this concept appeared designed to organise the United States, as well as all the other maritime nations, in an effective and perhaps decisive system of pressure on the Egyptian Government.

The SCUA scheme was a plan to which it was expected that the great majority of maritime and interested nations would adhere.

E

By organising the ships, operating the Canal, engaging the pilots and taking effective control of the Canal, it would deny the Egyptian Government both the prestige and the profits of their act of piracy. The essence of it was as follows:

> Britain and France and the U.S.A., and as many of the other London Conference Powers as possible, would join together in an association, whose ships would in concert sail through the Canal in accordance with their usual individual needs, employing its own pilots and other personnel to secure proper passage, and receiving the dues for passage. From the moneys received Nasser would be paid the share that they felt Egypt ought justly to have. They would seek Egyptian co-operation. If it were forthcoming, good; if not, they would pass through the Canal with the aid of their own pilots.[1]

But of course the sixty-four thousand dollar question remained. If the SCUA ships were stopped, what would the order be? Go forward or turn back? It was this fundamental issue which Dulles refused to face, and on which he allowed ambivalent interpretations to be placed.

On 10 September, a few days before the meeting of Parliament, the position was still obscure.

> I cannot help feeling that it's worth while to accept the House of Commons difficulty [about the United Nations] if we can really get the Americans to help with the 'Users' Club'. For if its members, including U.S., were really to sail their ships (with pilots) through the Canal disregarding Nasser, it would either cause Nasser to 'lose face' altogether, or get the Western countries, including U.S.A., into an 'incident' which would justify forceful action. But does Dulles really mean business? Will the Club act, and act quickly? Or will it negotiate with the Egyptians? We decided to send a telegram to Dulles to clear up these questions. The most important is that all dues should be paid to SCUA (including American and American chartered ships). This is the crucial test.[2]

When the French arrived on the same evening I sat next to the Prime Minister, Guy Mollet.

[1] Finer, pp. 207–8.   [2] 10 September 1956.

I asked Mollet whether he could not bring some influence on Gaitskell. After all, they were both Socialists. 'Yes,' replied Mollet, 'but this is a strange country. Here the Conservatives hold Socialist opinions and act accordingly; the Socialists are old-fashioned Liberals!'[1]

After much discussion the British and French agreed to the American plan. As Eden says, the decision whether to endorse this scheme was one of the most crucial that we had to face during the whole Suez crisis. The dilemma was a real one. Perhaps, had we known of the equivocal statements to be made by the President on the very day on which our decision had to be taken, we might have hesitated. We could, of course, have lost the goodwill of the United States had we rejected this plan out of hand and appealed direct to the United Nations on the terms of a resolution which Dulles had hitherto declined to support. On the other hand we would have avoided 'the long and dismal trail of negotiation in which we became involved in an effort to set up this Users' Club'.[2] In his own account Eden generously takes the main responsibility on himself for our decision which, in view of the meeting of Parliament the next day, had to be made urgently. He telephoned me early the next morning, with some natural doubts after a night of reflection. There was still an opportunity for further thought.

> The alternatives are still these: (1) Announce in the debate this afternoon that we are going to take the matter immediately to the Security Council; (2) Announce the formation of the Users' Club (SCUA). The Americans (who have been rather difficult in the latest exchanges) are against (1) and for (2). This will, of course, make trouble for us in Parliament. But it's worth while, to go for (2) now, since American support is so important—especially in the financial field. So this was agreed . . . and the speech was so designed as to be equivocal on (1).[3]

Although I was becoming somewhat disillusioned as to Dulles's intellectual integrity over this whole affair, I still hoped that we could obtain if not active support, at least the tacit approval of the Americans for any course which might be forced upon us. Of

[1] 10 September 1956.   [2] The Earl of Avon, p. 480.
[3] 12 September 1956.

course, by permitting payment of dues to Nasser they were allowing more than a third of the Canal revenue to reach his hands. But I had still hopes that this grave leak would in due course be stopped. On the other side of the picture, if the Americans would give reasonable support to sterling and help us in an emergency by paying for dollar oil, we and the European countries should be able to maintain our position even in the worst conditions. Of course, if the Americans were to sell sterling–officially or unofficially–and act not even as neutrals but in a hostile manner, we stood no chance. We had therefore little choice. We must accept a further period of delay, and trust in our friends. None of us could have foretold at this time the extraordinary *volte-face* which Dulles was to make and Eisenhower weakly to support.

One somewhat ludicrous source of confusion was caused by a phrase in one of Dulles's telegrams which shows the danger of a common language. He spoke of

> 'compensation' to be paid by the Users' Club to Egypt. This made British Ministers very indignant–until I explained to them that in America compensation refers to salary, wages, royalties, etc. It does not mean (as in English) payment in respect of a past injury by one party to another. This would be quite reasonable for SCUA to pay, if Egypt provides services, etc., and the use of the Canal for the new organisation.[1]

Actually I have always rather liked the phrase 'compensation', meaning salary or wages. It assumes a kind of permanent paradise in an unending *Concert Champêtre* of Giorgione which we have a right to enjoy. If we abandon it in favour of work we are entitled to obtain a corresponding indemnity.

Owing to Dulles's continued resistance to our going to the United Nations and the flow of argument which poured out from Washington against this course, we were forced, if we adopted SCUA, to restrict our attitude to the Security Council to a mere formality. We realised that if we were to accept the Americans' way of playing the hand, then it was no good doing so on half-hearted terms. Dulles, who was afterwards to become the champion

[1] 12 September 1956.

of the United Nations and play the role of an international Sir Galahad, was still violently opposed to France and Britain making any appeal to that body. There would be trouble in the House of Commons and the country. The Opposition leaders, forgetful of their own failure to get any United Nations support over the Persian oil dispute, were particularly strong in this demand.

In opening the debate the Prime Minister left Parliament and his allies under no doubt as to what he meant by the SCUA scheme.

> The Egyptian authorities will be requested to co-operate in maintaining the maximum flow of traffic through the Canal. It is contemplated that Egypt shall receive appropriate payment from the association in respect of the facilities provided by her. But the transit dues will be paid to the users' association and not to the Egyptian authority.[1]

He added these words:

> I must make it clear that if the Egyptian Government should seek to interfere with the operations of the association, or refuse to extend to it the essential minimum of co-operation, then that Government will once more be in breach of the Convention of 1888. In that event, Her Majesty's Government and others concerned will be free to take such further steps as seem to be required either through the United Nations, or by other means for the assertion of their rights.[1]

At this point there were, naturally enough, vigorous protests from the defeatists and demands for a more explicit statement. Eden has subsequently stated that he declined to make any further explanation of what he said, since the words had been deliberately chosen by the three powers. The messages and explanations that passed between London and Washington and Paris and Washington certainly support this claim.[2] It is only fair to the Ambassador, Winthrop Aldrich, to record that he was persistent in his warnings—he knew Dulles well.

In order to meet the susceptibilities of the devoted supporters of the United Nations, we adopted, with the approval of our French allies, a somewhat bizarre procedure. Eden made it clear that in the

[1] *Hansard*, 12 September 1956.   [2] The Earl of Avon, p. 482.

long run there was no question of excluding reference to the United Nations; meanwhile, while we were trying other methods, we had thought it proper, jointly with the French, to address a letter to the President of the Security Council informing him of the situation. One of our French friends contemptuously described this 'as leaving our visiting-card' upon this distinguished international figure.

On the whole, the debate went well.

P.M. made an admirable speech; he had a great ovation. Gaitskell was obviously taken aback by the 'Users' Club' plan and thrown off his balance. The rest of his speech was directed rather to getting off the patriotic line which he had inadvertently taken in August, on to the 'party' line.[1]

On the next day, 13 September, the Parliamentary situation was more difficult. In order to get the Americans thoroughly entangled in SCUA, we expected and indeed deliberately risked the criticism about our unwillingness to go to the United Nations.

We say that we are operating under Article 33. Our critics say, 'Will you promise not to use force without the consent of U.N.?' We say, 'How can this be, seeing that there is a Russian veto?' But, since there is this strange Anglo-Saxon mystique about U.N., they say, 'Yes–but *go* to U.N. all the same. Then you will have done the right thing.' Naturally, the Socialists pressed this hard yesterday and today. Equally naturally, the Liberals–Clem Davies and Co.–and the Archbishop of Canterbury (although they must have known why we chose SCUA, in spite of the delay involved) weighed in on the same side. This put us in a difficult position, especially as a good many Tories, mostly young and mostly sons of 'Munichites' . . . began to rat too. It was all the more annoying because we have every intention of 'going to the Security Council' . . . but have not done so, because Dulles has not yet agreed to vote against, or even to abstain on a Russian or Yugoslav amendment to our motion.[2]

Consequently this debate became more difficult to handle than that in August. On the second day Selwyn Lloyd moved a vote of confidence, condemning the Egyptian Government and welcoming the continued efforts of the British Government to find a solution.

[1] 12 September 1956.   [2] 13 September 1956.

Gaitskell had by now moved from his position of a few weeks ago, stimulated no doubt by the pressure in the parties of the Left. The Opposition continued to demand the immediate reference of the whole dispute to the United Nations. It was indeed a paradoxical situation.

Under all this pressure, P.M. naturally began to waver. On the other hand, the militant wing (Waterhouse–Amery) of the party might well turn nasty if he were to change his position too noticeably. Meanwhile, Foreign Secretary had moved the vote of confidence at 2.30–in a fine speech–but Sir Lionel Heald (an ex-Solicitor-General) had declared himself unwilling to vote for the Government, and other Tories were following suit. There was a meeting at 6 p.m. Butler was for giving the pledge–'no force, without recourse to U.N.' I was for standing firm, 'What I have said, I have said.' If P.M. were to 'climb down' under Socialist pressure, it would be fatal to his reputation and position. As we *are* going to Security Council–as soon as we can rely on U.S. support there–events, not words, will justify us. However, I thought the form of words which I (and Salisbury, Butler and Kilmuir) had agreed a day or two ago, would do. They should hold the position, from both angles. This formula was sent for, and approved.[1]

While the debate was proceeding, an account of an extraordinary Press conference given by Dulles was coming over the tape, at the very moment when the Prime Minister was winding up.

Dulles, who had made the *statement* on SCUA quite correctly, and strictly in accordance with the agreed terms, fell down (as usual) on 'supplementary questions'. He said that, if opposed, American ships would *not* repeat *not* 'shoot' their way through the Canal. No. They would go round the Cape.[1]

This was yet another example of the series of blunders by which the American administration seemed to take away with one hand what they had given with the other. Once again 'no comment' would have held the position and kept the Egyptians guessing. 'Of course, Gaitskell made great use of this in his wind-up speech . . . and P.M. was a little rattled.'[1] Gaitskell used the American pronouncement to

[1] 13 September 1956.

rub in his new policy—'Go round the Cape—order or build large tankers—put up with the extra costs.' As a result of all this, in reply to an interruption as to what would happen if this SCUA enterprise was forcibly interrupted, Eden was stung into saying, 'If the Egyptian Government are in default, we will take them to the Security Council.'

There was a roar of applause from the Socialist benches; silence on the Tories', except of course from the Waverers. . . . Fortunately, P.M. stuck [to] the tougher form of words . . . which formed the concluding passage of the speech. These words —although logically contradictory to what he had just said— seemed to hold the field, and had an air of confidence and determination.[1]

His final sentences were as follows:

I want to deal with the question: would Her Majesty's Government give a pledge not to use force except after reference to the Security Council? If such a pledge or guarantee is to be absolute, then neither I nor any British Minister standing at this Box could give it. No one can possibly tell what will be Colonel Nasser's action, either in the Canal or in Egypt.

Nevertheless, I will give this reply, which is as far as any Government can go; it would certainly be our intention, if circumstances allowed, or in other words, except in an emergency, to refer a matter of that kind to the Security Council. Beyond that I do not think that any Government can possibly go.[2]

I think that Gaitskell missed a great opportunity. Eden sat down at three minutes before 10 p.m. Gaitskell should have risen quietly, and in view of the assurances given by—or rather dragged out of— the Prime Minister, asked leave to withdraw his motion. He would have restored his reputation for patriotism by observing the tradition that an Opposition, in a time of national crisis, should do all it can honourably do to help the Government of the day. He had gained his point about the Security Council; and, by a strange paradox, he would have been helping the Government to do exactly what they had been wanting to do for the last six weeks.

[1] 13 September 1956.   [2] *Hansard*, 13 September 1956.

Gaitskell, following the debate, wrote a letter to *The Times* claiming that the Government's position about the use of force was contrary and obscure.

> P.M. rang me about it, and seemed rather concerned. I said that I felt very relieved that Mr. G. should take this line, as it entirely destroyed the argument that P.M. had 'climbed down'. My advice was that he should issue a statement that 'H.M.G. had nothing to add to what P.M. and Foreign Secretary had said in the debate'. The Press guidance might be that Mr. G. seemed a very naïve or a very unscrupulous politician. Was it necessary to tell Nasser beforehand how every card in the pack was to be played?[1]

With all this uncertainty the pressure on the reserves was naturally beginning to show itself. I had a number of meetings at the Treasury with my colleagues and various officials, including representatives of the Bank of England, and the immediate market situation was discussed.

> In spite of the heavy cost, it was decided to go on supporting 'Transferable Sterling'—at least till the meeting of the International Monetary Fund was over. The general view was that we must try to 'ride the storm' and use our reserves to do so. The second meeting (of much the same people) was on the question of 'claiming the waiver' on the American Debt settlement. Various plans were discussed—about which we can no doubt have some talk in Washington. But I cannot see that we can achieve much this side of 6 November [the American Presidential Election].[2]

The Second London Conference to establish SCUA was to meet in a few days. We were now feeling that we ought 'to go to the Security Council' as soon as SCUA got going, but we had to await Dulles's arrival on 18 September. On the same night,

> Dorothy and I dined at the American Embassy. Foster Dulles, Lord Salisbury, the Ambassador and I had a long talk after dinner. We did our best to convince Dulles of the need to take a very firm line. But I purposely did not divert his attention from

---

[1] 15 September 1956.   [2] 14 September 1956.

the great political issues by introducing the question of American money support, either by loan or aid. For to do so assumes that we have given up the idea of using the Canal (either by force or negotiation) and accepting the need to go round the Cape. It is vital that the Americans should not think that we are weakening, in spite of the Socialist Opposition and the other defeatist elements here.[1]

We had lost some $170 million from the reserves in the last three weeks, but the market now seemed to be steadier. Naturally, I feared that there would be a shock to City opinion when the figures were published.

I was to leave for America on 20 September for a meeting of the International Monetary Fund which it was my duty to attend as Chancellor of the Exchequer. There were also to be important discussions with the Commonwealth Finance Ministers. On the previous day the Prime Minister asked me to stay behind after a meeting for a talk alone.

> We cannot quite tell how SCUA will go; many of the countries have got cold feet. But it seems that Foster Dulles is doing his best to get it started. P.M. told me (in great secrecy, for he intends to tell no one else) that the Chief Whip reports a good deal of trouble in the Party. There are some who are opposed to—or afraid of—force even 'as a last resort'.[2]

I was struck by the quiet confidence which Eden showed when great issues had to be faced. His courage, moral and physical, triumphed over all his difficulties. It was only in trifling matters he was sometimes irritable or difficult. This was a supreme issue. He seemed quite determined. It was 1938 over again. He would not be party to any new appeasement.

We then had some talk about my visit to Washington. He seemed concerned that I should be away at such a critical time, but I told him that it would be bad for confidence if my journey were cancelled; to this he agreed. A day or two after I had left, the British Government came to the conclusion that it was now essential to refer the Suez question to the United Nations, and ask for a meeting of

[1] 18 September 1956.   [2] 20 September 1956.

the Security Council. In this decision the French Ministers con-
curred with their usual loyalty but with some unwillingness. They
were sceptical as to the result, but accepted the Anglo-Saxon view
that certain ritual motions must be gone through, however ineffective the ceremonies might prove. The Second London Conference had met on 19 September for two to three days; and it was
clear that a reference to the Security Council would be well received
by the other nations, to operate in parallel with the organisation of
SCUA. At any rate, our decision had the advantage of removing an
important bone of contention between the British Government and
the Opposition. Dulles was, of course, fully informed before the
actual decision was taken. At the time he seemed resigned, especially
since the SCUA plan still held the field. But he refused to allow the
United States to 'sponsor' the Anglo-French letter to the President
of the Security Council. This was despatched on 23 September and
asked for the matter to be put on the agenda for early discussion.
Most people assumed at the time, and many commentators have
subsequently asserted, that the delay in going to the Council was
caused by the reluctance of the British, or the refusal of the French.
This was not so. It was Dulles who objected from the very beginning,
and who was scarcely reconciled to the action when it was finally
taken two months after the seizure of the Canal.

I left for Washington on 20 September and did not return till
1 October. No event of great importance took place in my absence
other than the formal consideration by the Security Council of two
resolutions, one sponsored by Britain and France, and one by the
Egyptians. But the first stages were purely procedural.

I naturally took the opportunity, both in public and in private, to
make known both the anxieties and the determination of the British
Government and people. My first visit was to my mother's old
home in Indiana. We stayed the night at Bloomington, where I
received an honorary law degree from Indiana University on 22
September. The next day we were to go to the little town of Spencer
where my mother was 'born and raised', and where my grandfather,
Dr. Joshua Belles, was still remembered. But apart from a
sentimental pilgrimage my journey had another purpose. I was
determined, here in the Middle West, where the old tradition was

broadly isolationist and with all the memories or prejudices about 'colonialism', to state our case plainly and proudly.

At the university my speech was largely of a sentimental and family character, dealing with the ties of common effort and common suffering which joined our nations together. But when I spoke in the city of Indianapolis that evening, I did not hesitate to deal directly with the Suez crisis before an audience mainly of business men. I began with an explanation of the British economy and the immense efforts which we, almost alone among European countries, were making to pay our debts honourably and to earn our way in the world. At the present time we had a Budget surplus, and we were spending one-third of what we raised in taxation for the defence of the liberties not only of our country but of the world.

After setting out the situation of our island economy, with its dependence on imports of oil and raw materials to be met by exports of manufactured goods, I explained frankly and directly the immediate crisis:

> Behind what Colonel Nasser has done in seizing the Canal there lies a matter which is as vital to you as it is to us. Its immediate effect on us, of course, is much more serious.
>
> The operation, maintenance and freedom of navigation through the Canal touches the lives and affects the livelihood of everyone in Britain and, I would add, in Western Europe and East of Suez too.
>
> We used to be a coal economy; now we are becoming an oil economy. Our oil consumption has doubled in the last six or seven years. We cannot live without it. We are vitally dependent on Middle East oil supplies which amount to 70 per cent of our oil imports. The oil which comes through the Canal might, in theory, be replaced by taking oil from the Western Hemisphere; but this would mean a formidable addition to our dollar expenditure—an extra burden which we could not face.
>
> So the Suez Canal dispute is one which must be settled in such a way as not to threaten our oil supplies.

This might perhaps appeal to the hard-headed and practical men whom I was addressing. But I thought it was wise to stress the wider aspects of the issue and to show them how much was at stake.

Behind this dispute about ownership and running of the Canal lay something much deeper, 'and that is where you are in it as well as we'. America had helped to organise the great defence structures of NATO, SEATO and other similar groupings.

It is a trite, but nevertheless, true saying, that a chain is as strong as its weakest link, and if the economy of Europe were to be struck a serious blow NATO would itself collapse.

So that is the first reason why this is your affair as well as ours.

I turned then to the need for large-scale investment to lift the standard of living in the underdeveloped countries. This could best be done by Britain, Europe and, above all, the United States.

But in what conditions can you ask your people to make large-scale investment in these countries?

Surely this must depend, if it is to be a valid process, on the sanctity of contract. If these countries ask for our money they must give us good faith, and not act the way Colonel Nasser did in grabbing the Suez Canal. Without negotiating with us he tore up a couple of treaties.

This was as great a blow to the future of the underdeveloped countries as it was to the stability of more advanced nations.

I knew that Munich and appeasement were still dirty words in American opinion. I therefore made as my strongest point my personal experience of the dangers of weakness. Naturally I quoted Gaitskell's now famous phrase about Mussolini and Hitler, adding another warning given by the same statesman.

If Colonel Nasser's prestige is put up sufficiently, and ours is put down sufficiently, the effects in that part of the world will be that our friends desert us because they think we are lost.

Yes, it had all happened before. Hitler had established his position by a series of carefully planned moves.

First there was the occupation of the Rhineland—a breach of treaty—but many people said, 'Oh well, it is his own territory; why can't he do what he likes with it?'

Then there was the invasion of Austria, and the same people

said, 'Oh well, Austria is really German; if it wants to join Germany what's wrong with that?'

And then it was Czechoslovakia, followed by Munich. Then came Poland, and then war.

At every point there were plenty of arguments for delay; but delay had proved fatal.

I feel that all of us who went through those years—and I was one who did and can say with truth that I opposed this policy of weakness at every stage—are determined to see that this shall not happen again.

I then referred to the Berlin blockade and how this had been defeated by the immediate reaction of America and Britain. It might of course be argued that Egypt was a very different affair from Germany and Russia; a small country without any great resources. Would it matter, it might even be said, if Nasser got away with it? Indeed it would, for if contracts were broken and properties taken over without warning or negotiation, what would be the result throughout the Middle East, in Saudi Arabia, in Jordan, in Syria, in Iraq and the Sudan? New revolutions would begin by the same method and Communism would be strengthened.

The determination to seize other property—whether it be British-owned, American-owned, Dutch-owned or what you will—will be too great; and before we know where we are it may well be that the control of vital oil supplies, on which Western Europe at any rate must live, will be in the hands of powers which have in effect become satellites of Russia.

I then declared in the most solemn terms that Nasser must not get away with it. I could not believe that Britain and America would allow him to do so. I did not claim that if we failed there would be an immediate disintegration. It might take months; it might take years. But sooner or later unstable governments, or hesitating governments who would like to be friendly but who could be easily cajoled or bullied by a successful dictator, would be subverted or destroyed. So Nasser must be stopped—now.

My words were widely reported, not merely in the local Press but from coast to coast. They were addressed, at least in part, to the President and the Secretary of State.

On Sunday the 23rd, after a tour of the University,

> We motored to Spencer, mother's 'home town'. We were there received by an enthusiastic reception committee, including some old people who claimed to remember my mother and grand-father. The Methodist Church—rebuilt in stone since my mother's day but on the same site—was filled with a large congregation of all ages. I read the lesson—the parable of the talents—and made an address to the people about mother and her forebears. I found it rather difficult to get through without breaking down, and I really felt that my mother was there watching us and enjoying the satisfaction of so many of her hopes and ambitions for me. When I remember all that I owe to her, it's difficult to know how to express what she did for me. It was a most moving ceremony, and the people were extraordinarily kind and sympathetic.[1]

After the service I went to lay a wreath on my grandfather's tomb in the cemetery, where he and my grandmother and some infant children are buried in a family plot. The cemetery stands on the high banks of the White River, and no doubt was laid out very early in the life of this little community—probably about 1830.

I returned to Washington on 24 September, inspired by my short visit to the Middle West, and my contact with ordinary folk, to meet their rulers in Washington, in whose hands all our destinies largely lay.

Early the next morning I received a message asking me to come immediately to the White House. I was taken to the private entrance.

> The President seemed to me in very good health. I was quite astonished at this, for the photographs which we had seen made him appear very old and tired. But I believe that this is partly due to the faulty method by which photographs are telegraphed over. I saw photographs of Eden in the American papers which gave him a similarly haggard look. In any case, the President was in good heart. His colour was good; he was clearly active and interested—and very keen to win his election. Indeed, he was

[1] 23 September 1956.

anxious to hit back at his critics. He was going off to Iowa for a speech that afternoon.[1]

His manner could not have been more cordial. It was just like talking to him in the old days in Algiers at Allied Force Headquarters. He asked affectionately about Churchill, and talked at some length about 'the Grand Old Man'.

> On Suez, he was sure that we must get Nasser down. The only thing was, how to do it. I made it quite clear that we could *not* play it long, without aid on a very large scale—that is, if playing it long involved buying dollar oil.[1]

We then turned to defence and the cost of fitting out our Canberras to take atomic bombs. Next, to the question of rearming NATO. With necessarily smaller numbers of troops on our side, we needed superior armament. Hence the importance of tactical atomic weapons. Nevertheless there was a new and unwelcome development:

> Little countries could blackmail us, because we could not use the immense power of the H-bomb, and risk global war. This had happened in the Formosa trouble; in Indo-China; and was now our trouble in Egypt. All this needed thinking out again.[1]

He then referred to the United Nations.

> We had created something which was all very well as long as we could control it. But soon we might not be able to do so, even when we acted together. Anyway, U.S. had to pay a big price—in economic aid, etc.—for U.N. votes. What would happen in the next few years alarmed him. Why could not U.S., U.K., Germany and France form a group and try to settle all these things ahead of time—before they reached crisis stage.[1]

The President turned to domestic politics.

> He was 'mad' with some of his critics. They always said what had been done wrong in the past, or made wonderful promises for the future. But they never said what ought to be done now. (That's why they were not making Suez a campaign point. The Democrats had nothing to suggest.)[1]

[1] 25 September 1956.

Then came a familiar and delightful episode in which the President demonstrated one of the advantages of the White House garden.

It was a narrow 'fairway'–but outside the railings, there was a street lamp which he could aim at–about 270 yards. He could drive his ball at the lamp–but would not reach it.[1]

All this I, of course, reported to Eden on my return. I assured him of my strong feeling that the President was really determined to stand up to Nasser. When I explained to him the economic difficulties in 'playing it long' he seemed to understand. He accepted that by one means or another we must achieve a clear victory.

At 10.30 a.m. I attended a meeting of the International Monetary Fund. This lasted two and a half hours, chiefly taken up by an admirable review by its head, Eugene Black.

I made it clear that we were determined to maintain the strength of sterling. We were entitled to draw heavily from the Fund for this purpose, subject to the formal approval of the authorities. In addition, we were ready, in case of need, to use our dollar investments as collateral for a dollar loan from the Export–Import Bank or any similar source. There was no hint, at this time, of any difficulty being put in our way, or of financial backing to Britain not being available in full, whatever the circumstances.

Late in the afternoon I went to the State Department for a talk with Dulles. After a general conversation at which the British Ambassador accompanied me and Dulles was surrounded by advisers, he took me into a small private room in which we were alone. Since I had left London the formal Anglo-French request to the Security Council to put Suez on the agenda had been announced. I was therefore prepared for the outburst of indignation which followed. He really felt that he had been badly treated. He had understood when he left London that we had agreed to keep away from the United Nations a bit longer. He was, therefore, deeply hurt to find that we had taken this decision without further consultation. We should get nothing but trouble in New York; we were courting disaster. (From the way Dulles spoke you would have

[1] 25 September 1956.

thought he was warning us against entering a bawdy-house.) After a few minutes, he recovered his temper. He understood the pressure under which we were working and he would put the matter out of his mind. It was no use to 'go jobbing backwards'. We must just get out of the U.N. trouble the best way we could.

In view of the Secretary of State's subsequent actions, and the devotion to the cause of the United Nations which he was to express —at least in public—in almost passionate tones, this conversation, of which I have a careful record,[1] seems strange indeed. Dulles went on to talk about different methods of dealing with Nasser. He thought the new SCUA plan might prove successful. But of course it would take six months. At this point I said that I did not think we could wait six months, unless, of course, Nasser was losing face all the time. But our information from the Middle East was that he was not doing so. At any rate, if we were to 'play it long', the question of the payment of the Canal dues became of paramount importance. On this, I was given encouragement. American ships could certainly be got to pay to SCUA; and so, later on, could American-owned ships sailing under a flag of convenience.

Dulles next referred to the election. Naturally he hoped that nothing serious would happen until it was over, although he admitted that Suez was playing no part in the elections at the present time, since the Republicans didn't understand it, and the Democrats were frightened by it. The rest of the conversation was taken up by the problem of giving Britain financial aid. He thought something might be done on military lines, and added that he had rung up George Humphrey, the Secretary of the Treasury, to see what could be done to ease the terms of the post-war loan. On this matter of financial assistance to Britain, Dulles enjoined the deepest secrecy; he seemed very apprehensive lest anything of this kind were to come out during the election.

Except for the plea that we should try to avoid pressing the issue until the election was over, there was no hint in this talk that Dulles did not recognise our right and indeed our need to resort to force, if necessary. Perhaps I should have attached greater weight to the date of the Presidential Election. Although there was a

[1] 25 September 1956.

general opinion that it would be a 'walk-over' for Eisenhower, and the Gallup polls confirmed this view, yet there might have been some nervousness at Republican headquarters.

On the next day, 26 September, after a morning meeting of the I.M.F., I had a talk with George Humphrey. His chief purpose was to propose that I should come over, after the Presidential Election, to discuss the question of some alleviation in the loan arrangements to our benefit. He scarcely mentioned the Suez crisis. He referred to his friendly relations with Butler during the years that they had worked together, and hoped that we might co-operate with equal amity. The greater part of the interview was occupied by a monologue by Humphrey of considerable length. Its theme was the great danger which threatened the economy of the United States. They had lost gold every year for the last eight years. They were spending too much, both at home and abroad. Too many people were consuming goods and services without making comparable efforts in exchange.

This dark and almost tragic picture of the declining strength of the United States was accompanied by the smiling and easy manner which reflected the real buoyancy of Humphrey's character. His conversation was full of shrewd points based upon his experience in business. With an interesting explanation of the foundation of his family business and its wide diversification, and some observations about the problems facing the sterling area, the conversation continued in an agreeable way for about three-quarters of an hour. Humphrey had such charm of manner and such a jaunty, amiable way of expressing himself that I began to wonder what was the real purpose of the talk. But he now argued that our two Governments ought to think our global strategy out again. We were spending far too much, especially on aid and armaments. NATO would have to be 'rethought'. The next point was on the duplication of effort. I think the President or Foster Dulles must have spoken to him about this; for he began to develop the idea that we should try to act in a complementary, rather than a competitive, manner in certain types of weapons. Finally, he said in a most emphatic way that America must see the United Kingdom through any of her troubles. He realised the essential role of Britain; if we got into serious difficulties the whole of the security of America would be imperilled.

I was left feeling that in the Secretary of the Treasury we were likely to find a useful as well as a powerful friend. Since he made no reference whatever to the Middle East crisis which was so dominant in our minds, I assumed that he had no very strong feelings about it. In this I was soon to be proved tragically wrong.

The meeting of Commonwealth Finance Ministers took up the next two days. In addition to the main subject—European integration—there was a useful discussion on the financial and economic consequences of Colonel Nasser.

Before leaving for home I made calls on two old friends and colleagues—Bob Murphy and General Bedell Smith. Murphy was influential in the State Department and well liked by the President. I repeated the views I had expressed to him in London at the end of July. Bedell Smith was one of the President's most intimate friends. He had served him as Chief of Staff throughout the war, and no one had more influence at the White House. Bedell, incidentally, was no great admirer of Dulles. He listened sympathetically to what I had to say and no doubt passed it on to the right quarter.

I reached London on 1 October to find that SCUA had now been formally established at a meeting of the representatives of eighteen countries, presided over by the Foreign Secretary, Selwyn Lloyd. But, on the very same day, Dulles held a Press conference. After a good deal of talk about colonial powers—which seemed inopportune and in any case irrelevant, since the colonial powers were already engaged in giving freedom and independence to their imperial possessions—Dulles referred to the differences of approach to the problem between the Americans and the British or French traditions. This must lead to a degree of 'independence' in American policy while the 'shift from colonialism' was going on—a period which he unwisely estimated at fifty years. Dulles then delivered himself of a sentence calculated to destroy his own child. The question had been asked whether there was any real strength in SCUA; were there any real teeth in the plan?

There is talk about teeth being pulled out of the plan, but I know of no teeth in it, so far as I am aware.[1]

Even the normally impassive compiler of the *Annual Register* observes:

> Mr. Dulles at a Press conference in his own country seemed to have retreated so far from what had been supposed in Britain to be the purposes and powers of the Association that it seemed doubtful if it would serve any useful purpose.[2]

Nevertheless, with undeterred courage, Selwyn Lloyd, after presiding over a formal but ineffective meeting of SCUA, now doomed to decay, set out for New York, where he and Pineau, the French Foreign Minister, were to present our case to the Security Council.

The proceedings at the United Nations lasted for eight days. Although both the Press and the Foreign Office telegrams gave us a good picture of the public debate and the significance of the speeches, it was difficult to follow the intricacies of the private talks, even from the Foreign Minister's personal reports. At Dulles's request Selwyn Lloyd had agreed that in addition to the public sessions of the Security Council there should be meetings behind closed doors as well as private negotiation between the principals.

On the first day, 5 October, Selwyn Lloyd introduced the British and French resolution in public session with an admirable speech, which although couched in moderate terms was firm and determined. One phrase of his was to be repeated in an important statement by President Eisenhower a few days later: 'The United Nations Charter considers that there can be no genuine peace without the maintenance of justice and international law'. Pineau followed in similar terms.

During the next day or two there was a certain amount of fencing. Selwyn Lloyd repeated to Dulles his urgent plea to take action to stop payment of tolls to Nasser by American shipowners, whether flying the American flag or flags of convenience. But the Secretary

---

[1] The Earl of Avon, p. 499.
[2] *Annual Register, 1956,* pp. 49–50.

of State continued to prevaricate over this point. Although it is somewhere stated in Scripture that it is our duty to forgive our friends, I found it hard to understand or excuse his attitude. If SCUA could ever succeed, it could only be by Nasser being deprived of all the proceeds of his illegal action. Moreover, a decisive announcement of intention by the Americans would have had a considerable effect on the Egyptian delegate and his Government. Nasser would have been made to understand that he was in real danger of losing his advantage. Freed from this anxiety and observing the hesitations of the American Administration, he felt strong enough to resist and even to insult the Security Council. He announced in Cairo on 7 October that 'the United Nations would collapse if it supported the British and French plan for international operation of the Canal'.[1]

Nor did the Egyptians show the slightest compunction about the long denial of passage through the Canal to Israeli ships in spite of its clear illegality. According to some reports, we heard that they were resorting to taunts that if the Suez Canal was to be subject to international supervision, there were other similar waterways that well might be treated in the same way. This touched a very raw point with the Americans. There was in fact no comparison between the legal position of the Panama Canal and that of the Suez Canal. Yet the method of the former's acquisition, if used by one of the older nations, would certainly have been called an example of 'colonialism' or 'imperialism' in its crudest form.

The Franco-British resolution was in two parts, the first of which was ultimately passed unanimously by the Council. It laid down as requirements of any settlement six principles which were largely taken from Dulles's exposition at the first London Conference:

1. There should be free and open transit through the canal without discrimination, overt or covert.
2. The sovereignty of Egypt should be respected.
3. The operation of the canal should be insulated from the politics of any country.
4. The manner of fixing tolls and charges should be decided by agreement between Egypt and the users.

[1] Finer, p. 298.

5. A fair proportion of the dues should be allotted to development.

6. In case of disputes, unresolved affairs between the Suez Canal Company and the Egyptian Government should be settled by arbitration.[1]

The second part was equally important. It has been clearly and correctly summarised by Eden:

The second part of the resolution declared that the proposals of the eighteen powers corresponded to these requirements and invited the Egyptian Government to put forward its proposals to give effect to them. It requested the Governments of Egypt, France and the United Kingdom to continue their interchanges. It also laid down that in the meantime the canal should offer free passage to all shipping. . . . It further declared that the Users' Association should receive the dues payable by the ships of its members, and that the association and the Egyptian nationalized authority should co-operate to ensure the satisfactory management of the canal.[1]

Had this part of the resolution also received unanimous support, not only could a way have been opened for a test case on the banning of Israeli ships, but the first part could have been made operative and effective.

After the speeches of Lloyd and Pineau, Mahmoud Fawzi, the Egyptian Foreign Minister, made a skilful, if evasive reply, appealing to all the old anti-colonial prejudices. The struggle, he contended, was one between domination and freedom—between the old materialism of the nineteenth century and the new idealism of the twentieth. But he made a proposal which had some superficial attractions. He proposed that a negotiating body should be set up and discussions should at once take place to settle the composition and the place and date of its meeting. Of course this was mere evasion. After all these months it was an offer 'to negotiate about negotiation'. He had perhaps a stronger point in boasting the successful operation of the Canal since its seizure.

Fawzi, who was normally a smooth operator (indeed it was said of him that he was so slippery that compared to him an eel was like

[1] The Earl of Avon, p. 504.

a leech), allowed himself unexpected taunts against Britain and France and, above all, the United States. This seemed to show an unusual confidence. I had met Fawzi while I was Foreign Secretary and regarded him as a cautious diplomatist, unlikely to show truculence unless he was quite confident of his position. It was a Roman statesman who was quoted by Gibbon as describing the character of the Egyptians as 'insensible to kindness but extremely susceptible to fear'. What made Fawzi so sure of his ground? Neither the British nor the French Governments had concealed privately or publicly their determination to use as the last resort the measures necessary to secure their rights and those of the maritime nations, as well as to bring peace and order into the Middle East. The views of Commonwealth countries had been set forth forcibly by Menzies only a week before. Even the American President and Secretary of State had declared that the use of force could not be ruled out if all else failed. Yet Fawzi must have been convinced of two things—full support from the Soviet Government and the cracking of American nerve if and when the issue was put to the test. Indeed, Fawzi allowed himself especially wounding gibes against Dulles. I remember feeling disturbed when I read the account of his speech, all the more audacious because it was made in public. Nevertheless, he did throw out a vague plan of further negotiations, which he was to develop further in private discussions.

Shepilov, the Soviet Minister of Foreign Affairs, had treated his colleagues in the Security Council and his audience in the world outside to a particularly vicious example of Soviet invective. After a little experience of Russian methods of argument I had already learnt that many of these phrases so freely bandied about—corrupt exploiters, imperialists, colonialists, capitalist lackeys and the rest—were merely to be regarded like Homeric epithets, conventionally attached to their appropriate nouns. When it came to private conversation they used quieter, more normal language. I was therefore not unduly alarmed by Shepilov's vituperation. For some reason, the American delegation was sensitive to these attacks and kept issuing statements rebutting some of the Russians' accusations. American statesmen were then, and still are, strangely sensitive to outside criticism. They dislike being misunderstood. They long for sympathy. I have often told my American friends that now that the British Empire has come to an end in its old form and they have succeeded not only to our inheritance but to our burdens they must put up with being universally hated. This is at once the privilege and the penalty of a great power. I try to comfort them by reminding them that foreigners are now saying nothing worse about them than they have for years said about George III and those unlucky chests of tea that were thrown into the harbour at Boston. But, somehow, they still want to be liked.

However, from our point of view, both the Egyptian and the Russian combination of insolence and arrogance was on this occasion beneficial. For Dulles was stung into a stronger declaration, at least in appearance, than we had dared to hope. He replied on 9 October. After giving a list of the moves for peace and paying a tribute to the patience of the nations chiefly concerned, he gave us full support for our view of the position under international law. The Egyptians had repeatedly accepted this interpretation themselves, and he quoted with great effect a statement by an Egyptian representative at the Security Council as late as 1954 which admitted the whole case.

> The Canal Company, which controls the passage, is an international company controlled by authorities who are neither Egyptian nor necessarily of any particular nationality. It is a universal company, and things will continue to be managed that way in the future.[1]

In defending the statement which had been drafted largely by himself at the First London Conference, Dulles was earnest and effective. There was a phrase which made a great impression on those who heard it and on the world audience, hanging on his words. He said that if the Canal was used as a means of national policy—as it clearly had been against Israel—then every nation in the world 'would be condemned to live under an economic Sword of Damocles'. Nor did he fall for the insincere proposals of Shepilov and Fawzi for 'establishing a committee which is so constituted that we can know in advance that it will never agree'. He concluded his

[1] Finer, p. 304.

speech by announcing that the United States intended to vote for the British and French resolution.

The full debate was now adjourned, and the private talks and discussions began. So far all had gone well. Dulles had come out firmly in our support, and we had good reason to believe that we should have either the active support or the sympathy of the American people if and when the crunch came. It has been alleged by some critics that the British and French, obsessed with rage or the desire for revenge, missed an opportunity for a settlement. This is false. In effect, they made a great concession. Dag Hammarskjöld, who had joined in the private discussions (at which Dulles was present), did his best to obtain general acceptance of the six principles which should govern the operation of the Canal. To this end, the representatives of the eighteen powers who had formulated the London proposals met together to hear of the progress of the discussions and give their advice. Selwyn Lloyd showed himself an admirable and constructive negotiator and, in the sincere hope of reaching some solution, he now made on behalf of his Government a major concession. We accepted that the Egyptian Government should 'manage' the Canal, provided that there was a committee representing the users, with power to participate in the establishment and supervision of Canal policy on tolls, development, patterns of shipping, discrimination and the like; but on the understanding that the committee could take 'automatic' action if there were any failures of the accepted rules on the part of the Egyptian Government. The principles were admirable and unexceptionable. But what mattered was their implementation. The international committee must have power to act if these principles were disregarded or set aside. In other words, there must be some 'teeth' in the plan. The advisory body would mean nothing if there was no remedy for its advice being ignored.

This concession—to accept Egyptian management of the Canal and to disregard the right of the Canal Company—was a real one. It went further than some of our friends approved. But the most that Fawzi could be induced to offer in return was fair words.

It has also been alleged that the Egyptians might have accepted some appeal, in the case of dispute, to the United Nations or to the

International Court. On the Security Council they were quite safe, for a veto could be relied upon; and the International Court had no effective method of enforcing its judgments, which in any case were generally delivered only after protracted delay.

When, therefore, the Security Council resumed its formal sessions, there was little to be done except restate the positions of the different Governments. Selwyn Lloyd once again spoke effectively, demonstrating the moderation and restraint with which the British and French Governments had acted throughout. An equally impressive contribution was that of Spaak. The Australian representative spoke strongly in support of Britain's position. Dulles still hoped that something might be done with SCUA but evaded the vital issue as to the payment of dues. It so happened that at this final session Pineau was acting chairman. Accordingly, he contented himself with putting the resolution to the vote. This was taken on 13 October after Dulles had made the last speech.

The two parts of the Franco-British resolution were voted on separately. The first, the statement of principles, was passed unanimously. On the second nine countries voted in favour, two—Russia and Yugoslavia—voted against. This would have made both parts effective; and the Russians therefore interposed their veto. In the terse words of the *Annual Register:*

> The Security Council was thus relieved of the obligation to take any further steps in the matter and Egypt relieved of the obligation to pay any attention to the views of the majority.[1]

Meanwhile SCUA itself was making no progress. American shipowners were still paying their dues to Cairo. Nor had the organisation taken any effective shape. The American representative in London was still without authority to agree to the opening of a bank account into which Canal dues of other countries should be paid; nor had anything been decided as to how it should be apportioned. SCUA, Dulles's brainchild, unanimously accepted by the Second London Conference and from which much had been hoped, was gradually lapsing into a condition of impotence.

For many months Nasser had been pursuing his programme of

[1] *Annual Register, 1956,* p. 49.

Pan-Arabism which, in his mind, meant the union of all Arab countries and even of all Arabs within non-Arab states under his leadership. Many of the more experienced Arab leaders were suspicious both of his secularism and of his Communist ties. Rulers like King Saud were conscious that an Egypt without oil of its own was casting jealous eyes upon the vast wealth accruing from Saudi-Arabian oilfields. The King of Jordan, then as now, was torn by conflicting pressures; but the long connection of Jordan with Britain, and the fact that it was not in economic terms a viable state without British support, made him anxious to resist so far as practicable the dangerous Egyptian embrace. Syria was hopelessly divided. In Iraq alone could we have confidence in the King and his uncle, who had both inherited the fine traditions of their royal house, and in the wisdom of the Prime Minister, Nuri Pasha.

Throughout the area there had been many murmurings among the wiser Arabs about the Soviet arms deal in 1955. The seizure of the Canal in July 1956, while attractive to the public, was looked at with suspicion by the rulers. The strong action which seemed likely to result from the First London Conference confirmed these anxieties. It seemed clear that the Western powers would not allow Nasser 'to get away with it'; but the effects of the Second London Conference, and the obvious incapacity of SCUA, caused increasing doubts. These were confirmed by the impotence of the Security Council. Already, at the end of September, Nasser had succeeded in bringing both Saudi Arabia and Syria into a joint declaration of support. More ominous and more alarming was the increasing pressure upon Israel caused by attacks upon her territory, launched from all her neighbours, Syria, Jordan and Egypt. These had continued sporadically for a long time. They now became more intense. Moreover, the new form of attack by the so-called *fedayeen*, or voluntary infiltrators, was proving daily more formidable. It was clear that these raids were concerted between the three countries, under Nasser's leadership. Israel must retaliate or collapse. The danger of action taking the form of a military attack upon Jordan caused us deep anxiety. Unhappily many of the most dangerous raids were being launched from Jordan under Egyptian leadership. We had a treaty of obligation to defend Jordan, who had no effective air force but relied upon our fighter squadrons stationed in her territory. This situation Eden described as 'a nightmare which could only too easily come true; Jordan calling for support from Nasser and ourselves, Nasser calling for support from Russia, France lined up with Israel on the other side.'[1] On 12 October we were forced to give warning to Israel that, in the event of any serious attack on Jordan, Britain would be bound to come to the assistance of her ally if King Hussein invoked the treaty. At the same time we did our best to persuade the French, whose relations with Israel were much closer than ours, to warn the Israelis against the fatal result of formal military operations against Jordan, however much they might have been provoked by the raids launched from Jordanian territory. The activities of the raiders grew in intensity as the likelihood of Nasser's 'getting away with it' became more and more apparent. The *fedayeen* were now operating not only from Jordan and Syria, but from the Gaza Strip, where they were poised to make dangerous incursions into Israel, with corresponding results upon her economy and the lives of her people. Nasser now openly declared 'that he would choose the time and place for the final assault'. There was no doubt, even in the minds of the United Nations authorities operating in the area, that Egypt had now put herself into the position of the aggressor. It was clear that

> Egypt was gathering her allies, piling up Soviet arms and enlisting Soviet technical help, sharpening her propaganda and intensifying her raids. The risks entailed in the seizure of the canal having been safely negotiated, all was being got ready for the next objective.[2]

Meanwhile, Cairo Radio was pouring out its propaganda with increasing virulence.

The flow of Soviet arms was now reaching Syria, and although for the moment our friends in Iraq stood firm, yet obviously if Nasser succeeded in his declared aim of destroying the Israeli state, his prestige would be so great that they would not be able to stand. In the event they were to fall to assassination eighteen months later, inspired by Nasser's emissaries.

[1] The Earl of Avon, p. 512.   [2] The Earl of Avon, p. 516.

If we had our fears about our treaty obligations with Jordan, our French friends felt equal anxiety as to the effect of Nasser's propaganda upon their North African territories, especially Algeria. The fall of Nasser, by whatever means, would clearly relieve them of dangerous pressures, which indeed were to force even so strong a figure as General de Gaulle to surrender the French positions on the south shore of the Mediterranean Sea, so long maintained, and so important to French interests. At this time, when the French Government were determined to resist, they were naturally as anxious about Nasser's political operations outside Egypt as over the actual seizure of the Canal. In effect the two were closely linked. Like the Leader of the Opposition, the French saw the historic parallel with Mussolini and Hitler. If Nasser could succeed, first against the European powers by defying their protests against the seizure of the Canal, and secondly, in the destruction of Israel, then all the rest of the Arab world would fall easily into his grasp. The Kings and royal houses, the old established notabilities, even the more democratically elected Ministers—all these would fall into his hands, and with them the immense wealth from the oil-producing areas. This seemed to many at the time an exaggerated view. Time has shown that it was not.

Eden has described the anxieties from which he and those closest to him suffered in these critical days. The United Nations had failed us. The American Administration, although friendly, seemed incapable of following any clear and consistent policy. The President, naturally preoccupied with his health as well as with his election, seemed unwilling to give a lead. Whatever his intentions which, from my previous knowledge of him, I felt sure must be friendly, he seemed unable to make up his mind. I sometimes felt that both he and Dulles had lost their nerve and really believed that, if we were to act strongly, the Russians would intervene and the Third World War be launched. None of us at home had any such fears; nor were we led to think differently by the correspondence with the Russian leaders which Eden showed to us. They would do everything to annoy us at the United Nations and elsewhere; they would help Nasser with arms and money and public support; but they were as determined as the Western world to avoid a conflict from which neither side could emerge as victors. Only later, when they saw the United States turn against us, and Britain and France abandoned, did the Russian menace take a more violent form.

In the second half of October the problem was urgent. What then should we now do? Should the British and French send an ultimatum to Nasser and, if our demands were not granted, launch our troops to the occupation of Egypt? If we decided to act, should we announce our intentions to the American Government? Should we consult them; or inform them? Here, I admit that my judgement was wrong. I felt that the American Government, while publicly deploring our action, would be privately sympathetic, and thus content themselves with formal protests. We had learnt from many of our American friends that they were anxious to see the end of Nasser. Although this proved a wrong judgement on my part, it is curious how rapidly American opinion changed after the event, and how many of the most distinguished and reputable leaders of opinion in America reproached us afterwards for not forcing through the Suez operation to a successful conclusion. The alternative was, of course, to surrender altogether, not only the Canal, but Western prestige in the Middle East; and to abandon our old friends throughout the area — countries we had ourselves liberated by the defeat of Turkey in the First World War, many of whose statesmen and leaders of opinion had stood loyally with us. This would mean Pan-Arabism, dominated by Communism, and the right flank of Europe turned. This seemed to us unthinkable. It was in these circumstances, and with these considerations in our minds, that we took note of, and determined, after much thought, to take full advantage of, the situation now developing in the Middle East itself.

The sequence of events was rapid. On 23 October Egypt and Syria set up a joint command under Egyptian leadership which merely gave outward expression to what was already in operation. A day or two later, 25 October, Jordan acceded to this joint command. This was the final step in the pressure upon Israel, which was already suffering, not merely from an economic boycott but from a physical blockade. She could use neither the Canal nor her own port of Eilat on the Red Sea. She was now menaced by invasions. The stranglehold was complete.

The Israel reaction to the ring closing round them, and to the threats of extermination by the superior forces and armaments which Nasser now commanded, was not difficult to foresee. On 27 October Israel mobilised and on the 29th invaded the Sinai peninsula. Eleven years later the story was almost exactly repeated, when they launched and won the famous Six-Day War. Indeed, the parallel is remarkable. It was no doubt King Hussein's visit to Cairo in the summer of 1967 and the fraternal embraces with Nasser that caused the same powerful conclusions to be drawn by the Israelis with the same determination, shocking to many of their critics, not to await their fate calmly like animals in a stockyard, but to take pre-emptive action to preserve their freedom. As Eden grimly remarks about the earlier occasion, 'the marked victim of the garrotter is not to be condemned if he strikes out before the noose is round his throat'.[1]

The British and French Governments, who had already discussed all possible eventualities, had no difficulty in deciding on their course of action. It was to call upon both parties—Egypt and Israel—to stop hostilities and to withdraw their forces from the Canal. If either one failed to comply, British and French forces would occupy the key positions of Port Said, Ismailia and Suez. If at the expiration of twelve hours one or both Governments did not undertake to accept these requirements, the British and French forces would intervene in whatever strength might be necessary.

This ultimatum was given on 30 October; and Eden made a short statement at 8 o'clock that evening in the House of Commons. In a debate upon the adjournment, Gaitskell and the Opposition leaders confined themselves chiefly to pressing for an undertaking that no military action would be taken without further reference to the Security Council. Since Eden refused to give this pledge, a division was taken after two hours' debate, in which the Government secured its normal majority. Curiously enough, the Labour speakers at that time seemed mainly anxious lest we should be taking any action contrary to Israeli interests.

On the same day Eden despatched two telegrams, the first before and the second after the meeting with the French Ministers who had to come to London, warning the President of the United States

[1] The Earl of Avon, p. 523.

As Chancellor of the Exchequer, setting out to make the Budget Speech
'Rather like a school Speech Day—a bit of a bore, but something which had to be endured.'

With Lord Mackintosh, Chairman of the National Savings Committee

Eden and Mollet during the Suez Crisis, 10 September 1956

British paratroopers in Port Said, while oil installations burn in the background

of the action which we had decided to take and excusing himself for having operated so rapidly without full consultation, hoping that the American Government might give us general support. Eisenhower's first reply was not unhelpful. He expressed his disquiet, but thought it of importance that our two Governments should quickly meet and interchange their views. A further message arrived on 30 October when the President had learnt the terms of the British and French Notes to Egypt and Israel. Yet even in this message he only expressed his deep concern and his belief that peaceful processes would in the end prevail.

A resolution was rapidly proposed on 30 October in the Security Council in effect censuring Israel. It was moved by the American representative, Henry Cabot Lodge. It called on Israel to withdraw behind their frontiers and on all U.N. members to refrain from using or threatening force in the area. This resolution, for the first time in the history of British membership of the United Nations, Britain decided to veto. Of course, the whole might of the State Department was exerted, and seven votes were given in favour. We and the French voted against it; Australia and Belgium abstained. The Russians now, with some ingenuity, moved a new resolution substantially the same as the American draft but omitting the more offensive paragraphs. Our Ambassador's inclination would have been to allow this to pass; but since neither the British nor the French representatives were given any opportunity to consult their Governments, the French decided to use the veto, and for the sake of solidarity we acted together.

Our representative, Sir Pierson Dixon, maintained throughout remarkable dignity and resource. Meanwhile Cabot Lodge, the U.S. official representative, adopted a hostile and emotional attitude. He assumed a championship of the United Nations as ardent as it was unexpected. Some observers explained this devotion as an act of reparation for the part played in a previous generation by his grandfather, Henry Cabot Lodge. For it was he who took the leading part in the rejection of the Versailles Treaty of 1919 and thus prevented the adhesion of the United States to the League of Nations.[1] Others attributed the grandson's fervour to his New

[1] Finer, pp. 375 ff.

F

England and especially his Bostonian traditions. He was certainly prejudiced against Britain. He had not forgotten 1776. Like Mrs. Gummidge he seemed to be always 'thinking of the "Old 'Un" '– in this case George III.

On 31 October Israel accepted and Egypt rejected the Anglo-French note. Accordingly on that day military targets in Egypt were attacked by the British and French bombers operating from Cyprus.

Both the military and the political crisis was now fully launched. There followed a week of intense and violent emotion, one of the strangest and most testing in my experience. It was Munich in reverse.

Political issues rarely make a deep impact on the mass of the British people. They will put up with widespread industrial disputes, economic crises, swingeing increases in taxation, continual rises in the cost of living and a steady fall in the value of money, without more than the usual grumbles. Naturally they adopt their own remedies against these calamities: if they belong to the wage-earning and salaried class, by demanding more money; if they depend on pensions or so-called unearned incomes, by the expedient of selling their possessions, speculating on the Stock Exchange or, in the last resort, emigration. They shoulder these burdens in silence and respond without emotion. From time to time, however, there arise questions which seem to break through the stolid endurance of our people and stir strong and even passionate feelings. In past generations these crises were generally caused by religious disputes. The strongest and the most successful Government since the Revolution was destroyed by a sermon. All Marlborough's victories could hardly stand against Dr. Sacheverell's eloquence. Even in my lifetime I can dimly remember the bitter feelings raised by the objections to certain aspects of Mr. Balfour's Education Act of 1902, and the passive resistance movement organised by Dr. John Clifford, precursor to that carried out, on a wider scale, by Gandhi. But in recent years the occasions when the whole nation is plunged into bitter controversy, when whole households have been torn apart and long friendships broken, have been upon matters of foreign policy. From time to time, there arises a dispute on matters

THE ANGLO-AMERICAN SCHISM   153

so fundamental and involving such deep feelings as to cause temporary, and even permanent, rifts between old friends, divisions in families, heavy stresses on Party organisations, and implicating not merely those normally affected by political controversy but the whole mass of the population. Such emotions were caused by Munich and, nearly twenty years later, by Suez.

The House of Commons was in almost continuous and often tumultuous session for nearly a week. Sometimes the debates were on the adjournment; sometimes through votes of censure and sometimes by other procedural methods. On all sides feelings were bitterly inflamed. Ministers, especially the Prime Minister, were continually interrupted. On one occasion the Speaker was forced to suspend the sitting for half-an-hour to allow tempers to cool. Yet in spite of all their other preoccupations, both Eden and Selwyn Lloyd sustained the burden with remarkable resilience. During these fierce disputes I was largely engaged in Treasury matters and, in any case, was not required to take part in the discussions. There was little, therefore, that I could do except to sit upon the Bench, and give moral support to my colleagues. Outside the House, Eden delivered a broadcast on 3 November which had a deep effect. Gaitskell, who properly demanded the right to reply, made an equal impression by his sincerity, although to his opponents his performance seemed somewhat hysterical. He tried to tempt the Conservatives to bring down the Prime Minister by offering to support any successor who would agree to comply with the demands of the United Nations. Two junior Ministers, Anthony Nutting and Edward Boyle, resigned, and there were signs of a certain hesitation among some other members of the Party. We were correspondingly grateful for Gaitskell's rather too obvious snare into which even doubting Thomases on our side would be unlikely to fall. Meanwhile I was particularly unhappy about Edward Boyle's resignation, for he was an admirable and devoted colleague as Economic Secretary to the Treasury, and I had a deep respect both for his intelligence and his integrity.

On 3 November Churchill, who had never taken any part in any controversial issue since his retirement, published a letter which had a profound effect. He expressed his wholehearted approval of the Government's policy. Perhaps the most impressive sentence, which we hoped might have some effect upon the violent attitude now being adopted by the American administration, was this: 'I am confident that our American friends will come to realise that, not for the first time, we have acted independently for the common good.'[1] Such words rang true. In two world wars the first brunt had fallen upon us, to be shared later by the Americans. So it had been with Greece, when the State Department and most of the American Press violently opposed our action in 1944 to save Greece from Communism, yet, within a few years, America was to succeed to our responsibilities. So again it was to prove within a very few months over the Middle East.

The British Press was divided between support, opposition, and that assumption of neutrality based upon superior knowledge and more refined instincts which both sides in a fierce controversy find particularly irritating. As the situation in the United Nations unfolded, feelings were accentuated. Gaitskell accused Eden of defying the Assembly whose authority he regarded as more or less sacrosanct. Nowadays, even Labour Governments have learned to take little notice of these resolutions when they are disagreeable—for instance, when Britain is solemnly called upon to evacuate Gibraltar. But at the time he received strong and sincere support. Equally, as the American pressure grew and the strange coalition between Russia and the United States was revealed, indignation on our side rose to almost fever pitch.

In the few hours during which I could escape from the precincts of Whitehall, I observed that these acrimonious disputes had spread into premises where they are rarely found—in the clubs, in the pubs, in the streets, in the Underground. Wherever men congregated the argument was strenuously conducted—sometimes with courtesy and in polite language but more often in homely and simpler terms. The prevailing rancour spread to private homes and continued long after the end of the immediate crisis. As at Munich, personal quarrels disturbed the equanimity of private life, and in some cases, as I know to my own sorrow, led to permanent estrangement of old friends.

[1] *Annual Register*, 1956, p. 52.

The party positions were strangely reversed. The bulk of the Conservative Party, which had supported Chamberlain at Munich, were partisans of Eden. There were, of course, varying degrees of enthusiasm; I noticed that those Conservatives who had been the most violent opponents of the Munich policy were the keenest partisans of the Government's policy, while those who had been *Munichois* tended, logically enough, to be waverers or opponents. This was true not merely of those in active politics but of private individuals. Those especially who had been the depreciators and detractors of Churchill in the years 1935 to 1939 were now equally sneering about Eden. Although the social life of Britain had so greatly changed since the end of the Second War, yet in the houses where large social gatherings were still possible one could have heard twenty years later very similar opinions about the merits and demerits of appeasement to those current a generation before.

Perhaps the most curious reversal was in the Liberal and Labour parties, especially among the 'intellectuals'. The new doctrine about the infallibility of the United Nations, whether in the Security Council or in the Assembly, was declared by Gaitskell and his colleagues with all the infatuation of ultramontanism. Gaitskell in this respect resembled in 1956 Cardinal Manning in 1870. It seemed difficult to reconcile their demands for strong action in the years before the Second War with their repudiation of it today. Then the cry was 'Stand up to Hitler' or 'Don't let Mussolini get away with it.' This call to arms was reiterated at the time with all the fervour of devotees and re-echoed from the most normally un-warlike quarters. Day after day and month after month there poured forth from progressive politicians and the Left-wing Press of the thirties contempt for the policy of appeasement, and a demand for strength and resolution. Yet, judging from their attitude on this occasion, it is interesting to speculate what would have been the position had the Chamberlain Government accepted their advice. When Hitler remilitarised the Rhineland was the best, and perhaps the last, moment when he could successfully have been resisted. Yet, had the British and French Governments moved to prevent him by force, would their Labour and Liberal critics have followed their lead? Or would they have raised doubts as to the validity of our recourse to arms, and questioned our authority under the League of Nations, or international law? Would they not have said in excuse (as they did afterwards about Nasser) that Hitler was a national leader; that the Rhineland was his territory—his own backyard, was one popular phrase at the time—just as the Canal was Egyptian territory; that he was only pursuing legitimate national ambitions? We should have been lectured about offering friendship and understanding to the new national movements. Yet the failure to resist Hitler in 1936 probably cost twenty million lives.

Similarly Mussolini's attack on Abyssinia could have been prevented only by force. With the absence of American support, no economic sanction—even oil sanction—could be effective. Yet a naval operation cutting Mussolini's vital sea communications across the Mediterranean could easily have been effective. But that would have been an act of aggression, unsanctified by authority of the League. There was a moment in early August 1956, when Gaitskell seemed to have learned the lesson of history. But it was soon forgotten.

Yet perhaps because of these illogicalities, even with all the rigidities of the modern Party system, I sensed a certain uneasiness in the House of Commons. A number of the Trade Union Members by no means liked the virulence of their leaders and, from their inborn patriotism, were offended by their tone and temper. Moreover there were a number of Labour Members who had long and close connections with the Zionist movement, and deep sympathy with the Israeli Government and people. Soon after the military operations were ended, a by-election took place at Chester which seemed likely to provide a test on the effect on public opinion of all these troubles. Strangely, the result seemed to show that they had no effect at all. If anything the Conservative poll showed a slight recovery in November from a slight fall in June and July. The Gallup Poll equally seemed to demonstrate a wide public sympathy with the Government in its difficulties. Certainly, in these first days, in spite of clamour and alarm, we had no difficulty in sustaining our position, both in Parliament and in the country. We were confident that no internal pressure, however sincerely felt, or however strongly expressed, could deter us from the path on which we had set out after so much anxious thought, and with so deep a sense of responsibility. Nor were we unduly dismayed by blatant Communist threats. We had to endure something more distressing than division at home, or hostile menaces from our known enemies. For we were faced with impeachment by a traditional friend and powerful ally.

The British Cabinet certainly made a profound miscalculation as to the likely reaction in Washington to the Franco-British intervention. It has been argued that Eden should have told Eisenhower beforehand of the decision to deliver the ultimatum to Israel and Egypt. On the other hand, to be 'informed' rather than 'consulted' may be almost as wounding as to be kept in the dark. Moreover, since such information could not have been kept secret, there were strong military objections. Nevertheless, we altogether failed to appreciate the force of the resentment which would be directed against us. For this I carry a heavy responsibility. I knew Eisenhower well from the war years and thought I understood his character. I had also enjoyed during my short period as Foreign Secretary a close association with Dulles, having spent many days in his company in London, Washington, Paris, and Geneva. I believed that the Americans would issue a protest, even a violent protest in public; but that they would in their hearts be glad to see the matter brought to a conclusion. They would therefore content themselves with overt disapproval, while feeling covert sympathy. They could easily have followed this course. Indeed, on several occasions before and after the critical weeks many leading Americans, even in the Administration, expressed privately the hope that Nasser could be brought down and a new beginning made. This was undoubtedly the view of the Pentagon, acutely conscious of the dangers to NATO and ultimately to American interests if the position in the Middle East continued to deteriorate.

But our hopes were to be rudely dashed to the ground. The Secretary of State and, to a lesser degree, the President seemed to regard the action of Britain and France as a personal affront. They particularly resented the fact that we had acted on our own without American permission or concurrence. Dulles had all along regarded himself as the legal adviser in the Suez case. He had given much attention to the case and devised one contrivance after another. Now his clients had taken the matter out of his hands and acted on their own. This was an insult, almost a betrayal. Consequently, Dulles showed in the vital period a degree of hostility amounting almost to frenzy. There may have been other reasons. Perhaps the grim disease which was later to prove mortal had affected his psychological and intellectual equilibrium.[1] Perhaps the spectre of Soviet Russia, now armed with the terrible nuclear weapon, had begun to haunt his dreams. He clearly lost his temper; he may also have lost his nerve.

In any event, we and our French allies were now to face an attack, skilfully devised and powerfully executed, in which the protagonists were the Russian and American Governments, acting together in an unnatural coalition. We had the foretaste of the tone and temper of Washington in the resolution of 30 October which was vetoed by the British and French. But we still had reason to hope that this demonstration would content the Americans. After all, they had accepted the Russian veto upon the resolution of 13 October, reaffirming the Six Principles and demanding action upon them. The Egyptian Government had made no effort to comply. SCUA was fading away, and the Secretary of State seemed quite happy with the formal acceptance of the principles which he himself had devised and for which he had argued so powerfully at the first London Conference. He had, as it were, won the case in Court of First Instance; he had won again on Appeal. Whether judgement would ever be enforced was a matter of minor importance. But we were soon to be undeceived. When the British had wished to apply to the Security Council, he had argued strongly for delay. Now, he acted with almost hysterical precipitation. He resorted to a device which he had not thought fit to propose when the resolution embodying his own principles had been vetoed on 13 October. Indeed it was an expedient which had not been used since the time of the Korean War. This was to obtain an emergency meeting of the whole Assembly, based upon the 'Uniting for Peace' resolution of 3 November 1950. At that time, when the Soviet Government had absented themselves, it had been easy to

[1] Dulles suffered his first operation for cancer on 3 November.

persuade the Security Council to pass the necessary resolution to implement this plan and give it their unanimous authority. On this occasion, however, as Dixon was quick to point out, there was no legal authority for overriding a veto. Nevertheless, the British and French were unconstitutionally overruled. It is perhaps worth recalling that President Truman authorised American military and naval operations a day before approval of the Security Council had been obtained, and four months before confirmation by the Assembly. However, the fact that the precedent was not soundly based did not make it any less convenient.

Accordingly, the Assembly met on 1 November to discuss an American resolution demanding, *inter alia*, a cease-fire and with-drawal of all the forces engaged. The debate naturally gave an opportunity for the most violent diatribes against Britain and France from all quarters. It must have been somewhat galling, even for our keenest critics, to listen to the unctuous congratulations which the Soviet delegate showered upon his American colleagues.

The resolution was carried on 2 November by an overwhelming majority—64 votes against 5, the minority being made up of Britain, France, Israel, Australia and New Zealand. Among the abstainers were Canada, South Africa, Belgium, the Netherlands, and Portugal. But the verdict of the Assembly was not so impressive as appeared at first sight. When the United States and Soviet Russia, the great Capitalist and the great Communist powers, are combined, the Whips' task is not difficult. Twenty-six African and Asian states naturally voted against what they called imperialism; ten Communist states were solid in the lobby; and twenty Latin-American republics followed automatically the American lead.

The question naturally arose as to how far the decision which was taken by Dulles and supported less keenly and certainly less bitterly by the President represented the general view of the American people. We felt that a great part, perhaps the majority, of the American people in every walk of life felt a deep sympathy for the French and British, comrades in two world wars and linked by many ties of traditional affection. But these were vain consola-tions. We had to face the determined hostility of the American Government. Nevertheless, we had no doubt about our reply to the

F2

United Nations resolution. It was, of course, carefully concerted with our French allies, and the formal note was agreed by the Cabinet during the evening of 3 November. We were not prepared to halt our action. If and when an international force were created, as had been suggested by Lester Pearson, Canadian Minister for External Affairs, in the course of a speech explaining why he could not vote for the American resolution, we would, under certain conditions, be ready to make way. But these conditions must include an Arab–Israeli peace settlement and a satisfactory agreement regarding the Canal. Meanwhile our operations must continue. These must now be briefly described.

Our withdrawal from Egypt, which had begun in 1955 and was completed in the summer of 1956, completely altered, and worsened, the military difficulties. It was one thing to exert our will either upon Egypt or the Sudan when Alexandria was in our hands and we held a base in the Canal Zone. It was quite another thing to land forces from distant harbours and over long distances against defended territory. Cyprus, which the Chiefs of Staff had recommended as the alternative to the Egyptian base, suffered from the grave disadvantage of providing no deep-water port. Admirably adapted for aircraft, it was useless for naval forces. As a result, the initial airborne landing on Port Said had to be supported by seaborne forces starting from Malta nine hundred miles and six days' steaming time away. Further troops in support had to come from Britain or Algeria. The time factor immensely complicated the whole problem. It was necessary to eliminate the Egyptian air force as a first stage. We hoped to destroy many of the aeroplanes on the ground and the rest could be dealt with by fighter attacks from carriers and from Cyprus. We hoped also to put Cairo Radio out of action and to sink any Egyptian blockships which might be taking up positions in the Canal.

The Egyptian air force was destroyed on 2 November; but the main attack could not take place until the troops from the landing-craft were ready to support the paratroopers. In all the operation the French were to play a role conspicuous both for efficiency and gallantry. But it can readily be understood that the interval was an anxious one. The politicians were arguing at Westminster; groups of ageing intellectuals and earnest young people were clamouring in the Albert Hall; public meetings were being held in Trafalgar Square, denouncing the British Government with wild invective among Landseer's patient and unheeding lions; the Government of the United States at Washington was lashing itself into a high degree of moral indignation; the assembly halls and lobbies of the United Nations were filled with agitated delegates—all this time we sat in London waiting for the moment when the little armada would reach its destined point.

Meanwhile the wildest rumours circulated; the American Sixth Fleet had been instructed to intercept our forces in the long passage from Malta to Port Said; two Russian submarines had been sighted and reported to Lord Mountbatten, the First Sea Lord. At the same time the Soviet Government, which during the period when America was firmly backing Britain and France had stayed remarkably quiet, now came into action. A note from the Russian leaders to the Prime Minister was carefully made public before it reached him and was calculated to cause scare headlines in the Press, with the threat of an 'immediate resort to force to restore the situation in the Middle East'. Though these menaces caused some alarm in London, we did not find ourselves particularly impressed. The Russians were now running with the pack, and this was an agreeable sensation for them. Besides it helped their own situation. By concentrating on the mote in our eye they hoped to divert attention from the beam in their own; for the Hungarian revolution and its brutal suppression had by now come to the knowledge of the world.

On the morning of 5 November the British and French airborne forces were dropped in the neighbourhood of Port Said at dawn. By evening, Brigadier Mervyn Butler, commanding the 16th Parachute Brigade, announced the surrender of the town. Although further fighting followed, no doubt because of the wild rumours of Russian and even American intervention, yet General Sir Charles Keightley (C.-in-C. Middle East Land Forces) could certainly have carried out his original plan of occupying Ismailia and Suez by 12 November. While every weapon was being deployed against us by friend and foe alike—appeals, threats, diplomatic moves outside and within the United Nations—we were resolute upon one objective. Our men should get ashore and we should get a foothold, a *point d'appui*, as a basis on which to negotiate a genuine and constructive settlement.

On 4 November Lester Pearson brought forward a new resolution. It was based partly upon the proposal which he had outlined in broad terms in the previous discussion and partly on some words which Eden himself had used in the House of Commons on 1 November. These were:

> If the United Nations were then willing to take over the physical task of maintaining peace in that area, no one would be better pleased than we.[1]

The Canadian resolution asked the Secretary-General to draw up immediately 'a plan for the setting-up, with the consent of the nations concerned, of an Emergency International United Nations Force to secure and supervise the cessation of hostilities'.

Pearson had a difficult role to play. Canadian public opinion was both uninformed and divided. I got to know Pearson well in later years when he became Prime Minister of Canada. Apart from remarkable charm, he had all the diplomatic gifts—ease, tolerance, clarity of thought and expression, and a capacity for seeing both sides. He certainly could not be browbeaten by the Americans or the Russians, and in all his contributions to the various debates always took an independent line. His thoughts were framed in happy and idiomatic language. He could stand up to Lodge and Shepilov singly or jointly. To one of the latter's most extravagant statements he made a famous reply, accusing him of 'a verbal aggression on the truth'. He was helpful to us both at this stage and during the next period when he resisted the joint American–Soviet pressure to inflict upon us humiliation as well as retreat.

Pearson's resolution was passed in the early hours of the morning of 5 November and carried without opposition. Nineteen countries abstained. Our abstention was justified by Dixon on the ground that the resolution seemed in some respects to go too far and in others not far enough. It omitted any reference to the underlying issues.

[1] *Hansard*, 1 November 1956.

Nevertheless, it became a basis for future negotiation. Nor was Pearson to blame when Hammarskjöld, under American pressure, interpreted his authority to mean that on every disputed point Britain and France should give in to the Egyptians. Britain owes much to Pearson; had he been in a position to bring greater pressure upon the State Department, he might well have persuaded them to adopt a constructive policy and to use the opportunity to bring about a lasting solution of many if not all the Middle Eastern problems. But the country which he represented had not the weight of wealth or population to contend against the influence of the United States. At the same time, both by his personal powers of negotiation and by the respect in which he was held, he was able to exercise throughout the crisis a modifying and humanising influence.

The Cabinet met early on the morning of 6 November. After a long session it reached its fateful decision. This was announced in the House of Commons on the evening of the same day. Eden stated that the British Government had informed the Secretary-General that they would order their forces to cease fire at midnight unless attacked. This undertaking was subject to confirmation that the Egyptian and Israeli Governments had accepted an uncon-ditional cease-fire and that an international force would be sent, competent to secure and supervise the attainment of the objectives set out in the resolution of 2 November.

Many commentators and historians, then and now, have given a number of diverse, sometimes contradictory, sometimes inaccurate reasons which induced the Government to take so grave a decision. It has been stated that as Chancellor of the Exchequer I made an urgent plea that we should submit to circumstances and acknow-ledge our virtual defeat. I have often been reproached for having been at the same time one of the most keen supporters of strong action in the Middle East and one of the most rapid to withdraw when that policy met a serious check. 'First in, first out,' was to be the elegant expression of one of my chief Labour critics on many subsequent occasions.

It is quite true that the events of recent weeks and months had put a pressure upon our financial reserves greater than I had anticipated. Our losses were great, but by no means disastrous. In

September the reserves had fallen by $57 million and by $84 million in October. (This at the rate for the pound before the devaluation of 1967 was the equivalent of £20⅓ million and £30 million respectively.) These were tolerable figures, and no doubt confidence was sustained because the Americans seemed still to be active in our support. But when the critical moment came and it was clear that we had against us the whole pressure of the United States, both in Washington and in New York, the losses rapidly increased, and in November were to be $279 million largely, if not wholly, in the first few days. This was partly due to the effect on sterling of the clear split between the Allies. It may have been accentuated by the Russian demonstrations, which although they seemed to frighten our American friends much more than they alarmed us, had some effect on foreign holders of sterling. But the truth is that it was largely the result of speculation against sterling and heavy selling in New York. How far this was due merely to the desire to avoid loss and how far this followed the lead of the United States Treasury it is hard to know. But certainly the selling by the Federal Reserve Bank seemed far above what was necessary as a precaution to protect the value of its own holdings. I would not have been unduly concerned had we been able to obtain either the money to which we were entitled from the International Monetary Fund, or, better still, some aid by way of temporary loan from the United States. The refusal of the second was understandable; the obstruction of the first is not so easy to forgive. We had a perfect right under the statutes to ask for the repayment of the British quota. Accordingly I made the necessary soundings. I telephoned urgently to New York; the matter was referred to Washington. It was only while the Cabinet was in session that I received the reply that the American Government would not agree to the technical procedure until we had agreed to the cease-fire. I regarded this then, and still do, as a breach of the spirit, and even of the letter of the system under which the Fund is supposed to operate. It was a form of pressure which seemed altogether unworthy. It contrasted strangely with the weak attitude of the Americans towards Egyptian funds and 'accounts' after the seizure of the Canal.

Nevertheless, even our failure to obtain any financial support from America and the refusal of our own rights in the Fund would not have been decisive. We could still stand plenty of battering on this front, and if we had been able to show a conclusive military success confidence would have soon revived. Actually, the loss amounted to only one-eighth of the total gold and dollar reserves. The falling away of reserves was not in itself calamitous.

If they fall away because the fundamental trading position of a country is unsound, and if a country is not able to correct the unsoundness of the internal inflationary position, then the steady draining away of reserves is a very serious thing: but . . . if they fall away as a result of some temporary difficulties which occur, then that is what reserves are for, and that is what the reserves will be used for.[1]

Moreover, the Americans could not have permanently blocked our drawings from the Fund. They could, of course, have continued the pressure on sterling by resolute selling, but the more successful our policy the less effective this policy would prove. The oil position was indeed more dangerous, but not in the short term. Although, therefore, I did not conceal the seriousness of the financial situation, this was not the reason for our acceptance of the cease-fire.

It has equally been argued that we were frightened by Bulganin's threats. This is not true. We never took them too seriously. A nuclear attack on Britain must have led to a general nuclear war in which the Americans could not have failed to take part. At that time the balance of armaments in this field was overwhelming against Russia. Her leaders were quite aware that from a nuclear war they could gain nothing but destruction of their own people, with the minor consolation of being able to inflict considerable but not decisive damage upon their opponents. They might, of course, have put some Russian aeroplanes into the area, as they have since done on a great scale, but most of the current rumours and stories about this were regarded by us with scepticism and have since been proved false. At any rate, Eden found full support among his colleagues for the firm reply that he gave to Bulganin. The latter had accused us of waging war against the national independence of nations. Eden answered in words which certainly did not show any sense of alarm.

[1] *Hansard*, 12 November 1956.

The world knows that in the past three days Soviet forces in Hungary have been ruthlessly crushing the heroic resistance of a truly national movement for independence. . . .[1]

We, of course, at the time had no knowledge of how far these threats had affected Washington. In any event, they were no more the cause of our bringing the military operation to an end than the financial situation, serious as it might be.

The reason why we agreed to the cease-fire is inherent and springs directly from the basis upon which we embarked upon our military operations, namely our ultimatum to Egypt and Israel. Eden puts it very simply:

We had intervened to divide and, above all, to contain the conflict. The occasion for our intervention was over, the fire was out. Once the fighting had ceased, justification for further intervention ceased with it. I have no doubt that it was on this account more than any other that no suggestion was made by any of my colleagues, either then or in the hours which elapsed before my announcement in the House that evening, that we and the French should continue our intervention.[2]

There was no escape from this conclusion.

Although the advance was halted, Britain and France seemed to hold a strong bargaining position. In Eden's words,

We held a gage. Nasser had received a humiliating defeat in the field and most of his Russian equipment had been captured or destroyed by the Israelis or ourselves. His position was badly shaken. Out of this situation intelligent international statesmanship should, we thought, be able to shape a lasting settlement for the Arab–Israeli conflict and for the future of the Canal.[3]

We could not then believe that the United Nations, under the strong guidance of the United States, would nullify or ignore its own declarations regarding the future of the Canal and the settlement of the Middle East. We hoped that the United States would now pursue, if not a friendly, at least a neutral and perhaps even a constructive course. We could hardly foresee 'that the United States Government would harden against us on almost every point

[1] The Earl of Avon, p. 556.   [2] The Earl of Avon, p. 557.
[3] The Earl of Avon, p. 558.

and become harsher after the cease-fire than before'.[1] Once again, we had misjudged the mood of Washington.

We were now forced along a slow retreat on almost every point, accompanied by humiliations almost vindictively inflicted upon us at the instance of the United States Government. Yet, even in this process, there was vacillation or ambivalence. Immediately after the cease-fire Eden telephoned to the President, now safely re-elected by an increased majority. He at once agreed to Eden's suggestion that he and Mollet should come out for a general discussion. But within an hour, no doubt under pressure from the State Department, Eisenhower began to hesitate; and in a final telephone conversation made the excuse that he would be so taken up with internal affairs that the meeting had better be postponed. The proposal was not revived.

The Americans, not content with the 'cease-fire', were now demanding an immediate evacuation. Humphrey made it clear to me that he would maintain his opposition to any drawing from the International Monetary Fund or support by means of loan, until the British and French troops had left Egypt. But our resources were not so depleted as to make us yield to this new pressure. Our gold and dollar reserves were still over $2000 million. When I reported these discussions my colleagues felt a legitimate resentment. Yet we were driven back step by step. By the time the General Assembly met on 23 November we had agreed to admit an advance party of the United Nations Emergency Force into Port Said and to authorise General Keightley to enter into preliminary discussions with General Eedson Burns, the United Nations commander. We also made a token withdrawal of one infantry battalion. Beyond this we were not yet prepared to go.

At the meeting of the Assembly, approval was obtained by a large majority for granting full, if somewhat undefined, authority to the Secretary-General. The Russians now separated themselves from the Americans, at least temporarily. But already there seemed some reaction in our favour. Our old and esteemed friend, Spaak, put forward a constructive proposal. While calling for a withdrawal of British and French troops, he emphasised the urgent need for the

[1] The Earl of Avon, p. 561.

wider problems in the Middle East to be grasped and resolved by the authority of the United Nations. On this issue 23 votes rallied to us; against, 37; there were 18 abstainers, including the United States.

So the argument went on, and it now became complicated by the question of the arrangements for the clearing of the Canal from the obstructions caused by the Egyptians having scuttled a large number of ships. With the equipment and technicians included in our original force, we soon succeeded in clearing Port Said completely. But the Secretary-General yielded to Egyptian pressure in refusing to allow any clearance of the Canal itself until all Anglo-French forces had left. Nor would Nasser agree to the use of any of our salvage resources. He even refused permission for an immediate start to be made by the United Nations men and material. Nor was there any guarantee, as Eden reminded us, that he would agree to the clearance so long as any troops, even United Nations, remained on Egyptian soil. In all this Hammarskjöld showed an inexplicable pliability and weakness.

Through these tedious weeks Selwyn Lloyd, now present himself in New York, was fighting a splendid rearguard action with the able assistance of Pierson Dixon. But in Washington we were still, it seemed, more or less in quarantine. The President refused to receive the Foreign Secretary or the Australian Foreign Minister, R. G. Casey.

We were determined not to evacuate Port Said before we had some assurance from the Secretary-General as to the adequacy and intentions of UNEF, and the Canal's clearance. At last he met our requirements on the build-up of the force, and gave a clear undertaking that the United Nations should set about the task of clearance with all speed. Yet the failure to use our available resources was a foolish gesture. General Raymond Wheeler, in command of the United Nations salvage force, was making slow progress; what could have been achieved by us within a short period was correspondingly delayed for many months. In accordance with Nasser's demands, salvage work was not begun until 31 December. It was, however, agreed to make use of six Anglo-French vessels which had been engaged in Port Said harbour, on the understanding that French and British sailors should wear United Nations armlets! The Canal was finally reopened on 9 April 1957.

The United States Government never relaxed its pressure. At a meeting in Paris on 15 November which I attended, all assistance over oil, for which the plans were ready, was sternly refused. Not even the approaching threat to the economy of Western Europe moved the American representatives. Similar efforts by Sir Harold Caccia were brusquely repelled in Washington later in the month. It was a great moral issue, the Ambassador was told. Yet, curiously enough, Selwyn Lloyd about the same time reported to us that in the course of a private discussion Dulles deplored the fact that we had not managed to bring Nasser down, and reiterated his view that somehow Nasser must be prevented from 'getting away with it'.[1] This strange ambivalence is difficult to explain on any rational basis.

Finally, after we had reached the conclusion that we had made the best bargain available with the Secretary-General of the United Nations and comforted ourselves that we had obtained at least our minimum demands, we decided, on 3 December, upon withdrawal. The operation was to be phased according to a timetable to be settled between the two generals and was to have regard not merely to the smoothness of the changeover but to the military situation in the area. This decision was taken by the Cabinet in Eden's absence from London but with his full approval. The French agreed, although reluctantly, for they were even more sceptical than we of the good faith of the United Nations over the whole affair. The announcement was made on the same day to a somewhat turbulent House of Commons.

On 22 December, the last British forces left Egyptian soil. However wide the differences of opinion as to the wisdom of the expedition, there was universal admiration of its conduct, so far as the troops were concerned. The landings had been gallantly and skilfully carried out. No effort had been spared to avoid or reduce civilian casualties. During the seven weeks since the cease-fire, a high standard of control and discipline had been shown, under severe provocation.

[1] The Earl of Avon, p. 567.

Another vital aspect of the obligation of the United Nations was soon obscured or abandoned. It had indeed been agreed that negotiations on the future of the Canal should be taken up on the basis of the Six Principles approved by the Security Council. This was no great reason for satisfaction or encouragement from our point of view, since the Six Principles were ideals without any sanction. The eighteen-power proposals, of which Dulles had been the author and which later he seemed to discard, had some real strength. However, even the Six Principles were soon to seem obsolescent, and appropriately enough to be lost in the desert sand.

Before the end of the year Israeli troops were withdrawn from the greater part of the Sinai peninsula. They retained, however, their position in the Gaza strip, which seemed vital to their security. They also kept control of the Sharm-el-Sheikh Heights on the Tiran Straits. This secured passage from the Gulf of Aqaba and allowed the Israeli Government to take immediate steps to open up the port of Eilat. This development, in view of the unlikelihood of the Canal being opened for Israeli ships, was equally vital to their economy. The Israeli refusal to comply with the United Nations demand for complete evacuation led to acrimonious discussions and confused negotiations during the early months of 1957.

If the external difficulties which the Cabinet had to face during these critical months were baffling and painful, the internal situation in Parliament and in the country put an equal strain upon the Prime Minister and his principal colleagues. Long and often violent debates had preceded the announcement of the allied acceptance of the cease-fire on 6 November. But this decision gave us no relief. On the contrary, during all the tortuous stages of our struggle within the United Nations, Parliamentary discussion was accentuated rather than relaxed. Apart from an ever-increasing number of Parliamentary discussions from both sides, there was an almost continuous series of debates. Eden himself bore the greatest burden, and in his absence was ably supported by the Foreign Secretary. But at a critical time both of them were absent, one through ill-health and the other in New York. Then the main responsibility fell on Butler, supported by the rest of us, as best we could.

By an unlucky chance, the new session opened on the very day – 6 November – on which the cease-fire was announced. Consequently the debate on the Address, which traditionally lasts for nearly a week, afforded an admirable opportunity for criticism from both sides. On 8 November, Peter Thorneycroft, President of the Board of Trade, made a great impression by his robust defence of the Government's position. He boldly declared that the plans of the Russian Government had included a take-over of the Middle East, using Nasser's ambitions as their instrument. At least the Anglo-French intervention had stopped this in the nick of time. On 12 November the economic facts of the crisis came under review, and it was naturally my duty to reply. After stating that the military expenditure would be between £35 and £50 million, I added that in view of the estimated Budget surplus of £400 million this presented no great difficulty. But I admitted frankly the many economic hazards that we had to face, both because of the pressure on the reserves and the growing uncertainty about the supply of oil. I defended myself against the accusation of 'betraying the ordinary duties of a Chancellor' and neglecting to defend the economy against the dangers which our policy in the Middle East involved. I admitted that it was a great temptation to have recommended a less perilous course, all the more because in the short time that I had been at the Treasury we were clearly moving into an easier situation, with steadily improving prospects. All my interests had therefore been to follow what used to be called a policy of appeasement. Why had I not done so? It was because I had seen it all happen before. I had seen the drift to war in 1914 and again in 1936 to 1939. There was much talk now of our obligations to the United Nations Charter. But in those days what had we been asked to do?

We were asked to break all our literal, legal obligations. Had we gone to war with Hitler in 1936, 1937 or 1938 it would have been contrary to the Kellogg Pact, contrary to the League of Nations, contrary to all our obligations. We did not do it, and we drifted, drifted and drifted.[1]

I ended with these words:

[1] *Hansard*, 12 November 1956.

History alone will prove whether what we did was right or wrong. Ministers, if they are fortunate, can go through a period of office with the ordinary debates and the ordinary discussions – and they are plentiful, and quite agreeable – and never be faced with decisions like these. But when we are faced with them there are only two courses: one is to run away from them, and the other is to make the right decisions. I am sincerely convinced, having seen this happen twice in my lifetime, that the events of this period may prevent a third disaster coming to the world. . . . When these moments come,

'Then it is the brave man chooses, while the coward turns aside.'

Whatever may be the economic disadvantages or troubles – and they will be substantial – I believe that history will show that we have chosen aright.[1]

I find these sentiments still applicable after all these years.

The next day Butler wound up the debate on the Address with a vigorous defence of the Government.

There was now a short respite until 20 November, when it was announced that petrol rationing would be introduced on 17 December. The arrangements which we were able to make seemed likely to safeguard industrial needs and those of essential transport not only in Britain but throughout Western Europe. Nevertheless, motorists were limited to 200 miles a month, a not ungenerous ration compared with that enforced during the war.

On 5 and 6 December there was a further two days' debate which amounted to a post-mortem upon the Government's policy of intervention. On this occasion the Foreign Secretary, now returned from New York, opened with a firm and stout-hearted defence. Aneurin Bevan made one of his most effective contributions, all the more damaging because it was moderate and even sympathetic in tone. He seemed at least to understand the Government's difficulties. He showed all his wit and fire; but he clearly did not wish to press his thrusts too far. I thought it the most statesmanlike speech which had come from the Opposition side and ventured to say so. Philip Noel-Baker closed the debate for the Opposition and Butler for the Government. There had been some doubt as to whether the Con-

[1] *Hansard*, 12 November 1956.

servative group led by Captain Waterhouse and Julian Amery would be willing to vote for the Government's motion. They represented the disappointment and disillusionment of a large part of the Conservative Party. At one time it seemed likely that they would gain a large number of abstentions. But in the event the abstentions amounted to only fifteen.

Discussions continued until almost the last day of the year, and Eden defended himself in a speech on 20 December, which proved to be, unhappily, his last speech in the House of Commons.

This series of debates was on the whole conducted at a high level, Gaitskell being the most distinguished as well as the most persistent speaker from the Opposition side. He was ably supported by his chief colleagues. As so often, Aneurin Bevan was the most thoughtful and in some ways the most effective of our critics. Eden, Selwyn Lloyd and Butler carried the weight of the defence. I joined in, although my contributions were chiefly on the economic and financial aspects. But whenever possible I widened my arguments to the larger issues. Of the less well-known figures, James Griffiths and Philip Noel-Baker were effective on the one side as was Antony Head, the Minister of Defence, on the other. At certain times there were scenes which were denounced as unworthy of Parliamentary traditions. Eden, particularly, was subject to a continuous barrage of interruptions, catcalls and ironical laughter. But these are not uncommon symptoms of strong feeling at critical moments. There were undoubtedly occasions when the Prime Minister was subject to treatment which seemed to us unfair and ungenerous. The long debates on so many consecutive days naturally subjected him to an additional and distressing physical pressure. Yet he maintained throughout his gay and gallant demeanour. I shall always remember his slim, handsome figure, dealing with a mass of interruptions calculated to destroy the argument and obstruct the delivery of his speech. But he remained at the Box undaunted, armed with the same moral and physical courage that he had shown from early youth.

It was therefore a shock to me when on the evening of 18 November, while I was in my study at Number 11 Downing Street, Sir Horace Evans asked to see me. He explained that he had been forced to tell the Prime Minister that he must somehow obtain some respite, even for a limited period, if he was to avoid a serious physical breakdown. This, of course, was not due to any lack of mental or moral resistance; it was due to the recurrence of his old internal trouble which he had neglected in past years. Owing to his unwillingness to put aside important public duties for the necessary operation, at a time when it would have been easy and almost certainly successful, he had consequently had to undergo more than one remedial operation. But so far as we could see, he had made by the end of 1954 a complete recovery. The strain of the last few months had led to a return of some of the alarming symptoms; if a calamity was to be avoided, Evans insisted that he must have at least a few weeks of rest.

Lord Salisbury was with me, and we discussed the situation. It was clear that for Eden to leave England with so much still undecided might be misunderstood abroad and would place a heavy responsibility upon the Cabinet. But the doctor's decision could not be disregarded. The announcement was given to Parliament on 19 November, and a few days later he left for Jamaica. He returned on 14 December. During his absence the crucial decision had to be taken to withdraw altogether from Port Said. We were, however, able to communicate with the Prime Minister by cable and secure his approval.

Since the Foreign Secretary was also away during part of this time, Eden's absence made the task of his deputy, Butler, especially onerous. As so often happens in times of difficulty, the Cabinet rallied with conspicuous loyalty to their temporary leader. We all worked in harmony together. Butler asked me to act as his main confidant, and we laboured together in complete agreement. We had to secure the Cabinet's approval on many important questions. We had to defend our position in the House of Commons. Perhaps most difficult of all, we had to face the meetings of the 1922 Committee, that is, of the whole body of the Conservative Party, at sessions almost as frequent and sometimes almost as heated as those of the House of Commons itself. We made it a rule always to attend together and each to speak on the lines we had agreed. We did not allow ourselves to be separated either in private or in public. Thus we were able to hold the fort in the Prime Minister's absence and sustain as well as we could our position in Parliament and in the country. All the same, we were relieved to see the Prime Minister back, apparently fully restored to health.

Emotions were deeply stirred at this time. Those who sincerely believed in the illegitimacy of the use of force, whatever the situation, felt a passionate sense of indignation. Those who took a more realistic view seemed stunned by the attitude of the United States Government. As a result, there was a fierce outbreak of anti-American feeling in almost all classes of society. Our keenest supporters in the action which we took were naturally most disappointed at its apparent failure. When the arrival of the Christmas recess brought us a welcome respite, none of us could conceal from ourselves the danger in which we stood as a Government. In many foreign countries, as well as to many observers at home, it seemed impossible that the Government could survive. Yet perhaps the reason why we were able to resist such fierce attacks from all sides was the knowledge, shared even by our critics, that the country as a whole sympathised with our purposes and only regretted their frustration.

An unfortunate aspect of the Suez episode was the breach in Anglo-American friendship. There was an equal sense of disillusionment on both sides. It seemed as if the long tradition of close co-operation which had been brought to such a high degree of confidence and respect was now seriously, if not fatally damaged. In an attempt to restore the President's balance of view, Churchill sent a personal letter to him. I did not know of this until much later; it was a striking—and the last—intervention of the old statesman in world affairs. In the absence of Eden, the letter was passed through the United States Embassy, for Churchill did not want either the Foreign Office or the Secretariat at Number 10 to know of his action. He sent, however, a copy to the Queen. It is so deeply moving that I cannot refrain from quoting it in full.

There is not much left for me to do in this world and I have neither the wish nor the strength to involve myself in the present political stress and turmoil. But I do believe, with unfaltering conviction, that the theme of the Anglo-American alliance is more important today than at any time since the war. You and I had some part in raising it to the plane on which it has stood. Whatever the arguments adduced here and in the United States for or against Anthony's action in Egypt, it will now be an act of folly, on which our whole civilisation may founder, to let events in the Middle East come between us.

There seems to be growing misunderstanding and frustration on both sides of the Atlantic. If they be allowed to develop, the skies will darken and it is the Soviet Union that will ride the storm. We should leave it to the historians to argue the rights and wrongs of all that has happened during the past years. What we must face is that at present these events have left a situation in the Middle East in which spite, envy and malice prevail on the one hand and our friends are beset by bewilderment and uncertainty for the future. The Soviet Union is attempting to move into this dangerous vacuum, for you must have no doubt that a triumph for Nasser would be an even greater triumph for them.

The very survival of all that we believe in may depend on our setting our minds to forestalling them. If we do not take immediate action in harmony, it is no exaggeration to say that we must expect to see the Middle East and the North African coastline under Soviet control and Western Europe placed at the mercy of the Russians. If at this juncture we fail in our responsibility to act positively and fearlessly we shall no longer be worthy of the leadership with which we are entrusted.

I write this letter because I know where your heart lies. You are now the only one who can so influence events both in UNO and the free world as to ensure that the great essentials are not lost in bickerings and pettiness among the nations. Yours is indeed a heavy responsibility and there is no greater believer in your capacity to bear it or well-wisher in your task than your old friend

Winston S. Churchill.[1]

The President sent a long letter in reply, clearly of his own composition and in his own hand. I feel certain that Churchill's appeal was of material assistance when we had to begin in the following year the difficult task of re-establishing the old relations, without loss of dignity or retraction of our own positions, but with full sincerity and, happily, with full success.

[1] I am grateful to the owners of the Churchill copyright for permission to reproduce this letter.

On the more immediate issues the American Government was now ready to assist us. It was, of course, a little wounding to feel that we were to be given a 'reward' for our submission to American pressure. Nevertheless, I was not foolish enough to refuse, even though the conditions were somewhat distasteful. We received generous help to meet our urgent needs. In addition I was able to begin a negotiation with Humphrey which led to a revision of the American loan in our favour. The old and somewhat obscure waiver clauses were replaced by provisions giving the British Government the right to defer up to seven annual instalments in all, both of principal and interest, until the year 2000.[1]

On 12 December both Foster Dulles and Humphrey were in London. I had an interesting talk with Humphrey, of which I made a note at the time, on the general position; especially as regards the difficulties facing British and American companies in the Middle East.

I said that I felt that now was the time to get on with a long-term policy and try to get a fundamental settlement of all the problems. I expressed the view that this was the Achilles heel of the free world, and that the Russians would be much more likely to try and bring Western Europe down by bringing disorder into the Middle East than by trying a frontal attack on Europe itself. Mr. Humphrey agreed with this view. He then began to develop this following theme: The whole principle of American life was free competition—cartels, trusts and so forth were contrary to their philosophy. This was all right at home, but when they found themselves trading abroad it meant that their companies were at a great disadvantage. This was particularly the case now in the Middle East. Ten years ago the companies were the big shots and the sheikhs were very naïve. Now the sheikhs were the big shots and bullied the companies, who were terrified of them. The companies could not get together because of the Sherman Anti-Trust Law. If one oil man spoke to another, he was liable to be sent to gaol. The Government of the United States did not know what to do. He expressed the view that some new philosophy must be developed which, while preserving free competition and private enterprise in general, would put these

[1] *Annual Register*, *1957*, p. 373.

arrangements made in foreign countries under some governmental guarantee of authority. I then mentioned the Abadan
settlement and the strength which I thought the consortium had
given. He agreed. He also thought that what we had done in Iraq
had helped because the people saw some result of all its wealth.
The position in Saudi Arabia and the other sheikhdoms was much
weaker. I replied that I thought that we ought to get down to
studying this together and try to get a rapid settlement of the oil
and of the political problems of the Middle East. He liked the
idea of an Anglo-American study group in Washington, where
this could be studied both from the point of view of the oil companies, and so forth, and from the point of view of a longer-term
political settlement.[1]

We passed from that to financial questions, and our talks laid the
foundations for the agreement of the loan, ultimately concluded in
the following March.

Dulles also called to see me. We covered much the same subjects;
but he was discursive and vague.

> It was a rather painful discussion, and he was in a querulous
> and unhappy mood. He complained particularly about our
> having taken [away] Roger Makins. I said I felt sure he would
> get just as fond of Caccia as of Makins. But he was not willing
> to be comforted. He harped a good deal upon the lack of con-
> fidence, etc., between us all and did not know what would
> happen. . . .
> He went on to a long defence of himself and his policies. He
> was clearly hurt at the criticisms that had been made. He said
> that it was an error to believe that he and the President could be
> separated. He wrote most of the Presidential statements himself.
> When they had to be tough, they were made by the Secretary of
> State from the State Department. When they were idealistic, they
> were made by the President but written by the Secretary of State.
> He seemed very sensitive to any suggestion that there was a rift
> between them.[1]

Having listened to both Dulles and Humphrey, I summarised
the position as follows:

[1] 13 December 1956.

The President is wounded and rather mystified. Foster Dulles has the same feeling. . . . Humphrey, although very firm and in some ways toughest while the thing was on, will bear the least resentment and, I think, will do business with us in an ordinary frank way without it rankling.[1]

I ought to add that Humphrey at this time brought considerable pressure on Hammarskjöld; this proved successful at least to the extent that some of our ships were used in the work of clearing the Canal.

Although these conversations were not altogether discouraging, my visitors did not attempt to conceal the feelings of the American Administration. On my side, I made it clear how wounded British opinion had been, and how difficult it would be to restart the old relations. Nevertheless, I felt that some advance had been made, and that if we persevered – proceeding with patience but determination – it would be possible in due course to rebuild that close co-operation between our two countries which I have felt throughout my life to be essential for the peace and prosperity of the world.

[1] 13 December 1956.

CHAPTER V

The Change of Government

O N the morning of 9 January 1957 I was working at the Treasury when a message was delivered summoning me to Number 10 at 3 o'clock. I remember asking my private secretary to enquire what would be the main subjects of our discussion. The state of the sterling exchanges, the progress of the negotiations for financial aid, the estimates of the likely flow of oil — these were all matters on which I knew the Prime Minister would want the latest information. But from the nature of the reply which came from his private office, it was clear that he wanted a personal talk.

Eden was in the little drawing-room, the smallest of the three saloons which occupy the front of the famous house. All these face north and seldom see the sun; but in this room there is a window to the west, looking over the garden, and the afternoon and evening sun give it, even through the gloom of a London winter, a touch of warmth and glow. He told me with simple gravity, as a matter decided and not to be discussed, that he had decided to resign his office. The Queen had already been informed; this had been the purpose of his visit to Sandringham the previous day, which had generally been regarded as part of the normal routine, and not as marking any special occasion. He had already spoken with Salisbury and Butler. There was no way out. The doctors had told him the truth about his health and, though he was not doomed as a man, it must be the end of his political life.

I was deeply shocked, for I had not been at all prepared for this sudden and tragic end to the adventure on which we had set out so gaily some twenty months before. I had certainly learned from my talk with Sir Horace Evans of the nature and seriousness of Eden's malady; but the great doctor had seemed hopeful in November that a few weeks' rest, followed by the normal holiday at Christmas, would be sufficient. Indeed, when Eden returned from Jamaica in the middle of December, he had seemed almost, if not fully, restored. He himself 'had no suspicion of the advice the doctors were to have to give in January'.[1] Nevertheless, the doctors were inexorable, and there was nothing to be done but accept the verdict. Throughout our short and painful conversation he was as charming, as elegant and as dignified as ever. I could hardly believe that this was to be the end of the public life of a man so comparatively young, and with so much still to give.

We sat for some little time together. We spoke a few words about the First War, in which we had both served and suffered, and of how we had entered Parliament together almost at the same time. Although our paths had then diverged, in the great issues—especially the great external issues—we had been in full and fruitful agreement. I can see him now on that sad winter afternoon, still looking so youthful, so gay, so debonair—the representative of all that was best of the youth that had served in the 1914–18 War. That band of men had faced the horrors of the fearful struggle with something of an Elizabethan gallantry. The survivors of that terrible holocaust had often felt under a special obligation, like men under a vow of duty. It was in this spirit that he and I had entered politics. Now, after these long years of service, at the peak of his authority, he had been struck down by a mysterious but inescapable fate.

I walked sadly back through the connecting passage to Number 11, and waited almost stunned with the news. The Cabinet had been summoned for 5 o'clock, but nothing had leaked out. When, therefore, Ministers were told the truth for which they were wholly unprepared, they were dazed. On his return in mid-December all his colleagues had felt encouraged by the Prime Minister's buoyancy; he had conducted the last debates with all his old skill and command of the House. Attributing his illness to the mental stresses and strains of the last few months, they were ignorant of the true medical causes. It was a painful, and unforgettable scene.

Eden spoke shortly, and with great dignity. The doctors' decision was irrevocable. He must resign. Salisbury spoke—with

[1] The Earl of Avon, p. 574.

great emotion, almost in tears—of his lifelong friendship. Butler
spoke next—very appropriately. I said a few words. Then it was
all over. It was a dramatic end to an extraordinary and, in many
ways, unique career. What seemed so dreadful was that he waited
so long for the Premiership, and held it for so short a time.[1]

It would be disingenuous to conceal that for the last few days
some Ministers had been restless.

There had been many meetings—no intrigue, but great concern at the apparent inability of the P.M. or anyone else to take
hold of the situation. Outside the ranks of the Cabinet, etc.,
M.P.s have been meeting. There has been a general acceptance
of the fact that the Government could not go on. As soon as
Parliament met it would be in trouble; in a few weeks it would
fall. At the same time, no one has known what to do.[2]

Now a new blow had fallen. We had not only to face the House of
Commons with a Party bitterly disappointed at the turn of affairs,
and subject to all the pressures which any large group of men are
prey to in periods of uncertainty, but we had to go through all the
difficulties of a new leadership and a new Government. Yet, for the
moment, all these anxieties were forgotten. It was the human
tragedy which filled our minds.

I was one of the first to leave, making my way back to Number 11
unobserved. I heard afterwards that Butler left also, and that Lord
Salisbury, as senior Cabinet Minister, invited the remaining
Ministers to give their opinion about who should succeed to the
vacant and, in the circumstances, not very alluring post. The
Ministers were asked to see Lord Salisbury (the Lord President)
and Lord Kilmuir (the Lord Chancellor) one by one in the Lord
President's room in the Privy Council offices,

which could be reached without leaving the building. There
were two light reliefs. Practically each one began by saying, 'This
is like coming to the Headmaster's study.' To each Bobbety
[Salisbury] said, 'Well, which is it, Wab or Hawold?' As well as
seeing the remainder of the ex-Cabinet, we interviewed the Chief
Whip and Oliver Poole, the Chairman of the Party. John

[1] 3 February 1957 (recording events from 9 January).   [2] 3 February 1957.

Crowds of people and television cameras await the new Prime Minister in Downing Street, 10 January 1957

Returning from Buckingham Palace after his Installation as a Privy Councillor

Morrison, the Chairman of the 1922 Committee, rang me up from Islay the next morning. An overwhelming majority of Cabinet Ministers was in favour of Macmillan as Eden's successor, and back-bench opinion, as reported to us, strongly endorsed this view.[1]

There was no attempt by either Salisbury or Kilmuir to use what one might call a prefect's influence on the opinion of those they interviewed. They merely asked a question and received an answer. Since both were senior members of the Government and neither, from the nature of things, was a potential candidate for the Premiership, they acted with strict propriety in a difficult situation.

These two senior Ministers had agreed on this course before the Cabinet met. They were rightly anxious to preserve the Queen's Prerogative, and not to allow the election of a Prime Minister as the result of a Party meeting. This point had some importance because, in Gaitskell's absence in America, there was an attempt by Griffiths, the Deputy Leader, to object to the course which had been adopted. He even accused the Conservatives of having placed the Crown in a very difficult and embarrassing position. When Parliament returned, the Opposition would take the matter up and proceed to a vote of censure. However, Gaitskell was much too sensible to fall for this nonsense. No more was heard of any such protest. Nevertheless, in view of the controversy which was later to follow when illness brought my own tenure of office to an end, it is perhaps worth rehearsing the true story.

While this novel but not ineffective procedure was at work, Eden had gone to the Palace. In the evening, a bulletin signed by Sir Horace Evans and three other doctors was published in the following terms:

The Prime Minister's health gives cause for anxiety. In spite of the improvement which followed his rest before Christmas there has been a recurrence of abdominal symptoms. This gives us much concern because of the serious operations in 1953 and some subsequent attacks of fever. In our opinion his health will no longer enable him to sustain the heavy burdens inseparable from the office of Prime Minister.[2]

[1] The Earl of Kilmuir, *Memoirs: Political Adventure* (London, 1962), p. 285.
[2] *Annual Register*, 1957, p. 1.

G

At the same time the Queen's acceptance of her Prime Minister's resignation was announced.

My wife had come up on the same day from the country, and I had the comfort not only of her sympathy but her shrewd understanding. I was in a painful situation, for in the course of the evening some rumours reached me of the proceedings after I had left the Cabinet room. I could not, therefore, go to see even intimate friends or I would seem to be canvassing for support. I could not even—and this grieved me deeply—go over to talk to my old friend about his future, or give him what comfort I might from past reminiscences. My first instinct was to do so, but my wife reminded me that even passing through the connecting doors would be known to the messengers and Private Office.

The next morning I thought it wiser not to go to the Treasury.

I heard that Lord Salisbury and Sir Winston Churchill had been sent for by the Queen. But since no one had told me about what had taken place the night before, I had no idea of what advice they would give. It is since clear that Lord Salisbury did not give his own views. He merely informed the Queen of the general view among the leading members of the Party. . . . Since the Socialists afterwards tried to make out that this was a personal and private effort by the head of the Cecils, it is important to record that Lord Salisbury merely acted as a means of conveying to the Queen the general view inside the Party. I gathered from Anthony (whom I saw later on Thursday) that he had neither been asked for his advice nor had volunteered it.[1]

I passed the morning in the downstairs sitting-room, to which I had restored the picture of Mr. Gladstone, and I read *Pride and Prejudice* —very soothing. At noon Sir Michael Adeane rang up and asked me to be at the Palace at 2 o'clock. So it was settled.

We had then a small dining-room at the top of Number 11, which my wife and I used when we were alone. I sent a message to ask if we could have some luncheon at one o'clock, sharp. I had not told her about my summons to the Palace, but when I appeared in a tail coat, this unusual costume, combined with the insistence on punctuality, led her to make an accurate deduction.

[1] 3 February 1957.

The Queen received me with the greatest kindness and consideration. Although in various posts, especially as Foreign Secretary, I
had seen her not infrequently, yet this was the beginning of a quite
different relationship. The Prime Minister is above all the Queen's
First Minister. His supreme loyalty is to her. I could not disguise
from her the gravity of the situation. Indeed, I remember warning
her, half in joke, half in earnest, that I could not answer for the new
Government lasting more than six weeks. She smilingly reminded
me of this at an audience six years later.

After the resignation of a Prime Minister or of a Government
the Monarch has traditionally two alternatives. The statesman
selected can be invited to attempt to form a Government and report
later on his success or failure. Or he can be given the position of
Prime Minister and First Lord forthwith and accordingly 'kiss
hands' on his appointment. On this occasion the latter course was
taken.

As I drove back to No. 11, I thought chiefly of my poor
mother. The first little note which I got later in the afternoon was
from my sister-in-law (Mary, Duchess of Devonshire) with the
same thought. She understood and had a great affection for my
mother.[1]

On my return I immediately went to work in the Cabinet Room.
The urgent task was the formation of an Administration and to get
it into good working order before the meeting of Parliament on 22
January. I first saw Lord Salisbury and asked him to remain as Lord
President and Leader of the House of Lords. Although neither his
health nor his inclination made it very attractive for him to continue
in active politics, he willingly agreed, only stipulating for a fair
number of Peers in the Government.

This was a good start. I next saw Butler. I could imagine only too
well his feelings, for it was he who had carried the burden during
Eden's absence—a burden which I had tried to share with him to
the best of my ability. I realised that there would be plenty of gossips
and ill-wishers who would try to make trouble between us. I knew
that everything depended on our working closely together. I knew,

[1] 3 February 1957.

too, that the decision in my favour, for whatever reason, must have been a great disappointment to him. Yet in the perilous position in which the Government and the Party found themselves, our only hope lay in loyal and sincere co-operation. He must therefore have the right to whatever post he might choose, in addition to the leadership of the House of Commons. I was particularly anxious to keep Selwyn Lloyd,

> because I felt one head on a charger should be enough. Two was more than England's honour could support. Although Eden's illness is real, it will be thought in most countries to be 'diplomatic'.[1]

It was therefore a great relief to me when Butler chose the post of Home Secretary.

> He was very nice and reciprocated at once the attitude I took. We had preserved the Government by our loyalty and comradeship before Christmas—during Eden's absence in Jamaica. We must do the same now, or we should certainly founder.[1]

I was now free to ask Selwyn Lloyd, who had worked so hard and carried so heavy a burden, to stay at the Foreign Office. He seemed a little surprised, but at once agreed. These decisions unhappily involved asking one of my best and oldest friends, Gwilym Lloyd George, to make way for Butler. This was my first experience of the most grievous of all the tasks which a Prime Minister has to perform. Whether at the formation of a new Administration or during its lifetime, all Prime Ministers in turn have shrunk from the need to drop old friends and bring in new blood. It is rare indeed that such changes can be made without leaving some degree of ill feeling. Nor are there lacking plenty of so-called friends to stimulate later resentment. In this case, however, I was spared. I had received a characteristic letter, written on 11 January, from James Stuart, Secretary of State for Scotland. I had complete confidence in his wisdom—he had long been Chief Whip and enjoyed exceptional intimacy with Churchill. I found his frankness encouraging.

[1] 3 February 1957.

1. I think that *R.A.B.* will want the Home Office.
2. You may then prefer that *Gwilym Ll. G.* should 'depart in peace' to give you elbow room (unless you have some 'sinecure' job you *wish* to give him).
3. On balance—and without knowing how your plans are working out—I think that you would probably be wise to obtain all the 'elbow room' you can and want.

From this, I come to the conclusion that it might help you if Gwilym and I left together (being hardened *old* sinners) and prepared the way for the clever new boys.

Further, if Julian Amery is one of the new ones (and *I* am in favour of this) it may be a help if I, as a connection by a different generation, pass out. I mean by this that if any Conservatives should accuse you of nepotism . . . , you retort, 'Yes—but I have sacked J.S.'

He added:

you are right to widen your net to *Left* as well as to *Right* . . . . I would welcome a brief end to my time (already 33 yrs +) on a back-bench. It would prove that the *NON*-existent fruits of office do not necessarily matter to *all*—and this might not, I feel, be a BAD thing.

This generous attitude was equally shown by Lloyd George.

The Treasury was now vacant, for what even Mr. Gladstone found a difficult task in the nineteenth century when Prime Minister was obviously impossible for me to contemplate in the twentieth. Peter Thorneycroft gladly accepted the post and was succeeded at the Board of Trade by David Eccles. Walter Monckton, another old friend, was genuinely anxious to retire from politics. He had only remained during the last phase of the Suez crisis out of loyalty to Eden. It was not now thought necessary to retain his post of Paymaster-General in the Cabinet. To take the place of Eccles at the Ministry of Education I was fortunate in finding an admirable successor in Lord Hailsham. Lord Selkirk, who had previously been in the Cabinet as Chancellor of the Duchy of Lancaster, agreed to take the post of First Lord of the Admiralty, outside the Cabinet.

Encouraged by James Stuart's views I now brought in a completely new figure.

I had seen Percy Mills (rather by chance) at luncheon on the Wednesday. I got him to come in on Thursday afternoon (by the garden entrance) and offered him Ministry of Power. I got a message accepting on the Saturday.[1]

This meant moving Aubrey Jones to the Ministry of Supply. I had formed a high opinion of Mills's qualities first at the Ministry of Supply during the war and again when he worked with me at the Ministry of Housing. Although he was not a Member of Parliament, this was easily remedied by his acceptance of a peerage. This appointment, although something of an innovation, was well received. He was to prove a valuable addition to the Cabinet, commanding the affection and respect of all his colleagues. The chief difficulty was over the Ministry of Defence. Antony Head, by his long and intimate association with the Services and the admirable way in which he had carried out his task during the recent crisis, had a strong claim. Nevertheless, from the work which I had done as Chancellor of the Exchequer with the Service Departments I felt doubtful whether he would agree to the level of defence expenditure for the following year on which I would have to insist in view of the financial situation. After a frank discussion with him he decided that he was unable to agree to my proposals. Head accepted the situation with dignity and good feeling. I was happy indeed when I was able to persuade him, after the independence of Nigeria had been established, to accept the important post of High Commissioner in Lagos, a duty which he carried out with conspicuous success. In his place I selected Duncan Sandys. There were some who thought there would be too much opposition to so strong a character in a Ministry the duties and powers of which were still undefined.

I also wanted a 'directive' to increase the powers of the Defence Minister. Brook[2] (who is a tower of strength) drafted these, and I got the three Service Ministers to accept them *before* appointment. By moving Hailsham from the Admiralty to Education a possible danger was avoided. Also I think he will be

[1] 3 February 1957.
[2] Sir Norman Brook (later Lord Normanbrook), Secretary to the Cabinet.

a first-class Minister of Education. Anyway, he is one of the cleverest men in the country today.[1]

Henry Brooke was the obvious successor to Sandys at Housing and proved a very successful Minister. I also promoted Harold Watkinson to the Cabinet. I felt that in prestige the Minister of Transport must be on the same basis as the Minister of Power. Jack Maclay took James Stuart's place as Secretary of State for Scotland and this, together with the appointment of Charles Hill to the post of Chancellor of the Duchy, completed the Cabinet.[2]

The same evening, I made a visit to Churchill. I felt it right to pay my respects at such a moment to my old chief, from whom I had received, for so many years, many kindnesses and to whom I had long looked for support and inspiration. It seemed appropriate to seek the guidance of the greatest Englishman of this, and perhaps of all, time. He was almost paternal in his welcome. He grieved for Anthony; but he gave me a sort of blessing which was indeed heartening. Of course, this evening call somehow leaked out, and the photographers were on the doorstep. But there was no great harm in that.

The Cabinet was completed by Sunday afternoon (13 January), when the Queen came up from Sandringham to consider my proposals.

[She] seemed to approve the changes. She is astonishingly well informed on every detail. She particularly liked the decision about the F.O. and was interested in what I told her about Percy Mills.[3]

The Cabinet list was accordingly given to the Press for publication on the Monday (14 January) and got a good reception. On Monday I turned to

the next task—and rather a tricky one—the Ministers *outside* the Cabinet and Ministers of State. I was determined to bring back Ernest Marples, who did so well at Housing, but who was left out by Eden. He is delighted to be Postmaster-General. Reggie Maudling, with great good feeling and good sense, accepted to

[1] 3 February 1957.   [2] See Appendix 2.   [3] February 1957.

'The Middle Way'—*Cartoon by Vicky*

be Mills's representative in H. of C. and general deputy. He 'goes down' (nominally) in the hierarchy. But he really is in the interesting part of the game.[1]

He was soon to be used in a wider field.

I was particularly anxious to persuade Edward Boyle, who had been my Financial Secretary and resigned over Suez, to rejoin the Government. I had a very high regard for his talents as well as for his character. I think he was attracted by the Ministry of Education as well as by the partnership with Hailsham. After some hesitation he accepted the post of Under-Secretary.

We got the second group completed on Wednesday the 16th and the last—the Under-Secretaries and minor appointments—by Friday the 18th. The Queen had returned to Sandringham but was willing to approve the names submitted in a formal submission without an audience. The whole Administration was therefore completed in less than ten days. It was generally thought that the balance had been well kept.

The formation of a Government and the changes that from time to time become necessary are matters upon which it is very difficult to get advice, except to some extent from the Chief Whip of the day and perhaps the more senior members of the Private Office or the Cabinet Secretariat. It is difficult to discuss the merits or demerits of one colleague with another, especially where the higher posts are concerned. When it comes to the less vital but often equally perplexing task of filling up the junior ranks of administration, many considerations have to be borne in mind, apart from the merit or suitability of the candidate. It is important that different parts of the country should be represented, as well as different groups of opinion within the party. Loyalty should be rewarded, but remembering my own past I never felt that sincere disaffection should be held against a young Member. Senior Ministers are sometimes—and not unnaturally—insistent in pressing the claims of the young men who have served them. This makes the formation of a whole Administration, consisting of over eighty members, a difficult and complicated task not unlike a jigsaw puzzle. If one drops out, whether in the senior or the junior ranks, a whole series of alterations

[1] 3 February 1957. Maudling's official post was that of Paymaster-General.

G2

have to be made in the plan. Nevertheless, in this my first attempt, the chief objective was to make as little change as possible consistent with what seemed to me the needs of the moment. In all this I found Edward Heath, the Chief Whip, a most admirable assistant. Sir Norman Brook was always ready with advice when called on, and I had in Freddie Bishop, Principal Private Secretary, a tower of strength.

The staff at the disposal of the Prime Minister has grown from the very meagre allowance enjoyed up to the First War and has considerably increased since then. Nevertheless, it is minute in comparison with that provided for the President of the United States, and doubtless to the Heads of Administration in other countries. It is still small, and during all my time remained so. Its strength depends upon the Private Office, as it is called, consisting of three or at the most four Private Secretaries of modest rank in the Civil Service, who can all sit together and understand what each one of them is doing. The Principal Private Secretary held the rank of Under-Secretary, the others of Principals. I was admirably served first by Freddie Bishop and later by Tim Bligh at the head of this little group. Philip de Zulueta who dealt chiefly, though not exclusively, with Foreign Affairs, was a tower of strength and re-mained with me throughout. Others, especially Neil Cairncross, Tony Phelps and Philip Woodfield, dealt mainly with Home Affairs and were special masters in the art of answering Parliamentary Questions, including the essential 'Suggestions for Supplementaries'. Serving them were the Duty Clerks and what was called the 'Garden Rooms'—a series of admirable 'young ladies' (we inherited and confirmed Churchill's appellation), who were secretaries and typists of quite remarkable calibre. These were presided over by Miss S. A. Minto, of great experience and unswerving loyalty. To this list must be added the Parliamentary Secretary. I had in my time three—all devoted—Bobby Allan, Tony Barber and Knox Cunningham. This little staff, whether in London or at my own home in Sussex or at Chequers or on tour, gave me continual support and comfort as well as the most efficient service. I should add that I made in May 1957 an addition to the Private Secretaries in the person of John Wyndham (now Lord Egremont), who had served me in the Ministry of Supply, in the Colonial Office throughout the Mediterranean campaign, and in the Foreign Office. On and off he has helped me with his friendship and advice for a period of over twenty years. He acted without remuneration, but shared to the full in all the work.

Last, but by no means of least importance, was the official charged with what are euphemistically called 'public relations'. My Victorian predecessors would indeed have been puzzled and shocked by such an idea. Even in the first years of this century, the post was not officially recognised, whatever methods may have been used to secure the end in view. Today, with the vast extension of news—through the British, Commonwealth and Foreign Press, and through the new media of radio and television—it is important that those employed in these multifarious tasks should at least be given the facts. Propaganda is best left to Party organisations. But a Government has a right, as well as a duty, to secure that accurate information should be constantly available. I was indeed fortunate in obtaining the services of Harold Evans. He came at the start, and served to the end. He built up a remarkable reputation both for wisdom and candour. The 'lobby journalists' had complete confidence in his integrity. He trusted them; in return he earned their trust.

Parallel to the Downing Street staff, but not exclusive to the service of the Prime Minister, is the Cabinet Office. Its head acts as Secretary to the Cabinet, and he and his colleagues serve all Ministers alike. But necessarily, since all Cabinet papers are circulated by permission of the Prime Minister and since all the various committees of Ministers, permanent and temporary, are set up only with the approval of the Prime Minister, the Secretary to the Cabinet acts in effect both as co-ordinator and friend in a very special degree. It was my good fortune to have from the beginning the outstanding services of Sir Norman Brook. When he retired in 1962 he was succeeded by Sir Burke Trend, who gave me equal support.

This little band, with very few changes, were my colleagues and comrades throughout the whole adventure.

There was one other important, if unofficial and unpaid, member of the staff to whom I must refer. My wife not only kept us all happy and contented in our little society in Number 10, but she played in every aspect of my duties—whether in work for the Party or in entertainment of guests, public and private—a remarkable role. Nor did she neglect her obligations in our country home or the many charities for which she had worked so long. I was happy indeed when after my retirement she received from the Queen a reward which gave universal pleasure.[1]

At the time two main impressions were left upon my mind:

> First, the extraordinary efficiency of the Private Secretaries. Dorothy and I have received literally thousands of letters and telegrams, from everyone we have ever known or worked with— from a footman at Government House, Ottawa, or a driver in Algiers, to more exalted and distinguished friends. All these have been sorted out and traced (since many people sign only Christian names this isn't easy) and answers prepared. It has been a tremendous job for the staff and quite a heavy task for me to sign all the answers. The second thing that has struck me is how well everyone has behaved. Politicians are not really cynical and self-seeking. There has been a kind of 1940 spirit abroad. With very few (and rather unexpected) exceptions, everyone has put the public interest and the desire to help me above all other considerations. It has really been quite an exhilarating experience.[2]

Among the many messages that I received was a characteristic communication from Lord Beaverbrook. He reminded me that he had always hoped for and prophesied this event. Indeed, I found in my records a letter which he had written to me on 31 December 1952 when I was still at the Ministry of Housing:

> You have made an immense triumph, and for my part, I would be glad to see you Prime Minister in succession to the old gentleman who is my contemporary when he decides to retire—I hope not for many years.

His message now was: 'I told you so.'

Immediately after my appointment was announced, the President

[1] Lady Dorothy Macmillan was created Dame of the British Empire (Grand Cross) in January 1964.
[2] 3 February 1957.

of the United States sent me a formal message of congratulation, to which I replied in suitable terms. Both these were published. In addition, he sent a personal letter:

Dear Harold,
    This morning, upon learning of your designation by Her Majesty as the new Prime Minister, I sent you a formal message of congratulations, the kind that is approved even by State Departments. The purpose of this note is to welcome you to your new headaches. Of course you have had your share in the past, but I assure you that the new ones will be to the old like a broken leg is to a scratched finger. The only real fun you will have is to see just how far you can keep on going with everybody chopping at you with every conceivable kind of weapon.
    Knowing you so long and well I predict that your journey will be a great one. But you must remember the old adage, 'Now abideth faith, hope and charity—and greater than these is a sense of humor.'

                                        With warm regard,
                                                As ever,
                                                    D.E.

To both I made a suitable but not effusive reply. At this stage I thought it better to be the pursued than the pursuing.
    So far there had been only one hitch. On the evening of my appointment, 11 January, following a heavy day of interviews and discussions, I took the Chief Whip out to dinner, for our servants had not yet arrived from Sussex, and there were only skeleton arrangements at Number 11. Without thinking that I would already be followed, we went to the Turf Club, which I knew would be quiet. If there were any members dining they were not likely to be passionately interested in politics. We could not have gone to the Carlton Club, for obvious reasons. Unhappily, the news was obtained by some source or another, and as we came out our way was barred by all the usual paraphernalia of Press and television, to which I had not yet become accustomed. I thought that my guest and I were entitled after these strenuous events to a bottle of champagne and some game pie. The food, the drink, above all the place, were seized upon with avidity as the symbols of a reactionary

regime. Some of the critics suggested that a fatal choice had been made between the rival candidates. In Smith Square–the Butler home–there would have been plain living and high thinking.

On the evening of Thursday, 17 January, when the full list of Ministers had been completed, it was thought right for me to make a statement to the nation on radio and television. At this time the techniques were still primitive, and even the most practised politicians were not yet expected to be consummate actors. I gradually became inured to the need for these appearances, although I always suffered from extreme nervousness and never became at all expert. The chief problem appeared to be whether one should learn the statement by heart and deliver it as from the stage, or whether one should speak without a text, a method which had its own pitfalls, especially on any foreign issue. I proposed to the expert advisers who organised the performance that I should behave perfectly naturally and not be ashamed to look down at notes from time to time. This, however, was then regarded as a great breach of decorum. About this time there was invented a thing called a teleprompter, in which the written text went round and round. This had for me two disadvantages. First, being very short-sighted I could not see it; secondly, if I could just manage to read the words by screwing up my eyes, I presented the appearance of a corpse looking out of a window. My successors have been more skilful in the use of this instrument. In the end, I did what seemed to me sensible, delivered all I could by heart and looked at the notes when I had forgotten the next words. Although the professional critics were shocked, no one seemed to mind. The only passage that is perhaps worth recalling is my reference to America.

A lot of people are worried about relations with the United States. The life of the free world depends upon the partnership between us. Any partners are bound to have their differences now and then. I've always found it so. But true partnership is based upon respect. We don't intend to part from the Americans, and we don't intend to be satellites. I am sure they don't want us to be so. The stronger we are, the better partners we shall be; and I feel certain that as the months pass we shall draw continually closer together with mutual confidence and respect.

On this, as on all other occasions, I was fortunate to have the expert knowledge of Charles Hill, the 'Radio Doctor', as well as of George Christ, the brilliant political journalist who was already an intimate friend and valued colleague.

Like all Prime Ministers I started with the intention of reforming and perhaps improving our methods.

> I have tried to get the agenda into better shape—with one day foreign or colonial questions, and another domestic—financial and economic, etc. I have also tried to get the discussions less 'departmental'. We are, after all, comrades in a common enterprise, and stand or fall together.[1]

Naturally these arrangements could not be rigidly adhered to, but they had some effect.

Nearly a week had now passed. When the broadcast was over and with only the minor appointments to be finally resolved, there was a short opportunity for reflection. So far, I seemed to be living in a kind of maze. Had this actually happened to me? Was I really Prime Minister? How had it all come about? It seemed like a dream, or perhaps a nightmare. There was certainly attached to the whole affair a certain atmosphere of unreality and even absurdity. Perhaps because I had spent so many hours of my life in reading, and since my whole education had been based on the old learning, I was at any rate on one side of my nature and training what has been called 'a gown man': a product of a system which was intended to supply in the Middle Ages 'clerks' as priests and administrators, and in later times men to serve the Empire in its vast responsibilities —in the Home Civil Service, the Foreign Service, in the Army, the Indian and Colonial Services and, in addition, to provide instructors of the next generation. Even my family business had close connections with this quiet world of literature and art. The First War turned me unexpectedly into a 'sword man'. Action—harsh, brutal, compelling—ousted learning. The gown was exchanged for a tunic.

I have ever since been conscious of this duality. On the whole, it has been of some advantage to me. I could escape from the worst

[1] 3 February 1957.

moments of military dangers or political anxiety into the comforting world of books. I have equally been able to acquire a certain calm, not internally, for I have suffered from agonies of nervous apprehension, but at any rate externally—what was afterwards called 'unflappability'. Whether men who enjoy a more single personality, either as men of thought or men of action, have a happier and more successful career I cannot tell. I like to think that my two great heroes, Disraeli and Churchill, both had this combination of the thinker and the doer—the artist and the man of action. On a much lower scale this has certainly been the life which I have enjoyed or had to endure. It was at this moment that I wrote out on a piece of notepaper and hung upon the green baize door which separates the Cabinet Room from the Private Secretaries' Room the following quotation which I thought might serve as the guiding principle of the new regime: 'Quiet calm deliberation disentangles every knot.' This exhortation, later framed, became what is known in more exalted spheres as our 'signature tune'.

There were indeed difficulties and dangers immediately ahead. The first need was to restore the confidence of the people in their Government and in themselves. The events of the last few months had been a grievous shock both to those who approved and to those who were opposed to the last Government's actions. The fact that France and Britain, even acting together, could no longer impose their will was alarming. Never before in history had Western Europe proved so weak. The fact that they had been met by an unnatural combination between Russia and America was almost a portent. How then to restore any sense of security? Almost up to Christmas bitter recriminations and violent disputes had swept through Parliament like a tempest, and were only now suspended through the tragic illness and, as it were, political death of Eden as Prime Minister. A strange hush had followed—almost a silence— but as soon as the 'funeral' was over the truce would end, and the battle would be launched with unremitting bitterness against the new heir. Parliament would soon meet, and then would come the test. The breaches in the Conservative Party, in and out of Parliament, had somehow to be healed. Much would depend upon the Press —so far friendly and generous; much depended on my power to use the new methods—of which I had little experience—of radio and television. Yet the future was unpredictable.

Secondly, there was all the aftermath of Suez. The clearing of the Canal, the indignities which would, no doubt, be imposed upon us and which we must struggle to resist. There was the problem of oil and the dangers of fresh interruptions in the flow, and the question of whether, when the Canal was ready for use, the Egyptian authorities would accept sterling in payment or try to demand gold or dollars. Then there was the impending question of compensation for British subjects for losses incurred in the fighting, or by Nasser's appropriation of their assets. The unwinding of all this tangle must offer at every stage a flank both to the Right and to the Left.

Thirdly, how were we to treat the United States, and to re-establish that alliance which I knew to be essential in the modern world? Nor would it be worth arguing whose fault it was. Somehow, without loss of dignity and as rapidly as possible, our relationships must be restored. The fact that there were already the first signs of a reversal of opinion in Washington as to their obligations in the Middle East was encouraging. Here I felt would perhaps be the least baffling of all our problems.

Fourthly, there was the economic situation. We had recently succeeded in getting help from the United States, and the position had unexpectedly improved in other ways. Nevertheless, as I knew from my year in the Treasury and was to learn for the rest of my active life in politics, to maintain the British economy at the right level, between inflation and deflation, balancing correctly between too much and too little growth, was a delicate exercise. All the clever young economists and journalists and all the armchair experts could not resolve it. There were so many imponderables, and so many uncertainties. It was not a subject to be solved by mathematical formulae, or exact calculation. It was like bicycling along a tightrope.

Fifthly, defence. There were lessons to be learned from the Suez expedition. The true value of Cyprus had to be re-examined. Still more important, as I knew from my short months as Minister of Defence, a reappraisal of the relative importance of conventional and unconventional weapons had to be made. Most difficult task of all, if reliance was to be placed upon the nuclear deterrent, was to achieve the removal of the ban on information which the Americans had imposed upon us by the McMahon Act. Yet, in the present atmosphere of Washington—at least so far as the Administration was concerned—this seemed an almost hopeless ambition.

Finally, there was the future of the Commonwealth. In the Suez crisis, so far as I could judge, the old Commonwealth countries had stood splendidly firm with loyalty and understanding. India, in spite of her natural dislike of force as an instrument of policy, had shown sympathy and good sense. So had Pakistan and Ceylon. There would have to be a meeting of Commonwealth Prime Ministers in the next few months, and it would need careful handling. But what of the future? I reflected that in the coming year both Ghana and Malaya were due to become independent. This process was bound to continue. Could it be resisted? Or should it be guided as far as possible into fruitful channels? Was I destined to be the remodeller or the liquidator of Empire?

In the short intervals for reflection which were possible in these hectic first days, I pondered over all these prospective obstacles which we would have to surmount as best we could if the new Government was to survive. Meanwhile there were two immediate hurdles which must be taken as lightly as possible.

The first hurdle was the Party Meeting—the usual constitutional meeting of all sections of the Conservative and Unionist Party, held in those days formally to elect the Leader of the Party and ratify his earlier selection. The Party Meeting was made up of all Conservative Members of the House of Commons taking the Whip and prospective candidates, Peers who take the Whip and the Executive of the National Union of Conservative and Unionist Associations in the country. In all it amounted to about one thousand men and women. They met on Tuesday, 22 January, in Church Hall, Westminster, at noon. The proceedings were in three stages. In the first two we took no part; my wife and I were kept in a waiting-room outside. Lord Salisbury presided and moved a resolution, accepting with regret Eden's resignation. This was seconded by Walter Elliot, the senior Privy Councillor present in the absence of Churchill. I heard afterwards that he delivered, as I would have expected, a most eloquent and moving speech. Walter Elliot was one of those political figures whose memory has perhaps faded among the general public, though treasured by many old and dear friends; for he made a large and valuable contribution to the development of Tory philosophy.

The next item on the agenda was to propose my election as leader. This again was done by Lord Salisbury, the seconder in this case being Butler, who was, very properly, received with great applause. After him Sir Eric Errington, as Chairman of the Executive Committee of the National Union, supported the motion, which was carried unanimously.

Meanwhile Dorothy and I waited in a little room behind the platform, attended and comforted—and even stimulated—by the Chief Whip, Edward Heath. When the time came, he led us to our places, and the third phase of this ritual ceremony began. Fortunately the choice of time—12 noon—for the meeting limited all the speeches, including my own. Indeed, the whole affair was concluded in fifty minutes. Naturally I began by my own tribute to my predecessor:

> I have been a friend of Anthony Eden's for over thirty years. In addition to the personal affection which has grown up between us, I have learned to respect his two salient characteristics; courage and integrity. When all the clouds of controversy have cleared away, it is by these two outstanding qualities that he will long be remembered.

I next referred to my election to the leadership as at the same time inspiring and humbling. Inspiring because of its traditions; humbling because of the immense burden of responsibility placed upon my shoulders. Happily I would not be alone. All through these years, with many ups and downs, I had had the support of my wife without whose help I could have achieved nothing. Apart from being one of the most expert and devoted canvassers,

> she serves to remind me of the realities of life. These are so often concealed in White Papers and Departmental briefs. You learn quite a lot from having four children and eleven grandchildren. If I show signs of becoming remote from those everyday problems

that perplex people in their homes, for that after all is what a great deal of politics is about, then my wife brings me back to fundamentals.

I next spoke of the loyalty of the Party and especially the growing strength of the Young Conservative movement. From this I passed to the formation of the Government which

> of necessity involves sad partings from old friends, as well as the recruiting of new blood. I should like to pay a tribute to the spirit which everyone has shown in putting the cause before the individual.
>
> I think we have a good Cabinet and a good Administration. I certainly could not have accepted my task without the help which Mr. Butler has given me in true loyalty and partnership.

Turning to the rank and file of the Party, I recalled that it was thirty-four years since I first stood as a candidate, and that I had fought altogether ten contested elections. I had visited a large number of constituencies all over the country.

> The chief thing I have learned is what I would call the warmth and friendliness of our Party. You know, it isn't those who are always addressing each other as comrade who necessarily show the most brotherly feelings.

Since there had been a good deal of talk in the Press about the Right and Left of the Party, I thought it best to make some reference to the different elements which it comprised. Although I had spent all my political life on what I suppose would have been called the Left of the Party, and had even resigned the Whip between the wars, I was now regarded as belonging to the Right. I could not help feeling slightly amused at the short memories of political commentators.

> I hear a lot of silly talk about the Left and the Right. To the broad stream of our philosophy there are many tributaries. Indeed we are always adding to this flow as the Parties of the Left break up into a kind of delta of confusion. And so our great river flows on triumphantly to the sea. We don't believe much in expelling people. I think that is a good thing; because I, no doubt, would have been a candidate for expulsion many years ago.

But tolerance did not mean that we had no strong principles. We tried to apply them pragmatically or, in other words, with common sense. We did not accept or reject old ideas merely because they were old; nor did we accept or reject new ideas merely because they were new. The only test was would they work to the common good.

To use Disraeli's phrase, we must be conservative to conserve all that is good and radical to uproot all that is bad. So it is that we have never been, and I trust that while I am your Leader we never will be, a Party of any class or sectional interest.

Men and women had both rights and duties. Rights for themselves and families, and duties to the Crown and fellow subjects. This philosophy had governed our views about social problems.

There are some people in this country who are persuaded that social reform began in 1945 with the Socialists. That is not true. Our structure of social services has been built up by centuries of conservative and liberal thought and action. What distinguishes both these points of view from the Socialist is this. We believe that unless we give opportunity to the strong and able we shall never have the means to provide real protection for the weak and old.

Perhaps it was this last phrase which caught the most attention in and outside the meeting. It is the true distinction still between the parties.

Finally, I declared that as at home so it must be abroad. We had our rights which we were determined to maintain, as well as our duties to our partners and allies which we would not shirk.

This all seemed to pass off very well, and I was not sorry that the next test to be made was in the House of Commons that same afternoon. Although I was nervous, making my first entry as Prime Minister, it all went well. I was received by what one of the papers called 'a dutiful rather than an enthusiastic cheer'. It was warm enough but not over-enthusiastic. It was clear that on such an occasion the main purpose was to pay a tribute to our former Leader, with not more than a restrained reception for his successor. The Labour Party, who had been accustomed to make a good deal of noise in the last few months, confined themselves to a reasonable amount of derisory shouting and laughter.

After Questions, Gaitskell rose to pay a tribute to the former Prime Minister. He did this, as was his custom on such an occasion, with outstanding grace. It moved both sides of the House by its generosity, as well as by the fine language in which the tribute was clothed. In his last paragraph he made a graceful reference to my succession, offering his congratulations 'and strictly personal good wishes'.

> I cannot say that we wish him to have a long tenure of office. Nor can I hold out any hope that we shall give him an easy time— he would not wish it . . . . We shall be happy to relieve him of the burden of office whenever he likes. But, meanwhile, at the beginning of what may be a series of stormy Parliamentary battles, we extend to him these few words of personal good will.[1]

Jo Grimond then said a few words about Eden, followed by David Grenfell, the oldest Member in the House. I made a reply, contenting myself with a few paragraphs. In my tribute to Eden I repeated what I had said before. He had two great qualities—courage and integrity; he had always done what he thought was right, and no greater tribute could be paid to any man. As for the Leader of the Opposition, I thanked him for his welcome, although I knew that the kind things he had said about me were to some extent 'the stylised preliminaries to combat, like the salutes between duellists'. Nevertheless I was grateful. I would promise to serve the House as a whole to the best of my ability.

My wife was in the Gallery, and together we walked back to Downing Street. Our thoughts turned naturally to Anthony and Clarissa on the long voyage to New Zealand. I thought, too, about the immediate future and our prospects. Much would depend on the Party and the House of Commons, and to what extent the extremists on either side were prepared to push their views. Much, too, would depend upon the firmness of my Cabinet colleagues. In any case, I remembered the traditional encouragement which Lord Melbourne—reluctant to accept the Premiership on the ground that

[1] *Hansard*, 22 January 1957.

it was a 'damned bore'—had received from his friend Tom Young. 'Why, damn it all . . . such a position was never held by any Greek or Roman: and if it only lasts three months, it will be worth while to have been Prime Minister of England.' On this Melbourne had replied, 'By God! That's true.'[1] I had only promised the Queen six weeks.

[1] David Cecil, *Lord M.* (London, 1954), p. 111.

CHAPTER VI

Aftermath of Suez

HOWEVER short and precarious our tenancy might prove to be, my wife and I now moved to No. 10.

It is very comfortable. I have a good room as a study, next to Dorothy's 'boudoir'. (She has arranged a working sitting-room upstairs.) The house is rather large, but has great character and charm. It is very 'liveable'.[1]

A few days later Churchill came to luncheon alone.

> It seemed strange for me to be entertaining him at No. 10. He has aged, but is still very well informed and misses little that goes on.[2]

He was pleased at my having come to see him immediately on my appointment and was full of goodwill and almost patriarchal blessings. Shortly afterwards, he sent me a note by one of his Zionist friends. The point of its argument was that in denying free passage for Israeli ships through the Canal since 1949 and in refusing to allow the Gulf of Aqaba to be treated as an international waterway, Egypt and the other Arab states were claiming that they were still at war with Israel. They were therefore merely exercising belligerent rights. At the same time they complained that Egypt had been the victim of an aggression by Israel in November 1956. Yet, if the Arab contention was right, this Israeli invasion of Sinai was not an aggression but an ordinary military offensive. In sending me this memorandum on 24 February he added, 'I am astonished at Eisenhower and America's State Department.' I was glad to have his moral support and to know how deep and persistent an interest he took in these great affairs.

[1] 8 February 1957.   [2] 14 February 1957.

In the third week of February my wife and I made our first visit
to Chequers.

[This house] has been so often described that it is not worth
doing so again. It is certainly a fine house, but it has been rather
spoilt. The great hall (made out of an open courtyard) is a failure.
There is a lot of fine furniture and some good—and [some]
indifferent—pictures. But there seems too much of everything.
However, it's very comfortable—well heated, with plenty of
WAAFS as servants.[1]

I was to find Chequers of great value during my years as Prime
Minister. It was a truly noble gift. Unhappily, although adequately
endowed by the donor with the income necessary to maintain a
house and estate of this character in 1917, it now required a large
subsidy from the Treasury. The garden was well designed and well
kept; the lawns sloping up behind the house, where the unspoilt
Elizabethan north front presents a fine appearance, form a specially
attractive feature. The path leads up through a little wood to the
hill, with the great mound reputed to have been the fortress of King
Cymbeline. Here there is a wide and splendid view over the great
plain below. The south side of the house has been much altered,
and there are too many stone terraces and modern gazebos in the
Elizabethan style. Nevertheless, Chequers is a splendid national
possession and plays a most useful part in modern political life. It is
as admirably equipped for carrying on public business as for private
recreation. The house is especially well adapted for entertaining
Commonwealth Prime Ministers and Ministers, as well as foreign
notabilities. I used it almost entirely for two purposes—either to
receive a large number of public guests, or to spend a short time
alone where I could work quietly and ponder over special problems.
My wife never liked the place. It had no attractions for her, whose
chief relaxation was gardening. But such, no doubt, are the weaknesses of human nature that gardening is not much fun when it is
someone else's garden, and you are never quite sure whether you
will be there to enjoy the shrubs and flowers in the spring and
summer that have been planted in the previous autumn. Accordingly,

[1] 17 February 1957.

I used to lend the house for long periods to one or other of my colleagues, especially to Selwyn Lloyd.

Meanwhile we had begun to settle down in No. 10. No doubt each successive occupant of this famous house gives it the particular flavour of his life and character. My wife brought to it her own special gifts. She soon learnt the names and shared the interests of everyone, from the Private Office and the Garden Rooms – the secretaries and typists – to the messengers, the policemen and the telephone-girls. One of the charms about the house is that there is no back door. There is the garden gate, by which distinguished men or secret visitors are sometimes introduced. But normally the milk bottles and all the rest are left outside the front door, and various stores of food and drink seem to arrive in the same manner. But now, added to all the usual impedimenta, were bicycles, tricycles, scooters, as well as an occasional perambulator. These were the belongings of the various members of my large family. Dorothy, who moved frequently between London and Sussex, always arrived in a Ford or Austin van filled with vast quantities of vegetables and flowers and packages of all kinds. Since she generally appeared about the time that the flow of Ministers and other notabilities was beginning, some confusion ensued. I had to try to persuade her to time her arrival, and unloading, to a more appropriate hour. Similarly, I had to tell some of my grandsons that if they wished to play draughts or dominoes with the policemen, to which I had no objection, they should do so in a way which would not obstruct the arrival of Ambassadors or Cabinet Ministers. All this, however, began to provide in these early months a certain warmth and geniality to the new regime and even promote a sense of confidence.

Although I had, of course, realised the multifarious character of a Prime Minister's work, it was something of a shock to find the difference between my new life and past experience. A Minister, however important his Department, is able to concentrate almost his entire attention upon a limited range of problems. This was certainly true of the Ministries in which I had served. In Supply the problems were varied and baffling, but all upon one theme–the arming of the nation. In North Africa, with all the complexities of the situation, I had to deal only with Mediterranean problems. Moreover, the French problem was almost concluded before I passed to Italy or Greece. Housing was a single-purpose operation, although with varying aspects. This also applied to Defence; and although in my short tenure of the Foreign Office there were many different questions covering the world, I paid little attention to the House of Commons or to public speaking and, living quietly with my own advisers, concentrated upon my own work or undertook a number of interesting journeys. As Chancellor of the Exchequer I was back once more in dealing with matters which, although difficult, were bounded by definite limits and ran along a more or less single track. Now I found myself alone, solitary (for very few people ask to see a Prime Minister except those he does not much want to see), only leaving my house to go to the House of Commons (since the house itself was my office); seldom if ever going to a club; and working in one way or another for very long hours. The day was spent largely in interviews or meetings—Cabinet, defence or special committees of Ministers to discuss a particular subject. Parliamentary Questions took me to the House of Commons for an hour or so; but the rest of the time was the study of papers, preparation of telegrams and the multifarious and complex series of difficulties, all of which in the end seemed to come to me to settle.

On 9 February, a month after I had taken over, I made this note:

In thinking over our immediate problems, they seem to be

(a) *U.N. and Israel.* As long as Israel refuses to leave Gaza, etc. U.N. will declare her in default and may try sanctions. U.K. opinion will *not* stand for this. But if we stand out, Arab opinion is still more inflamed against us. The Americans are behaving very weakly over this, with legalism and pedantry.

(b) *Syria and Egypt* . . . Owing to (a), Syria will not allow the Mediterranean pipeline to be mended and Egypt may close the Canal.

(c) *Nasser and the Canal.* He may refuse passage to British and French ships.

(d) *Canal dues.* Nasser will claim full dues. If we refuse, we don't get our oil. If we accept, we lose face terribly. (We might even lose our majority in the House.) Here again Dulles uses fine words but does nothing.

All this makes the prospects for the next few weeks pretty grim. If we can get over these immediate troubles, we might manage fairly well.[1]

But even this did not complete the story, for there was still the publication of the Estimates, including the great rise in the Civil Estimates which would certainly give a shock to confidence. There was the Farm Price Review—an annual headache, always a danger, where feelings sometimes ran high and resignations threatened. In addition, we were determined to present a new and startling defence policy, based on the nuclear concept. Finally, we had to repair and restore our relations with the United States.

A fortnight later nothing had changed.

We have at present more 'balls' in the air than I can remember. In *Foreign Affairs*, these are (*a*) Israel–Egypt; (*b*) Clearance of Canal (now held up by Egypt); (*c*) Canal dues–short term; (*d*) Long-term Canal settlement; (*e*) Syrian pipelines. In *Commonwealth*, (i) Indian–Pakistan disputes over Kashmir. Indian threat to leave Commonwealth. (ii) Discussions with *Malta*, about to founder on Mintoff's intransigence.

In *Defence*. (1) British Forces in Germany, and our desire to reduce, resisted in W.E.U. and NATO. (2) German support costs; the Germans are wriggling out of the £50 m. agreement which seemed 'in the bag' a week or two ago. (3) Cuts in Forces– and new pattern of Forces.

In *Home Affairs*. (1) High Civil Expenditure. (2) The doctors' claim to £20 m. (3) Old Age Pensions. (4) Budget prospects.

If *everything* went right, we should still have difficulties. But of course, hardly anything ever goes right.[2]

Then, of course, there were the inevitable by-elections, all of which were bad, some worse than others; there were the depressing calculations of the psephologists–the astrologers of democracy– which, in the stern judgement of the *Annual Register*, 'indicated with varying degrees of emphasis that the Conservative Party no longer enjoyed the degree of support that had carried it to victory

[1] 9 February 1957.   [2] 25 February 1957.

in the spring of 1955'.[1] The swings against us were sometimes 4, 5 and even 7 per cent. Yet, curiously enough, this swing was no more marked than in the by-elections before Suez. Perhaps the public did not worry about Suez at all and were more concerned with the Rent Bill.

With all these preoccupations we had now to face the threat of devastating strikes throughout industry. On returning from Paris one Sunday night in March I noted:

A mass of work on my return – all troubles! The shipbuilding strike, to be followed by a strike throughout the engineering industry, seems almost certain. Then the railways! There is complete confusion about UNEF and the Gaza strip, and Nasser's insolence to U.N. goes unreproved by anyone. The President is ill; Dulles is in Singapore; and Hammarskjöld is as weak as water.[2]

It was not easy to analyse the cause for the strikes which suddenly seemed to hit so many industries – shipbuilding, the whole of general engineering and now a railway strike, probably to be followed by the power stations and the docks. One of my colleagues was

convinced (from what he has heard in the lobbies of the House of Commons) that this is a political plot, between the Communist and extremist union leaders and the Parliamentary Labour Party. Since they cannot get the Government out by Parliamentary means, and since they have not been able to get us 'rattled' by ordinary methods or even the swing of Gallup polls and by-elections, they hope to finish us off by creating an untenable industrial situation.[3]

I was sceptical of this somewhat romantic explanation.

I think the unions have got their own way for so long (since 1939) that they cannot imagine that there is any point at which they can meet firm resistance.[3]

There was soon to be added the indiscretion of one colleague (which had to be defended in the House of Commons) and the resignation of another, a senior Minister and old friend (which

[1] *Annual Register, 1957*, p. 8.   [2] 10 March 1957.   [3] 15 March 1957.

seemed likely to shake the stability of the Government). By 31 March I noted:

The Press foretells the early collapse of the Government, as the result of Lord Salisbury's resignation; the Suez failure; Makarios and Cyprus; the strikes; and the general sense of malaise. The *Sunday Express* is particularly virulent. I always felt that these would be the critical weeks. If we last the summer, we shall stay the course.[1]

So it was to go on from my first appointment for some four months. It was not until after the final debate on the aftermath of Suez on 15 and 16 May that I felt we had turned the corner. We should now be able, with ordinary luck, to run till the normal end of the Parliament. And so it was to prove.

When I became Prime Minister the most urgent questions facing us were: the clearing of the Canal from physical obstructions; the terms upon which it should be reopened, especially the terms that would be imposed upon British and French shipping; the position of Israel, whose troops were still in occupation of the Sinai peninsula, including the Gaza strip, as well as the vital Sharm-el-Sheikh heights on the Gulf of Aqaba; the opening of the Syrian pipeline which had been put out of commission in the previous November; and, finally, the changing and incalculable moods of the American Government.

All these were interlocked. Although after much dispute the British salvage fleet had been allowed to operate for a few weeks, General Wheeler, who was in charge of the United Nations operations, had demanded, no doubt under American instructions, the withdrawal of the last of our ships by the end of January. This resulted in a considerable and unnecessary delay. Although by the end of March a channel was cleared for ships up to four thousand tons, it was not until May that the task was finally completed. This work was retarded partly by the reluctance to use British resources, partly by technical difficulties and partly by obstruction by Nasser, who continued to refuse to allow the tug *Edgar Bonnet* to be removed from the channel until his other demands were met.

[1] 31 March 1957.

Meanwhile an important development was taking place in American policy. While maintaining, at least outwardly, an almost fanatical devotion to the infallibility of the United Nations in all questions great and small, whether of faith or morals, they now began to develop what was soon to become known as the 'Eisenhower Doctrine'. At the very beginning of the year the President, seeing the power gap which was developing in the Middle East and realising at long last the danger of growing Russian infiltration, asked Congress for authority to fill this dangerous breach in the defences of the free world. The unnatural flirtation, amounting to a liaison, if not a legal marriage, between the Russian and American representatives at the United Nations was now beginning to cool. The State Department seemed to realise the danger, and even to reproach us, in private, for not having persisted in our military occupation of Egypt. There were two main aspects in the new doctrine as presented by the President. First, he was to have power to use the armed forces of the United States

> to secure and protect the territorial integrity and political independence of any [Middle Eastern] nation or group of nations requesting such aid against overt armed aggression from any nation controlled by international Communism.[1]

Secondly, a further $200 million was voted, apart from any other appropriations, as additional aid to such countries as were under pressure.

This gallant effort to shut the stable door after the horse had bolted was welcome to us, for it at least marked a return to the world of reality. The conditions were, of course, limiting. An American intervention had to follow an invitation; but with all the resources of diplomacy, overt and covert, this should not present too great a difficulty. The precise meaning of 'aggression' even as interpreted by Dulles's explanations in Committees of Congress was obscure. Was the subversion of a Government by the usual Communist methods to be regarded as an act of aggression? The recent cases of Czechoslovakia in 1948 and of Hungary in 1956 were in all our minds. How would they have appeared in terms of this new

[1] *Annual Register*, *1957*, p. 195.

theology? These questions were often asked and seldom answered. Nevertheless, as a whole, the Eisenhower Doctrine was greeted by Western Europe with a certain wry satisfaction. At least it avoided the vetoes of the Security Council or the resolutions of the Assembly. All the precious dogmas which had hitherto been sacred were now, it appeared, made subservient to the real interest of the United States and her allies. We had no objection. Yet we could not help observing that the promulgation of this new tenet on 5 January and its acceptance by the House of Representatives on 30 January and even its final endorsement, after much controversy, by the Senate at the beginning of March did not change the attitude of Washington in regard to past events or towards actions taken by their allies. Dulles, somewhat to our amazement, declared: 'Unless we move quickly into the area the situation will be lost.' But that applied only to American troops, navies and armies. Here a certain latitudinarianism was allowable; other nations must adhere to the full orthodox creed, first formulated at San Francisco after the war, and now enshrined in the vast glass temple of the United Nations in New York.

Yet all this dealt with unknown and uncertain events, lying in the future. The immediate need was for the reopening of the Canal and, of lesser but considerable importance, for the restoration of the Syrian pipeline. The trouble was that while these were matters of great significance to us they did not seem so urgent to our American friends. As early as 6 January, Cairo Radio reported Nasser's declaration that British or French ships would not be allowed through Suez so long as Israeli troops remained in occupation of Egyptian territory. The British and French Governments naturally replied by calling in aid the assurances against any such discrimination given by the Secretary-General of the United Nations before they agreed to the final withdrawal of their forces. Heavy pressure was brought upon the Israelis at the United Nations in the debate of 17–19 January. By the 22nd they agreed to a complete withdrawal from Sinai except from the Gaza strip and from Sharm-el-Sheikh. As the Israeli troops withdrew those of the United Nations occupied the territory behind them. But the Israelis were naturally unwilling to abandon these two vital positions without some equiva-

With Churchill
'My old chief, from whom I had received, for so many years, many kindnesses, and to whom I had long looked for support and inspiration.'

With Hailsham and Butler

Hailsham 'created great enthusiasm both in the Party and throughout the country. He was not afraid of novel methods of publicity.'

Butler—'I knew that everything depended upon our working closely together.'

Leaving for Paris with Selwyn Lloyd

'I was particularly anxious to keep Selwyn Lloyd, because I felt that one head on a charger should be enough.'

lent guarantees. A double process of intimidation was now applied. In Cairo, Nasser tried to use his control of the Canal to ensure support from the maritime powers; in New York, Cabot Lodge tried to overwhelm the Israeli representative by a hysterical combination of reproaches and appeals.

This situation was naturally a cause of extreme anxiety in London. Public opinion both in Parliament and in the country would find it intolerable if Egypt were rewarded for her illegalities and breach of treaty by continuing to use Gaza as a base for the guerrilla attacks on Israel, threatening a renewal of a war 'to drive the Israelis into the sea', and also to cut off Israeli shipping from the Gulf of Aqaba. They were already in breach of the 1888 Convention by preventing Israeli ships from using the Canal. Was it to be tolerated that they should continue to prevent them using their own harbour of Eilat? The Americans seemed now to be demanding economic or even military sanctions against Israel if they did not comply with the United Nations demands. Such a course was described by one of my advisers as 'unthinkable'. I remember observing that this phrase usually meant that it would happen. At the same time, complete intransigence by Israel could lead us into equal difficulties. Even the friendly Nuri Pasha, Prime Minister of Iraq, let us know that he regarded the withdrawal from Gaza, under some guarantees no doubt, as essential. If the British and American Governments pursued a common policy, they could now regain the confidence of Iraq and other Arab countries and strengthen their hands against Egypt. We were thus placed in a disagreeable dilemma. We could use our influence with Israel to agree to a compromise. But we could not in honour or in equity agree to sanctions. Yet if no concessions were made, the Canal would not be reopened and the Syrian pipeline would remain severed. Unhappily, neither of these issues was of any particular interest to the Israeli and the American Governments.

After much discussion, our colleagues broadly approved the line which Selwyn Lloyd and I had worked out:

This is (*a*) we cannot vote for sanctions against Israel; (*b*) in order to put ourselves as right as possible with Arab world, we

H

shall try to get a 'moderate' motion sponsored by (say) Canada, which would call for a fair settlement.[1]

If the Israelis were adamant, the Americans were clearly apprehensive.

The Americans, now 'up against' realities, are angry and puzzled. Our only line is to sit back a bit. The State Department has called us into consultation, together with the Canadians, and there is talk of a possible compromise being made at the last moment.[2]

I still felt that some form of guarantee to Israel could be devised. Of course Egypt might well react by preventing General Wheeler from finishing his work of clearing the Canal. Equally, until Israel's terms could be agreed, there seemed little hope for the Syrian pipeline. This must entail heavy losses for us, and also for Iraq, whose oil was exported through Syria and whom we would have to support in some way in order to keep Nuri Pasha in power.

President Eisenhower, who has been on holiday for the last month or more, golfing and quail-shooting, has returned to Washington. The situation regarding the Israel–Egypt dispute over Gaza and Gulf of Aqaba is getting more and more confusing and dangerous. The American Administration is at last being brought up against realities, and poor Foster Dulles is floundering more and more. We too are about to be placed in a most difficult position, if there is another Afro-Asian 'sanctions' resolution against Israel.[3]

Unhappily, Eisenhower on his return to Washington delivered a broadcast in which he demanded unconditional withdrawal by Israel.

The Israeli Ambassador came to see me on 20 February, and I impressed upon him the need for some gesture. I told him that British public opinion was clearly in favour of a 'package' deal, combining a withdrawal with adequate and effective guarantees.

At Question Time, it became clear that feeling was running rather high, on both sides of the House, about the President's

[1] 11 February 1957.   [2] 18 February 1957.   [3] 19 February 1957.

speech on the radio last night. His approach to the Israel problem seems to us all very legalistic and one-sided. Of course, we can't say what we are doing behind the scenes, so we get all the blame. Our honour and our interest are in conflict. We want the Israelis to retire as soon as possible—so that the Canal clearance can continue and pressure be turned on Nasser. We are anxious about the oil-producing countries if 'sanctions' are imposed— whichever way we vote ourselves. We could not easily vote for sanctions, for we don't think Israel has had a fair deal. Even abstention must injure us in the Arab world and might shake our position at home. So, at all costs, we must work for a settlement.[1]

We finally decided to put our weight behind a resolution to be proposed by the Canadians and try to make some amendments to it. Certainly we were not prepared to vote for sanctions whatever happened. We would vote, or abstain, in accordance with the way in which things were going. It now became necessary for me to state our position clearly, and publicly. I did so in answer to a question from Emanuel Shinwell, in these words:

> We believe that the Gaza Strip should be evacuated by Israel. We equally believe that it should be made a United Nations responsibility and that United Nations Forces should be stationed there. We believe that the Israeli forces should retire from the west shore of the Gulf of Aqaba. We equally believe that coupled with that withdrawal it should be made clear beyond a peradventure both by the United Nations and by leading maritime countries that they regard access to these waters as free to the world.[2]

Subsequent exchanges made it clear that all sides of the House were agreed.

Since the President was fond of appealing to the opinions of the 'common man', I decided to send him a personal message (on 22 February) which I thought might have some effect. In this I asked him, as an old friend, to study my appeal with sympathy and understanding. In his broadcast he had paid tribute to his British and French friends and allies for the immense contribution they had made to world order by withdrawing their forces. He had gone on

[1] 21 February 1957.   [2] *Hansard*, 25 February 1957.

to say that this put the world under a heavy obligation to see that these two countries did not suffer. Our people, apart from our own interests, could not agree to Israel being asked to do what seemed to them wrong. Most people here, I declared, would think it reasonable that they should withdraw their forces from Gaza and the Gulf of Aqaba if there were a clear understanding that Egypt would not be allowed to continue to break international law or the armistice agreements. So far as Gaza was concerned, this could best be guaranteed by the United Nations forces moving in immediately, and it should not be impossible to devise some arrangement for the civil administration. So far as the use of the Gulf of Aqaba was concerned, which was vital to the life of Israel, it was not unnatural that the Israelis should be hesitant, since Egypt had been in default over the resolutions dealing with Israeli shipping in the Canal for many years without any sanctions being used against her. There could be a resolution of the United Nations or, better still, a guarantee by the United States, to which other countries might adhere, securing to Israel the right to use the Gulf of Aqaba. It might be wiser for the United Kingdom not to take the lead at the United Nations; but I felt sure Canada would be willing, if this plan seemed the best course to adopt.

The President replied that he thought a condemnation of Israel and a vote of sanctions would be wrong, at any rate at this time. Perhaps a single resolution combining the withdrawal orders and the assurances to Israel might be acceptable; but he did not think that the required votes could be obtained without some intimation of the consequences to Israel if she refused to comply. This message, although faulty in logic, at least showed some understanding of the real question at issue.

On 1 March, the Israelis, relying on Dulles's private assurances that their conditions would be enforced, announced in the United Nations their willingness to withdraw both from Gaza and from their position on the Gulf of Aqaba. At the same time, we made a formal declaration in New York, stating that we regarded the Straits of Tiran at the entrance to the Gulf of Aqaba as an international waterway to which all nations had rights of passage. This view was supported in the United Nations by the American representatives.

In the House of Commons it was clear, from the questions asked, that all parties were becoming more and more critical of the United Nations and the United States because of their equivocal and even unfair attitude. Syria and Egypt on 7 March insisted that neither pipelines nor Canal would be restored until Israel complied with their terms. But on the same day, relying on Dulles's assurances, the Israeli evacuation took place. The administration of Gaza was handed over to the UNEF and within a few days the pipelines were restored. The position seemed therefore to be gradually improving.

At this juncture I had to make a short visit to Paris in connection with our defence arrangements. Mollet and Pineau gave me

a most vivid and entertaining account of their visit to Washington. According to them, the President was very much the master when large decisions had to be taken. He was like a king, and the courtiers intrigued for his favour. Pineau gave a most precise account of the final stages of the Israel agreement to withdraw from Gaza and [the Gulf of] Aqaba. It seems that Foster Dulles double-crossed the Israelis—or else that Cabot Lodge took a line in U.N. without regard to the State Department.[1]

Of course I took all this with a grain of salt, but it was a vivid picture.

Unfortunately, no sooner had the United Nations forces entered Gaza than they handed over the civil administration to the Egyptians. The *fedayeen* raids immediately began again. Nevertheless, the Israelis showed considerable restraint. They refrained from massive reprisals, and they were to some extent encouraged by the growing emphasis on the Eisenhower Doctrine. At any rate, the presence of UNEF in both Gaza and on the Gulf of Aqaba gave them some sense of security.

The first step, therefore, in the restoration of something like normality had been achieved in spite of many and apparently insuperable obstacles. The Canal would be ready for use by the end of March, at least for smaller ships, and larger vessels would be accepted a few weeks later. A second problem, however, had now to be faced. On what terms should we and other maritime nations be 'allowed' to use the Canal?

[1] 9 March 1957.

Before this formidable obstacle had to be met, one minor, though important, hurdle was successfully negotiated. We had been advised earlier in the year by Charles Johnston, our Ambassador in Amman, that, in view of public feeling in Jordan, we should probably gain rather than forfeit the goodwill of the people if we were to agree to replace the existing Jordan treaty by a new arrangement, involving the gradual withdrawal of our troops, leaving behind certain military installations for which Jordan would pay us. Accordingly, on 16 January we informed the Jordanian Government of our willingness to enter into discussions with a view to the termination of the old treaty. Within two months a new agreement had been reached. This was not something in which we had been forced to acquiesce, but rather an operation which promised certain tangible advantages. The old treaty had little or no strategic importance for us, particularly since the signing of the Baghdad Pact, which itself involved us in onerous and expensive commitments. Indeed, as we were later to learn, the presence of British troops was of much greater value to the King and the Royal regime in Jordan than to us. We continued to maintain friendly relations with Jordan, and to do all we could to help in developing the economy. We even, when they were in financial trouble, agreed to postpone the agreed payments. We recognised the difficulties in which the King was placed, subjected to pressure from all sides. He faced them, as later, with patience and gallantry. I was happy indeed that in accomplishing all this we did not sever, but indeed perhaps strengthened, the traditional friendship for Britain which was still widespread among the Jordanian people.

While awaiting the final and critical stages of the 'Suez crisis', I had my first experience of the distractions and complications which a Prime Minister has to endure, sometimes from the consciences, sometimes from the indiscretions, of his colleagues. As the years pass, one becomes inured to these occupational hazards of Premiership. But when they struck me at such a delicate moment I was hardly yet prepared for them. The first arose at the end of February out of a remark made by Sir David Eccles, President of the Board of Trade. Eccles first made his mark during the years of Opposition. Later he served with success as Minister of Education in Eden's

Government, and I appointed him President of the Board of Trade when I formed my Administration. He thus held, next to the Treasury, the most important office among the economic Ministers. A chance and unprepared reply to a supplementary question on the connection between the levy on film distributors and the future of Entertainment Tax was solemnly elevated into a 'Budget leak'. When the matter came up on 28 February a great row seemed to be threatened. Even the Press joined in, and some of my supporters were gravely disturbed.

I had a rough time after questions—Gaitskell, Bevan, Wilson— all joining in the 'hue and cry'. I felt sure that they were going to use this as an extra piece of pressure against a Government which is going through a bad patch. The by-elections all show a swing away from us. . . . Eccles's slip is a very small and venial one, and I was determined to protect him by drawing all the fire on to myself.[1]

I was now faced with a formal vote of censure for not having demanded his resignation :

the younger members of our party (and most of the Press) thought that I was too unyielding and counter-attacked too vehemently. But I felt that Bevan's pretended moderation was a trap. (His indignation when I didn't fall into it proved this.) B. wanted Eccles to apologise. I remembered that Dalton apologised —the first day. On the second the hunt started again and he was out.[2]

On 4 March a long debate in the House of Commons took place on the Eccles affair.

Gaitskell opened—very weakly. [The] Chancellor of Exchequer replied (not very well) and then the debate degenerated into *opéra bouffe*. It was brought back by Harold Wilson, in an able, witty and effective speech. But there was really nothing in it all, and I had no difficulty in demolishing the Opposition case in winding up.[2]

The truth was that, as so often happens, in the interval of a few days the heat had gone out of this synthetic indignation. The Press,

[1] 28 February 1957.   [2] 4 March 1957.

including papers like the *Manchester Guardian*, the *Observer* and the *Star*, turned against the Opposition. We therefore won the division by an easy majority and our Party seemed pleased by my speech. On reflection, the House realised that a statement made openly in Parliament, whether prudent or not, can scarcely be termed a 'leak'.

The most curious feature of the debate was a pathetic (and very 'shy-making') contribution from Dr. Dalton, who described (almost like the prisoner in a Russian trial) his own fall from grace.[1]

This minor episode is scarcely worth recalling except as an example of the strange squalls which blow up so suddenly and subside so quickly in the life of the House of Commons. Eccles was an able Minister, who had never been afraid to show his intellectual contempt for his opponents. One of the motives, therefore, for this attack upon him may have been a personal desire for retaliation. There was also no doubt another purpose. If a new Prime Minister could be rattled into abandoning a colleague, it would help to discredit a Government already in grave trouble. There was perhaps a more general advantage to be gained.

On thinking over the Dalton episode (which was really nauseating) this seems the only possible explanation. The Opposition want to pretend that the 'Eccles indiscretion' is of the same order as Dalton's famous 'leak'. (Of course they are utterly different.) So D. is made to do this terrible act of political Buchmanism, and the public are supposed to draw the conclusion that under Socialism the strictest rules of moral conduct are enforced, while the Tories are lax. It's quite possible that the public will be deceived; but the scene of Dalton's 'confession' was very unpleasant.[2]

A few weeks later I was to suffer another, and much more serious, blow. On 27 March, the night of my return from a short visit to Bermuda to meet President Eisenhower, I heard that Lord Salisbury was about to offer his resignation. Thus, within three months of the formation of my Administration, one of its great props was withdrawn. Yet we still had to face the main test. This storm had blown

[1] 4 March 1957.   [2] 5 March 1957.

up very rapidly from the Eastern Mediterranean. It was not, alas, the warm and soothing breeze that one expects from the Cytherean isle, but a chilly and, at this moment, a particularly ill wind.

Since my unsuccessful attempt to bring about a settlement of the Cyprus question by the London Conference[1] and since my transfer from the Foreign Office to the Treasury in December 1955, I had had very little to do with Cyprus, either directly or indirectly. I knew that the new Governor, Field-Marshal Sir John Harding, was determined to get a settlement if it was at all possible, and when I left the Foreign Office negotiations had begun and were continued throughout January and February 1956. But unhappily these efforts were met by mounting terrorism and disorder. I was very ready to see the famous formula[2] modified if this would help Archbishop Makarios, and to this the Turks agreed with good grace. At the time I had noted:

The talks will now be renewed and we shall see whether the Archbishop is really prepared to risk reaching an agreement with us. I feel that the precise terms are not so important as the fact. For a large number of Communist and extremist groups will turn against the Archbishop (whatever the terms of any agreement). These forces are revolutionary and cannot be appeased.[3]

So anxious was Eden to reach some settlement that he even thought of going out himself. But it was clear on consideration that this would only lead the Archbishop to raise his price.

By the beginning of March 1956, from whatever cause, the talks had broken down. As soon as one point seemed to be settled another arose. Although various approaches were made through unofficial representatives and with the assistance of the Bishop of Chichester, Dr. G. K. A. Bell, no progress was made. Furthermore the Governor became convinced that both Makarios and the Bishop of Kyrenia were implicated in the terrorist activities. The two dignitaries were arrested and deported to the Seychelles on 9 March. This decision was followed by debates in Parliament in which the Socialist and Liberal leaders expressed the utmost indignation. Eden made a fine

[1] See *Tides of Fortune*, pp. 664 ff.   [2] *Tides of Fortune*, Appendix 5.
[3] 12 January 1956.

H2

speech in defence which had given great comfort to his Party. In the House of Lords,

> The Archbishop of Canterbury made a nimble, balanced, equivocal speech, worthy of Cranmer. The Bishop of Chichester . . . made a woolly, sentimental and unrealistic speech, and was terribly and rightly castigated by Salisbury.[1]

Nevertheless, I knew well from the history of all such movements, notably in Ireland, that coercion alone could not be the answer. The troubles of Ireland had ultimately led to partition; but Cyprus was small, and the areas occupied by Turks or Greeks were by no means homogeneous. Yet partition in some form might prove the only solution.

> On Cyprus, the problem of finding a solution acceptable both to Greece and Turkey remains just as intractable as I found it last summer at the Tripartite Conference. This fundamental difficulty cannot be resolved by verbal formulae, however cleverly devised.[2]

Negotiations of some kind were still continuing, and in the middle of July Lord Radcliffe was appointed to draw up the terms of a constitution granting internal self-government. On 16 August EOKA, the Greek Cypriot revolutionary organisation, announced a temporary suspension of violence 'in order to facilitate a settlement'. But when the Governor issued his terms, these were not acceptable, and violence began again, becoming more and more intense during the autumn and winter months. On 19 December, Lord Radcliffe's proposals for a constitution were published.[3] These were favourably received in Britain and America, the State Department even declaring that the Radcliffe Plan 'could be a first step toward an eventual peaceful and generally acceptable final solution'. But however ingeniously drafted, including a system of diarchy to reassure both communities, these proposals were immediately rejected on the familiar ground that they did not provide for self-

[1] 16 March 1956.
[2] 19 June 1956.
[3] These provided for internal autonomy with a legislative assembly composed of both Greeks and Turks.

determination. It must be Enosis or nothing. But Enosis, as we well knew, meant war between Turkey and Greece.

So the matter rested at the turn of the year. But with terrorism waxing and waning with varying intensity, there seemed no end to the hideous situation. The needs of our base in Cyprus could no doubt be adequately preserved; but the insoluble question remained – Turks and Greeks could not be reconciled. Coercion achieved partial success, and at the end of December the emergency regulations were relaxed. But this phase was followed by a new plunge into cold-blooded murder. Soldiers and civilians were killed in the shops and the streets, and scarcely a week passed without some new outrage.

A few days after becoming Prime Minister I sent a minute to the Foreign Secretary, reverting to the possibility of a settlement on the lines of partition. This had indeed been hinted at in the autumn by the Colonial Secretary, Lennox-Boyd, whom I also consulted. I also asked that the Minister of Defence should set up an urgent inquiry into our military needs, and whether the base could be carved out of the territory without too much difficulty and effectively defended. All Ministers were working on this possibility when unexpectedly a new move was made by the terrorist leadership.

On 15 March we were informed by the Governor that EOKA was offering to call off terrorism if Archbishop Makarios were released. Leaflets were widely distributed to this effect. Their somewhat sophisticated language suggested that they had been prepared in Athens. It was evident that the terrorists were being slowly mastered by the forces of law and order. Nevertheless this move could not be disregarded.

Of course, the Press here and the Archbishops and Bishops here, with their usual sentimentality, will regard this as a 'change of heart', and a 'conversion to constitutional methods' and so on. What we have to do is (a) not to relax the pressure on the terrorists at the critical moment; (b) not to lose Turkish support; (c) to satisfy home and foreign opinion (and especially *The Times* newspaper) that we are dealing with the new situation in an 'imaginative' way.[1]

[1] 15 March 1957.

The recent hanging of a young man, taken in possession of firearms, had caused a good deal of complaint on both sides of the Atlantic. Critics seemed to have overlooked the fact that he had admitted to a number of brutal murders. However, it was clear

> that the hanging had no effect on the EOKA decision, which is either the result of the desperate position into which the gangs have been driven, or just a ruse to get time to reform.[1]

In spite of the obvious objections to anything like a deal, I was anxious somehow or the other to reduce our liabilities.

> I am not persuaded that we need more than an airfield, either on long lease or in sovereignty (like Gibraltar). Then the Turks and Greeks could divided the rest of the island between them.[1]

About the same time Lord Ismay, as Secretary-General of NATO, offered his services as a conciliator. I felt that we should build on this initiative.

> This gives us a more respectable entry into a new position than the EOKA pamphlets. I rang up Lord Ismay in Paris, and arranged with him to send his letters to the U.K., Greek and Turkish representatives at NATO forthwith.[1]

I also called together those of my colleagues who ordinarily dealt with colonial affairs and prepared a document for the consideration of the Cabinet, to be used, if Ministers agreed, as a basis for a communication to the Turkish Government.

> I think it is about right. We accept the NATO offer; we 'assume' that the Archbishop will now recommend the end of violence—in which case we will release him from Seychelles (but *not* yet let him go back to Cyprus). But I feel that (*a*) the Turks, (*b*) some of the Cabinet, will jib at this.[1]

When the matter came up for discussion, it was clear that there was a division of opinion. Everyone agreed that we should accept the NATO initiative, but nobody seemed to know what to do about the Archbishop. Most of us felt that we could not detain him

[1] 15 March 1957.

indefinitely in the Seychelles, where he had been for nearly a year. We did not want him to go back to Cyprus to take the lead in a terrorist campaign. He would be troublesome in Washington, New York or London. Nevertheless, after much deliberation, there was a general agreement that, if the Archbishop would make a declaration opposing violence by EOKA, we would be willing to end his detention. The new approach to NATO, coupled by a cessation of terrorism, seemed to create a situation of which we ought to take advantage.

This was agreed before I left for Bermuda on the evening of 19 March, and I was cheered to receive a telegram next day from Butler, who presided over the Cabinet during my absence, reporting that Lennox-Boyd, the Colonial Secretary, had made a statement on these lines in the House of Commons which had been well received. During the next six days I was in Bermuda, in conference with the President, and I did not leave until midnight on 26 March. During this time what I had feared took place. The hope that the Archbishop would make a clear statement was always too sanguine. His declaration was equivocal, although there were plenty of fine sentiments about a new start. He tried to bargain with us. He wished to hold us to the abolition of the emergency regulations, which we could not accept. I still felt that his evasiveness ought not necessarily to mean that we must keep him in the Seychelles. What we must be sure of was that we did not appear to accept the conditions which he was seeking to impose.

It was difficult indeed to deal with a situation of this kind in my absence. But I made it clear to my colleagues that I favoured the release of Makarios, so long as it was not related to any action concerning the emergency regulations.

A whole sheaf of telegrams have been arriving—personal from Butler; personal from Lennox-Boyd; personal from Lord Salisbury. The first two (supported by Governor Harding) want to accept Archbishop's statement as satisfactory; let him out from Seychelles; and announce changes to mitigate emergency regulations. The last strongly disapproves, and in fact threatens resignation.[1]

[1] 24 March 1957.

Selwyn Lloyd, the Foreign Secretary, was fortunately with me, and we agreed a line which we thought most Ministers would support.

(*a*) Say Archbishop is – as usual – equivocal and logic-chopping; (*b*) say we can make no bargain with him or EOKA – the emergency regulations will be mitigated as and when Governor decides; (*c*) all the same, let him go; (*d*) inform Turks; (*e*) no commitment to be given in Parliament about 'negotiating' with Makarios.[1]

I got home on the morning of the 27th. There was to be a full Cabinet the following day. Salisbury came to see me after dinner – as charming as ever – but I felt that he was determined to resign about something. He seemed in one of his resigning moods. The weight of opinion was clearly in favour of the course recommended by Lennox-Boyd, the Colonial Secretary, and by the Governor, Sir John Harding. And on 28 March the Colonial Secretary made a statement on the lines agreed which had been carefully drafted to avoid, as far as possible, the various pitfalls.

With his usual consideration Salisbury agreed to postpone the interchange of letters until the following day, 29 March. In those days the courtesies of public life were still preserved. He sent me two letters – a formal letter for publication, addressed to the Prime Minister giving his reasons for resignation, and an informal letter in which he expressed his gratitude for the patience and consideration which I had shown, and his regret at the difficulties which his action would cause me. He also undertook, if the formal letters were published, not to raise the question in the House of Lords. In my formal reply I repeated shortly the arguments in favour of an act of statesmanship which I hoped would reap its reward. But I admitted that only events could prove which of us was right. I added an expression of the regret which I and all my colleagues felt on losing his services. My personal letter was as follows:

Dear Bobbety,
     I cannot tell you with what grief I got your two letters. It was a blow which, although not altogether unexpected, was none the less severe.

[1] 24 March 1957.

You will hardly realise (because of your modesty) what a sad loss you will be to all your colleagues, who look to you for wide advice, based on great experience. But to me, of course, it means much more. I have taken on a very difficult job, in circumstances almost unparalleled in political history. I wish you could have been with me to see it through.

In addition, we have worked together (and I think with general sympathy of outlook) for very many years.

One thing comforts me—you refer to our old friendship. That we can surely keep.

Yours ever,
Harold

It was indeed a sad event. A note in my diary recalls it all to me.

A terrible day. I worked from 10 a.m. till 7.30 p.m. in the Cabinet Room. We have rewritten the White Paper [on defence]; had a long discussion about the strikes; accepted Lord Salisbury's resignation (with interchange of letters); appointed Lord Home as Lord President and Lord Hailsham as Deputy Leader in the Lords; written a speech for Monday's debate [on Defence].[1]

Naturally the loss of so old a friend was a personal sorrow to me. Moreover, Lord Salisbury's own distinction in politics, and his high standard of integrity, were impressive and widely recognised. He had resigned with Eden in 1938, as a protest against the policy of appeasement towards Mussolini. He had not only a fine political career, but he was also the bearer of a name distinguished in history and unique in the Conservative annals of the last century.

The resignation caused far less sensation than I had expected. Indeed, it seemed to me then that he had chosen an issue on which no strong public opinion would be aroused; more especially as we were supported by the man on the spot. But there were other dangers looming ahead. Now that the Israeli withdrawal had been completed, it was becoming urgent to reach a decision as to the terms on which the Suez Canal would reopen. It was more than likely that we should be gradually forced from one position to another. I could not tell what humiliations we should have to

[1] 29 March 1957.

undergo. I felt, therefore, that, sad as it was for me on personal grounds, the resignation of so outstanding a statesman might have taken place in a way to cause me even greater anxiety.

As regards Cyprus, the President sent me a message of sympathy to which I could only reply that the world now recognised that Cyprus was an international problem. I did not believe that the Archbishop had changed his views, but I still felt that, in the long run, a solution would be found. In the next few months little progress was made. The United States seemed now to have abandoned their original support for Enosis, or union of Cyprus with Greece. But the manœuvring of all parties was destined to continue for many months, and indeed it was not until nearly two years later that agreement was finally reached between Britain, Greece and Turkey, followed by the return of Archbishop Makarios to Cyprus.

After overcoming these preliminary difficulties, we now faced the major crisis over the future of the Canal. On 18 March the Egyptians stated that Canal dues should be paid in advance to the Egyptian Canal Authority. The British and French Governments, with United States support, proposed that the dues should be paid to the United Nations or to the International Bank. Discussions were accordingly opened between Nasser and Hammarskjöld. The House of Commons naturally became restive, more especially since we were not in a position to give any clear direction to British ship-owners. Finally, on 29 March, Nasser set out his full terms to the United Nations. While reaffirming the readiness of the Egyptian Government to abide by the 1888 Suez Convention, guaranteeing freedom of passage, he insisted that dues should be paid to the Egyptian authorities. He requested that his memorandum, which covered a number of other points, should be deposited as an inter-national instrument with the United Nations. The question was now raised as to how far the Egyptian Government's terms could be reconciled with the Six Principles adopted by the United Nations in October 1956.[1] Negotiations were next opened by Raymond A. Hare, the United States Ambassador, with a view to harmonising the two declarations, but without real success. One encouraging

[1] See above, p. 145.

development at least became possible. The flow of oil now allowed us to abolish the rationing of diesel oil on 1 April.

Although the Canal was officially clear for small ships, we were still advising shipowners to hold off. This naturally led to our being pressed as to whether our objection was on political or technical grounds. All we could do was to continue to stall. The American negotiations were making some progress in detail, but few concessions of substance could be obtained. Long discussions took place among Ministers at the beginning of April

> about what I call 'the water-jump'—i.e. the Suez Canal. More by good luck than by good management, we seem to have scrambled over the other hurdles. But I don't see how we can fail to take a toss at the canal hazard. The best we can hope for is to pull the horse, rather vigorously, to the other side and then scramble back into the saddle. But it will be touch and go![1]

I could only reflect that it was probably more advantageous to have faced the Salisbury resignation over Cyprus than over Egypt.

On 8 April the clearance of the Canal was virtually completed. We must soon face the problem. If there was no settlement, British shipping would be seriously handicapped. It was already rumoured that some firms were considering re-registering their ships under Liberian or other flags. The Americans were again working closely with us, but the harm had been done; although some minor concessions had been obtained there seemed very little hope of further progress. Should we go to the Security Council? Should we appeal to the Assembly? Should we revive SCUA?

> Our real problem is how to use the Canal with the minimum of short-term loss of face.[2]

In view of this critical phase in the life of the Government, I kept the Cabinet fully informed on every detail. The Americans were willing to accept our plan for the next steps, but was there anything which could be more than face-saving? Finally we agreed

> that we must try to cover our decision to use the Canal (if Nasser is willing to accept transferable sterling) by (a) appeal to Security Council; (b) recommendation of all maritime nations in SCUA.[3]

[1] 3 April 1957.   [2] 8 April 1957.   [3] 9 April 1957.

I reported the decision at some length in a telegram to Menzies, explaining our dilemma. Our competitors were beginning to use the Canal. We were doing all we could to persuade the Americans to exert the maximum pressure in their negotiations. But if these failed we must face either a boycott of the Canal or recourse to the Security Council. A boycott would be damaging to our commercial interests and seemed unlikely to be watertight. If the matter were taken to the Security Council we would consider advising users to pay the dues under protest. In reply, the Prime Minister of Australia recommended that we should try to place the responsibility of finding a settlement upon the United Nations. They had taken the matter up and they should not be allowed to shuffle out of their self-imposed burden.

But a new difficulty began to cause us concern. Quite apart from the now somewhat theoretical question of reconciling the famous Six Principles with Nasser's new proposals, on what conditions would these ships be allowed to pass? So far we were supporting the Americans in their negotiation.

Mr. Hare (now called Mr. Tortoise), the American Ambassador, is conducting this in a leisurely, but able manner. Meanwhile, we are trying (not without success) to keep the ships of all countries out of the Canal.[1]

But we must now consider

not whether we ought to send British ships through the Canal, but whether Nasser will allow us, except on absurd terms—for instance, compensation for damage at Port Said. (No one in the Press or Parliament seems to realise this.)[1]

Although we could not yet abolish petrol rationing we were able to increase the basic ration by 50 per cent on 17 April. This at least was a sign of progress in the general problem of oil. Lord Salisbury now entered the controversy by a letter in *The Times*.

It is critical of the Government about Suez and will increase the danger of a split in the Party. I don't think it is really meant as a bid for power. But I have no doubt that many people will regard it as such.[2]

[1] 15 April 1957.   [2] 18 April 1957.

A number of Tory Members, about fifteen in all, were encouraged to put down a motion on similar lines. The signatories soon rose to thirty. I still felt it wiser not to force the issue. Although a large ship had passed through the Canal, the main maritime countries were continuing the boycott.

The Suez affair goes on slowly—just as I should wish. Even if we have to give in to Nasser, in a sense, we must not lead the rest—we must follow.[1]

When the Security Council met on 26 April at the request of the United States, Cabot Lodge, although critical of the Egyptian terms as not fully meeting the Six Principles, could only suggest giving them a trial.

The Security Council went more or less according to plan. SCUA will meet on Tuesday. The 64-dollar question is whether Nasser will accept transferable sterling if and when we want to send our ships through the Canal.[2]

SCUA met on 30 April, and although it took the view that the Egyptian proposals were insufficient, the intention to resume the use of the Canal clearly emerged. But the vital negotiations from our point of view on the question of payment had now to begin. These were to be conducted at Basle, but there was a preliminary hitch.

[The talks] will not start till tomorrow (Monday). This is a great nuisance. It is not clear whether this is deliberate or just bad luck. First, the Governor of the Bank of Egypt (who should have gone to Basle on Friday) got 'influenza'. Next, three of his colleagues were to arrive Saturday and talk on Sunday. Then they failed to turn up till Sunday evening. Meanwhile, how are we to hold back the other maritime countries? We have managed to keep them back for two or three weeks after the real breakdown of the American negotiations with Nasser. But they are getting very restless. It is impossible to foresee what line Nasser will take. But I feel sure that if he accepts transferable sterling it will only be after much haggling concerning the No. 1 account.[3]

It was our purpose to keep the large sterling balances blocked in the No. 1 account and to persuade the Egyptians to accept payment of

[1] 25 April 1957.   [2] 28 April 1957.   [3] 5 May 1957.

the dues in transferable sterling which would be made available for each transaction. I had to leave for Bonn on 7 May, returning on the 9th, but to my immense relief I received a telegram while I was there to say that the Basle negotiations between the Bank of England and the Bank of Egypt had gone unexpectedly well. Under this plan a special transferable sterling account would be opened for Canal dues and other outgoings in connection with shipping. This removed one great headache. In the Security Council we had only been able to put on record our continued protest against the illegality of the seizure of the Canal, at the same time agreeing to give *de facto* recognition of the situation and thus giving Egypt's six-point plan a trial. This was damaging in the sense that it recognised the failure of our long struggle to assert our rights and thwart Nasser's ambitions. The French held out for another month, and proposed a further reference to the Security Council. But when this took place, the result was negative, and on 12 June they too were to authorise their ships to use the Canal. There could be no argument against the realism of our policy. What would have been intolerable would have been a demand to pay in gold or dollars, or to unblock the Egyptian No. 1 account. The French reservation was tiresome, but the main danger was overcome. Accordingly, on 11 May we privately informed the Commonwealth Governments that we would no longer bar United Kingdom shipping from the Canal. In spite of the unsatisfactory position I added this phrase: 'We have . . . every intention of doing what we can to put ourselves in future less at the mercy of unilateral action by [Nasser].' This was the beginning of the new tanker and storage policy.

On 13 May I publicly announced that shipowners would no longer be discouraged from using the Canal, and I explained the terms of the Basle agreement. I emphasised the point that the new special account did not in any way change the position of the No. 1 blocked account, where large sums of money still remained under our control. The future of this must rest upon satisfactory arrangements concerning our financial claims. Discussions would in due course take place in a neutral centre. Naturally this statement was not agreeable or easy to make; I phrased it in as simple and matter-of-fact [terms] as I could. There were many fewer questions, from either side of the House, than I expected. But there was rather a tense calm—like that just before a storm.

The Tory dissentients are beginning to organise themselves . . .[1]

The next day I noted that

Lord Salisbury has 'joined the rebels', with rather a bitter statement in the House of Lords about the Suez decision. But I do not think myself that it will 'cut much ice'. (What a blessing he went over Makarios !)[2]

The scene was now set for a full-dress debate, with a growing sense throughout the Party of difficulty and even peril. One practical step I had already taken. In a minute to Lord Selkirk, First Lord of the Admiralty, thanking him for the work that had already been done for the transport of oil from the Middle East, I drew his attention to the importance of stockpiling. At the same time I was fortunate in obtaining the services of Sir Matthew Slattery as special adviser for considering the whole question of the tanker programme. He was to co-ordinate and press forward plans to build more and larger tankers and provide harbour and repair facilities for them; to construct pipelines and ensure adequate supplies of steel for this purpose. I wanted our share of the world tanker fleet and of tanker building to be as high as possible. All this, of course, was to be done with full and timely consultation with the interests concerned. It was not till more than two and a half years later that he completed this task. Admirable results have flowed from his work, for which the country owes him a great debt. When the prolonged closure of the Canal followed the June war of 1967 the nation was to reap the reward of these precautions.

In the House of Commons the discussion covered two days, beginning on the afternoon of 15 May and ending in the evening of the 16th. Final abolition of petrol rationing was announced on the first morning. As so often happens on these occasions the debate proved one of fluctuating fortunes and high tension.

It is difficult for those who only read of the doings of Parliament

[1] 13 May 1957.   [2] 14 May 1957.

and the speeches of the chief protagonists to realise the extreme degree of nervous strain involved. I worked hard upon my speech, on which so much depended. I even sat up until 2 a.m. in the morning of 15 May to complete its preparation. Yet I was wholly unprepared for the ordeal which awaited me. Gaitskell opened, with a motion skilfully formed to attract both opponents and supporters of the Suez operation. The first half of his speech was scarcely an attack; the second half more effective. As a whole, although ably and well argued, it was rather muted in tone. When I got up it was clear to me that the Opposition were determined to throw me off my stride.

So they kept up a sort of wave of laughter, jeers, cat-calls, etc. – just not enough for the Speaker to interfere, but very disconcerting. This quite spoiled the serious parts of the speech – especially the long passage on the future transit of oil – and made me rather fumble other parts. But all I could do was to go on – as manfully as I could – till I got to the end. It was not a success.[1]

The material was good enough for the record, but it did not meet the Parliamentary situation. On that first evening the position looked bad. It seemed the Tory abstentionists would number twenty, or even thirty. More than the so-called 'Suez Group' they were naturally encouraged by the French 'fight to the finish' attitude. With a majority of only fifty, such a figure would be serious, even fatal. I realised that everything would depend upon the winding-up. and began to think about it before going to bed.

On the next morning, 16 May,

The Press is not bad on the matter and substance of the debate. My speech is called 'below recent form' by the *Manchester Guardian*, which criticises also certain phrases as banal. The *Express* is violent, and in spite of Lord Beaverbrook's dislike of Lord Salisbury has started to laud Lord S. to the skies. 'The Suez Betrayal' is Max's line. 'Eden was deserted by his colleagues' (which . . . is strange!), *Times* was correct and quite fair. *Daily Telegraph* did its best.[2]

[1] 15 May 1957.   [2] 16 May 1957.

By an extraordinary chance, before the debate was resumed, public opinion was to some extent diverted into an altogether different channel.

> The H-bomb was successfully exploded yesterday. (I got the news last night.) This has filled the papers today . . . to the great advantage of the Suez situation![1]

On the second day, after an able but bitter speech from Kenneth Younger, Selwyn Lloyd followed.

> He did very well and got a good sympathetic reception from most of our people. The Press, the Socialists, and the dissidents are making a dead set at him and trying to force me to ask for his resignation. (He has offered this to me, but I have, of course, refused it.)[1]

The debate remained upon a high level. Aneurin Bevan wound up for the Opposition. His speech, which

> was to have been absolutely devastating, failed completely. He spoke for 45 minutes—was rather dull and made a great error in resting too much of his case on the Bulganin letters to Eden. (Even the Socialists, after Hungary, don't much like Bulganin's Pecksniffian lectures.) It was rather like my speech yesterday, though (I think) worse. He had two good jokes, and that was all.[2]

When I rose at 9.30, I realised how much depended on my reply. By some miracle it was as great a success as that of the day before had been a failure. Curiously enough, although I merely repeated the arguments of the day before, somehow I was able to strike the right note, and was listened to almost in silence. I tried to cast the balance sheet fairly, with gains and losses. We could not disguise our failure to dislodge Nasser or force him to disgorge. Against this, we had the Eisenhower Doctrine, which had been welcomed by Gaitskell as a valuable contribution to peace. Here there was an opportunity for a little Parliamentary fun. So I reflected that

> the President's request to Congress to use troops if necessary was described by the Leader of the Opposition as a 'very wise and courageous step'. But the right hon. Member for Ebbw

[1] 16 May 1957.   [2] 17 May 1957.

Vale [Bevan] condemned it as loudly as his Leader applauded it. This is what he said about the Eisenhower Doctrine:

'It doesn't add up to any coherent policy at all.'

He went on, in a radio statement, to say that the main attack on the British Government by himself and his hon. Friends had been that they had acted outside the United Nations; and then he said,

'The President seems to be inviting the American nation to do the same thing.'[1]

I commented that these two Opposition leaders should really try to get on better terms. Then there was the attitude of the Commonwealth which had rallied well, and had become more and more sympathetic and helpful. There was the position of the Arab States and the steadiness of the Baghdad Pact Powers. In addition, Egypt had suffered a humiliating military defeat, which would not be forgotten throughout the Middle East. In any case, although the terms of the Motion merely expressed concern at the Government's Suez Canal policy, it was in fact a vote of censure.

It raises, therefore, as all Motions of censure must do, the one simple but over-riding issue, upon which I hope the House will ponder, of whether, in the opinion of the House . . . the prestige and economic interests of Britain would be in safer keeping if they were transferred to the hands of the party opposite. That is the only question upon which we shall be voting.[1]

In the event, the Motion was defeated by a majority of 49, with only 14 Tory abstentions. When the figures were announced,

the whole Tory party stood up and cheered me. At the Speaker's chair, I turned and bowed. It was an extraordinary and spontaneous act of loyalty and touched me very much. How odd the English are! They rather like a gallant failure. Suez has become a sort of Mons retreat. Anyway, we're through this particular trouble—at least for the moment.[2]

This view was shared by the Press. Every newspaper regarded the new Administration as having passed successfully through the first big test. I felt that, come what may, we should now be able to carry on until the Parliament reached its natural close.

[1] *Hansard*, 16 May 1957.   [2] 17 May 1957.

Nearly two years followed in which our relations with Egypt were mainly concerned with financial negotiations. Progress was very slow. Although discussions began on 24 May 1957, they broke down within a few weeks. In September, the Egyptian Government seemed willing to re-start the talks. Fortunately the United States Government remained firm about the Egyptian dollar reserves, which were still blocked, and in early October negotiations began again in Rome. But it was not until after the Shell company had made a private settlement in December 1958, and after the intervention of Mr. Eugene Black, that the financial treaty was finally initialled on 17 January 1959. Even then, new complications arose over the distinction between British property which had been 'sequestrated' and that which had been 'Egyptianised'. At last, on 28 February 1959, the agreement was signed, and at the end of the year, on 1 December, diplomatic relations were re-established at the level of chargé d'affaires. It would be tedious to discuss the ups and downs of this long and complicated controversy, but it was finally concluded.

More troublesome problems arose out of the system of *ex gratia* payments which we decided to set up to meet the losses of British firms and citizens. This led to many difficulties, since the plan which we adopted, while giving full compensation to the smaller claimants, necessarily involved substantial reductions in the case of large sums, affecting both companies and individuals. Moreover, there were awkward moments throughout all this period in Parliament, especially in the House of Lords. Nevertheless, as a result of the devoted work of the board appointed for the purpose, broad justice was done, without too heavy a burden being placed upon the Exchequer. Not unnaturally, some claims were put forward in a wholly exaggerated form.

So ended the Suez controversy so far as this Parliament was concerned; nor did it play any role in the ensuing Election. I have often wondered about this—perhaps the reason was a general disinclination of all Parties and individuals to re-open old wounds. Moreover, the changing kaleidoscope, both in the Middle East and throughout the world, raised new hopes and involved new disappointments. The fundamental problems and dangers of the Middle East remain.

CHAPTER VII

A New Strategy

HE most urgent, and at the same time the most delicate, task which confronted me on becoming Prime Minister was to repair and eventually to restore our old relationships with Washington. With this was closely linked the new defence organisation and strategy for the United Kingdom, which must now take full account of the impact of nuclear weapons. It was clear that any attempt to restore our amicable co-operation with Washington must be carefully handled. I was not at all in the mood, nor were my colleagues, to appear in a white sheet or put ourselves, however great the prize, in a humiliating posture. We felt that we had been let down, if not betrayed, by the vacillating and delaying tactics which Dulles had pursued in the earlier stages of the Suez crisis and by the viciousness with which he and his subordinates had attacked us after the launching of the Anglo-French operation. There might come a moment when my close ties with America and my former association with the President could be usefully exploited; but I was in no mood to make the first approach.

I did not have long to wait. On 22 January the American Ambassador called with a private message from the White House to which the greatest secrecy was to be attached. The President was anxious to see me. Would it be possible for me to come over between the 21 and 24 March? He would either receive me in Washington or meet me in Bermuda if I thought that preferable. As regards the subject for discussion he would like to make it clear, when the time came for an announcement, that the talks were to cover all the great issues confronting the world, not merely those of the Middle East. I told the Ambassador that I would give a reply after consultation with some of my senior colleagues. But I raised at once the question of an invitation to Mollet, the French Prime

Minister, and I was told that the President was considering this, but had not yet reached a decision.

For my part, I was naturally pleased by the President's message, couched in such friendly terms. But I had not relished the idea of going to Washington. It did not seem that this was the moment for a pilgrimage to Canossa. I was therefore touched by my old friend's delicacy in proposing Bermuda. After some negotiations about the arrangements which the French would prefer, it was agreed that the French Ministers would make a visit on their own to Washington, and that the Bermuda Conference should take place on an Anglo-American basis. Mollet, with his usual good sense, seemed quite happy with this plan, which seemed to suit him well enough. For us, Bermuda—British territory—made the whole difference. The formal announcement of these visits, which made it clear that the invitations came spontaneously from the President, was made on 11 February.

I had many indications that the American Government itself was distressed and anxious to repair, if possible, the harm they had done. For instance, on 23 January, the day after I received Eisenhower's message, I had a visit from Arthur Hays Sulzberger of the *New York Times*. What he told me was encouraging. His paper, which had taken a line throughout the crisis hostile to Washington and friendly to London, had added a hundred thousand to its circulation. This at any rate was an indication of what the public were feeling. The President, whom he had recently seen, was determined to restore full Anglo-American co-operation, and like other members of the Administration, had begun to realise the dangers of the United Nations as it was now developing, with its growing Afro-Asian representation.

During these weeks Duncan Sandys had been in Washington as Minister of Defence and had taken a very firm line in a talk with Dulles. The latter had given him an opening by making a somewhat laboured excuse for his 'regrettable remark' to the Senate about not wishing to have a British and French soldier on either side of him in the Middle East. Sandys had underlined the widespread and deep anti-American sentiment which prevailed in Britain. America's best friends had been sadly disillusioned. We had felt badly let down, and it would need a big effort by the Americans to restore our confidence. Dulles, although embarrassed, seemed to accept these criticisms without any serious protest and agreed that we must now at any rate try to revive the old working system. I applauded Sandys's firm position, but was interested to hear that the President had asked to see him and had expressed a desire to do all in his power to mend the broken fences.

I was naturally delighted that this first stage had been so rapidly concluded, and on the President's own initiative. In my message to him on 25 January, therefore, I now felt able to revert to our old friendly relations. He had already been to the Mid-Ocean Golf Club in Bermuda, and I felt sure that this would be an agreeable as well as a valuable meeting. My message ran as follows:

I must tell you again how much encouragement I have got from your suggestion of a meeting so early in my tenure of my new responsibilities. I am so glad you like Bermuda. We shall there be unencumbered by speeches, dinners and all the rest of the paraphernalia of official visits. It will be fine to revive the atmosphere of the talks we had in old days, before these immense burdens had descended on you, and now, to a lesser extent, on me. . . .

We shall have to settle the range of subjects to be discussed. We might exchange a list of headings. I do not expect that either of us will want too many papers: what we want to do is to go over the canvas with a broad brush. But I certainly see this as an opportunity for joint decisions on broad issues of policy. The smaller and more intimate we can keep the party the more progress I think we shall make.

At the same time I sent telegrams to the Prime Ministers of the Commonwealth countries, informing them of the forthcoming conference. By 9 March, I was able to give them an indication of the subjects which I hoped to discuss. These would include the future of the United Nations, in view of recent developments; disarmament; our relations with Russia and the satellites; Suez and Palestine; United Kingdom relations with Europe and especially the proposed European Free Trade Area; the more general problems of the Middle East and Africa in view of recent Soviet moves; China and East–West trade. Since I would not be reporting even to my own colleagues during the crowded hours of the Conference itself, I hoped the Prime Ministers would be content to rely on a full report when it was finished.

The Minister of State for Colonial Affairs, Jack Maclay, had reminded me of the opportunity for protesting against the American attitude towards British colonial policy, largely based on ignorance. While I was not anxious to discuss colonialism as such, I was certainly determined that the Americans should be made to understand the rapidity with which our policy was developing and note the dangers as well as the benefits involved.

Before leaving for Bermuda, I interchanged some useful messages with Menzies. He was rightly concerned about the illegal but effective authority which the Assembly of the United Nations seemed now to have arrogated to itself. In a long telegram, he told me of a recent discussion with Dulles on the dangers ahead. He had argued that the great powers seemed to be losing their authority, while the Assembly was trying to usurp that of the Security Council. Although Dulles had replied that this diagnosis was an exaggeration, yet, in Menzies's opinion, he was clearly becoming anxious about the djinn which he and Cabot Lodge had incautiously unloosed from the Afro-Asian bottle. Accordingly we might now be reaching the psychological moment for putting pressure upon a somewhat repentant Administration. The Americans were certainly having second thoughts and becoming increasingly aware of some of the real problems with which we were all faced. Yet the President seemed still to regard faith in the United Nations as a substitute for a foreign policy. Somehow he must be disabused. As I told Menzies in reply, the firmness and frankness of his talk with Dulles certainly made a good preliminary to the Conference. Meanwhile the promulgation of the Eisenhower Doctrine, however vague and shadowy, was at least evidence that the American Administration had realised the dangers in the Middle East and the importance of not allowing a power vacuum to be filled by subversive and Communist forces.

I had come to the conclusion at the time of forming the Administration that a complete review of our defence policy was now essential. The first question was one of machinery. When appointing Duncan Sandys as Minister of Defence I informed the Service Ministers that I proposed to bring some reality into the task given to the Minister under Section 1 of the Ministry of Defence Act, 1946. This made him responsible for 'the formulation and general application of a unified policy relating to the Armed Forces of the Crown as a whole and their requirements'. Accordingly his immediate tasks were to be to work out a new defence policy in the light of present strategic needs which would secure a substantial reduction in expenditure and manpower; at the same time to prepare a plan for reshaping and reorganising the armed forces. For this purpose he would have authority, subject of course, to the Defence Committee and the Cabinet as a whole, for deciding all questions on the size, shape, organisation and disposition of the forces, as well as their equipment and supply, their pay and conditions of service. In order to bring some greater order into the discussion of these affairs, individual Service Ministers and the Minister of Supply when putting proposals to the Defence Committee on any matters within this definition, were to make the approach through the Minister of Defence, who would be provided with a Chief of Staff—in this case Marshal of the R.A.F. Sir William Dickson—to act both as Chief of Staff to the Minister of Defence, and as Chairman of the Chief of Staffs Committee. Equally important, the Minister could call into consultation any officers or officials of the Service Ministries and the Ministry of Supply, and look to them for full advice and assistance.

I took the precaution to get the general approval of the new Service Ministers before their appointment or confirmation in the new Government. Accordingly, when the formal directive, embodying detailed proposals worked out in consultation with the new Minister, was circulated on 18 January, there was little resistance —although naturally some grumbling in high places. I was well aware that without a complete reorganisation (such as I was not able to undertake until much later) this new system would depend on a reasonable degree of goodwill and co-operation. On the whole this proved to be forthcoming; although naturally there was a good deal of heartburning when particular issues arose. I could not, in the time available, do more; but I was determined, by all the influence that I could bring to bear, to make the Minister of Defence's position as strong as it must be if the purposes which Parliament had in mind were to be effectively carried out. I was confirmed in my opinion a few days later by a characteristic and enthusiastic letter from Lord Montgomery:

Hurrah! The step you have taken in the Defence reorganisation is admirable. Duncan Sandys now has the power given him by you, to give orders; and, being the man he is, he will see his orders are carried out. A further point is that Dickson is now *his* man and can give him professional military advice without having any obligation to clear it with the Chiefs of Staff first—as he has had to do in the past. Sandys can order that his Chief of Staff takes the chair at meetings of the Chiefs of Staff Committee—as representing him (the Minister of Defence).

I had often discussed this whole problem with the Field-Marshal during my short term as Minister of Defence. Now I was at last in a position to make a start in bringing into being a new structure, on the need for which we were both agreed.

As part of the new strategy, I was determined to maintain the credibility of the British contribution to the nuclear deterrent. I therefore decided that we should press ahead with the nuclear trials on the Australian range as soon as possible, and sent out instructions accordingly on 1 February.

While Sandys was making a visit to Washington at the end of January, a new proposal from the Americans was suddenly brought forward. This was to deploy a number of intermediate range ballistic missiles (IRBMs) in Britain, the sites to be manned by British personnel as soon as they were trained. The weapons and specialised equipment would cost us nothing, although of course we would undertake to provide site works. This would give us a rocket deterrent long before we could hope to produce one ourselves; moreover it would provide full training for our own men in these new and sophisticated armaments. The details were finally settled at Bermuda, and the official announcement of this vital agreement approved in the communiqué. It was generally hailed as a triumph for British diplomacy and an outward proof of our restored relations.

Sandys worked hard and rapidly on the reorganisation of our defence system. By the middle of February, he had completed a comprehensive plan, for the radical reshaping and redeployment of our armed forces. This was approved at a weekend meeting of senior Ministers at Chequers on 23 February.

The plan included a proposal to reduce our army in Europe from 80,000 to 50,000 men. It soon became clear that this was the most distasteful aspect of our proposals from the point of view of our allies. I warned the Foreign Secretary that in negotiating this change—as we had to do in view of our commitments[1]—we must be careful not to be drawn into new engagements, nor, so far as Germany was concerned, were we to make their share of our costs automatically reducible unless, of course, our total involvement ever fell below the agreed German payment. Curiously enough, in view of later developments, it was the French who raised the strongest objection to the reduction of our troops in Europe. I was anxious, if possible, to bring the private discussions with France and Germany as well as the negotiation in NATO and in W.E.U. to an end before the Bermuda meeting. The timing and tactics were not easy to devise with all these interested parties to be soothed or satisfied. There was rather a stiff exchange of messages between me and Adenauer on the subject of support costs. I thought it wise to answer him frankly, without any attempt to disguise or minimise our firm intention. For I knew him to be too shrewd to be deceived by anyone, even by himself. Owing to Mollet's indisposition, I was not able to see him until 9 March, which was unfortunate, with the date fixed for Bermuda so near. Meanwhile the Ministers of W.E.U. met in London on 26 February.

I gave a large dinner (32 people) for the Foreign Ministers attending the Western European Union meeting. I gather that the reception of our plan for cutting our forces was pretty chilly.[2]

However on 3 March

---

[1] See *Tides of Fortune*, p. 482.   [2] 26 February 1957.

Bermuda Conference, March 1957: Selwyn Lloyd, Eisenhower, Macmillan, Dulles

'The President seemed very well—bronzed and alert.... He told me very frankly that he knew how unpopular Foster Dulles was with our people and with a lot of his people. But he must keep him. He couldn't do without him.'

With Selwyn Lloyd in Paris for a meeting of NATO, March 1957

On a visit to Germany for talks on the Common Market
'The atmosphere was very friendly and the Chancellor [Adenauer, *right*] in good form, sometimes serious, sometimes gay.'

With Eisenhower at the NATO Conference, 16 December 1957

One piece of good news—the negotiations with Germany about 'support costs' have finished successfully—at the official level. The Germans have agreed to recommend a payment of £50m for 1957–8. We have now to get agreement from W.E.U. (and NATO) to our proposed reduction to 50,000 men (from 80,000). I think . . . the Germans will support us. It is the French who are going to be difficult.[1]

President Eisenhower now began to express concern about our proposed cuts; but I explained to him that it was vital to keep our economy solvent, and that we would mitigate the immediate effect for General Lauris Norstad and NATO by every possible device, including a system of phasing the cuts over a period. Since all this had to be settled under a close timetable, with the Defence White Paper and the Budget so near, I begged the President not to oppose us when we got to the NATO discussions. I made a similar appeal to Louis St. Laurent, the Prime Minister of Canada, pointing out the urgent need to take final decisions. He made it clear that his representative would be ready to give us their full support. After a confused talk on the telephone with President Eisenhower, I sent him a firm telegram setting out the modifications which we were prepared to make.

We have made a great effort to meet General Norstad's views by agreeing that only a half of our proposed reductions shall take place during the financial year 1957–8 and that the second half will take place during the financial year 1958–9. We have further agreed that of the 1957–8 reductions a major part will take place in the first quarter of 1958 rather than the last quarter of 1957. Norstad seems satisfied, and by extending our reductions over a longer period I hope that we have done a lot to diminish the risks which you fear.

Early in the morning of 9 March, Selwyn Lloyd and I left London for the NATO meeting in Paris. Mollet had just returned from his visit to Washington, and the first part of the discussions was taken up with a brilliant if somewhat burlesque account of his experiences. But when we came to the formal session with officials present,

[1] 3 March 1957.

I

We had a very long, and rather unpleasant, argument about our force reductions in Europe. Although the French military, and even the Quai d'Orsay officials were quite understanding, both Mollet and Pineau were bitterly hostile. This is chiefly due to an imminent debate in the Assembly, and Mollet's fear that he will be attacked by Mendès-France as having 'betrayed' the Paris agreement.[1]

After nearly two hours of arguing we passed from the subject without any real progress. That same night, after a formal dinner at the Quai d'Orsay,

> Selwyn Lloyd and I had another go at Pineau about our forces and I think made some impression.[1]

In the event the NATO meeting passed off fairly well. The Western European Union discussions proved more difficult.

> We have got [Dr. Walter] Hallstein and [Herbert] Blankenhorn (the leading Germans in this field) more or less on our side. But Adenauer (like Mollet) is bitterly opposed to our scheme. The sly old fox is very anxious; he is thinking chiefly about the next election in Germany. (It's a pity that *all* Elections, in every country, cannot be synchronised! There is, nowadays, always one going on somewhere.)[2]

On 18 March I had to go to Leicester for a public meeting, leaving just after lunch. There was a packed audience of 3,000 or more and, except for 400 Young Conservatives on the platform, it was not a 'ticket' meeting.

> The audience gave me a tremendous reception, both at the beginning and at the end. We had a supper in the hotel (drink and sandwiches) for about 200 or so of the workers, which lasted till 11.30 p.m. or so.[3]

I then went to my room, to which a scrambler was installed, and at midnight,

> I got a message from London that the W.E.U. talks were going pretty well. Just before going to sleep (about 1.30 a.m.) the news came of a complete agreement.[3]

[1] 9 March 1957.   [2] 14 March 1957.   [3] 18 March 1957.

A NEW STRATEGY 249

My speech that evening was largely confined to the home situation. There had been a number of plans for a solution in the shipyard industry, now in the throes of a damaging dispute, and a foolish argument had raged about whether 'arbitration' or 'conciliation' should be used. I declared that the principle of 'arbitration' was really part of the process of 'conciliation'; and pleaded for an early settlement. If our great industrial nation was to avoid these self-inflicted wounds, of which the only beneficiaries would be our competitors, a new spirit must emerge. 'A fight to the finish' was a bad slogan; nobody could win the fight, and it was the whole nation that would be finished.

When I returned to London the next day we were able to reach an agreement which at least looked like avoiding a threatened railway strike. In spite of the serious industrial situation in other fields, I felt sufficiently encouraged not to take the drastic step of cancelling the visit to Bermuda. I had complete confidence in Butler, who presided over the Cabinet in my absence, and Macleod, the Minister of Labour. They would work loyally and tirelessly on the lines that we had agreed. To have cancelled the Bermuda Conference would have over-dramatised the industrial difficulties at home.

In the course of my Leicester speech I had said, 'Our object at Bermuda is to clear up any differences between Britain and the United States, and to restore Anglo-American relations as a cornerstone to world peace.' Nevertheless, although I had expressed confidence about the outcome, I must confess that I faced this first meeting with the President and the Secretary of State with some apprehension. There was one encouraging sign, which I was able to emphasise in the House of Commons on my return :

> The meeting took place not at my suggestion, but on the proposal of President Eisenhower. It was he, also, who suggested that it should take place on British soil. I would like to express my appreciation of his action in both respects.[1]

We timed our arrival so as to allow ourselves the morning and early afternoon free before the President was due to arrive. The Mid-Ocean Club repeated the gesture which they had earlier made

[1] *Hansard*, 1 April 1957.

for a meeting between Eisenhower and Churchill, and the whole building was made available for the Conference. I was accompanied by Norman Brook and Freddie Bishop with the usual team of secretaries and typists, and I left the others behind in London to look after the many problems at home, and ensure rapid communication. As it turned out this was essential, partly because of the situation in Cyprus and partly because of increasing dangers on the industrial front, where it now seemed likely that a railway strike would be added to our other difficulties. Selwyn Lloyd brought with him Patrick Dean—a lion-hearted man, who was later to make a splendid Ambassador in Washington.

The dining-rooms and smoking-rooms of the Club had been arranged for our purpose, and the Governor, Lieutenant-General Sir John Woodall, extended generous hospitality, and put all his staff at our service. The President came by sea and reached the island at 4 p.m.

> The Governor met him first and presented his wife and daughter. Then President and I shook hands. The usual guard inspection, etc., followed, after which I drove with him in his 'bubble car' to the Mid-Ocean Club.[1]

The bullet-proof 'bubble car' had been brought earlier, together with a vast number of guards, F.B.I. men, and all the rest.

> The whole population, white and black, of the island seemed to join in the welcome. The President seemed very well—bronzed and alert. He had rather a tiresome cough; but as I have caught a shattering cold myself, we are evenly matched in this respect. Foster Dulles flew in from Washington about the same time.[1]

During the twenty minutes' drive the President

> talked very freely to me—just exactly as in the old days. There were no reproaches—on either side; but (what was more important) no note of any change in our friendship or the confidence he had in me. Indeed he seemed delighted to have somebody to talk to! In America, he is half King, half Prime Minister. This means that he is rather a lonely figure, with few confidants. He told me very frankly that he knew how unpopular Foster Dulles

[1] 20 March 1957.

was with our people and with a lot of his people. But he must keep him. He couldn't do without him. Nor could he find a substitute. Governor Herter (now Under-Secretary) was a fine man, but with poor health.[1]

At 7.30 the four of us dined alone, the President, Dulles, Selwyn Lloyd and I.

After dinner, we really got down to it—a broad review of the general situation in the world. Nothing very startling was said and nothing settled; but the atmosphere was very good—I thought; in view of all the circumstances, surprisingly so. They did most of the talking; we were more reticent. But it is clear that we are not going to be the 'suppliants' or 'in the dock' at this conference. It is rather the other way round.[1]

The next day, 21 March, the Conference began at 10.30; and, as the host, I was entitled to make the opening statement. I have kept a copy of the very full notes which I had prepared.

1. Grateful to President—
receive as host; greet as old comrade; welcome as head of the greatest and most powerful nation in the world.
2. Critical time in history—
In short time, tremendous problems of Suez Canal and Middle East, on which life of Europe depends.
Also critical in secular struggle against Communism; and future of United Nations.
League of Nations failed because it placed peace before justice and so lost both.
3. Some general reflections—
Balance of power changed; so quickly difficult to grasp.
When I was a child—Queen Victoria's Concert of Powers—i.e. *European* powers.
Austrian, Hungarian and Turkish Empires have gone.
Large part of Europe and Asia balkanised.
Europe destroyed itself in two internecine struggles.
The immense powers of U.S. and U.S.S.R. dominate whole world.
Many countries in Europe are tempted to give up struggle.

[1] 20 March 1957.

Neutralism (disguised sometimes as Third Force. Concept).
I must frankly admit recent events have revived this in Britain.
But I believe you cannot be neutral in a war between two
principles, one of which—Communism—is evil.
With change in balance of power, change in position of Western
and Christian civilisation.
For about 2,500 years Whites have had it their way.
Now revolution: Asia/Africa.
Bound to be immense stresses and great power vacuums over
great areas.
Who is to fill these voids? Russia, China or free alliance.
The number of uncommitted countries must increase, as they
emerge from colonial or other dependence to independence.
We in Britain cannot stop; but we might now and then control
this process.
In ten to fifteen years, India, Pakistan, Ceylon, Burma.
Now Ghana, in August Malaya; next Singapore.
Same process going on in French territories: Tunisia, Morocco,
soon Algeria.
Indonesia.
Within ten to fifteen years of mutually destructive European
war, these immense territories have become in effect neutral.
In the Middle East countries more or less under guidance have
become more restless and obsessed by Moslem and nationalist
propaganda.
In this confusion, Europe is divided between those who wish
to watch from the sidelines—for a change—and those who are
ready to play their full part.
I believe Britain—I know my Government—will be for staying
in the game and pulling our weight.
That is why I welcome full restoration of confidence and co-
operation between our two countries.
Partly sentiment, though sentiment may work both ways—
there are people who still seem to be harking back to that Tea
in Boston Harbour.
Partly interest—powerful as you are I don't believe you can do
it alone.
You need us: for ourselves; for Commonwealth; and as leaders
of Europe.
But chiefly because without a common front and true partner-

ship between us I doubt whether the principles we believe in can win.

... I hope you will forgive me if I make in conclusion some observations on an urgent issue with that frankness which true partnership and comradeship not only allow but, in honour, require.

We can discuss what we are to do in the longer term about many issues.

What we are to do about the Far East; about a Palestine settlement; even about how to manage the United Nations.

(Sometimes an ideal, sometimes an embarrassment)

But there is one issue in the immediate future on which our people feel passionately, and on which my country's power to be of service to our common efforts may well depend.

That is Nasser and the Canal.

Let us be frank.

I don't suppose that either of our Governments or peoples has any love for Nasser.

After all, he is just a self-elected dictator, who plays off the West and the East—but is more and more sold to the Communist.

It's like Mussolini—he started, in a way, as an Italian patriot.

He ended as Hitler's stooge.

Let me be frank again: your Government and many of your people think we acted foolishly and precipitately and illegally.

Our Government and many of our people think that you were too hard on us—and rather let us down.

Well, that's over—spilt milk.

Don't let's cry over it—still less wallow in it.

But the Canal remains.

I hope you will do everything you possibly can ... to get a Canal settlement, short and long,—especially regarding dues—which we can claim as reasonable, if not quite what we would like !

But if we can't get it—if Nasser is absolutely obdurate ... if we all have, in the *short* run, to eat dirt and accept a bad and unjust settlement, I hope you won't say in public or in private that it's a good settlement.

I hope you will denounce Nasser and all his works in the strongest terms.

Bring every pressure—political and economic—upon him.

If we have to accept a humiliating defeat don't let's call it a victory or even a draw.

Let's make it clear that we'll get him down—sooner or later.
Our people have been through some bad times in the first half of the century for progress.
They have learned, I think, patience: how to wait.
But they can't be fooled.
Funnily enough—for they have about as great a sense of fairness as of self-interest—the British people and Parliament feel as strongly about Gaza, Aqaba and treatment of Israel, as about the Canal and Canal dues.
It's rather embarrassing to us, the Government, because of the oil-producing countries, and the risks involved, but it is so.
Anyway, I do hope that if we have to accept a *bad* settlement in the short term, you will make it clear that it is a bad settlement, foisted upon us . . .
Any other course would I fear cause such a rift between our countries and people as would take much longer to repair than the urgent needs of the world allow.

The President took up the point about the British people feeling let down by America rather sharply. Nevertheless his reply

was very gracious and very fair. But I think we managed to take the offensive at the start.[1]

We next discussed the procedure to be followed until the end of the Conference. After general talks between the four of us, the President and I would leave the Foreign Secretaries to deal with all the points separately. Naturally the Foreign Office and my own staff had produced an admirably documented set of briefs, and neither Selwyn nor I had any doubt as to what were the main points on which we sought to reach agreement. But I knew well from the old days in Algiers that the President would not wish to take part in all the discussions himself. He would like to let the staff hammer out the answers and then bring him conclusions for approval. Accordingly in the afternoon of the first day, and the morning of the second day, 21 March, he and I spent the time either in recreation, or in general and informal talk. The admirable golf course was also available, and although the weather turned unpleasant, the President was able to get out to play a few holes.

[1] 21 March 1957.

Meanwhile telegrams kept pouring in from London chiefly about the strikes. The Cabinet was clearly uncertain as to what to do with the railways. We could avoid a strike by paying 5 per cent instead of 3 per cent, but it was clear that my colleagues

asked for my decision—or at least, guidance. I felt no doubt. We really cannot stand a railway strike, probably followed by a mining strike. Our economy is too weak; anyway, all these disasters weigh more in the balance than 2 per cent.[1]

Friday the 22nd was in a sense the critical day. My cold was very bad and had gone to my chest, and I therefore stayed most of the day in my room fortified by some potent drugs produced for me by General Howard Snyder, who had, for many years, looked after the President's health. Snyder showed me the greatest kindness, and dosed me very successfully. Eisenhower and I spent over an hour together on the morning of 22 March which was usefully employed

partly going over old ground and partly breaking new. He repeated very strongly what he had said the first night and again yesterday. He regarded the Conference as a very great success and he felt that it had re-established complete confidence between himself and the Head of the British Government. That was his firmest purpose. He felt that our peoples would only gradually realise this fact. There were so many people on both sides of the Atlantic who would like to have it the other way. He suffered from foolish speeches by Senators and Congressmen, and foolish articles in the newspapers. For himself he never read the newspapers or listened to the radio, but Mr. [James] Hagerty told him about it. He quite realised that attacks upon him and Foster in our papers were natural. He thought that this could only gradually be put right, but the first step was confidence between us. I said that of course this was so, but that he must realise that my difficulty was that it was the most patriotic and traditionalist elements in our country which were the most disturbed. The extreme Left did not particularly want England to be a great country any more, but the elements on which I had to depend were sensitive.[2]

The next day, 23 March,

[1] 21 March 1957.   [2] 23 March 1957.

12

About 10 a.m. I was sitting in my room, in pyjamas, feeling rather bad, with this vile 'sirocco' blowing, when President came in. He stayed an hour. At 12 noon I went to his room. He enjoys these talks very much—he does most of the talking. He feels that he can escape from it all—at least that's my impression.[1]

We then began to talk about the communiqué, which is far the most important part of any Conference.

I observed that I thought the long communiqué was often an attempt to conceal very little result. I also made it clear to him that I could not stand for general propositions in communiqués. The British people were tired of these. The President seemed to think that in America people liked them very much.[1]

But we got our way. The American experts produced

a frightful 'draft' communiqué, full of the usual high-falutin' verbiage about United Nations, self-determination and whatnot —with no relation whatever to what we had in fact discussed, either in private or plenary sessions.[1]

I persuaded the President to cut all this out, and to have a short communiqué of two to three sentences, with a list of the agreements reached and the subjects discussed in an annex. He agreed to this procedure, and this part of the communiqué was now referred to as the *protocol*. This idea, which Selwyn and I worked out, brought us back to a procedure much more like the great war conferences. Moreover, by this method some real work was accomplished, either agreements, or by agreeing matters for further study. The immediate effect of a conference like this might well be considerable. But unless it was specific and quickly followed up, it would be fleeting.

During the course of these conversations, apart from the great issues, President Eisenhower talked to me constantly about his Cabinet:

He wanted to bring in younger men so that there might be men of Presidential calibre to succeed him. . . . He brought Nixon into every Cabinet committee, Defence committee, etc., and whenever possible sent him round the world to improve his experience.[1]

[1] 23 March 1957.

He told me at length about his long visit from Nehru, and summed up his impressions shrewdly. Nehru had talked to him at immense length and on a high idealistic note. Nevertheless, the President thought he could be pretty tough when it came to action; for instance over Kashmir. We also talked at length about our defence plans for Britain, for which the President, with all his experience, had great sympathy. He had learned from Churchill the danger of all forces becoming top-heavy, and was always fighting a battle with his own people on this.

Among one of the agreeable features of these days was to find my old friend Bob Murphy among the State Department delegation. We had some useful and illuminating private talks. He had a deep affection for the President, but found Dulles difficult.

By dinner-time on the 24th the *protocol* had been agreed, and the President and I signed the various documents embodying the various agreements, and the text of the communiqué was also approved, including the agreement on nuclear tests. At dinner that night the same four met.

We had a long discussion on the United Nations—its use and future. I found Ike much less dogmatic about this than I expected. He has a sort of semi-religious faith—but it is not blind faith. He seemed very much oppressed by America's abandonment of the old League of Nations—a sort of sin for which they must try to make amends. Foster was more cynical. He just thought there was no way of doing without U.N. but thought that if, in future, U.S. and U.K. policies were thought out beforehand and brought closely into line, we could probably still manage the majority there. I think the general conclusion was that we *must get* working together again at U.N. I said that this involved Cabot Lodge being willing to co-operate with Dixon (U.N. representative) which he doesn't do at present.[1]

Eisenhower spoke very sincerely about the danger of perpetual criticism of America by Europeans :

He was pained at the reactions in England, although he seemed to understand them. He had quite a lot of trouble in getting Congress, and other elements in America, to go on spending so

[1] 23 March 1957.

much money for the benefit of Europe, and the feeling might easily grow that they had better get themselves clear of it all and reduce their taxes and so forth. He would fight that as much as he could as long as he had authority. But he felt that too much criticism in England merely added fuel to these isolationist tendencies, which were always present in the United States.[1]

One of the most valuable outcomes of this meeting was our arrangement to write to each other—perhaps once a week or once a month—frankly and freely on any subject on which we thought we should know each other's view. These communications he would keep to himself, showing them only to Foster Dulles.

The President, who was not very keen on Press conferences, suggested that as I was the host, I should hold a conference for all the Press, including the British and American. He accordingly left quietly on the Sunday morning, the communiqué having been published that same morning.[2] It was my first experience of facing so varied a collection of Pressmen, but it passed off well enough. The weather had now returned to its normal warmth and sunshine, and everyone seemed very gay and happy.

Although I was not able, because of pressing demands at home (the problem of the Canal, the Defence White Paper, and the Budget), to go, as I had hoped, to Ottawa, Louis St. Laurent and Mike Pearson, his Foreign Minister, had kindly agreed to come to Bermuda. They arrived for lunch on Monday the 25th, and we had three hours' talk in the afternoon. We went over the whole ground that we had already covered with the Americans, and sustained a full day of talks with them on Tuesday the 26th. I told them my intention to hold a Commonwealth Conference in the summer. At 6.30, the Canadian Prime Minister and I had a joint Press conference. I got the impression that he was a little concerned at not having stood more firmly by our side over the Suez affair, and was anxious to be particularly helpful now. Many hours of continuous discussion, spread over nearly two days, gave me an insight into the character of this courteous and distinguished statesman. He seemed to treat me with almost paternal kindness.

[1] 23 March 1957.
[2] *Final Communiqué from the Bermuda Conference*, Cmnd. 126 (H.M.S.O., March 1957).

The broad results of the Bermuda Conference and our talks with the Canadians now had to be sent out to our Commonwealth colleagues, a task which was completed before we left. We also were able to convey an impression of the reception by the Press, both in Britain and America.

My first duty was to report to Parliament. I could reasonably claim that the Bermuda Conference had succeeded in its main object, which was to restore Anglo-American relations:

> Both sides spoke with absolute frankness and sincerity to each other, and this was wise, because it is only by complete frankness that we can hope to rebuild and strengthen a partnership so vital to the future of the world.[1]

We covered a wide range of topics—eleven in all—and had reached a number of decisions, some of them for immediate application and some reserved for further study. There were issues such as that of trade with China on which we were not in agreement, and further consultations would be needed. There were other points which were rather matters of approach than of immediate decision, especially regarding the future functions of the United Nations.

> I made plain our view that just trusting to the United Nations is not a substitute for a foreign policy.[1]

The problem of European unity had been discussed in detail and the Americans as well as the Canadians accepted our hopes for the development of an international free trade area which would include the six Powers in a wider plan.

I had to admit that it had not been possible to reach any final conclusions on Egypt and Israel. The future here remained dark and uncertain. Nevertheless we had done much to explain our anxieties to our American friends. Moreover, in the light of the so-called Eisenhower Doctrine, we had considered in some detail how best to protect our 'oil supplies and the peace and stability of the oil-producing areas'.[1] Meanwhile we had reaffirmed the need for the United Nations Emergency Force to remain in the Gaza strip and the right of innocent passage for all ships passing through the Gulf of Aqaba.

[1] *Hansard*, 1 April 1957.

The presence of the United Nations Force at Sharm-el-Sheikh is an added guarantee that this rule will be respected.[1]

Apart from these broad conclusions, there were three specific points on which definite agreements had been reached. The first dealt with the decision of the United States to join in the work of the Military Committee of the Baghdad Pact. This was a cause of special satisfaction to me, since I had laboured so hard and so long during my period as Foreign Secretary to persuade the American Administration to give open support to this Pact.[2] I was happy that the Americans now recognised the Pact's role and the staunch way in which its members had held together in recent troubled times.

We also found the Americans fully appreciative of the role we are playing in the Persian Gulf and of the importance of our policy of keeping faith with the States and Rulers with whom we have treaty relations and to whom we have strong and binding obligations.[1]

The second agreement dealt with the decision to supply us with guided missiles. These would soon be available and would prove an important addition to the deterrent power already based in the United Kingdom and to the strength of NATO as a whole. There had already been some controversy about the control of these weapons. So long as the warheads were provided by the Americans they would of course be under control of the American authorities in the same way as the American bombers armed with the kiloton and now the megaton bomb. But the agreement provided that these should not be used without the consent of both Governments.

[The rockets] will be the property of Her Majesty's Government, manned by British troops who will receive their prior training from American experts. The rockets cannot be fired by any except the British personnel, but the warhead will be in the control of the United States—which is the law of the United States—and to that extent the Americans have a negative control; but it is absolutely untrue to say that the President and not the British Government will decide when these missiles will be launched and at whom.

[1] *Hansard*, 1 April 1957. [2] See *Tides of Fortune*, pp. 632 ff.

So long as we rely upon the American warheads, and only so long, that will remain a matter for the two Governments.[1]

An interrupter at this point denounced this plan as a humiliation for Britain. I could only reply that it was the same agreement as already governed the American bombers which had been negotiated by Attlee. Meanwhile we were free to develop both British-made warheads and rocket systems.

Warned by the questions which had been asked in the House of Commons before the debate, I devoted the greater part of my speech to the third specific agreement, that for the continuation of nuclear tests. This tactic had two advantages. It switched the debate almost entirely into this field and away from the dangerous subject of the Canal, where we were not yet on any firm ground; it also served to exploit the split of opinion on this matter in the ranks of the Opposition. Gaitskell and all the other Labour speakers accordingly became entangled in a hopeless web of confusion. I spent much time in dealing with the medical risks involved in the tests and the very natural and widespread anxieties of the general public. This subject of external radiation and the hazards that might follow had been dealt with by a recent report of the Medical Research Council in great detail and continued to be a subject of controversy for many years. The contribution to the external radiation hazard from bomb tests was up to that time very small, almost negligible. But I myself felt a deepening anxiety as the tests grew in number and, in the case of the Russian tests, became more dangerous in character. It was not till almost the end of my Premiership that I was at last able to achieve an ambition that now formed itself in my mind; that is, an agreement between the three nuclear powers to ban all atmospheric tests. At the time, however, there was no real chance of this. All I could say was summed up in the following words:

While we must not underestimate these risks, whether of external or internal radiation, we really must not exaggerate. It would be wrong not to give the closest and most continuous study to the problem and continue our efforts for a practical

[1] *Hansard*, 1 April 1957.

system of limiting the tests which I have described already; but it would be equally wrong to try to excite hysterical or unbalanced fears; and to do so for political purposes would indeed be to plumb the depths of cynicism.[1]

One further advantage that we had gained in Bermuda was that the Americans fully understood the new defence policy on which we were working, especially regarding the reduction of our forces in Germany.

In general, the debate was successful, although it placed upon me a heavy task, particularly on the details of the nuclear problem:

An enormous team of 'Eggheads' arrived at No. 10 and we worked through the speech with their help. The work was only finished at 1 p.m. I lunched alone and then rested till 2.45. I have never been so strained or nervous before a speech. According to the Press, the continuance of the Government and the unity of the Party depend entirely on my performance.[2]

Looking back upon it, I felt that we were indeed fortunate, for the situation was certainly not encouraging. As an article in one of the newspapers stated, all the advantages appeared to be with the Opposition:

Suez and its aftermath, abstentions by Conservative voters at by-elections, the continuance (on Monday) of the shipbuilding and engineering strikes, Lord Salisbury's week-end resignation—in Labour eyes the Prime Minister must have looked like a man about to be 'butchered to make a Roman holiday' for them. . . .
What happened in the first part of the debate destroyed all such notions. By the time that Mr. Gaitskell resumed his seat at half-past five the tables had been turned almost completely.[3]

The truth is that during the last few months he had been so long accustomed to thrust that he had forgotten how to parry.

One interruption I was able to make during Gaitskell's speech. It was to challenge him to answer unequivocally whether or not the Opposition would cancel the joint Anglo-American tests about to take place at Christmas Island. Gaitskell, although normally an

[1] *Hansard*, 1 April 1957.   [2] 1 April 1957.   [3] *Western Mail*, 5 April 1957.

agile speaker, fell into the trap and exposed beyond doubt the lack of any clear policy on the Labour side. I noted in my diary:

12 midnight. The debate is over. By some miracle, the speech went *very* well and our boys were delighted. I ended with the Tories (temporarily) united and the Socialists split in two. This was by devoting a great part of the speech to the Bomb and the Bomb testing and challenging Gaitskell to say whether he would continue or abandon the tests if he were in my position. He faltered; wobbled; hedged–and so lost both wings of his party. So we have got over this particular fence. The water-jump (the Suez Canal) is still to come. On this we shall very likely fall. Meanwhile, we are alive![1]

All these emotions, vivid and compelling as they are at the time, are soon forgotten. Yet in reading these faded papers and records the old scene comes back to my mind. There was a lively discussion in the Press at the time as to whether the burden placed on Ministers, especially on Prime Ministers, was becoming intolerable. I read it with some interest. I had only been three months in office, yet I felt that in retrospect the anxieties of this period left a mark upon me. Nevertheless, since they were all in the field of great public affairs they were tolerable. They were not as painful as some personal issues were destined to be in later years.

Our next task was the final revision of the Defence White Paper. The Minister had worked with commendable determination, as well as speed, during the few weeks since he had received my directive. By 28 March his proposals were approved at a full meeting of the Cabinet and published on 4 April. They constituted the biggest change in military policy ever made in normal times. Although Eden had considered some of these matters during his short Premiership, the stresses of 1956 had prevented their being brought to fruition. There had, therefore, been no complete or radical review of policy in the light of post-war conditions.

We were now determined to put forward a scheme of inter-related changes to be carried out during the next five years. Although the actual reduction in defence expenditure might not seem dramatic,

[1] 1 April 1957.

amounting to only £78 million in the first current year, it was a
notable achievement. For years the defence budget had increased
annually, yet we had held the inevitably increased cost of modern
weapons within a decreased total allocation. The first objective, as I
claimed in a speech at Sheffield on the day after publication, was 'to
give us forces more mobile, better trained and better equipped.
They will, in due course, be smaller; but they will be more efficient.'
This new system must depend 'on our readiness to base ourselves on
the deterrent power of nuclear armament'. I declared that we had
been bearing, during recent years, more than our fair share of the
defence burden of the West. The reduction of the British forces on
the Rhine from 77,000 to 64,000—the figure accepted by our allies—
had already been announced. In making this change we scrupulously
followed our obligations, both to W.E.U. and to NATO; and in
winding up the debate on 17 April, I expressed my gratitude to the
various Governments for the understanding which they had shown.
In addition, President Eisenhower had immediately expressed his
admiration for

> the courage and nerve which this country had shown in drawing
> up this plan, and that it represented an effort to bring our military
> establishment into line with the military facts of today and to keep
> our economy viable.[1]

We admitted that Britain and, indeed, Western Europe could
not be effectively protected against nuclear attack. The over-riding
principle, therefore, must be to prevent war, rather than prepare for
it. Accordingly aircraft of Fighter Command were to be substantially reduced, their role in the United Kingdom being limited to
defending the deterrent bases. We hoped that they would in due
course be replaced by a system of ground-to-air guided missiles.
The means of delivery of the deterrent which we were now ourselves
manufacturing were mainly the V-class bombers which would
remain in service for many years. These were to be supplemented
by ballistic rockets initially of American manufacture, but we hoped
to rely eventually on our own production. All this had been made
possible by the Bermuda agreements.

[1] *Hansard*, 17 April 1957.

But the main and most startling proposal was to bring National Service to an end after the end of 1960, so that by the end of 1962 the armed forces would be composed solely of regular voluntary recruits. The total, which still, in 1957, reached the staggering figure of 690,000, would be reduced to about 375,000. But a stern warning was given that, if voluntary recruitment proved inadequate, a compulsory system of some kind would have to be introduced.

I am not one of those who thinks that there are no compensating advantages in the system of National Service. There are. But it also has great weaknesses and great wastefulness. There are too many people under this system learning and then leaving when they have learned, and there are too many people teaching.[1]

At this time there was no difficulty in filling the ranks of the Navy or the Air Force, nor indeed of the front-line element of the Army. Trouble would no doubt arise in some of the subsidiary and service elements—the 'tail' rather than the 'teeth'. But we felt hopeful that they could be overcome.

The tactical air force in Germany would be approximately halved, at the same time as the troops were withdrawn. But a big expansion of R.A.F. Transport Command would enable us to move reinforcements quickly to trouble spots. Equally the Navy's contribution to NATO was to be substantially reduced, although the nine cruisers of the active fleet would be replaced by three *Tiger* class cruisers which were under construction. Many ships in the reserve, including four battleships, were to be disposed of or scrapped. East of Suez our strength was to be kept undiminished, although the main elements were to be based on a small number of aircraft-carrier groups.

The main human problem which arose from these changes was the prospect of absorbing officers and other ranks into civilian occupation. The Minister of Labour, Iain Macleod, made a deep impression on the House by his speech describing the methods he proposed. Yet, as a whole, the credit for working out the 1957 White Paper, which, for good or ill, marked a revolution in

[1] *Hansard*, 17 April 1957.

post-war military thinking, rests with Duncan Sandys. He showed throughout all his notable characteristics: thoroughness, tenacity and immense application. The Service Ministers rallied splendidly, and the presentation of the White Paper–to quote the impartial words of the *Annual Register*–'undoubtedly raised the somewhat battered reputation of the Government'.[1]

Much of the debate, both in Parliament and outside, turned naturally on the new weapons and their uses in various types of war. Once again the Opposition were in a difficulty, owing to the division in their own ranks about the reliance on nuclear weapons. Many of the back-benchers were altogether against their production or use. I noted at the time :

> Since the Defence White Paper makes it clear that *all* our defence–and the economies in defence expenditure–are founded on nuclear warfare, it throws the Socialists into still greater confusion. Gaitskell's position becomes more and more humiliating. Meanwhile, however, the political side of their campaign has dangers for us all. The sentimental appeal is very strong. The worthy people of all types and ages are particularly easy prey and of course they will be cynically exploited.[2]

In the debate, which Sandys opened with an admirable exposition, I naturally concentrated upon the dilemma in which the Opposition were placed. We regarded nuclear power as a deterrent against massive attack. Many members had tried in the defence debate two years previously–the last in which Churchill had spoken–to force us to define what would be the occasions on which we should rely on conventional resistance, and what would be a situation when all-out war would be necessary.

> This is very dangerous. We had it two years ago in a famous debate on a White Paper, and I venture to repeat what I said then–to define too closely seems to be almost to incite and invite aggression.[3]

In any case, it was fundamentally the function of NATO to reassess this position from time to time.

[1] *Annual Register, 1957*, p. 20.   [2] 5 April 1957.
[3] *Hansard*, 17 April 1957. See also *Tides of Fortune*, p. 579.

The Opposition attempted to meet their dilemma by an amendment pressing the postponement of nuclear tests while a last-minute attempt was made to secure their abandonment by the United States and Russia. Apart from the fact that this was a forlorn hope, since the Russian and the American Governments were about to carry out a series of massive tests, any such postponement would be particularly serious from the British point of view, for our own tests were vital to the development of our own independent warheads.

On the general issue, while expressing sympathy and understanding for the true pacifists, it was not difficult to submit the Opposition's proposal to effective dissection. Full disarmament might come one day, and a test-ban treaty was not impossible. But it was a mistake to believe that 'banning the bomb'—even if it could be agreed and effectively policed—would solve the problem of European security.

> We are not in favour of the abolition of the unconventional, that is the nuclear, weapon without such corresponding reductions in conventional forces as will make Europe secure from Soviet aggression.[1]

Indeed I went on to observe:

> I have been through two major wars fought by conventional weapons. Some people now talk as if those were quite harmless and quite respectable operations.[1]

As for the compromise amendment, it amounted to this:

> We are to rely on the nuclear deterrent—but not unduly. We are to postpone our bomb tests—but not for very long. We are to ask other powers to agree to abolish all bomb tests, and if by any chance they should agree, then presumably they would be left with the fully tested bomb and we should be left with a bomb which had not been tested at all. So, of course, we should have to rely on American nuclear power for our defence. In the same breath the same hon. Members tell us that it is humiliating to obtain, whether by gift or purchase, an American rocket because the warhead is under American control until we can make our

[1] *Hansard*, 17 April 1957.

own. Then, to crown it all, the House is asked to withhold its
approval from a policy which lacks firm decisions.[1]

On the first day of the debate the most notable speech on the
Opposition side was delivered by George Brown.

> Considering the absurd position which the Opposition have
> got themselves into over the Bomb, I thought he made a gallant
> effort. Of course, he had to go back on his robust broadcast
> statement. The Opposition amendment is contradictory and
> ridiculous, for it attempts a compromise between two diametri-
> cally opposed views.[2]

The Press, who had already given a generous welcome to the
White Paper, recognised that, on the nuclear issue, the balance of
the argument weighed heavily in favour of the Government. But,
alas, great difficulties still remained. The complexity and expense of
modern weapons, together with the heavy risks involved with novel
and untried devices, were to prove, during the years that followed,
a perpetual source of difficulty and disappointment. On the wider
issue, although the world seems to have become accustomed to a
situation in which the great powers have the capacity to destroy
themselves and their neighbours, yet the very magnitude of the
disaster has produced a certain sense of stability, and even security.
But under the cover of this 'balance of fear' new conflicts of a minor
but dangerous nature have developed in many parts of the world.
I had no doubt that the part that Britain should still play, even in
the changing world and with new Commonwealth responsibilities
replacing her old imperial power, could be adequately performed
by the kind of forces which were then designed.

[1] *Hansard*, 17 April 1957.   [2] 16 April 1957.

CHAPTER VIII

Arabian Nights

T HE second half of 1957 brought us fresh anxieties in different parts of the Arab world. In spite of the troubles of 1956, the greater part of the Middle East settled down with remarkable and unexpected ease. The halting of the Anglo-French operation at Suez, coupled with the violent attacks on Britain and France at the United Nations, with the Afro-Asian pack in full cry, led on by the United States and Soviet Russia as joint masters, undoubtedly prejudiced the power and prestige of the European powers throughout the area. On the other hand Nasser's humiliating defeat by the Israelis undermined the Egyptian dictator's strength and influence and was to curb his pretensions for over a decade.

The meeting at the beginning of June of the Permanent Council of the Baghdad Pact, with which the Americans were now prepared to be associated, was certainly a success for British diplomacy. This alliance was an important contribution to stability, and the programme for regional co-operation prepared by its economic committee showed the strength and vigour of the Pact. The United Kingdom increased their contribution by £500,000, as well as providing £2 million for technical assistance and the improvement of communications. The Americans were equally generous. The Foreign Secretary reported to his colleagues that perhaps the most valuable by-product of the June meeting was the friendly and hopeful atmosphere which prevailed.

The Americans were helpful and robust throughout. The contribution of their 'observer', Loy Henderson, was particularly valuable. Altogether this meeting proved that the spirit and purpose of the Baghdad Pact had remained unshaken by the events of the previous year. Selwyn Lloyd described our co-operation with the Americans as 'first-class', although there was the usual difficulty in reducing a verbose communiqué to proper shape and form. But we were deeply grieved to learn of Nuri Pasha's decision to resign as Prime Minister of Iraq owing to ill-health. Nevertheless he was to remain confidential adviser to the King, and there was every reason to believe that the character of the regime and government would remain unchanged. Alas, these hopes were destined to be cruelly disappointed.

There now arose a new complication in another part of the Arab world which, although of minor importance, faced the British Government with something of a dilemma. In Muscat and Oman a revolt broke out, the Imam, Ghalib bin Ali, attempting to supplant the Sultan, Said bin Taimur, whom we had a moral duty to protect. The movement was confined to Oman and was led by the Imam's brother, Talib. The revolt, originating in the mountains and barren districts, spread to the more fertile areas, threatening the settlements in the plains. The Sultan slowly and deliberately began to rouse himself to meet the danger, and made the journey from Muscat to Oman. But his troops were weak and helpless, and he now appealed for our assistance to restore his authority. Since British friendship and support had been afforded to the Sultan for more than a century, to have withheld our assistance at this critical moment would have involved a grave loss of confidence among all the friendly Sheikhs and Rulers throughout the Gulf.

Moreover, although no oil had yet been proved, two companies were actively carrying out exploration throughout this area. We had, therefore, an additional reason to support our ally.[1]

In the Buraimi operation of 1955, which I had recommended to Eden when I was Foreign Secretary and which had been carried out successfully with the full support of the Labour Opposition under Attlee, the invading forces had suffered a severe setback; the Sultan's forces had occupied the mountainous area of the country, and it seemed as if the prospects for peace were reasonably good.[2] However, the Saudi Government had resented our intervention, and the Imam's brother, Talib, had little difficulty in obtaining,

---

[1] Oil was subsequently discovered, and the oil income of this previously impoverished state had, by 1968, reached £35 million per annum.
[2] See *Tides of Fortune*, p. 641.

during a tour of Saudi Arabia and Egypt, not only the sympathy of their rulers, but a substantial supply of arms and money. A 'Free Oman Movement' propaganda office was opened in Cairo, and the usual violent attacks launched by radio upon British imperialism and exploitation.

By the summer of 1957 the insurgents had driven the Sultan's officials and garrisons from the central Oman towns and had proclaimed its independence under the Imam. The Sultan's forces were scattered and demoralised. Although any operation to restore the position would be on a small scale, yet for the British Government after the events of 1956 to embark single-handed upon a further military enterprise, even of a modest character, seemed at first to some of my colleagues hazardous and even foolhardy. Apart from critics at home and in the United Nations, we would again be risking the disapproval and opposition of the United States.

On the other hand Ministers agreed that our position in the Gulf would be greatly, perhaps fatally, jeopardised if we were to abandon an old ally in distress. It was agreed to give various kinds of 'unprovocative' support, such as the supply of stores and arms by air to the Sultan's troops as well as the use of the Trucial Oman Scouts under British officers. A second frigate was also to be despatched to control the coast. But we could not avoid the vital question: should the R.A.F. be used to attack the positions held by the rebels? The United States and the United Nations would no doubt express their disapproval. We should be accused of inhumanity and 'frightfulness'. We might alienate Arab states at a time when Arab sympathy with Egypt was generally diminishing. Nevertheless the Cabinet agreed to run the risk, although using rockets and not bombs, and only making raids on their defended posts in the hills after profuse distribution of warning leaflets.

After the Cabinet meeting, I decided to send an immediate message to the President, setting out our difficulties. I made it clear that although the present insurrection had obviously been organised and armed from outside, we proposed to say as little as possible about the Saudis in our statements and to press forward with an attempt to bring the Sultan and King Saud into better relations.

But our duty was clear, both from the narrower and the broader aspects:

> The Sultan has appealed to us to help him, and the obligations of friendship seem to us to demand that we should not desert him in times of trouble. Moreover, there must be a risk that if the troubles in Muscat are not contained and disposed of as soon as possible, they may spread. I hope that it will be possible to restore the Sultan's authority quickly, by dealing, with the help of limited air support from us, a speedy blow at the confidence and prestige of the rebel leaders.

In his reply to my message of 22 July, the President was sympathetic and seemed chiefly concerned to deny the current rumours that the troubles in the Sultan's area had been fomented by some of the American oil companies in order to damage their British rival who had obtained concessions in that region. We naturally accepted these disclaimers, and I hoped from the President's answer that we could rely on his support.

The R.A.F. carried out a number of rocket attacks on military targets, preceded in every case by warnings to the civilian population. Nevertheless

> The Imam's rebellion in Muscat continues. Whether we can put it down or contain it seems doubtful; we cannot operate by land (it is too hot) and we have to be careful about air attacks. However, we have made a start.[1]

At this critical moment Secretary Dulles's restless nature made him propose an immediate trip to London.

> There was a lot of telephoning, over a message from the President, announcing the arrival of Foster Dulles in London on Monday. I was very anxious about what might be read into this, and rather annoyed at the abrupt way it was all done. However, we straightened it out all right, and I think the public will accept that he is coming here to talk about disarmament (which will be good) and *not* about Muscat (which would be very bad).[1]

I was naturally concerned that the rebellion should be brought to an end as rapidly as possible, yet the remnant of the Sultan's soldiers

[1] 27 July 1957.

were at present untrained and incompetent. We had only a few hundred troops; the area was large and mountainous, and the climatic conditions bad. I had, however, confidence in our chief agents on the spot, both of whom I had known from war days.

[Sir Bernard] Burrows (Political Resident) and [Sir Laurence] Sinclair (Air-Marshal) are both good men, and I am glad to see them sending us *joint* telegrams (as Field-Marshal Alexander and I used to do from Greece and Italy).[1]

On 29 July a full statement was made by the Foreign Secretary in the House of Commons. He made it clear that although we were under no treaty obligation to assist the Sultan, yet in view of our long friendship we had a moral duty to help him resist subversion or aggression. With the Gulf Rulers, of course, we had formal and binding agreements, but

The difference between a formal obligation and the obligations of a longstanding relationship of friendship is not readily apparent to the local Rulers and people. If we were to fail in one area it would begin to be assumed elsewhere that perhaps the anti-British propaganda of our enemies had some basis to it and that Her Majesty's Government were no longer willing or able to help their friends.[2]

Rather to my surprise this statement was accepted by the House, and the leaders of the Opposition took no exception to our decision. One Member asked whether there was anything to suggest that the rising had been supported or inspired by the Government of Egypt, or the Government of Saudi Arabia. The Foreign Secretary wisely replied that he had made no allegations against specific Governments. Nevertheless it was 'Evident . . . that these anti-tank guns and machine guns were not produced in Central Oman itself.'[2] It was now clear that so long as the operation was successfully and rapidly carried out we had little to fear in Parliament.

On 5 August, I expressed my concern to the Minister of Defence at the way things were going. There seemed a good deal of confusion and great delays.

[1] 30 July 1957.   [2] *Hansard*, 29 July 1957.

The air transport system seems to have broken down completely. We cannot even get one company of British troops from one place to another. Considering the ludicrously small size of this operation, it makes one wonder why we spend £1,500 million on the Services to get so little out of it.

I sent a similar protest to the Secretary of State for Air:

What has happened to the transport aircraft? There seems to be great trouble about them in the Persian Gulf. I would like a report as to (1) what is the state of Transport Command? (2) what is available for this area? (3) how much has been out of service? and so forth. At first sight it seems rather a sorry story.

Actually some of my complaints were rather unfair and the Ministers concerned were able to make reasonably convincing replies. But my anxiety for a rapid conclusion was justified. We had to bring the matter to an end before criticism could develop at home and abroad.

In the absence on holiday of the Minister of Defence, I assumed the direct responsibility for the Ministry and for the Oman operation. By the middle of August the revolt seemed almost at an end. The towns in the plain had been cleared and brought under the Sultan's authority. There only remained the difficulty of dealing with some of the rebels in the mountains, where amid the rocks and caves they enjoyed an advantage over the small body of troops trying to chase them, which will be familiar to the readers of Scott's *Rob Roy*. On 13 August, perhaps somewhat prematurely, I noted:

Oman seems to be over. I am much relieved. The operation has been brilliantly conducted, when one considers the difficulties of terrain and climate—with only three companies of Cameronians and very second-rate Arab troops.[1]

But on 3 September I had to record:

The Oman affair drags on—in the sense that the rebel leaders (with some of their supporters) have fortified themselves in a mountainous position (4,000 or 5,000 feet up). The choice is (*a*) to blockade them, (*b*) to try to 'winkle' them out. Both courses have their objections. There is public opinion; the United

[1] 13 August 1957.

Nations; the nervous state of the Arab world; the British Press; the danger of the infection spreading; the problem of air attack.[1]

The next day we decided to go ahead at least for a limited period.

If the operations against the remaining rebels failed (owing to difficulty of terrain, supply, etc.) to lead to early success, it would be best just to blockade them in the mountains. The troublesome thing is that (in these days of radio communication, etc.) they may be able to claim that they exist as a 'movement' or even as a separate state.[2]

Although at the end of the year there were still some tribesmen holding out in the hills, and the elusive Talib had still evaded capture, yet so far as the greater part of the country was concerned the rebellion could be considered at an end. The story, however, was not finally completed until several years later. Sporadic outbreaks continued, and during the rest of this Parliament, and even at the end of 1959, the rebels had not been completely suppressed. Some important military lessons were meanwhile learnt by us from this affair. Accordingly I insisted upon suitable plans being immediately prepared in the event of similar difficulties arising in any part of the Gulf, particularly in Bahrain or in Kuwait.

Another question, however, gave me much concern. The British troops were now withdrawn from Oman territory. Although we had regular forces available for a new emergency, we must try to reach a satisfactory agreement with the Sultan both as to the organisatio of his own forces and the establishment of a firm political control over the interior.

The Sultan was a strange figure, with considerable charm, great mental agility and a degree of patience which often merged into obstinacy. Nor did he approve of innovation in any form. I sent out Julian Amery, Under-Secretary of State for War, to see whether we could bring the Sultan to accept a reasonable arrangement. I chose Amery because I knew him to have great capacity for a negotiation of this kind. He was both patient and resolute. After long and difficult discussions he was able to obtain an agreed minute to serve as the basis of a more formal agreement. As so

[1] 3 September 1957.   [2] 4 September 1957.

often happens in Oriental affairs, further delays ensued, and it was not until September 1958 that full accord was finally reached. At the same time the Sultan voluntarily ceded Gwadar, his small possession on the coast of Baluchistan, to the Government of Pakistan. Amery carried out his task with a skill and success which encouraged me to use him later on a similar and even more difficult negotiation.

Meanwhile, although British opinion remained steady, we still had to face the usual troubles in the United Nations. On 12 August the Political Committee of the Arab League decided to call for a Security Council meeting to discuss British aggression in Oman. I noted at the time, perhaps a little unfairly, that

> The Americans are behaving outrageously to us about Oman. They haven't the courage to vote *against* inscribing the item at the Security Council. I talked with the Foreign Secretary, and I think I shall have to send a stiff telegram to the President.[1]

On 20 August I recorded: 'I have had some exchanges of telegrams with the President during the weekend. He answers agreeably enough, but does nothing.'[2]

During this month many equally urgent problems crowded in upon us—the position in Syria and the pressure on sterling following the collapse of the franc. However, since some of my leading colleagues were on holiday, this at least simplified the administrative problems: 'As I am now performing the functions of Foreign Secretary, Chancellor of the Exchequer and Minister of Defence, I am in a strong position.'[3]

In spite of our efforts the meeting of the Security Council took place on 20 August. The most that I had been able to persuade the American Administration to do was to 'abstain'. The President argued that this would probably be as useful as a negative vote. He proved right, for the Arab request failed to obtain the necessary seven votes, in spite of Russian support. The question therefore fell to the ground and was not discussed.

I have thought it worth while to tell the story of this minor but significant episode. It was commonly said at the time, and has been

[1] 16 August 1957.   [2] 20 August 1957.   [3] 22 August 1957.

repeated since, that the Suez operation in 1956 was the last time that any British Government would have the strength to support its own interests, or to protect a client, even in alliance with another power, without appealing to the cumbrous and frustrating machinery of the United Nations. Naturally there were hesitations and doubts in many quarters, even among our own advisers. But my colleagues in the Cabinet, in spite of the many difficulties confronting the Government, were commendably firm. Once again we had to operate without full American assistance. In addition we risked reviving some of the emotions of the previous autumn, stimulated by all those forces in Britain which were only too eager to denigrate the actions of their own Government and country. The successful operation in Oman helped to restore confidence in that part of the Arab world, especially throughout the Gulf. For it proved that the British Government remained unshaken by the misrepresentations of its policies, at home and abroad, or alarmed by the parrot-like accusations of 'colonialism' and 'imperialism'. As a result we were able in subsequent years to operate in Jordan and Kuwait both to protect our friends and to defend our own national interests. It was at least some encouragement to feel that we had not lost our nerve. I felt satisfaction in drafting for the Queen's approval an appropriate paragraph in the Prorogation Speech:

> In view of the long-standing ties of friendship between Muscat and Oman and the United Kingdom, My Government took prompt action in response to a request from the Sultan for armed assistance in quelling a rebellion in his dominions.[1]

While the Muscat–Oman operation was running its course, we were confronted during the summer with a much more serious problem in the Levant. This arose from the serious Communist infiltration into Syria. Here we had the full, almost embarrassing, support of our American friends. Indeed, paradoxically enough, our function proved not to stimulate but often to restrain the impetuousness of the State Department, which was interpreting the new 'Eisenhower Doctrine' with all the enthusiasm of recent

[1] *Hansard*, 1 November 1957.

converts. In this evangelistic mood, Dulles seemed ready and even anxious to consider measures which a few months before he would have denounced as shocking and immoral.

Our information was indeed disturbing, although we did not feel that the position was yet critical or irremediable. Since the beginning of the year left-wing army officers had been promoted, while others of longer service and stability had been purged. Treason trials had been staged against many of the moderates, with vague and trumped-up allegations of plotting against the regime. As a result many of the centre and right-wing figures took refuge in flight. The Soviet Embassy was quite openly organising these sinister developments. There were many similar indications of the rapid growth of Communist strength in the country and growing, almost decisive, Russian influence.

Apart from our desire to rescue Syria from the throttling hug of the Northern Bear on political grounds, our own interests were closely involved. The oil pipelines passing through Syria could handle some 25 million tons of oil a year from Iraq and a further 12 million from Saudi Arabia. We had therefore two important and sometimes conflicting objectives. While we did not want to allow this oil complex to fall under Russian control, we equally did not want to provoke Syria into cutting these pipelines. At any rate, if we were to take immediate risks we must be assured that America would persevere to the end, with an effective settlement for the Middle East as a whole. We could not afford again to be pushed forward by Dulles with some attractive plan and then left in the lurch. Apart from our own needs for oil, Iraq's economy would suffer, and the position of the friendly King and Government would be threatened if the pipelines were cut for any length of time. Moreover in certain circumstances oil supplies through the Canal might once more be interfered with. All the immediate risks would fall to us to carry—the interference with our economic recovery and the strengthening of our currency and reserves. Yet, if we could be sure of the sincerity and firmness of American policy, we ought to play our full part in devising and applying any pressures which might prevent Syria falling, almost without a struggle, into Russian hands. These anxieties, of course, were shared to the full by many of

Syria's neighbours, especially those enjoying monarchical and conservative regimes.

After some weeks of discussion through ordinary diplomatic channels, I received on 22 August a long personal message from Dulles. He was still in a comparatively cautious mood. I could not help being slightly amused by the last paragraph of his letter. After putting forward, in somewhat obscure terms, a tentative plan, he continued:

> I would be glad to get your own thinking about this solution. I think it important that not only Israel but the Western countries should avoid any initiative but that if Syrian developments carried a threat to Syria's Moslem neighbours they should know that they would have our moral support in any defensive measures they might feel called upon to take.

At the same time he informed me that he was sending Loy Henderson to Turkey and other friendly countries to assess the situation. In my reply, although concerned both about Syria becoming a Communist state—a dangerous example which might easily spread—and about the control of the pipelines, I felt that in the first instance we should try to act through our friends.

> I am sure that the Western powers should not seem to take over the lead in opposing the Syrian regime. We should, however, try to encourage the friendly Arab states and Turkey to consult together about the situation and give them all possible support. If the other Arabs could attack the developments in Syria as a betrayal of the Arab cause it would at least be a beginning. The essential point is that the other Arabs should expose the pretensions of the present Syrian regime to be good Arab nationalists and should denounce them for what they are, namely Communists or Communist stooges.

Even if these immediate efforts were to fail, a purely Communist Syria might awaken the Middle East, especially the devout Moslems and the Royal regimes, to the dangers involved.

On 27 August

> I gave the Cabinet a broad picture of the messages which I had received from Washington [on Syria] and the draft of my

K

proposed reply. This question is going to be of tremendous importance. The Americans are taking it very seriously, and talking about the most drastic measures—Suez in reverse. If it were not serious . . . it would be rather comic.[1]

The situation was now becoming clearer. The Soviet Government, deterred from open aggression by the nuclear threat and the appalling results of any major conflict, were proceeding by stealthy subversion. What were the counter-measures? Should we imitate the Russians and bribe the armies of the other countries in the Middle East by providing them with weapons?

The problem is *not to discourage* the Americans, if they are really serious and will see through any action to the end; at the same time *not to stimulate* them to do something which (if it goes off at half-cock) will be fatal.[2]

Dulles was now pressing urgently for a personal talk. Could some secret meeting-place be arranged? Neither I nor the Foreign Secretary felt that this was possible at the present time. It was therefore arranged that my Principal Private Secretary, Freddie Bishop, whom Dulles had met and liked, should go to Washington immediately. His visit proved a great success, since Bishop's charm and intelligence made a great impression upon the Secretary of State. Nevertheless the situation in the Middle East was not improving. Lebanon had warned the United States Government that they could hardly hold out against Syrian pressures unless something could be done to assist them. But the other neighbouring countries seemed unwilling to play the part for which they had been cast by the United States Government.

Iraq (without Nuri) has a weak Government; Jordan is weak too (and the two Royal families have had a tremendous quarrel); Lebanon is a frail plant. The Turks would probably play up, but then what about Russia?[3]

I took a few days' holiday in Scotland and awaited the results of these new discussions. A message arrived from Dulles on 5 September:

Both he [the President] and I have given thought to the possibility of one or other of us working out a personal meeting with you. We both much share your thought of how good it would be if we could be in the same room and talk all this over as we have done before. However, so far, our ingenuity has proven unequal to overcoming what seemed to be the risks that such a meeting would build up into a public spectacle that would be exaggerated and misinterpreted.

I am delighted that Bishop is staying on for a few days more.

Whether all this collaboration or even collusion should be regarded as a proof of the so-called 'special relation' between Britain and America I do not know. In any case it suited me well enough.

Yet in spite of this close and happy co-operation between Washington and London, the solution of the problem seemed no nearer. I told Dulles that in my view we needed some more examination of the methods open to us. On 6 September I again explained the whole situation at great length to the Cabinet. While we were unwilling to be committed to any overt action, we were quite willing to consider in detail proposals for encouraging the states bordering on Syria who had so far resisted or had not been subjected to the Soviet pressures.

My colleagues were impressed by the importance of not discouraging the Americans (now they are in this mood) and I think recognised the immense stake. For unless Russian influence in Middle East can be stopped, Britain and Europe 'have had it' (as they say). Only the Americans can bring the power to bear (*a*) to stop Arabs, etc., from falling, (*b*) to risk the consequences—i.e. Russian threats to Turkey, Iraq, etc., (*c*) to stop this degenerating into global war—by the American air threat to Russia—still at its strongest moment in history. (In ten years—or less—the transcontinental rocket will alter the balance.)[1]

On 10 September Nuri Pasha came to see me.

He looked much better. Three months out of office and his 'cure' in England have done him good. He was not very hopeful about the situation. But we felt that if nothing were done, the

[1] 6 September 1957.

whole of the area would gradually slide into Communism. He is going back to Iraq and will do his best.[1]

I had intended to take a week's holiday as John Morrison's guest in Islay, but I now decided to abandon my plan. The countries bordering on Syria were becoming more and more restless. The American proposal was to assure them that they would be supported in the United Nations and given full financial and economic help. If Russia intervened, which seemed very unlikely, they would be defended militarily. For myself I doubted whether such messages to the Middle Eastern countries would be framed in a way to give them encouragement without offering them a blank cheque. We must not incite them to do more than we were ready to defend and reinforce.

The Foreign Secretary, with whom I had discussed every move, returned about this time from a short visit to Yugoslavia. He reported a great friendliness towards us, but growing anxiety lest Middle Eastern unrest might bring about a clash between the two giants, the Soviet Union and the United States.

The Foreign Secretary next went to Washington and had many long conferences with Dulles, with whom he had reached an excellent understanding. The chief problem now became how to assist those states who might appeal for help. This would be quite a different matter from trying to bring pressure on a Government like Syria's with the hope of bringing about its fall. This would be a case of answering an appeal. Eisenhower recognised the need for quick action, and thought that the 'Eisenhower Doctrine' could cover subversion, whether from within or without. In fact it was to be so applied a year later.

Dulles accordingly contented himself with a message to the countries concerned which amounted to a reaffirmation of the 'Eisenhower Doctrine'. This was followed on 9 September with a substantial delivery of arms to Jordan to which much publicity was purposely given.

The Russians now intervened openly; they asserted that the Turks were concentrating troops against Syria, and warned Turkey that

[1] 10 September 1957.

Russia might reply by a similar mobilisation on the Russo-Turkish frontier. Bulganin—still the ostensible head of the Russian Government—followed this by a direct appeal to Turkey not to associate herself with the American designs on Syria. The Turkish Government replied by a firm statement that her preparations were purely defensive.

I had already sent a full account to the Prime Ministers of the Commonwealth of the development in the Middle East, warning them of the dangers which seemed to lie ahead. I now supplemented this with further messages to put them more fully in the picture. I was encouraged by the general support of old friends like Menzies and Holyoake, as well as by a helpful message from Diefenbaker.[1] Equally gratifying were the understanding and reasonable sentiments expressed by the leaders of the more recent additions to the Commonwealth. Nehru, while not objecting to our desire to stem Russian expansion, expressed his doubts whether recent developments in Syria were really Communist; he saw them as symptoms of a nationalist movement activated in part by fear of 'encirclement' by the Baghdad Pact. I was not much impressed by this argument— which we had heard *ad nauseam*, though in a different context, before both world wars. Menzies's reply of 19 September was characteristic:

> I think you have achieved a great deal by establishing this confidential contact with the Americans, and I entirely agree that your policy of giving broad moral support to them has been a wise one. It would be completely wrong for us to hold back now because the Americans have not been sufficiently understanding and helpful in the past, and I am glad you take that view.

Throughout September the interchange of telegrams and messages between Washington and London continued almost daily, and what was now called 'contingency planning' was carefully co-ordinated between our military as well as our political experts. No one could tell what might result from this critical position, and every possibility must be provided for. The Foreign Secretary, who

[1] Keith Holyoake was Prime Minister of New Zealand in the autumn of 1957, and John G. Diefenbaker had become Prime Minister of Canada in June 1957.

had returned from Washington, came to see me on 26 September with a full account of his talks with Dulles.

I noted:

> I'm afraid we aren't making much progress with Syria. But it's a great comfort to be working so closely and with such complete confidence with the Americans.[1]

The King of Saudi Arabia now made a three-day visit to Damascus, from 25 to 27 September, which had a calming effect; and the Syrians began to repudiate any question of undue Communist influence or threat to Turkey.

On 8 October an insignificant border incident was made the pretext of a protest by the Syrian Government to Ankara and a complaint to the United Nations against the Turkish provocation. Something like panic and hysteria now prevailed in Damascus. Charges and countercharges were made not only between Turkey and Syria but also between the American and Russian Governments.

One curious incident in this war of nerves is perhaps worth recalling. On 13 October Gaitskell, accompanied by Aneurin Bevan, came to inform me that they had received a letter from Khrushchev addressed to the National Executive Committee of the Labour Party, from which they read a short extract. (They were however unwilling to give me the full text.) It seemed that Khrushchev had addressed similar communications to the Socialist parties in Norway, Denmark, France and Italy, and perhaps to others. (The Norwegians kindly supplied us with the text which the leaders of the Opposition were unwilling to provide.) Bevan added that when he visited Khrushchev recently the latter had asserted that he · had full evidence that Loy Henderson's visit to the Middle East in September had been in order to organise a political *coup d'état* in Syria. Sabotage and wrecking operations such as a cutting of the pipelines would be arranged as a pretext for invoking support from the surrounding Arab countries and from Turkey. Naturally I assured them that so far as I knew there was no truth in this story. Henderson's purpose had not been to organise a counter-revolution in Syria, but to provide some reassurances for Syria's neighbours

[1] 26 September 1957.

who were much alarmed by the latest Soviet intervention. I could not help feeling that Khrushchev's technique had marked similarities to that employed by Hitler before the war. The leaders of the Opposition would remember that when Hitler organised a *coup* he always denounced any reactions to it as provocative. It might well be therefore that we must expect a further Soviet move against Iraq, Jordan or even Saudi Arabia. On the other hand it was possible that the Russians would follow the traditional Russian methods, whether Tsarist or Communist; having gained a little ground they might well be prepared to call a halt and wait for the next move. Gaitskell did not make any reply; indeed, he seemed rather unhappy. But Aneurin Bevan (who was an old friend) talked on at considerable length, on a wide variety of topics. This I encouraged him to do, partly because his talk was always interesting, and partly because I realised that Gaitskell found it embarrassing.

On 16 October Syria made a formal appeal to the United Nations, and with strong Russian support referred the 'Turkish threat' to the General Assembly. Dulles in reply declared that if the Soviet Union attacked Turkey the United States would not restrict itself to a 'purely defensive operation', and Russia would not be left in the position of a 'privileged sanctuary'. The affair now appeared to be reaching a critical point. On 10 October King Saud, on a state visit to Lebanon, offered to mediate in the Turkish–Syrian dispute. This was accepted by Turkey, and in the first instance by Syria, who then withdrew her acceptance. The Arab states now began to hesitate and compete with each other in declarations of the solidarity of the Arab world. Lebanon, Saudi Arabia, Iraq, all made the same protestations, but all were equally alarmed and anxious to see the Russian aggression halted by some means or other.

On 29 October after all these months of anxiety the bubble burst. Khrushchev at a party given by the Turkish Ambassador in Moscow made a jovial admission that there was no threat in the Middle East at all and that the whole affair had been misunderstood. Two days later the Syrians, no doubt on Russian instructions, withdrew their complaint from the agenda of the United Nations and did not even press for the commission of enquiry which they had suggested.

Thus to all appearances the whole matter came to an end. Dulles appeared satisfied with his experiment in brinkmanship.

It seems difficult today, when the Western world has been forced to accept not merely increasing Russian influence in Syria and Iraq, but the almost complete control of Egypt supported by a considerable fleet, to realise the concern which was felt in Washington and London at the first serious manifestations of Russian penetration into the Eastern Mediterranean. With all our efforts, we achieved at this period no conspicuous success. But this change in American policy from the autumn of 1956 to the summer of 1957, if belated, was at least dramatic.

Both these episodes, the Imam's rebellion in Oman and the Russian infiltration into Syria, occupied an immense amount of my time and labour. The handling of Oman was at least our own affair, and we had only the duty of explaining and justifying our action to the outside world. On Syria long and complicated messages from Dulles arrived daily, and at one time almost hourly, with occasional letters from the President. All these had to be dealt with, either with the help of the Foreign Secretary or, in his absence, the Permanent Secretary, Sir Frederick Hoyer Millar. The American affection for position papers and the study of almost every conceivable circumstance or contingency that could possibly arise out of the main question, or in connection with any of its ramifications, led to a vast interchange of telegrams, occasionally varied by telephone conversations. Naturally I did not complain of this, I was indeed glad to feel that we were back upon the same terms as we had been before the disastrous attitude taken by the Americans in the previous year. But it certainly made it a hard and testing summer and autumn, during which I allowed myself only a few days' holiday.

I received throughout the most splendid support from the Foreign Secretary and, in the first episode, from the Minister of Defence. Selwyn Lloyd had been not unnaturally shaken by the strain of the events of 1956 and the intricate questions to be resolved during the aftermath of Suez. Yet throughout all these trials he showed both flexibility and resolution; I felt sure that I had been right to ask him to stay as Foreign Secretary in the new Government. Moreover, not only was he fertile in ideas and resourceful in proposing solutions to tangled and baffled difficulties, but he was always good-tempered and friendly. He did not at all mind the President sending me personal messages or even Dulles doing the same. Naturally I showed him everything; but he recognised that this co-operative attitude towards me shown by both the President and the Secretary of State was based on old friendships, and was of real advantage.

Both episodes had their moments of trial, but also their compensations. The first restored our confidence in ourselves; the second proved to us that the vows of friendship and comradeship renewed in Bermuda were sincere and could stand the test.

CHAPTER IX

Russia and the Bomb

A FEW days after I became Prime Minister I was reminded
that in the previous July an understanding had been reached
between Bulganin and Eden that the latter should pay a
return visit to Moscow early in May 1957. But the political
atmosphere, comparatively unclouded when Bulganin and Khrushchev came to England in the spring of 1956, was now overcast and
even menacing. The Soviet Government's threats at the time of the
Suez crisis were fresh in our memories. Although the British
Government rated them at their true value, they caused widespread
concern and alarm throughout great masses of our people, conscious
of our isolation at a time when Moscow and Washington appeared
to be in alliance against us. Moreover the terrible events in Hungary
and the brutal suppression of the popular movement in November
1956 produced a wave of revulsion against the Soviet leaders, which
affected even those elements in Britain ordinarily sympathetic to
Russia. I therefore thought it right to send on 28 January a message
for our Ambassador to deliver to Bulganin reminding him of the
arrangement made between him and my predecessor, and proposing
some delay in its fulfilment.

I feel it courteous to let you know that owing to my many
preoccupations I fear that I shall not be able to contemplate a
visit to Moscow at that time.

I hope that a situation may develop when a visit would be both
welcome to you and timely from the world point of view.

Bulganin replied in the following terms:

I have received your message of 28 January. My colleagues
and I still attach great importance to personal contacts with
British statesmen which are regarded as an important factor in

the relations between Great Britain and the Soviet Union. In doing this we proceed from the fact that these relations should develop in a favourable way in the interests both of our countries and of the improvement of the international situation in general.

It goes without saying, that the agreement formerly reached with your predecessor Sir Anthony Eden about the visit of the Prime Minister of Great Britain to Moscow remains in force and we would welcome you in Moscow this May. However if you are not able to visit the Soviet Union at this time we would like to know your considerations about some other time for your visit more acceptable to you and which could be additionally agreed upon.

We have no doubt that a meeting with you in Moscow would give an opportunity for a fruitful exchange of opinions on questions directly concerning Anglo-Soviet relations as well as on other questions of mutual interest to both parties.

I still hoped that I might at some time attempt an improvement in the relations between the Eastern and Western blocs. But it was clear that for such an adventure the time was not now propitious.

On 20 April I received another personal letter from Bulganin. This communication was indeed a formidable document.[1] It covered, from the Soviet point of view, the causes of international tension and the wide range of developments in the Middle East, Near East and elsewhere throughout the world which had added to these stresses. It emphasised the need for disarmament and for Anglo-Soviet co-operation over the whole field of these immense problems. The document was nearly ten thousand words in length.

A careful examination of the text of Bulganin's letter showed that the Soviet Government was determined to regain the moral position which it had lost through the Hungarian repression, by concentrating upon the need for what was described as 'the most burning, the most essential international problem . . . disarmament'. They called first for

an immediate prohibition of atomic and hydrogen tests, in so far that this solution is not connected with any complicated administrative arrangements and under the present state of scientific

[1] *Correspondence between the Prime Minister and Mr. Bulganin, April 20 to September 2, 1957*, Cmnd. 380 (H.M.S.O., February 1958).

development could be safely supervised. The Soviet Government is of the opinion that this issue should be separated from the general disarmament problem and solved independently without subjecting its solution to the reaching of agreement on other aspects of the disarmament problem.

He went on to propose that, if the British and American Governments were not ready for an immediate banning of tests, there should be a suspension for a specified period with a view to facilitating an eventual agreement. This was followed by something like a menace:

> It goes without saying, that one cannot disregard the fact that Governments insisting on the continuation of tests of these weapons of mass extermination are assuming a heavy moral and political responsibility and place themselves in a position contrary to the unanimous demand of peoples as well as Parliaments and Governments of numerous countries of the world including, by the way, members of the British Commonwealth.

Bulganin declared that his Government was actuated by the highest motives; they were only putting forward this proposal 'because, according to our convictions, statesmen who are responsible for the future of their peoples should not gamble with the fate of these peoples'. (The fact that the Russians had just completed an immense series of tests was conveniently overlooked.) The letter went on to make some general reflections about the dangers of military blocs and especially the situation created by the organisation of NATO, aggravated by the admission of the Federal German Republic, and the building of American bases armed with nuclear weapons in many parts of the world.

> While peoples more and more persistently demand that atomic weapons be prohibited and destroyed intensive preparations for an atomic war are being carried on in the NATO grouping.

There followed a critical reference to the recent Anglo-American agreement at Bermuda by which rockets were to be stationed in the United Kingdom. This was a dangerous development:

> We do not think, however, that such measures can lead to strengthening the security of Great Britain. In the atmosphere of

an armaments race they will rather bring opposite results. As I understand a lot of people in Great Britain realise this.

In contrast to these Western provocations 'the Soviet Government has no thought whatsoever of entering the path of intimidation'. (With the memories of Czechoslovakia and in view of the recent brutal repression of Hungary, this was hard to accept at its face value.) Finally, after some compliments to the recent British decision to reduce their forces in Germany and a tribute to the prestige of Britain throughout the world, the concluding paragraphs referred again to the need for the improvement of relations between the Russian and the British peoples, about which so much talk had already taken place at the Geneva Conference in 1955, so far with little practical result.

I sent copies of the letter to Eisenhower, Mollet and Adenauer. Since I was to meet Adenauer in a few days, I sent him in addition a short covering letter:

> I am in some doubt about the meaning of this letter and about the way to handle it. I look forward to discussing this with you when we meet at the end of next week. You can be sure that in any case I should not act on it without the closest consultation with my friends. I am sending a copy of the letter to President Eisenhower and also to Mollet and asking for their comments.

As can be imagined, the great range covered by the Russian document, as well as the critical issues raised by the specific proposals, led to a considerable discussion between the Allies. It was not until 13 June that I was able to make a complete and formal reply. Moreover the position was complicated by a number of other urgent questions. The first of these in order of time, and almost of importance, was to obtain the sympathy and support of the German Chancellor for our new defence plans. I had already arranged a visit to Bonn for 7 May. I realised, from the Foreign Secretary's account of what had taken place at the NATO meeting a few days before, that I should have a difficult passage. Selwyn Lloyd had explained the main anxieties of the Germans. Apart from the problem of nuclear disarmament, they were anxious that the so-called shield should be strong enough to prevent Germany and the Low Countries being overrun by a conventional attack, and they still seemed to believe that it would be possible to organise NATO defences on conventional lines comparable to the armies which Russia could put into the field.

Fortunately, the Foreign Secretary was able to come with me and proved of immense assistance throughout. At our first meeting on the afternoon of 7 May the subject was, as I expected, defence:

Adenauer, Hallstein, [Franz-Josef] Strauss (Defence Minister) and General Halsinger; on our side, myself, Selwyn, Sir Richard Powell. In addition, the usual number of ambassadors, Foreign Office advisers, etc. But the room was not too large or too crowded, and the talks could be intimate and frank. There was no temptation to make speeches.[1]

It was clear to me from the start of the talks that the Germans, especially the Chancellor, were profoundly suspicious of our new policies. They also seemed ill-informed:

Their military concepts were based on those of the past—large number of divisions, on both sides, armed with conventional weapons and waging a long-drawn-out war. Naturally the British 'cuts' have alarmed them. They foresee a dangerous period between the British reductions and the creation of the new German Army. They excuse, but cannot explain, the slowness with which the Germany military effort has developed.[1]

I was absolutely frank and explained the military concepts which lay behind our Defence White Paper as well as my view that Europe could never be protected by conventional means alone; all we could hope to do was to provide a period of delay with what some people called a shield and others a trip-wire, so that there might still be an opportunity for discussion at the highest level, before resort to the nuclear deterrent—the only ultimate defence. It was for this reason that I had always opposed nuclear disarmament unless this was accompanied by conventional disarmament on a scale which would result in a reasonable balance between East and West. The Germans seemed shaken, without being wholly convinced. I therefore took advantage of the formal dinner which was

[1] 7 May 1957.

given by the Chancellor in my honour on 7 May to deliver a speech of considerable length and unusual seriousness dealing with the history of Europe through the last hundred years; our failures, our follies, and now our opportunities. I began by referring to the important changes which had taken place in the last three years since I had first visited Bonn, changes so rapid that we had almost forgotten how impressive was the ground which had been gained.

The formal termination of the occupation regime was only the official recognition of a development which had been going on a long time before. I think I can say with truth that my country under successive Governments took a lead in the transformation of our relations.

In spite of the economic progress of Western Germany there were many problems still to be resolved. I fully realised that uppermost in their minds was the reunification of Germany. Without this there could be no final settlement in Europe. Indeed when we talked of the unity of Europe we must never forget the many peoples on the other side of the Iron Curtain, forced to live under regimes which they abhorred.

We have admired the firm resistance of the Germans who are gripped in this iron vice. Many years ago Voltaire said to the Poles:
'If you do not know how to prevent the Russians from swallowing you, you must at least prevent them from digesting you.'
I am confident that Eastern Germany will neither be swallowed, nor digested.

I then dealt frankly with Britain's position; her difficulties as the Head of the Commonwealth and her long tradition, if not of isolation, at any rate of avoidance of definite external commitments. Now there had been something like a revolution in our thinking.

It has come about insensibly without great controversy. But it marks a profound change, and we now approach all these problems, whether of defence or economic co-operation, in quite a new spirit. We recognise that we cannot stand alone in either of these spheres. The frontiers of the United Kingdom do not lie any longer in the Channel, or the North Sea, and there is no defence possible to us, except as members and partners in a great alliance. On the defence side of course it is an essential part of it that we should keep in our alliance the Atlantic Powers, the United States and Canada.

At the same time we must not blind ourselves to the real yearning of the civilised world for some end or limit to this vast production of destructive weapons. Sometimes these genuine feelings were exploited by Communist propaganda; sometimes they were put forward in all good faith by pacifists and idealists.

I always remember the fable of the wolves who offered to make peace with the sheep provided they would send away the dogs. You and I know what happened to the sheep. But many of our countrymen would like to shut their eyes to these dangers. Moreover, the forces ranged against us are very intelligently manœuvred. It is worth remembering that the Russians are the best chess players in the world. And chess is a game where the keen player does not mind how long it lasts, and where in addition he is always ready to experiment with different openings.

All this made it all the more important that we should hold frequent consultations in order that our policies and purposes might be kept in harmony.

On what principles then was the defence of Europe to be based? It must always be twofold.

Against minor incidents or calculated risk that might be taken by the enemy for infiltrations and erosions into European territory, there must be sufficient conventional forces to repel a minor attack and to ensure that it cannot succeed upon a basis of avoidance of the main risks.

Secondly, if such an attack developed, or if it should be the prelude to an all-out aggressive purpose to invade and seize free Europe, then there must be sufficient following action by forces tactically armed with the strength to hold them at bay until such time—it may be only a question of hours or days—until the full strategic counter-attack can be developed. So long as there is no doubt left in the Russian mind that this reaction will be inevitable there is little danger that the Russians will risk an attack upon us. Thus peace depends both on the shield and the sword.

Turning to the economic unity of Europe, which we were then trying to promote by the development of a wider Free Trade Area, to include the Common Market countries, I made a plea for sympathetic consideration of our proposals. For it indeed would be a tragedy if a Europe already divided should be subjected to a new division.

It is said that the moon has no atmosphere because it is not big enough. I believe that Europe is not big enough to play her role for which history intended her in the full development of the world if she divides herself again. She is already split into a free Europe and an occupied Europe. We have already lost great territories and great civilisations. We cannot afford to make a fresh division of what remains.

I ended with a tribute to the personal contribution which Adenauer had himself made, a contribution which would place him high in the role of international statesmen.

A speech of this character, delivered at a dinner of this kind, was perhaps unusual. Nevertheless it was worth while; for it seemed to make a considerable impression both on the Chancellor and his principal colleagues.

The next day the Chancellor was far more relaxed, and the discussions turned on Bulganin's letter and the best way to frame my reply. In the evening when we resumed talks we discussed

the European Common Market and the proposed Free Trade Area. We are very anxious about all this—but the Germans were, or professed to be, entirely on our side. They would regard the union of the six Messina powers as a disaster if it were *not* followed by the Free Trade Area.[1]

A communiqué was agreed without great difficulty, and the visit ended with a dinner at the British Embassy. This time Adenauer made a long and friendly speech. After dinner, Adenauer and I adjourned to an adjoining room, where we had a long conversation.

[1] 8 May 1957.

The atmosphere was very friendly, and the Chancellor in good form, sometimes serious, sometimes gay.

He told me 'I don't know how it is with you, but there are at least four members of my Government who think they would be better than I am as head of it—and two of them are sitting on that sofa!' He talked a great deal about Germany and the Devil. He believes in a personal Devil. He said that no one who had lived through the years of Hitler could fail to believe in the Devil. He said, 'I tell you, what I could not say to any German, no one realises the harm that Nazism has done to the German soul. It is by no means cured yet. We have got rich again too quickly. I don't want us to get strong again too quickly. I hate uniforms, the curse of Germany. You will see that our Generals in conference are like yours, in civil clothes. I see great dangers ahead. That is why I yearn so for European unity and (in view of France's weakness) for British participation.'

A. told me that when he was in prison, his cell was immediately above the Nazi torture chamber.[1]

On 15 May came the successful explosion of the first British H-bomb, which took place at Christmas Island in the Pacific. It cleared the atmosphere in the political sense, even if it may have polluted it physically to a small degree.

On the same day I received some suggestions from the President about the proposed reply to Bulganin which were helpful. In thanking him I observed:

Now that our bomb has gone off, and our debate has gone off—both satisfactorily from the Government's point of view—I must get down to the job of working out the best answer. Your many comments will be of the greatest help.

The Bulganin letter was disingenuous but exceedingly able. It marked the beginning of a propaganda offensive which was subtle and seductive. By blandly professing the most respectable concepts of international co-operation and by alleging that their only interest in the Near East and Middle East was to assist the developing nations to attain their full national freedom and economic progress;

[1] 12 May 1957.

by drawing a veil over the past years of Soviet aggression carried out both in the West and the East in the spirit of Tsarist imperialism; by even seeming to obliterate as a 'non-fact' the atrocity of the oppression of Hungary, and by concentrating upon the needs of disarmament and the dangers of the new nuclear weapons, the Russians skilfully exploited the fears as well as encouraged the hopes of a very large number of the British people always ready to forget the past and look hopefully to the future.

It is difficult now to realise the genuine anxiety about nuclear arms, amounting almost to hysteria, which had started to develop and was to continue for several years in certain sections in Britain. Processions, demonstrations and deputations began to pursue me in and out of season, and were to continue almost to the end of my Premiership. Deputations of worthy intellectuals from the universities and elsewhere were treated by me with the deep respect due to the eminence as well as the sincerity of their members. But there were embarrassing moments when young partisans of passive resistance began to lie down in front of my car, for my wife had a robust contempt for such antics, and when she was driving me accidents were with difficulty avoided. However in the contest of wills she was generally successful.

Much of the fear was based upon the obvious danger which confronted the world, and with this I was deeply in sympathy. As the years have passed we seem to have learnt, like the villagers on the slopes of Vesuvius, to live with danger; or perhaps the scale of destructiveness involved in a nuclear war has somehow seemed a guarantee against its outbreak. At this time, as young boys and girls began to organise marches from Aldermaston, I began to realise how profound and how widespread was the concern, and how easily it could be exploited.

At this period the British public's growing apprehension as to the dangers of nuclear warfare seemed to blind them to the hopelessness of our position should the 'bomb' be effectively 'banned', and Western Europe with its tiny armies left to face the overwhelming conventional forces of the Soviet Union. I now made up my mind that when the immediate controversy was over and the battle of words which followed Bulganin's letter was ended, I must try, when the moment seemed ripe, to make an effort, however quixotic it might appear, to make at least some indent upon the Iron Curtain, partly in the hope of some genuine *détente* and partly to satisfy public opinion at home. Such an adventure could not be embarked upon hurriedly without preparation. Britain herself had to be sure of her nuclear capacity with her weapons tested and efficient. We must wait to see what would emerge in Russia. We must above all confirm our close alliance with the United States which had been partially but not completely reconstructed at Bermuda. We must if possible command, if not the approval, at least the sympathy of our European allies.

The dangers of allowing the Opposition to exploit the position were considerable. The announcement on 16 May of our first thermonuclear explosion roused no particular comment from the Leader of the Opposition. I now had to announce a further test which took place on 31 May. This led Gaitskell, prompted by the return of Aneurin Bevan from abroad, to take a much more hostile line, almost demanding that we should immediately fall into the Russian trap. Bevan intervened with emotion and almost with violence.

A flaring row, started by Gaitskell, continued by Bevan, and directed at me about the H-bomb. This is the first time that Bevan has really declared himself. He was away when we had the big debate. It's clear to me that he thinks the H-bomb can be an electoral winner for the Socialists and worked up into a sort of Peace Ballot Campaign. I fear that he is right.[1]

Accordingly I sent a minute on 5 June to Charles Hill (Chancellor of the Duchy of Lancaster), who was in charge of our 'publicity':

I have been meditating during the last day or two about the by-elections and the swing of opinion from us. It is the fashion to say that it is the revolt of the middle class against the cost of living, coupled with the fear of the Rent Act. . . .
I wonder . . . whether all this propaganda about the bomb has really gone deeper than we are apt to think. This, combined with Suez, has drawn away from us that wavering vote with vague

[1] 4 June 1957.

Liberal and nonconformist traditions which plays such an important role because it is still the no-man's land between the great entrenched Parties on either side.

I was very much struck by Bevan's intervention yesterday—clearly much to Gaitskell's disgust. He has obviously thought a lot about this. He was away in India when we had the debate in the House on the bomb and therefore is up to now uncommitted. He had obviously decided to go violently anti-bomb . . . and out-manœuvre Gaitskell, who still has some . . . qualms of conscience and is forced by intellectual pride, if for no other reason, to take a reasonably middle position. Bevan is by nature a Radical rather than a Socialist and not at all in sympathy with the intellectual Socialists. He is an old-fashioned Radical, who 50 years ago would have been Lib./Lab.—anti-Church, anti-landlord, anti-Royalty and anti-militarist. I believe that he senses all this and thinks that the bomb will be the great grappling point. After all, it presents many features useful to the agitator. It has an appeal for the mother, the prospective mother, the grandmother, and all the rest, and every kind of exaggeration or mis-statement is permissible.

I next took the step of writing a carefully argued letter to a constituent, which was published both in the local and the national Press and had some effect in steadying opinion. Nevertheless I was conscious of the danger of our position internally and externally. At home we were subjected to agitation of growing strength, concentrating on the demand that we should abandon the series of tests that we had planned, which were absolutely essential if we were to become an effective nuclear power. Externally we were now to suffer a new blow from an unexpected quarter.

The United Nations Disarmament Commission had, in 1954, set up a sub-committee of five powers, U.S.A., U.S.S.R., U.K., France and Canada. Inconclusive negotiations had proceeded, and were re-opened at Lancaster House in London on 18 March. The Chief of the Russian delegation was Valentin Zorin. Governor Harold Stassen led the American team with the somewhat grandiose title of 'President Eisenhower's Special Assistant on Disarmament'. In April both the American and the Russian delegations put forward proposals for the reduction of non-nuclear weapons, first by 10 per cent and then by a further 15 per cent. The Americans followed up their plan with a scheme for depositing condemned weapons in internationally supervised depots. There were also detailed discussions as to the reduction by stages of man-power in the American and Soviet forces. All this caused us little anxiety, largely because the Americans seemed to make a prior agreement on many political issues, including the reunification of Germany, a precondition of any final treaty. (I had learned from Algiers days, as well as from my year as Foreign Secretary, the vital role of that word *'préalable'*.)

Stassen, burning with enthusiasm and ambition, and anxious to bring off a dramatic success, now became guilty of a serious error. He devised, at the beginning of June, and allowed to be filed as an American proposal, a scheme for nuclear disarmament without any prior consultation with his British, French or Canadian colleagues, although they had hitherto worked together in the closest co-operation. It seemed even doubtful whether the State Department had themselves been informed or approved the details. Some of his suggestions were indeed harmless; but there was one which from our point of view could be fatal. The problem of nuclear disarmament divided itself into two; the question of tests and that of fissile material. On the first the Western proposals had hitherto included the exchange of information on the number of recent tests in order to see how many were detectable at long distances, and the advance registration of any future tests. All this was quite acceptable to us for there would be no interference with our planned programme. But on the question of fissile material we were much more vulnerable. To our amazement the Stassen memorandum proposed an early end to the production of such material by any of the great powers. This plan came to be known as the 'cut-off'. For us, this would be fatal. It would involve the abandonment of our nuclear ambitions. I heard of this on 1 June.

> Mr. Stassen (U.S. Representative at the Disarmament Sub-Committee) has filed an extraordinary set of proposals, without telling us or the French—or, it seems, the State Department. Nor has he given copies to anyone except the Russians! Is this America's reply to our becoming a nuclear power—to sell us

down the river *before* we have a stockpile sufficient for our needs? Some of my colleagues suspect this.[1]

Whatever his motives, Stassen's action in parting with the text of this document to the Russians without even providing a copy for his allies was singularly inept.

It seems that Stassen returned from America without instructions. He kept hesitating and delaying. Some instructions must therefore have come for him before he saw the Russians. Stassen told Moch[2] (whether truthfully or not) that he had never intended to give any paper or memorandum to the Russians. He had meant to read over his ideas, which were informal and did *not* bind the American Government. But after he had been through the memorandum orally with the Russian delegates, he was asked for copy in writing—and weakly gave it.[3]

Since the memorandum was about thirty pages of typewritten material and cast in official language suitable to the Heads of a Treaty, this explanation struck me as rather thin. The true difficulty arose from the failure of the great powers to get together and work out a plan to which they could all agree. This had allowed the disarmament committee to develop a kind of life of its own without sufficient control from the Governments concerned.

After consulting some of the Ministers and officials chiefly concerned I sent a personal message to the President which he has reproduced in his own reminiscences.[4] I expressed my surprise that Stassen had taken this action apparently on his own account.

This is, after all, the greatest issue that faces the civilised world; it is one on which the freedom and survival of our island may depend: and, as we correspond on so many questions very freely, I would have hoped that we could have examined together the possible consequences of these proposals before they were put forward. I would not be straight with you if I tried to disguise a certain feeling of distress that we were not told in advance that this document was to be given to the Russians.

[1] 2 June 1957.
[2] Jules Moch was the French representative at the disarmament talks.
[3] 3 June 1957.
[4] Dwight D. Eisenhower, *Waging Peace* (London, 1966), p. 473.

What made Stassen's action even worse was that he had spoken fully to the NATO representatives on this question only three days before, without disclosing anything about his new move. I went on to explain to the President the difficulty which this might make for us; for amidst the whole series of complicated proposals the vital new point of Stassen's plan was that there should be an early date fixed when the production of fissile material for military purposes would be banned. This plan would

> raise some tremendous difficulties for us and for our European friends. A cynical critic might say that, at the end of the process which they envisage, two great nuclear powers would remain: the United Kingdom would be prevented from developing the nuclear strength which she is just beginning to acquire: and all the other countries of Europe would have signed away their right to defend themselves with these weapons for the rest of time, whatever changes may take place in the political conditions of the world.

However, I assured the President that like him I never thought it worth while to job backwards. The question was what were we to do next? Of course the Russians might reject the plan *in toto*, but I doubted whether they would do so.

> Their usual habit, once they have got a document, is to deal with it like a dog with a bone. They never surrender any bit of it which is in any way to their advantage. It is I think more likely that they will give it partial support. Indeed, there are great gains in it for them, especially as the conditions for inspection and control which they have always particularly disliked, have now been relaxed to a point at which evasion would be easy.

In the final passage of my message I reminded him that we already had received from the American Government what amounted to an undertaking that, whatever agreements might emerge, 'the development by the United Kingdom of nuclear weapon resources adequate to her needs should not be prejudiced'.

On 3 June, Moch called to see me. He shared my concern and amazement at Stassen's action, but I had to admit that whether we liked it or not a new situation had been created. We could not face

Parliament once Stassen's proposals were known without putting forward a proposition of our own. I hoped it might be Anglo-French or better still Anglo-French-Canadian. As I told our representative at the disarmament talks on 3 June,

> I was ready to take the risk of waiting a few days until we saw whether the Stassen proposals were in fact published, as they might well be either by the Russians or as the result of the NATO meeting on Wednesday, or indeed by Mr. Stassen's friends. If that happened although the document would not be an official paper before the Committee it would be taken by the world as the American proposals, and I felt that we could not be in a position of having no proposals of our own.

The difficulty was that at the moment there was no French Government. A serious crisis had led to the fall of Mollet's Government on 21 May. Mollet was an old and loyal friend and I thought it right to send him a personal letter of sympathy. It was three weeks before a new Government could be formed. If therefore we put in a British document not supported by the French, the Russians would think that a further wedge had been driven between the allies.

On 6 June the President's reply arrived. It was in the following terms:

> Dear Harold:
> I have just received your cable of June 3 and to say the least I am disappointed to learn of the developments you describe. They took place without the knowledge or authorization of us here in Washington. When Governor Stassen was here a number of meetings were held to outline positions as a basis for a possible future agreement that would be acceptable to us provided they were satisfactory to our Allies. We had assumed that these positions would not be conveyed to the Russians as a statement of the United States position before they had been fully discussed with you and the French Government and with NATO. (Also of course the Federal Republic of Germany is deeply interested in some of the possible implications of this disarmament matter.)
> I am particularly distressed if matters have not gone ahead along this line and if the Russians have been informed on at

least an 'informal memorandum' basis prior to the Allied consultations which we had envisaged.

I assure you that the co-operative spirit so obviously present at the Bermuda Conference is something I regard as of the greatest value as between our two countries and I shall do my best to preserve it and live by it. Already, before your letter was received, the State Department and other Departments involved have been studying the matter with a view to seeing what corrective measures were possible and Foster is working on that this afternoon.

I realise that once the Soviets have a piece of paper in their hands from the Head of the United States Delegation, it puts you and our other Allies in an awkward position, one that is not easy to redress, but we shall do the best we can.

With warm regard,

D.E.

Foster Dulles also telephoned to apologise at length about Stassen. His apologies were all the more sincere because I knew he disliked Stassen and was jealous of his semi-independent position.

But the question remained: what was to be done? So far I had only consulted a few colleagues especially concerned—Butler, Selwyn Lloyd, Lord Home and Sandys. Fortunately Sir Edwin Plowden[1] with a number of experts was in the United States at this time, and I decided to wait until his return in a few days' time. On 12 June Plowden gave us a full account of his visit and of his talks with Admiral Lewis Strauss, the Chairman of the United States Atomic Energy Commission. Although Plowden could throw little light on the Stassen mystery, it was clear that the indiscretion involved a serious danger for Britain. Incidentally it made it necessary to amend my proposed letter to Bulganin. The Russians never miss a trick.

As I fully expected, the Russians have made full use of Stassen's rather naïve diplomacy. They now propose suspension of *all* nuclear tests, and agree to a plan for policing this suspension. They say nothing about production of fissile material *or* of weapons. This puts the Americans, who have always insisted on

[1] Chairman of the Atomic Energy Authority.

linking tests and production, in a hole. (Incidentally it puts us in a *political* difficulty also, but it saves us from the fatal 'cut-off').[1]

I now despatched my reply to Bulganin's letter. My answer was naturally the work of many hands, and I had to ensure that nothing I would say would cause trouble among any of our major allies. With these limitations it was nevertheless possible to emphasise my main point. It was one which I had already put forward publicly at the beginning of April and had stressed on many occasions. For instance, speaking at Sheffield on 3 April, I had used these words:

> I would not be doing my duty if I did not say quite frankly that, much as we desire disarmament and hard as we will work for it, this must cover both the new weapons, the unconventional weapons as we call them, and conventional forces.
>
> Any other course would leave Europe and the free world at the mercy of Soviet power.

In my reply to Bulganin, despatched on 13 June, I insisted that the crux of the problem was the achievement of international agreements on both conventional and nuclear disarmament. Nor were any agreements of value without an effective plan for control. History proved that paper agreements prohibiting the use of particular weapons were valueless. There was no 'substitute for a wider agreement covering both the conventional and the nuclear field in proper systems of control'.[2] I added that I did not believe that we would obtain any substantial reduction of forces without some reduction in political tension. Mr. Bulganin had complained of the aggressive character of NATO: but that was not true. NATO was a defensive organisation only brought into being by Soviet aggression in Eastern and Central Europe. Nevertheless in spite of the strong position which I felt bound to take, I tried to introduce a friendly note which might in due course lead to the *détente* I had already in mind. The very first phrases of my letter emphasised the dangers which oppressed us all.

> The first and most important question that faces us all is how to dispel the threat of war. You and I have lived through two

[1] 15 June 1957.
[2] *Correspondence between the Prime Minister and Mr. Bulganin*, Cmnd. 380.

world wars. We have seen their terrors. We must wish to preserve our children and grandchildren from a third and perhaps final tragedy.

Since Bulganin's letter to me had been published by the Russians, we thought it right that the answer should be made available within a short period of its receipt in Moscow. The British Press was understanding and regarded the reply as moderate and friendly. But it had been so long delayed that it had been overtaken by events—first Stassen, and next Zorin. On 14 June, Zorin formally proposed a two or three years' moratorium on tests with supervision by an international agency stationed at various monitoring posts throughout the world, including Russian territory.

The situation was somewhat complicated by a long letter from Chancellor Adenauer on 7 June, in which he argued that German reunification must precede any real disarmament, and asked for a four-power conference of the four Foreign Secretaries. But I was more concerned with the immediate dangers. Our technical position at this period was weak. Our problem was not to expose this weakness and yet to obtain American help. 'I have now prepared three drafts of a message to the President, but so far despatched none of them.'[1]

On 18 June Harold Stassen and Selwyn Lloyd came to dinner.

I took a very tough line with Stassen and I think he was a bit shaken. Anyway, he has agreed to alter the text of his reply to the Russians, in order to make it less difficult for us. The tests and the 'cut-off' (of material) are the fatal things for us if they come too soon.[2]

I now thought it necessary to give the whole Cabinet a full account of the whole affair.

I read to my colleagues my correspondence with the President and tried to give them the whole background, as well as make clear to them the terrible dilemma in which we find ourselves, between the Scylla of test suspensions and the Charybdis of 'cut-off' of fissile material.[3]

[1] 17 June 1957.   [2] 18 June 1957.   [3] 24 June 1957.

Of course the public did not appreciate the danger of the 'cut-off' proposals and the plan for an abolition or suspension of tests seemed attractive.

This affair, coming just before the arrival of the Commonwealth Prime Ministers for the Conference (26 June to 5 July), caused me a degree of annoyance and even anger, which I must have success-fully concealed from my American colleagues. President Eisen-hower's account of my reply to his soft answer is as follows: 'The Prime Minister cheerfully accepted this explanation, and the diplo-matic squall blew over.'[1]

Naturally the Russian proposals for a two or three years' mora-torium on tests was widely welcomed. It would not be easy to find the right answer. Nevertheless by 2 July a joint statement was made on behalf of the four powers. This was announced in the House of Commons on 3 July. It began by welcoming the Soviet acceptance of the need for

> inspection posts with appropriate scientific instruments, equip-ment and facilities, to be set up for the purposes of control and detection of nuclear testing. This is an essential requirement which the four delegations had long proposed and upon which they had insisted.[2]

It went on to say that the acceptance of this principle now made it possible to consider a temporary suspension of nuclear testing, 'as part of an agreement for a first step in disarmament'.[2] Such a first-stage agreement should include other provisions to halt the growth of armaments. The four powers proposed that a group of experts should prepare plans for an inspection system. Within a few days the Americans proposed that, subject to certain conditions, we should recommend an initial suspension of nuclear tests for ten months. On 11 July we announced that Britain would support this last proposal to which the French and the Canadians had already agreed.

In the meantime a startling development had taken place in Russia, involving the expulsion of Molotov, Malenkov and Kaganovich from the Presidium.

---

[1] *Waging Peace*, p. 473. [2] *Hansard*, 3 July 1957.

The sensational changes in the Russian Government leave us rather uncertain as to where we stand on disarmament. Our proposals have had a fairly good press, and the fact that U.S.A., U.K., France and Canada are united is good. When they were put forward by the F.S. on Monday, the Russian delegate (Zorin) was very 'cagey'—we did not know why at the time, but we assume because of the Palace revolution going on in the Kremlin. Molotov, Malenkov, Kaganovich and Shepilov have been ousted. (A few years ago, they would have been shot; but this seems not obligatory any more.) The position of Gromyko (who has always been one of Molotov's men) is obscure. B. and K. are more firmly established than ever—with the help of the Army, under Zhukov. On the whole, it may mean a more flexible policy towards the West. But it may be more a personal struggle for power than a conflict of policies.[1]

I must confess that I rather regretted the eclipse of Molotov. I had enjoyed our meetings in Vienna, in San Francisco and in Geneva. I also had a sincere respect for his abilities.

In late July Bulganin renewed our correspondence with a somewhat acrimonious letter, which skated over the questions I had raised in order to concentrate on what the Russians clearly thought the most fruitful and productive field of propaganda. The Russians' plan now became abundantly clear. All the wide range of European political problems were to be put on one side. On disarmament the question of reduction both of conventional and unconventional weapons was disregarded. The Soviet Government was clearly now to plug a single theme—the suspension of nuclear tests regardless of all other aspects of disarmament or the settlement of political difficulties. This was a simple, but effective, tactic calculated to attract the maximum of support in the free world. Nevertheless when the disarmament debate took place in the House of Commons at the end of July, we had no great difficulty in maintaining our position.

The debate on disarmament went pretty well. Selwyn Lloyd made a competent and Sandys a really impressive speech. Bevan was quite good. He was in his statesmanlike mood—which is always rather dull.'[2]

[1] 5 July 1957.   26 July 1957.

The relations between Washington and London were now becoming very intimate as a result of the Syrian crisis. I was therefore pretty sure that Dulles would not allow any further steps to be taken at Geneva without the fullest consultation with us. Indeed in the best Russian tradition, whether Tsarist or Communist, towards the middle of July he sent over an old friend of mine, Julius Holmes, formerly on General Eisenhower's staff, now a member of the State Department, to keep an eye upon Governor Stassen.

As an old comrade from A.F.H.Q. days in Algiers, he was both friendly and forthcoming. My impression was that he was much less confident than Stassen appears to be about the chance of any agreement with the Russians.[1]

Dulles's arrival in London at the end of the month was publicly connected with the disarmament negotiations, although his main purpose was to discuss the situation in the Middle East. Dulles could never keep out of the air; he must have flown hundreds of thousands of miles in the course of his journeys from one crisis point to another. How far this benefited his work it was hard to tell, but it gave rise to a quip in the United States which I first heard at this time. 'I heard they are inventing an aeroplane that can fly without Dulles! They hope soon to get it into production.'[2] He made it clear to the Foreign Secretary that he now intended to resume proper control of the talks in Geneva. As a result, at the beginning of August, Stassen was authorised to put forward a new set of so-called 'package' proposals agreed by the four Western powers. These included the cessation of tests for one year as soon as a control system could be agreed, and cessation for a further year if detection machinery was working by the end of the first year and if the Russians agreed to a control of the production of nuclear weapons. These proposals were linked to some reductions in conventional arms, to the establishment of an international committee to work out a plan for the peaceful use of outer space missiles (this was an idea about which the President was especially enthusiastic) and finally to some system of aerial and ground inspection zones. These proposals were not acceptable to the

[1] 15 July 1957.   [2] 14 August 1957.

Russians, and this was made clear at the end of August by the Soviet representative. At the same time the Russians announced the testing of their first intercontinental ballistic missile. So the matter rested, and at the beginning of September the disarmament sub-committee adjourned.

Meanwhile, the British at least preserved the opportunity to perfect their own experiments. I informed both the Australian and the New Zealand Government that we should be making another test in the autumn. As I expected, both Prime Ministers, Holland and Menzies, proved co-operative. At the same time the Australian Government showed themselves ready to help in every way with the tests that we were to make in Australia.

Only one matter remained—to answer Bulganin's letter of 20 July. This I did on 26 August, dealing as courteously as possible with the points raised in his last communication. I could not refrain from confessing to some disappointment that he had not answered some of the fundamental questions which I had posed in my earlier reply.

> As regards European security, I note that you suggest that European States and the U.S.A. should 'jointly bind themselves not to afford military or economic assistance to any State violating the peace of Europe'. Perhaps you have overlooked the fact that this undertaking has already been given, voluntarily and uni-laterally, by the Governments members of NATO, on October 23, 1954, when they associated themselves with the Declaration by the Governments of France, the United Kingdom and the United States made on October 3, 1954. A similar obligation to withhold support from an aggressor was contained as the second provision in the Outline of Terms of Treaty of Assurance put forward by the Western Powers at the Geneva Conference of Foreign Ministers in 1955.[1]

To Bulganin's assurance that the only consideration which guided Soviet policy in Middle Eastern affairs was the desire to contribute to ensuring lasting peace I replied as follows:

> I welcome this declaration but I must frankly say that the actions —especially the recent actions—of the Soviet Government have

[1] *Correspondence between the Prime Minister and Mr. Bulganin*, Cmnd. 380, p. 25.

appeared in a somewhat different light. Nevertheless the British Government is always ready to co-operate with other Governments either through the United Nations or in other ways to promote peace and harmony in that area.

As regards Anglo-Soviet trade, while admitting certain restrictions which the British Government thought it necessary to impose in the interests of their own security, I pointed out how wide was the range of goods freely exported from the United Kingdom to the Soviet Union. Here was certainly a field for further expansion to our common benefit. I welcomed proposals for 'cultural contacts'. There were some hesitations which had naturally followed from the fact that British public opinion had been deeply shocked by the Soviet intervention in the Hungarian uprising, but I hoped that political conditions would improve, and free exchange of persons and information between our countries would gradually become possible. I concluded as follows:

> Please do not think that we are any less anxious than you are to find ways of improving our relations. You know that for the British people actions mean more than words. I am very glad that we are making real progress in trade and cultural matters. I am sincerely convinced that we shall achieve results with at least some of the problems which remain to be solved if both sides wish for this. But we must approach this task with sincerity and tolerance, if we are to reach understanding. It is sometimes better that disagreements should be openly expressed, not camouflaged in obscure wording. In this way, we may find a basis for agreement. These considerations have been uppermost in my mind during my study of your letter.

Although the Press and the public seemed to read this correspondence with interest, I hoped myself that it would be discontinued, or at least suspended. So far our letters had been interchanged with courtesy, but on a healthy basis of mutual distrust. Nor was there very much to be learned from Bulganin's lengthy epistles. There was little in them that I did not already know or disbelieve. A final resolution of the fundamental disagreements between the Communist and the free world could not be foreseen in the near future. As a great Russian revolutionary, Alexander Herzen, wrote,

L

'reconciliations are only possible when they are unnecessary'. It might be that, over the years, by an evolution of Communism in Russia and by progressive changes in the economic and social systems prevailing in the Western world, there would be a steady reduction of the great gulf that separated the two groups. In pondering over the events of these summer months I felt convinced that neither the interchange of a long and argumentative correspondence, nor the almost interminable detailed discussions of the disarmament sub-committee in Geneva would prove the real road to progress. The Summit meeting in Geneva in 1955 had been disappointing. Nevertheless something had been gained. I now began to consider means by which a new effort could be made. Clearly more preparations both personal and diplomatic would be required, and patience as well as a bold initiative would be necessary. Meanwhile these thoughts remained dormant, but not inactive, at the back of my mind.

CHAPTER X

Honeymoon at Washington

I N spite of Russia's brusque rejection at the end of August of the 'package' proposals put forward by the Western powers, the whole question of disarmament was due to be debated again by the United Nations Assembly in the autumn. The public were deeply concerned by the prospect of increasing nuclear armaments and their possible spread into less responsible hands. Nevertheless even left-wing opinion felt that the Russians had been wrong in their refusal even to consider the Western plan. This was soon to be exemplified by a significant incident at the Labour Party Conference in October. Aneurin Bevan, who had only a few months before violently opposed the manufacture of the H-bomb by Britain, unexpectedly delivered a passionate defence of the very policy which he had so recently denounced. For this retractation he was able to secure the support of the leading trade union leaders. His conversion, if less dramatic in its details, was almost as significant in the narrow sphere of politics as that of St. Paul.

The *Daily Telegraph* has a leader headed 'Bevan into Bevin'. The Bevanites are furious; the rank and file of the constituencies voted pretty solidly against him and the platform. But the unions (in spite of [Frank] Cousins, who was voted down in his executive) voted solidly *for* the Bomb![1]

Although I had already sensed this change in opinion, I was anxious that we should not appear before the United Nations without some definite and 'constructive' plan. The Foreign Secretary was in Washington at this time and discussed with Dulles a memorandum which I had prepared on 18 September on one aspect of the vast disarmament problem. I proposed that we should make a gesture, which would be both practicable and imaginative:

[1] 4 October 1957.

First, we would undertake to declare [all tests] . . . beforehand
and register them with the United Nations, or some other body.
Second, we would undertake to limit our explosions during the
next two years unilaterally, whether the Russians agreed or not.
Third, that the limit of our explosions would be such as would
create an amount of radiation, etc., which would not exceed a
specified figure.

Selwyn Lloyd discussed the whole question at length with Dulles.
Since he returned to Britain for a brief spell before the disarmament
debate was likely to open in New York, I was able to receive from
him a full report. At the same time the President sent me a message,
promising to discuss my ideas with Admiral Strauss. He seemed
attracted by the plan:

> We have, together, already moved quite a distance in the
> direction you suggest and perhaps by putting it all together, and
> putting it in a fresh package with some little addition, it could be
> made into what would catch the popular imagination.

The successful launching of the Russian Sputnik on 4 October,
followed by another satellite on 3 November, was received with
mixed feelings in the West. On the first occasion, the British public,
with characteristic generosity, paid full tribute to this wonderful
technical achievement. The Americans were not unnaturally
alarmed by so striking a proof of Russian scientific and technological progress. The second experiment, however, in which a small
dog was sent up into the upper atmosphere, shocked the British
profoundly.

> The Russians have launched another and larger 'satellite'
> (with a 'little dawg' in it) which has created much alarm and
> despondency in U.S. The English people, with characteristic
> frivolity, are much more exercised about the 'little dawg' than
> about the terrifying nature of these new developments in
> 'rocketry'. Letters and telegrams were pouring in tonight to
> No. 10, protesting about the cruelty to the dog.[1]

[1] 5 November 1957.

Admiral Strauss came to see me in London on 9 October, and as a result of our talk I sent messages on the following day both to Foster Dulles and to the President. Apart from all the minor questions of tactics at the United Nations, on which we could easily agree, we must now face realities. To Dulles I wrote shortly on 10 October,

> There is an ominous note of confidence and truculence in the recent statements of Russian policy. This has led me to send some thoughts on our joint defence efforts to the President which I have no doubt he will show you.

In my long message to the President on the same day I pleaded that we should now re-examine our ability to meet the Russian challenge on every front, military, political, economic and ideological. Ten years after the Atlantic Pact, we needed a new approach. The countries of the free world should try to pool their resources to meet the increasing threat. Acting together, the Western nations could easily achieve their purpose. But at present their efforts were often sporadic or dissipated. The United States must give the lead; if they took the initiative other countries would surely follow.

> Each of the countries of the free world has its contribution to make—it may be military or scientific or economic or political. Surely these resources if purposefully directed will succeed where unco-ordinated effort is bound to fail.

From the British point of view, if we were to resume full co-operation in the atomic field this would necessitate repeal of the McMahon Act (passed in 1946) which effectively prevented the development of any common programme.[1] If we had to plod along a path already trodden by our American friends, this would involve grievous expenditure of money and effort. Our British scientists and technicians could do the job—but at a heavy cost. I did not yet venture to raise this delicate issue, although I was determined to do so at the right moment. Meanwhile it was better to deal in generalities.

The President replied immediately giving a generous welcome to my ideas.

[1] See *Tides of Fortune*, p. 566.

As you know, I have long been an earnest advocate of closer ties between our two countries. I believe that the nations of the free world cannot possibly carry the burdens and sacrifices necessary in the preservation of free systems of government unless they can have the confidence that those to whom they look for world leadership are bound together by common convictions, purposes and principles. I believe that all countries that fear themselves threatened by communism or any other form of dictatorship look primarily to your country and to ours for the leadership they need. I think, therefore, that it is necessary not only that the highest officials of our two countries are close together in these matters, but that this understanding and agreement should, to the greatest possible measure, extend to our two peoples and indeed to as many more as we can reach.

Within a few days I received a telegram from the Foreign Secretary, now back in Washington, reporting a talk with Foster Dulles. He said that Eisenhower was very anxious to discuss all these matters personally with me and asked if I could not come over on some pretext or other. I was particularly encouraged by Dulles observing that if anything was to be done which would require Congressional action the 'processes' would have to be started by 1 December. Our meeting therefore should take place as soon as possible. This, of course, meant that the repeal of the McMahon Act was not ruled out. Indeed a few days later Selwyn Lloyd reported that Dulles had stated quite firmly that the McMahon Act was 'obsolete'.

A large number of telegrams have come in from the Foreign Secretary (who has gone to Washington to be with the Queen). Foster Dulles and the President want me to come over for a talk, if it can be arranged without attracting too much attention or causing alarm. I have replied, offering to go next Tuesday. But I don't think any 'cover plan' (they suggested a degree or a lecture) would hold water at such short notice, and I said so.[1]

Both the Chancellor of the Exchequer and the Foreign Secretary fully agreed with my decision. I told my colleagues that I would strive in Washington for the repeal of the McMahon Act and the

[1] 16 October 1957.

mobilisation of a genuine collective defence, and—on a wider front—an unobtrusive establishment of machinery by which our two countries could study the political, military and economic issues arising from the Soviet threat and devise means for rallying our friends in the Commonwealth, in Europe, and throughout the free world.

Meanwhile I thought it right to send a message to Adenauer inviting him to London later in the year to discuss the whole situation, including the economic and financial dangers which threatened the stability of Europe. Adenauer, while fully understanding these problems, remained somewhat mistrustful of our ability to put up a strong front against Russia. This was partly due to his criticism of 'weak leadership in America' and partly to his anxiety about the confusion in French political life with its short and unstable Governments. Adenauer, in spite of his unbroken record of success, was always something of a pessimist.

By this time there had been a dramatic reversal in the relations between London and Washington. A year before they had reached a low ebb. Whatever the causes and wherever the blame might lie, all confidence between us had been shattered. At the end of 1956 there was thus not only misunderstanding but bitterness on both sides. The Bermuda Conference in March 1957 had gone a long way to restore mutual confidence, without apologies or retractations on either side. I remembered Churchill's words—'the past should be forgiven even if it cannot be forgotten'.

Even the British decision at the end of May to abandon the special restrictions which had been imposed on trade with Communist China and to substitute a much smaller list based upon that which regulated trade with Soviet Russia did not lead to any new breach. Selwyn Lloyd had warned Dulles of our intention, and the President sent me a message on 18 May protesting against our proposed move and asking me to reconsider our decision. His apprehensions were chiefly caused by the strong feeling in Congress. I replied on 21 May:

> Of course I always want to work in the closest harmony with you. But this Chinese business has become almost as much an

318   RIDING THE STORM

obsession with us as it appears to be with your Congress. Quite between ourselves as old friends I do not think there is much in it. You say that if we get what we want the Chinese will only switch their trade from one item to another. That may very likely prove true, but traders never think like that. Each individual firm and industry believes that it can increase its own sales, and of course in our country, which only lives by exports, this is quite an important factor.

To this the President made only a mild answer, more in the nature of an appeal than a reproach. In my reply of 29 May, I hastened to bring the matter to conclusion:

I should reply at once about the Russian–Chinese trade question. I am very glad that you understand our special difficulty about this matter. As you realise, the commercial interests of our two countries in this are not at all alike. We live by exports— and by exports alone. So I feel that we cannot any longer maintain the existing differential between Russia and Chinese trade and we shall be making a statement to this effect in Parliament tomorrow.

I added that the Russian list of exclusions was quite extensive, covering 250 items; thus trade with China would still be severely limited. In my view most of the other countries would feel that we had taken a right step, as indeed proved to be the case. I also declared that I felt it was better to get this difference settled rather than allow it to drag on and poison our relations. We had many far more important problems which we must face together. Largely due to the President's influence this Chinese affair, which had caused me much concern, was not elevated by the American Government or Press into a great issue. The State Department contented itself with a statement that it was 'disappointed'. In the last paragraph of a letter of 3 June dealing mainly with other matters, Eisenhower with his usual fairness observed:

while there was some unfavourable comment here in the States, both political and editorial, I am relieved to note it has not caused the furore that could have taken place.

It was therefore in a hopeful mood that I set out on another journey. In March the President had come to meet me in Bermuda on British soil. This time it seemed right for me to go to Washington. It is generally wise before a meeting of this kind, which is necessarily short, to reach some preliminary agreement about the subjects for discussion. But on this occasion I thought it wiser to follow whatever the Americans might propose. In sending his invitation Eisenhower had used almost my own words. If we could meet we should be able to reach some general conclusions on which could be based a joint directive to our staffs.

It was equally necessary to send telegrams to all the Commonwealth countries to inform them of the meeting and the scope of the discussions to be expected. I also arranged for the Heads of the German and French Governments to be told in general terms of what I had hoped to achieve. For I was already conscious that closer American–British relations might raise suspicions among some of our European friends; they might feel that we were moving away from the concept of Europe which many of us cherished. Wisely and discreetly handled, I did not believe then–and do not believe now–that there is any inherent contradiction between Anglo-American friendship and Britain's full co-operation in Europe. Indeed one of the assets which Britain has to contribute as a member of a European community, apart from the Commonwealth connection, is close understanding with the United States. Only those who take a jealous and inward-looking view can regard these traditional relationships with a jaundiced eye. More generous leaders of European opinion would welcome this contribution which Britain might make to the strength and prosperity of Europe.

In the timing of this conference, I was fortunate indeed; for the whole country was still enthralled by the visit of the Queen. She had arrived in Washington accompanied by Prince Philip only a week before, after taking part in the 350th Anniversary of the founding of the colony of Virginia. Our Ambassador, Harold Caccia, 'told me that the Queen's visit has made a tremendous effect here. She has buried George III for good and all.'[1] I could certainly have chosen no more suitable a moment; for both in official and unofficial

[1] 23 October 1957.

L2

circles I sensed a friendly and even enthusiastic mood. In addition, 'The Russian success in launching the satellite has been something equivalent to Pearl Harbour. The American cocksureness is shaken.'[1]

We reached Washington at 9.15 a.m. where we were met by Foster Dulles and the Foreign Secretary; all the Commonwealth Ambassadors were there, together with a number of other notabilities.

Foster Dulles soon began to reveal the new ideas with which he is struggling. He realises that America cannot stand alone, still less 'go it alone'. I responded, with quite a romantic picture of what U.S. and U.K. could do together. . . . But I added that our unity must be not to rule but to serve the world. Foster said this represented the President's inmost thoughts. The problem was how to do it. We continued our talk till luncheon.[1]

During the interval our Ambassador gave us a clear picture of the political situation which certainly seemed favourable to our hopes.

The President is under severe attack for [the] first time. Foster is under still more severe attack. His policies are said to have failed everywhere. The administration realises that their attitude over the Canal issue was fatal and led necessarily to the Suez situation. The atmosphere is now such that almost anything might be decided, however revolutionary.[1]

After luncheon we had a further meeting with Foster Dulles, this time with five or six 'advisers' on each side.

We went over all the ground—but rather skated over it. I was not pleased with this conference. The Foreign Secretary was excellent, but Foster seemed to be retreating a bit. On reflection, I felt that he was rather inhibited in the presence of so large a meeting. I don't think he is quite sure what line the President will finally take.[1]

At 7 p.m. we went to the White House. There were present only the four of us—the President, Dulles, Selwyn Lloyd and I.

[1] 23 October 1957.

Drinks, etc., with mostly reminiscent chat till dinner. The President seemed much better than at Bermuda. He was brisk, confident, and seemed more sure of himself. He complained a good deal about 'politicians' and the attacks upon himself. (This is a new experience for him. Up to now, he has been immune.)[1]

After dinner the real talk began.

I felt that Foster was rather feeling his way. So I let him make the running. The conversation was rather scrappy, and the President, while agreeing to the need for full co-operation in principle, seemed unwilling to discuss just how it was to be done in practice. However, Foster was persistent, in his slow laborious way and at one time I thought we should get down to real business. But we didn't.[1]

Rather unfairly, I could not help thinking of the criticism of another statesman—'his speech was slow, but it easily kept pace with his thought'. Although everything was very friendly, yet there seemed to be no real progress.

The only point which seemed to get home was when I told the President that if we couldn't get all this done in the next two or three years, with all the advantage of our close friendship, it was unlikely that our successors would be able to do the job.[1]

When I got back to the Embassy I was exhausted; for we had had a long day following immediately upon a night flight. I was also rather depressed. I desperately wanted two things out of this conference; first the repeal of the McMahon Act and second a renewed impetus to Western co-operation against Soviet aggression or infiltration. For this we could only lay down the broad principles. The implementation would require both imagination and patience. So far there had only been the most general talk about the second; the first had not been mentioned.

Selwyn Lloyd took a more hopeful view than I did, and Norman Brook tried to comfort me, but I was worried and anxious, and slept hardly at all. However, by the next day, I reached the conclusion that it would be best to let the hand play itself. We would ask for

[1] 23 October 1957.

nothing, but see what they had done for us. At 10 o'clock there was a 'plenary' meeting at the White House in the Cabinet Room, a fine and dignified apartment, in size and character not at all unlike that in which we met in Downing Street. 'The Americans start early, for a meeting of the National Security Council was just ending as we arrived.'[1]

We fielded our full team, the Foreign Secretary, Sir Norman Brook, Sir Richard Powell (Permanent Secretary of the Ministry of Defence), and Sir Edmund Plowden, as well as Pat Dean of the Foreign Office. The Americans, in addition to the President and Foster Dulles, brought with them the Secretary of Defence, Charles Wilson, as well as Allen Dulles (Head of the Central Intelligence Agency), Admiral Strauss, and Douglas Dillon of the State Department. The two Ambassadors, John Hay Whitney and Sir Harold Caccia, were also present.

> The President opened with a little speech—perfect in form and very good in substance. He went very far—further than I dared hope last night. Then I spoke—a little 'sentimentally'—but I think they liked it none the worse. (I had prepared nothing, but trusted to the spirit moving me. I thought how pleased my mother would have been to see me, as British Prime Minister in the American Cabinet Room, addressing a meeting presided over by the American President.) Foster spoke next, very well. Then Selwyn Lloyd—short, clear and effective. Then the President asked Allen Dulles to give his appreciation of Russian military strength and future potential.[1]

At this point the President produced a directive obviously prepared by Dulles and approved at the National Security meeting before we arrived. It set up two committees, one to be headed by Sir Richard Powell to deal with collaboration on weapons, the other under Plowden and Strauss on nuclear collaboration. This was agreed, as well as a communiqué to be given immediately to the Press announcing the formation of these two committees, which were to report the same night.

> I could hardly believe my ears—such rapid progress, to be publicly announced. This done and agreed, the President

[1] 24 October 1957.

adjourned the meeting, and we left the White House at about 11.30.[1]

Dulles came to luncheon at the Embassy. We had a talk afterwards, and he produced the draft of a declaration to be called the Declaration of Common Purpose. 'I glanced at it, and saw, embodied in a lot of verbiage, para. 3–the end of the McMahon Act–the great prize!'[1] The Americans certainly move quickly once they have made up their minds. The relief to me was immense. We could now proceed with our work in the atomic field and remain a nuclear power without the appalling waste of effort involved in slowly arriving by our own efforts at the point of development which our American allies had already reached. At any rate for the next decade Britain's problems in this immensely expensive and complicated area of scientific development of weapons were resolved. The way was clear. After luncheon, I went to bed and slept soundly for nearly three hours.

At 6 p.m. I

went to see Dulles in his house, for half an hour, before going to the White House for dinner. He said he got on much better now with Selwyn, but would like to feel that he could sometimes approach me, either direct or through the President. He seemed very happy at the way the talks were working out. 7.00 p.m. at the White House–drinks and talks before dinner. All the same party as at the plenary session. Another committee (in addition to the two technical committees) had formed itself–Norman Brook and Livie Merchant.[2] By dinner, a redraft of the Declaration was available; and later (after dinner) the reports of the two technical committees, as well as one on *general* co-operation, through working parties, over the whole field of our relations–political, economic, propaganda, foreign policy, etc.[1]

I now raised the question of how we were to avoid the jealousies of other countries, whether in the Commonwealth or among our allies, especially the French and Germans. We must make it clear that we were not trying to set up a kind of Anglo-American hegemony. On the contrary, our sole purpose was to mobilise our affairs

[1] 24 October 1957.
[2] Livingston T. Merchant, United States Ambassador to Canada.

in the best way and share our efforts with all those countries of like mind with us. I would send full information about our meeting to the heads of the leading Commonwealth countries. Both the President and I would do our best to explain our purpose to the French and Germans, as well as to the other NATO powers.

In the long interval which was devoted to that generous consumption of alcohol which normally precedes an American dinner and compensates for the iced water that follows,

there was a lot of chaff between us all about the Declaration. I suggested 'Declaration of Inter-Dependence' as the title. The President rather liked the idea—but on reflection we all thought it a little too dramatic. Fortunately, both he and I had made some very similar amendments in the draft. But everything of substance remained.[1]

I had heard that there was some anxiety among the American advisers regarding paragraph 3, which dealt with the repeal of the McMahon Act.

But I have high hopes that the President and Secretary Dulles will stand firm. Incidentally, at the plenary session this morning, the President rather shocked some of his people by referring to the McMahon Act as 'one of the most deplorable incidents in American history, of which he personally felt ashamed'.[1]

The plenary meeting was fixed for 10.30 a.m. on 25 October. It was clear within a few minutes that the President had decided to stand by his words. The Declaration was finally approved with a few verbal changes, and the agreements on general weapons and nuclear co-operation were agreed and initialled.[2] Other personal commitments were entered into by the President with me regarding some of our overseas anxieties which I considered to be of the greatest value.

By a happy chance M. Spaak, now Secretary-General of NATO, whose duty it would be to organise the next NATO meeting, was in Washington. He came to the White House at 2 o'clock for a full discussion. Spaak was an old and valued friend, and his presence at this moment was most fortunate. We showed him the communiqué

[1] 24 October 1957.
[2] 25 October 1957. For the text of the Declaration see Appendix 3.

and called his special attention to those paragraphs which referred to the NATO meetings. Spaak immediately agreed to set about the plan for making the December meeting one of 'Heads of Government', not merely of Foreign Ministers. Over this proposal he was enthusiastic, especially when he heard that the President, if invited, would come himself.

Before leaving I sent a personal letter to the President:

Dear Mr. President,

I cannot leave Washington without sending you a few hurried words to express my gratitude to you. It has been of tremendous value for me to have had these quiet unofficial talks with you and Foster.

Although at one time we both thought it very difficult to arrange such a meeting, it somehow seems to have gone off without causing any undue trouble or alarm. I hope that this means that we may be able to have further meetings with the same informality. Of course if the NATO plan comes off and you are able to come to England in the course of it, it will be another chance for at least a short talk.

However, this is not really my purpose in writing. What I want to say, but find it difficult to express, is the sense of inspiration which these last few days have given me, and, I think, all our associates. The whole spirit of our talks together at the top seems to have spread right through all our colleagues and assistants. We have got a pretty difficult job, but it is fine to feel that we are setting about it with such confidence through all our efforts all over the world, and I am very grateful for the theme which you developed that our two countries are working together not to rule or to impose our will, but to serve.

Yours very sincerely,
Harold Macmillan

I also wrote to the Secretary of State:

My dear Foster,

I cannot leave Washington without sending you just a few lines to thank you. I know how much we owe to your friendship and to your courage. This meeting which we have looked forward to so much has proved a tremendous success. I feel quite a new spirit, and a good many of the difficulties and troubles seem well worth while, for we are putting our hands to a great task, and I somehow think that we have found the right approach to it. I and all my colleagues feel a real debt of gratitude to you for your wisdom and far-sightedness. I hope that you will not hesitate to let me have at any time any of your thoughts on any aspect of the work which you think might be helpful.

I think that when we look back on these few days we shall feel we have done a lot. I shall go home not only content but, what is more, rather excited, for it is really a great adventure on which we are embarked, and with God's will we may hope to leave behind us something really firm and fruitful.

Yours ever,
Harold

I sent accounts of the talks to Commonwealth Prime Ministers with full details to Menzies and Holyoake, both of whom were especially interested owing to the use of Christmas Island for our atomic tests. All the necessary telegrams were drafted and despatched before we left by the remarkable efficiency of my small staff aided by that of the Embassy. I had already experienced at Bermuda not merely the skill and devotion with which Prime Ministers are served at such conferences, but the remarkable rapidity with which these civil servants are able to act in spite of all distractions. It has since become the fashion somewhat to disparage these leading members of the 'establishment'. Nobody who has had the advantage of their quality can share in this ignorant, if popular, denigration.

We next went to Ottawa, arriving in the evening of 25 October. Diefenbaker received us with his usual enthusiasm and hospitality.

It was rather thrilling . . . to stay at Rideau Hall. I went there in 1919; Dorothy and I were engaged there in the first months of 1920. I sent her a telegram (it is sad that she is not with me) before leaving.[1]

The next day, 26 October,

At 10 a.m. we had a meeting of selected ministers and officials (British and Canadian). I gave an 'exposé' of the Washington talks, and the mood and purpose of our American friends.

[1] 26 October 1957.

Diefenbaker... resisted any expressions of 'jealousy' and seemed to appreciate the high plane to which I tried to raise the whole affair. Foreign Secretary was excellent at questions. At 11.30 a.m. Foreign Secretary and I saw the whole Canadian Cabinet, in the Cabinet Room. There was a general discussion—Washington, Trade, Middle East, etc., etc. This meeting ended at 12.45 p.m.[1]

We went for luncheon out to the Country Club in Hull, across the river. It was here that thirty-four years before we all used to go to dance on Saturday evenings, when I was an A.D.C. at Government House. Some of my old dancing partners were there, married and staid. There were short speeches and a very happy atmosphere.

I had two other duties before the reopening of Parliament offered me an opportunity to give a full account of the Washington conference. I had to explain to my Canadian, Australian and New Zealand colleagues that in view of the importance of getting the McMahon Act repealed, I had acceded to the United States request to send observers to Christmas Island, if they could arrive within the next few days, for the H-bomb test which was about to take place. Since we had made no provision for observers and could only with the greatest difficulty accommodate two, I hoped that they would understand why we had decided to give the only available places to representatives of the United States. In addition to the formal telegram I sent this message to Menzies.

I hope you will understand [my difficulty]. It is a very big fish hooked, but not yet landed. I don't want anything to go wrong.

It only remained to thank Admiral Strauss, since I felt under a considerable debt of gratitude to him for his generous help. It was he who had first suggested these talks when we had met in London some weeks before.

It was after your encouragement that I wrote to the President and began to outline some of the large ideas which we discussed last week. It was also largely due to your interest and sympathy, I feel, that the general meeting of minds in Washington took, in the end, such a concrete form of expression.

Strauss has remained a close and valued friend ever since.

[1] 26 October 1957.

The speech which a Prime Minister makes on the Opening of the Session presents considerable difficulties to the orator. This was the first time I had been confronted with this task.

I have, by tradition, to make a long speech expanding all the items in the Queen's Speech, more or less seriatim. This makes a dull speech—and mine was pretty dull.[1]

However, I was able to expand in greater detail the aims on which the President and I had agreed in the Declaration of Common Purpose. For myself I preferred the phrase 'Inter-Dependence', for it seemed to summarise the facts of life in the world today. There have sometimes been doubts as to the true position of the United States!

We have heard from time to time suggestions that the United States could, if necessary, write off Europe and either relapse into isolationism or decide to go it alone. We did not grudge, although we might have envied, our American friends this relative security. All the same, with the best will in the world, there can be absolute confidence in an alliance only where all the partners are more or less at equal risk.

Naturally, the United States is bound for years to come to enjoy a vast superiority over the other countries of the free world and to be relatively safer; but the resources of applied science and technology have somewhat changed the situation and, to be frank, the American people are no longer confident that even their great country can do everything itself without allies to secure its own survival and still less to secure the survival of the ideals for which they stand. . . . This new situation in the United States, will be of far-reaching importance to us all.[2]

We had therefore, at Washington,

first, common agreement that the free world could not afford any longer to waste its resources in skill and money but should some-how find means to make its joint effort truly co-operative; secondly, the President accepted wholeheartedly what he and I called the doctrine of inter-dependence and he was as anxious as I was to give this concept practical meaning.[2]

[1] 5 November 1957.   [2] *Hansard*, 5 November 1957.

We were not, and it was vital to emphasise this, trying to set up an exclusively Anglo-American alliance or partnership. The fact that the Secretary-General of NATO had been present in Washington had been a great advantage and I was now able to announce that the meeting in December would be one of Heads of Government, including, of course, the President of the United States. I recognised that the agreements reached in Washington had been attacked from both sides. The isolationists here alleged that we had sold out to Washington. I did not think there was any fear of that. What we would gain would be the co-operation between our scientists and technicians and those of the United States, especially in the nuclear field. We had much to contribute. In this 'co-operative effort, if we are allowed to achieve it, we shall not go empty-handed to this exchange ; but I do not think that we shall lose by it'.[1] There had, of course, been an attack from another quarter—the Communists and the fellow-travellers. Aneurin Bevan was not present at this debate, but I recalled that he had described our discussions at Washington as 'sterile'.

He is certainly not helping them to be fruitful. I see that on 18th October, he said in *Tribune* . . . 'I feel bound to say that if Nikita Khrushchev did not sincerely believe all that he said to me he must be a supreme actor or I am very credulous.' The antithesis seems to me somewhat artificial. It is quite likely that both propositions are true.[1]

I could not help sympathising with the Leader of the Opposition, Gaitskell, in the delicacy of his position.

It is not so bad when his right hon. Friend is in this country. At Brighton, for instance, he was a reformed character. He talked quite good sense about the deterrent and the bomb, and so forth. He was altogether off the heady wine of demagogy—he hardly touched a drop. Now that he has gone abroad, there has been a relapse.[1]

One advantage at any rate of the close working between Washington and London was already clear. We had little more trouble in

[1] *Hansard*, 5 November 1957.

New York; for the United Nations Assembly on 14 November passed a resolution endorsing the proposals for disarmament which the Western powers had already put forward. These linked nuclear disarmament both with inspection and with reduction of conventional forces.

The meeting of NATO in Paris was fixed for the middle of December. My own hopes were high.

> The more I think about the 'inter-dependence' theme (which is really only a variation of the Churchill speeches after the war) the more I feel the vital importance of the NATO meeting in December. This will set a pattern. The chief problem will be to get practical measures going.[1]

Meanwhile

> one of the most urgent things is to get a really good agenda for NATO. The Germans are very shy about nuclear and want conventional armies. The French seem in a rather dazed condition—until Algeria is conquered, evacuated or conciliated, they are immobilised. Spaak is working hard on the right lines. But it won't be easy to get down to brass tacks. If we could get ourselves into a better posture, there might be another meeting with the Russians. But it is too early yet. I believe I could get the idea into the President's head that it should happen while we are both in command.[2]

This thought of reviving in some form the direct talks with the Russian leaders which had been initiated in Geneva was never out of my mind. There was still some preliminary work to be done. Unhappily Adenauer's visit to London had been cancelled owing to the Chancellor's illness, although Heinrich von Brentano and Hallstein came in his place. We had long and useful talks, and the atmosphere was good. 'But the shadow of our financial weakness and the problem of "support costs" hangs [over] everything.'[3]

Before the date fixed for the NATO meeting I was able to make a short visit to Paris. I found the French, who had been without a Government for five weeks, in a somewhat nervous mood. The new Prime Minister, Félix Gaillard, was inexperienced and unsure of

---

[1] 10 November 1957.   [2] 11 November 1957.   [3] 4 December 1957.

himself. Moreover the atmosphere was clouded by an unhappy dispute about the recent delivery of small quantities of British and American arms to Tunisia. The French, with some reason, suspected that any arms given to Tunisia, now an independent country, might be used to support the Algerian rebels. The last French Government had before its fall proposed a Franco-Tunisian Conference; but in the long interregnum this plan had lapsed. It was patent that the Tunisian Government, if they could not get supplies from the West for the purposes of internal security, would accept offers from Russia, either direct or through Egypt. In these circumstances we had agreed with the American view that it would be better to make some small deliveries to Tunisia on the understanding that they obtained none from any other country. The French authorities were fully informed throughout. Nevertheless I think we made a serious error, at a critical moment when France was already nervous and uncertain. It would have been wiser to take the risk of Soviet infiltration, in order to keep the French sweet.

The French Press was naturally working up this minor affair into a large issue.

All kinds of usual accusations about *perfide Albion*. We and the Americans were accused of (*a*) trying to dominate NATO, (*b*) doing the French out of the oil exploitation in Sahara, (*c*) preventing France becoming a nuclear power–etc. etc. However, although it was rather sticky to start with, I think the Paris meeting did good. I like the young and energetic P.M. (Gaillard), and I felt that he was a man of considerable power and character.[1]

At the time I did not fully realise the true situation in France. The continual changes of Government and the growing weakness of the Fourth Republic had produced a sense of 'alarm and despondency'. Even the future of the regime seemed uncertain. Indeed the return of de Gaulle to power was only six months away. By the time the NATO meeting took place the situation had somewhat improved, and the arrival of the Heads of Government in Paris caused a renewed interest in the alliance. At any rate we had done our best to work in concert with both our French and German friends.

[1] 1 December 1957.

At the beginning of the month a sudden panic developed in Britain led by the *Daily Mirror* about the H-bomb being carried in the American bombers based in this country. The public were led to believe that American bombers flew all over Britain with the bomb in a loaded position without any safety devices which would prevent an accidental explosion.

All the pro-Russians and all the pacifists and all the senti-mentalists (inspired by the clever politicians) have tried to work this up into a sort of 'finger on the trigger' campaign.[1]

However, the explanations which I was able to give were regarded as satisfactory by the more responsible parts of the Press, and this storm, like so many others, seemed to blow itself out. I was amused to find in his next letter to me (of 11 December) Bulganin made skilful use of this incident.

Before we left for Paris a definite decision had to be taken about a new series of tests and the future of Christmas Island.

It is *just* possible that (if the McMahon Act is repealed) we shall get the knowledge we require from America. But one of the main reasons that we have made so much progress with the American administration is that we *are* a nuclear power on our own. I felt that to stop now would be like giving up 'in the straight'. Ministers agreed.[2]

Accordingly we agreed to continue the plans for the 1958 pro-gramme and thereafter to maintain the base at Christmas Island in a satisfactory condition.

At this time I had two other visitors. René Massigli, a true and loyal friend of the Anglo-American alliance, came to see me on 4 December.

He was very gloomy about France. He thought the Tunis arms incident more serious than we supposed, but only as a symptom. France was back in a self-critical and hopeless mood, which expressed itself (as I had known so well in de Gaulle's time) by being as tiresome as possible to everyone else.[3]

On 12 December Churchill came to luncheon. We were alone, and although we discussed some large issues, he seemed unusually quiet.

[1] 1 December 1957.   [2] 6 December 1957.   [3] 4 December 1957.

His memory remains remarkably good, especially about his early days. He talked about his father, to whom he is very loyal.[1]

We had all been deeply distressed by the news given to the world on 25 November that Eisenhower had suffered what was called officially 'a cerebral occlusion'. This somewhat obscure phrase we took to mean a slight stroke. At first I feared that he would not be able to come to the NATO meeting. This would be a real disaster since so much depended on his personal leadership and prestige. I was accordingly delighted when I received a personal letter dated 4 December, which struck a more cheerful note.

Dear Harold,

My recovery from my sudden illness of ten days ago has apparently been steady and rapid. The earliest symptoms of my indisposition were sufficiently slight that the doctors did not class the difficulty as a 'stroke'. However, I did suffer a marked 'word confusion,' with also some loss of memory of words alone.

In all other respects, I was not aware of any physical impairment, and within twenty-four hours I began to improve. While I still speak a bit more slowly and will occasionally mispronounce a word, I am sure that the doctors are most optimistic of my complete recovery.

All this means, as of this moment, that I am planning to be at the NATO meeting in mid-month. It is possible that I will try to avoid any lengthy public addresses, but otherwise I see no reason for curtailing my normal activity. . . .

I believe that the first meeting is to be Monday noon. In order that I may have a reasonable period of rest after my transatlantic trip, I may plan on reaching Paris about Saturday noon. I might use this interval not only for some rest and additional briefing, but I should like also if possible, to take a short visit to SHAPE just to see how my old headquarters has prospered. It would be fun to see the place once more.

Looking forward to seeing you in Paris, and with my warm regard,

As ever
Ike.

[1] 12 December 1957.

I reached Paris early on 14 December and stayed at the Embassy. Selwyn Lloyd and Duncan Sandys came with me.

Foster Dulles came at 11.30 and stayed to luncheon. He seemed rather vague about this NATO meeting, and to be wondering now whether we had been wise in 'writing it up' so much. He seemed to think it could be just a sort of 'jamboree'. We would accept the American nuclear rockets, give three cheers for ourselves and one for Uncle Sam and then go home.[1]

I agreed that the meeting might fail to produce all the detailed results for which we had planned in Washington. There would be hesitations, doubts and weaknesses, affecting one country or another. This would probably be reflected in any communiqué that could be agreed. Yet if we thought of this as only the first stage in a long struggle we ought not to be depressed. Actually I felt that Dulles was chiefly worrying about Eisenhower and his health.

The President duly arrived on the afternoon of 14 December and 'had a great reception from the people of Paris. He stood up in the open car, waved his arms to the crowd and generally delighted them all with his manner.'[2] On the same evening

Gaillard came to a small dinner at the Embassy. He was much relaxed since I was in Paris a few weeks ago. We had a long and intimate talk about the Conference and agreed that it must be taken more seriously. We must have political, as well as military discussions. The French Prime Minister was much more forthcoming (and moderate) about Algeria than before. He feels more firmly established, having successfully got the *Loi Cadre* through the French Parliament. He hopes to get his Budget voted this week–he will make it a *question de confiance*. After that, he should be safe for some months, unless the foreign exchange problem becomes too difficult.[2]

On Sunday, 15 December, Adenauer called to see me and I had a good talk with him alone. Apart from the perpetual question of 'support costs' about which the Germans were always promising to do something without much actual result, the conversation was not difficult. But I thought the Chancellor in a rather confused mood.

[1] 14 December 1957.   [2] 15 December 1957.

On the general question of NATO, the Germans were reserved. They don't want the I.R.B.M.s in Western Germany. But they don't want to have to say this openly. They would like a decision on 'military' grounds, which in fact was against West Germany as a suitable site. I said I thought that if this decision really was sound, some price should be got for it. What would the Russians pay?

Although it struck me that the Chancellor had aged he still seemed in every sense the master of his Government and Germany. He seemed however very anxious about the future.

He would like to see West Germany definitely bound up with the West–through NATO or other means. That is why he was so keen on E.D.C., the European Army, the Six-Power Common Market plan, the Free Trade Area–in a word, everything which would range Germany in the ranks of the civilised countries. But he knows how his people (ever since Bismarck) hanker after Eastern dreams. When he is dead, he fears that his people will fall for the bait–unified but neutral Germany. Some will accept it from genuine patriotism–to get unification. Others will see the advantages of neutralism–and hope to play off one side against the other. Others again will just be weary of all these struggles. With all this in mind, Adenauer is not saying much–especially to his colleagues.[1]

The next day at 10 a.m. I called upon my old friend. I found the President

sitting in a large room, on the first floor of the American Embassy, and . . . very pleased to see me. We had nearly an hour's private talk–if a talk can be called so, when the large folding doors on the landing outside are wide open, and the police, G-men, Hagerty (Press) and others are lounging about this gallery. However, the President seemed to take no notice of them–so I decided to conform to this.[2]

He told me a good deal about his illness. He had been determined to come to Paris. If the doctors had forbidden him, he would

[1] 15 December 1957.   [2] 16 December 1957.

immediately have resigned his office. This, of course, explained the anxiety and pessimism which Dulles had shown.

The President next

> talked about France. He is anxious to help them, but they make it difficult by being so truculent. I said I thought they were more relaxed than a few weeks ago. We must not forget their great inherent strength and the important role they must play in NATO.[1]

The Conference officially opened at noon. The formal speeches were made by an old and valued friend, Joseph Bech of Luxembourg, and by Spaak, the Secretary-General. The President also made a formal speech of welcome. Then lunch—an important and lengthy item. The discussion in open session began at 3.30. Eisenhower spoke, without apparent difficulty, but handed the second half of his speech to Dulles to read out. Everyone made the usual prepared speeches. On the whole the tone was good, yet no one seemed to have any ideas as to how the Conference was to go on. Accordingly, after all my colleagues had spoken,

> I made a speech, like a wind-up in the House, from notes which I had made during the discussion, supplemented by some prepared passages. The effect of speaking in this way was electrifying. Everyone listened and the contrast between this method and the droning along of the prepared texts seemed to enchant them.[1]

It seemed that this was an unusual procedure in these gatherings.

> I ended by saying that instead of a peroration—and, I added, I have a lovely one all ready—I will make two practical suggestions. First, let an agenda be prepared—political and military—one for Tuesday; the other for Wednesday. Let it be discussed on the morning of each day by the Ministers of Foreign Affairs [and] in the afternoons or evenings by the Heads of Governments. Secondly, let us decide to stay till Thursday—when we can agree the communiqué.[1]

These proposals were unanimously agreed. The main practical decision which we wanted from this Conference was the agreement to the stationing of American rockets, I.R.B.M.s, in the different

[1] 16 December 1957.

Western countries of the alliance. At that time the inter-continental weapons (I.C.B.M.s) had not been perfected. It was therefore of great importance to arrange for the short-range protective nuclear weapons on which the deterrent depended to be distributed in advanced positions. To balance this decision and to make it more palatable to Parliaments it was proposed to make an offer to the Soviet Government of another conference of Foreign Ministers 'to break the deadlock'. This plan was brought forward for discussion on the afternoon of Tuesday, 17 December by the Heads of Governments, after it had been proposed at the Foreign Ministers' meeting in the morning. The Americans did not much like this plan, but finally agreed.

> I talked it over with Dulles behind the scenes and he behaved very reasonably. I told him that I thought this was necessary if we were to get acceptance of nuclear weapons by the NATO alliance.[1]

I reported this decision to Butler, adding that this view had been supported by the French, and the Canadians, and finally accepted by the Americans.

The next day, 18 December, the same procedure was followed. The Foreign Secretaries and the Ministers of Defence met in the morning and in the early afternoon. The Heads of Government were not summoned until 5 o'clock.

> But everything went through satisfactorily. The Scandinavians behaved quite well. They accepted that the alliance should be armed with rockets, but they don't want them in their own territories.
>
> The Germans were very non-committal. They don't take a great part. They are watching to see how things work out. The preparation of the communiqué will be a great problem. But we managed to get agreement to a small committee of officials to make a draft. Since Norman Brook is one of these, I feel fairly confident.[2]

Meanwhile it was necessary for me to make some reply to an appeal to abolish nuclear tests which had been openly made by Nehru at a Press conference. I was not very anxious, nor was the

---

[1] 17 December 1957.   [2] 18 December 1957.

Commonwealth Secretary, to indulge in diplomacy by Press conferences. But I thought it wise to send a soothing message to Delhi
reminding him that all this had been discussed at the Commonwealth Prime Ministers' Conference in the summer at which the
British position had been made quite clear. I also said how much I
looked forward to talking to him about all these great issues during
my forthcoming visit to India.

On 19 December the full plenary session took place at 11 a.m.,
and by 1.15 p.m. the communiqué had been agreed. We then broke
up in great relief rather like schoolboys at the end of term. Although
the communiqué was cast in the somewhat platitudinous language
which is necessary to get agreement, yet in fact it contained more
than the sceptics realised. I certainly felt satisfied that this first full
conference had lived up to the doctrine of 'inter-dependence'. At
any rate we could congratulate ourselves that without our practical
proposals the whole procedure would have broken down.

> We have got the Americans to take a more realistic view of the
> psychological and political situation in Europe. We have got the
> Scandinavians off their moral high-horse. There is *no* division
> between NATO countries who approve the rockets and those
> who disapprove—at least, on ethical grounds. Nor, I think, will
> there be much opposition to the sites which the High Command
> are likely, in practice, to select.[1]

On the broader issues

> We are beginning to get the Europeans out of the 'Maginot
> Line' complex and begin to look to their flanks. Suez—although
> a tactical defeat for us—is in this sense beginning to be vindicated
> strategically.[1]

Moreover both the Americans and the Europeans fully realised the
importance of the Middle East and the Near East, where new
dangers were beginning to threaten. There had also been a welcome
recognition that economic penetration and political subversion by
Russia constituted an even greater danger than military aggression.
Finally, and this was of supreme importance, the suspicions aroused
by the Washington meeting had been dispelled. Undoubtedly

[1] 19 December 1957.

beneath the somewhat uninspiring terms of the communiqué there was a real sense of renewed purpose and practical approach. I felt therefore satisfied. 'Altogether, the conference has been a success. The American and French Press (whom I saw yesterday) have been very generous to the British leadership.'[1]

On 20 December there was a debate in the House of Commons on the recent Ministerial meetings in Paris. The Foreign Secretary and I decided, with the agreement of the Chief Whip, that the debate should be held on a formal motion for adjournment. This had the advantage of not forcing the Opposition, who seemed to want to divide the House, to appear to vote against the unanimous decisions of the NATO partners. Although it would have been easy for us to frame a motion asking for approval of the decisions required by the communiqué, I did not want to force the Labour Party into an apparent position of hostility to the defence system upon which the life of Europe depended.

It was indeed fortunate that I had persuaded the Americans to agree to the inclusion in the communiqué of an offer of further direct discussions with the Soviet Government. Although the prospect of disarmament, so long as the Russians refused our two conditions, inspection and control and the reduction of conventional as well as unconventional forces, might seem rather remote, nevertheless public opinion in Britain was deeply concerned about the dangers, particularly of nuclear warfare. An agitation had already blown up against the placing of the missiles in Britain and this was skilfully exploited by all the defeatist elements. To the existing scare about the danger of the bombs in aeroplanes there was now added the fear that the missiles, wherever they might be placed, would be targets for Soviet attack. In addition there were a few of our extreme right-wing members who had not forgotten the events of 1956 and seemed unwilling to swallow the reconciliation between London and Washington. They even argued that the missile bases ought to be under our sole control.

[The] debate began at 11 a.m. with a speech by Foreign Secretary. He was not at the top of his form; but considering the

[1] 19 December 1957.

work he has done during recent days and the short time available for preparation, it was adequate. Anyway, he made no mistakes and took a tough line about Russia. Bevan followed—with a rambling speech—some good phrases—the chief purpose of which was to make as much mischief as possible while trying to unite the essentially divided opposition, some of whom are pro-Russian, others defeatist and others sound loyal supporters of NATO and the Bevin tradition. George Brown (who belongs to the last group) wound up as best he could. I did not feel that his heart was in it.[1]

The best speech was that made by Shinwell. It was a splendid contribution, honest, robust and well delivered. In concluding the debate I contented myself with making a few obvious but nevertheless salutary points. Bevan had been very critical of the Foreign Secretary for relying on Communist statements to give a picture of Communist ambitions. In reply I observed:

I think that it is a great mistake not to take some of these things that are said and written at least at some value. I remember that we made that mistake before. Mr. Hitler wrote a very long and a very dull book. Very few people read it, but it would have been a good deal better if we had read it, because what in that book he said that he intended to do, he, in fact, did.[2]

Certainly the situation had changed; but it had largely changed because of the organisation of NATO and the powerful armaments contributed by the United States. It was these that Russia feared.

I summed up our position as follows:

Our policy, therefore, is really two-fold, and I think in essence simple. It is a firm and powerful N.A.T.O., from the military point of view, but always ready to discuss and to negotiate on a practical basis to obtain practical results.[2]

In a single phrase it could be described as 'arm and parley'.

We had a bad division (39 majority) with some sick (unpaired) and some deliberate abstentions (Lord Hinchingbrooke and the rump of the Suez group). Altogether, it was rather dampening—after all our labours. We thought (in Paris) that we had done

[1] 20 December 1957.   [2] *Hansard*, 20 December 1957.

pretty well. But we had a cool reception at home! This often happens, but it's rather discouraging.[1]

During the next two days some of the Press worked themselves into an orgy of defeatism.

The *Daily Express* has joined the hunt, with the *Herald* and *Chronicle*. I am said to have lost touch with public opinion in England, because I have not already set out for Moscow to see Khrushchev. All this is pure Chamberlainism. It is raining umbrellas.[2]

There were plenty of other difficulties to which I had to turn my attention. At the same time I felt not altogether dissatisfied with the diplomatic efforts of this year. At the beginning of January, I had found our friendship with the United States destroyed, the European alliance almost shattered, and dismay and uncertainty in many parts of the Commonwealth. While great problems remained, the Commonwealth leaders seemed reassured; and the Paris meeting of NATO marked the reconstitution of the Western world and its determination to maintain its liberties and freedom by all the means in its power. I had established a good relationship with Chancellor Adenauer; and the French Government, although frequently changing and subjected to many pressures, were co-operative. Thus, in spite of some misunderstandings, the old alliance remained firm. With President Eisenhower I had instituted a close system of constant communication on a basis of absolute frankness. This was to last throughout his Presidency, and indeed till the end of his life.

[1] 20 December 1957.   [2] 21 December 1957.

CHAPTER XI

Money and Men

O N 4 January 1957, a few days before I became Prime Minister and without any foreknowledge of the destiny which awaited me, I circulated to the Cabinet a memorandum on the state of the economy at the beginning of the year. The opening paragraphs dealt with the immediate situation. Suez had been a tactical defeat; it was our task to ensure that like the retreats from Mons and Dunkirk it should prove the prelude to a strategic victory. We must therefore face the realities of our situation, and our policy at home and abroad must be based upon our actual resources. Our task was to increase these by stimulating investment and production and increasing exports. Overseas, we must deploy our efforts at the points where there was most to be gained. A broad analysis of the position then followed, in terms which have recently become familiar. We had been right to mobilise our reserves to meet the Suez crisis. But we could not use them to defend, month by month, a sterling rate which seemed threatened by doubts about our ability to manage our own finances. We must therefore rebuild the reserves. At the same time we had to meet new commitments, including the additional costs for oil development programmes in countries wishing to draw on sterling balances. We still had a role as world bankers. Our aim must therefore be to achieve a balance of payments surplus averaging from £300 to £350 million a year, instead of the £50 million, which was the most we could expect for 1956. In considering the forthcoming Budget it was, therefore, essential to avoid 'inflationary measures'; but the estimates showed an increasing deficit 'below the line' and a reduced surplus 'above the line'. To some extent the gap might be bridged by savings, which were still doing well as the result of the new measures. Taxation was already so high (or so it seemed to us at the time) that it was stifling enterprise and the urge to work and save. Some economies 'above the line' in expenditure must therefore be achieved however disagreeable the process might prove. So far as 'below the line' expenditure was concerned we must bear in mind the need to build up our basic economic strength and productivity, especially in view of the growing challenge from Europe, from the Commonwealth, rapidly becoming industrialised, from the Soviet bloc and from the United States. This required increasing investment, both public and private; but we must concentrate on the most productive projects and reduce or eschew altogether the least fruitful. An important aspect of this endeavour would be the extent to which the nationalised industries, which were devouring so much capital investment, could find some of their own finances from profits.

Before I left the Treasury, I circulated a paper suggesting where economies might be made. As usual there were hostile reactions from Ministers as regards their own departments, and from some who felt that the cuts in defence might well fall below the level on which any effective foreign policy was possible.

As the argument proceeded in subsequent discussions, all possible remedies were considered. Devaluation; deflation; a wage freeze, or at least a low norm for wage increases, and a concerted effort to increase productivity by moderating the overfull employment resulting from restrictive practices and by making the best use of machinery. Doubts began to be expressed as to the capacity of the Welfare State to be indefinitely financed on the existing system, based on flat-rate contributions and ever-increasing benefits. A deficit was emerging in the National Insurance Fund which it soon became necessary to meet by a separate and higher contribution in respect of the Health Service. Saving could also be made by increasing the charge for school meals and welfare milk.

Meanwhile the cost of the railway modernisation plan, already announced, as well as the demands of other nationalised industries, were beginning to rise alarmingly. Yet if we were to take too stiff an attitude to any wage increases, a series of strikes might result, dealing a serious blow at the British economy.

Fortunately the pressure on sterling soon began to ease; indeed Peter Thorneycroft, the new Chancellor of the Exchequer, was

M

able to recommend a reduction of the Bank Rate from $5\frac{1}{2}$ to 5 per cent.

> In spite of the oil cuts, industry is going on pretty well. Yesterday, because of market conditions and considerable funding by the Bank—£200m. in the last few weeks—we knocked $\frac{1}{2}$% off the Bank Rate.[1]

Meanwhile

> We have got the Cabinet to agree to about £15m. cuts in Civil Estimates and a new 'Health Stamp' to bring in (say) £34m. and give back some of the insurance character to the Health scheme.[1]

I was by now pretty confident that the new defence plans would eventually be approved by my colleagues. But to give an idea of the heavy pressure of manifold anxieties while trying to deal with financial and economic problems, I reproduce an extract from my diary of the same date.

> Every sort of other trouble boils up—Israel and Egypt and the absurd behaviour of Senator Cabot Lodge (apparently quite uncontrolled by the State Department) in U.N. Then there is the Canal. Then there is oil. . . . Altogether, a lot of problems. However, Ministers are working well and I am admirably served in the Private Office. One of the more agreeable aspects of my new job is the weekly audience. This is usually on Tuesday evenings. The Queen is not only very charming, but incredibly well informed. Less agreeable, are visits and letters from the Archbishop of Canterbury. I try to talk to him about religion. But he . . . reverts all the time to politics.[1]

On 19 February the Chancellor of the Exchequer informed the House of the Government economies, including the increases in the prices of welfare milk to 4*d*. a pint and of school meals from 10*d*. to 1*s*., as well as the increases in the National Health Service stamp from 10*d*. to 1*s*. 8*d*. The total saving would be £57$\frac{1}{2}$ million. The Opposition responded by demanding an immediate dissolution, but compromised by tabling a vote of censure. The Cabinet were in a determined mood, and in addition to other measures, decided, in

[1] 8 February 1957.

spite of the unpopularity which must ensue, to go ahead with the Rent Bill, providing for the decontrol of many houses in the following year and permitting substantial increases in controlled rents.

A serious engineering strike was now threatened. The Minister of Labour, Macleod, handled this with great skill.

> The ridiculous and . . . very widespread strike, starting at Briggs, extending to Fords, and perhaps reaching eventually to half the engineering industry seems to have been called off, at least temporarily, by his efforts. If this proves a firm settlement, it will redound much to the credit of the Government.[1]

By-elections continued to go against us, first North Lewisham and then Wednesbury. In the first we lost a Conservative seat and in the second the Labour majority was greatly increased. The Parliamentary Party, however, was reasonably steady and when the vote of censure came in the middle of March, it was easily repelled. Boyd-Carpenter replied to the debate in an admirable speech. Even the *Economist* could scarce forbear to cheer. I found Thorneycroft an admirable partner, full of resolve and contrivance. Even the usual disagreement of the Farm Price Review, involving long meetings between the Ministers concerned, proved capable of compromise.

> I had made up my mind to go for the 'agreed' settlement, in spite of the embarrassment about milk (which is technically wrong). But, really, we have so much trouble coming to us that we must try to have some friends and preserve the firm agricultural base of the party, in the House and the country. Actually, £14m. (with this almost derisory ¼d. on milk) will be thought a tough, not a weak settlement. It would not be understood if we had failed to get agreement for so small a sum as £1m.[2]

The Chancellor of the Exchequer proved throughout firm but understanding.

> I think he really felt that it was the right decision from the wider political point of view. But it helped him, as Chancellor, to have the Cabinet take the decision collectively and after three full discussions.[2]

[1] 25 February 1957.   [2] 14 March 1957.

The industrial situation in this month of March was indeed gloomy. On 5 March the shipbuilding employers announced that they would not raise wages, and a strike both in this industry and in engineering seemed inevitable. The railways now joined in, and as I was about to depart to Bermuda, it was an anxious period.

There seems little hope that the shipyard unions will accept the offer of arbitration. They are to go to the Ministry of Labour this morning. But it is clear that it is a 'war of nerves'. The unions feel sure that H.M.G. will bring a last-minute pressure on the employers, as they have so often done before. The truth is that we are now paying the price for the Churchill–Monckton régime–industrial appeasement, with continual inflation.[1]

The power stations were likely to be included, and something like a General Strike might easily develop. On the afternoon of 15 March I went through all the emergency plans so as to be prepared for the worst.

The emergency organisation is working well; the regional organisation is being re-activated; we have quite enough troops (soldiers, airmen and sailors) without bringing back any from Germany. But it will be a fierce struggle.[1]

The shipbuilding strike began on 15 March. On the 19th, before leaving to meet the President, I had a private discussion with some leading employers, of whom Sir Colin Anderson of the British Employers Federation was the most helpful. It was generally agreed that we should try to settle the railways at any reasonable figure, 4 or 5 per cent. Sir Brian Robertson was assured that

he would *not* be regarded as having sold the pass by private industry if he did this. On the contrary, it was essential to get this out of the way as soon as possible.[2]

On the same day the engineering unions announced their strike, and all through the Bermuda meeting, as already described, a stream of telegrams flowed between Butler and me. Finally the railwaymen were settled at 5 per cent, and by 2 April the ship-building and engineering strikes were called off. 'This is very good. Another hurdle surmounted–and no concessions.'[3]

[1] 15 March 1957.   [2] 19 March 1957.   [3] 2 April 1957.

These complicated manœuvres were for me a novel and harassing experience. Moreover the industrial situation was still worrying.

> Although the men have gone back to work pretty well, there is an ugly feeling in the industrial world. This is political, and inflamed by the Communists and left-wingers.[1]

I held long discussions with Macleod as to how this might be overcome. I did not feel much hope that we could persuade the T.U.C. to urge the postponement of wage-claims or to agree to compulsory arbitration. As I wrote to Macleod there seemed

> more hope of their co-operation in the campaign for greater productivity; and the better productivity is, the less objectionable are the wage claims.
>
> There is another line of action which would be protective and constructive at the same time. This would be to renew our campaign for a new industrial charter, including the right of the workers to be given a month's notice before their employment can be terminated.

If many of these questions are still the urgent issues of the day, on others real progress has been made.

By the time that Thorneycroft introduced his first Budget, the situation was definitely improving, and, with the full approval of his advisers at the Treasury, he was able to put forward an agreeable and even encouraging set of proposals amounting to a reduction of taxation by £100 million or £140 million in a full year. Even so the current surplus would be substantially increased. The extra 1s. per gallon petrol tax, imposed in the previous November, was removed. It had served its purpose by the restriction of petrol during the Middle Eastern crisis. I had argued strongly that the time had come to make some relief in surtax. When in 1920 this tax had been extended to include incomes of £2,000 that figure amounted to a substantial income or salary. But by 1957 its value had been more than halved. The Chancellor of the Exchequer was now able to make some alleviation. At the same time the income tax allowances were increased for children, and higher exemption rates were introduced for old people. There was a cut in purchase tax on a

[1] 4 April 1957.

number of articles entering into daily household use. Investment allowances on new ships were raised from 20 per cent to 40 per cent. Finally, there was an important tax concession for companies operating abroad. This had been recommended by the Royal Commission on Income Tax, and in the previous year I had promised that it would be implemented as soon as practicable. Some subsequent critics objected then and since that this concession would result in additional strain on the balance of payments. This objection, although superficially persuasive, misses the real point. The greater the investment abroad and the greater the success of companies operating overseas, the greater in the long run becomes the strength of our island economy.

On the day before the Budget we had the usual Budget Cabinet.

The Chancellor of the Exchequer explained the financial and monetary position very clearly and then expanded his proposals. Ministers were very pleased. It will be fascinating to see what the Press, the House, the Party and the public will say. The Opposition will naturally attack the surtax reductions violently.[1]

On the next day he opened the Budget to a crowded House.

It was an admirable speech—well constructed and well delivered. We have kept pretty well to the plan. Apart from minor changes in Entertainment Tax (living theatre and sport freed; £6m. relief to cinemas, balanced by £1 [from £3 to £4] on T.V. licences) the 'give-away' is £100m., divided in 4 equal parts—£25m. for overseas trading companies, £25m. for surtax relief, £25m. for children's allowances, £25m. for Purchase Tax cuts. The Opposition seemed rather dazed; our chaps were very pleased.[2]

The Budget had a good Press on the whole, although naturally the surtax concessions were attacked by some of the papers. This of course soon became the line of the Opposition in Parliament, in which Harold Wilson, in a brilliant speech, argued that the concessions to the owners of big incomes were not necessary. Battles, he said, were not won by generals. The analogy was not perhaps very happy and was easily answered. On the morning after the Budget

[1] 8 April 1957.   [2] 9 April 1957.

I received a visit from Sir William Haley, editor of *The Times*, 'who seemed to approve of the Government but nevertheless lectures us daily in the best grandmotherly style'.[1]

Unfortunately this relatively favourable economic atmosphere was soon to be clouded over, and in the last days of May, I received a minute from the Chancellor of the Exchequer, expressing alarm at what seemed a dangerous situation. I sent the following reply:

> When you say that our liabilities are £4,000 million and our assets are £830 million, this deals of course with the external position. In other words, as bankers we owe our customers four times the working capital of the bank. I have always wondered whether the bank business was worth while, but nobody has ever found a way of stopping it. If we wound it up we would only pay five shillings in the pound.
>
> One of the main reasons why people get out of gilt-edged is the fall in the value of money and the attraction of gambling in equities. This has affected even Archbishops: buying equities to the ecclesiastical mind has all the fascination of gambling without its moral guilt.
>
> But there is another reason and that is the perpetual feeling about Consols and the sense that those who bought irredeemable stock have been swindled. I am sure this has done a great injury to our credit. It might even be worth while fixing a redeemable date, however far ahead, for the present irredeemable securities.
>
> Of course we are spending too much and we must go on with the credit squeeze. But I think we must also be selective.

I then went through all the various suggestions, some of which were adopted.

In the course of the summer there was a growing sense of anxiety. The big drop in the Conservative majority in the Hornsey by-election at the end of May, coupled with the new Rent Act, added to the political pressures.

> The Press yesterday and today has been very bad. The recent by-elections have shaken them. Lord Beaverbrook's *Daily Express* has a leading article attacking me personally (for the first time). The *Sunday Times* attacks the Party machine. It's very

[1] 10 April 1957.

queer what bad nerves the English people have got in this politico-journalistic world.[1]

Throughout the month of July the Press and other commentators added their pressure for action, but as usual often struck a somewhat hysterical note. *The Times* in particular demanded that it should be made 'possible for the monetary system to support higher wages' and called upon the Government to take action accordingly. Even Lord Beaverbrook, who came to lunch with me alone on 12 July, seemed to be in an unusually deflationary mood. As always he was personally helpful and friendly, but most of our conversation was confined to reminiscences of the past.

July is always a bad Parliamentary month, and if, as so often happens, there are financial difficulties at the same time the Government finds itself more than usually harassed.

> On the whole, the House of Commons situation is *not* as good as a few weeks ago. . . . The Party in the country is *not* in a good mood. But I think we shall get through to the end of the session without disaster. If we *can* do that, it's more than I thought possible six months ago.[2]

The increase of salaries to M.P.s and Junior Ministers did nothing to dispel the growing criticisms. Even the increase in the salary of the Leader of the Opposition from £2,500 a year to £3,750 caused no satisfaction outside a tiny circle.

On 20 July I had to make a speech at Bedford to a large crowd in a football ground. This was well reported in the Sunday Press and helped to steady things. My chief purpose was to warn the people of the dangers of inflation, however prosperous things might appear at the moment. It was here that I first used, without exciting any particular comment, a phrase which afterwards became notorious.

> Let's be frank about it; most of our people have never had it so good. Go around the country, go to the industrial towns, go to the farms, and you will see a state of prosperity such as we have never had in my lifetime—nor indeed ever in the history of this country. What is beginning to worry some of us is 'Is it too good to be true?' or perhaps I should say 'Is it too good to last?' For,

[1] 2 June 1957.   [2] 19 July 1957.

amidst all this prosperity, there is one problem that has troubled us—in one way or another—ever since the war. It's the problem of rising prices. Our constant concern today is—can prices be steadied while at the same time we maintain full employment in an expanding economy? Can we control inflation? This is the problem of our time.

At this time the phrase 'we have never had it so good' was not misrepresented, misquoted and taken out of its context, as proved its fate in subsequent years. The speech at Bedford contained a further warning.

The great mass of the country has for the time being, at any rate, been able to contract out of the effects of rising prices. But they will not be able to contract out for ever, if inflation prices us out of world markets. For, if that happens, we will be back in the old nightmare of unemployment. The older ones among you will know what this meant. I hope the younger ones will never have to learn it. What folly to risk throwing away all that we have gained.

I pointed out finally that this problem of full employment and inflation was a constant anxiety and not a sudden crisis nor was it peculiar to this country. It seemed to me that it must be dealt with by practical steps in a practical way and not by an extreme dogmatic approach.

Like everything else in this world, it is a matter of balance—the middle way. The first lesson I had about this was as a child when I read *Alice in Wonderland*. I did not know then that it was about inflation, but it shows the point.

'One side will make you grow taller,' said the caterpillar, 'and the other side will make you grow shorter.' 'One side of what? The other side of what?' asked Alice. 'Of the mushroom,' said the caterpillar.

And there you have it. If you have too much deflation, you will starve yourself. If you feed yourself up on inflation beyond what your system will stand, you will suffer from the effects of over-growth.

Although by nature and temperament an expansionist, I could not resist the argument that this was a moment for at least a temporary pause in the general advance. Some of my colleagues accused me of levity by using this simple illustration, but many people understood the point. At any rate I could not accept the Socialist view, now being confidently put forward, that after mismanaging the country for six years they should be given another chance by peddling the old prescription.

I once heard of a young man who sat for his matriculation exam, and failed. He sat twenty times, and every year he failed. But was he discouraged? Not a bit of it. He set up in business as a crammer, and advertised: 'Coaching for the Matric—Twenty Years' Experience.' And I believe he did very well. Afterwards he set up as a Socialist leader.

However great our anxieties, I was determined at this moment to adopt, if I did not altogether feel, an appearance of confidence and even of jauntiness.

The next week there was a debate in the House of Commons on inflation. The Government had recently put forward a plan for an independent Council on Prices, Productivity and Incomes, but it had made little appeal to the trade union leaders. The Chancellor of the Exchequer made it clear during the debate that, despite all discouragements, the Government intended to go ahead with its plan. The members of the Council, 'The Three Wise Men', whose appointment was announced later, were Lord Cohen, Sir Harold Howitt and Sir Dennis Robertson—a judge, an accountant and an economist. This was the forerunner of similar attempts to obtain what one might call 'restraint without tears'. We hoped to obtain, and largely succeeded in achieving, our objectives by willing assent without recourse to statutory and compulsory powers.

About this time a bus strike began and ended with only a modest award from the appropriate tribunal. The Covent Garden porters went out on strike without any marked effect and returned to work a month later without winning any advantage.

The Covent Garden strike is likely to be over. [Frank] Cousins has had a rough ride, but seems to have got a small majority for going back. The 'terms' represent a complete defeat for the strikers.[1]

[1] 15 August 1957.

Yet all through July and August the long discussions continued in Government circles as the pressure on the pound increased and the industrial wage-demands showed little sign of relaxation. At this point I asked the officials to consider what was the true economic cost of industrial dispute, and circulated a memorandum to my colleagues expressing the view that apart from certain key positions such as electric power stations, mining, railways and docks, the granting of higher wages at his moment was more damaging to the economy than stoppages. The investigation was prolonged and carried on by officials of many departments. On 30 July I summarised the conclusions to my colleagues as follows:

> We should try to correct the view which has recently gained ground among the public and the Press that it is the Government's duty in the interests of the national economy to prevent strikes at almost any cost. Obviously the Government's attitude to a strike must depend on the circumstances in each particular case and cannot be decided as a matter of general principle in advance. But it seems to me that we should emphasise the economic damage of cost inflation rather than the economic damage of stoppages of production.

Amid all these distractions I was able to give one little piece of comfort to Thorneycroft, although perhaps in rather a cynical mood. The free distribution of orange juice to children of all ages invariably appeared among the list of possible 'cuts' presented to successive Cabinets in the search for economies. Plagued and harassed by continual attacks upon the nuclear tests and the effect of fall-out upon children all over the world, I was delighted to see in a medical journal an unexpected but apparently authoritative view that orange juice could present grave dangers to health. I therefore sent the Chancellor of the Exchequer the following minute:

> You will remember that we argued for days and even weeks about orange juice. I see now that the doctors say that it has a most deleterious effect on the children, almost worse than strontium 90. No doubt you will take full advantage of this.

By the end of August the pressure on the pound was increasing and expected to continue. A run on the gold reserves began on almost conventional lines. Although this was attributed by some observers to 'a bout of speculation', the underlying cause was the probable devaluation of the French franc and the strong rumours of a revaluation of the German mark. (Economic history certainly repeats itself.) Funds began to move rapidly out of London, and all the usual phenomena with which we are now familiar ensued. But at the worst moment the total loss did not amount to as much as £200 million. I was not too much concerned with this aspect of the question. After all, in recent months gold and dollar reserves had been rising, and the exports remained buoyant. What worried me was the apparent inability of production to rise at the expected rate. Certainly the purchasing power of the community because of wage-increases had begun to increase beyond the rate which production could support; prices therefore had inevitably risen. Yet I did not feel that we ought to panic.

> The collapse of the franc and the tremendous rise in the mark has meant a very bad month for us on the exchanges–the worst since Suez. But the actual balance of payments position is good and so is the trade balance. So we must hold on.[1]

Corrective action, if timely, could be relatively slight. Of course, if delayed until too late, more drastic cures would prove ineffective. I was therefore quite willing to agree to some of the remedies which were proposed after much careful discussion.

The diagnosis of the situation was clear. The public must learn to appreciate the connection between rises in prices and rises in wages, if these were unaccompanied by genuine increases in productivity, but the degree of direct control which the Government could exercise was much smaller than most people realised. At a time of rising profits and general upward movement in the private sector, employers competing for scarce labour (especially skilled labour) could hardly be deterred from raising wage-rates. In the public sector, many wages and salaries were fixed by procedures of arbitration over which neither the government nor the employers had any direct control. The government could, and did, tell public employers, nationalised industries and private industry,

[1] 4 September 1957.

formally and informally, that wage-increases unrelated to increases in production were damaging to the economy.

At the Trades Union Congress early in September the delegates carried by acclamation a motion rejecting wage-restraint in any form. The motion was put forward in a speech by Cousins, who declared war on everything and everybody. It was interesting, however, that the General Council gave no advice on this matter and offered no collective opinion. *Plus ça change* . . .

It was useless to have a head-on confrontation with the unions if an inflationary situation was at the same time creating an ever-increasing demand for labour. Demand must be reduced by reducing the money available. Money and credit must be controlled through the banks, either by the method of rationing or by direct control of advances. At the same time we must somehow reduce ordinary Government expenditure, 'above the line', by a reasonable amount.

Through the first weeks of September the argument went backwards and forwards between all the various authorities concerned. Encouraged by my old friend, Roy Harrod, I still resisted the idea of deflation as a permanent or even prolonged policy. Indeed Harrod argued that the economy needed in many respects to be 'bucked up' rather than 'damped down', so that men would work overtime and production rise. But the short-term problem had to be faced.

By the third week in September Ministers were ready to reach a conclusion as to the immediate steps to be taken. Both the Chancellor of the Exchequer and I had gained special help from the wise counsel of my old and dear friend, Lord Mills, who combined the natural desire for expansion and development of a man who had spent all his life in industry, with some of the caution drawn from experience. September was obviously going to be a bad month on the exchanges, perhaps worse than August. Accordingly

The Treasury wanted to relate [our plan] primarily to the attack on the £. I have resisted this stoutly—and successfully. What the British people are waiting for is the answer to the $64,000 question—how to stop rising prices and fall in value of money. They will (perhaps) accept measures to deal with these problems. But they regard our exchange crisis (which they do *not* understand) as some kind of a swindle organised by foreigners.[1]

After much discussion informal and formal, inside and out, the broad lines of the Chancellor of the Exchequer's proposed statement were finally approved. These included proposals which by a curious by-path were to lead to new troubles. 'The Bank want to raise Bank Rate by 2%—a thing practically without precedent (5%–7%). After much argument, this was left for me and Chancellor to settle.[1] We met on the next morning. I was very unhappy about the rise in the Bank Rate, having argued strongly against this in a minute only a few weeks before.

> If we reduce the volume of money by direct controls (for that is what the plan is), there is no need to use indirect controls. It would be foolish to combine the old system with the new. When I was Chancellor of the Exchequer I was persuaded to use the orthodox weapon, the Bank Rate. But that was at a time when we did *not* control—in any direct way—the volume either of public or private expenditure on capital account. If we are using the measure of quantitive control, what is the purpose of a high Bank Rate? None whatever. So far from raising it, it should be reduced, and thereby you gain in three ways. You gain on the exchanges, you gain on the Budget and you gain politically.

However, after much discussion, I yielded to the pressure brought upon me. Peter Thorneycroft was convinced, as were all his advisers, that a spectacular rise in the Bank Rate was the only way to deal with the run on the reserves. I argued that this situation was already better and was not really the main issue. It was the internal economy that mattered, and this could not be cured by attracting hot money through a competitive Bank Rate. If an internal squeeze was necessary, this could be done better by selective control through the banks.

I deeply regret that I did not stick to my point. But I reflected that the Chancellor of the Exchequer was carrying the burden and must be allowed, at any rate for the present, to play the hand as he and his advisers demanded. Nevertheless I stored up this incident

[1] 17 September 1957.

in my mind and was determined not to yield indefinitely to pressure. The financial measures were formally announced on 19 September. In addition to the exceptional rise in the Bank Rate, which was justified because of the 'heavy speculative pressure against sterling', public investment and bank advances were both to be held down and the 'credit squeeze' intensified. A few days later it was announced that $550 million had been lost to the reserves. On 20 September I noted:

> Naturally all stocks and shares fell rapidly, from the best 'blue chips' to gilt-edged. The Chancellor gave a short T.V. message. This morning, so well was the secret kept that the Press seemed dazed. On the whole, the serious papers give full support. *Daily Telegraph* excellent; *Times* quite good; *Yorkshire Post*, very good. What is interesting is that the *Daily Mirror* has no reference at all to the whole subject. The Opposition will, I think be cautious. Since they aspire to office (and no doubt feel confident about the next election) they will try to be 'statesmanlike'.[1]

My confidence was justified since Harold Wilson issued a statement supporting the increase in Bank Rate as a short-term measure designed to deal with speculative movements, and expressing the hope that it would prove successful. Naturally he added his anxiety lest there should be any general cut-back in the level of production and employment. In this situation there was once more wide discussion, even among ourselves as well as among our supporters, of alternative courses which we might have pursued. Should we have devalued? Should we have allowed sterling to float? All this was discussed at the time, and is still being discussed, sometimes with, and often without, much knowledge. However, we had taken our decision. It was therefore vital that Ministers and all those who could influence should stand upon it. Accordingly I issued the following instruction to Sir Norman Brook:

> I would like the following Minute distributed to the Cabinet:
> To all Ministers, in or outside the Cabinet.
> 1. The Government have taken their stand to defend the pound, and the measures which we have adopted have received generous approval, both at home and overseas.

[1] 20 September 1957.

2. It is of vital importance that no doubts should be thrown upon our determination.

3. Whatever the theoretical arguments for or against a particular course at a particular time, we as a Government have now nailed our colours to the mast. I trust, therefore, that we shall not show any wavering in our own ranks, or allow idle or foolish talk among those whom we have the power to influence, whether officials or unofficials.

4. It is of course an attractive intellectual exercise to discuss alternative policies; but the moment is certainly not opportune.

On 26 September I received an encouraging message from Thorneycroft, who was in Washington. He reported there was solid support for sterling, but it was important that rumours of devaluation, or any other unorthodox approach, should be scotched. At the same time we must not allow exaggerated accounts of our decisions to be circulated. Some people were speaking as if investment in the public sector had been altogether halted. In fact it would run at the level of about £1,500 million a year this year and next.

Meanwhile Gaitskell, as Leader of the Opposition, had written to me asking for an early recall of Parliament to discuss the financial and economic position. I did not feel that this was necessary and composed a letter refusing an emergency meeting. In my answer I said that I thought our discussions would be more fruitful if they took place after the situation had had an opportunity of developing. I also 'reminded him gently that [a meeting of Parliament] was, of course, necessary in 1931, when the £ was devalued!'[1] The Press accepted my decision. The situation seemed not unfavourable.

Although the public opinion polls continued to go against us, and support seemed to be drifting away, there was an undercurrent of firmness. Since we had taken our position in defence of sterling, public opinion might be expected to rally in due course, if the policy proved successful. The Chancellor of the Duchy of Lancaster, Charles Hill, was in charge of information and carried out his task excellently. I sent him the following message on 30 September:

I think one method of rallying opinion would be to get people interested in the battle for the defence of sterling. This has both

[1] 24 September 1957.

a moral side and a practical side; a moral side because one should not default upon one's debts, and a practical side because to default would bring us ruin and unemployment. No doubt on the Party aspect you could consult with Lord Hailsham and others how this might best be put across. I am wondering whether it would not be legitimate to get a certain amount of [publicity] through the Central Office of Information to get a purely objective picture of what defence of the pound means. The Opposition could hardly object to this because they themselves say that the pound ought to be maintained at its present value. Will you think over this.

At the Conservative Party Conference which followed at Brighton ten days later I devoted the greater part of my speech to defence and foreign affairs, leaving my colleagues to explain and support the recent economic policy. I did, however, use words which seemed to me to summarise our purpose.

At home we have reached, so far as the mass of people are concerned, the highest standard of living in our history.

I see that Mr. Bevan called the people 'an embittered and frustrated industrial mass' ...

Has he never seen any of those six million T.V. aerials which have gone up since 1951? Has he never run across any of the extra two million cars and motor-bikes?

Does his view not embrace any of those houses he didn't build but we did?

Let us be frank. The wage-earner and the businessman find wages and profits go far above prices.

It is the pensioner, the retired man, the people on fixed or nearly fixed incomes, who have borne the burden ...

We have a clear duty to those sections of our people who have not shared in this general prosperity and that duty we intend to discharge.

When the Cabinet met on 14 October, Thorneycroft told me that, although in the previous two months the gold and dollar reserves had fallen to a figure of £650 million, that is two-thirds of the level at the end of 1954, nevertheless the pound was now beginning to stabilise. We were beginning to take in money, and foreign opinion seemed to be satisfied as to the firmness of our decision to defend sterling. The Commonwealth Finance Ministers were themselves adopting a more helpful and realistic point of view in their attitude towards sterling. Fortunately the so-called Kuwait gap—a loop-hole which had cost the reserves very large sums—had now been effectively closed. Most of us felt that the management of our economy was in the long run more important than the sudden if alarming fluctuations in the reserves due to technical reasons, such as the weakness of the franc or the strength of the mark; conditions which might, if pursued too long, threaten the whole concept of fixed exchanges which had dominated world economy since the war. So long as we were sure that we had some hold upon the inflationary situation at home, surely the reserves were there to be used.

One of our main difficulties, much discussed, was how we were to deal with wage-demands in the nationalised industries or in the public service. In opening a debate on the economic situation at the end of October, Thorneycroft told the House that he had informed the Transport Commission that the Government would not advance a bigger railway deficit in 1958 than that of 1957. This should be in the minds of all those who had to deal with wages, including arbitrations. Although attacked as a direct violation of established custom, this declaration, combined with the refusal of the Minister of Health on 1 November to confirm a Whitley Council agreement to give a 3 per cent increase to the clerical staff of the service, was taken to prove that the Government was in earnest.

One sentence that the Chancellor of the Exchequer used in the House has lately been given a new significance.

> The value of the pound at home and the value of the pound abroad is, in the last resort, the same thing, and one cannot tamper with the one without affecting the other.[1]

This seems in sad contrast to a later and more progressive attitude to devaluation, when we were told by the highest authority, 'It does not mean, of course, that the pound here in Britain, in your pocket or purse or in your bank, has been devalued.' Nevertheless I

[1] *Hansard*, 29 October 1957.

continued to search for some means other than deflation, hankering
still after an alternative method. Alas, this search, although continued to the end of my Premiership—and beyond—has so far
proved fruitless. My anxieties and hopes were illustrated in a
minute to the Chancellor of the Exchequer sent on 28 October.

> Following my last minute to you about the economic situation,
> we discussed before what is to be the future of the sterling area.
> For the moment it hangs upon the slender thread of the high
> price of wool in Australia and a 7% Bank Rate in London. In
> the course of the next few months we must really search for an
> answer to some of these fundamental questions. It haunts us at
> every point and makes foreign policy, defence policy and home
> trade policy very difficult to carry on. It may be that we must
> resign ourselves to being permanently in this position, but I am
> bound to say that I view with much apprehension the last six
> months of this Government, when the money will be running out
> of this country at the same rate that the sands are running out of
> our power.

The chief difficulty at the time lay over the wage-increases.

> It is going to be very difficult to hold the balance between
> firmness and truculence. A great deal depends upon the tone
> which we adopt. If the trade union leaders think that there is any
> chance of weakening, they will press forward. On the other hand,
> they will seek to make a grievance of our intransigence.[1]

Although, when the House met, I had a great number of reports to
present, mainly arising from my recent visit to Washington and my
approaching visit to Paris, it was of course necessary for me to deal
with the economic situation, although leaving the main burden of
the debate to my colleagues. Mine was an adequate but not inspired
performance. Our general line was now becoming clear; in dealing
with our own employees we would accept arbitral awards, but the
money must be found within the particular vote or from the total
Government expenditure. In nationalised industries we would
require the boards to make savings to balance any wage-increases
resulting from arbitration. They must not increase wages of their

[1] 31 October 1957.

own volition. In private industry we must expect the monetary policy to exert a healthy check on unreasonable wage-demands. I tried to express our plans in a simple phrase in my speech on 5 November (incidentally a strange day on which to summon both Houses of Parliament to assemble in Westminster). Increases of wages must come from greater productivity, but not from increased supplies of money.

Meanwhile the situation was by no means discouraging.

The 'wages' problem is easing. Of course, we don't know what the unions will do. But it's clear that no one is really 'spoiling for a fight'.[1]

The next day

I lunched with 5,000 'directors' (the Institute of Directors) and addressed them afterwards in the Festival Hall. I spoke 'off the cuff' for 10–15 minutes. I think it was just what they wanted to hear—it certainly went very well. When 5,000 men who have had 30% chopped off their holdings (gilts and equities) and are paying 8% for money stand up and cheer, it's quite a sign of good feeling and understanding.[2]

By the middle of November it was clear that so far as sterling and the reserves were concerned we were over the main crisis.

The £ is responding to treatment, but at a very high price. The trade unions are being fairly cautious. But the transport claims are gathering—buses, railway clerks and the N.U.R., etc. The timing is as bad as possible for me—with my proposed visit to Australia in January.[3]

However, in November the leaders of the Engineering Union wisely accepted a refusal of their demand for a 40-hour week, while those of the Transport and General Workers Union showed similar restraint following rejection of the London busmen's claim for an extra 25s. a week. Equally the railway wage-claim was not pressed.

By the middle of December the civil estimates for the following year became available. The Cabinet had all along agreed that steps

[1] 6 November 1957.   [2] 7 November 1957.   [3] 11 November 1957.

must be taken to limit current Government expenditure. In the event supplementary estimates for £100 million would be needed at the beginning of 1958, while the civil estimates submitted for 1958-9 were £250 million higher than the original estimates for 1957-8, or £150 million higher than the out-turn. Although the reserves were now improving, and the growth in the gross national product seemed likely to be satisfactory, the Government could not afford to fail in its own sphere. I knew therefore, when I saw these figures, that it would not be easy to steer my colleagues to a unanimous decision.

I went to Paris about this time for the NATO meeting, which President Eisenhower attended, and reflected sadly upon our situation.

The mass of peasants and bourgeois classes have (under their beds) more gold than the gold and dollar reserves of the Bank of England and H.M.G. The French Government and Bank have nothing. The French 'rich' classes have two or three times this wealth in Switzerland, and are continuing to export capital. Here, it is the opposite. Such wealth as we have, the Bank and the Government get hold of—and dissipate! Which country, France or England, is intrinsically the stronger?[1]

Meanwhile the Chancellor of the Exchequer naturally argued that the civil estimates should be cut. He wished to hold them at the same level as 1957-8, involving a reduction of £153 million. The question now became urgent. How?

On the evening of Sunday, 22 December, I had a useful talk with the Chancellor of the Exchequer.

He is very worried about the civil estimates, which show a great rise for 1958-9. . . . Most of this is due to inescapable causes—the old (being pensioned), the young (at school) and the agricultural subsidies which rise automatically as world prices fall. (This, of course, is a gain to the balance of payments but a loss to the Exchequer.) The Chancellor wants some swingeing cuts in the Welfare State expenditure—more, I fear, than is feasible politically.[2]

[1] 15 December 1957.　　　　[2] 22 December 1957.

The next day a small group of Ministers held a prolonged discussion, lasting nearly four hours, partly about future policy of the party, but largely about immediate financial problems.

The Chancellor is feeling in a very determined (also resigning) mood. The rest are bitterly opposed to his main proposal, which is to abolish the children's allowance . . . (second child only). I summed up impartially, but laying most stress on the need to win the battle on the wages front. We must not be deflected from this.[1]

It was hoped that of the £153 million reduction in the civil estimates which the Chancellor of the Exchequer demanded as much as £40 million might be saved by normal Treasury scrutiny. On 1 January 1958 I circulated a minute to my colleagues supporting this first demand:

This would be a useful instalment towards the total saving which we must secure. I realise that economies of this order may involve forgoing the introduction of new projects or the improvement of existing services which, on merits, are desirable. They may also involve the reduction of expenditure on existing services. But in our present economic circumstances it is essential that the Government should be seen to be applying to its own expenditure the same disinflationary discipline as it is imposing on the rest of the economy.

Accordingly I asked all Ministers in charge of departments to co-operate to the full in this preliminary task. As to the larger sum, there was long and painful argument. Members of all Governments, of whatever party, must have experienced similar and equally agonising consultations. The search for economy in this or that item tends to produce a state of acute mental weariness and irritation as the same points are considered and reconsidered in the dreary run of continual—and repetitive—discussions. Sometimes these arguments lead to compromise; sometimes deadlock is reached. Yet a few weeks later, few of the Ministers concerned could probably recall what exactly had caused the threatened resignation of Ministers and even the dissolution of a Government. It was a difference about a comparatively trivial amount on the naval estimates

[1] 23 December 1957.

in 1894 that led to the end of Mr. Gladstone's Fourth Administration and his final retirement from political life. A similar crisis threatened to disrupt the great Liberal Government in 1909, again upon the naval estimates. Here the solution was quaint but effective:

> In the end a curious and characteristic solution was reached. The Admiralty had demanded six ships: the economists offered four: and we finally compromised on eight.[1]

I could not however hope to emulate such a miracle of accommodation, but could only go wearily on with the search for a solution.

As the discussions continued through 3, 4 and 5 January, it became apparent that the Chancellor of the Exchequer, whether consciously or not, was making a demand which could hardly be sustained by reason but required an act of faith. That any excess, of whatever size, over the previous year's expenditure, was to be regarded as unacceptable was a dogma, not a policy. Even an equal sum in money terms amounted to an actual reduction in real terms. But his colleagues did not press this last point with any vigour. They accepted honourably their obligation to give all the help they could to the Treasury at this time. As a result of prolonged discussions, economies amounting to £100 million were agreed. In addition Sandys agreed to find another £5 million on the defence vote. Innumerable combinations and permutations of further savings were discussed, but even after the most rigid search and the acceptance of some very unpleasant and awkward cuts there was still a gap of some £50 million. The Chancellor of the Exchequer held to his view with almost fanatical rigidity. The additional £50 million had to be saved by other measures, such as deferring rises in basic rates of Service pay, abolition of family allowances for the second child, and other cuts in social services. But the intention to improve Service pay had been announced in the Defence White Paper of 1957 and postponed under stress of that autumn's financial emergency. Further delay would be politically indefensible and would retard the prospects of reaching an adequate level of voluntary recruiting. To abolish the family allowance for the second child would mean withdrawal of more than half of the main post-war

[1] Winston S. Churchill, *The World Crisis—1911–1914* (London, 1923), p. 37.

social service which a Conservative government could claim to have created. If National Health Service contributions were raised, it would be the third time in twelve months. The charge for welfare milk had been increased from $1\frac{1}{2}d$. to $4d$. a pint on 1 April 1957. To impose full charges for school milk would be resented by the teachers. These were indeed formidable difficulties.

At these and other meetings I reminded my colleagues that the main issues were psychological. Sterling had regained much of the ground lost in 1957. The next step was to recreate confidence in the internal administration of the country by keeping Government expenditure within reasonable limits. This was a critical point in our term of office. In our first year, we had been more successful in restoring the British position than we might have hoped at the outset. If we could surmount this difficult period, further opportunities were in prospect.

Broadly, while I felt that the Chancellor was entitled to ask his colleagues to show that they were determined to support his policy as a whole, yet if deflation were enforced to the point at which it created a stagnant economy or provoked undue industrial unrest it would be self-defeating. Against this, throughout the discussions, Thorneycroft argued,

> that the expenditure for this year (including supplementaries) should *not* be exceeded 1958–9. Thus our policy would be complete and logical, in its three aspects. Capital investment and Bank advances are already to be held to 1957–8 levels. Government expenditure should be the same. This sounds very well in principle, but has considerable difficulties in practice.[1]

At the Friday Cabinet, which lasted four hours, little progress was made. Indeed I had some difficulty in preventing some of my colleagues bursting out in their indignation against what they felt was an over-rigid and even pedantic attitude shown by the Chancellor of the Exchequer. The meeting had been adjourned for a short interval, and after it was resumed I said that I thought we should pledge ourselves to achieve as nearly as possible the saving which the Chancellor wanted, but I doubted whether a precise arithmetical

[1] 6 January 1958.

equilibrium could be achieved. If we could reduce by £100 million, which I thought to be within our grasp, the residue could be no more than one per cent in the Exchequer's outlay. A figure of this order, largely attributable to factors over which the Government had no control, such as increases in the numbers of children to be educated in the schools or pensioners to be supported in their old age, surely could not be represented as any weakening in the Government's determination. But the Government would equally be condemned by their supporters and by world opinion if as a result of their inability to agree and their failure to resolve a minimal difference of opinion, they faltered and thus abandoned the great enterprise on which they had embarked a year before. On this note we adjourned on Friday night 'on the understanding that we would take up the work on Monday, after a small meeting of Ministers on Sunday evening'.[1]

On Saturday, after a good day's shooting at home, I returned to No. 10 to deliver a broadcast on foreign affairs and defence. Although this was well received, it seemed strange to speak on these large topics to a vast number of listeners while concealing the threatened disruption of the Government itself.

On Sunday 5 January,

> I saw the Chancellor at 10.30 a.m. and made an appeal to him—on personal and public grounds—not to threaten us any more but to tell the Cabinet that he would work along with his colleagues and accept the collective view. The defence estimates could be finalised (as was necessary) at once, and further discussions about the civil estimates could continue for at least another three weeks. This work could go on during my absence overseas and results agreed by telegram. He looked uncomfortable; said he had not finally made up his mind; but I got the impression that he had made up his mind to resign, unless he got his full demand.[1]

I then motored to Chartwell and lunched with Churchill.

> I told him what was going on. He was very indignant with Thorneycroft and promised his full support. He could hardly

[1] 6 January 1958.

believe in a resignation. (The parallel with Lord Randolph Churchill is curious !)[1]

The Cabinet met on the Sunday evening. The Chancellor repeated his demand. The £50 million to make up the full £153 million must be drawn from defence or other estimates or both.

> Duncan Sandys (by really remarkable efforts) has got the defence estimates *below* last year, and that to include £35m. of extra pay, allowances, etc., and £20m. of once-for-all compensation to officers, etc., compulsorily retired. He has now made further offer of £18m.[2]

But in view of the technical difficulties involved, it became clear that the only two effective or practical measures would be either another health stamp or a severe cut in children's allowances.

> But the new stamp (fixed by legislation in the autumn) only starts in February. And to abolish the second child allowance affects 3–3½ million families—amounts to a 10% wage-cut in low-paid homes—and seems hardly a wise start to the wage struggle which confronts us.[2]

Many Ministers felt doubtful as to whether Thorneycroft would press his resignation, although most agreed that he was being egged on by the Treasury Ministers, Nigel Birch and Enoch Powell.

The Cabinet met at 6.30 p.m., and the meeting, though less painful, was no more fruitful than before. Most Ministers took part in the discussion. I adjourned at 8.30 p.m. and asked the Cabinet to reassemble at 10.30 p.m. the same evening.

> Dorothy was with me at dinner (having come up from Birch Grove). We also had Butler, Macleod, and Heath (Chief Whip). We discussed the position—still confused as the Chancellor had left the door open. Sandys was very keen that if he went it should be clear that he went on 'family allowances', 'welfare milk', etc. Macleod thought he was obsessed and dominated by Powell. Butler was really shocked at the irresponsibility by which

---

[1] 6 January 1958. Lord Randolph Churchill resigned as Chancellor of the Exchequer in December 1886, being unable to agree to demands upon the public purse made by the Ministers for the Army and the Navy.
[2] 6 January 1958.

Cabinet was asked to make great changes of policy at a few days'
notice, without study or preparation. I still thought he would
retreat, if we could get him a few more economies to save his face
(I was proved wrong).[1]

At the adjourned meeting, which lasted about forty minutes, at
which of course the Chancellor of the Exchequer attended, I
summed up the situation, and the Cabinet quietly dispersed.

> Most thought that my statement (which I tried to make fair
> and balanced, as well as very flattering and generous to the
> Chancellor) would succeed in avoiding the crisis.[1]

Later that night, in thinking over the situation, it became clear to
me

> that the greater danger was the complete disintegration of the
> Cabinet—Treasury Ministers; Defence Ministers; Labour and
> Social Ministers—all might resign (for different reasons) and
> there would be no alternative to the resignation of the Govern-
> ment; a Labour administration; a dissolution; an election in
> which the Conservative Party would be in a hopeless and even
> ridiculous position, without policy or honour. This must at all
> costs be avoided.[1]

The next day, 6 January, proved eventful, if somewhat exhausting. I was due to leave for my Commonwealth tour on the following
morning. I had therefore to act quickly. The crisis now reached its
culmination point.

> As far as I can see, carefully planned by the Chancellor of the
> Exchequer and the Treasury Ministers. As far as I can judge,
> the Treasury officials have had no hand in it and have dis-
> approved of it.[1]

At 10.30 a.m., I was given a letter from the Chancellor of the
Exchequer offering his resignation. It was accompanied by letters
from Birch (Economic Secretary) and Enoch Powell (Financial
Secretary).

There was no covering note expressing personal regret. It was a formal and somewhat contemptuous document. It ran as follows:

> I write to ask you to accept my resignation from the office of Chancellor of the Exchequer. My reason can be shortly stated.
>
> I am not prepared to approve estimates for the Government's current expenditure next year at a total higher than the sum that will be spent this year.
>
> Your proposed departure from this country on the 7th January has made it essential that a decision of principle upon this matter be taken now. It is clear that in this proposal I do not have your support or that of a number of colleagues. In the circumstances, and since the level of Government expenditure is central to my responsibilities as Chancellor of the Exchequer, resignation is the only course open to me.
>
> In the sterling crisis of last summer restrictions were placed in money terms upon the level of public investment and of Bank advances. The Government itself must in my view accept the same measure of financial discipline as it seeks to impose on others.
>
> I recognise that in order to achieve my aim some combination of politically unpopular courses would have been necessary. I nevertheless regard the limitation of Government expenditure as a prerequisite to the stability of the pound, the stabilisation of prices and the prestige and standing of our country in the world.

The terms of this communication, unless firmly rebutted, were calculated to do serious injury to sterling, for the writer sought to give the impression that he alone in the Cabinet stood against inflation. I therefore thought it essential for the protection of our national interests not to content myself with a mere formal acknowledgement. Before the end of the day I had prepared and despatched a full reply with the purpose of correcting any false impression:

> I was sorry to receive your letter this morning offering your resignation as Chancellor of the Exchequer. I particularly regret that you should think it necessary to take this step when the difference between you and the rest of the Cabinet is such a narrow one.
>
> The policy upon which we are all resolutely determined is to check inflation and to maintain the stability of sterling. In this

context the limitation of Government expenditure is certainly of the greatest importance. But we must regard the policy as a whole.

We have two objectives, one to restrain the supply of money, the other to hold back pressure for more rewards, including wages and salaries. You say that the estimates for the next year must be the exact equivalent of the sum spent this year. The rigid application of this formula, to be carried out immediately and without regard to any other consideration, would do more harm than good. For, as became clear in our discussions, to apply it literally must involve cuts in vital services, including those especially affecting certain aspects of family life—and this without any regard to the effect upon the industrial front and on the task of those who have the responsibility of working for wage-restraint.

This is not a matter of popularity. We have never shrunk from unpopular measures. This is a matter of good judgement.

In view of the terms of your letter, I feel it necessary to put on record that throughout the twelve months in which this Government have been in office you have had the full support of the Cabinet in the financial and economic policies which we have worked out together.

When, only a few days ago, the estimates were put before us, the Cabinet decided to pursue by every possible means the policy of keeping Government expenditure substantially the same as last year. We were faced initially with estimates which, as they were first presented, were considerably higher. Many of these increases were unavoidable, partly because of the larger number of children at school, the expansion of secondary and university education; and partly because of the provision that has to be made for the increasing number of old people. Nevertheless, as a result of our work together, the Cabinet was able to reduce this excess to something less than one per cent of the total of current Government expenditure. Moreover, we agreed to review our policy during the coming year in order to provide a greater measure of control over expenditure in certain sectors on the civil side which can only be dealt with as a longer-term problem.

I therefore cannot accept that there is any difference of principle between the rest of the Cabinet and yourself. Resignation is always a difficult decision. It is, in my view, justified only on matters of principle. I must add that your resignation at the present time cannot help to sustain and may damage the interests which we have all been trying to preserve.

The economic and financial measures which we adopted during the past year are, I believe, beginning to bear fruit. The Government are united in their determination to pursue them resolutely to the end. I am therefore sorry that you have chosen this moment to leave us.

Nigel Birch, the Economic Secretary, and Enoch Powell, the Financial Secretary to the Treasury, also resigned their offices. In my formal replies I referred them to my full reply to their chief. In writing to Nigel Birch I added these words:

> I cannot accept the implication in your letter that the Cabinet could not accept the reductions in expenditure proposed because of their fear of the results of the electorate. This Government has already proved that they are not afraid of unpopularity.

Both these men, although nominally subordinate to the Chancellor of the Exchequer, were, in my view, largely responsible for leading him, by their powerful advice and influence, to this final step. Although I had great personal admiration for their gifts, I distrusted their judgement, since they seemed to have introduced into the study of financial and economic problems a degree of fanaticism which appeared to me inappropriate. If they did not actually welcome martyrdom, they did nothing to avoid it and seemed rather to seek and enjoy the crown.

When the Cabinet met at 11.00, I read out the Chancellor's letter and told my colleagues that I intended to make a full, and I hoped convincing, reply. The rest of the day, since Dorothy and I had to leave for our Commonwealth tour early the next morning, was somewhat hectic.

> After the Cabinet, I offered [the] post of Chancellor of the Exchequer to Heathcoat Amory, now Minister of Agriculture. He was rather hesitant, but accepted. By 6 p.m. (when I saw the Queen) I had got this post filled; also Hare to Minister of Agriculture (from War Office). Soames to W.O. Jack Simon to be F.S.T.—no E.S.T., but Maudling (now Paymaster-General) to help with Economic work of Treasury. This has only left a few

minor posts to be filled. We also had composed a reply to the letter which Thorneycroft wrote to me . . . as well as listening for an hour (3–4) to a deputation from T.U.C. about H-bombs. This remarkable feat was due to the way in which everybody helped me. Butler has been excellent throughout. The Chief Whip superb. Freddie Bishop works quickly and efficiently. And Sir Norman Brook is always a tower of strength. I took my list of new Ministers to the Queen for approval—also text of two letters. The Queen was very sympathetic.[1]

On returning from the Palace, Dorothy and I gave a sherry party for the Commonwealth High Commissioners and their wives. On 7 January,

> We started off from London Airport . . . as planned. I felt sure that this was the right course to follow. Almost the whole Cabinet came to see me off. This was intended, obviously, as a mark of respect and loyalty.[1]

In speaking to the B.B.C., T.V., Press, etc., I made a short and carefully prepared statement about the Commonwealth trip. In doing so I referred to 'some recent difficulties' in our affairs at home which had 'caused me a little anxiety'. However, 'I thought the best thing to do was to settle up these little local difficulties and then to turn to the wider vision of the Commonwealth.' I was conscious of seeming to minimise the crisis. Nevertheless, I was sustained by the conviction that we had nearly turned the corner. Sterling stood at the highest point in relation to the dollar since May 1956. The Exchequer returns for the first nine months of the financial year showed that, while Government spending had been only fractionally above the previous year, total revenue was coming in at a rapid rate. Industry, including the mining industry, seemed to be going ahead satisfactorily and prices reasonably stable. Indeed I was already beginning to wonder whether we were in danger of pushing the deflation too far and to meditate about the wisest method of relaxation when the time came.

A fortnight later, in the aeroplane from Singapore to New Zealand, I still felt optimistic.

[1] 7 January 1958.

Butler, Chief Whip and all the others seem to have kept things going very well. There is, of course, great confusion and perplexity in the Party. The Press has naturally exploited the sensation of the resignation to the full. Nevertheless, I have a feeling (from the reports) that the worst is over. The trouble is that ordinary people cannot understand how a responsible Minister could resign over so small an issue (as things go today).[1]

This estimate proved to be correct. Fortunately no lasting personal division remained. Before I surrendered my office as Prime Minister I was happy to include both Thorneycroft and Powell in the Administration.

Another cheering message also reached me. David Eccles, President of the Board of Trade, was away during the crisis. I kept him informed, and he immediately expressed his support. A few days later he added, 'You may like to know that your decision not to delay your departure greatly impressed the American bankers and held their confidence in sterling.'

All the same, it had been quite a wearying business, and I was not sorry to sink my cares, like other holidaymakers, in the pleasures of travel.

[1] 19 January 1958.

Thorneycroft (Chancellor of the Exchequer) speaking at the Conservative Party Conference, watched by Lady Dorothy Macmillan, Eccles and Powell (Financial Secretary to the Treasury), 10 October 1957

Three months later Thorneycroft resigned. 'Macleod thought he was obsessed and dominated by Powell' who had 'introduced into the study of financial and economic problems a degree of fanaticism which seemed to me inappropriate.'

Commonwealth Prime Ministers' Conference, 26 June 1957. Standing: De Silva (Minister of Justice, Ceylon), Macdonald (Minister of External Affairs, New Zealand), Louw (Minister of External Affairs, South Africa), Welensky (Rhodesia). Seated: Nkrumah (Ghana), Nehru (India), Diefenbaker (Canada), Macmillan, Menzies (Australia), Suhrawardy (Pakistan).

'I found little difficulty in establishing a genuine sense of harmony even among many views, some of which were naturally divergent.'

CHAPTER XII

Commonwealth Tour

ALTHOUGH I had attended in various capacities several conferences of Commonwealth Prime Ministers, that which met
from 26 June to 5 July 1957 was the first over which it was
my privilege to preside as Prime Minister of the United Kingdom.
It was admirably timed. The Middle Eastern troubles, culminating
in the events at the end of 1956, had undoubtedly presented the
Commonwealth with its first major crisis since the Second World
War. Moreover it came at a time when the old structure was under-
going rapid changes. The Dominions, founded and dominated by
British settlers, had long achieved their independence. To the
countries that had come to be known as the old Commonwealth—
Canada, Australia, New Zealand, South Africa—there had recently
been added as separate and independent nations, India, Pakistan
and Ceylon. Others both in Africa and Asia were soon to
reach a similar status. Indeed Ghana was admitted at this very
meeting.

The Middle Eastern conflict had therefore come upon the
Governments and peoples of the Commonwealth at a time of
transition. They had broadly shown gratifying support for, or at
least understanding of, the policy of the old country. Menzies, the
Prime Minister of Australia, had taken a leading part in the attempt
to induce Nasser to agree to some reasonable solution. Sir Sidney
Holland, who had preceded Holyoake as Prime Minister of New
Zealand, had been equally robust. Canada, through Lester Pearson,
Minister for External Affairs, had played an important and helpful role at the United Nations. The South African Government,
conscious of the importance of the Canal, had given all necessary
help. India and Pakistan had shown remarkable sympathy in spite
of their natural doubts. Neither Nehru nor Shahīd Suhrawardy,

N

whatever their views of the wisdom of the decisions taken by the British Government, had indulged in recriminations. Nevertheless, when the Conference met, I was not without some apprehension. At any rate, the interval of some six months had provided an opportunity for reflection.

Outside the formal discussions I was able to see most of the members of the Conference for private conversations. When I had to summarise the general discussions on foreign policy at the end of the morning session on 28 June I found little difficulty in establishing a genuine sense of harmony even among many views, some of which were naturally divergent. 'I took rather a robust line, to stiffen our real friends, and I think did so without offending India, although obviously Nehru did not [altogether] agree.'[1]

There were the usual luncheons and dinners and similar entertainments, culminating in the Queen's formal banquet. This, by her own happy suggestion, was held for the first time at Windsor. It was a splendid and moving opportunity for the Head of the Commonwealth to welcome its leaders. I was also fortunate in being able to have talks with many of the Prime Ministers over the two weekends both at Birch Grove House and at Chequers.

On 2 July

Dorothy and I gave a great dinner–60 people–on Tuesday. Churchill came, which really 'made' the evening. There was a reception afterwards. We live, in between the plenary sessions, in a perpetual series of luncheons, dinners, receptions–and private talks. The last are the most useful.[2]

At the final meeting on 5 July there was less difficulty over the communiqué than I had anticipated. There was certainly no desire to dwell upon past events. All the countries were thinking more about the problems and opportunities of the future.

The Conference has gone on all the week, morning and evening–and, on the whole, has gone well. The discussions have been frank and candid. There has been a good deal of disagreement–but a wide measure of agreement as well.[2]

[1] 28 June 1957.   [2] 4 July 1957.

Two new issues were introduced which were the source of much discussion. The British Ministers chiefly concerned set out in some detail our hopes of being able to organise a European Free Trade Area. In considering this novel and to some extent disturbing project, the Prime Ministers and Ministers proved 'sympathetic and sensible—though naturally vigilant'.[1] But perhaps the most dramatic intervention was the invitation of the new Canadian Prime Minister, Diefenbaker, to the Finance Ministers of the Commonwealth to meet in Ottawa in December 'in order to make arrangements for a Financial and Economic Conference of the Commonwealth'. Diefenbaker, who had just won an election by which his party had returned to office after many long years in the wilderness, was a newcomer to these meetings. Having arrived almost straight from the hustings he seemed

> still the victim of his election oratory. He is a fine man—sincere and determined; but I fear that he has formed a picture of what can and cannot be done with the Commonwealth today which is rather misleading.[2]

(Perhaps this had something to do with Lord Beaverbrook's influence.) Some doubts were expressed as to the danger of raising false hopes. Menzies put forward this view with his usual directness.

> An economic conference, if it were to be held at all, could only succeed if great and expert preparation preceded it. If it were written up to great importance and then failed, it would be a major disaster. (All this, of course, is true, but poor Mr. Diefenbaker looked first puzzled, then pained, then indignant.)[2]

Nevertheless, a compromise was reached without much difficulty.

> After some discussion a formula was agreed to say that 'The Prime Minister of Canada had invited the Commonwealth Finance Ministers to have their *normal* meeting (after the International Bank Meeting) this year in Ottawa'. Although this did not, of course, give Mr. Diefenbaker what he really wanted, he seemed much relieved and accepted the compromise. After it was all over he thanked me most warmly for my help.[2]

[1] 4 July 1957.   [2] 5 July 1957.

The final communiqué welcomed Ghana's representation 'as further practical evidence of the progress made by the United Kingdom in pursuit of her policy of encouraging constitutional development in dependent territories'. As regards international relations some differences of view had been expressed but there was 'a broad similarity of approach and purpose'. There was a reference to the need for strengthening the United Nations and an expression of 'grave concern at the tragic events in Hungary'. On economic questions, after a reference to the need for co-operation in the use of nuclear energy for civil purposes and the need for paying special attention to the impact of development programmes on domestic economies and on the sterling area, the Canadian Prime Minister's suggestion for a meeting of Commonwealth Finance Ministers at Ottawa in the autumn was accepted in accordance with the terms agreed.

Even the formal terms appropriate to these declarations proved to the world that any wounds caused by recent events in the Middle East had been satisfactorily healed. *The Times*, not usually a friendly critic, summed up the result on 6 July as follows:

> The Conference has been a personal success for Mr. Macmillan. The tributes rendered to him yesterday were undoubtedly sincere. The clouds of mistrust engendered in some quarters by Suez may have been dispersing of their own accord, but last week has blown them away even more swiftly.

After the dispersion of the members of the Conference, I reflected deeply over all that I had heard and learned. What was now to be the future of the Commonwealth? On the constitutional side it was clearly entering upon a new phase. The addition of India, Pakistan and Ceylon, had marked the end of the old all-white Commonwealth. It was now to be followed by the progressive dissolution of the Colonial Empire and by a rapid increase in the number of independent nations, great and small, which would, year by year, join as full members. This must not only change the character of the organisation as a whole, but alter the conditions and form of these Ministerial Conferences. The nations of the Indian sub-continent had already been followed by the addition of Ghana.

Indeed it was my first duty, when the Conference met, to welcome Dr. Kwame Nkrumah to our ranks as Ghana's first Prime Minister. Others were almost waiting in the wings. Sir Roy Welensky sat by courtesy as representing the recently established Federation of Rhodesia and Nyasaland. Whatever the future was destined to bring to those territories, I knew that from every part of the world there would be countries, large and small, ranging from the vast territories of Nigeria to the little island of Cyprus, which might soon be sending their Heads of Government to these gatherings. This development was an inescapable evolution. But it was also, in a sense, revolutionary. The old *Pax Britannica* which had for so many generations brought to about a quarter of the globe the inestimable advantage of order and good government, under which the social, political, and economic development of their peoples could be peacefully pursued, was now being replaced by a new and untried system. Although this recognition of the sovereignty of its members dated back into the period following the First World War,[1] yet so long as the Commonwealth was restricted to the peoples of British descent, the change seemed small. Now that independent countries were to arise throughout Asia, Africa and the Caribbean, we were embarking on a new and untried adventure from which a series of new and baffling difficulties would inevitably ensue. The old Commonwealth and Empire had been able to maintain a strong centripetal attraction, politically, economically and above all in defence. Now equally powerful centrifugal pressures would begin. Moreover, in the intoxicating atmosphere of independence it was doubtful how far we could hope to maintain the mystique which had held the old organisation together, under a common allegiance to the Crown. Although these developments, inherent in the policies pursued by successive British Governments, had moved at an accelerated pace from the end of the Second World War until the time when I assumed responsibility, the stream of gradual change was now to be augmented into a fast-flowing river, which might soon break its banks through its torrential force. Where in all this were we to find the unifying principle to make a reality of the Commonwealth in all the spheres of human endeavour? It was not

[1] *Winds of Change*, p. 112.

unnatural that I should brood over these dangers. Yet I felt inspired at least to try to guide these disparate forces into a common faith.

Before the Conference began, Nkrumah, the Prime Minister of Ghana, had called to see me. 'He was in a very merry mood and certainly has considerable charm.'[1] He showed a justifiable pride and even enthusiasm at being admitted as the first African to this unique assembly of statesmen. It was natural that he should be thinking mainly in terms of his own local problems and needs, although he was to prove by no means unwilling to take full part in all discussions on wider subjects.

The Prime Minister of Ceylon was unable to attend, but was represented by M. W. H. de Silva, an old and experienced Minister. Here certainly it was concentration upon his immediate difficulties that prevented the Head of the Government from appearing in person. De Silva explained to me the situation: 'His Prime Minister is engaged in trying to prevent the bitter controversy about the language question from reaching the point of civil war !'[2]

Similarly the tension between India and Pakistan was undisguised even at formal meetings. After the last session on 5 July, Nehru stayed to luncheon with me.

> He seemed more relaxed. He likes to talk alone and he speaks more freely and less circumspectly in this way. He pressed me again to come to India after Christmas.[3]

It was after this invitation and one equally urgent from Menzies to pay a visit to Australia that I began to consider seriously whether I could not undertake a tour of the Commonwealth in the New Year. At any rate, if I should succeed in hazarding an absence of five or six weeks amidst so many troubles at home, it would be the first time that any Prime Minister in office had embarked on such an adventure.

After luncheon Nehru and I sat in the garden at No. 10. It was a lovely summer day, with that perfect English weather which is all the more welcome because of its rarity. In the quiet walled garden, sitting in the shade of the holm oak and protected from the noise of traffic, we might have thought ourselves in a country parsonage or the restful precincts of a cathedral dignitary.

[1] 24 June 1957.   [2] 25 June 1957.   [3] 5 July 1957.

[We] were soon joined by Suhrawardy (Prime Minister Pakistan). Since these two men are on the worst of terms and *never* meet—in India or in London—this was rather a risk. But the talk—which lasted an hour—went off very well.[1]

Here at any rate there might emerge a function for the Commonwealth as a whole; a role which especially the old country might usefully play in the capital city, outside the fevered corridors of the United Nations. Here in these gatherings might be an opportunity, no longer for authority, but for mediation.

Two great sources of dispute divided the successor states to the old Indian Empire. The first was the bitter struggle over Kashmir. Equally urgent was the solution of the controversy concerning the resources of the great Indus River. This meeting might perhaps prove a start, and, whether successful or not, seemed to mark a fruitful activity by which the underlying respect and even affection for Britain might be put to good use.

> I have just a hope that they may reach some settlement about the Indus Waters and both agree to accept the International Bank's proposal. If they could only get this question cleared up, it would make the approach to Kashmir much easier.[1]

Agreement on the first of these was at last reached by the signing of the Indus Water Treaty in September 1960 and its ratification early in the following year. On the second a long and bitter dispute continued to resist all methods of mediation from whatever source, and was later destined to lead to the terrible catastrophe of two Commonwealth countries becoming engaged in open conflict. Although the war was preceded, according to the tradition of civilised nations, with the most solemn protestations that each party was sincerely desirous of peace, this was an impressive reminder of the lost unity of the sub-continent following the disappearance of the British raj.

I soon decided to accept the invitations which had been extended to me at the Conference, and the tour was now planned to include Pakistan and Singapore as well as India, Australia and New Zealand. My main purpose, as I said at London Airport on 7 January,

[1] 5 July 1957.

was to listen, to see and to learn; to meet many old friends and to make many new ones; and in a series of informal talks, as well as by public appearances, help co-operation and understanding between the countries of the Commonwealth. I added :

this is a community of nations of a quite unique character, and perhaps in this confused world it has a special role to play. Its very diversity gives it an authority that more compact alliances or organisations do not have. In addition I wish to take with me a message of goodwill and friendship.

To conclude, I read out a heartening telegram put into my hands a few minutes before boarding the aeroplane 'from the greatest of living Englishmen, Winston Churchill'. It ran as follows: 'As you start on your long journey to our Commonwealth friends I send you my support and my warmest good wishes.'

At that time I could express the confident belief that the Commonwealth stood for a recognisable philosophy of social and political action. This I tried to summarise in a farewell broadcast delivered on 28 January at the end of my visit to New Zealand:

The strength of our unique association is founded in our common belief in principles and institutions which are fundamental to human freedom. We all believe in the tolerance, the mutual give and take of our system of Parliamentary democracy. We believe in justice for everyman, we believe in liberty of conscience, we believe in the freedom of the individual, freedom of speech, thought and action within the law, and we believe that the purpose of the State is to enable the individual to live a full life in peace and freedom. These are the principles on which our national institutions are founded.

Admittedly we were soon to learn that we had been too optimistic in believing that the system of Parliamentary Government, developed over many centuries in our own country, could be expected to survive the strains and stresses affecting some newly emerging nations. Nevertheless we may perhaps regard these lapses as the growing pains of youth. Similarly, while at that time only one of the countries of the Commonwealth, India, adopted a formally neutral position in the East–West struggle and eschewed the various military alliances into which great areas of the world were marshalled, yet there was and remains every hope that the 'unaligned' countries of the Commonwealth would resist the dangerous advances made to them by Communist countries, whether from Russia or from China. In a speech at Sydney, on 3 February, I referred in some detail to the problems of defence.

We have throughout the world a number of regional defensive alliances—NATO, the Baghdad Pact, ANZUS and SEATO— but the threat is by no means wholly—or even primarily—a military threat. The dangers of political pressure and economic penetration are even more serious. Therefore, in this, all the international organisations of the free world have a part to play. And first among them is our own . . . Commonwealth, which is founded on those very principles of freedom which it is our object and purpose to defend. . . . Let me remind you . . . how our Commonwealth is linked with all these international organisations. We are of course all members of the United Nations. Canada and the United Kingdom are members of NATO. Pakistan and the United Kingdom are in the Baghdad Pact. Australia, New Zealand, Pakistan and the United Kingdom are in SEATO. Australia and New Zealand are members of ANZUS. Canada is an observer at the organisation for European Economic Co-operation. And, finally, no less than eight out of the ten independent countries of the Commonwealth are members of the Colombo Plan. . . . If we think of the world as a huge circle of which our Commonwealth Club is the centre, we are in a unique position to ensure that the principles and ideals which we hold in common, and which we cherish and develop through our own Commonwealth association, can spread outwards from the centre to all those other countries with whom we, severally and individually, associate on the periphery.

Recognising the free decisions of each Government on this issue I declared at Melbourne on 5 February:

There are some of us, however, who are unwilling to join in any military alliances . . . not, I am sure, out of any sympathy for the Communist doctrine, but because they believe that military groupings and alliances, even for defensive purposes, are wrong. We do not agree with that view, but we can, and should, respect it.

N2

At any rate it was my purpose, which I carried out throughout the tour, to preach a broad picture of a future in which the Commonwealth, Old and New, could look back with pride upon the past and with confidence to the future.

My wife and I had now set out upon a journey which was to prove a fascinating and exhilarating experience. We were accompanied by an admirable staff which included, with the usual secretarial staff, Sir Norman Brook, Morrice James (Under-Secretary, Commonwealth Relations Office), Harold Evans (Chief Adviser on Public Relations), and two Private Secretaries, Neil Cairncross and John Wyndham. We flew over 33,000 miles in 120 hours. We travelled in addition 1,500 miles by road. Four nights were spent in flying, and thirty-four other nights at different centres. We left on 7 January 1958 and reached home on 14 February.

We landed first at New Delhi, where we spent four crowded days, of which not the least interesting parts were the times set aside for private talks with the Prime Minister. It was clear that Nehru intended not merely to show himself an attentive host in private, but to demonstrate in public his sympathy and pleasure.

His home was organised with the traditional comfort of large Indian establishments, which the British had copied. It was the house previously occupied by the British Commander-in-Chief. His daughter, Mrs. Indira Gandhi, took special pains to make my wife's visit agreeable. We lived in English style—a substantial breakfast, which seemed much to the taste of the only other guest, President Achmed Sukarno, the head of the Indonesian Government. I formed the impression that Nehru was not particularly pleased with this somewhat flamboyant phoenix, who had risen from the ashes of the Dutch Empire. His curious costume, a uniform of blue velvet, with silver stars—apparently a cross between those worn by little Lord Fauntleroy and Liberace—was in strange contrast to his host's simple dress. Moreover his habit of carrying about a sort of Field-Marshal's baton (putting it on the sideboard during meals) was, I could see, not altogether appreciated. But I was glad to meet this remarkable man, who talked well and with considerable knowledge on a wide range of subjects.

Nehru showed us throughout exquisite courtesy.

We stayed at his own house—instead of staying at the President's palace, formerly Government House. This is a very unusual compliment. We had two good evenings of quiet talk—especially the last. . . . He came to the High Commissioner's party—this is very rare. He drove with me and back three times—on arrival and departure—(these are most unusual).[1]

The 'Civic Reception' at the Red Fort proved a most spectacular affair. A vast audience of tens of thousands, all the humanity that could be squeezed into the space, greeted us with enthusiasm. Indeed this was the highlight of the visit, for the Fort was wonderfully illuminated and the great mass of applauding and seemingly happy people could not but touch the heart. Nehru made a generous speech of welcome, to which I made an impromptu reply, throwing away my prepared text.

Another equally fascinating evening was spent at the Viceroy's House, which I had visited in Lord Wavell's last days there.[2] It was strange indeed to return as a British Prime Minister to this huge Imperial Palace which had been the vital centre of undivided India under British rule. All the etiquette and ceremony were preserved according to the old style. The plate and china remained, with their arms and heraldic devices. The pictures of the Viceroys were on the walls. Indeed my wife sat exactly opposite a portrait of her grandfather, Lord Lansdowne, who had been Viceroy more than half a century before. The military guards and the servants were in the old picturesque costume, dating from the days of the Moguls.

All the pomp and circumstance [are] unchanged. We were also the chief guests at a garden party there—also in the old style, with the old Viceroy's guard in their splendid uniforms, the trumpeters, the military secretary, and A.D.C.s [all in military full dress].[1]

On one afternoon we had a trip into the countryside, visiting a number of 'Indian villages, where thousands of people turned up, danced, sang and cheered my speech to the echo !'[1] The warmth of our reception surprised us all, including the Indian Ministers and their friends, but it was certainly genuine. 'Each time we appeared, the welcome grew. It could not have been "inspired".'[1]

[1] 19 January 1958.   [2] *Tides of Fortune*, p. 245.

When Nehru had urged me in London to come to India he had promised me a good reception. It certainly surpassed anything that I could have expected. Even the inevitable Press conferences, although presenting some difficult questions, were marked by much friendliness and considerable sense of humour. The private talks with Nehru were carried on in a reflective and relaxed mood. He summed them up in a public statement in the following words:

Ii is true we do not agree about some matters, but the chief thing is to understand each other and to approach our problems in a friendly way. It is this friendly approach which makes all the difference, and the Commonwealth association is most valuable because it encourages such friendly contacts.

Apart from the wide range of our talks, I recorded two points which particularly struck me.

Nehru, who is a curious mixture of advanced thought and old-fashioned opinions, deplored the Americanisation of India. He said that he was very unpopular because he would not allow American dance bands and crooners on the radio without there being a large proportion of Indian traditional music.[1]

On a more serious matter:

He told me at this discussion something of his visit to China. He holds certain theories about the division that may come between China and Russia, who are not spiritually, or even traditionally, friends, and there is always a good deal of friction.[1]

On Kashmir little progress was made. Nehru

said that it was impossible to deal with the Pakistan Government—they never stayed in office for more than a few months; they had no sound democratic system; there was nobody who could settle any agreement—in fact he was not at all hopeful. I did not pursue the matter because I did not want to get involved in the familiar arguments about Kashmir.[2]

I thought at the time that Nehru tended to under-rate the economic problems that confronted India, especially in view of the

[1] 8 January 1958.   [2] 11 January 1958.

growing population. He seemed to pin his faith on the 'Five-Year Plan' with an optimism which seemed to me little justified. But of its political importance I was easily persuaded.

It is clear to me from what Mr. Nehru said that the Five-Year Plan is absolutely essential for two reasons; first, Five-Year Plans are an essential feature of a developing community today. He is faced with the Communist pressure, which is undoubtedly growing in India, industrially as well as politically. He must put up as good a show as the Russians or the Chinese—perhaps the Chinese more especially because they are a community more similar in character to the Indians. The second reason is that the Congress Party is in a sense in the position of the Irish Party after Home Rule—it cannot just live on the claim that it made the revolution. In the same way, the Whig Party could not continue indefinitely on fear of Jacobitism. The Five-Year Plan is part of the new political attraction the Congress Party is putting before the people, and since it is in our interest to prevent Communism, I think we ought to do everything we can to help them with the Five-Year Plan and encourage America and Germany to do the same. A serious breakdown in the Five-Year Plan could not be to our advantage commercially, and certainly not politically.[1]

I had some meetings with the leading economic Ministers, including Morarji Desai, which were quite illuminating. In addition, Norman Brook held discussions with the various heads of departments, which were of considerable value and certainly helped to make some of the points and requests for assistance more precise.

As regards international issues, Britain's relations with Russia and my recent correspondence with Bulganin were in everybody's mind. He had sent me two more long epistles, one in December and one in January, and the possibility of Summit talks was beginning to emerge. Another reply had to be prepared, and at this time I saw the chance of some progress if I myself offered to go to Moscow to discuss with Khrushchev the agenda and the procedure of such a meeting. Accordingly I drafted a telegram for the consideration of the Cabinet, which, although it did not altogether please my

[1] 8 January 1958.

colleagues at home, was the germ of a plan which I was to carry out in the following year. The Bulganin correspondence, and particularly these last letters to which I had not yet replied, seemed to be of deep interest to the people of India, judging from the number of questions asked on all sides.

The four days of our visit passed all too quickly, crowded with colour and even excitement. It was sad to be allowed so short a time. Nehru seemed genuinely distressed at our departure and loaded us with presents of all kinds.

On 12 January we left for Pakistan. In the aeroplane, I noted some impressions:

First, of India after ten years of independence. The country is much more sure of itself. So are the Government. . . . They have learned a good deal about practical politics. After years of opposition—when they had nothing to do except oppose the Government, by argument or force or both, they now have to deal with intractable problems—like religious strife, the language question, Communism in the trade unions, administrative corruption, etc., etc. . . . They also realise that the fact that the country can be governed at all they owe to the British. The Company organisation, and then the [Indian Civil Service] . . . set up a machine of government; the broad structure remains.

Moreover, since the British proportion of I.C.S. was very small, a highly trained body of administrators (Indian) existed, ready to hand, to serve the Congress Government.

The legal system, civil and criminal, is an inheritance from British rule. The whole judiciary also. The army is British, and is treasuring most religiously the old regimental traditions. The Parliamentary and 'democratic' system is ours—and so is much of the ordinary way of living. All this, now that the bitterness of the struggle is over, even Congress men are beginning to remember. There is also the contrast between the way the British made the 'transfer of power' and what was done by the French and the Dutch.

The second impression is of the supremacy of Nehru.[1]

Nehru certainly dominated the scene, and in spite of the many difficulties which threatened him, he seemed confident of the future. But I thought he was rather repetitive in his ideas.

[1] 19 January 1958.

His speeches (or monologues) are . . . well-tried records—the rise of Asian nationalism; the new Communism in Russia, and its renunciation of war, etc. Nevertheless, he is able, full of charm, cultivated and ruthless—all great qualities in a leader.

The third feeling I had was the very strong position of the British—especially business men. They are liked and trusted. They have to compete for business, but that does them no harm. Socially, they stand higher than under the old regime, which was dominated by soldiers and civil servants.[1]

On arriving, some days later, at Singapore I received a letter from our High Commissioner at Delhi, Malcolm MacDonald, a sympathetic but a discerning observer. He wrote, in enthusiastic if perhaps too generous terms.

You and your wife's visit to Delhi was a huge success. You made a tremendous impression on Nehru, his Cabinet colleagues, and various other leading personalities who met you. You also greatly touched the crowds of ordinary Indians who gathered everywhere to greet you, by your sincerity and friendliness as well as your distinction. I knew that your visit would do a lot of good, but if I may say so, the excellent results have exceeded even my expectations . . .

Many visits here by V.I.P.s leave only a short, transitory impression; and your visit might conceivably have been one of these. Delhi receives so many Heads of States, Prime Ministers, Foreign Ministers and others in these times that people here are liable to welcome them warmly when they appear, and then to forget them amongst the crowd of their successors. I have been delighted to learn on my return that the impression left by you is quite different. It is lasting. Every day people speak to me and my colleagues in the High Commission about your visit, saying how much they liked you and your wife, how much they appreciated your speeches and statements, and how much good the visit has done to relations between the U.K. Government and the Indian Government.

These, whether justified or not, were encouraging words, for which I was and remain grateful.

[1] 19 January 1958.

In Karachi there were none of the large public demonstrations of popular goodwill which were such a feature of our visit to Delhi. But, as other events of the tour amply showed, the apparent indifference did not denote any absence of friendly feeling. Personal contacts with individuals were easier and more relaxed than in India. For, apart from Nehru, official Indian society was rather intense and highly intellectual. In Pakistan everything was on a less exacting basis. I could not help observing that going from one capital to another was rather like leaving Hampstead or North Oxford for the Shires.

We were met on Sunday morning, 12 January, by the Prime Minister, Sir Malik Firoz Khan Noon, and his principal colleagues. After the usual ceremonies at the airport we drove to the residence of the President, Iskander Mirza, who entertained us with princely hospitality. He and his wife, a Persian lady of great grace and dignity, proved charming hosts.

Among the many contrasts between the two parts of the old Indian Empire was the stability of the political leadership in India under the Congress Party led by Nehru, compared with the frequency of political change in Pakistan and the precariousness of the constitutional regime, which the President did not conceal from me.

> Pakistan is poor; politically unstable; in a state of religious turmoil (the Mullahs have large though rather uncertain power) without a 'political' class—without so large an I.C.S. tradition as India, and practising corruption on the grand scale.[1]

From this last criticism Iskander Mirza specifically excepted the new Prime Minister, Noon, a distinguished Indian civil servant under the British regime, who had lately taken the place of Suhrawardy.

> The one stable element in the situation is the Army. The Air Force and Navy are also reliable. East Pakistan, more advanced and richer, is drifting to Communism—or may easily do so. The old Moslem League, orthodox and rigid, is supported by the Mullahs, but less and less by the people. The Services—especially the Army—are excellent. I saw something of them all. The men

[1] 19 January 1958.

werc smart, and the officers (especially in Air Force) young and intelligent.[1]

I did not of course realise at the time how short would be the President's career, and how soon would follow the political *coup* by which Mohammed Ayub Khan took control and brought the Parliamentary system to an end. Nevertheless it was clear enough that there was as yet no firm base on which democratic institutions could be solidly built.

In Karachi there were the usual entertainments, with dinners and speeches. Here at any rate I could enlarge frankly on the defence role of Pakistan, as a member of the Baghdad and SEATO pacts. It was also easy to dwell upon the ties which linked Pakistan's Army, Navy and Air Force with British tradition, and the close connection still maintained between the British and Pakistani armed forces. There was naturally a Press conference, at which I was struck by the high standard of the questions and the interest shown in Commonwealth and world affairs. An air display, followed by luncheon in the officers' mess, a meeting with the United Kingdom business community, and a tour of the harbour with the Commander-in-Chief and the senior officers of the Navy filled the first two days. I was glad to be able to pay my tribute to two great men by laying wreaths at the tombs of Mohammed Ali Jinnah and Liaqat Ali Khan. Both of these, in their different ways, played a vital role in the history of Pakistan. Had Jinnah lived he might have held Pakistan together as its founder with some of the authority exercised by Nehru. Had Liaqat Ali Khan escaped the assassin's bullet he might have guided the nation along sound lines; he would certainly not have brought constitutional government into disrepute by any lack of moral integrity.

Amid these ceremonies plenty of time was allotted to private discussions with the President himself and with the Prime Minister, Noon. One difference between Pakistan and India was very marked. Whereas in India the difficulty had been to induce the leading figures, including Nehru, to discuss Indo-Pakistani differences, in Pakistan both the President and the Ministers seemed able to think or talk of little else. Of course, this reflected Pakistan's acute

[1] 19 January 1958.

sense of being at a disadvantage. Consequently, apart from some discussion of cotton imports and plans for economic aid, almost the whole of our talks were taken up with the questions of Kashmir, the Indus Waters and the supply of arms. On the first the Prime Minister seemed to see little hope of a settlement. 'None could be reached by direct talks between the strong and the weak.' On the Indus Waters there appeared to be more chance of eventual agreement. As regards defence, Pakistan wanted more arms, especially tanks and bombers. While I promised to consider these requests and pointed out that both India and Pakistan, like other Commonwealth countries, were free to purchase arms from private industry in the United Kingdom, if they so wished, we as a Government were anxious not to aggravate the arms race. To this Noon sorrowfully replied that 'India's intentions are evil.' It was sad to witness the bitterness of leading Pakistanis. Partition had indeed dealt a terrible blow to the sub-continent.

The highlight of our short visit was the trip to the North-West Frontier. Leaving early on 14 January, we flew in our Britannia aeroplane to Peshawar, enjoying in perfect weather the grand view of the Himalayas. At 11 a.m. we left by car for the Khyber Pass, stopping on the way for a tank demonstration by the 4th Cavalry. At Jamrud Fort, the entrance to the tribal area, we were met by many tribal Maliks who had travelled to meet us and present us with the traditional presents of sheep. (I was also given a locally manufactured rifle.) We then drove through the Khyber Pass as far as the Afghanistan frontier. It was indeed a thrilling experience. This was the historic scene of great conflicts throughout history. Above all it was moving for us to see recorded the names of almost every British regiment, which had fought and suffered in the great defile. It is indeed a tale of tragedy and triumph. For those who knew the great Imperial story this seemed almost a sacred way.

We lunched at the officers' mess of the Khyber Rifles, where I was glad to see everything unchanged since 1947–the regimental silver–the portraits of past British officers–even the pipe band.

Here all goes on as before–Khyber rifles; medals; regimental H.Q.; polo; even the Hunt. The tribesmen are all armed– several 'Maliks' were paraded for us, armed to the teeth. But they are quieter now, and many of their sons come in to the new University at Peshawar. This situation is partly the patriotic reaction of the Border tribes against the intrigues of Afghanistan.[1]

Greatly as I enjoyed my visit to Pakistan, I did not leave it without some foreboding. Outwardly the position looked strong enough, with the fighting services in fine fettle, with well-trained officers and good discipline. Yet the structure seemed to me fragile, while the President, who certainly towered above all others, appeared hampered rather than strengthened by his loyalty to constitutional principles. Only a few months were to pass before the process of degeneration forced Iskander Mirza to make way for a successor who was to abrogate the constitution and rule by martial law. This was the first breach in the inherited structure of the Parliamentary system in any Commonwealth country.

We left Karachi at 8.30 a.m. on 16 January and arrived at the Katunayake Airport at 2.30 p.m., where we were met by the Prime Minister of Ceylon, S. W. R. D. Bandaranaike and other Ministers. We drove from the airport to the city in a colourful procession amid laughing and apparently enthusiastic crowds. Scarcely ever have I seen such merry faces. Indeed during these two days we made an almost royal progress through Ceylon. Whatever their motive, the people seemed to seize the opportunity of giving a smiling and cheerful greeting to an apparently distinguished visitor, uncertain as many of them might be as to who he was or what he represented.

Dorothy and I and some of our staff were the guests of the Governor-General, Sir Oliver Goonetilleke.

Ceylon has not yet declared herself a Republic, so there is still a Governor-General, in whose charming and antique home (Dutch by origin) we stayed in great comfort. The Europeans bow or curtsey to him—and some of the Ceylonese. He does the job well.[1]

Sir Oliver was a shrewd and experienced politician, with an intimate knowledge of the domestic situation in Ceylon. Although his group or party was no longer predominant, his influence was great. He explained to me how the present Prime Minister had been largely successful in mobilising the forces of the Buddhist monks and

[1] 19 January 1958.

priests on his behalf. He thought, however, that he was in danger and that they might soon turn against him.

Ceylon had recently suffered from serious floods as the result of the bursting of some of the historic 'cisterns', on which the population still mainly relies. Fortunately, both the Royal Navy and the Royal Air Force had been able to give immediate and substantial help. In addition the fighting Services had supplied medical and other necessary stores. In my speech at a dinner given in my honour by the Ceylon Parliament on 17 January, I was able to promise additional aid, both in the short and in the longer term. This entertainment was organised by the Senate and the House of Representatives; I was thus able to speak to my hosts as a colleague. After referring to the principles of freedom which must lie behind any system of democratic government, I added these words:

> These principles which we ourselves accept are in many parts of the world under challenge. All this was well expressed by your Prime Minister, Mr. Bandaranaike, when he spoke recently of the golden thread of the tradition which binds together the members of the Commonwealth.

In the course of the afternoon and evening I had two long conversations with the Prime Minister. He showed deep interest in world affairs, especially the possibility of some fruitful negotiations with Russia. He also spoke at length about China, and told me he had had a number of private conversations with Chou En-lai. In Bandaranaike's opinion, although the Chinese leader bitterly resented his 'ostracism by the West', he would not accept a place in the United Nations at the price of recognition of the Nationalist occupation of Formosa. Bandaranaike was much concerned about the situation in Indonesia.

> He thought that President Sukarno had got himself into trouble by failing to deal firmly with the extreme elements. It was significant that the attempt on his life had been made by Muslim extremists. It was likely that the more moderate elements in Indonesia had advised Sukarno to go away for a time, and that this was the real reason for his present journey.[1]

[1] 16 January 1958.

It was clear from what the Prime Minister said that there was little sympathy between these two men, of very different types. Sukarno, for all his flamboyance, was a man of action; Bandaranaike was, essentially, a sentimentalist—one a sword man, the other a gown man.

When we got on to the subject of economics,

I told him that he could 'socialise' or 'nationalise' . . . port and harbour companies and the like without much harm. But I begged him to let alone the rubber and tea estates, on the efficiency of which the whole economy of the island depends. (The deterioration and almost disintegration of the Indonesian economy now going on is a useful object lesson for Ceylon politicians.)[1]

In its broader aspects I found the structure of Ceylonese politics intriguing.

The Prime Minister . . . is [a] sort of local Nehru—except that he has only just got into office and had nothing to do with Ceylon obtaining Independence. He clearly models himself on Mr. N.; dresses like an Anglo-Catholic priest at the altar, stole and all; is a very rich man and the son of a very rich man; is Westernised (he was Secretary and Treasurer of the Oxford Union, when he was at Christ Church); makes friends with everyone, and is himself partly Conservative and partly advanced Socialist, as is his Government.[1]

No regular Party system on modern British lines had developed.

In a curious way, the political life is more like that of Whig politics in the eighteenth century than one would suppose. The leading figures have a 'following' (like the Bedfords or the Rockinghams). But the Government . . . comprises men of very different points of view.[1]

All this was in itself harmless and agreeable, but I could see that

the danger here (as elsewhere throughout the East) is the collapse of the agreeable, educated, Liberal, North Oxford Society to whom we have transferred power, in the face of the dynamism of Communism, with all the strength of Russian imperialism behind it.[1]

[1] 19 January 1958.

In Ceylon there was an additional complication resulting from the strength of the highly organised body of clerics. This introduced a new and uncertain element absent from the period of the Whig domination, although powerful in the previous century. Indeed my poor friend Bandaranaike was to fall a victim to the murderous attack of a fanatical monk less than two years later.

On the next day the Prime Minister took us both by car to Kandy, and we were allowed to make a visit to the famous Temple of the Tooth. This ancient and well-known shrine has often been described and clearly still commands respect and veneration. It was a curious contrast on the return journey to visit the University of Ceylon, where I received an Honorary Degree with the full ceremonial of Oxford and Cambridge, including gowns, hoods and mortar-boards.

Our visit to Ceylon, although so limited in duration, was happy and seemed successful. We took away a sense of genuine friendliness.

Our next stop was at Singapore, where we arrived at 4.30 on 18 January after a flight of seven hours. Since we were to return to Singapore on our way home we had no public engagements on this occasion. This gave a useful opportunity for dealing with the London telegrams. Lim Yew Hock, the Chief Minister in the semi-independent Government, on its last lap before independence, came privately to dinner. 'A wise little man, but I have doubts whether he will hold out against Communism directed from China.'[1] Indeed the pressure against him was already mounting.

Before leaving, I was fortunate in being able to attend the final session of the Annual Conference held by the Commissioner-General for South-East Asia, Sir Robert Scott. This

> was an interesting conference of Ambassadors, Governors, High Commissioners, Generals, Admirals, Air Marshals, etc., etc., going on at the Commissioner-General's house where we were staying. These are periodical gatherings, and my presence seemed welcome and useful.[1]

Bob Scott was a man of remarkable ability who had served originally in India and was now to have a fine career in the Foreign

[1] 19 January 1958.

Service. Sir William Goode, the Governor of Singapore, was clearly a wise and experienced administrator. General Sir Francis Festing (afterwards Chief of the Imperial General Staff) was a tower of strength, combining commonsense and imagination. Hoyer Millar, the Permanent Under-Secretary of the Foreign Office, had come out especially for the meeting. I was greatly struck by the quality of the representatives and the value of their contributions. In any event, it was fortunate for me to have attended this Conference, since I was to hear much about the defence of South-East Asia both in New Zealand and in Australia.

In spite of the rapid movement towards independence about to take place throughout the area none of us at that Conference had any doubt of the importance of maintaining the authority and prestige of the United Kingdom by a substantial military presence. Nor were there any fears that this would be unwelcome to the successor governments. On the contrary, for many years to come the emerging territories, such as Malaya, would feel increased confidence if they could rely on our firm support. Total evacuation was never contemplated at that time. It would have seemed an inconceivable and unworthy act of defeatism, to which Britain could never be reduced.

We left Singapore after luncheon on 19 January. With only a short stop for refuelling at Darwin in the Northern Territory of Australia, we continued direct to Auckland, arriving at 4 o'clock in the afternoon of 20 January—a long and exhausting flight. Unfortunately I had caught a severe chill at Singapore with a high temperature; but with the help of appropriate drugs I managed to sleep during most of the journey. Although a kind delegation of Australian notabilities came to greet me at Darwin, in the middle of the night, Norman Brook was resolute in keeping me to my bunk. At Auckland we were met by the Prime Minister, Walter Nash, and Arthur Harper, the Secretary for Internal Affairs, who was responsible for our whole tour. To be transported so rapidly from the tropical heat and exotic scenery of the East to the temperate climate and familiar surroundings of New Zealand was indeed a change. To be greeted by the friendly faces of English and Scottish people was like coming home.

The authorities had so planned our tour as to allow us to see as many people and visit as many places as possible within the allotted time in both the North and South Islands. The rest of the hours available were spent in long conversations with the Prime Minister. I was also able to make some headway in dealing with the large number of messages which kept arriving from London, both on internal and external affairs. 'Rab' Butler, who presided over the Cabinet and acted as my deputy during my absence, was, fortunately, discriminating as well as conscientious in deciding what ought to be forwarded, whether for action or for information.

My Moscow plan did not please the Cabinet. But it has persuaded them that we must, in the next reply to Bulganin, be a little more positive about the 'Summit meeting' on the basis of proper preparation. We can, I think, by this means test the Soviet sincerity. If they refuse all preliminary work, it will show that all their peace talk is really propaganda. Even Gaitskell has said that careful preparation is essential if any real business is to be done.[1]

There had been a General Election in New Zealand two months before our arrival, resulting in the return of the Labour Party with a majority of two over their opponents. Apart from Nash himself, the Cabinet lacked experience; they were also confronted with the familiar problem of how to redeem their election promises, which included reductions in taxation and increases in social benefits, when faced with a formidable economic crisis and a rapidly worsening balance of payments.

They are in temporary financial trouble, because during the last few years of high prices for wool and dairy products—as well as meat—they have had a terrific buying and spending spree. Now they have no sterling reserves and have been forced to make import cuts. But the [high] prices could not last indefinitely, and even at present levels the farmers are doing very well. Wool prices seem to be recovering (except merino) and the British market still absorbs a vast export of milk products and meat.[1]

Nash himself was an old-fashioned radical, rather than a socialist. His hero was Gladstone, not Marx. Somewhat 'vain and talkative,

[1] 24 January 1958.

but sound and loyal. I have found him very easy to get on with.'¹ He was passionately fond of political history and had read widely.

I formed with Nash a close friendship which continued until his death. He represented a fine tradition of English radicalism of the last century based upon sincere idealism and genuine piety. In the pursuit of what he thought right he was both persistent and fearless. Although he was deeply interested in foreign policy, and much of our talk was occupied by a survey of the world situation, the main items for serious discussion were naturally economic. The proposed European Free Trade Area for industrial goods did not concern him or his colleagues unduly, even if some adjustments of the Ottawa agreement were involved. They were chiefly concerned with maintaining the market for agricultural production.

It may be possible to help them to some extent by our new 'anti-dumping' legislation. They do not complain so much of our British production as of the sale of foreign produce below (as they allege) cost price in the British market.¹

On 23 January I attended a meeting of the New Zealand Cabinet which lasted nearly two hours. Apart from the immediate economic difficulties, on which I assured them that British exporters would understand the need for temporary import controls, Ministers seemed chiefly interested in the questions of defence. In particular, they expressed anxiety about developments in Indonesia and the future of Malaya. Fortunately for me the Prime Minister conducted the whole affair off his own bat and filled up the greater part of the time with his own exposition. In the evening I had another private conversation with him which lasted until the early hours of the morning. All this was both useful and informative, if somewhat repetitive. Nash was fond of talking, and when he found another Prime Minister ready to listen to the arguments which he thought it right to expound, he enjoyed to the full 'the rare felicity of uniting, in the same pursuit, his duty and his inclination'.

The chief purpose of the tour was that we should show ourselves and see as many people as possible in the time available. The 'civic receptions' were almost tumultuous in their warmth. People in all

¹ 24 January 1958.

walks of life showed themselves extraordinarily friendly and loyal. Some variation was introduced by a Maori gathering at a place called Ngaruawahia and by a visit to the Wairakei Geyser Valley, where we saw this wonderful natural phenomenon with interest and almost with awe. The plans to harness these natural resources to the production of power were explained to us by the experts in charge. We arrived at Wellington on the evening of 22 January and stayed at Government House. 'Lord Cobham and his wife were delightful hosts in Wellington and are clearly very popular. Their eight children appeal to the people.'[1]

I was relieved to get a message from home about the economic debate following Thorneycroft's resignation. This had apparently passed off well, ending in a majority of sixty-two.

> Meanwhile, the Cabinet seems to have been working well and loyally on the 'estimates' problem. It has been agreed that the stamp should be increased by 8*d*.–but no cuts in the welfare services.[1]

At Dunedin I had a welcome which any man of my name and descent might expect to command; but I have never seen so many Scottish people so enthusiastic. It was an unforgettable tribute which seemed to come from the heart. Perhaps the most enjoyable day was the drive from Dunedin to Christchurch, with various stops which gave us a good view of the countryside and a useful picture of the life of the people. 'At Christchurch I had [to make] a speech to the Chamber of Commerce–the only financial and economic speech of the New Zealand trip.'[2] The luncheon was really a social occasion. But the audience accepted the need for an address of some kind with respect and resignation.

In my public speeches I naturally emphasised the major role which Britain's private investments were playing in New Zealand. I explained the policy behind the European Free Trade Area proposal. I accepted loyally the need for Commonwealth countries to develop their own firm links with the United States, and of the complete compatibility of these with membership of the Commonwealth family–this was, in fact, to accept ANZUS without cavil.

[1] 24 January 1958.   [2] 31 January 1958.

But I dwelt equally on the value of British military strength in the Far East. At the same time I urged the people of New Zealand, as one of the old Commonwealth countries, to recognise the rapid changes now taking place in the Commonwealth structure. It was vital that they, together with the people of Australia, Canada and South Africa, should understand and encourage the part in world affairs which India and other new Commonwealth countries might be led to accept.

Both my wife and I thoroughly enjoyed our visit to New Zealand. As we travelled round we felt that although no country could be farther away from home, there was none which resembled Britain more closely. This applied both to the nature of the country itself and to the character and traditions of the people. Since neither of the islands had yet developed more than a certain amount of light industry, in driving through the countryside one could easily imagine what Britain must have been like before the sprawling growth of towns and disfiguring tentacles of industry had clawed away so much of our beautiful land. The rivers, like ours in old days, were unpolluted and full of fish. Indeed there was hardly a stream in which some of the best trout fishing in the world could not be obtained for a few shillings. The mountains of the South Island were reminiscent of Scottish scenery, and full of deer, imported perhaps a little improvidently by some enthusiast. The chief difference seemed to be that while in Scotland stalking deer is a rich man's sport, here in this blessed isle you were paid for shooting them. Partly because of the clemency of the climate; partly because of the fertility of the soil, with a luxuriant growth of grass providing throughout the year for vast flocks of sheep and herds of cattle; partly because of the immense distance of these islands from the main centres of world population, not yet compensated for by the rapidity of modern communications, the people seemed, if not parochial, at any rate satisfied with a relatively static society. Yet in a world more and more dominated by a pitiless national and individual determination to excel at almost any cost, these delightful islands and these friendly folk seemed an oasis set in the cruel desert of modern life. If New Zealanders appeared at that time a little unwilling to adapt themselves to new conditions and a little prone to depend on the protective arms of the mother country, they were none the less building their future without some of the hideous mistakes and crimes which have been committed in more ruthless times.

We left Christchurch with much regret on 28 January, arriving in Canberra in the afternoon of the same day. On arrival we were met by the Prime Minister, Menzies, a number of other Ministers, and Lord Carrington, the High Commissioner. We drove immediately to Government House, where we were received by the Governor-General, Field-Marshal Sir William Slim, and Lady Slim. 'The Governor-General is obviously liked and respected. He is a strong character.'[1] Indeed scarcely any Governor-General has commanded such genuine admiration. His splendid war record and the affection of those Australian troops who served under him naturally added to his prestige. In addition his simplicity, wisdom and dignity deeply impressed all those with whom he came in contact.

Telegrams were pouring in from home, and occupied us until the early hours of the morning, after the formal dinner at Government House had come to an end. Selwyn Lloyd was in Ankara at a meeting of the Baghdad Pact countries, and I judged that the Foreign Secretary was having rather a rough time.

> The Americans have suddenly turned very nasty about our proposed reply to Bulganin. They do not seem to understand the feeling either in our country—or perhaps their own. They are now pressing for a very negative reply from me to B.'s last letter. They are almost threatening. With so much at stake (e.g. financial support, McMahon Act, etc.) it is difficult to know quite how to handle the situation. I am now awaiting Selwyn Lloyd's appreciation (he is discussing it all with Foster Dulles) which I hope to get when I arrive [in] Brisbane.[1]

Canberra in 1958 was scarcely more than the ground plan of the noble city which it has since become. The extensive lake, now the most splendid feature of the capital, was as yet unfilled and presented only a dry and repellent acreage of mud. Some buildings had, of

[1] 31 January 1958.

course, been erected; but of these many were only temporary. Yet it was already clear what a magnificent example of architectural and town-planning design Canberra was soon to prove. I was fortunate enough to be able to pay a visit ten years later. Although many buildings and houses had yet to be completed, I could see and admire the miracle which had been performed.

Since our aeroplane had touched down for an hour at Sydney Airport for refuelling, I had already undergone the severe test of an Australian Press Conference. Another now awaited me. During the following two or three days there were the usual ceremonies, of which the most important was the Parliamentary dinner on the evening of 29 January. Menzies had warned me that a speech of some importance would be expected. The introductory passages at any rate seemed to meet with general approval.

This is a new experience for me, and a very great honour. As a Parliamentarian of nearly thirty-five years' experience I know how great an honour it is. It seems to be quite incredible that so many members of both Houses of Parliament should assemble in the Recess, coming long distances and, so far as I know, unwhipped. If the Whips had been put on I would have thought you would have all paired. I do thank you for the honour that you have done for me and through me to the Old Country. I cannot of course claim to be the first Scotsman to come to Australia; but I can claim, as your Prime Minister said, to be the first British Prime Minister in office to visit Australia.

I went on to refer to the strong links which bound us together.

Ties of common origin, common loyalties and, as I was so poignantly reminded when I was taken to that beautiful war memorial in your city this morning, common sacrifices.

On the material side, I added :

Britain is Australia's most important trading partner. Britain's investment in Australia is far higher than that of any other country and indeed higher than all the countries of the world put together. There is a steady flow of, I like to think, a good character of British immigrant who come here to make their careers in what they rightly believe to be a land of ever-increasing opportunity.

It was natural, therefore, that we should regard really vital matters from the same point of view.

All the same, like brothers or partners or members of a family, it may happen that although we have so much in common we may sometimes forget that we each have separate problems. Placed as we are on the opposite sides of the world . . . we must always remember . . . that what we call the Far East is to you the Near North, and you for your part must not forget that Britain is geographically part of Europe, geographically and historically as we have learnt to our sorrow twice in my lifetime, and that therefore we have important political and economic interests in Europe which we cannot ignore without disaster.

It was so much the fashion to denigrate the old country that I thought it right to refer also to Britain's achievements since the end of the Second World War and went on to give a factual account of our successes over many fields. I had been warned that many Australians were feeling some concern about Britain and her place in the councils of the world, as well as about the ability of Western nations to provide effective international leadership. I therefore tried to give reassurances which seemed to be both acceptable and convincing.

Apart from this Parliamentary dinner there were the various receptions and entertainments, varied by a visit to the Australian National University where I was met by and received an Honorary Degree from Lord Bruce, the Chancellor and a former Prime Minister of Australia.

On the political side, the most useful parts of my visit to the capital were the long discussions both with the Prime Minister alone and—on two occasions—with his Cabinet.

Bob Menzies is by far the outstanding figure here, and quite dominates the political scene. I had a morning with the Cabinet, trying to give them a general picture of our international problems.[1]

Apart from consideration of the forthcoming Commonwealth Economic Conference in Ottawa, our talks were mainly concerned with two subjects—defence and the new proposals for European

[1] 31 January 1958.

integration. On both of these, although strenuously cross-examined, not only by Menzies but also by all his Ministers, I was able to give sufficient assurances to satisfy the Australian Cabinet. With his usual generosity, in a joint Press Conference which we held before I left, Menzies expressed himself as fully satisfied and in complete agreement with me on the many problems on which we had taken counsel together.

On Menzies's suggestion I had a long talk at Parliament House with Dr. Herbert Evatt, the Leader of the Opposition. Evatt was a remarkable and indeed unexpected figure in Australian politics, brilliant, but, as it seemed to me, somewhat undependable. He reminded me of Stafford Cripps. He was a lawyer of deservedly high reputation and a politician of great energy, with occasional bursts of genius. Nevertheless, I could not help remarking to Menzies after our talk that I thought he was uncommonly lucky in his principal opponent. For Dr. Evatt, regardless of the fact that the Labour Party counted among its adherents a very large number—perhaps even a majority—who were Roman Catholics, had succeeded in quarrelling bitterly with the Hierarchy and the Church. This split continued for a long time, and for many years I remained envious of the good fortune of my Australian colleague in this respect.

On Friday 31 January we flew to Brisbane, where we were received by the Administrator of Queensland, Sir Alan Mansfield, and Lady Mansfield, and the Premier, Francis Nicklin.

Brisbane was very enthusiastic—a splendid 'civic reception' and so forth. The new Premier (there has been a change of Government after twenty years or more) is a Liberal.[1]

Fortunately we spent Saturday and Sunday resting in the country as guests of Mr. and Mrs. Bridle at Banyak Suka, where apart from a 'barbecue' meal and other pleasant entertainments we could see something of the countryside.

From Brisbane we flew to Sydney where we were met by the Premier of New South Wales, John Joseph Cahill. Here again there was a luncheon and a dinner and more speechifying. We were most fortunate in staying at Kirribilli House next to Sydney Harbour

[1] 3 February 1958.

—a guest-house maintained by the Commonwealth Government—opposite Admiralty House. Here, apart from the beauty of the view, there was the thrill of seeing the great ships seeming to pass within a few feet of the garden wall. 'The house (an old one, just done up in excellent Regency style) is very comfortable. Lovely weather—hot, but not too hot.'[1] By the kind thoughtfulness of our hosts, Dorothy and I were alone with one or two of our own staff. On the next morning we made a tour in one of the launches of perhaps the most magnificent harbour in the world. A first visit to Sydney is certainly a revelation, both as to the marvels of the scenery and the lively and enterprising character of the inhabitants.

In my speeches, both in the Town Hall and at the Parliamentary dinner, I referred at some length to defence and to the Russian problem. Everywhere I went there seemed to be unexpected interest in East–West relations. At the first of these ceremonies on 3 February I used these words:

> After the bitter experience of these last ten years we now realise that this contest between East and West, between those who believe in the free society and those enslaved by Communism will be a long and a difficult struggle.
>
> We are fighting it, not for any reasons of ambition or self-interest, but for self-defence; so that we may preserve in the free world our democratic way of life. And I believe that, because freedom is highly prized by man, its cause will in the end prevail.
>
> Eventually, it may be that, as education spreads among the masses of the people who are now held in the grip of the Communist system, more of them will come to understand the human values on which our competing system is based. . . . If that happens, Marxist materialism will begin to lose its appeal. But there is no room here for wishful thinking. This transformation, if it comes at all, will not come for many years—certainly not in our lifetime. . . .
>
> Meanwhile, though we may be able to reduce tensions here and there from time to time, the great struggle and conflict of ideas will continue. We must 'lean up against them'—steadily and firmly—and hold on to our own way of life and preserve it fully for all those in the free world who now enjoy its benefits.

[1] 4 February 1958.

Leaving for the Commonwealth Tour, 7 January 1958
'Almost the whole Cabinet came to see me off.'

With Nehru in New Delhi, January 1958

*Commonwealth Tour, Singapore,
February 1958*
'The situation was somewhat tense as
a result of the left-wing triumph in the
municipal elections. . . . However, all
went well, and the people seemed
pleased to see us.'

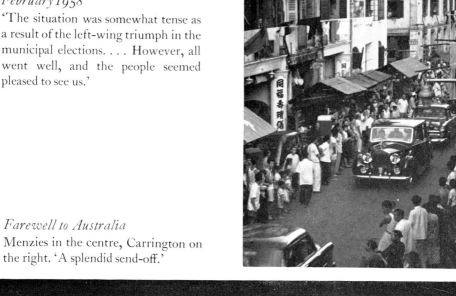

Farewell to Australia
Menzies in the centre, Carrington on
the right. 'A splendid send-off.'

From Sydney we flew to Melbourne, arriving in the afternoon where we were met by the Premier of Victoria, Henry Bolte. On the long drive from the airport to Government House the streets seemed crowded, people streaming out of house after house. I was delighted with this large gathering of onlookers, and observed to the Premier that I thought it was a great courtesy that they should have turned out in such numbers. He was too polite to disillusion me. John Wyndham later put me right. No doubt some were anxious to greet the British Prime Minister, but the reason for the crowds was at once more simple and more natural. At this time the licensing law was severe, and all the beer-shops closed at 6 o'clock. This simultaneous exodus of drinkers had by a happy chance coincided with my arrival in the city.

Our hosts at Government House were Sir Dallas and Lady Brooks, who had already served for more than one term and had an intimate knowledge of local affairs. There were the usual entertainments—dinner with the Premier of Victoria; a meeting with the senior officers of the defence services, followed by a reception given by Sir Philip McBride, the Federal Minister of Defence ; luncheon at the Victorian Chambers of Commerce; a meeting with the Mayor for a formal presentation; and finally a dinner given to a number of leading citizens by the British High Commissioner, Lord Carrington, in the famous Melbourne Club. This was followed by a civic reception at which a large number of guests attended. All this meant more speeches—necessarily variations on the same theme. At the State Dinner on 5 February I was able to make a reference to my own situation which seemed to please the company assembled.

By the way, as I was coming along tonight I felt what a remarkable man Lord Melbourne was. He gave his name to the greatest city next to London in the whole of the British Commonwealth. He was also a very encouraging sort of man. First of all, he did not want to be Prime Minister, secondly, no one expected him to become Prime Minister, and thirdly, everybody agreed that when once there he would not last more than a few months. But in fact he stayed on for years.

o

A thrilling, even inspiring, incident took place after the reception at the Town Hall—something I will never forget. All the guests and a great part of the population waited for us to come out. It was a hot but not stifling night, and the whole crowd was in a hilarious mood. It was clear that before we could leave a further speech of some kind was required. This naturally had to be extempore, and as luck would have it proved to meet the mood of the people. I spoke from the heart, being myself much moved; all the experience of recent weeks seemed to culminate in this great audience. It was one of those occasions when one becomes gifted with something like true eloquence. Much to the relief of my staff (who had a healthy suspicion about speeches off the cuff), no record seems to have been made nor, since the event was altogether outside the authorised programme, did any account appear in the Press.

Early on the morning of 8 February we left for Hobart. Those who have visited Tasmania will remember the beauty and the charm of the island. The ceremonies were not exacting. Luncheon with the Prime Minister, Robert Cosgrove, was followed by a reception at Government House. I was delighted to find in the Governor, Sir Ronald Cross, an old House of Commons colleague. Sunday was a day of rest, with no engagements except to read the lessons in church. Since this was my ordinary practice at home, it was not an imposition. The next morning we spent with the Mayor and civic authorities of Hobart and left in the afternoon for Canberra, arriving in the evening of 10 February.

> Back at Canberra, after a very pleasant weekend in Tasmania. Everyone seems to think that the Australian tour has succeeded very well.
> My sixty-fourth birthday![1]

I was beginning to feel the disadvantages of so long an absence from London with so many problems to be resolved. The Foreign Office had prepared a new draft for a reply to Bulganin, to which I was willing to agree, subject to its being formally submitted to the NATO council.

[1] 10 February 1958.

It should meet the American anxieties without abandoning my own position. (Actually, now that the Americans have successfully launched their own 'sputnik' they will be in a better temper.) We found, on closer examination, that the new draft followed very closely my original draft. I do *not* suggest any particular date for the Summit meetings, but I do suggest that the 'preparatory work' (whether by Foreign Secretaries or diplomats) should start forthwith.[1]

Having established my chief point, I was content. On the day that I returned to Canberra our reply had been dispatched and published. 'Reply to Bulganin is published and seems to have had a good press.'[2] At the same time the situation at home was not altogether discouraging in spite of some troubles.

We seem to get excellent majorities in the *House*—62, 64, 69. But it is *not*, alas, the same in the country. We shall lose Rochdale, I fear, by a lot. The Liberal intervention in all these by-elections is very annoying.[2]

By now I was getting anxious to return.

On the evening of our second visit to Canberra, Lord Carrington gave a dinner in my honour at his own house which was a remarkable gathering of old and new friends. On the following day Menzies and I had our final talks, both in the morning and the afternoon, followed by a joint Press Conference. In the evening we left for Singapore after a splendid send-off.

On the morning of 12 February we arrived at Singapore. I had further discussions with Lim Yew Hock, the Prime Minister, and these were followed by a Press Conference.

Singapore was interesting. The present Government (of Lim Yew Hock) is moderate and sensible. But the 'Leftists' or 'semi-Communists' have won the municipal elections, and there is an atmosphere of uncertainty and alarm. I made it quite clear that we would go through with our undertaking to give 'internal independence'. But I made it also clear, in a public statement, that we expected any Singapore Government to carry out its side of the bargain.[3]

[1] 3 February 1958.   [2] 10 February 1958.   [3] 13 February 1958.

Since I had previously been to Singapore only as a bird of passage
I took the opportunity to make this a more formal visit. In view of
the extreme heat it was not until the late afternoon that the ceremonies began. We went first to the Town Hall, where we were
received by the Mayor, signed the visitors' book and took tea with
the members of the Town Council. The situation was somewhat
tense as a result of the left-wing triumph in the municipal elections
and there was some doubt as to whether the Mayor would be willing
to receive me. However, all went well, and the people seemed
pleased to see us whatever their political opinions. We drove
through the crowded streets of the city for over an hour. This day
marked the formal end of the tour.

On my way home I felt that, whatever the future might bring,
we could at least feel that the effort had been worth while.

There is no doubt that the tour has been a great success—far
greater than I or any of my advisers thought possible—so far as
the various Commonwealth countries are concerned. What is
unknown to me is whether it has had any impact at home.
People at home seem to be in a very cynical and defeatist mood
about everything.

My fears, however, proved groundless, for besides the Press of the
countries which I had visited, in the British Press the recognition
of the success of the tour was full and generous. When I got home
I found that there had been very wide coverage throughout our
journey and considerable space had been allocated both in letter-
press and in pictures.

Our success was largely due to the wonderful support which my
wife gave to me throughout. Besides carrying out an appropriate
programme especially arranged for her in each country, she had at
once conquered the hearts of the people by her own special gifts.
Naturally reserved, and even shy except among those whom she
knew well, the unexpectedly enthusiastic welcome which she was
given seemed to have affected her deeply. She had always been both
loved and respected in the circles where she was known, especially
in Stockton and Bromley, as well as in Sussex, and by all those with
whom she was thrown in contact. But this was her first experience

of an almost royal progress, and it seemed to bring to the surface some of the hidden qualities of her deeply sympathetic character. The remarkable powers which she had of making herself understood and loved had hitherto only been exercised on a restricted scale; now they had found their opportunity. She was more interested in people than in things; she made everybody realise that this was a sincere feeling and not adopted for the occasion. Thus among the old and the young, the important and the unimportant, all whom she met were enchanted. She returned happy, and, for all her modesty, conscious of having succeeded.

In the same way, so the critics said, I appeared to have grown in strength and authority. I certainly felt inspired with a new ardour and a new faith. Indeed those sections of the British Press which were normally only too glad to use against me the weapons of criticism and even of ridicule now seemed almost adulatory. I might easily have had my head turned had it not been for the salutary operation of British democracy. The people, to use Alan Breck's immortal phrase, have 'a grand memory for forgetting'. In my absence, they had certainly managed to forget any need for electoral gratitude. Thus it was not necessary for me, like an Eastern potentate, to be followed by a slave to remind me of the fickleness of fortune and the mortality of man. The remedy is as easily supplied by the English by-election system.

> We arrived at London Airport about noon, having been away nearly six weeks. Rab (Lord Privy Seal), Alec Home, and one or two other Ministers were [there] to meet me. The Rochdale by-election (on Wednesday), where our vote fell [from 26,518 to 9,827] and we were behind the Liberal (who polled 17,000), has been a tremendous shock. I was, of course, asked a question by the B.B.C. and I.T.V. interviewers. I said that the Government would continue to carry on its work and that a single incident in a campaign did not settle the issue.[1]

We were back home all right—with another 'little local difficulty'.

> I drove back to London with Rab; he stayed an hour with me at No. 10; then the Chief Whip; then the Foreign Secretary. All the same problems—all important, and all insoluble![1]

[1] 14 February 1958.

Although I was soon to be immersed in the daily round, I thought much about my recent experiences. As one of the papers not unkindly said: 'Whatever Macmillan may have done for the Commonwealth, the Commonwealth has certainly done something for Macmillan.' It certainly led me to try to reflect upon the lessons to be learned even from so hurried a tour.

It was clear that, more than ever before, the future of the nations linked together through the Commonwealth tie must depend upon personal as well as formal relations. Not only must the new opportunities of rapid travel be used to bring the leading figures of the old country in frequent touch with the governors of the newly emerging states, but equal care must be taken to maintain the closest co-operation with the older members—Canada, Australia, New Zealand and South Africa. So far as the choice rested with us, future Governors-General must be of the highest calibre. I had seen two outstanding examples of how beneficial their influence could be. In Field-Marshal Slim, Britain had a representative of all that the Australians most admired; in Lord Cobham we had chosen a man equally attractive to the people of New Zealand. But it was likely that fewer and fewer Governors-General would be appointed from Britain. It was therefore upon the High Commissioners that we must depend. In their choice, as in the Foreign Service, the principle must be reasserted that the man should be chosen most likely 'to do the Queen's business'. Above all there must be no appointment without careful consideration of the personal characteristics, foibles, and even susceptibilities of the Government to which our High Commissioner or Ambassador was to be accredited. Above all no question of seniority should be allowed to interfere with the object in view. There must be no 'Buggins's turn'.

In India we had in Malcolm MacDonald a most practised diplomatist, with a profound knowledge and a genuine love of Asia and the East. In New Zealand the genial figure of George Mallaby made him well adapted to his role. The fact that he always appeared in a bowler or billycock hat on every occasion, whether suitable or not, seemed to endear him to all classes. In Australia we were served at this time by perhaps the greatest envoy that we have ever sent—

Lord Carrington—loved then and still loved by every class and rank throughout that vast territory.

Nevertheless the personal qualities, however important and sometimes decisive, could not alter the great changes now beginning. In 1958 the transformation from the old Colonial Empire to the new Commonwealth had, with the exception of Ghana, been restricted to Asia. Yet it was clear that the process must begin soon both in Africa and the Mediterranean. In other words the dilemma would soon be presented to us either to allow the rest of the Colonial Empire to follow the same course or to try to maintain the old system by force. If, as seemed certain, we were to choose the former alternative, by what means could we hope to maintain the reality of a unity amidst so diverse and so numerous a group ranging from minute territories to sub-continents? We must, of course, do our best to interest the older members of the Commonwealth of British descent in those newly joined countries in Asia or Africa. Yet it was clear that the main task of giving economic aid and political guidance must fall upon Britain. There could at any rate be no question of going back. We could only go forward, in faith and hope.

When I reported on my tour to my colleagues in the Cabinet it was on the whole a cheerful picture that I could present. In Australia and New Zealand I had found strong evidence of real loyalty to the Crown and to Britain. There was a widespread desire that immigration should be mainly British—the Pommy was sincerely admired if sometimes laughed at—and economic development should be, as far as possible, supported by British capital. There were naturally misgivings in these countries about the admission of Asian and African members to the Commonwealth, indeed there was less interest than there ought to be in this aspect of Commonwealth development. Britain therefore had a duty to interpret the new members to the old. As to the Asian countries that I had visited, I reported my admiration of the balanced view taken by the leaders of opinion on the value of the British connection past and present. At any rate, whether or not the practice of Parliamentary democracy would prove successful, all the members of the Commonwealth were so far united by a common belief in its principles and by a determination to maintain individual freedom. This unique association of nations had therefore an important role to play in the world struggle. The rapidly changing situation inside and outside the Commonwealth presented a challenge to imaginative statesmanship. Might not the vision of co-operation between peoples of so many different races and creeds make as great, if a different, appeal to the youth of today as it had to past generations? These were, of course, the hopeful sentiments encouraged and fostered by what I had just seen and heard. In spite of many disappointments they seem to me still applicable to the needs and opportunities of today.

CHAPTER XIII

The Strange Case of
the Bank Rate 'Leak'

THE drama of political life oscillates between tragedy and comedy. Indeed it is in the interplay of these that much of the human interest lies. From time to time, to the general amazement of the spectators, it degenerates into melodrama or even farce.

One of the most whimsical examples of such exhibitions was provided at the end of 1957 by the 'Strange Case of the Bank Rate Leak'. In this Harold Wilson played the role of Sherlock Holmes, complete with pipe and almost seeming to sport a deerstalker, supported by an admiring if somewhat reluctant Watson in the shape of Hugh Gaitskell. However, this case proved, in spite of a promising start, one of the great detective's failures. Or perhaps Transport House, while equal in imagination, was unable to match the analytical skill of Baker Street.

The story begins with the appointment of Lord Hailsham as Chairman of the Conservative Party in succession to Oliver Poole. During the summer of 1957 the state of the Party and the current of public opinion still moving against us made me reflect deeply about our prospects. In Parliament our strength was growing and almost consolidated. But in the country we were still weak and divided. It seemed to me that the best chance lay in a change in the chairmanship which would be sufficiently dramatic to create something of the improvement effected by Lord Woolton after our electoral disaster in 1945. Hailsham appeared to have all the qualities required.

I talked all this over with Poole, who proved in complete agreement with this idea. Oliver Poole had sat for some years in the House of Commons and now held an important position in the

O2

City. He was an admirable organiser as well as a most loyal and devoted supporter of the Party. He had been appointed to the Chairmanship by Eden in 1955 when Lord Woolton resigned. It was typical of Poole's selflessness that it was he himself who suggested that a somewhat more spectacular head of the Party organisation was required for this period when a General Election must take place within two years and might come even sooner. Poole by his own admission was no great speaker, and found himself far more suited to the work of day-to-day management of a complicated machine than to appearances before large audiences, whether in London or in the provinces. He not only willingly agreed to the change, but also promised to continue to give Hailsham his full assistance. Accordingly on 27 August,

> I . . . offered the Chairmanship of the Party to Quintin Hailsham (coupled with Lord President and Deputy Leader of the House of Lords). He professed—quite genuinely—inability to do so great a job. But he will think it over.[1]

On 29 August I noted that Hailsham

> has accepted, if Oliver Poole can be persuaded to stay on and help. This is just what I want. I saw Poole later in the day, who has generously agreed to become Deputy Chairman. He will do 'organisation'; Hailsham political leadership and ideas. This should make a very good combination.[2]

On 30 August I wrote formally to Hailsham as follows:

> I have had a good talk with Oliver Poole this evening. With characteristic loyalty and sense of duty he is very willing to give you any help he can. He is perfectly ready to accept the position of Deputy Chairman of the Party to which I have the right to appoint him (which is in fact not a new post but one which has existed in the past). He thinks that he could be of assistance to you on the organisational side. Personally I feel that you and he together would make a splendid partnership and it will impress the public with the sense of team spirit which we are all ready to show.

Hailsham's appointment involved his transfer from the Ministry of Education. He was replaced by Geoffrey Lloyd, an experienced

[1] 27 August 1957.   [2] 29 August 1957.

politician and administrator. These changes were announced on 17 September. After this curtain-raiser we had not long to wait before the opening scenes of a new thriller destined to run successfully throughout the winter months.

The Chancellor of the Exchequer's measures, intended to sustain the value of sterling and combat inflation, were published on 19 September. Although the greater part of these were not unexpected, the increase in Bank Rate by 2 per cent was exceptional, if not unprecedented. Indeed, I was only finally persuaded to agree on the day before the announcement. So large a rise certainly came, as Thorneycroft intended, as a shock to public opinion. Wilson immediately published a statement giving a general, if qualified, support to the proposals as a whole. A few days later, on 24 September, I was informed that he had written to Enoch Powell, the Financial Secretary to the Treasury (the Chancellor of the Exchequer was in Washington), asserting that there were indications of a leakage of information prior to the publication of the new Bank Rate which called for urgent investigation. The story can perhaps best be told from my own record at the time:

> A new row. It is alleged that there was a 'leak' about the intention of the Government to raise the Bank Rate. Since I only agreed to this on Wednesday morning, and since the dealings on Wednesday evening (after the Stock Exchange had closed) were very small, I think this improbable. We have had careful enquiries made; but no trace can be found of any irregularity. Harold Wilson has written a letter to the Financial Secretary, demanding an official, or rather a judicial, enquiry. In the absence of the Chancellor of the Exchequer, Enoch Powell came to see me to discuss his reply. The Governor is quite happy—so is the Chairman of the Stock Exchange—that we should refuse. I therefore authorised the F.S. to send his reply and publish it at once (as Wilson had done). The Lobby were seen and took the decision (with background explanations) well enough.[1]

I had of course been in communication with the Chancellor of the Exchequer by telegram. He readily agreed to the course which I proposed.

[1] 26 September 1957.

Wilson at once published a further protest and said it would
be raised when Parliament met. No doubt there will be trouble
in some of the newspapers tomorrow. It is, of course, true that
the Chancellor saw a few newspaper editors (*Times*, *Manchester
Guardian*, etc.) about the *general* policy (investment cuts; restriction of credit base, etc.). But he naturally never mentioned the
Bank Rate.[1]

As I expected, Wilson's detective instincts had now been aroused
to an intense pitch of excitement. He was not to be thrown off the
trail by any denials, official or unofficial. He returned to the charge
on 4 October in a letter to Powell in which he stated that '*prima
facie* evidence has been brought to my attention suggesting that the
leak emanated from a political source'.[2] Certainly he seemed determined to get the greatest possible publicity out of this affair for

He published the letter on the tape and wireless at 6 p.m. After
consulting Norman Brook, Bishop and Chief Whip, I got my
reply (F.S.T. was away) to him, to B.B.C., and to press by 9 p.m.
I rejected his general demand for a roving enquiry into vague
rumours. I went on to say that he now made a specific allegation,
for which he said he had evidence. If he would send it to me, I
would refer it to Lord Chancellor for advice as to whatever
further investigation was called for.[3]

Accordingly on 7 October

Before the Cabinet, Mr. Harold Wilson, accompanied by Mr.
James Griffiths (vice Mr. Hugh Gaitskell) called. I had the Lord
Chancellor with me. They seemed rather nervous, but produced
a story about a Mr. X (who was under my 'patronage') and a
conversation with a Mr. Y (who was under my control). Mr. Y
had claimed that he had full knowledge of the Bank Rate decision.
I assumed from this that Mr. X must be a civil servant or a
bishop, and Mr. Y an employee of the Conservative Central
Office.[4]

Wilson demanded that a judge should make the preliminary
enquiry and not the Lord Chancellor, Lord Kilmuir, as I had

[1] 26 September 1957.   [2] *Annual Register*, 1957, p. 57.
[3] 4 October 1957.   [4] 7 October 1957.

proposed. However, I stuck to my decision. On 9 October Holmes and Watson, or rather Wilson and Gaitskell, came to see the Lord Chancellor. This at any rate seemed something of a climb-down.

> They are still very unwilling to produce Mr. X. The Lord Chancellor, however, pressed them, and they undertook to see Mr. X and ask him whether he would give his story to the Lord Chancellor.[1]

So the matter rested until we all set off on 10 October for the Conservative Party Conference at Brighton.

Meanwhile I was under no illusions as to the broad political situation:

> What will happen during the next two years, no one can say— or even if we can keep the Government going for that time. At the moment, the whole thing is swinging *away* from us. But has it swung to Labour? Gaitskell is trying to attract the middle vote. But will he lose the enthusiasm of the Left? (The H-bomb is perhaps the real test.) I think he will probably succeed—but he has made a tactical mistake in trying to get his troops rallied too early. If I can [postpone the] battle . . . it is quite likely that they will quarrel again. My problem is, of course, very similar. If we cannot bring back the traditional strength of the Party to the fold—small shopkeepers, middle class, etc.,—we have no chance. But we also need at least three million trade union votes. We too have a war on two flanks.[2]

The Conference, however, did much to restore Conservative confidence. It was made memorable by Lord Hailsham's first appearance in his new part. He had already stirred the country on 5 October by a fine broadcast. He now appeared in the more exuberant role of 'cheerleader' and created great enthusiasm both in the Party and throughout the country. He was not afraid of novel methods of publicity. Undoubtedly he became the hero of the Conference. Early every morning he was seen and photographed in a bathing-costume upon the Brighton beach—in itself an impressive sight—and the famous bell with which he roused the delegates to a high pitch of emotion became a symbol of national revival. Even the

[1] 9 October 1957.   [2] 5 October 1957.

editor of the *Annual Register* in recording these events was stirred into an unusual romanticism by describing the new Chairman of the Party as

unflaggingly strenuous, clubbable, provocative, and amusing. It really looked as if Lord Hailsham enjoyed himself among the 4,000 delegates, and that was what the 4,000 delegates liked about him.[1]

Indeed so successful was Hailsham's conduct of the Conference and so eloquent his final speech that some of the Press and other commentators felt that the new Chairman had put the Prime Minister somewhat into the shade. I had, of course, no feelings of reproach, but with characteristic sensitivity, Hailsham sent me a letter of explanation. This crossed one of thanks which I had already despatched. His was in the following terms:

My dear Harold,
I think we can write down Brighton as a modest success. The troops came a little down in the mouth, and they went away heartened.
But there has been one thing which has grieved me, and that is the tendency of the Press to dramatise me. This is all the purest ballyhoo. Do not be misled into thinking that the sober statesmanlike speech from the Prime Minister need suffer from the campanological eccentricities of the Party Manager. People like people to be themselves; they were satisfied with their Prime Minister who acted like a Prime Minister, but I hope that they also had a warm spot for the Party Chairman who sent them away with a cheer on their lips and a good belly laugh. Incidentally I gave them on Thursday a serious political disquisition which I hope they may read.
I had hoped that the photographs of my navel would suffice to disabuse anyone of the belief that I had ideas above my station. But I write this simply to say again what I am sure you never doubted (1) that you have my unqualified loyalty and support and (2) that I am not quite such an ass as I seem, and I must be allowed to attempt this task in my own eccentric way. The Opposition must continue twittering with rage, and our sup-

[1] *Annual Register, 1957*, p. 53.

porters cheering and laughing. In the meantime you will win the vote of the serious.

y.e.

Q.H.

Before the Conference ended I heard that Kilmuir had started his investigation into Wilson's charges.

He has not told me about it, except that it will take him some days to complete. This affair has been a great nuisance, and distracted the attention of a lot of people from their work. I hope it will turn out all right.[1]

On 18 October he delivered his report: 'Although it completely exonerates all concerned and quite definitely advises me *against* a formal enquiry, it is not easy to decide the next step.'[2] After consultation with some of my colleagues, I decided to inform Gaitskell of my decision not to proceed further. The Leader of the Opposition immediately issued a statement that an enquiry by the Lord Chancellor was no substitute for one conducted by 'an independent judicial person'.[3] At the same time he somewhat enlarged the issue by declaring that he and his friends knew

beyond any shadow of doubt that certain circles in the City as well as certain people in the Press were aware on the Wednesday afternoon that the Chancellor of the Exchequer was going to make a grave statement on the Thursday morning which would 'put the screws on' and intensify the credit squeeze.[4]

To this I made no reply. I left for Washington and Ottawa on 22 October and did not return until 27 October. Three weeks then passed, and the matter seemed likely to pass into oblivion, as indeed it should have done. But I noticed on 31 October that 'According to the *Daily Herald*, Wilson is to go on asking questions about "The Bank Rate Leak" and thinks he has fished out something to our discredit.'[5]

Of course I was aware of the guidance which the Chancellor of the Exchequer had thought it right to give, in accordance with normal practice, regarding the main restrictive measures which the

[1] 12 October 1957.   [2] 18 October 1957.   [3] *Annual Register, 1957*, p. 57.
[4] *Annual Register, 1957*, pp. 57–8.   [5] 31 October 1957.

Government intended to take. For this purpose he had himself seen a number of leading journalists as well as the Director-General of the Federation of British Industries. He had also given similar information to Oliver Poole in order that the necessary preparations might be made to explain and defend the Government's policy. He had authorised the Minister of Labour to see representatives of the Trades Union Congress and the British Employers' Confederation. Similarly the Minister of Power had communicated the broad outline of the Government's plans to the Chairmen of the Central Electricity Authority, of the Gas Council and of the Coal Board. In none of these interviews or communications was there any mention of the decision to raise the Bank Rate. Nevertheless I felt it would perhaps be possible to create prejudice on account of these perfectly legitimate interviews which were thought desirable in order to mobilise the greatest possible support at home and abroad. I was therefore not altogether surprised when on 12 November the matter was raised by a question in Parliament from Sir Leslie Plummer, a Labour Member who had been intimately connected with the Beaverbrook Press. His intervention followed the line of an article which had already appeared in the *Daily Express*. In the course of supplementary questions a direct reference was made to Oliver Poole by both Plummer and Wilson. Indeed Wilson allowed himself to refer sneeringly to Poole's 'vast City interests'.[1] I was not in the House at the time; but Thorneycroft very properly refused to answer any questions as to the people whom he had seen, contenting himself with a reference to the Lord Chancellor's enquiry. I received a full account of what had taken place in the House of Commons later in the evening.

As I had feared, the storm broke at Question Time in the House of Commons, when more or less direct charges of falsehood and/or corruption were brought against the Chancellor of the Exchequer and Mr. Poole. (The latter was, for the first time, mentioned by name.)[2]

The next day I received a letter from Poole asking for a formal enquiry. It seemed intolerable that he should be brought into dis-

[1] *Hansard*, 12 November 1957.   [2] 12 November 1957.

credit by statements in the House of Commons without any opportunity of reply.

On reflection, I reached the view that we must now set up the Judicial Enquiry into the alleged 'Bank Rate Leak'. Although no *prima facie* evidence has been produced to me *or* to the Lord Chancellor, there has now been an imputation against the honour of distinguished men. Oliver Poole has written me a letter 'demanding' an enquiry. Thorneycroft is in the same mood. We discussed all this during the morning and my conclusion was upheld by the leading colleagues whom I had in [for consultation].[1]

Accordingly on 13 November I announced the decision to set up an enquiry under the Tribunals Act.

In making this announcement to the House, I began by referring to the correctness of the Chancellor of the Exchequer's refusal to give information as to individuals whom he had seen on the day preceding the Bank Rate announcement as it was

contrary to precedent and damaging to the conduct of public business to disclose the confidential discussions which are frequently held in advance of an announcement of Government policy.[2]

But I now felt that, in view of the interpretation that had been placed on his reply, the information should be given. While repeating the categorical assurance that at these interviews no information had been disclosed by the Chancellor of the Exchequer or any other Minister about the intention to increase Bank Rate, I gave a full list of the persons whom he and his colleagues had seen on that day. All this, of course, had been put before the Lord Chancellor, and he had reached the conclusion that I had already announced. I continued:

No new evidence of any leakage of information has been adduced. But in the course of the supplementary questions yesterday imputations were made–or, at any rate, implied–on the honour of my right hon. Friend the Chancellor of the

[1] 13 November 1957.   [2] *Hansard*, 13 November 1957.

Exchequer and on the character and probity of Mr. Oliver Poole. These are serious imputations, and my right hon. Friend and Mr. Poole have both represented to me most strongly that they should be given an opportunity to rebut them.

Mr. Poole, who is no longer in a position to defend himself in this house, has sent me a letter . . . asking that an inquiry should be held for this purpose. In the circumstances which have arisen, I have decided that this is now the right course to take.[1]

In reply to questions I asserted:

This is a completely changed situation. This is now an attack on the honour of two gentlemen, and I think it right that they should have an opportunity to rebut this attack upon them, which, at an earlier stage, was mere tittle-tattle.[1]

On the following day, in proposing the motion to set up a Judicial Enquiry, I further justified my previous refusal and the reason for my changed decision.

While I felt it right to determine the matter by the exercise of my own judgment, in accordance with precedent, at the point where everything was still in the realm of vague rumour or even prejudice, once an accusation is made which touches the honour of a member of the Government or of an individual outside a different situation arises. Parliamentary Privilege is a treasured right of the House of Commons, but we should not forget that it stems from the days of relationships between the Executive and Parliament very different from those which now exist. Privilege was intended to be a buttress of liberty. It should not be used as a protection for defamation.[2]

I concluded by regretting the circumstances which had led me to propose the motion that I thought the House would agree that the Government had acted all through in accordance with precedent and propriety and, in their final decision 'in accordance with something which over-rides both–the right of men, even in the highest places, who have been attacked by name, to defend their honour'.[2] The Opposition affected to criticise this robust attitude, but it

[1] *Hansard*, 13 November 1957.   [2] *Hansard*, 14 November 1957.

seemed to be well received by the Press and the country, as well as by the Government's supporters in and outside Parliament.

The Tribunal was appointed forthwith. It was presided over by Lord Justice Parker, assisted by two distinguished Queen's Counsel, Edward Milner Holland and Geoffrey Veale. It began its work on 2 December and completed its hearings by 20 December. It covered an enormous field, hearing evidence of the most detailed kind. Information was given of almost every transaction in gilt-edged stocks, large and small, before the rise of Bank Rate by a great variety of individuals who might be supposed to have some prior information or even be vaguely aware of some rumours. Although I felt sure that the evidence given had really destroyed and almost turned into ridicule the case that Wilson had made, there might be some consequential question arise as to the position of part-time members of the Court of the Bank of England and their possible conflict of interest. I was confident that any question of improper disclosure would be altogether swept aside and the personal honour of Ministers, the Governor of the Bank and others would be completely vindicated. But I felt sure that the Opposition, thwarted in their original purpose, might try to ride out on this quite different issue. Accordingly I sent a minute to Butler and to Thorneycroft on 28 December calling their attention to this problem of the Directors of the Bank and making some suggestions as to how it should be dealt with. At the same time I was anxious not to allow Wilson or even Gaitskell to escape too lightly. When the Bank Rate Report was finally published on 21 January and all the charges were proved wholly false and altogether unsubstantiated, I could not resist sending an encouraging message to Butler from Canberra.

I have now seen London Press comments on the Parker report. These are very favourable. My refusal to agree to a tribunal until the honour of individuals was attacked seems to receive general support. Even on the position of outside Directors of the Bank there now seems to be no serious pressure for any early change. *The Times* is for once entirely on our side. From here therefore it looks as though we should take a pretty firm stand in the debate with the aim of showing that the attitude and tactics of the Opposition were wholly unjustified. A robust attitude would, I think, encourage our people. Harold Wilson should be shown up . . . Gaitskell should never have yielded to him. Even on the position of outside Directors I would think that as things have turned out there is no need for haste and that this might be left to be considered by the Radcliffe Committee as part of their review of the whole system.

In every case the Tribunal found those individuals against whose probity accusations had been made or suggested, whether by direct charge or innuendo, to be completely exonerated from any possible charge of misconduct. In the case of Oliver Poole, who had been the main target of attack, the Tribunal used these words:

> After full inquiry, we are satisfied that there is not a shred of evidence that Mr. Poole made any disclosure either in regard to the Bank Rate or the restrictive financial measures to any person connected with the companies with which he is associated, or that he made use of any such information for the purpose of private gain.[1]

Its general conclusions were summarised as follows:

> It will be seen from what we have said above that we have unhesitatingly reached the unanimous conclusion that there is no justification for allegations that information about the raising of the Bank Rate was improperly disclosed to any person.[2]

Not content with this sweeping and complete exculpation, the Tribunal expressed approval of the Chancellor of the Exchequer's conduct throughout.

> We have found the occasions on which and the circumstances in which prior disclosure was made by Ministers of the proposed restrictive financial measures. We have also found that in every case the information disclosed was treated by the recipient as confidential and that no use of such information was made for the purpose of private gain. . . . The propriety of such disclosure is a matter for Parliament alone. We do, however,

[1] *Report of the Tribunal appointed to Inquire into Allegations of Improper Disclosure of Information relating to the Raising of the Bank Rate*, Cmnd. 350 (H.M.S.O., January 1958), para. 83.
[2] Ibid., para. 115.

understand and appreciate the reasons for the decision of the Chancellor of the Exchequer, with the approval of his Cabinet colleagues, to explain in advance to Press representatives, the Conservative Central Office and representatives of industry the nature of the intended restrictive financial measures, having regard to the serious financial situation, and the urgency created by his imminent visit to Washington.[1]

Scarcely ever has any public enquiry of this kind led to so sweeping and overwhelming a rejection of the charges made. Yet an immense machine of investigation and heavy expenditure both to the nation and to individuals, as well as considerable danger of discredit to the financial system of the City at home and abroad, had been made necessary by the persistence which the leaders of the Opposition showed, basing their accusations on the flimsiest evidence and on gossip or malice. When we examine the slender foundation on which all this massive edifice of allegation and insinuation was actually based, we change from melodrama to pure farce. Now at last the identity of the mysterious figures, X and Y, already known to Gaitskell and Wilson as well as to the Lord Chancellor and myself, were revealed to an astonished public. This was the story, in the words of the learned judge and his colleagues:

On Wednesday, the 25th September, 1957, on the 9.8 a.m. train from Woking to Waterloo, a conversation took place between Mr. J. L. Pumphrey, a Civil Servant, and his cousin Miss Chataway, then employed in the Press Department of the Conservative Central Office. It was this incident which gave rise to the following statement by Mr. Harold Wilson in the Memorandum forwarded to the Lord Chancellor on the 9th October, 1957:

'A man holding an important public position whose integrity, intelligence and sense of responsibility can be vouched for by a number of well-known persons, including Lord Attlee, will state that on 25th September he was told by an employee of the Conservative Central Office that they had known "about this Bank Rate business" before the announcement on 19th September. The employee said jocularly that they were expecting the

[1] Ibid., para. 116.

police in any day! He reported this to a friend who informed Mr. Gaitskell. Subject to the assurances asked for in my covering letter, this man, with whom Mr. Gaitskell and I have been in touch, is willing to supplement this statement by oral evidence and answer any questions the Lord Chancellor may wish to put to him.'

In connection with this incident, we find the following facts:

'Miss Chataway, then 18 or 19 years of age, had been employed by the Press Department of the Conservative Central Office only since the 16th September. She was a learner, whose duties on the 16th, 17th, 18th and 19th involved such elementary secretarial work as the typing of hand-outs, preparation of envelopes and packing into envelopes. The conversation with Mr. Pumphrey, which took place in a crowded compartment, covered family matters and Miss Chataway's new job. Mr. Pumphrey, who was more than twice Miss Chataway's age, admittedly joked about the new job. He suggested that she must be able to give a lot of inside information, in particular to her brother, who is a television commentator. She replied in similar vein "Oh yes, the lot." She went on, jokingly, to say that the office were expecting the police any day about "this Bank Rate business." We are quite clear that this claim to prior knowledge was made by Miss Chataway in jest, as part of a conversation begun by Mr. Pumphrey in jest. How he came to take her remarks seriously is difficult to understand. In any event we are satisfied that Miss Chataway had no prior knowledge of a rise in the Bank Rate.'[1]

An equally slender case was based upon another incident also reported to the Lord Chancellor.

On Friday, the 20th September, 1957, about 9.30 a.m., at Watford Station, a conversation took place between Mr. L. Goodman, a principal in the Ministry of Housing and Local Government, and Mr. McIntosh, Principal Information Officer to the Ministry of Labour, which was overheard by a Mr. Loftus, a reporter on the staff of *Reynolds News*.

It was this incident which gave rise to the following passage in Mr. Harold Wilson's Memorandum to the Lord Chancellor:

[1] Ibid., paras. 97–8.

'It has also been reported to me, admittedly at second-hand, that a person who can be vouched for, but who may not be willing to come forward, overheard a conversation between a Treasury official and the P.R.O. of a Government Department (not the Treasury) during which the latter categorically stated that he was aware of the forthcoming increase in the Bank Rate which called forth a very critical observation from the Treasury official who said he had no right to know such a thing.'

This incident also gave rise to an article in *Reynolds News* of the 22 September stating:

Last night came information that the Cabinet's decision was known to more than one Treasury official—not of the top rank—twenty-four hours before the announcement.
Many Whitehall officials are shocked that anybody should be given advance information.[1]

Here again the likelihood of a principal in the Ministry of Housing and Local Government having prior knowledge of the Government's decision seemed in itself remote, and the Tribunal had no hesitation in dismissing Mr. Goodman's impressions as arising 'out of a misunderstanding'.

We think that Mr. McIntosh only intended to convey that he had received prior information of the restrictive financial measures, and was using the phrase 'Bank Rate' loosely and inaccurately to indicate these measures. He was not intending to claim prior knowledge of the increase in the Bank Rate. We were, however, surprised that Mr. McIntosh, who realised that Mr. Goodman was taken aback by something he had said, did not appreciate that Mr. Goodman thought he was claiming prior knowledge of the increase in the Bank Rate and immediately correct that impression.[2]

Finally, in summing up their view of this incident the Tribunal declared

In any event, we are satisfied that Mr. McIntosh had no prior knowledge of the proposed increase in the Bank Rate.[2]

[1] Ibid., para. 99.   [2] Ibid., para. 100.

Thus out of a conversation in a railway carriage with a young lady of nineteen, engaged by the Conservative Office for less than a week before the crucial date, and out of some foolish tittle-tattle between two minor officials, the great Bank Rate Leak case was blown up into a formidable balloon and then with infinite care and effort, but at heavy public cost and much private inconvenience, decisively and finally pricked. *Solventur risu tabulae.*

I was on my Commonwealth tour when the consequent debate took place in the House of Commons. Perhaps if Wilson had expressed his regret and made some suitable apology, explaining his action as a proof of his zeal for the public welfare, the ending of this affair would have been more agreeable than the beginning. He did not choose this course, preferring to answer Butler's formidable speech condemning 'the political weapon of the smear' with an amendment altogether irrelevant to the main issue. The discussion was violent and uproarious throughout; indeed such was the confusion that the Opposition not only voted for their own amendment but against the motion thanking the members of the Tribunal for their labours.

The 'Great Bank Rate Scandal' had turned out to be a 'mare's nest' after all.

CHAPTER XIV

The Wooing of Europe

THE Eden Government, before it came to a premature end through the unhappy illness of the Prime Minister, had at least completed an important stage in the long struggle towards the economic co-operation of the countries of Western Europe. After a year's devoted work by the officials concerned and through the close understanding between Peter Thorneycroft and myself which ensured the full co-operation between the Board of Trade and the Treasury, the British Government had succeeded in completing and depositing its own plan by the beginning of October, 1956.[1] This—the famous Plan G—had not merely obtained the agreement of the Cabinet but secured the acquiescence, if not the enthusiastic support, of the Party in the House of Commons. Since the outcome of the negotiations originated at Messina in the previous year between the six countries of Western Europe was still more than doubtful, there was every reason to hope that our formula for an association between the Six and the other countries of Europe which would ensure a Free Trade Area for all goods other than foodstuffs might prove an acceptable and practical compromise. The events of the winter, traumatic as they were to prove, increased rather than diminished my hope, when I became Prime Minister in January 1957, that the recent close and friendly co-operation between France and Britain might make our partners as sympathetic and helpful in the economic as they had recently proved themselves in the diplomatic and military spheres.

When we began to recover from the somewhat breathless operations involved in the formation of the new Government and the aftermath of Suez, the first indications seemed encouraging. We were in close and intimate relations with Paris. Selwyn Lloyd

[1] See above, p. 77.

reported from Rome on 18 January that the Italian Government was well disposed and seemed fully to understand our position. Much of course would depend upon the attitude of the members of the Organisation for European Economic Co-operation. At the beginning of February this body reported that a European Free Trade Area was a practical concept. However opinions might diverge as to whether agriculture should or should not be included, the technical problems in its exclusion seemed by no means insuperable.

On 7 February 1957 the British Government submitted a further memorandum, which was also published as a White Paper. In this we reaffirmed our view that an industrial free trade area could be established in Europe and proposed that formal negotiations should now be undertaken in O.E.E.C. to that end, based on the assumption that the six Messina powers were approaching a successful conclusion of their own discussions. We pointed out that although our special interests and responsibilities in the Commonwealth precluded the acceptance of arrangements which would make it impossible for Britain to accept agricultural imports from the Commonwealth on terms at least as favourable as those applying to Europe, yet we could co-operate fully in an industrial free trade area. We believed that other European countries not included in the Six would be ready to do the same. We argued that the establishment of a European Free Trade Area would raise industrial efficiency by encouraging increased specialisation, large-scale production and new technical developments. It would thus strengthen the economy of Western Europe; and from this improved position we could all begin the movement to reduce or remove restrictions on imports from outside. There would therefore be no conflict between the establishment of such a free trade area in Europe and the recently agreed aim of developing a wider system of multilateral trade and payments. This formal and public declaration was warmly welcomed in Europe, both by the six Messina powers and by the other O.E.E.C. countries which would be prospective members of the European Free Trade Area. The French showed none of the hostility which was afterwards to develop; indeed they seemed more anxious about the obligations and difficulties involved in the proposed Common

Market Treaty. René Massigli, who had recently retired from the Embassy, told me that Mollet was altogether friendly and that in his opinion his government 'will last quite a bit—but we must hurry with our plans for European unity'.[1]

When the Council met in February it proved wholly favourable to our ideas and readily agreed that the negotiations should be set in motion. I was anxious, however, that this task should not be restricted to officials. I therefore proposed to Thorneycroft that a Committee of Ministers should be formed representing the Governments interested in the scheme who would give a continuous impulse to the work of the officials which might otherwise drag on indefinitely. This was agreed. I also thought that we needed inside the United Kingdom an unofficial committee of industrialists, trade unionists and others, whom we could consult from time to time. This too was agreed. I was fortunate in having in the Chancellor of the Exchequer an enthusiastic supporter of European unity. His successor at the Board of Trade, David Eccles, was an old colleague from Strasbourg, who threw into the movement both his brilliant intellectual powers and all his moral enthusiasm.

The British Press was on the whole favourable,

except the *Express* which demands an immediate General Election and has a bitter personal attack on me. I'm afraid this is the beginning of what will be a sustained campaign. It's all the result of the European Free Trade policy, for which Lord Beaverbrook has a fanatical hatred.[2]

On 20 February I spoke to a meeting of industrialists who seemed fully satisfied with the policy which we were pursuing. When I went to Paris in the beginning of March, I was not so happy. The French, with their customary skill, had now succeeded, during the concluding stages in their discussions with the Common Market group, in including the French Colonial Empire on the most favourable terms. Satisfied themselves, they were now less sympathetic to the needs of others.

Although the Paris talks were mainly concerned with our proposal to make substantial force reductions in Europe, to which

[1] 8 February 1957.   [2] 17 February 1957.

Mollet and Pineau showed extreme hostility, yet when we came to the economic discussions they were in a calmer and more relaxed mood.

> The French have got what they want, but they have put *us* in a great difficulty. If it had not been for the question of our forces in Europe, I would have attacked the French for the way in which they managed the last stages of the negotiations for the Common Market, especially the inclusion of the French Colonial Empire. This was got through at the last minute, and makes great difficulties for us.[1]

On 25 March the Messina powers after much hard bargaining signed the famous Treaty of Rome, which, if ratified by the Parliaments concerned, would come into force on 1 January in the following year, 1958. This historic event was to prove for good or ill a landmark in the history of Europe. It brought into being the European Economic Community with all its complicated administrative and judicial arrangements, thus constituting into a group those whose geographical borders were roughly those of Charlemagne's Empire. The opportunity for the extension of French influence and authority was not to escape the new ruler of France destined to emerge within a year. Yet on the surface, at any rate, the Common Market powers seemed still ready to proceed with the negotiations for the wider area of Free Trade.

In writing on 15 April to my friend, Edward Beddington-Behrens, about his plan for a public meeting in support of our ideas, I felt bound to state my anxieties.

> Any predictions about the progress of our negotiations are bound to be speculative; but what I think possible is that the official negotiations in Paris for a marriage between the Common Market and the Free Trade Area may have reached an impasse by the end of May. In order to make progress, as we must, it will probably be necessary for the Foreign Secretary, the Chancellor or me to take some political initiative with the Ministers of the other countries. We are unlikely to be able to do this before the early part of June.

[1] 9 March 1957.

Equally in writing to another friend on 18 April, I expressed the same doubts:

> What I chiefly fear, and what we must at all costs avoid, is the Common Market coming into being and the Free Trade Area never following. . . . However I will do my best.

All through this period I kept my Cabinet colleagues fully informed of the problems. On 2 May I warned them that the situation was serious. I was soon to make a visit to Bonn, and I intended to speak frankly to Adenauer about the political implications of an attempt to create a customs union excluding the possibility of an industrial free trade area of the kind which the United Kingdom had proposed. This must lead to the disintegration of any large European policy, eventually involving the collapse of NATO and of the existing system of defence. After my meeting with Chancellor Adenauer and the talk which Thorneycroft had with some of the French Ministers, we received assurances that as soon as the Treaty of Rome had been formally ratified, they would renew discussions with us about the formation of the Free Trade Area. Both the French and the Germans expressed sympathy, but seemed determined upon a policy of procrastination. This was due partly to a genuine anxiety about obtaining ratification in their respective Parliaments and partly to suspicion of each other. The Germans were becoming conscious of their strength and their ultimate superiority, but always fearful of being 'outsmarted' by the extraordinary skill of French diplomacy, equally agile and resourceful in victory and in defeat.

In spite of the argument that no progress could be made until after the Treaty of Rome had been formally ratified, I sent a minute to the Foreign Secretary at the beginning of June as follows:

> We ought to make a forward movement on the constitutional aspect, e.g. we ought to make it clear that we would accept a Council of Ministers and a majority vote on a limited field of decision, e.g. matters affecting the Free Trade Area. What I am not so sure about is how this hand ought to be played. The present line is to let everything go along without effort until after the ratification. The dangers of this plan are (*a*) that the French

may not ratify; (*b*) that when the Six have ratified they may snap their fingers at the Free Trade Area and leave us in the lurch. In some ways I should be less worried about (*a*) because then we might be able to do an exercise as we did after E.D.C. [European Defence Community] to pick up the pieces.

Similarly I felt that ELEC (The European League for Economic Co-operation), an unofficial body which commanded the respect of leading economists and statesmen throughout Europe and had some real achievements to its credit, ought to be able to help us. I appealed for help to my friend, Lady Rhys Williams, who set about this task with her usual energy.

At the Commonwealth Conference, as already described, there was much discussion on the whole question of European integration, both formally and informally. The Prime Ministers and Ministers showed themselves generally sympathetic. Since under our proposals the agricultural interests of the Commonwealth countries would be fully preserved, even the violent opposition of the Beaverbrook Press caused me little anxiety. Indeed my personal relations with the proprietor were never disturbed; with all his delight in controversy, Beaverbrook had a strong sense of loyalty to those who had served him in however remote a past.

What more could the British Government do? After considerable reflection I sent my ideas to Thorneycroft, the Chancellor of the Exchequer.

I feel sure that the pressure for European integration, though expressed in economic terms, really derives from the strong desire of many European countries for some form of closer *political* association. We should take advantage of this, since, while we are in something of a straitjacket as regards economic integration, we may well be able to show Europe that we are prepared for a closer political association. The following points ought to be considered urgently:

1. As I foreshadowed in my broadcast after the Commonwealth Prime Ministers' Meeting, we might agree that the management of a European Free Trade Area should be left to a European managing board. This might well be called a 'supra-national' institution. But does it matter?

2. We cannot afford to wait till November. Some earlier initiative, on a high level and with a political connotation, seems to be necessary.

3. For this purpose, it might be necessary to entrust our interests in this matter to a special Minister, who would co-ordinate the activities of, and be helped by, all the Departments concerned (principally the Treasury, Foreign Office and the Board of Trade).

4. We must not be bullied by the activities of the Six. We could, if we were driven to it, fight their movement if it were to take the form of anything that was prejudicial to our interests. Economically, with the Commonwealth and other friends, including the Scandinavians, we could stand aside from a narrow Common Market. We also have some politico-military weapons.

What the above amounts to is this: that we must take positive action in this field, to ensure that the wider Free Trade Area is more attractive than the narrower Common Market of the Six. We must take the lead, either in widening their project, or, if they will not co-operate with us, in opposing it.

Both the Chancellor of the Exchequer and the Foreign Secretary agreed with the idea for a Minister specially charged for the negotiations, and on the 22 July I sent a further memorandum to the Chancellor of the Exchequer defining my plan.

This Minister should be charged with collecting all the material, guiding all the studies, and being answerable to a group of Ministers consisting of myself, the Foreign Secretary, the President of the Board of Trade and yourself. The Colonial and Commonwealth Secretaries should be included in this group for purposes of major decisions but not necessarily for day-to-day discussion. . . .

One of [the] important duties would be to travel between now and the beginning of the great negotiations. It would be very important to travel both among the Six and among the Eleven. On the whole, it is as important to hold firm the Eleven as it is to break into the Six. He should therefore be something of a St. Paul: not merely the Jews but the Gentiles should be his care.

Now I come to who this Apostolic figure should be . . . I propose [Reginald] Maudling. . . .

Of course Maudling would still be Paymaster-General, but would be given these special duties. There is another argument, that I do not particularly want to have a Minister of State for Europe.

Thorneycroft readily agreed to my choice, as did those Ministers with whom Maudling would be working most intimately. I was careful to consult Butler before taking a decision. Although as Home Secretary he had little departmental interest, it was right for him to be closely associated with any important step. Moreover I always found his advice of special value in matters where the feelings of the House of Commons and the Party must be specially considered. Butler had a remarkable flair for scenting political mischief which might lie ahead, especially in a matter such as this where the Party as a whole was by no means enthusiastic.

The appointment was announced on 7 August and was well received. *The Times* referred to Maudling as 'one of the outstanding younger men in the Government'. I was indeed grateful to him for accepting what must be an onerous, and might prove a fruitless, task. Yet in these summer months of 1957 we could not foresee the long and dreary negotiations which were destined to be brought to a sudden and almost brutal conclusion at the end of 1958. Maudling began his work immediately and pursued it with an impressive combination of acute, even brilliant, capacity to seize the vital points and an unruffled calm, however great might be the disappointments or obstacles.

By the late summer of 1957, it had become clear that the Free Trade Area negotiations would not succeed if the United Kingdom kept up a completely negative attitude on foodstuffs. The other European countries insisted that, in exchange for the eventual entry, duty free, of British manufactured goods into their markets, they should gain easier access to our market for their own agricultural products. The European countries did not favour free trade in foodstuffs, but rather an evolution towards a system of managed markets. We could either offer to undertake obligations in respect of foodstuffs in general, or negotiate concessions on the imports of specific agricultural commodities. We might also offer not to increase unreasonably our domestic agriculture's share of our own market.

It appeared that the Six, in asking us to enter into an arrangement about foodstuffs, were not chiefly interested in the United Kingdom as a market for low-priced food exports. They were more concerned to secure our association with their own managed market arrangements based on minimum prices. Closer British association with Europe was therefore not likely to damage the agricultural interest at home.

All these matters were discussed at a full meeting of the Cabinet at the beginning of October, when Maudling explained the situation with a remarkable combination of clarity and brevity. Indeed he fully justified the decision which I had made a fortnight before to include him as a full member of the Cabinet.

Maudling felt no doubt that we could count on considerable support among the six countries, signatories to the Treaty of Rome. Germany, Belgium and the Netherlands would undoubtedly be favourable to our plan. Italy, though not anxious to expose her economy, which was then very weak, to further competition, was nevertheless attracted by the project for political reasons. The French Government although distracted by many internal conflicts was in the main not unfriendly on the same grounds. Nevertheless they would no doubt repeat the tactics by which they had managed to secure substantial concessions in favour of French domestic industry in the course of the negotiations leading to the Treaty of Rome. So far as the other members of O.E.E.C. were concerned, the Scandinavian countries, Switzerland, Portugal and Austria favoured our plan. Denmark was faced with special problems in respect of her agricultural exports. Unless she could obtain some satisfactory concessions regarding her trade in foodstuffs in the proposed Free Trade Area, she might be forced to apply to join the Six. Turkey and Greece were favourably disposed, at least in principle. This equally applied to Eire and Iceland, but they would no doubt wish to postpone the date in which they would have to accept the full obligations of membership.

As regards British agriculture, our plan involved the exclusion of foodstuffs from the scope of the Free Trade Area. Nevertheless it seemed wise to go forward at least with the discussion of possible methods of European co-operation in this field. There would be

P

considerable complications about the question of the origin of raw materials. This, however, was likely to cause real difficulty only if the Six intended to impose high tariffs on raw materials. There was considerable discussion of the possibility of using the technique of bulk purchase on long-term contracts (which were a feature of the policy of the Six), both as regards Commonwealth countries and our own agriculture. I pressed that we should pay special attention to the formal aspects of the Free Trade Area and tried to secure that its institution should be invested with dignity and authority. These economic questions had to be elevated to the plane of major policy. Our purpose was to consolidate the political and economic resources of all Europe in the common stand of the free world against Communism and disruption.

On 16 October the Council of O.E.E.C. declared their determination to promote the establishment of a European Free Trade Area, and an Inter-Governmental Committee was appointed to conduct the negotiations. Maudling was elected as Chairman. The formal constitution of the European Economic Community—the Six—came into being on 1 January 1958, but there was no sign at this stage of any breakdown in the wider discussions.

During my Commonwealth tour early in 1958 I devoted much time to expounding, privately to the Ministers of the different countries which I had been visiting and publicly through Press conferences and speeches, the objectives which we were seeking to secure. The reception was sympathetic. Meanwhile Maudling conducted the affair with skill and patience. Nevertheless it was clear by the beginning of March that the agriculture problems were not the real cause of the difficulties. This was largely due to the fact that the Six were themselves very uncertain about the type of agriculture arrangements which they intended to set up within the Community. Having reached no clear position of their own intentions it was difficult for them to bring strong objections against the proposals for co-operation which the British had put forward. In later years, after the Community had at last reached some agreed basis with all its difficulties for the control of their own agriculture, this became a major obstacle. But in 1958 it was not a serious difficulty. Nevertheless as the agriculture problem came to seem less and less important,

French opposition to the whole principle of the Free Trade Area began to develop.

> Long talks with Maudling and Selwyn Lloyd about the negotiations for the European Free Trade Area. The French are being very difficult.[1]

Behind the French opposition lay two fundamental arguments, or rather fears. The first arose from the growing anxiety of French industrialists that in addition to suffering heavy pressure from German competition they would have to face free entry of British goods. Conscious of the relative inefficiency of French industry, they were becoming more and more opposed to having to meet this double danger. The other objection was different. Federalist opinion in France, which influenced many of our old friends and colleagues in the European movement, was much more concerned with the political than with the economic integration with Western Europe. It was for that reason that I was anxious that the Free Trade Area, although consisting of two parts—the Six and the Eleven (as they were commonly then described)—should develop an institutional basis within which the ideals of United Europe could be fostered and developed.

It had been agreed, at Maudling's suggestion, that July should be regarded as the deadline for decision—at least in general terms. Reductions inside the Six were timed to come into force on 1 January 1959, and if the tariff cuts in the Common Market and in the wider Free Trade Area were to be introduced simultaneously, at least six months would be required for the technical arrangement.

At the beginning of March the French proposed two major modifications to the Free Trade Area which were completely unacceptable to the British; one was that agreements between the Common Market and other O.E.E.C. countries should be made on an industry-by-industry basis, and that hard-pressed industries would have to wait until conditions of competition had been 'harmonised'. The other feature of the French proposals was that preferential tariffs in overseas Commonwealth countries should be extended to a certain quota of Continental European goods.

[1] 21 February 1958.

On 17 March Maudling came to see me to explain the state of the game:

> It looks as if the French are determined to wreck it—partly out of weakness, but mostly out of jealousy and spite. The French Government are not unfriendly—but as in the case of Tunis, it is the prisoner of the Right.[1]

There now arose a new complication due to American intervention concerning North Africa. I did my best to prevent this, and, as already described, only agreed to a very small, almost a token, delivery of arms to Tunisia. But the opponents of M. Gaillard's Government were quick to seize upon this grievance. I warned Dulles that if the super-sensitive French were upset they might well use this excuse to wreck the prospects of the European Free Trade Area. My anxiety was to prove justified. M. Gaillard's Government resigned on 16 April and there followed a long and painful interval before a new Administration could be formed.

On 16 April Adenauer made a visit to London.

> The Queen gave a dinner at Windsor to which Dorothy and I were bidden, and the Germans thoroughly enjoyed themselves. The old Chancellor sat between the two Queens, and flirted with both.[2]

Our talks covered three days, the first two being mainly upon the questions of Russian policy, Summit talks and the rest. On the third morning, 18 April, we discussed the negotiations for a European Free Trade Area. The Germans seemed deeply distressed by the fall of the French Government and what seemed to many the imminent collapse of the Fourth Republic. Adenauer promised to help us with the French, and I had little doubt that his protestations were sincere. The whole visit gave him real pleasure, especially his reception by the Queen. It ended with a dinner at the German Embassy during which the Chancellor was in a merry mood. For it seemed now that the whole unhappy past was forgiven, if not forgotten.

> Adenauer seems to be delighted with the visit and feels that it has been an immense success. It has certainly helped to counteract the poison which the French have been pouring into his ears.[3]

[1] 17 March 1958.   [2] 16 April 1958.   [3] 19 April 1958.

The French political crisis dragged on. It was not until 14 May that Pierre Pflimlin was able to form a Government. On the next day there was a

> Meeting of Ministers concerned (that is almost half the Cabinet) to hear from Maudling the latest state of play on European Free Trade Area. The confusion in France (they have had no Government for six weeks or so, and now they are threatened with a *crise de régime*) makes progress very slow. We shall have to make some concessions—the question is how far we are to go. Maudling, who is admirably clear and lucid in his explanations, obtained general approval for his ideas.[1]

The day before Pflimlin became Premier of France the European population of Algeria demanded a committee of public safety to be headed by General de Gaulle.

> There has been a great flare up in France, still in a state of political confusion. The Generals in Algiers have set up a committee of public safety. Whether it is to be followed by an attempt at a *coup d'état* in Paris is obscure. M. Pflimlin is forming a Government. No doubt the politicians will now rally, in fear of the Army.[2]

It is strange now to remember that the agitation both in Algeria and in France led by the Army but supported by a great number of citizens of the centre and the right had for its purpose the recall of General de Gaulle to power to restore order in Algeria and to defend to the last this proud possession of France's Colonial Empire. The General himself was less specific.

> De Gaulle has made an equivocal statement, but one which has terrified the French politicians. It is cast in his usual scornful, but enigmatic language.
> France is in a turmoil—no one knows whether it will lead to the collapse or the revival of the Fourth Republic.[3]

The French Prime Minister, however, did not give in at once. He was a man of considerable strength and determination.

[1] 15 May 1958.   [2] 14 May 1958.   [3] 16 May 1958.

The news from France is still obscure. It looks as if Pflimlin was holding pretty firm against the Generals—at least for the moment.[1]

Four days later I noted:

The French situation is still obscure. The P.M. (Pflimlin) seems to be putting up quite a fight. But de Gaulle has taken up a pretty good strategic position.[2]

On 24 May French parachute troops from the Algerian insurrection landed in Corsica, and it soon became apparent that a 'takeover' in Paris with de Gaulle's triumph could not be long delayed. Pflimlin resigned on 28 May, and de Gaulle accepted the President's invitation to form a Government. On 1 June he received a vote of confidence from a large majority of the French Assembly. The stage was now set for the opening of a new act in the long drama of France's constitutional history.

I had been keeping all the Commonwealth countries fully informed as to the progress of the discussions of the Inter-Governmental Committee, sometimes by formal telegrams and sometimes by less official communications. Now the prospects of any practical steps towards European unity on a wide basis depended upon France and France alone. With the *coup d'état* in Paris it seemed likely that all the previous discussions so carefully prepared and carried on with such detail and patience would fall to the ground. Both the European Community of the Six and the larger concept of the Free Trade Area would depend upon the unpredictable decisions of the new ruler of France. I had to confess to myself that the prospects did not seem very favourable. I knew from my many intimate talks with de Gaulle during the war how obsessed he was by his almost insane hatred for Roosevelt and even for Churchill; by his jealousy of Britain, and by his mixture of pride in France's splendid history and humiliation by her ignoble fall in 1940. It would indeed be difficult to lead him away from the nostalgic concepts of France's position in Europe towards the new picture of what a United Europe might mean in a changed and changing world. I could only

[1] 17 May 1958.   [2] 21 May 1958.

hope to make at least some use of my association with the General at a most critical moment in his own career.[1]

Accordingly I despatched a message to the new Prime Minister in the following terms :

I send you my warm congratulations and good wishes on the occasion of your investiture as President of the Council of France.

It will be a great happiness to me to be able to renew our war-time friendship, founded in the days when as President of the Committee of National Liberation you were leading France to victory.

Recalling those days and the indissoluble ties of friendship and interest which bind our two countries I look forward to working with you in our common causes.

To which he replied with his usual courtesy.

The good wishes in your friendly letter have deeply touched me. They correspond entirely to my own feelings about the relations between our two countries.

I too have the happiest memories of our personal collaboration during the war which Great Britain and France waged together for the freedom of the world.

We shall, I know, have much to do together and I look forward to this.

I then thought it wise to write a further letter, the chief purpose of which was to inform him of my approaching visit to the United States, for I had not forgotten his old prejudices against America and it seemed prudent to inform him of my plans rather than let him hear about them indirectly.

I was very touched that in the midst of all your preoccupations in forming your Government, you found time to respond so quickly and in such generous terms to my message of good wishes. I am also glad to see that you have been able to get on so fast with forming your Government and that your full powers have been duly granted.

I realise that you will be very occupied in the immediate future in working out your policy, particularly towards North Africa. I

[1] See *The Blast of War*, chaps. 8–16.

am myself, as you know, setting off for America next Friday for a week's stay in the United States and Canada. This is primarily a private visit to receive a degree at a university which my maternal grandfather attended. But I shall also have some informal talks with the President and Dulles, as well as more formal conversations with the Canadians.

Had it not been for my feeling that you would wish to concentrate for the moment on your own problems, and for my previous engagement across the Atlantic, I would have suggested that we might meet very soon. I always find that there is no substitute for personal contact; it is the only way of really discussing things frankly and avoiding misunderstandings or misrepresentation. I hope we shall perhaps be able to meet when things are a little easier for both of us, possibly towards the end of June or in early July. I could then give you some account of the impressions I had gathered during my visit to the United States and Canada and we could discuss some of the many international problems with which, along with the other Western countries, we are confronted—such, for example, as our relations with the Soviet Union; the proposed Summit meeting; disarmament; European security; the Middle and Near East; the world economic situation and the relationship between the United Kingdom and Europe.

In the meantime, I venture to send you my best wishes for the success of your visit to Algeria. I hope this visit may lay the foundations for a satisfactory settlement of the North African problem. If you can achieve such a settlement you will indeed have rendered a notable service, not only to France, but to the Western Alliance as a whole, whose interests are so bound up with the peaceful development of Africa and Asia. We in this country will certainly watch your efforts to bring about an improvement in the situation in North Africa with every sympathy. We feel that any solution of the North African problem must take into account the leading role which France has played in that part of the world and have regard for France's special responsibilities and interest.

On 7 June I left for America and Canada and did not get back until 14 June. At de Gaulle's suggestion I went to Paris on 29 June, in a hopeful though not a confident spirit, taking with me the

Foreign Secretary. Outwardly everything seemed friendly and the omens hopeful. I made a full record in my diary of the two days which give my impressions at the time.

On arrival at Orly, we were met by General de Gaulle. There was a guard of honour; a band; and a very large crowd. The General—whom I had not seen for many years—was all affability and charm . . . I made a little speech in French (which seemed to please him). He was accompanied by Couve de Murville (his Foreign Minister), [Louis] Joxe [Ministry of Foreign Affairs], and Ambassador [Jean] Chauvel. It was a beautiful Sunday afternoon— and a very large crowd was out the whole way from Orly to Paris. They all seemed very relaxed and in a most friendly mood. . . . I have never seen a French crowd cheer in such a friendly way. (The last time I was in Paris we were not at all well received. It was when poor M. Gaillard was Prime Minister and we had supplied arms to Tunis.)
At first I thought that all this was laid on by order—then that it was all for the General. The latter was partly true, except that he was not in our procession. I think really it was a sign of the popular feeling of hope. At the moment, everyone is confident that the General's policy will succeed. No one knows what it will be—all the same it commands general confidence.[1]

We drove to the Embassy, where the Ambassador, Sir Gladwyn Jebb, gave me a vivid picture of recent events and of the situation in Paris. We then

set off for the Matignon. We had a conference for an hour before dinner—two a side (with advisers making four or five). The talks were partly in French—partly in English—with running translations where necessary. Dinner was then served—simple but excellent. After dinner, de Gaulle took me for a walk in the garden of twenty minutes or so, before resuming the conference. Here he talked simply but impressively, about himself—and his hopes and difficulties. Two issues fill his mind—Algeria and French constitutional reform. We left at 11 p.m.
June 30. It was arranged that the Foreign Secretary should meet with Couve de Murville at 10. I went for a talk with the

[1] 29 June 1958.

General alone at 11. At noon, we had a final meeting of the full conference. . . .

The chief subjects were: (1) Russia–the future of NATO–the desire of France to join the nuclear club–tests, etc.; (2) Middle East–especially Lebanon, Algeria and North Africa–Far East; (3) European institutions: the Community of Six–the European Free Trade Area.[1]

It was a remarkable occasion for me, remembering the last time I had talked with the General in Algiers:

It was astonishing to me to see de Gaulle in his present mood. He has, of course, aged a lot. He has grown rather fat; his eyes are bad and he wears thick spectacles; he no longer smokes chains of cigarettes (indeed, he does not smoke at all). His manner is calm, affable, and rather paternal. But underneath this new exterior, I should judge that he is just as obstinate as ever. I spoke very strongly to him about the Free Trade Area, and the fatal political results which would follow the present French attitude. But he clearly was neither interested nor impressed. I decided to leave a . . . letter behind and told him I would do so. . . . De Gaulle, like so many soldiers of his type and period, cares nothing for 'logistics'. (This is one, but not the main reason for the French failure. The chief reason in 1940 was a moral, not a financial or economic collapse. De Gaulle knows this.) His present view is that France is rich, if confidence can be restored. (That also is true.) . . . I am very apprehensive about European Free Trade, for M. Pinay (whom de Gaulle has made Minister of Finance) is . . . completely dominated by the French 'patronat'. As regards the new French constitution . . . de Gaulle says that the plebiscite will be held on it on 30 September or 1 October. No one seems (including de Gaulle or Mollet) to know what it will be–but it will no doubt try to create a greater stability for Governments–perhaps by placing the power of dissolution in the hands of the Prime Minister and/or by giving greater power to the President. Many people think that de Gaulle will then go himself to the Elysée.

De Gaulle told me that *all* French citizens will take part in the plebiscite–including Algerians. Then Algerian deputies will be elected–some by separate, some by common voting lists. When

[1] 29–30 June 1958.

they have been duly elected, he will deal with them. He will offer them integration, autonomy, or any other plan. He will put the burden of choice on them. If they choose integration, it will be expensive for France in the short term, but the great potential wealth of the Sahara will make it bearable in the long run.[1]

Before leaving the Embassy I sent a letter putting forward the arguments for the Free Trade Area in the strongest possible terms:

I feel I ought to emphasise the very grave issues which we feel are bound up in the question of the European Free Trade area. The negotiations have been going on a very long time. At the request of the French Government we held them up until the Treaty of Rome could be concluded. When the negotiations began last October the French Government made reservations, and after some months undertook to produce counter-proposals. These have not yet reached the Committee of Seventeen Nations. In effect the negotiations have been at a standstill for some time. While of course I understand the difficulties of former French Governments, I am hoping that this period of hesitation will now be over and that a period of decision will have begun. The matter is becoming very urgent, for unless real progress can be made in the course of July there is no hope of introducing a Free Trade Area in parallel with the Treaty of Rome on January 1, 1959. The consequences of this failure may be very serious. If there are any special French problems that need a solution I am sure that they can be met, but I do not believe that a system of piecemeal arrangements would do. In any case I am told that as regards the two main difficulties to which you referred, agriculture now presents no real obstacle and it seems most improbable that the French Overseas Territories could suffer any damage. On the contrary, there may be some disadvantages for our own Overseas Territories. However, what I hope you will support is a broad agreement in principle which would allow detailed negotiations to continue on any special points.

What really concerns me is not by any means only the financial and commercial problems. I have no doubt that in some way or another Great Britain would be able to overcome these by alternative groupings. But this could hardly be done without bringing

[1] 30 June 1958.

to an end all that progress towards general European co-operation to which I personally attach so much importance. It would split Europe yet again.

Like you I am not very enamoured of elaborate constitution making, but I think that the Free Trade Area could be more simply organised without losing effectiveness. I hope that this is in line with your general thinking.

In a word, what really worries me is that I do not see how one can divorce economic and political grouping. Europe is already tragically divided from Stettin to Trieste and I am very anxious to avoid any further division.

I hope you will not mind my putting these thoughts very frankly before you. While I realise your great anxieties about Algeria and other matters, this is urgent and a mistake now might have tragic effects.

On the evening of 4 July, Maudling came to see me. He had just returned from Paris.

He could make *no* progress at all with his European Free Trade negotiations. Pinay is hostile; Couve de Murville is waiting on de Gaulle's decision. I fear it looks as if the whole of this great effort will break down, foiled by the . . . insularity of the French.[1]

De Gaulle's reply reached me the next day. It was in his usual rather vague style.

Thank you for your letter of 30 June which I have studied with care. Our conversations, of which I have the happiest memories, allowed us to clarify the position of our two Governments on the question of the Free Trade Area. I had the opportunity of saying to you—and I want once again to underline this— that France is not at all unfavourable, quite the contrary, to an enlargement of economic co-operation in Europe, in which Great Britain is naturally included. My preoccupations, as to the end to be attained, are therefore close to yours. But we must find means of arriving there without destroying the equilibrium of France's economy and finances to which my Government attach, as you will readily understand, an over-riding importance, and without basically putting at issue the agreements existing between the six member countries of the European Common Market. You

[1] 4 July 1958.

and we will have to make an effort of imagination and of will. Please rest assured that I shall follow this matter personally in the spirit of close friendship which characterised our conversations.

To this I sent an answer, pressing him at least to agree in principle to the proposals which had been put forward before the Inter-Governmental Committee.

I was very glad to receive your letter of 5 July about the Free Trade Area. I am most grateful to you for the personal interest which you are taking in this. For it is certainly one of the most important questions with which we must deal at the moment; on its successful solution may depend not only the economic prosperity of the Continent, but also its political cohesion.

I was particularly glad to note that you are favourable to an enlargement of economic co-operation in Europe and that we are therefore aiming at the same goal. Of course I understand the preoccupations which naturally affect your Government; I am sure that they can be met. I feel that what is required now is an agreement in principle in accordance with the farseeing statesmanship which you advocate. To this end Mr. Maudling, as Chairman of the Inter-Governmental Committee, has circulated a paper which offends neither of the conditions you lay down in your letter and, I hope, will give your Government the opportunity of contributing to a general move forward. I believe that, if this was possible, the detailed negotiations could proceed, and the experts could work out a satisfactory detailed plan.

I hope you will not mind my setting out my thoughts frankly to you in this matter, but I believe that honest and friendly exchange of views between us can be of great help in solving the problems with which our two countries are faced.

But the French attitude in the negotiating committee continued to be unhelpful. I did not feel that we wanted to take any precipitate action amounting to a definite rupture in the negotiations. On the whole it seemed best to seek a temporary pause which could perhaps be related to the imminent Commonwealth Economic Conference at Montreal.

I thought it prudent to inform Adenauer of the state of affairs by a personal message. In addition I referred to my conversations with de Gaulle.

As regards the Free Trade Area, I found that the General still regards this very much as an economic problem and did not perhaps fully appreciate the political implications. However, he did assure me that he would take a personal interest in this subject on which I spoke to him with all the emphasis that I could command, and I already see signs that our talk has borne fruit. I think that the General is still preoccupied with the economic dangers which he fears for France in the Free Trade Area, although he is in general receptive to plans for greater economic co-operation in Europe.

A few days later, 4 August, Adenauer sent a friendly reply:

With regard to the Free Trade Area, the results of the last sessions of the Maudling Committee indicate that the prospects for a generally satisfactory solution of outstanding problems have definitely improved. I have no hesitation in ascribing this progress to your conversations with General de Gaulle.

The Commonwealth Economic Conference at Montreal lasted for nearly ten days and passed off satisfactorily from the point of view of our European negotiations. The relevant resolution declared:

It is our conviction that an outward-looking Free Trade Area, in which trade would be increased rather than merely re-channelled, would contribute to the objective of an expanding world economy.

On 8 October at Adenauer's suggestion and in the hope of getting the Germans to give more active help I made a visit to Bonn. I arrived with my small staff at Wahn Airport in the morning; after luncheon at the Embassy with Sir Christopher and Lady Steel, I paid a formal call upon President Theodor Heuss. Our Conference began at 3.30 and lasted until nearly 7.00. The Foreign Minister, von Brentano, was present during most of the time. A great part of the Conference was taken up by discussion of the situation created by an unexpected action by President de Gaulle. This is best described by my own words recorded at the time.

The most serious question raised at our talks, both before and after dinner, was the memorandum which General de Gaulle sent privately to President Eisenhower and myself regarding the present organisation for the defence of the free world. In this (which was given privately and secretly to us both a few weeks ago) the General sets out his ideas for reform. He is rightly critical of NATO, which may well turn into a kind of European Maginot line, regardless of its flank. But he suggested a world organisation, under an Anglo-American–French triumvirate. NATO would be the European branch of this; other parts of the [free] world similarly. Of course, the whole purpose is to claim for France 'as a coming nuclear power' a special position, with Britain and America.

The President and I have kept his confidence scrupulously. But . . . the General gave a copy to Spaak – on a personal basis – and allowed the *German* and *Italian* ambassadors in Paris to see it. Although none of the other NATO governments . . . have actual copies of the memorandum, they have a pretty good idea of its contents and are naturally enraged. Knowing that this had happened and that I would be put in a difficult position when I saw Adenauer, I asked de Gaulle what I was to do. He replied that I could certainly discuss with Adenauer his (de Gaulle's) ideas in general terms. (He seems still to be quite unaware of the effect of his action.)

I found the Chancellor very concerned. In the afternoon, with the various officials present, he tried to control himself – after dinner, in a small group, he showed his disgust and resentment. He had trusted de Gaulle. They had met for confidential talks only a few weeks ago. De Gaulle had seemed to be loyal and open. Now he had struck this cruel blow at Germany and at the Chancellor's policy of Franco-German friendship, etc., etc. I tried to calm him as much as I could. I had a much longer experience of de Gaulle than almost anyone. He was apt to treat his friends with this curious ineptness and rudeness. It was because of his mysticism and egoism. But I felt sure that the best way to deal with this, before it went too far, and caused real trouble in NATO, was to get the General to write another memorandum, leaving out the offensive parts, which could be circulated and discussed in NATO. The President and I would have to consider how to deal with his request for the Anglo-American–French 'directorate'. Probably we should say that since there was no Anglo-American 'directorate', there was nothing for the French to join. Of course the United States and the United Kingdom had rather special relations—arising from history, language, the last war, the Churchill–Roosevelt and now the Macmillan–Eisenhower friendship. But we had never tried to 'institutionalise' this. Nor would we do so.

One of Adenauer's staff had asked (before dinner) of Sir Anthony Rumbold whether I would give Adenauer a copy of the memorandum. I did not think I could do this honourably. I could not go beyond the letter and spirit of de Gaulle's agreement as to what I should say to Adenauer. So I told this straight out to the Chancellor, at the beginning of the talk after dinner, and I think he understood and respected my scruples. Moreover, Adenauer might wish to write me 'private and personal' letters. He would not do so with confidence if I had acceded to the suggestion that I should give a copy of a similarly *private* memorandum from de Gaulle to another person. Of course, the great *gaffe* which de Gaulle committed was to give a copy to Spaak. Yet (as I told the Chancellor) this was a proof of clumsiness but also of innocence.[1]

In spite of the diversion from our agenda caused by this incident, the dinner was both agreeable and merry.

The Chancellor, who is a great expert on wine, produced one bottle after another of Rhine wine, and made me take a glass from each, explaining at the same time the different qualities.[1]

On the next day we met at 10 a.m. and by 11.30 a.m. had covered the whole field and a communiqué was easily agreed.

In a restricted session, Adenauer showed me a draft letter to Spaak—very discreet, especially about me—saying that all this would soon leak in public, and asking Spaak to discuss with de Gaulle how the position could be regularised—perhaps by circulating another, but inoffensive, memorandum, as soon as possible. The Chancellor is still very hurt and angry.[2]

My chief purpose in this visit was, of course, to try to persuade Adenauer to help us over the Free Trade Area. I had been alarmed that in view of the growing Franco-German *rapprochement* Adenauer might have been urged by the German officials to take a less friendly

[1] 8 October 1958.   [2] 9 October 1958.

view towards our plan. This meeting certainly helped—so did de Gaulle's unexpected move. Nevertheless if the negotiations for the Free Trade Area proved fruitless and we found ourselves excluded and perhaps damaged by the economic union of the Six, we must now begin to consider what action we would take. Should we turn our back on Europe or should we make an effort to organise the other countries, equally excluded from the Treaty of Rome? All these ideas were passing in my mind and embodied in Minutes to the Chancellor of the Exchequer and the Foreign Secretary.

Meanwhile my anxieties continued to increase.

> The outlook for the European Free Trade Area seems bad. The French are determined to exclude United Kingdom. De Gaulle is bidding high for the hegemony of Europe. If he could get peace in Algeria and hold on to the Sahara oil, he might achieve it.[1]

On 31 October I held a meeting of the Ministers chiefly concerned.

> Maudling has handled the whole affair with great skill and patience. He thinks that the French must soon declare their hand. At present, they have just wasted time. But even the Five (their partners in the Treaty of Rome Six Powers) are shocked and angry at French insincerity and trickery. We must wait till the end of November. If the French make no move we should break off the negotiation. We must consider what, if anything, we and the other powers (Scandinavia, Switzerland, Denmark, Austria) can or ought to do, either in the political or economic sphere.[2]

On 3 November Adenauer sent me an encouraging message ending with these words.

> I personally tend to the view that the European Common Market Commission could make an even more useful contribution than they have done in the past. I would in any case do all in my power to assist them, in order to further the successful outcome of the negotiations.

Following a negative meeting with Couve de Murville, who came to see me on 6 November, I decided to send a further letter to the General.

[1] 26 October 1958.   [2] 31 October 1958.

I am deeply disturbed at the position we have reached in our negotiations for a Free Trade Area. We have always well understood that France had specially difficult economic problems. We have also understood and admired the efforts of France, through the Treaty of Rome, to achieve a measure of economic unity which would lay a sound basis for political harmony in Europe.

But the Treaty of Rome, taken by itself, can easily lead to a division in the European ranks rather than a bond of union. If the industry of the other Western European countries is progressively excluded from the markets of the Six, how can we prevent political antagonisms as well as economic rivalries from springing up?

We thought the idea of a Free Trade Area provided the solution. We saw it as something which in no way interfered with the aims of the Common Market. We recognised that special attention would have to be paid to damage which might be caused to individual industries in individual countries. But, within these limitations, we did see it as providing for substantial freedom of trade between the seventeen countries of Western Europe without forming a purely protectionist bloc against the outside world. It is on this conception that we have been negotiating for almost two years. And this is, I am confident, the aim which has inspired the other participants in the negotiations.

It has been all the greater shock to have it brought home to me in the last few months, and most clearly of all during the visit of your Foreign Minister, that France is not after all aiming at the same objective. Monsieur Couve insisted not only that France is not prepared to stand a régime of free trade in Europe (in spite of the safeguards we are all prepared to consider) but that such a régime must inevitably destroy the objectives of the Common Market. If this is really so we have been negotiating at cross purposes. In less than two months' time, an economic cleavage will occur which the present negotiations will be powerless to prevent. This is because, to put it bluntly, France is operating on a conception quite different from that of her partners. It is no secret that even among the Six the conception of a large free-trading area in Europe is generally welcomed for its political sake alone.

Nobody has striven harder than I to put Europe in its rightful place in the world. Nobody has made greater efforts to find the means whereby Britain can be brought closer to Europe. The best solution to these two problems I can find—and it is one which has been almost universally accepted in the world—has been the Free Trade Area with the meaning which that phrase denotes.

I beg you not to regard this as a technical issue. I hope you will give your close attention to it in its broadest political aspects. I am convinced that we are already in a crisis which has the seeds of disaster for Europe in the long term. In the short term, the political consequences will start to become acute on 1 January. If before then we cannot do something to prevent the erection of barriers between two halves of Europe, I am fearful of the consequences.

I am sure you will not mind my taking advantage of our old friendship to speak quite frankly to you.

May I add how glad I am to hear from our Ambassador's report of his talk with you yesterday that there is a good hope of your coming to visit us early next year?

Unhappily, this appeal had little effect. On 14 November an official statement was made on behalf of the French Government declaring that

it is not possible to create a Free Trade Area as wished by the British—that is, with free trade between the Common Market and the rest of the O.E.E.C. but without a single external tariff barrier round the seventeen countries, and without harmonisation in the economic and social spheres.

De Gaulle's letter, although not so brutal as the official statement, was obscure and unsatisfactory:

Your letter of 7 November showed me, clearly and once again, the importance which, in all respects, might be attached to, on the one hand, the entry into effect of the Treaty of Rome, and, on the other, the problems to which it gives rise as regards trade between the Six of the Common Market and the eleven other countries of Western Europe.

I have been particularly struck by what you say about the misunderstanding which could be at the root of the negotiations between the two groups. Without going into the allegations which have been made—without effect—from both sides in the course of these long discussions, it seems to me that we have reached the point where the intentions which have been declared so far, as well as the procedure and the framework which have been used, offer little chance of achieving practical results. And I am inclined to think that, in this matter, it is practical results which are in question.

These could not, evidently, consist of the establishment of a Free Trade Area in the conditions proposed by the Eleven. The very existence of the Common Market, the obligations it imposes on the member States, the actual state of their economy, in any case the economy of France, would be incompatible with the area as suggested. But I am convinced that steps could be taken with a view to a progressive easing of the trade between the Common Market and the eleven other powers of Western Europe.

In my view, it would be as well to consider that problem from this angle. As you have been so good as to tell me of your anxieties, I think it is my duty to tell you that my Government would be ready to enter into contact with yours for a first examination of the real possibilities, it being understood that we should, for our part, have to act in liaison with our partners of the Common Market.

Although, in my view, it would be as well for such conversations—should you feel so disposed—to take place shortly, I do not think that they ought to take place in a hurry which might risk compromising them. It is true that 1 January is the date fixed for the entry into force of the Common Market. But, as you know, the entry into force will not, initially, result in any profound change in the actual pattern of trade.

If your wishes correspond to ours, we have time enough to take the matter up again. I assure you that, so far as we are concerned, we earnestly hope, for the sake of the harmony of Europe and the friendship of our two countries, that it will be possible, in the end, to reach agreement on this great matter.

In my reply I did my best to keep my temper and the situation open, as far as possible.

Thank you for your letter which I received yesterday after I had seen M. Soustelle's declaration.[1]

[1] Jacques Soustelle was Minister of Information July 1958–January 1959.

I cannot conceal from you my concern over the situation which has developed from the breakdown of these prolonged negotiations, and especially the effect upon Western Europe. The growing tension in Europe and the world makes me feel that it is imperative that a solution should be found. My colleagues and I are considering the situation which has arisen, with all its implications.

As regards the French President's proposal of bilateral discussions after the French elections in January, my colleagues agreed:

The right tactics for the moment seem to be to hold off for a bit and let other countries bring pressure on the French. The first hurdle is 1 January. If the French act in a discriminatory way against us and the other eleven countries, I fear this must mean the disintegration of O.E.E.C. and other European institutions. But they *could* easily avoid this in one of two ways. They could claim their escape clauses, and lower their tariffs *neither* to the five nor to the eleven. (Similarly with quotas.) Or they could extend their concessions to all Europe.[1]

Accordingly Maudling made a statement in the House about the situation in moderate terms which was well received by all Members, including the Opposition.

I still feel that we should hold off until after the French elections, and until some more pressure develops on the French. If 1 January comes without any proposal and if discrimination against the eleven actually develops, there should be an emergency meeting of O.E.E.C. The French have so far shuffled, and prevaricated, and wasted time. Now that they have spoken the truth (through Soustelle) Europe had better understand and ponder on the prospect.[1]

So ended the first stage in what has proved to be a long and sterile negotiation. It was not in effect until after our own General Election in October 1959 that we were able to bring an alternative, if less ambitious, plan to fruition.

[1] 17 November 1958.

CHAPTER XV

The Two Worlds

A FEW days before Christmas 1957, while still wrestling with financial problems at home which were about to lead to the resignation of all the Treasury Ministers, and busily preparing for an arduous Commonwealth tour, I found time to reflect on other urgent questions. I summarised these in a Minute to the Chief Whip:

> I am anxious about the misunderstandings in our Party on foreign policy.
>
> There are three main troubles: first, the anti-Americanism of many of our supporters, which of course reached its culminating point at Suez but has not yet died down. It is partly based on real apprehensions and partly, I am afraid, represents the English form of the great disease from which the French are suffering more than any other people—that is, looking backwards to the nineteenth century, instead of looking forwards. . . .
>
> The second form of this isolationism is directed against Europe, and of course inspires Beaverbrook and his followers. So we are reaching a position in which the English people of fifty million, who in material terms are quite unequal to the new giants, will move neither towards Europe nor towards America. It is a stultifying policy.
>
> The third problem, not I think so much in the Party but in the country, is all about the H-bomb, the American bomber bases, the fatigue and worry of the long-drawn-out struggle against Russia, the clever Russian propaganda for peace, and all the rest.
>
> I feel that before I go I ought to try to write and deliver a serious statement on all these great issues. Can I find before 7 January a suitable platform? Something might be arranged. Alternatively I might try a sound broadcast.

Accordingly on 4 January 1958, while still waiting for the Chancellor of the Exchequer's final decision, I used the occasion of a Party Political Broadcast to discuss the problems of peace:

Our work for peace is dominated by the problem of how well we can get on with the Russians. And yet over Russian policy hangs a kind of question-mark. They often speak fair words; they spoke many fair and friendly words to us on New Year's Day. Are these professions of respect and friendship really genuine? Or are they saying a number of things they think we would like to hear in order to weaken our resolve? We can't yet be sure of the truth; and it is a terrible responsibility for any Government to have to choose to act either upon this interpretation or that without being absolutely certain. Let me give you an example. There have been repeated proposals for the abolition of nuclear armaments, atom bombs and hydrogen bombs. Suppose that we worked out an agreement for the abolition of such weapons and the prevention of their manufacture – because that would be very attractive, for many reasons, and among others, because it would save us a great deal of money and effort. But, suppose that as a result of such an agreement we found ourselves virtually defence-less before the greatly superior weight of Russian conventional arms, men, guns, tanks, aeroplanes, surface ships and sub-marines? If that happened wouldn't we bitterly regret the loss of our nuclear deterrent, the one weapon that must give pause to any enemy however powerful he may be in other respects?

I went on to use words which shocked some of my hearers, but were on the whole well received, about the benefits as well as the dangers of the nuclear arms. At that time this approach, now so trite, was almost novel:

In a curious way the knowledge of the immense devastation which would follow a world conflict does now deter aggressors. The hydrogen bomb is a protection, for in a nuclear war neither side can win a victory. The fact that our sure defence lies in our ability to destroy an aggressor as cruelly as he destroys others is, of course, a horrible idea. I know that, but we daren't let our revulsion from the idea of the H-bomb deprive us of our best guarantee of safety from attack and so really the best guarantee of peace.

This is one of those truisms which may still be true. It was at that time still necessary to remind a British audience how all this had come about.

> In 1945, after the last war, we were all hoping for a period of prolonged peace and friendship. We had learned here to admire the courage and fortitude of our Russian allies. Although we differed profoundly from them in their attitude towards life and liberty we were confident that we could live in harmony together; indeed if we'd thought of the phrase then we would have said, in 'peaceful co-existence'–that really means live and let live. But, alas, our hopes were soon dashed; the Soviet Union which had already swallowed the Baltic States brought most of Eastern Europe into subjection and finally, the seizure of Czechoslovakia led to the formation of the North Atlantic Treaty Organisation– NATO–now in its tenth year of life. This alliance of fifteen countries was born from the bitter experience of aggression and the determination to halt it. In that purpose it has so far succeeded.
>
> And if therefore we have now reached a stalemate, well, it's no bad thing, for at least it means that world conflict is much less likely, perhaps even impossible.

I then referred to and defended the American contribution:

> It may be, of course, that it has been to their own interest, but if their interest and ours coincide, and we both see it, all the better for us both. If we had had this sort of co-operation with America after the First War, we might not have had a second war. And every Government that we have had in Britain since 1947, whatever political Party, has welcomed and worked with the American allies. In 1948, for instance, American bombers arrived in Britain by an arrangement entered into by Mr. Attlee, then Prime Minister. This arrangement was later reaffirmed by Mr. Churchill. The Americans came to join in the protection of the free world–they are part of our joint defences. Of course their bases cannot be used for war–warlike operations–except by agreement between our two Governments. We have a veto, and they have a veto. The early American bombers were armed with the atom bomb, now they're armed with the hydrogen bomb. . . . None of these bombs could be or would be used except by deliberate military order given upon the instruction of both the

British and the American Governments acting in agreement. We ourselves have an absolute veto on the dropping of these bombs from any plane based in this country—there is no doubt about this whatever.

As regards the future there were only two ways to preserve the peace of the world; these were not opposed but parallel, indeed complementary:

The first is to maintain the full strength of our alliances. There may be some who would seek to open old wounds, to stir differences between us and to incite jealousies. These people serve their own generation ill.

But there was a second way just as important.

The way of negotiation, of conciliation; don't let's be dismayed by the failures up to date. We must go on with it, we must go on trying. We intend to go on trying to get some agreement with the Russians for disarmament and for the relief of tension in the world.

After referring to the disarmament plan put forward by the United Nations Commission in the previous year and regretting its collapse, I declared that we must not give up but try again. I then made a proposal which was soon to cause something of a storm in Washington although it seemed to me harmless enough.

We can start by a solemn pact of non-aggression. This has been done before, it will do no harm, it might do good.

I went on to urge progress towards an agreement about tests of nuclear weapons, their manufacture, their use and their numbers, which must include the parallel reduction of conventional arms. I added:

Reduction in all forms of weapons must be so planned as to reduce tensions and not to increase apprehensions. And then there is one condition which is vital to every plan, the agreements must be subject to an effective system of inspection and control in all the countries concerned. We on our side would agree to inspectors ranging over our countries, so long as inspectors could do the same without hindrance in the Soviet bloc.

Nobody had tried harder than the British Government to reach agreement with Russia. For example

I have been myself at two high-level meetings with the Russians. One of Heads of Governments, the other of Foreign Ministers. I have watched the work of the Disarmament Conference. We couldn't get an agreement, but I don't despair, and that is why at NATO last month we made it perfectly clear that we were ready and anxious to make a new effort to break the deadlock. For my part I don't mind whether we make it through the United Nations or at some smaller meeting. Whether it is done this way or through diplomatic channels, or a combination of both, the object would be to clear away the rubble of old controversies and disagreements, and then perhaps to get the path ready for a meeting of Heads of Government.

Meanwhile messages had passed backwards and forwards between Washington and London as to the proposed reply to Bulganin's latest note delivered in December 1957, which reiterated Russian suspicions of the West's aggressive intentions, and called again for an immediate ban on nuclear tests.[1] I suggested to the President that we should try to work out a joint policy on disengagement based upon the demilitarised zone which had been proposed by Eden at the Summit meeting in 1955 and had now been elaborated by the Poles in the Rapacki Plan. An agreement on disengagement must be linked with an efficient method of inspection; but, as Eden had so often urged, an experiment in a small zone might be later extended to cover a much wider field. Eisenhower in his answer sent me a draft of a very full reply intended as a public restatement of the whole Western position. At the same time he showed a certain anxiety about my broadcast reference to a non-aggression pact.

I had a more practical and immediate preoccupation. The British Government could only agree to an abolition of tests if the United States had amended the McMahon Act in order to allow us access to their nuclear knowledge. The President was frank in telling me that he could not guarantee that Congress would permit the full

---

[1] *Correspondence between the Prime Minister and Mr. Bulganin, December 11, 1957 to February 8, 1958*, Cmnd. 381 (H.M.S.O., February 1958).

disclosure of nuclear information to the United Kingdom. But he promised to do his best and had every hope of success. I was indeed relieved to find that the amending legislation would give him full discretion to pass on all information which, in his judgement, it would be in the interests of the United States defence to supply to their British allies.

Since Nehru made a speech, when I was in Delhi, strongly welcoming my suggestion of a non-aggression pact and in view of the fact that this idea had been blown up to unintended dimensions, I felt that the wisest course was to try to get general agreement for my plan. However, in the vast accumulation of correspondence which passed between the allied capitals on wider and more vital issues it fell to a second place.

A second letter from Bulganin was delivered on 9 January while we were still discussing in NATO the reply to his first. It was sent to nineteen states with copies to all members of the United Nations. Although disingenuous, it was skilfully composed. Bulganin contrasted the pacific attitude of the U.S.S.R. with the growing nuclear armaments of the West. He now proposed a meeting of leading statesmen to discuss the suspension of nuclear tests, the outlawing of nuclear weapons and the Rapacki proposal for a demilitarised zone.

While the reply to the first letter was still to be sent the President rather unexpectedly intervened on 12 January by writing himself to Bulganin accepting the idea of a Summit Conference in principle, provided that preliminary diplomatic exchanges gave 'good hope of advancing the cause of peace and justice in the world'. He added another proviso of equal importance—that our Foreign Ministers must show some measure of accord and make some progress on the outstanding questions before a meeting of Heads of Governments could be useful.

My reply to Bulganin's first letter was sent off on 14 January. The chief points made were as follows. If the Soviet Government was earnest about disarmament, especially nuclear disarmament, would they agree to the experts starting work immediately on the technical details of control? I went on to say that in addition to studying the Polish proposals we would take up the question of a high-level meeting in replying to their second letter. Telegrams then passed backwards and forwards between my small staff, as we found

ourselves in various Commonwealth cities, and the great machine of
Whitehall. I thought the first draft too cold and not likely to be well
received by an anxious public. We must not appear to be dragging
our feet. Accordingly I telegraphed from Singapore to the Foreign
Secretary the text of a possible reply which I thought might both
touch public imagination and bring the Russians to the point.
Whether the Americans would agree, and what would be the
attitude of the French, Germans and NATO generally, I could not
tell. But I wanted to frame my answer somewhat in these words:

> I must frankly say that I do not feel that this method is getting
> us very far—if, as I hope, our purpose is not propaganda, but to
> achieve some practical result. I would, therefore, make the
> following proposal. Everyone agrees that somebody ought to
> discuss something at some level. *I would be willing, if you are
> agreeable, to come to Moscow at a time convenient to us both to discuss
> only two points:*
> (*a*) the agenda for further discussions, and
> (*b*) the procedure for further discussions.
> If we reach agreement on these I would certainly recommend
> it to my friends and colleagues in the Governments with which
> my country is in alliance or active co-operation. I make this
> suggestion in the sincere hope that it might at least help to clear
> the first hurdle. I shall not publish this letter until I have your
> reply, which, I earnestly hope, will be favourable.

In sending this draft I told the Foreign Secretary that since the
meeting could not be for six weeks or more we should work out with
our allies ideas for an agenda and procedure. I added:

> Somebody will try to break the log-jam one day. Why shouldn't
> we get the credit? If, as is very probable, it all ends in failure to
> agree, we shall at least have gone through the necessary moral and
> intellectual exercises to strengthen our resistance. In any case,
> whatever I answer now, we and our allies should be working out
> our ideas on agenda and procedure. At present we have done
> nothing since Paris.

I was not altogether surprised by Selwyn Lloyd's answer. My
colleagues did not much like my plan nor did they think it would be
acceptable to our allies, or to our supporters at home.

On 22 January Khrushchev made a threatening speech at Minsk. I continued to exchange possible drafts with the Cabinet until 24 January, when a text was finally agreed. In accepting the Cabinet rejection of my own plan I made the comment that while I was quite prepared to abandon my particular proposal for the present, I still thought that some such initiative would be necessary. More than twelve months were to pass before I could put it into effect.

Meanwhile Selwyn Lloyd had been having long conversations with Dulles in Ankara, where the members of the Baghdad Pact were meeting. Dulles made it clear that neither he nor the President liked the idea of a Summit meeting unless there were some grounds for thinking it would be productive. To raise hopes only destined to be dashed to the ground was always dangerous. A meeting which broke down would be a disaster. Even if an agreed communiqué resulted, little would be gained if it contained nothing but platitudes. Indeed the vigilance of public opinion in the free world might well be undermined. The Soviets were already making dangerous use of this new game of sending simultaneous letters to the various allied governments and then exploiting any difference which resulted from microscopic examination of their answers. My reply, which had still to go the rounds of the various allies, was not finally despatched and published until 10 February. Bulganin, on 1 February, had written to the President altogether rejecting the plan of a Foreign Ministers' meeting. Hammarskjöld had intervened on 5 February suggesting private negotiations within the United Nations framework, and the last draft of my reply to Bulganin's second letter was an attempt, after all these comings and goings, to reach a fair balance between all the different opinions. It was dated 8 February and ran as follows:

When I replied to your letter of December 11 I promised to send a separate answer to your further letter of January 8. This, after full consideration with my colleagues, I am now in a position to do.

I should be willing to participate in a meeting of Heads of Government which I think must be preceded by adequate preparations. I must say to you, as I have already said in public, that such a meeting will not be fruitful unless the ground has been thoroughly prepared in advance and it is clear from this preparatory work that there is broad agreement on the nature and order of the agenda and a real desire among all who participate in the meeting to make practical progress towards a settlement of the differences between us. There must be a reasonable prospect of achieving concrete results on specific issues. Otherwise we should run the risk of a fruitless meeting which might make matters worse and not better. I remember very well our meetings at Geneva in July and October, 1955. In looking back at these discussions I am convinced that one of the main reasons why we then achieved so little was that the ground had not been sufficiently prepared before the Heads of Government met.

In drawing up the agenda it would, of course, be necessary to consider not only the proposals in your letter but any other proposal which might be put forward by other Governments concerned. There are, for example, the suggestions in the letter addressed to you on January 12 by President Eisenhower which I fully endorse. Despite the comments which you have made on them, these suggestions must clearly be considered further in the preparation of any agenda for a meeting of Heads of Governments.

At their meeting in Paris in December the member Governments of NATO put forward the proposal that there should be a meeting of Foreign Ministers to try to break the deadlock in the disarmament discussions. This meeting of Foreign Ministers might well extend its scope and be a preliminary to a meeting of Heads of Government. Thus we might hope that the Heads of Government would be able to concentrate on the solution of specific problems. In order to make some immediate progress I therefore propose that a meeting of Foreign Ministers should take place in the near future. As a matter of convenience it might be best that this meeting should consist of the Foreign Ministers of the Governments represented at Geneva in 1955. But this does not prejudice the ultimate composition of a subsequent meeting of Heads of Government. I have put forward this proposal for a meeting of Foreign Ministers in the knowledge that you have already commented adversely upon it. Nevertheless I believe it to be the best way in which to begin.

An alternative method would be to make these preparations

through confidential diplomatic exchanges. The first method I have proposed would, I think, improve the prospects for a meeting of Heads of Government. We could agree to either method, but of course we could not presume to speak for other Governments.

If either of these proposals proved acceptable to the Governments concerned, the detailed arrangements for a Foreign Ministers' meeting or for the diplomatic exchanges might best be made without delay through their diplomatic representatives in Moscow.

If we can adopt this approach, progress may well be made towards a better understanding between us, but it is right that we should recognise from the outset that on some of these issues there is between us a considerable gulf to be bridged. To ignore or to minimise this fact would be unrealistic and therefore in the long run unhelpful to the end that we have in view. This is the reason why, as stated above, I attach such importance to adequate preparation.

In all this we must remember that our peoples are anxious that something concrete in the way of agreement should be achieved. My anxiety is that their hopes should not be raised only to be disappointed. Nevertheless in spite of our different approaches to some of the issues outstanding between us we undoubtedly have one thing in common, namely a very strong interest in the preservation of peace. I believe that each side recognises that the other has this same interest and on this basis it ought to be possible for us to have a useful meeting and to obtain positive results.[1]

This document was well received by the Press and the public. Both *The Times* and the *Manchester Guardian* were complimentary. The latter summed up the situation as follows:

No polemics—that seems to have been the principle which Mr. Macmillan set himself in his further reply to Marshal Bulganin. May this example prove infectious. The less that the propagandist aspect of a public correspondence is emphasised, and the more that Heads of Governments stick to practical points, the greater will be the hope of progress. Mr. Macmillan turns resolutely—and rightly—to the business of arranging a conference.

[1] *Correspondence between the Prime Minister and Mr. Bulganin*, Cmnd. 381, pp. 26–8.

The *Daily Express* was equally friendly.

His new letter shows his willingness to meet the Russian point of view without in any way losing faith with his American allies. Never has Britain's role as intermediary power proved more vital. It gives the whole world an early promise of a better prospect for peace.

The next day Dulles made an important concession. He stated that he did not regard the meeting of Foreign Ministers as a necessary preliminary for a Summit, certainly not a *sine qua non*. He only insisted that there should be adequate diplomatic preparation. As usual with the Secretary of State, this declaration was made at a Press conference, and without previous notice to his allies. Nevertheless I welcomed it wholeheartedly.

On 15 February I received a long and helpful letter from the President in which he expressed himself fully satisfied as to the way in which we had handled the Bulganin correspondence. In his final paragraph he said:

> I believe that all our efforts should now be directed toward laying the best possible foundation on which a Summit Conference may be based. Preliminary conversations with the Soviets at the diplomatic level might well be initiated soon as a step toward determining those areas in which some substantial results might be achieved. Along this path I think we can proceed in sufficiently ordered manner toward a truly promising Summit meeting.

On 19 February there was a two-day debate in the House of Commons on foreign affairs. In answer to criticisms of the slow progress achieved through all these discussions I repeated that it was clear that unless a Summit Conference produced some good, it might do actual harm; hence the importance of serious preliminary work. At some risk of being accused of frivolity I thought it right to give Parliament and the country some description of the difficulties and dangers of wholly unprepared meetings.

> For those who advocate this, I should like to give the House a picture of what happened at the first Geneva Conference, at

which I was present. . . . Each of the four Powers was represented by four or five leading figures in the front row, and
supported by 20 or 30—or sometimes more—experts in the rows
behind them. We met in an immense room in the old League of
Nations building, at a table which, I would guess, was roughly the
size of about three or four billiard tables put side by side, all
equipped with the familiar mechanism of microphones, speakers
and translating equipment. There were, in addition, a considerable number of spectators of various kinds, who seemed to
be around in the back benches of the hall.

In effect, the members of the conference did not confer. They
made a series of speeches to each other, in a strict rotation, each
taking the chair for one meeting. These speeches were nominally
secret, but immediately at the end of each session, by some
mysterious means, the full text of the speeches made by each
delegate reached the three or four thousand journalists assembled
in Geneva. There were, of course, a good many very pleasant
photographs taken, and some agreeable dinners organised.
Indeed, it was only at the dinner parties that anything like discussions began to take place, but as they were usually bilateral
that also had its limitations on the idea of a conference. There
was only one occasion when we did—and I remember it yet—
move into a smaller room and something like the kind of conference I would like took place; and this—if I remember aright—
was an attempt to break a particular deadlock on procedure that
had arisen.[1]

This sketch, or vignette, of the famous Geneva meeting, however
whimsical, seemed to amuse my audience.

Gaitskell answered with a statesmanlike speech which gave
general satisfaction except to that section of the Labour Party which
supported the popular movement for unilateral abandonment of
both nuclear tests and the manufacture of nuclear weapons. His
response certainly justified my determination to keep my speech
'moderate in tone and with, I think, a good balance between realism
and hopefulness'.[2] On the second day Aneurin Bevan made a speech

[1] *Hansard*, 19 February 1958. For a fuller account see *Tides of Fortune*, pp.
615–17.
[2] 19 February 1958.

Q

which the author of the *Annual Register* criticised with unusual vigour. This

> long and incoherent oration seemed to show that he did not know his own mind, or rather that he did not know which section of his own divided party he would do best to support.[1]

Bevan made the great error of trying to explain away the famous speech which he delivered at the Labour Party Conference at Brighton in 1957 when he declared that a Foreign Secretary must not enter a conference 'naked'. He now explained that by this expression, which was generally taken to mean 'deprived of nuclear power', he only intended to say 'that we could not possibly throw aside all our allies, all our obligations and all our friends and negotiate with other nations, with Great Britain having no friends anywhere in the world'.[2] This flimsy evasion was received with mixed incredulity and indignation by the sophisticated audience to which it was addressed.

The Foreign Secretary, who followed, contented himself with delivering the somewhat formal speech which he had already prepared; a more agile Parliamentarian could have torn Bevan to pieces.

> He [Selwyn] had a wonderful situation and opportunity, and failed altogether. He is *so good* in the work that I really cannot think of anyone who could be more efficient. But he has—for the moment—lost his nerve in the House.[3]

Accordingly I decided to 'wind up' on the second day instead of entrusting this task to one of the Under-Secretaries at the Foreign Office.

> I spoke for twenty minutes only—had a completely quiet House —and got great applause from our side. We got a good majority— sixty-six. Poor Selwyn is very distressed, and I did my best to comfort him. He is *so* good and *so* loyal.[3]

I had hoped that the debate would pass off without a division, but the Opposition insisted on putting down an amendment. I therefore had no qualms in using my opportunity to underline the essential difference between the views stated officially by the Leader of the Opposition and those by which the Labour movement kept up an agitation in the constituencies.

[1] *Annual Register, 1958*, p. 7.   [2] *Hansard*, 20 February 1958.   [3] 20 February 1958.

There now arose one of those foolish agitations in the Press and among the weaker brethren in the Parliamentary Party to demand Selwyn Lloyd's replacement.

> I had a talk early this morning with Foreign Secretary. The Press is loudly demanding his resignation—all except the *Daily Telegraph*, which is behaving admirably, and *The Times*, which is aloof and grandly ignoring everything—with 'leaders' on racing, or education, or anything but the great issues.[1]

The next day I noted :

> The Press is 'gunning' for Selwyn in a most unfair way. They are all speculating about his successor. All this is (*a*) just malice; (*b*) an attempt to bring down the Government. Salisbury, Thorneycroft, Selwyn Lloyd—with all the by-elections, culminating in Rochdale—the calculation is that I could not stand the pressure.[2]

I naturally resisted what seemed to be a most unfair attack on a Minister who had carried out his work efficiently and loyally. In the course of a television interview on the night of 21 February in answer to a somewhat truculent question from one of the new class of cross-examiners which has since become so popular, I took the opportunity to say,

> I think Mr. Selwyn Lloyd is a very good Foreign Secretary and has done his work very well. If I did not think so I would have made a change. I do not intend to make a change as the result of pressure. I do not think that is very wise and it is not my idea of loyalty.[3]

Nevertheless it was not easy to bring comfort to my colleague.

> I have had two or three very difficult days with Selwyn Lloyd. He feels that his position has been so weakened (*a*) by his failure in the House, (*b*) by the attacks upon him, that he is of no use to the Government. He sent me a letter offering his resignation. I think he is very sensitive and cannot bear the charge that he is 'clinging to office'. But I really cannot have another resignation—although from a different cause. Selwyn is quite sincere and

[1] 21 February 1958.   [2] 22 February 1958.   [3] *Annual Register, 1958*, p. 8.

most friendly. But he is definitely shaken in nerve. . . . However, after a lot of talk and a formal letter, the incident is over—for the moment—and Selwyn has agreed to go on.[1]

Commentators and even historians are apt to under-rate the physical and mental pressure which falls upon Ministers in high office who have had to go through a series of difficult crises. They often forget the nervous tension under which modern Governments have to face the most intricate and exhausting problems, enduring a permanent criticism from the Opposition in the House of Commons, from nerveless members of their own Party, from the Press, sometimes mercurial and always patronising, and now from the radio and television. Happily this incident was rapidly closed by a friendly exchange of letters.[2]

The Anglo-American agreement on the stationing of inter-mediate-range ballistic missiles in Britain was now published and caused little hostile comment. Fortunately we had insisted on including an important clause making it clear that the decision to launch missiles was one to be taken by the two Governments jointly. It was indeed lucky that this clause was drafted in such unequivocal terms. For the week was not out before an embarrassing incident took place resulting from an exuberant speech from an American Colonel of the Air Force who claimed to have—apparently in his own hands—'full operational control' of the rockets and rocket bases in the United Kingdom.

> There was a great 'flap' this morning over an extraordinary statement by a certain Colonel Zinc—an American 'Eagle Colonel' of the Air Force—who claims to be about to take over *operational* command of the rockets and rocket bases in England. As this is in direct contradiction to (*a*) the terms of the agreement published last Monday, (*b*) what we told Parliament on Monday and in the debate yesterday, Colonel Zinc has put his foot in it on the grand scale![3]

At first sight this name seemed improbable; it seemed more like an international organisation or an agency of the United Nations. But the facts were soon checked, including the startling claims of this metallic warrior. Happily our Washington Embassy rose to the occasion.

[1] 26 February 1958.   [2] See Appendix 4.   [3] 27 February 1958.

I saw the paragraphs in the paper at 8.30 (2.30 a.m. Washington). At noon (6 a.m. Washington) we telephoned the Embassy. The State Department issued a *démenti* by 3.30 p.m. London and 9.30 a.m. Washington time, which was produced in the House of Commons during [Geoffrey] de Freitas's speech at about 3.45 p.m. I have sent my congratulations to the British Ambassador. The American alliance is continually being put in jeopardy by the folly of American officers, in all ranks.[1]

I added in my record some prophetic words: 'Americans will feel quite differently about all this when their own country becomes a target.'[1]

The arguments about a Summit meeting continued for the next few months. On 28 February the Soviet Government agreed to a Foreign Ministers' Conference to prepare for a Summit, but only on conditions which would nullify its value. For they would only be allowed to discuss 'technical questions and not matters of substance'. This, it seemed, meant they must agree on the place of meeting, its date, its composition but not what it was for. This would be turning the Summit into a propaganda phantom, an argumentative quiddity. The NATO powers now began to join in the discussion, and on 4 March I asked my old friend M. Spaak, now Secretary-General of NATO, who chanced to be in London, to call for a talk.

I told him about the messages which were passing to and from Washington. He is, like me, anxious about the way the hand should be played. Actually, the situation of the different countries in NATO is strange. The French are not much alarmed about the H-bomb. They do not think it will be used or that the Russians will dare attack so long as the Americans have their bases. The Italians *don't* want 'Summit talks' at all — for they are about to have elections, and the Christian Democrats have to take the line that Communism is an accursed thing and the Communists untouchables. The Benelux countries are resigned. U.K. and Scandinavian countries are *for* Summit talks, in the hope of some good coming out of them. American public opinion is definitely *against* talk; Canadian neutral.[2]

My colleagues seemed on the whole to favour a more positive approach; but the Americans contented themselves with replying

[1] 27 February 1958.   [2] 4 March 1958.

that the Foreign Ministers must consider substantial matters as well as mere questions of how to organise a Summit meeting. This somewhat dreary interchange was interrupted by a strange interlude:

> A ridiculous and tiresome night. The House sat late—till nearly 4 a.m. After midnight, the first editions of the morning papers began to come in. The *Daily Herald* had a most circumstantial story—in the headlines—saying that Duncan Sandys (Minister of Defence) was to go to Moscow on my instructions to try to deal direct with Moscow, by-passing Washington and the NATO alliance, and reach a separate arrangement with them. This of course was given to the *Daily Herald* by the Russian Embassy and they fell for it. Unfortunately Sandys could not be found anywhere. He had gone home after a broadcast and gone to bed and neither by telephone nor by going to the house could he or his housekeeper be roused. Finally we got the story, early on Friday morning.
>
> *7 March.* Chief Whip, Sandys, Harold Evans, Hoyer Millar (F.O.) came round at ten to discuss *l'affaire Sandys*. It seems that, while I was on my tour he got an invitation to Moscow—as other Ministers often do. Since 'Hungary', these were not accepted, until quite recently. After consultation with Foreign Secretary, he 'accepted in principle' with no date fixed or likely to be. We drew up, with some difficulty, a statement to Press, which I hope will 'kill' the story. But it was a bore to be deprived of sleep for practically one whole night on this account.[1]

It was a storm in a teacup; but in politics we sail in paper boats.

Meanwhile the NATO meeting passed off well enough; the constituent countries being satisfied with the way in which we and the Americans were handling the question of the Summit. They certainly did not want to be rushed, and in spite of their geographical exposure to danger their populations seemed less emotionally involved than ours in the nuclear nightmare. Some delay also suited us; for if there was to be any question of stopping tests or a 'cut-off' of the essential material as the result of any agreement, we must be covered by the definite repeal of the McMahon Act. The French, with whom we were in close consultation throughout, were anxious

[1] 6–7 March 1958.

to avoid the argument becoming an exclusively Russian–American affair. Finally in March Pineau, Dulles and Lloyd, who were together in Manila for a SEATO meeting, agreed with varying degrees of enthusiasm to start new discussions. These should, if possible, lead to a Foreign Ministers' meeting and finally to a Summit.

When Selwyn Lloyd returned to London he gave me a full account of his recent talks with Dulles.

> On the Summit, it is evident that the President plays little or no part – Foster Dulles will decide. He is very anxious to help us, if he can do so without injury to what he believes the broad Western interest. So far, he has not reacted too favourably to my idea of a short statement – three or four paragraphs – of the Western position on the Summit talks, which the people would understand in every country and on which we could rest.[1]

Accordingly I sent a letter to the President on 17 March in the hope of influencing the American attitude.

> Selwyn Lloyd has just returned and told me of the useful talks which Foster and he have had together at Manila on many subjects. In spite of the strain that these gatherings cause to Foreign Ministers they are certainly very useful in giving opportunities for consultations without too much public attention being called to them. . . .
> It was also very useful to have Pineau there who has learned a lot in the last two or three years and is fundamentally a moderate and sensible man. . . . We must try and keep the French along the right lines if it is possible to do so. We both know from experience how sensitive they are and how difficult to guide.
> Now about the Summit. I think so far we are in quite a good posture, but we always have to keep ahead of the Russians and not fall into any of their traps. I am sure you and Foster both recognise the danger of the Russians trying to run out and putting all the blame on us. Some of Khrushchev's recent speeches make me feel that he may be preparing for this, or at any rate keeping this open as a fall-back position. On the other hand he may be willing to bargain about the agenda. . . . What I am anxious about is that we should come forward as soon as possible with a

[1] 16 March 1958.

constructive proposal that will put the burden firmly back on the Russians and be understood to do so. Selwyn will send to Foster against his return a suggested statement of the Western position which we are trying to work out. I think the vital points are the following: that there ought to be a meeting if there is reasonable hope of agreement, even a limited one; and if there is also proper discussion of the main problems, whether agreement is likely or not. For myself, I think now that it will be best to use the Ambassadors to start the work and that when they have made some progress there should be the meeting of Foreign Ministers. Since the Foreign Ministers' meeting was our original proposal at NATO, which the Russians first refused and now seem to accept, I feel we cannot go back upon it. After all, it is a bit of a climb-down for the Russians who I suppose refused the Foreign Ministers' meeting because they knew Foster would be too strong for them. But I quite agree that it would be best to start with the diplomatic exchanges. This way we get serious work done and yet maintain our original position. We should, of course, make it clear that neither the Ambassadors in their first examination nor the Foreign Ministers at a later examination are supposed to reach decisions or agreement on substance. What they have to do is to prepare this twofold agenda, first, the subjects, where we might make some progress, however small, and secondly, the subjects which must be seriously discussed if a Summit meeting is to be worthy of the name. I think it is important that we should get this statement out as soon as we can, for once we have got a position we have something to guide us in all future negotiations. We shall, of course, have to discuss it in NATO, but I should have thought this could be done in the course of this week.

It is difficult now to recall the condition of anxiety, and in some cases almost panic, which was sweeping across the country regarding the nuclear threat. The more extreme and excitable members of the public organised pressure-groups and demonstrated under the somewhat disingenuous slogan of 'ban the bomb'. What exactly this phrase meant was obscure. To some it meant the abandonment of our efforts to develop a British deterrent. Others apparently thought that Russia and the United States would equally respond to this demand. Of course the Soviet Government exploited these fears with considerable skill, knowing full well that any disarmament agreement which merely covered nuclear weapons would leave them with an overwhelming superiority.

Bulganin now launched another long epistle more calculated to delude the weaker brethren than to inaugurate any real move.[1] He repeated his proposal that the Foreign Ministers should start work at once, but only apply themselves to what he called 'organisational aspects'. Even at a Summit meeting the reunification of Germany was not to be open for discussion. It was a matter for two sovereign states, East Germany and West Germany, and therefore not a matter involving other countries. But progress could be made on disarmament if there were cessation of nuclear tests, a ban on nuclear weapons and the elimination of foreign bases. He also declared that his Government were not convinced of the sincerity of the Western powers, especially in view of the recent Anglo-American agreement regarding medium-range missiles.

In the absence of the Foreign Secretary in Holland, on a state visit with the Queen, I sent an urgent message to our Ambassador in Washington to tell Dulles that I was anxious that this prolonged correspondence with Bulganin should now cease. Unless we were careful more and more letters would be showered upon us which would create new confusion at home and throughout Europe. We must have a statement of the Western position; but Dulles should be warned that it was important

> that we should not pose as speaking for NATO. There are two reasons for this. First of all United States and United Kingdom responsibilities go much beyond NATO, e.g. the Bomb which protects the Middle East and the East as well as Europe. Secondly, we must not pose as NATO's representatives or we shall end up with not a Summit talk but a conference between NATO and the Warsaw powers.

I was also anxious lest the Soviet Government might jump the gun and announce a unilateral suspension of tests. Our own attitude towards this was complicated by the fact that the repeal of the McMahon Act had not yet passed through Congress. On 27 March the news came of Bulganin's resignation and Khrushchev's

[1] *Correspondence with the Soviet Union on Summit Talks*, Cmnd. 423 (H.M.S.O., May 1958).

Q2

succession. Although we knew little at the time of the long and devious methods by which Khrushchev had reached the aim of his ambition, it was clear that we had to deal with a man who, if he had not the authority enjoyed by Lenin and Stalin, had achieved something like presidential powers. Happily on this occasion Western diplomacy worked rapidly; on 29 March I was able to send Khrushchev the text of the three-power statement on behalf of the United States, France and Britain. It was clear and short. If the Soviet Government would agree to our proposals we might divert our energies from conducting a lengthy public correspondence and get down to serious preparatory work without delay. The message ran as follows:

1. The present international situation requires that a serious attempt be made to reach agreement on the main problems affecting the attainment of peace and stability in the world. In the circumstances a Summit meeting is desirable if it would provide opportunity for conducting serious discussions of major problems and would be an effective means of reaching agreement on significant subjects.

2. It is clear that before a Summit meeting can meet in these conditions preparatory work is required.

3. This preparatory work could best be performed by exchanges through diplomatic channels leading to a meeting between Foreign Ministers.

4. The main purpose of this preparatory work should be to examine the position of the various Governments on the major questions at issue between them and to establish what subjects should be submitted for examination by Heads of Government. It would not be the purpose of these preparatory talks to reach decisions, but to bring out by general discussion the possibilities of agreement.

5. The Foreign Ministers, assuming they have concluded the preparatory work to their satisfaction, would reach agreement on the date and place of the Summit meeting and decide on its composition.

6. If this procedure is acceptable to the Soviet Government it is suggested that diplomatic exchanges should start in Moscow in the second half of April.[1]

[1] *Correspondence with the Soviet Union on Summit Talks*, Cmnd. 423 (H.M.S.O., 1958).

As I expected we were only just in time. On 31 March—two days later—the Soviet Government announced its decision to abandon nuclear tests unilaterally and called upon all other powers to follow suit. I noted in my diary the somewhat hectic events of that weekend.

1. Gromyko has announced the unilateral decision of the Soviet Government to suspend all nuclear tests. (As they have just completed a large and accelerated series, this is a bit thin as propaganda for ordinary folk, but has naturally had a great effect on people like the Editor of the *Daily Mirror* and on the Radicals and Socialists generally.)

2. After weeks of arguing, the U.S. Government and now *all* the NATO Governments have approved our idea of sending a short and clear reply to Russia about the Summit meeting. I actually drafted this paper myself some weeks ago and telegraphed it to Foreign Secretary at Manila. At that time Dulles did not like it at all. But he changed his view—just in time, after a good deal of coaxing. (The President, judging from his messages, has been more flexible all through; but of course he generally bows to Dulles in the end.) Then we had to get NATO support.

For the substance, this was easy enough—only one or two amendments being made to our text. But then came the problem: who was to deliver the note to Moscow? On this, the NATO representatives argued for several days; Italy, Turkey, Greece, Belgium—all wanted to join. For Italy, owing to a General Election, this had some importance. Finally, it was agreed, after a lot of telephoning and telegraphing, that the *note* should be *delivered* by the Geneva Conference Powers—U.K., France, U.S.—but that this would be without prejudice to the question of what powers would actually take part in a meeting of Foreign Secretaries or Heads of Governments.

Gromyko's speech was Monday afternoon. The Allied note was given in on the same afternoon and published at 5 p.m. (6 o'clock news). It was 'a damn close-run thing'. Actually, I think our notes about the Summit almost cancelled out the propaganda effect of the Russian decision on tests. I had, of course, to explain all this to the Cabinet, and get their general approval for the line I would take in House of Commons—that is, to stand quite firm on *tests*.[1]

[1] 1 April 1958.

Twice a week I was subjected in Parliament to an interrogation, not to say cross-examination, about atomic 'fall-out', nuclear tests and the path to the Summit. The preparation of the answers to the printed questions and of possible supplementary points which might arise involved a bi-weekly meeting with expert scientists who painfully but patiently tried to coach me in the profound mysteries of atomic theory. Unfortunately my knowledge of these high matters stopped at Lucretius. But I found that like a recitation—or 'saying lesson' as it was called at Eton—I could remember enough to get through any particular bout of questioning. However, as soon as the ordeal was over, I forgot it completely, and the process had to be constantly repeated. Fortunately for their reputation and peace of mind, judges are expected to know nothing outside the law—even matters of common repute. Ministers are not so lucky. They are required to be omniscient.

On this occasion, as I expected, the new Russian announcement was received with enthusiasm by the left of the Labour Party, some of whom were genuine pacifists and others who were commonly regarded as 'fellow-travellers'. In such situations I always looked to see if Shinwell was in his place. If so I could confidently leave this impulsive but patriotic figure to administer an appropriate rebuke. Gaitskell did his best to maintain a central position. Although it was necessary for him to criticise the Government for their missed opportunities, he was too prudent and too public-spirited to allow himself to be gulled by the patent insincerity of the Soviet offer. The Russians had just completed a long series of large and 'dirty' tests without regard to the wider question of general disarmament. They now asked that all tests should be suspended.

Questions went pretty well. Since the Labour Party are trying to cover their deep internal divisions on the whole question of defence by a compromise—'no more tests till the Summit' they were outwardly in a strong position. However, I stoutly maintained our position and got a general support from the House. All the patriotic Labourites had seen through the cynicism of the Russian propaganda line. Three megaton tests in a week—then, no more tests.[1]

[1] 1 April 1958.

Nevertheless I had already begun to think of some method of making a forward movement. If we could not make much progress on disarmament, what about trade? I had always felt that the restrictions on trade in items of so-called 'strategic' importance were exaggerated. Accordingly I enquired of the Foreign Secretary:

What is happening . . . about Russian trade? When do you think it will be safe to take a strong line with the Americans? I suppose not until the Amendment Bill for the McMahon Act is through. I think the abolition of all these restrictions is one of the few things we might really get out of a Summit meeting.

If so, we ought to prepare a good case on it. My view is that the President and Dulles are really on our side; it is Congress that they fear. However, our experience over bringing the China list into line with the Russian was that the pressure groups were more or less inactive.

On the same day, 1 April, Hammarskjöld came to dinner. He was on his way back from Moscow.

Hammarskjöld was very pleasant and quite interesting, but he speaks so indistinctly as to be barely comprehensible. . . . Khrushchev is supreme, without challengers, and very confident of his own and Russia's strength. He will make no concessions. We must have Summit talks, but we shall achieve nothing serious, except perhaps on tests—that is, if we are ready to stop. On most weapons and scientific development—especially in 'space science', the Russians are ahead of the West. Thus Hammarskjöld— (incidentally confirming what our own Intelligence Services tell us).[1]

Khrushchev was not slow in getting off the mark. On 4 April I received a letter which was a curious combination of appeal and menace. It was skilfully devised to frighten the timid and attract the idealists.

One knows [he wrote] the anxiety with which the continuation of atomic and hydrogen weapon tests is regarded by the British public circles realising the disaster which an atomic war can bring to Great Britain in view of her geographic position alone.

He went on to point out the dangers to health.

<hr />

[1] 1 April 1958.

Systematic explosions of atomic and hydrogen weapons for experimental purposes already now in times of peace are harming the health of peaceful, unsuspecting and completely innocent inhabitants of different countries. It is stated in the petition signed by 9,235 scientists from forty-four countries, including many eminent scientists of Great Britain and the Soviet Union, and submitted last January to the Secretary-General of the United Nations, that each nuclear bomb test increases the amount of radioactive fall-out over all parts of the world, thus inflicting harm to the health of people throughout the world and threatening the normal development of coming generations.

After a reference to the difficulties of common agreement the letter went on to express the noble intentions of the Soviet Government.

Guided by a desire to make a practical beginning to the universal ending of atomic and hydrogen weapon tests and thus to take a first step towards the final deliverance of mankind from the threat of an annihilating atomic war, the Supreme Soviet of the Union of Soviet Socialist Republics has decided to end in the Soviet Union the testing of atomic or hydrogen weapons of all kinds.

There then followed a formal declaration.

In pursuance of this decision by the U.S.S.R. Supreme Soviet the Soviet Government *has resolved to end unilaterally as from 31 March 1958 the carrying out of atomic and hydrogen weapon tests of all kinds.*

Not unnaturally there was an escape clause. If other countries failed to respond, the Soviet Union would be 'clearly left with no other alternative but to consider itself free from the obligation it assumed with regard to ending nuclear tests.'

This new Russian move was swallowed either genuinely or for political reasons by a large part of the Labour Party; even Gaitskell thought it necessary to declare that there was a widespread desire in the country that we should make an effective response and indicate our willingness to suspend tests. Bevan was more direct: 'Why could not the Prime Minister act with a little more moral courage and accept the offer.' The reply was not difficult:

I am as anxious for advance as any other hon. Member, but I am also anxious that it should be properly negotiated, properly tied up, and effective, without endangering our own security. As for moral courage, the House must judge.[1]

Public opinion although anxious remained firm. Even the more excitable critics realised the need for the British Government to consult its allies before making a formal reply to the Soviet proposal. This was all the more necessary because both the Americans and ourselves had test programmes arranged for the immediate future; our policy therefore must be strictly co-ordinated, and if there were any question of the suspension or abolition of tests and still more of a cut-off of material then I must ask for a fresh confirmation of the President's promise 'to see us through'.

Harold Caccia, our Ambassador in Washington, reported Dulles's scepticism about any fruitful negotiations with the Russians. He regarded this new gesture as pure propaganda. He did not believe that the Russians intended to reach any agreement at the Summit. He was accordingly unwilling to make any concessions in order to reach a Summit. Eisenhower replied to Khrushchev on 8 April by renewing the proposal for expert discussions on the practicality of an inspection system to control the suspension of tests. Some days later, 21 April, I made a statement in similar terms.

The Soviet Government now proposed ambassadorial meetings, provided that these were confined to a discussion merely of the time, place and composition of any Summit meeting. Although this marked no real advance the Western powers accepted. There followed an argument of almost Byzantine intricacy as to whether the ambassadors should be received by Gromyko jointly or severally.

Adenauer, who was in London on 16 April, thought 'the Russians . . . can best be tackled and shown up by making "controlled disarmament—conventional and unconventional" our main demand'.[2]

On 21 April I sent a further message to Khrushchev urging him as strongly as possible to agree to a meeting of experts.

Since your letter to me of 4 April on the subject of nuclear tests, talks have begun in Moscow which may, we hope, prepare

[1] *Hansard*, 1 April 1958.   [2] 17 April 1958.

the way for a Summit Conference. Despite certain difficulties of procedure, of which I am sorry to learn, I trust that satisfactory arrangements will soon be made leading to a meeting of Foreign Ministers, to be followed by a meeting of Heads of Governments. It seems to me that the question of nuclear tests must be one of the subjects, together with other problems of disarmament, which will be discussed. Any practical agreement in this sphere must depend of course upon an agreed system of inspection and control. I wonder therefore whether we could not press forward now with the proposal which has already been made, namely, that technical experts should meet in order to work out the kind of arrangements which would be necessary for such a system.

But before my message could have reached him he reiterated his rejection of the experts' talks.

While these labyrinthine negotiations dragged wearily on, we did our best to co-ordinate action between London, Washing' jn and Paris.

A good deal of telephoning yesterday and today, the Russians having made a further proposal about the Ambassadors' talks, preparatory to the Summit. They now want to add Poland and Czechoslovakia. Neither U.S. nor France will willingly accept this, though I see little harm in it.[1]

This proposal was eventually refused, and the President continued to reiterate his request for a meeting of experts to discuss the possibility of effective control of tests. I took the opportunity on 25 April at a Primrose League Rally in the Albert Hall to steady opinion by giving a clear statement of our policy and the arguments on which it was based. In addition, I thought it right to counter-attack by exposing the ambivalence of the Labour Party leaders over defence:

In all this controversy, I find the position of the Labour Party very confusing. It seems to be more directed to the preservation of unity within the Party than to the defence interests of Great

[1] 27 April 1958.

Britain. I can understand and respect the views of those people who are genuine pacifists—who feel that strict Christian duty enjoins no more than passive resistance and that any form of self-defence is wrong.

I say I respect but I do not agree with these views. Nor do I think they are ever likely to be the foundation of policy by any Government in this country. But the mass of the Socialists are not conscientious objectors in this sense of the word. Yet their attitude to the whole problem of the nuclear weapon is equivocal and weak. The majority now say that Britain should have the bomb and should not abandon it unilaterally. I agree with that. But if I had followed their advice we should not now have the bomb—or rather we should only have a bomb which was completely untested and whose effectiveness was therefore quite unknown.

This time last year, before our very first experiments were made, before we really had a bomb at all, the whole Labour Party led by Mr. Gaitskell censured me for continuing with the tests and a great campaign was got up through the country to prevent the tests taking place. Great pressure was brought upon me, from many quarters. Much came from very sincere and worthy people, and moved me greatly. Some was not so respectable. But had I yielded to this, Mr. Gaitskell's present policy would be even more foolish than it is. Now he says that Britain must have the bomb and use it to bargain with at the Conference. Even Mr. Bevan says not to do so would be to go naked into the Conference —though he has since tried to explain away this momentary lapse into good sense.

Last year the Opposition moved a formal vote of censure. I venture to repeat my words in Parliament in reply—'We are to rely on the nuclear deterrent—but not unduly. We are to postpone our bomb tests—but not for very long. We are to ask other powers to agree to abolish all bomb tests, and if by any chance they should agree, then presumably they would be left with the fully tested bomb and we should be left with a bomb which had not been tested at all. So, of course, we should have to rely on American nuclear power for our defence. In the same breath the same Hon. Members tell us that it is humiliating to obtain, whether by gift or purchase, an American rocket because the warhead is under American control until we can make our own. Then, to crown it all, the House is asked to withhold its approval from a policy which lacks firm decisions.'

However, Mr. Gaitskell has, it seems, learned nothing since then. He is still, officially, as Leader of his Party, against any further British tests.

I referred to the latest turn in this tortuous argument.

> The Russians, having just had some of the greatest tests in history, have asked us to call off tests without any firm agreement for inspection or control and in isolation from other measures of disarmament. This is as if in a football match, one side having scored two goals asked the opposing team not to play any more. Mr. Gaitskell says that I should suspend the tests at least until the Summit Conference. If the object is to appeal to Khrushchev's better nature or to avoid wounding his susceptibilities I think that this is an unrealistic, indeed a fantastic view. But that, of course, is not the true purpose of Mr. Gaitskell. He is not so interested in Mr. Khrushchev's feelings as in Mr. Bevan's feelings. He has managed, temporarily at any rate, to give an appearance of unity in his own party. He sits side by side with Mr. Bevan on the Front Bench. It is true that they don't look very happy in that position but there it is—and Mr. Gaitskell has Mr. Bevan temporarily at any rate on his best behaviour.

> Mr. Gaitskell is trying to stake a claim to be regarded as a responsible statesman who could be entrusted with the defence needs of our great nation. But I say that his campaign against finishing our current series of tests is not statesmanship—it is pure opportunism. It is to paper over the cleavage in the Opposition not to strengthen the foundations of the British Empire and Commonwealth.

On 29 April I heard that the latest British H-bomb test had been carried out satisfactorily on the previous day. This news was immediately published to the world. I expected a great row in the House, but in fact Gaitskell's protests were ineffectual and confused. But much was still at risk.

> The Americans are beginning to think in terms of suspending tests under certain conditions. Our test last week was very successful and we are advancing the dates for our next test to

1 September. This will conclude this series. But we shall still depend on the amendment of the McMahon Act.[1]

On 9 May Khrushchev made a new move:

The Russians have made a tentative proposal about a scientific committee to enquire and report on the practicality of detecting nuclear tests. This is at least a small move forward, as we proposed this ourselves nearly a year ago and have repeated it since.[2]

The situation was now becoming clearer. The British Government and especially the British people wanted a Summit under proper conditions in the hope that some agreement might be reached on disarmament generally which we could accept without danger. In this move forward the British Government were ready to take the lead; they certainly had no intention of introducing obstacles. Nevertheless so far as tests were concerned there was a complication, all the more embarrassing because it could not be referred to publicly. On 29 May I explained the situation to a meeting of those Ministers mainly concerned:

Our last test (a few weeks ago) was successful. Nevertheless it is absolutely vital for us to complete this series in September. If all goes well, we shall need only two explosions; but if (as is very possible) we have a failure in the new and very special system which we want to test, we shall need two more. We should complete everything by 31 October (at latest) and probably before. Can we hold on against (*a*) the public and political pressure now; (*b*) the extension of this pressure which is likely to follow U.N. report on medical effects? These are the questions we must face. But if we give up now we shall *not* have a reliable weapon or one which the enemy cannot neutralise. This last is really the vital point. Yet (until McMahon Act is amended and a new agreement made with U.S.) we cannot even discuss the problem with them. However, the news about this is good. The Amending Bill has passed the Committee stage and there is just a chance of an agreement being concluded in time to lie thirty days on the table *before* Congress adjourns. But it will be a race against time. And everything depends on it! For, if we get a really good working agreement, it is unlikely that we shall need any more tests—except

[1] 1 May 1958. [2] 17 May 1958.

perhaps just this last series, to put us in a better bargaining position. However, *with* American working arrangements made, our autumn tests are not a 'must'. Without these, these are absolutely vital to the safety and strength of Britain and we must go on.[1]

Meanwhile on the broad question of a Summit meeting Adenauer's position, no doubt under internal pressure, was becoming modified. He wrote to me on 23 May as follows:

> All of us, I believe, know the difficulties which seem to stand in the way of a successful Summit Conference. But it is my opinion that we should try to overcome these difficulties. It would appear to me to be dangerous if we were to leave to the Soviet Union the effective propaganda thesis that it was she who tried to have at least clarifying talks at the highest level, that the realisation of this intention, however, was made impossible by the unwillingness of the West. In our endeavours to arrive at an effectively controlled disarmament of nuclear and conventional weapons and thereby also at a political *détente*, we should all the more be careful not to let Soviet propaganda get the better of us, as we cannot exclude out of hand the possibility of achieving at least some acceptable partial results. I think I can also detect some common point of departure in the readiness expressed in principle by the Soviet Union to take part in negotiations in which the question is to be examined how, as a beginning, such controls could be established with regard to the testing of atomic and nuclear weapons.

On 31 May, after much telegraphing between London, Washington and Paris, Llewellyn Thompson, the United States Ambassador in Moscow, handed to Gromyko the Western proposals. These outlined general headings for the agenda for a summit meeting, together with suggested 'sub-topics'. Khrushchev did not reply for nearly six weeks.

Meanwhile I had begun to prepare for another visit to the United States. I was to be given an honorary degree at my grandfather's old university, DePauw, at Greencastle in Indiana. I was also to visit Washington, and I was anxious that discussion should not be

[1] 29 May 1958.

limited to the immediate political and disarmament problems which faced the Western alliance. After all, these high hopes lay in the future, and might well prove illusory. But another problem, if not more grave at least more urgent, faced us all. In Britain, we had been forced to defend our sterling reserves and strengthen our balance of payments by restrictionist methods which, although not extreme, were to me distasteful. Other nations were in a similar predicament. The United States was passing through a phase of industrial and commercial recession and had adopted a cautious, even deflationary, monetary policy.

In order to try to turn the Americans' minds from the rather narrow, not to say reactionary, attitude which they took to the problems of trade and liquidity I sent Eisenhower a long message containing my thoughts. Apart from all the other matters which had filled our minds, there were two issues which seemed to me vital. The first was how to organise the economic aid which could be given, especially to the underdeveloped countries; to supervise how this was shared out, so that these countries could plan ahead without extravagance, and be encouraged to use our assistance for peaceful purposes as well as for legitimate defence.

The other was how to make sure that enough financial credit was provided for a steady expansion of trade. It would be a tragedy if the productive capacity of the free world was held back because we had failed to provide the necessary financial machinery. Work and production were the best defences against Communist subversion. Of course, the sterling system was at present an indispensable part of the world credit system and was playing a particularly important role in the maintenance of world trade. With its growing surplus, the United Kingdom ought to be able to take a full share in helping with the problem of international liquidity. In other words our increasing reserves would be a buffer for the rest of the sterling area countries, so that they would be less likely to be drawn into a decline in world business. But all this would be of little avail if the United States Treasury were to continue its so-called orthodox policies. The world needed a large supply of money. It must somehow be provided.

I had, as yet, no precise proposals to put before the President.

But I felt, instinctively, that in the period which lay ahead the struggle against Communism would shift more and more into the economic field. So long as we maintained the alliances and did not lower our guard, the Communists could not launch a hot war. But the cold war in all its forms would grow in intensity. A recession in world trade would be a staggering blow to the stability of the West.

These thoughts were to fall on stony ground, but I was able to revive them with Eisenhower's successor.

I had informed both Adenauer and de Gaulle, as well as the heads of the Commonwealth Governments, of my forthcoming visit to Washington, and on 7 June I set out upon this new journey. Before I left I had a characteristic letter from Lord Montgomery, who was then acting as Deputy Supreme Commander of NATO, describing his recent visit to the United States and his talks with Dulles. He had told the Secretary that he

> reckoned American foreign policy was inconsistent. The United States had worked with the Western powers in Europe and against them in the Middle East, the Far East, and in Africa.

Whether because of the Field-Marshal's representations or for other reasons, Dulles was now about to make a dramatic change in policy.

At the pressing invitation of the President, Dorothy came with me and proved of great comfort and value to our little party of friends. Norman Brook proved, as usual, invaluable; for he commanded both trust and affection. The usual team of secretaries and typists was headed by Freddie Bishop and Philip de Zulueta.

> We arrived at Washington about 10.30 a.m. Foster Dulles was there to meet us, as well as Harold Caccia and his wife. Almost immediately on arrival we got down to work—there was a lot to be done to prepare the agenda, etc. Sir Edwin Plowden arrived for talks about the proposed agreement to be made in pursuance of the amended McMahon Act . . . it will be a tight squeeze, since Congress is expected to rise at the end of the first or second week in August.[1]

The next day was Sunday, and since the ceremony at Greencastle, Indiana, was the excuse if not the reason for my visit, Harold Caccia

[1] 7 June 1958.

and I, with Bishop and de Zulueta, left Washington in the Britannia, arriving at Indianapolis airport about 1 p.m.

There we were met by various dignitaries—including the Governor and the Mayor, as well as by Mr. [Eugene C.] Pulliam, the owner of the *Indianapolis Star* and other newspapers. We drove from the airport to President [Russell J.] Humbert's [the head of the University] house at Greencastle. All the route, about thirty to forty miles, was lined with people, who gave me a tremendous welcome. There were banners with 'Welcome Mac', or 'Welcome Home' across the streets in the villages. It was really most touching. There was rather a wind; otherwise a fine day and not *too* hot—about eighty degrees. At President Humbert's house were assembled all the faculty of the University of DePauw. Finally, about 3.45, we left in an open car for the stadium. A large crowd was gathered in the streets; and in the stadium were about 6,000–7,000. After the playing of the National Anthem, etc., the 'Commencement Exercises' began. This meant the conferring of degrees on some four hundred 'graduating' young men and women and of some M.A.s and doctorates on a few more advanced worthies. Finally, punctually at 5.30, began a ceremony which was on a more or less nationwide T.V. hook-up. (It is said that at least twenty million people will have seen it—perhaps forty to fifty million!) The Dean read the citation and Dr. Humbert introduced me and conferred the degree. My speech began at 5.35 and had to end at 5.59 precisely. We had taken a lot of trouble about the content—and also about the *length*. The speech ended at 5.59—just in time. It was well received by the local audience. But of course, all depends on its effect upon the larger audience—the whole American people—to whom it was addressed.[1]

The theme of the speech was the interdependence of nations one upon the other. Mr. Pulliam gave a dinner to about thirty guests.

Mostly 'publishers' and editors of local and neighbouring newspapers. Mr. [William D.] Maxwell—who has succeeded the redoubtable Colonel McCormick—was there, representing the *Chicago Tribune*. Kansas was well represented also. It was a pretty good collection of those who both make and reflect Middle Western opinion. After dinner, they asked questions for nearly

[1] 8 June 1958.

an hour. I am bound to say that I was amazed at the change in the 'isolationist' Middle West since the old days. Moreover, where they are changed, they will stay changed. For they are folk who are fixed in their ideas. Mr. Pulliam gave me a beautifully framed portrait of my mother (an old photograph, really) which had been found somewhere. It was a kind gesture.[1]

On the afternoon of 9 June we were received by the President at the White House. The Ambassador, Caccia, Norman Brook and Bishop came with me. There were also present for part of the time Pat Dean, Edwin Plowden, and Con O'Neill. The conference lasted until 6 p.m. and was very relaxed and friendly.

Among other things, the President and I initialled an agreement about the use of bombs or war-heads under *joint* control. So far as the bases are concerned, which the Americans have in England, this regular agreement replaces the loose arrangement made by Attlee and confirmed by Churchill. We have also negotiated an agreement (in provisional form) which can be submitted to Congress (to lie thirty days on the table) as soon as the Bill amending the McMahon Act is through. There seems a good hope now that this will be by 1 July. Since Congress is expected to go on till the first week in August, we may just do it. But it will be a tight squeeze. If we can't get the atomic agreement this summer, the opportunity has gone till next February. All this naturally has a tremendous effect on our policy on tests.[2]

Eisenhower seemed pretty well, although he told me that he got tired as the day went on; but then his day started very early. He was always at his desk at 7.45 a.m.

The Americans seem quite happy. I think they feel stronger in popular opinion than a few months back. This, however, makes them rather stiffer over Soviet affairs, especially as regards Summit talks.[2]

On the next day, 10 June, President Eisenhower took me by helicopter to Baltimore, where we arrived about 10.45.

We drove in an open car to the campus of Johns Hopkins University. The Commencement ceremonies were in progress,

[1] 8 June 1958.   [2] 9 June 1958.

the conferring of degrees on students who had just graduated was completed. The President and I were received by the President of the University, Dr. Milton Eisenhower (brother to Ike).

After the usual ceremonies, in the course of which both Ike and I were given honorary degrees of doctor, speeches were made. Both the Eisenhowers said very nice things about me. My speech was shorter than the DePauw one—about fifteen minutes—but on the same general theme. In spite of the anxieties of the British Treasury, I think it's as well to go on 'plugging' the same point: 'Economic interdependence is every bit as necessary as military.'[1]

After consultations with the Ambassador, I also introduced a reference to the Summit. It ran as follows:

We must maintain these alliances—our sure shield—but I am not without hope that we may succeed little by little, if not all at once, in making some progress towards the relaxation of tension in the world.

Naturally I do not believe that at a Summit, or at any other meeting, five or six men can in four days bridge the immense chasm between these two concepts. It would be folly to suppose so. But, if conditions are favourable, and if the will is there, they might make first a little progress here, and then a little there, and so bring us out of a condition of stalemate into one of negotiation. They could do that, but only if both sides are willing. We on our side are certainly willing. That is why we have held in both our countries that some beginning could be made in controlled disarmament of both nuclear and conventional weapons. Control is really the essence. Once both sides agree to experiment in this we shall have really made a start. We shall have established a beginning of confidence and confidence means peace.

Meanwhile, while accepting and welcoming progress to these ends bit by bit, we must stand firm. Anything else would be a betrayal.

We flew back to Washington, and I went to luncheon with Senator T. F. Green on Capitol Hill. There was a distinguished body of senators there, including Senators William Fulbright and Alexander Wiley. After luncheon I was taken on to the floor of the

[1] 10 June 1958.

Senate. There had just been a count called, and when all the Senators had returned I was told to address this august body. This was rather an alarming task, since I had been given no notice. However, I told them that my mother had once declared to me that to be an American Senator was the height of human endeavour and felicity. This seemed to please them.

At 3 p.m. we went to the State Department for a further spell of discussion. This time it was interdependence in fields *other* than military—i.e. economic and propaganda. Mr. [Robert B.] Anderson (U.S. Treasury) was interesting, genial, well-briefed, but not inspiring. He succeeded George Humphrey, and has (I fear) succeeded to some of H.'s rather conventional ideas. But the movement will be too much for him. American public opinion is moving towards my conceptions. Even the Middle West, once so anti-British and isolationist, is changing. After a good session with Anderson and his assistants, when Doug Dillon was very helpful, we changed to Allen Dulles and his team. I think we made some progress here towards co-ordination of Anglo-American effort in propaganda and counter-subversion.[1]

In the evening I received all the Commonwealth Ambassadors, and then went to dine at the White House, a men's dinner.

On 11 June I had a long talk with Dulles at the State Department, and after the usual luncheon and speech to the Press Club I went to the White House.

Here we had a talk for an hour—four of us, President, Dulles, Caccia and I. Dulles put forward some very far-reaching ideas about the future, on which we must really do some work and have another meeting to discuss. What he wants to work towards is a unified system of Government for the free world. Both he and the President feel that, while this sense of unity and understanding exists between us, we should try to create something definite to leave to our successors.[2]

Alas, these ideals are easier to put forward in conversation than to bring into practice. Apart from all other difficulties we had not yet realised the bar to progress that would be presented by de Gaulle's insularity and nostalgic dreams.

[1] 10 June 1958.   [2] 11 June 1958.

After this useful and even inspiring visit we left for Canada, arriving at the airport before dusk. After the usual ceremonies we drove to Government House.

Dorothy had not been to Ottawa since she and I left, an engaged couple, in 1920. She dined with Vincent Massey (Governor-General). Brook and I went to dine with Diefenbaker and a few of his chief Ministers.[1]

The programme for the following day was as follows:

9.15–10.15: talks with Prime Minister and a few colleagues. 10.30: T.V. interview. 11–1: I spoke to the whole Canadian Cabinet. The atmosphere was *very* friendly and helpful. After a luncheon alone with Governor-General, back to Parliament buildings. Talks resumed with different groups of Ministers, lasting till 7 p.m. Finally, dinner at Country Club for Dorothy and me, given by Canadian Government. Prime Minister Diefenbaker made a short informal speech, to which I replied — quite a day![2]

On the morning of the 13th I was received in the Canadian House of Commons. The Chamber was packed, since Senators as well as Members of Parliament attended.

The Speaker of the Senate made a short introductory speech, followed by the Prime Minister. I spoke for twenty-five minutes. The speech, which was partly in French, was very well received. We had taken a lot of trouble with it, and I really think it was a good speech.[3]

We lunched with Sir Saville Garner, the High Commissioner, at Earnscliffe,

once the house of Sir John Macdonald, now the residence of the U.K. High Commissioner. It stands on the banks of the Ottawa River, just below Government House.[3]

At 5 p.m. we left. The Prime Minister, Diefenbaker,

has been very kind and helpful. Before leaving Government House I rang up the former Prime Minister at Quebec. Mr. St. Laurent seemed very pleased by this attention.[3]

[1] 11 June 1958.   [2] 12 June 1958.   [3] 13 June 1958.

I reported to the Cabinet the results of my visit to Washington. I was able to assure my colleagues that the President had reaffirmed the practice, if not the principle, of close Anglo-American co-operation on all matters of common concern. This was intended to cover economic as well as military problems. As regards formal relations, France was already included in the 'Standing Committee',[1] and consultations both with France and Germany should be frequent and friendly. With regard to the Summit and to the question of suspension of tests a good deal must depend upon the forthcoming meeting of scientists at Geneva who were to consider the technical problems involved in establishing a system of control and inspection. If we could obtain even the beginning of such a system it would be well worth making an offer for suspension of tests. For all disarmament, whether conventional or unconventional, hung upon the essential pivot of inspection.

As regards the Middle East the Americans had made it clear to me that they were moving rapidly towards a policy of supporting our friends in the Arab world, while maintaining a correct but cool attitude towards Nasser. Nevertheless it was something of a surprise to us all when the Americans some six weeks later decided upon a much more drastic intervention.

On questions of world currency and liquidity I had to admit that my efforts were politely but frigidly received. It was clear that the United States Government were not likely to take any steps to counter the recession, nor were they prepared to abandon the most orthodox financial policies. At the best, the seed that I tried to sow could only lie dormant, at least for the present.

I made a brief statement to the House of Commons and sent full reports to the Commonwealth Prime Ministers and to Adenauer. At the end of June I made a short visit to de Gaulle[2] in which I was able to give him an account of what I had learnt in Washington.

On my return from Canada I had found awaiting me the text of a long letter from Khrushchev comprising eleven closely typed foolscap pages. Stripped of its verbiage, the argument ran as follows:

---

[1] The Committee in Washington of American, British and French officers, to which the Commander-in-Chief of the NATO forces was responsible.

[2] See page 447 above.

It seems quite simple to end world tension—everyone should stop tests, renounce the use of nuclear weapons, establish a denuclearised zone in Europe, and come to a Heads of Government meeting without wasting any more time on preliminary exploratory talks. Since the West does not accept this simple programme, can it be because they do not really want talks?

In my answer, sent at the beginning of July, I thought it right to point out to him as courteously as possible that there seemed to be a real difference of approach:

Yours is to simply convene a Summit Conference. Ours is to negotiate a settlement of some of the differences which divide us. We want a Summit Conference because we want an effective means of making progress in negotiation.

At present we had not yet been able to agree on an agenda for any conference, nor had Mr. Gromyko replied to the proposal which we had made.

To persist in refusing to consider any compromise method of reaching agreement on this is bound to create the impression that you are not really interested in the success of, but only in the demand for, a Summit Conference. I must add that this impression also arises from your action in publishing our confidential exchanges without even consulting us before doing so.

At the same time I still had the feeling that some progress might yet be made. I therefore concluded as follows:

Although I must admit to feeling discouraged by your letter I have no intention of abandoning the hope that we may still be able to get the negotiations started. We shall certainly not relax our efforts and I ask you most sincerely to make your contribution by accepting our procedural proposal in a spirit of compromise or to let us hear of some alternative suggestion.

In spite of these rather discouraging communications the eight-power conference of experts on the detection of nuclear explosions opened in Geneva on 1 July. I now began to consider a plan by which we might get some agreement for the suspension of nuclear tests by Russia, America and Britain for a period of two years from

1 January, while allowing the French, should they wish to do so, to carry on their experiments. This seemed fair, since the French had started behind all the others. But this plan, like so many others, never even came to the starting gate.

On 2 July I received news that the President had signed the repeal of the McMahon Act and this fundamental difficulty was at last resolved. It was to be followed on 4 August by the formal coming into force with the approval of Congress of the Atomic Bilateral Agreement. The interchange of information on the most precious secrets began from that moment and was carried out with absolute sincerity on both sides. I was only too glad when we were able to give immediate assistance on certain technical problems on which we had made advances in which the American scientists were anxious to share. This happy occasion was marked by an interchange of messages between the President and myself.

Dear Harold,

Yesterday I took satisfaction in signing into law the amendments to the Atomic Energy Act. I was gratified to be in a position this morning to authorize the Secretary of State to sign the bilateral agreement between our Governments which our representatives have successfully negotiated. We have acted at once to get this agreement before the Congress.

With warm regard,

As ever,
Ike

My dear Friend,

Now that the Atomic Agreement between us has been signed I must tell you how grateful I am for the help you have given us over this right from the beginning. I am particularly grateful that you saw our difficulties over the preamble about which I telegraphed you last week. I trust that Congress will enable the Agreement to become effective.

This agreement will be regarded as a further symbol of the partnership which we both want for co-operation between the countries of the free world.

With warm regards,

Yours ever,
Harold Macmillan

All through these months, much wearisome argument had gone on between London and Bonn about the perennial question of support costs. It is one which has continued in various forms ever since. The Americans, so far as they were able, were helpful and sympathetic. At last a temporary agreement was reached. For 1958 Germany would make a contribution of £12 million, plus £22½ million as an advance repayment of those instalments of the German post-war debt which would normally fall due in the years 1962–4. In addition, Germany would deposit £50 million as an advance payment for defence equipment. In 1959–60 and 1960–1, the German Government would continue the annual contribution of £12 million. It was agreed by Germany that British troops should be reduced in 1959 from 55,000 to 45,000 and before the end of the summer this was accepted by our NATO allies.

During the first half of 1958 the main interest in foreign affairs, so far as British public opinion was concerned, was thus concentrated upon the question of nuclear tests and the possibility of a new Summit meeting between the heads of the three Western powers, the United States, France and the United Kingdom, and the head of the Soviet Government. These negotiations were still continuing, when in mid-July the action was once more suddenly shifted to the Middle East.

CHAPTER XVI

More Arabian Nights

I N the Middle East, the year 1958 opened ominously. During a meeting of the Ministerial Council of the Baghdad Pact in Ankara in January, which was otherwise encouraging, not least because the Americans now offered an additional $10 million of economic aid, the news came of a new and threatening move. On 1 February Egypt and Syria announced their agreement to form a union to be known as the United Arab Republic. This proved the signal for a period of confusion and even anarchy in which the Western powers were to become progressively involved. Some indication of a general unrest in the Arab world had been given at the end of January by the request of the Yemen Government for the withdrawal of our *chargé d'affaires*. No reason was vouchsafed; but those who had followed the peregrinations of the Yemeni Crown Prince Muhammad al Badr through Europe and the Far East were not surprised. Already his flirtations with the Communist powers had resulted in a five-year agreement with China signed in Peking on 12 January. This was accompanied by a pompous declaration in which the Crown Prince joined with Chou En-lai in condemning 'colonialism' and 'imperialism', now almost ritual words. Similar coquettings with Moscow followed. But perhaps the most fatal of all the errors committed by the Government of the Yemen was the decision, announced on 8 March, to enter into a federation with the United Arab Republic. A heavy price was to be paid for this folly in subsequent years. All that the Council of the Baghdad Pact could do was foster closer co-operation between Iraq, Jordan and Saudi Arabia. In this they were partially successful. On 14 February King Feisal of Iraq and King Hussein of Jordan formally proclaimed the union of their states in an Arab Federation.

Nuri Pasha, the veteran statesman of Iraq, came to London in the middle of February. I was very glad to meet again so distinguished and loyal a friend, but I felt on this occasion that he was in an unusually excitable mood.

He is going back to Iraq today and expects to take on the Premiership again. He is full of plans—some of them rather dangerously vague—for detaching Syria from Egypt. He wants us to get the Ruler of Kuwait to join, in some form, the Iraq–Jordan union. The problem we have is to head Nuri off impossible or dangerous schemes, which are bound to fail, without losing his confidence or injuring his will to resist Egypt and Russia. The Americans (according to Nuri) have given him promises of 'support'—but his story does not quite tally with what they have told us. However, we will clear this up.[1]

The one certain thing was that the Syrians, if spurred on by Nasser, were poised to do great damage to their Iraqi neighbours by interrupting the flow of oil. Accordingly early in March I asked the Chancellor of the Exchequer to work out a plan of guaranteeing at least part of such losses.

Nuri has told [Sir] Michael Wright [British Ambassador in Baghdad] that in such circumstance he would like to be able to call on an appropriate credit which, in his view, would be anything from five million pounds to twenty million pounds. I should be grateful if you would examine urgently the possibility of indicating to the Iraqis that if the Syrians take action which results in a further short-fall of Iraqi oil revenues, the Iraqi Petroleum Company would be prepared to extend further assistance. This would be by way of loans up to the unexpended balance of the top limit of twenty million pounds agreed upon for similar loans in 1957–8. Clearly, we should first have to discuss this with the I.P.C. To get their agreement, we shall presumably have to promise a parallel extension of H.M. Government's own guarantee to the Company.

This would be all against the, I hope, unlikelihood of the pipelines being cut again and I think that help here would have a very considerable effect, even though, with luck, we should not in fact have to spend any money at all.

[1] 17 February 1958.

R

Nuri had another scheme which did not seem to me so happy. He was anxious that we should give up our position in Kuwait, according her complete independence and thus allowing her to become an additional member of the Iraq–Jordan union. The Foreign Secretary reported to me a discussion with the King and Nuri on this matter and expressed a good deal of doubt, which I shared, as to the wisdom of such a plan. After all it was not at all impossible that the Kuwaitis might be persuaded to join Egypt instead of Iraq, against whom they entertained certain jealousies, from which was later to develop a menacing situation. While we had no objection to an association of a friendly kind, the union now proposed was too obviously intended to allow Iraq and Jordan to lay their hands on the immense revenues of Kuwait in order to nourish their own resources. As Lloyd frankly told Nuri there seemed to be a certain illogicality between the concept of declaring the independence of Kuwait and at the same time ordering her to join the Iraq–Jordan union. It was surely wiser to maintain our protection of Kuwait as well as the other Sheikhdoms in the Persian Gulf. Meanwhile what we could and did do was to provide assistance in arms and money to Iraq to the best of our power and at the same time persuade the Americans to give generous aid.

Trouble now began to appear in another quarter. Aden was a vital outpost of British power. From its geographical position and the strange mixture of races by which it was inhabited it was also a continual source of trouble. During April the Aden Protectorate was subjected to frequent minor attacks on its border villages and tribal forts. These culminated on 27 April in an attack by a thousand rebel tribesmen on Fort Assarir. We had already authorised the Aden Government to order the arrest and removal of the well-known Jifri brothers, prominent political agitators operating mainly from the protected state of Lahej. I had fortunately heard of this trouble before it reached its peak.

> We . . . had to face a most difficult situation in Aden. One of the Sultans in the Protectorate looks like going over to Nasser. We are authorising the Governor to take strong action and have sent reinforcements.[1]

[1] 15 April 1958.

Unhappily only one of the brothers was found; the others in due course escaped to their spiritual home.

At the beginning of July the position was still deteriorating. The Governor was therefore summoned to London for a conference with the Colonial Secretary, Lennox-Boyd, who combined with firmness and resolution a deep sympathy with oriental peoples.

At 9.15 a.m. meeting with Secretary of State [for the] Colonies, Governor [Sir William] Luce of Aden, and various officials. Emergency action has to be taken in Lahej (one of the largest of the Aden Protectorates). The young Sultan has gone over to Nasser . . . and some of his people have already crossed into Yemen. He will have to be deposed. The other sultans or chieftains appear to be loyal.[1]

This action was fully justified, for it was obvious that the Sultan of Lahej, one of the largest states, had not only refused to co-operate with the Governor in trying to control the activities of the Jifri brothers, but had in addition connived at the defection to the Yemen on 25 June of the Commander of his State Forces together with a large part of the army and the sum of £10,000. With the usual generosity of colonial governments, we made no attempt to keep the Sultan in duress. He too found his way to Cairo. The rest of the Protectorate rulers came to London at their own request, partly to assure us of their loyalty and partly to open discussions as to a possible federation of the states.

Meanwhile a wave of unrest began to spread across Lebanon, which has always been one of the most developed and civilised of the Levant states. In the first weeks of May the split between the Moslems and Christians as well as between the pro-Western and pan-Arab sections seemed to be widening. The balance between the two religious communities had hitherto been scrupulously maintained. The President, Camille Chamoun, was a Maronite Christian. His Prime Minister, Sami es-Solh, was a Sunni Moslem. But the frankly pro-Western ideas of the President and his Foreign Minister, Charles Habib Malik, were being fiercely attacked by many Moslems and especially by the pan-Arabist enthusiasts. The formation of the U.A.R. had a disturbing influence on the more excitable

[1] 6 July 1958.

sections of the public. Allegations were freely made, and deemed well founded, of massive Egyptian infiltrations, sometimes across the frontiers and sometimes across the sea, with corresponding imports of arms and money. Guerrilla forces were being openly recruited. By the middle of May a state of something like chaos began to develop. The pipelines were cut by some saboteurs; and although these were rapidly repaired, no one could foresee what the next phase of anarchy would bring.

In his distress President Chamoun enquired of the British and American Governments whether they would be prepared to provide military assistance within twenty-four hours of receiving his appeal. If we could not do so, Lebanon would in his opinion collapse as an independent power and be forced to join the U.A.R.

> Nasser is organising an internal campaign there against President Chamoun and his régime. This is partly Communist and partly Arab Nationalist. Russian arms are being introduced from Syria, and the object is to force Lebanon to join the Egyptian–Syrian combination. In other words, after Austria–the Sudeten Germans. Poland (in this case Iraq) will be the next to go.[1]

Thus once more we were faced with an aggressive action by Nasser threatening the stability of the whole Middle East. With the loss of our positions on the Canal and the outcome of the military intervention at the end of 1956, we were far worse placed from a military point of view. On the other hand the Western world had learnt much in the last two years and we no longer stood alone.

> Fortunately the Americans have learned a lot since Suez, and the Bermuda and Washington visits are beginning to show results.[1]

After a long discussion and with the full realisation of the dangers internal and external

> the Cabinet agreed that we would join with U.S. in saying to President Chamoun that if he decided to ask for military help to preserve the independence of Lebanon we would give it.[1]

I remember as a curious example of the pressure of life in Downing Street that while my colleagues and I were discussing this

[1] 13 May 1958.

dangerous and difficult decision, we were interrupted by a message from Sir Brian Robertson to say that the threatened railway strike had now reached a critical position and asking for authorisation to make a modest offer which might lead to a settlement. It was only after this short interlude we could get back to the main business of the day and prepare the necessary messages.

There were a number of defence problems to be settled urgently, and as usual between allies there was some initial confusion.

There has been a hitch in the military planning for Lebanon, because the American admiral here (who is to be in charge) had received no instructions. I rang up Harold Caccia [in Washington] and tried (so far as one can on the open line) to get him to push things along. I heard later in the day that this had been cleared. We will, of course, accept an American commander for any expedition, because we hope to contribute the smaller force. But our forces – probably airborne – must come in together.[1]

On the same day I sent full information about the threat to Lebanon and the proposed Anglo-American response to the Prime Ministers of the Commonwealth. Both the President and I still hoped that the promise of support might enable Chamoun to calm the situation.

The news from the Lebanon is better. Our assurances seem to have put new heart into the Lebanese Government. But the situation is very tricky and the loyalty of the army uncertain.[1]

By the 16th I felt more cheerful. The railway strike at home had been settled and

Lebanon still holds. Our forces are in readiness in case the request for help comes.[2]

Although the forces that we had to assemble were not large, I was pleased to learn that all the preliminary steps had been taken. Unfortunately, on the afternoon of 17 May, Selwyn Lloyd rang me up to say

that the news of the proposed Anglo-American military help to the Lebanon has leaked in Washington! It seems that Dulles

[1] 14 May 1958.   [2] 16 May 1958.

had a confidential talk with the Senate leaders. One of them must
have talked and it is all in the morning's *Washington Post*! We
have decided to tell all the 'spokesmen' of Foreign Office and
Service departments to refuse to say anything. We are enquiring
from Washington as to what Dulles is going to say. But I have no
doubt that there will be a storm on Monday in the House of
Commons.[1]

Unexpectedly this dangerous time-bomb, which I feared would
explode with devastating effects, appeared to be a dud.

> The House of Commons is unaccountable. We expected
> yesterday great trouble. . . . As regards Lebanon, in spite of the
> American leak, there was no trouble. It seems to be generally
> known that we and the Americans have given some guarantee
> to President Chamoun and that troops are ready to go. But for
> some reason even the extreme Left of the Labour Party have
> made no protest.[2]

A few days later, on 22 May, the Lebanese Government turned
to the Security Council to ask them to take account of the massive
measures of intervention in Lebanese affairs by the United Arab
Republic, and on 11 June the Security Council authorised the
despatch of an observation group to Lebanon.

When I was in Washington at the beginning of June, I naturally
discussed this serious situation in full and particularly urged upon
the Americans to afford greater financial help both to Jordan and
Iraq, whose 'Arab Federation' had just held its first meeting of
Parliament. This was agreed on 10 June. Our share was to be $4
million, and the Americans would undertake a considerably larger
commitment. It certainly was not financial difficulties which were to
lead to the tragedy which took place in Iraq a month later.

About the same time there was an unexpected approach by the
Egyptians to Hare, the United States Ambassador in Cairo, which
was told to me by Dulles himself in Washington. It seemed to
suggest that some compromise might be reached. Chamoun could
remain President until his term expired but should not stand again.
General Fuad Chehab, whose loyalty was very doubtful and who was

[1] 17 May 1958.   [2] 20 May 1958.

indeed generally regarded as in direct opposition to the President, should at once become Prime Minister. Nasser, of course, denied providing any support from Egypt, but he promised, in the event of this compromise being reached, to use his influence to bring the rioting and fighting in Lebanon to an end. Both we and the Americans felt that Chehab had not put his heart into the fight against the insurgents, and if he were now to become Prime Minister, Chamoun's position would become impossible. Nevertheless it was not clear what were Nasser's motives. Did he fear an Anglo-American intervention? Had the Russians warned him to avoid this at all costs? When I met the President he expressed unwillingness for the United States Government to act as Nasser's 'lackey' in his matter. Finally it was agreed that the best course would be for the United States Government to instruct their Ambassador in Beirut to tell Chamoun frankly what had happened, but to emphasise that he was making no recommendation whatever about the course which Chamoun should follow. At the same time it should be made plain to him that the American assurances already given still stood.

On 19 June,

> Gaitskell, Bevan and Griffiths came (at their request) to see the Foreign Secretary and me about Lebanon. Bevan was more robust than the others. I refused to give any pledge that we would *not* intervene in any circumstances. (They really accepted that such a *public* pledge would be a fatal encouragement, to Nasser and his party in Lebanon.) Anyway, the Secretary-General of United Nations was now in the [Middle East] and we must await his return to New York.[1]

During the course of my visit to Paris on 30 June I was able to have a full discussion with de Gaulle about the Middle East in general and especially about Lebanon. He seemed both friendly and sympathetic. It was clear to me that he was much more concerned with North Africa than the Middle East.

For the next few weeks the situation continued to deteriorate without any marked incident. Hammarskjöld carried out a tour of Middle Eastern capitals and seemed to confirm the view of a group

[1] 19 June 1958.

of observers, consisting of representatives of Ecuador, Norway and India, that the scale of infiltration had been exaggerated. This somewhat academic report seemed, however, an insufficient solution of a position where something like civil war had in fact broken out. All these various disorders were now overshadowed by the tremendous events which took place in Baghdad on 14 July.

Early on the morning of Monday 14 July, Selwyn Lloyd rang me up to say that there had been a revolutionary *coup* in Baghdad. The information was scanty, but it was feared that the King, Crown Prince and Nuri Pasha had been murdered. On arrival in London I found that there was still little news: 'Some said that the Crown Prince was still alive and fighting and that Nuri had escaped.'[1] Alas, when the full account reached us it was clear that the tragedy was complete. The rest of the country seemed calm; indeed the Foreign Secretary was able to tell the House the next day that the Iraq Petroleum Company reported that everything was quiet at Kirkuk and at Basra, and that no attempt had been made to interfere with our military and air force establishments at Habbaniyah. The sudden and unexpected revolt in the capital city with all its attendant horrors had been caused by two brigades of the army which had been improvidently allowed, contrary to the usual practice, to march through Baghdad on their way to another encampment. We had known that there were revolutionary plots among the discontented section of the army, but neither our Ambassador nor the Government had felt any undue alarm. So confident had the King and his uncle been that the situation was in control that they had planned to leave the next day on a visit to Turkey.

This small body of troops in fact ran amok. The King was brutally murdered as well as the Crown Prince and other members of the Royal Family. We were to learn later that Nuri had escaped in disguise, but on the next day was caught and not only killed but treated with the utmost barbarity, his body being dragged naked through the streets for the delectation of the lowest section of the mob. So ended the Iraqi Hashemite monarchy, which had served the people so well and so courageously since the end of the First World War.

[1] 14 July 1958.

We also learnt that the Embassy had been invaded by the mob, a British officer killed, and the Ambassador and his staff forced to seek safety in a neighbouring hotel. All this was devastating news, destroying at a blow a whole system of security which successive British Governments had built up, greatly to the interests of the Iraqi people and supported with generous aid in money, skill and experience. By a cruel irony no Arab Government had striven harder than that of Iraq to invest prudently the resources arising from oil in their own country as well as from outside aid. These had been used not for the vainglory or luxurious expenditure of the few, but for the improvement of the conditions of the many.

Thus when the Cabinet met on the evening of 14 July all was uncertainty. All that we knew was still rumour, but not, unhappily, likely to prove exaggerated. I saw Gaitskell before the Cabinet to tell him such news as we had, and did not disguise from him the possible development of events in Lebanon. We now heard that President Chamoun had informed our Ambassador that he would call on the United States and the United Kingdom within twenty-four hours to honour their undertaking to intervene with military forces along the Syrian frontier. It seemed that the Americans intended to respond favourably to this appeal and were prepared to 'go it alone'. This was indeed a strange reversal of the situation only eighteen months before.

If the Eisenhower doctrine of 1957 represented a marked change from the attitude of the American Administration in 1956, the interpretation now to be given to it in 1958 was not merely in words but in deeds, a recantation—an act of penitence—unparalleled in history. Of course, the Americans, who could still control the United Nations, were able to arm themselves with at least a modicum of acquiescence from its various organs. Moreover, since they were operating in response to an appeal by the constitutional head of Lebanon, their action could perhaps be justified under the normal rules of international law. Nevertheless, apart from these niceties, the new American policy could hardly be reconciled with the Administration's almost hysterical outbursts over Suez. In any event the British must now try to assess what would be the effect throughout the whole area. It was impossible to isolate Lebanon.

R2

The general feeling was uncertainty as to what the American policy really would be. Nothing could be more fatal than for the Americans to go to the Lebanon and rest content with that or soon retire in favour of a U.N. force. *We* had to carry, on our economy, all the evil effects that might follow—in Iraq, Syria and the Gulf. Our sterling oil might dry up and what real guarantee had we from U.S.?[1]

After I had seen Gaitskell, I called my colleagues together at the House of Commons.

The Cabinet ended at 8.45 p.m.—in a good state of morale, but naturally very worried. During the Cabinet the American telegrams began to make it clear that U.S. were inclined to land troops in Lebanon, in answer to Chamoun's appeal.[1]

At 10.45 p.m. I had a long telephone conversation with President Eisenhower. The mechanisms by which such conversations could be protected had not yet been developed, and for practical purposes one might assume that the line would be tapped by hostile as well as by friendly listeners.

It soon became clear that the Americans had taken the decision, and the fleet was approaching Beirut. I said 'You are doing a Suez on me', at which President laughed. The conversation became almost impossible to carry on with an open line. All the same, I think I made it clear that we really must expect the Americans to stand by us and to see the thing through. I then drafted a telegram to put all this into proper words and we got it off by about 2 a.m.[1]

In my telegram, while agreeing that intervention in Lebanon in response to President Chamoun's appeal seemed to be all the more necessary because of the events in Iraq, and that the President could justify it as an action to support the independence of a small state, I tried to expand what I had attempted to make as clear as possible on the open telephone line. There would certainly be a lot of trouble. The various oil installations at Tripoli could not be immediately protected and would probably be destroyed. The pipelines through Syria would certainly be cut. There might also be attacks upon other

[1] 14 July 1958.

oil installations throughout the whole area, all of which would inflict great loss upon the international companies and particularly upon countries which depended on sterling oil. Nevertheless my colleagues and I were quite prepared to accept the risks if it were part of a determination to face these issues; to protect Jordan as well as Lebanon, and broadly to see the crisis through. In that event we would give all possible support in our own Parliament, throughout the Commonwealth and in the United Nations. With regard to Lebanon, since the President had suggested that we might be wiser to preserve our forces, we were inclined to agree that this was the proper course, for they would certainly be needed elsewhere.

While the Cabinet was sitting we had received a message from Hussein that he was determined to maintain his position, but making as yet no formal request, only asking to be informed of our intentions. While I was drafting the telegram to the President, I heard the news that the King had subsequently asked for an assurance both from the United States and from Britain that we would come to his immediate assistance if he thought it necessary to preserve the integrity and independence of Jordan. I therefore sent a further telegram in the early hours of the morning which I knew would reach the President on his breakfast-table. In this I impressed once more upon him that an operation confined to Lebanon entailed much greater risk to us than to the Americans. I felt sure that we should soon be receiving a final appeal from King Hussein; indeed it might well be better to act in both places rather than to let the situation drift. I repeated my anxieties that the position in Jordan might rapidly deteriorate until all hope of action was past. When the Cabinet met on the following morning, 15 July, we knew that the United States Government had decided to land troops at Beirut using the Sixth Fleet and without British assistance. At the same time they informed the Security Council and requested the establishment of a United Nations Emergency Force to which the American Army could hand over its responsibilities in due course. I also had to tell my colleagues that neither the President nor Dulles had really given full consideration to the position in Jordan. The President had not yet sent me any comment about the need for King Hussein to make a formal request for American and British military aid. The news from Iraq remained confused, but it seemed that the insurrection was confined to Baghdad. We did not yet know whether Nuri had escaped. We had warned the rulers in the Gulf to be on their guard. Altogether the position was full of anxieties. Dulles seemed once again to be providing himself with a line of retreat. Nothing could be worse for our position in the Middle East than to find ourselves first exposed and then abandoned, as we should indeed be if we responded to King Hussein's request, only to find the United States forces had left Lebanon and handed over to some shadowy and insufficient United Nations group.

All we knew for certain was that the United Nations Security Council had been summoned at the request of the American Government, who asked the Council to arrange to protect Lebanon. The Soviet Government had countered by putting forward a resolution requesting the Americans to withdraw their troops. The next twenty-four hours were indeed confusing and even alarming. Eisenhower had not replied to my telegrams directly. Dulles seemed still to be hesitating. As regards Jordan he expressed some doubt as to whether intervention would serve its purpose. Might it injure rather than strengthen King Hussein? All therefore that we could do on 15 July was to send warning and explanatory telegrams to all the Commonwealth Prime Ministers and to state publicly in Parliament our moral support for the action of the Americans. I saw Gaitskell before the House met to tell him the situation.

> Foreign Secretary made statement after questions. There was a good deal of feeling among the Opposition, especially below the gangway. But I thought many of them were uncertain as well as unhappy. Our side were sensible and subdued. It was agreed to debate it all tomorrow.[1]

Selwyn Lloyd contented himself with the bare statement that the United States forces were landing at Beirut that afternoon at the request of President Chamoun. He added:

> Her Majesty's Government have been in close consultation with the United States Government throughout the present crisis. They were informed in advance of the United States Govern-

[1] 15 July 1958.

ment's intentions. They believe that the United States action is necessary to preserve the independence and integrity of the Lebanon in this very uncertain situation. This action has Her Majesty's Government's full support.[1]

The President's statement, which was published in *Hansard* in full,[2] emphasised the menace to Lebanon's independence; deplored the revolutionary action and the barbarous assassinations in Baghdad; noted the reference to the U.N.; and declared that the measures being taken by the American Government would be terminated as soon as the Security Council had itself taken action to maintain international peace and security. All this was satisfactory enough from the juridical point of view and certainly eased the political situation at home. But it did not go to the root of the matter. We should equally be entitled under the Charter of the United Nations to help Jordan if required. But unless the new American policy was really going to be carried through with determination and not content itself with legal niceties, we might well find ourselves at the end in a position of virtual isolation. One helpful suggestion came from Washington. Would the Foreign Secretary go immediately to discuss the situation with the President and the Secretary?

The next day, 16 July, proved long and exciting.

Among other things, we arranged for Selwyn Lloyd to go to Washington to discuss the whole situation with Dulles. Much more encouraging telegrams have come from America. I feel sure that the Americans realise how much we have at risk. It would be good for Selwyn to have frank talks about how they are to be defended. He will take [Sir William] Dickson (Chief of the Defence Staff) with him and leave tonight—before the end of the debate.[3]

The Cabinet had met in the morning and approved this plan as well as the general lines upon which the discussion in the House of Commons should be conducted.

The debate was opened by Selwyn, in an excellent speech— short, objective, and well expressed. It was very well received. Bevan followed with a weak speech. Gaitskell wound up for the

[1] *Hansard*, 15 July 1958.   [2] *Hansard*, 15 July 1958, cols. 1021–2.   [3] 16 July 1958.

Opposition, and I for the Government. There was *no* vote. The whole atmosphere, though charged, was different to Suez. Apart from it being merely a matter of moral support to an American 'intervention', the Opposition made little attempt to challenge the legality of the decision. It was a matter of its wisdom. Of course, they kept trying to extract promises that British troops would not be used. But I avoided, or evaded, this.[1]

The Opposition seemed to be in some difficulty as to the line they should take.

> It seems that there was a tremendous dispute in the 'Shadow Cabinet' and in the Labour party meeting about voting. Gaitskell (who is clearly trying to 'live down' his Suez performance) seems to have carried the day against Bevan. So there was no vote. I think my 'wind-up' speech was well received in all parts of the House. I tried to argue the case very objectively and to keep the temperature as low as possible.[1]

But, when the debate ended, the day's, or rather the night's, work was only just beginning.

As I went to my room behind the Speaker's chair, where Dorothy, who had been in the Gallery, was to meet me in the hope of going home together for supper, Freddie Bishop

> gave me a telegram from Amman—it had just arrived—it was written out in longhand—not typed yet. It was soon followed by another. One was a message from the King, sent through our Ambassador; the second, a further plea, still stronger and more poignant, from almost the last survivor of the Hashemite family.[1]

It was now just after 10 p.m., but I immediately decided to call the Cabinet and to add the Service Ministers and the Chiefs of Staff. Everyone was finally collected by about 11 p.m.

> There followed a very remarkable—and perhaps historic—Cabinet meeting in my room in the House of Commons. I don't think I have ever been through anything of the kind.
> The political, diplomatic, Commonwealth, United Nations, Middle East difficulties were all put over and over again by me

[1] 16 July 1958.

and Lord Privy Seal [Butler]. The Staffs described what could be done—and it was precious little. Two battalions of paratroops to be flown in from Cyprus to Amman, to hold the airfield and give succour to the King. But militarily—as I kept telling Ministers— an expedition without a [line of communications]; with a supply by air only if the Israelis agree to overflying; no sea base; no real purpose or future—since we cannot attempt to invade Iraq—and even if we wanted to do so, it would not be through Amman.[1]

During the three hours' discussion I had two telephone conversations with Dulles and asked his frank opinion as to whether we should respond to the King's request.

Dulles thought it rash but praiseworthy. He could not promise troops, but would give *moral* and *logistical* support.[1]

In the course of the long discussion I made each Minister in turn express his view without any lead from me. I was determined that if this adventure was attempted and proved a disaster there could be no question of any Cabinet Minister, including the Service Ministers not in the Cabinet, not having been properly informed. 'As at recent Cabinets—on the Lebanon—I had the Attorney-General [Manningham-Buller there] all the time.'[1] From the military point of view the Chiefs of Staff's views were vital, and I asked them many questions in order to test the difficulties. In the absence of the Foreign Secretary, the Foreign Office was represented by a Junior Minister and the Permanent Under-Secretary. The latter

seemed quite sure that the Israeli consent would be forthcoming. ... [He] had seen the Ambassador. It would be almost a matter of form.[1]

The argument was nicely balanced. In favour of immediate intervention was the fact that if the airfield at Amman fell into the insurgents' hands, the opportunity for effective intervention would be lost and King Hussein's will to resist seriously undermined. Jordan would then in all likelihood pass into the orbit of the United Arab Republic and our position in the whole area would be threatened. The long-term political difficulties of such a situation

[1] 16 July 1958.

would be even worse than the short-term difficulties if we took action. Nor would delay render it any more likely that we should receive operational support from the United States.

As regards the juridical position, there was no difficulty. We were fully entitled to support an ally who asked for our assistance. On the other hand, any force we could send into Jordan would be small and ill-equipped. Their arrival, far from strengthening the King, might provoke such hostility that we should be overwhelmed unless the United States supported us at least by supplying heavy weapons and equipment.

It was now after 2.30 a.m., and a decision must be reached. I asked for ten minutes' interval and went with Butler and Norman Brook into another room.

> We all thought the Cabinet were determined to do this rather 'quixotic' act and that we would not forgive ourselves if the King were murdered tomorrow, like the Royal Family of Iraq. Moreover, the Arab world (on the Gulf, etc.) might be more moved by our inaction than by some reaction to the loss of all our friends in Iraq.[1]

When I returned I summed up all the difficulties and advantages. There would be no scope for exploiting such an operation in the longer term; it was hard to see that it would serve any purpose beyond that of stabilising the existing regime in Jordan and denying the country for a time to the United Arab Republic. The operation would cause a sharp division of opinion at home. On the other hand, failure to respond, and absorption of Jordan by the United Arab Republic, would gravely weaken our political position. Probably the older Commonwealth countries, including Canada, would support action; as would Pakistan and other Baghdad Pact countries. It would strain relations with India, Ceylon, Ghana and Malaya. If we went forward, we must ensure that our action was regarded as comparable to that of the United States in Lebanon. It should be reported at once to the Security Council. We might offer to withdraw our forces as soon as other effective arrangements could be made to safeguard the integrity and independence of Jordan.

[1] 16 July 1958.

I had told Dulles in the second talk that we were disposed to move. He undertook in that event to give full support in public and at the United Nations; and, on his own authority, promised 'logistical' support as the situation developed. He again said that no operational support could be considered until Congress leaders were consulted.

I told the Cabinet about my telephone conversations and repeated that this would be a quixotic but honourable undertaking. The political risks at home were nicely balanced. It was impossible to foresee the end of the operation. It might have grave consequences for the nation and for the Government.

> Then I went round the room. All were 'for'. So I said 'So be it.' The Cabinet dispersed about 3 a.m.[1]

There was much still to be done.

> Commonwealth Office, F.O., Chiefs, all had to get on with the immense amount of work to be done—some consultative, some informative, some executive that follows such a decision. Norman Brook undertook to co-ordinate the work. In fact, he did not go to bed at all that night. I got to bed about 3.30 a.m., having been assured that everything would be done that needed to be done.[1]

The events of the next day are perhaps best told from my own diary.

> One thing—alas—had *not* been done—or too lightly done, with too much taken for granted. This mistake—which I am convinced would never have happened if the Foreign Secretary had not been away in Washington—nearly led to a terrible disaster, which would (I think) have resulted in the collapse of all our policies and the fall of the Government.
>
> I was woken up at 8—and told that we had started the flight from *Cyprus, over Israel, without* obtaining the permission of the Israeli Government. Some machines (with about 200 men) had gone into Amman. Then the order was given to stop and other machines had to go back. At 10 a.m. Gaitskell was coming—fortunately he put this off himself till 1. We had tried telephoning (poor Norman Brook spent three hours trying to get through).

[1] 16 July 1958.

We had tried telegrams. But nothing seemed to get through, and certainly nothing came back.

Cabinet at 11. I told them only a little of the difficulties, and then left Rab to carry on the routine business. In addition, all our telegrams to Commonwealth countries, and to NATO countries had gone (when we thought—as F.O. said—that it was a mere form). All had to be stopped, or withdrawn, or halted, or explained away.

What was I to say in the House? I must announce the facts at least, at 3.30. But what were the facts? No one seemed to know. I waited throughout the morning in my study—trying to deal with other work and hide my sickening anxiety. All we knew was that the Israeli Government was still sitting. Brook (who thought it was his fault) was almost in tears. F. Bishop and the other P.S.s were very kind and sympathetic.

Gaitskell came at 1 p.m.—alone. I was just beginning to tell him about the political situation in Amman; the . . . information which we had got about the Cairo plots in Jordan, when a small bit of paper was brought to me. 'The Israeli Government has agreed.'[1]

My urgent appeal to David Ben Gurion had been supported by the United States Government, who assured them that our intervention had their full support. Perhaps, seeing how much the life and economy of Israel depended on America, this may have turned the scale. This was immediate and vastly welcome relief.

I told Gaitskell what we had done (trying to look as calm as possible) and asked how he would like it handled. Perhaps he and his two friends (Griffiths and Bevan) could come at 2.45 and we could agree how to handle it in Parliament. This was agreed.[1]

I spent the luncheon interval in composing the terms of my statement. The Chief Whip, Ted Heath, had wisely suggested that we should ourselves offer the adjournment at 7 p.m.

This avoids the 'motion' under the Standing Order, with all the Opposition standing up in support—a dramatic gesture which we should be able to avoid. When Gaitskell and his friends came, I suggested this. A short statement; not too many supple-

[1] 17 July 1958.

mentaries; a debate at 7. This was accepted. So it was my job to make a statement at 3.30, with about quarter of an hour of supplementaries; an opening speech at 7 p.m., and a 'wind-up' at 9.45 p.m.[1]

Greatly to my relief,

More by good luck than good management, it all turned out pretty well—from the Parliamentary angle. Gaitskell was quite good, and very restrained, following me. Bevan, who had asked for thirty-five minutes, sat down after twenty minutes, having completely lost the House and a large part of his reputation. The Opposition, having decided *not* to vote yesterday—on the American intervention in the Lebanon—very unwisely decided to vote today. My last words at 9.58 were 'I ask myself this question. If it was not right to vote against America yesterday, why is it right to vote against Britain today?'[1]

This final sentence gave a satisfaction which was not altogether confined to the Tory benches. Nevertheless

It was the only 'partisan' thing I have allowed myself throughout the crisis. But it is a phrase which will stick. We got a majority of sixty-two in the division—Liberals *against* us; some Labour (notably George Brown) *abstained*. All the Conservatives (and some Labour) stood up in my honour as I walked out of the House—under the clock—into the Members' Lobby.[1]

When I got back to No. 10 there were more telegrams, more troubles and more meetings.

But, anyway, I feel the House of Commons is in a good mood. There is none of the rancour of Suez. I tried (and I think succeeded) in making them *feel* how difficult and balanced was the decision which we had to take. In the country generally I think there will be a sense of the gravity of the situation—but I hope also a sense of unity.[1]

On the next day the news from Washington was reasonably satisfactory. We would not be likely to obtain any practical help in Jordan unless real fighting began, but there was every hope that the

[1] 17 July 1958.

stationing on the airfield of the two battalions which we sent in
would be sufficient to maintain the King's authority and to prevent
the insurrection which was being planned and fomented by the
United Arab Republic to promote internal disorder and to overthrow the regime. Our two battalions arrived within twenty-four
hours; their tasks were to hold the airfield, protect the King and
Government and safeguard the main Government installations at
Amman. If necessary two battalions of Foot Guards could be
despatched in support. There would be no heavy weapons, but it
was hoped that the Jordanian Army, which was supplied with
British armour, would be trustworthy.

The next task was to send in my own name full telegrams explaining the action which we and the United States had taken, both to
the important Commonwealth leaders and to our chief European
allies. Nehru had already sent a message expressing his anxiety lest
the situation should be allowed to drift into war. To this I could
only reply in soothing terms. All the public statements, whether in
the Commonwealth or Europe, seemed to show understanding and
appreciation of our motives.

At the same time there was some danger of further disturbances.
The Sudan Government asked whether we could send help if they
were attacked by the Egyptians. The Turks, as usual very determined,
were ready to bring all possible pressure including military action if
necessary upon Iraq. All this had to be calmed down. In the Sudan
the chief danger seemed to be internal revolt rather than external
invasion.

In Iraq it was impossible to restore the old regime, whose chief
representatives had been so brutally murdered. The British had in
Iraq heavy commitments, military and commercial. The detach-
ment of the Royal Air Force formed part of the strategic defence of
the Middle East, and it was doubtful whether it could be able to
maintain its position—indeed it was at considerable risk. Our oil
interests were very large and must be protected. All we could hope
for was to work as well as we could with the new Government. This
at the time seemed not impossible. But there was still much to
decide at the various meetings of Ministers and Chiefs of Staff,
which took place almost continuously.

The Gulf is very uncertain – but we have plans for Bahrain and Kuwait, in case of need. But there is the usual dilemma. Shall we go in now? If so, it is 'aggression'. Shall we wait? If so, we may be too late.

Kuwait, with its massive oil production, is the key to the economic life of Britain – and of Europe. The 'Ruler' is an enigmatic figure. He is in Damascus 'on holiday'. Will he return? He has seen Nasser. Has he sold out to Nasser? No one knows. We have *no* troops at all in Kuwait. So we might lose the airfield, which means fighting our way in. Can we get the Ruler to ask for a battalion or a ship now? All these questions are asked, but not resolved.[1]

As might be expected, many discussions both public and private were taking place at the Security Council, with many suggestions, all of which fell to the ground. The Russians vetoed the Japanese resolution proposing that the Secretary-General should organise a United Nations force which might make possible an Anglo-American withdrawal. In the debate the British delegate made it clear that we were ready to explore with the Secretary-General some form of United Nations action.

On the evening of 19 July, Mr. Khrushchev proposed that Summit talks should take place immediately on the Middle East situation. This somewhat panic action, demanding a meeting within three days, led not unnaturally to considerable confusion at home and abroad.

The *Mirror*, *Herald*, etc., have lost their heads, screaming for immediate acceptance of Mr. K.'s threatening demand for a meeting on Tuesday![2]

A great deal of consultation between the various capitals took place during the last days of July over the possible time and place for such a Summit, which Mr. Khrushchev thought India should be invited to attend.

On 21 July I received a somewhat petulant complaint from Ben Gurion that the permission to overfly was being abused.

[1] 18 July 1958.   [2] 21 July 1958.

I have tried a 'soft answer'. The truth is that an extreme party in Israel thinks that Jordan had better 'collapse' and that they can then seize all territory up to the west bank. Others are frightened by the Soviets, or sympathetic to them. I am trying to get logistic aid from Americans – both for oil supplies for Jordan and for our own troops.[1]

Meanwhile I insisted that we must open the sea route from Aqaba and a line of communications from Aqaba to Amman. This was immediately set in hand. For although the Israelis were merely protesting and not stopping the airlift, without a proper supply-line I realised that Jordan might soon wither away. By the end of the month further action was needed.

It is clear that we need another battalion – partly to strengthen our position in Amman, and partly to secure the new l. of c. for Aqaba. I agreed to this – rather reluctantly, for I hate committing our troops in penny packets all over the place. But there was a long argument – not resolved till midnight – as to the means of transport – by air, or by sea? We finally agreed to ask Ben Gurion for permission to 'overfly', giving as a reason for despatching this battalion the opening of the new l. of c. (which he will like). The position in Jordan is precarious and may blow up at any moment. God grant that we can avoid a disaster. But, of course, our force is too small for any real conflict – if, for instance, the Jordanian Army deserts the King. Its only use is to strengthen the hand of the Government and provide an element of stability. The danger is that it might be overwhelmed. I do not think a mob could do this. But if the Jordanian armoured division went over to Nasser, we should have difficulty in extricating our troops. So it is – and will be – a continual worry, until we can get a U.N. force in their place.[2]

The Russians began to bring extreme pressure on the Israelis.

The Russians have sent a note to the Israelis protesting against Anglo-American violation of their air space (they have sent a similar protest to Italy). The Israelis, partly out of fear of the Russians, but more (I think) to try to force a 'guarantee' of some kind out of U.K. and U.S. Governments, have ordered us to

[1] 21 July 1958.   [2] 1 August 1958.

cease the airlift at once. The Israeli Cabinet meets this morning to consider its reply to the Soviet note. Much telephoning and telegraphing to Washington and Tel Aviv went on during the night. We must have two objects: (*a*) to continue the airlift if at all possible; (*b*) *not* to let the Soviet Government get the immense propaganda victory involved. It is a most difficult and dangerous situation. That in Amman is bad enough, without this extra problem in Tel Aviv.[1]

I had continual talks with the Foreign Secretary, who had now returned, and as the telegrams began to come in on 3 August, it was clear that the result of all these communications was not encouraging.

(1) The Israelis have insisted on the airlift stopping tonight. The Americans have agreed—so we have had to agree. (2) The Americans are *not* anxious for us to send a cruiser from Cyprus with the troops to Aqaba, since this means going through Canal. They asked us to send [a] merchant ship. But the news is better in this sense:

(1) The Israelis look like not answering the Russian note for a day or two.

(2) The Americans have strongly urged them to reject it.

(3) We have about a month's supplies (or more) at Amman, and so long as we can use and develop Aqaba, this l. of c. should be all right.

On the other hand, we shall need to resume flights for personnel—sick and wounded—if we can. We must press the Israelis for this later on. After our final talk, we decided to send the extra battalion from *Aden*, thus avoiding the risk of trouble in the Canal.[2]

I was much relieved when I heard on 8 August that the battalion of Cameronians had safely reached Aqaba, and perhaps more important that the United States Globemasters were now undertaking to carry supplies by direct route from Cyprus to Amman. I should add that through this anxious time the Israeli Ambassador in London proved helpful and understanding.

Meanwhile it became necessary to consider an agreed reply to Khrushchev's proposal for a Summit. On 22 July I explained to my colleagues

[1] 2 August 1958.   [2] 3 August 1958.

the plan which Dulles has suggested to Foreign Secretary. Let there be a so-called Summit meeting—but let it be held in U.N., in New York, or under Article 28 (to which, fortunately, Arthur Henderson specially drew my attention yesterday in the House). This article allows special meetings of the Security Council to be attended by Heads of Governments.

In addition, of course, there could be informal meetings, which would amount to a sort of private Summit 'on the side' and without anything like the publicity.[1]

Since this seemed to meet with general approval, I immediately asked to see Gaitskell and suggested to him that the Foreign Secretary might open the debate which he had asked for on foreign affairs and outline our plan. To this he readily agreed. The

Foreign Secretary made another excellent speech. Bevan followed in a rambling, meditative, and quite harmless speech—taken from an article in last week's *Observer*. The Foreign Affairs debate droned quietly on until 10. No division![1]

The next day we heard that Khrushchev now accepted our idea of a meeting of the Security Council 'providing India and the interested Arab States should attend'. I acknowledged this with the suggestion that the permanent representatives in New York should start preparations for such a meeting, to agree who was to be invited and when the meeting was to be held. I did my best to keep General de Gaulle fully informed and to persuade him to share in our planning. I also sent full messages to Adenauer.

All yesterday I struggled (to no avail) with the French, who have now sent a reply to Moscow on quite different lines to that which we and the Americans have sent. The French *don't* want the Security Council concept; *don't* want to go to New York; but *do* want the original Russian proposal—a meeting of five Heads of Governments (India included) at Geneva. But even this they *don't* really want very much and only at leisure, after 'calm preparation'. On the other hand, U.S. and U.K. (who have troops in Lebanon and Jordan) *don't* want delay but *do* want to press forward with some short-term solution to L. and J.[2]

I was now anxious for some kind of Summit, which

[1] 22 July 1958.   [2] 27 July 1958.

attached to or running alongside the Security Council meeting is the only hope of getting an 'unvetoed' plan through the U.N. None of us really knows what to propose. I am rather keen on a sort of 'Austrian' settlement for Lebanon. The Russians—if they are afraid of war—*might* agree to this. The great thing in our favour consists of the American Army—11,000 strong—in Lebanon. We must *not* let the Americans take this body of men out of the country in response to some fake U.N. gesture. Although Foster doesn't say much in the presence of his vast team of advisers, I feel sure that he is determined to hang on in the Lebanon (by hook or crook) until something decent emerges from all this confusion. I emphasised the need for a longer-term policy, which would take account of Arab aspirations. Nasser cannot now be won over by kindness—or even money. But I still doubt whether he wants to be sold out—body and soul—to the Russians.[1]

General de Gaulle now definitely proposed that the Five-Power Summit should meet in Geneva on 18 August. I had no doubt that Khrushchev would exploit to the full this difference between the French reply and that which we and the Americans had made.

In spite of all my efforts with the French Government throughout Saturday, de Gaulle had insisted on replying in a totally different way to us and the Americans. He had swallowed the Soviet bait, hook, line and sinker. He accepted a Summit meeting of five, at Geneva. This is partly his dislike of U.N.; but chiefly the desire for a European meeting, where he can play a larger role and make France (in the absence of Germany) the recognised leader of Continental Europe.[1]

Chancellor Adenauer expressed to me considerable alarm as to de Gaulle's attitude and seemed inclined to interpret his action as an intention to make a separate deal with Russia, but I did my best to reassure him. Adenauer was always extremely sensitive to any separate negotiation with Moscow by any of his allies unless he were fully informed. This was due to his anxiety to prevent any general recognition throughout the Western world of a constitutional position for East Germany. In reply to Adenauer I stated that

[1] 27 July 1958.

there have been suggestions that the General might wish to do some independent deal with the Soviet Union. I myself very much doubt if this is so. Certainly I have no evidence for believing it; and it seems to me intrinsically unlikely.

But perhaps the old Chancellor was more astute than I. De Gaulle had not yet shown his hand, and I had not fully realised how increasingly isolationist his position would become or how nostalgic his conception of France's role. Alas, he was never to learn the truth of the phrase 'history does not turn back; life is rich in materials and never needs old clothes'.

Meanwhile Foster Dulles and the other Ministers of the Baghdad Pact powers had come to London for a full meeting. Iraq was missing, but all the other members, with the Americans as observers, were still present. After a short tribute which I made in public to the King and Crown Prince of Iraq and Nuri Pasha, we met all through 28 July in closed session.

> The subjects really amounted to this: (*a*) Middle East situation generally; (*b*) future of the Pact; (*c*) future of Iraq. On the whole there were quite robust sentiments expressed. But the critical decision was taken by Foster Dulles in the course of the early afternoon. After discussion by telephone with Washington and the President, he devised a formula by which (in effect) U.S.A. becomes a full member of the Pact, making separate arrangements with each of the countries. This the President can do without a treaty (which only the Senate can make) resting on the authority given him recently by Congressional resolution. Naturally this public declaration was the real highlight of a meeting otherwise darkened by failure and tragedy.[1]

Brigadier Abdul Karim Kassem appeared to have established some kind of order. I could not disagree with the decision reached by all the other members that it would be right to recognise the new regime.

> As regards Iraq, everyone wants to 'recognise' the new Government. The Moslem powers will begin; we will follow.
>
> The future of the Pact—now much fortified by American

[1] 28 July 1958.

adhesion—will not be pressed to a definite conclusion as regards Iraq. We shall not *expel* them; we shall wait for them to retire (which they can legally do with six months' notice) or to resign (without notice). This seems wise.[1]

Khrushchev was not, of course, slow to act. On 28 July in a seven-page epistle marked with a good deal of truculent and even offensive attacks upon the President and America he declared his preference for the French idea of a Summit meeting outside the United Nations. It was fortunate indeed that Foster Dulles was in London at the moment, for the Foreign Secretary and I did not find it difficult to agree with him a line of reply.

We shall stick to the meeting under the aegis of the Security Council, but with 'informal' talks as well. We would prefer New York, but would go to Geneva. Telephone talk with President Eisenhower confirmed this. It was a great help having the Russian reply (which came over the tapes as we were conferring) before Foster left to get his plane.[1]

There now began to be trouble with the NATO powers about our proposed reply to the last Russian note. They

are naturally distressed to see the rift between the Western powers. But I explained—in a special letter, telegraphed to Spaak—that, since Parliament had to pass the adjournment motion tomorrow, I could *not* postpone my reply later than 3.30 that day (Thursday).[2]

The answer was upon the lines agreed, proposing a special meeting of the Heads of Government at the Security Council on 12 August at whatever place might be generally agreeable.

I got Gaitskell to my room at 2.45 and showed him my reply to Mr. K. (which I read out at 3.30 to the House). He seemed satisfied. I also showed him the statement on T.V. for opening of Parliament, to which he also agreed. The reply to Khrushchev (which I read in full) was well received in all quarters of the House. So was T.V.[3]

Before Dulles left I had sent him a note in the following terms:

[1] 28 July 1958.   [2] 30 July 1958.   [3] 31 July 1958.

It was grand to see you in London and to have a good talk about all our problems. They do not look like decreasing, but it is fine to feel that we face them together.

I was reading a life of Lord Palmerston the other day and found this passage written in 1853. It was contained in a minute to one of his colleagues.

'The policy and practice of the Russian Government has always been to push forward its encroachments as fast and as far as the apathy or want of firmness of other Governments would allow it to go, but always to stop and retire when it was met with decided resistance, and then to wait for the next favourable opportunity to make another spring on its intended victim. In furtherance of this policy, the Russian Government has always had two strings to its bow—moderate language and disinterested professions at Petersburg and at London; active aggression by its agents on the scene of operations. If the aggressions succeed locally, the Petersburg Government adopts them as a *fait accompli* which it did not intend, but cannot, in honour, recede from. If the local agents fail, they are disavowed and recalled, and the language previously held is appealed to as a proof that the agents have overstepped their instructions.'

Things have not changed much in 100 years.

I had fully expected Khrushchev to continue his attempt to divide the Western powers. It was clear that the recognition of the new Government of Iraq under General Kassem, which had been strongly urged upon us by all our partners in the Baghdad Pact, had removed his fear of any military action by Turkey. On 3 August he had finished a short visit to Mao Tse-tung in Peking and, no doubt under Chinese pressure, he now executed a sudden and almost spectacular retreat. He went back altogether on his original proposal for a Summit. It was suspected that the Chinese, then his close allies, had strongly objected to the inclusion of India in any conference. Instead he called for an emergency meeting of the General Assembly of the United Nations.

About midnight Foreign Secretary rang up and said that Washington was about to accept, with a Presidential statement

(Dulles was in Brazil). Since there was already an American appeal to General Assembly on the 'order paper' regarding Lebanon, I said we would agree if the motion (which will have priority over any new Russian motion) could be amended to include Jordan.[1]

In accepting the last Russian proposal I could not resist the temptation to remind Khrushchev of the continual changes in his proposals and our readiness to accept under agreed conditions the kind of meeting he had suggested. My message, which was published, was as follows:

On 31 July I proposed that we should meet on 12 August in New York, Geneva or any other place that might be generally agreeable. I said that I would be there on that date and hoped that you would be there too.

I therefore regret that in your letter of 5 August you have withdrawn your agreement, very clearly set out in your letter of 23 July, to a Special Session of the Security Council to be attended by Heads of Government. May I remind you of your words: 'Considering the need for taking urgent decisions in the interests of maintaining peace the Soviet Government considers that the form of meeting of the Heads of Government in these circumstances cannot have any decisive significance. . . . We share your views about the approach to a discussion of this question at a special meeting of the Security Council with Heads of Government participating'; and of your further words: 'We learnt with satisfaction that you, Mr. Prime Minister, are ready to go to New York for a special meeting of the Security Council with the participation of Heads of Government; so far as the Soviet Union is concerned . . . . the Soviet Union will be represented at this session by the Chairman of the Council of Ministers of the U.S.S.R.'

You now propose instead that there should be a special meeting of the General Assembly. This had, of course, been proposed by the United States on 18 July, but action had been suspended because of your view, which both the United States and United Kingdom Governments approved, that the matter should be discussed by Heads of Government and in a more limited circle.

[1] 5 August 1958.

A special session of the General Assembly would be acceptable to Her Majesty's Government. I do however still think that more progress could have been made on Middle East questions by a meeting of the Security Council, especially one where the Heads of Government could negotiate as well as debate.

As to the 'Summit' meeting of the larger character about which we have corresponded since last January I fail to understand the suggestion in the last paragraph of your letter that you are awaiting a further move from me. On the contrary it is I who am awaiting from you an answer to my letter of 1 July. I reminded you in this letter that we had had no response to the suggestions made to you as long ago as 31 May for resolving the difficulty created by the fact that each side had put forward a different set of proposals about which to negotiate. I have always made it abundantly clear that I am anxious for such a meeting under conditions which are acceptable to all of us.

It was now becoming clear that the new crisis developing in the Far East over the Offshore Islands had also affected Khrushchev's decision. Five pages of his reply sent on 10 August was nothing but a verbose attempt to justify his change of position.

I left England on 6 August and did not return until the 12 August. These visits were necessary because of the situation in Cyprus. When the General Assembly met on 13 August, after numerous resolutions had been canvassed which were acceptable to nobody, an unexpected Arab resolution was unanimously adopted on 21 August. This was a great triumph for Selwyn Lloyd, who worked with assiduous and skilful diplomacy. The resolution asked the Secretary-General to make 'such practical arrangements as would adequately help in upholding the principles and purposes of the Charter in relation to Lebanon and Jordan'. It asked him to bear in mind, in carrying out his task, renewed assurances that the Arab countries would respect each other's systems of Government, and all United Nations members' obligations not to interfere in each other's internal affairs. This was what both the Americans and we wanted. For things were quietening down in Lebanon and even in Jordan, and we were anxious at some point within the near future to be able to use the United Nations in these improved conditions to allow our forces to withdraw after the completion of their task.

This final resolution at any rate placed upon the Arab Governments the obligation not to intervene in each other's affairs and gave us some prospect of bringing our military intervention to an end before the end of the year. Yet the position in the Middle East remained very disturbed, and alarming rumours continued to reach us. For instance I noted on 1 September as regards Iraq, 'The return of Rashid Ali (our arch-enemy) bodes no good.'[1] Happily a plot with which he and his friends were associated was discovered and suppressed with many arrests. In Lebanon the position was beginning to improve following Hammarskjöld's visit in September. By 15 October a coalition Government was successfully formed. As for Jordan, Foster Dulles had, under continued pressure from the Foreign Secretary, at last agreed to increase substantially American aid.

I think we shall be able to get our troops back from Jordan, and leave the régime with as good a chance of survival as we can give it by any method short of permanent and large-scale occupation.[2]

Since the new President of Lebanon, President Chehab, had been forced to appoint Rashid Karami, the leader of the former opposition party and a friend of President Chamoun, as Prime Minister, the United States troops decided to begin their withdrawal. This was completed by 25 October. We too decided to withdraw from Jordan and all our troops left successfully by 2 November. The first stage of this operation could be said to be completed. President Eisenhower sent me a message early in November which, however it might be criticised as taking too optimistic a view of the long-term effects of what we had done together, certainly gave me pleasure as showing the spirit of co-operation which had been re-established between our countries.

Now that the missions of the British forces in Jordan and the American forces in Lebanon have come to a close, I think that your country and mine can take deep satisfaction in the successful accomplishment of undertakings of wide and historic significance. Without firing a shot in anger, and in close and friendly

[1] 1 September 1958.   [2] 9 October 1958.

collaboration with the local authorities, our forces have achieved what they were sent to Lebanon and Jordan to do, at the request of the respective governments. They have preserved the independence of these two small countries against aggressive subversive forces directed from outside. Our actions have proved to the world, and especially to the smaller nations, that we stand by our pledges and that we have the courage to carry out our solemn undertakings, regardless of the threats made against us. No matter what political developments may in the future take place in Lebanon or Jordan the effect of our actions will remain valid. I consider this development of the highest significance to the free world. If we had not acted as we did, the determination of the smaller nations to stand firm against the forces of aggression would have been gravely undermined, with all this would have meant for the positions of the United States and the United Kingdom.

We can also take special satisfaction in the complete understanding and splendid co-operation which was evident between our two governments in these undertakings. Both of us are, of course, dedicated to promoting the health and vigor of this spirit, but it is good to feel that in a difficult situation it was effectively applied.

I wanted to let you know what a source of high personal gratification all this has been to me.

In thanking him I used these words.

I have no doubt that there are further difficulties and troubles to be faced, but so long as your country and mine continue to act together in spirit and in deed, as we have over the last months, I am sure we can deal successfully with any eventuality.

The short-term results of the Anglo-American intervention in Lebanon and Jordan were not unsatisfactory. Indeed, in spite of all the varying pressures of their neighbours, including the perpetual intrigues of Nasser, both Lebanon and Jordan succeeded in maintaining internal stability for another decade. The tradition of compromise, strongly developed in Lebanon, enabled her people and Government during all these years to resist the temptations either of Russian infiltration or fanatical Pan-Arabism. Even in Jordan, King Hussein was able, until 1967, to preserve his position intact.

Then he was unluckily swept along by the irresistible pressure of Egyptian chauvinism into the fatal war with Israel, only to find himself abandoned and betrayed by Nasser, and as a result despoiled of half his territory.

But in Iraq the situation began rapidly to worsen. By the spring of 1959 the Government seemed to be moving rapidly towards Russia and Communism. This now began to disturb even Nasser. An anti-Communist but pro-U.A.R. revolt was organised by his agents in March 1959 but failed signally.

The 'Nasserite' revolt in Iraq has failed. But this may mean that the present régime will go more and more Communist. We are in a bad position here—between the devil and the sea.[1]

About the same time the United States Government signed formal defence agreements with Turkey, Persia and Pakistan, thus giving effect to the change of policy announced in July 1958. Nevertheless the situation in Iraq continued to deteriorate, and short of a direct military intervention there seemed no way of countering the lapse into Communism or anarchy. At this time Iraq formally announced her withdrawal from the Baghdad Pact. She also repudiated her military agreements with Britain. Consequently by 31 May the last of the R.A.F. detachments left the famous base at Habbaniyah. Iraq also signed cultural and scientific agreements with East Germany, Poland, China and Russia. Even King Saud now became seriously alarmed, and sent me, through an unofficial intermediary, a passionate appeal for Anglo-American armed intervention. I could only suggest in reply that a return to normal diplomatic relations between Britain and Saudi Arabia, which had been broken off at the time of the Suez operations, would facilitate mutual consultations. As far as the oil in Iraq was concerned, the general view was that rather than seize or nationalise the installations the Iraqi Government would continue to squeeze the company for more money.

I dined last night with Lord Mills. He was full of wisdom. He is worried about Iraq, but still doubts whether the revolutionary Government will altogether destroy I.P.C. They are more

[1] 11 March 1959.

S

likely to squeeze the company for more money. Up to a point, that is tolerable.

Early in May it seemed that if Communist pressure on Iraq was intensified their Government might collapse. Anti-Communist countries in the Middle East might then try to intervene, in which case Russia would certainly react, possibly in Iraq, but more likely in Iran. All these anxieties were to continue, nor were we or our American allies disposed to repeat in Iraq the intervention of the previous year in Lebanon and Jordan. However, the situation dragged on without flaring into a dangerous crisis. Meanwhile the ruler of Kuwait became seriously apprehensive of aggression from Iraq. In May therefore he asked for a definite assurance of help in the case of any threatened aggression. This we gave, being now reasonably certain that we would receive full moral support and perhaps some practical help from our American friends in protecting Western interests in the Gulf if serious trouble were to break out. Indeed, so long as we held the vital position of Aden, the Gibraltar of the Red Sea, we were able to exert some control on the situation in the Middle East and the Gulf. Nor did it later prove difficult so to arrange affairs that the chief losers by dabbling in the politics of Yemen were Nasser and his unlucky Egyptian armies.

In spite of continuous efforts to concert a definite plan for the maintenance of Western influence and prestige throughout the Middle East, I was never able to persuade the President and the Secretary of State to do more than give what help they could as each crisis arose. Thus, while we had considerable success in concerting with the Americans to meet any pressing dangers, we never succeeded in agreeing on a long-term policy for the Middle East. Although Selwyn Lloyd pressed him hard, Dulles seemed strangely unwilling even to embark on such a study. While I do not believe that either the President or I would have accepted the loss of authority and power not only in the Middle East but in the Mediterranean, which has been the result of recent policies, American interest in the Middle East seemed to be becoming all the time more fitful and uncertain. This was no doubt because they were increasingly concerned at the dangers which they saw developing in the Pacific. To the vast populations of the Western States, the new movements in the Far East appeared considerably more menacing than any of the complicated intrigues and rivalries among the successor states of the old Turkish Empire. Red China had already begun to haunt the fears and obsess the imagination of the American people.

CHAPTER XVII

Chinese Puzzle

THE earliest of scientific historians long ago called attention
to the difference between the causes and the occasions of war.
If this distinction was true in antiquity, applied to simpler
quarrels and ambitions, it is still more relevant to the dark and
complex divisions underlying the highly organised civilisation of
modern times. Thus it is that so often in our history names and
places hardly known before leap into a sudden and dangerous significance. This was so even in the rivalries of nationalities and empires
of my youth based upon traditional jealousies and historical anti-
pathies and hatreds. It is still more true of the bitter ideological conflicts which now divide the world.

A few days after Khrushchev suddenly abandoned his proposed Summit meeting in favour of a resolution at the General
Assembly of the United Nations condemning Anglo-American
aggression in Jordan and Lebanon, there arose in the Far East a new
and dangerous development of a situation long dormant. In November 1954 the Chinese Communist Government had threatened to
attack Chiang Kai-shek's Nationalists in the islands of Tachen,
Matsu and Quemoy, presumably as a preliminary to an invasion of
Formosa. President Eisenhower had thought it necessary to reply
with a formal declaration that Formosa and the Pescadores islands
would be defended against attack. This incident had been followed
by Chou En-lai's declaration in January 1955 of China's determination to 'liberate' Formosa, yet no serious event took place. On the
contrary the United States Government decided to help the Chinese
Nationalist forces to evacuate the island of Tachen, one of those in
dispute, leaving only two remaining, neither of any serious military
value, although both of considerable psychological significance.[1]

[1] See *Tides of Fortune*, pp. 550 ff.

At the time these events caused little public emotion. But now suddenly the world was startled by the decision of the Chinese Communist Government to begin a heavy bombardment on these two so-called 'off-shore' islands. This measure was assumed to be a preliminary to a full-scale attempt to assault and destroy the Chinese Nationalist forces wherever they might be. The public both in America and Britain was alarmed, and the names of Matsu and Quemoy were to become in the next few weeks almost as much household words in every British family as Fashoda in my childhood or Agadir in my early youth. Happily this particular outbreak of the fires underlying the hatreds of the world was not to prove more than a symptom; and after some months of anxiety the volcano which threatened to burst forth with devastating fury gradually ceased its activities and simmered slowly down into its normal condition of an occasional efflux of smoke and a few ashes, in a petulant rather than a destructive mood. As I had seen Vesuvius in the Second War flare up and die down again in the Bay of Naples, so it was to be with the outbreaks that threatened the peace of the world from the distant waters of the China Seas. Meanwhile there was a lot of trouble to be faced.

The emotion felt in Washington and shared by the whole American people about the course of recent history in China seemed to most foreign observers unnatural and strained. Those with only a superficial knowledge of American life and history found it difficult to realise the deep feelings aroused in almost every American home. Although the American people flattered themselves, in spite of certain incidents in the Philippines and Panama, that they had been freed from the evil side of colonialism and imperialism with the defeat of George III's armies, yet, sprung from the same race and inheriting the same traditions as the people from whom they had broken away, they accepted with enthusiasm all the more respectable elements that composed the white man's burden and the obligation to bring teachers, doctors, hospitals on an ever-widening scale to the undeveloped world. For this purpose, excluded from Africa and India, they chose China. To bring help and enlightenment, and of course trade, to the Chinese had been the task which the American people had set themselves for many years. Their universities, their schools, their libraries, their medicine and technical institutions and, above all, their missions, were spread all over China. These were not supported by Government finance nor even by those rich individual donors who water the rivers of American charity with ever-swelling streams of benevolence. The American work in China was largely the product of and sustained by the savings and donations of ordinary folk, in large cities and small townships, through the churches and chapels, whose congregations would bestow their gifts with deep and genuine enthusiasm. The British people might boast of the civilising work which followed in the train of armies in conquered Indian or African territories ; but China would yield without violence or authority to the embracing arms of American goodwill and charitable purpose.

This simple but sincere view of the actualities of Chinese life and politics was fostered by the American leadership. Indeed during the Second World War many of us felt that President Roosevelt had made himself something of a nuisance about the Chinese. Their representatives were brought in great state to the Cairo Conference in 1943, where they arrived too early and stayed too late. The President insisted on elevating China, then largely in the hands of Chiang Kai-shek and his supporters, into a world power. The Chinese leaders must share all the secrets, and be made privy to all the plans, of the Western allies. When the war was over they must hold the position of a Founding Member of the United Nations, with a permanent seat on the Security Council. China, under American guidance and no doubt supplying considerable opportunities for American business as well as American benevolence, would thus complete the group of leading nations, the allies of the war – Russia, America, France and Britain – who would form a twentieth-century Holy Alliance under which peace would be preserved and prosperity extended throughout a grateful and applauding world. When this somewhat ingenuous plan broke down in respect of Soviet Russia, the American Government and people were startled and disappointed. But they soon became reconciled to the situation, and once they had recovered their nerve were the first to take steps to redeem the mistakes of their previous policy. But when Mao Tse-tung, the Communist leader, utterly destroyed the forces of Chiang Kai-shek and drove his armies out of the mainland, this was a grievous blow not merely to those Americans who took an interest in strategical and military appreciations, but to all Americans, from the most sophisticated to the humblest home. China, for whose people they had so long collected dimes and dollars to put into the bag or plate in church and chapel; China, for the benefit of whose troubled and suffering millions they had for so many years made such great sacrifices; China, to which they had sent their missionaries, teachers and doctors from every state, city and township throughout the United States; China, for which so much had been done and from whom so much was hoped—had turned against them in sullen contempt. This was a bitter blow to American pride.

The attitude of American public opinion was faithfully reflected by successive Administrations. The Government of 'Red' China was not officially recognised, even *de facto*, still less *de jure*. In Britain, until recently, recognition of a foreign Government was not regarded as a kind of diploma or certificate of respectability but was based upon more pragmatic considerations. The purpose of a diplomatic mission was solely to 'do the Queen's business' and protect or advance the interests of her subjects. With this in mind Attlee had recognised the Chinese Communist Administration as early as January 1950. Within a few months the Korean War broke out, in which the American Government and people bore the brunt. This not unnaturally strengthened the American attitude towards China. But the Americans not only refused to recognise the Government in Peking, or Peiping as they chose to call it, but insisted upon the exiled Nationalist Government of Chiang Kai-shek retaining the Chinese seat both in the Security Council and in the Assembly of the United Nations.

The Nationalist forces, to the number of some half million, had crossed the Formosa Strait and settled in the beautiful island of Formosa or Taiwan. Here, with American support, General Chiang had developed a powerful stronghold and almost founded a dynasty. The Americans did all in their power to assist him and to make him and his troops acceptable to the existing population by a generous flow of aid of every kind.

America's attitude was resented by some of her allies as unrealistic and almost childish. For no one seriously supposed that, unless continental China were to collapse into civil war, the comparatively small armies of Formosa could reconquer the mainland. At the same time the Americans fought strongly, and on the whole successfully, to persuade all their Western allies to avoid trade with China or to limit it by excluding all the items on the well-known 'China list'. This dispute was a continual source of friction. Although most of the countries of the free world accepted the policy of refusing to supply strategically important manufactures and materials, yet they resented Washington's pressure to ensure that almost all articles of commerce should be classed under these elastic headings. While ready to control the supply of arms, I used always to argue that the best way to subvert the Communists was to make them as rich as possible, when they would fall into all the enervating vices inseparable from capitalist society. Somehow or other my American friends did not find this reasoning acceptable.

Equally distasteful to many was the insistence of the Americans, who still more or less controlled the voting in the United Nations, that Chiang Kai-shek's representatives should continue to sit in the Security Council as the representative of six or seven hundred million people, when he, in fact, merely exercised a military rule over an island with a population, including his own exiled armies, of barely ten million. This was a matter which was continually being raised by the Opposition in the House of Commons, and I found that some of the Commonwealth Prime Ministers, particularly Nash in New Zealand, felt strongly about it. In the course of my visit earlier in the year he had discussed this question with me, explaining, more than once and at some length, the reasons why he would like to recognise Communist China. At the same time he was very anxious not to offend the United States Government. I was obliged to tell him that I did not think that our recognition, although based upon sound tradition, had done us much good. Indeed rather the reverse, since we had failed to follow up recognition by support-ing their claim to the Chinese seat at the United Nations. I had equally to admit to Bandaranaike in Ceylon that I did not believe the Communist Government would accept the compromise which was widely supported in Britain, by which the mainland would be represented by the Communist Government and Formosa by the Nationalists. Chou En-lai almost certainly would regard this as adding insult to injury. The Prime Minister of Ceylon seemed to agree, following his recent talks with the Communist leader. In the event the Americans were able without difficulty to rally support in the United Nations to reject by one means or another the recurring resolution in favour of the transfer to Communist China of the Chinese seat.

Meanwhile the Americans stood firmly by the guarantee to protect Chiang Kai-shek from any attack from the mainland which they had reaffirmed in the winter of 1954–5. Their purpose, of course, was to build up a barrier against the advancing hosts of Chinese Communism with the help of Formosa itself and the string of islands known as the Pescadores. Whether this pledge of President Eisenhower's included the three small islands lying just off the Chinese coast was not altogether clear. One of them, happily, had been evacuated; but two remained. The Nationalist leaders had reinforced Matsu and Quemoy with as many troops as their small size would allow. They seemed determined to defend them by all possible means; but whether as an oriflamme of freedom or as a convenient method of bringing pressure upon the State Department was still obscure.

When, therefore, on 23 August 1958, the Chinese Communists suddenly started a heavy bombardment of Quemoy after nearly three years' quiescence there was considerable alarm in Washington and London. We were still embroiled in Lebanon and Jordan and expecting to face a full debate in the Assembly as a result of Khrushchev's latest manœuvres. The news reached me on 27 August, after a long day's discussion on Cyprus with three or four of my colleagues mainly concerned.

> Now a new trouble is developing–in the Far East. The Chinese are threatening to attack the famous 'off-shore' islands about which we used to hear so much in 1955. This puts the Americans –and to a lesser extent ourselves–in a difficult situation. If the Americans abandon the Chinese Nationalists, it will be a great blow to their prestige and may even endanger their hold on the Pescadores and on Formosa. If they help the Chinese Nationalists

to repel an invasion (the island [of Quemoy is] only a couple of miles from Amoy) they may fail, if they stick to conventional weapons. If they attack the Chinese airfields with nuclear weapons, the fat may be in the fire with a vengeance. Our dilemma also is great. Our own view is that the Chinese (Communists) have an unanswerable case to the possession of these islands (we distinguish—apparently on good juridical grounds—between these and Formosa, etc.). Eden stated this view in 1955, and Churchill took the same line—(in private, he wrote very strongly to the President). But if we abandon the Americans—morally I mean, they need no active support—it will be a great blow to the friendship and alliance which I have done so much to rebuild and strengthen. If we support them, the repercussions in Far East, India and through the Afro-Asian group in the Middle East may be very dangerous. At home, Parliament and public will be very critical of any change from our public position three years ago. So there we are![1]

Naturally Khrushchev's recent visit to Peking and the sudden change of policy that followed seemed highly suspicious.

It is said by some that Khrushchev arranged all this (or agreed to it) during his recent visit to Peking. Since the Communist bloc seemed to be losing the initiative somewhat in the Middle East, the plan is to regain it in the Far East. Also, seeing that British and American policy is united and firm in Middle East, a wedge can be driven in over these wretched 'off-shore' islands. Another view is that the Russians do not like this at all and are seriously alarmed of it leading to war. Nuclear war would destroy Russia; but the Chinese are said to have reminded them blandly that it could not do much harm to China. Two or three hundred million people might be killed; but that would be tolerable and rapidly put right. Such are the divergent explanations of the experts.[2]

Secretary Dulles was away on holiday when the bombardment began, and I thought it wiser to wait until his return before sending any message either to him or to the President. In replying to an anxious appeal from Nehru I could only say that, while we were looking with anxiety at the situation in the Far East, it was hard to tell how

[1] 28 August 1958.   [2] 29 August 1958.

much it was a real threat to peace and how much bluff. On 3 September I thought it prudent to approach President Eisenhower direct.

I see that you are going to discuss with Foster tomorrow this new trouble which has loomed up in the Far East. In these two years since I have been Prime Minister you and I have faced a good deal of worry, and you know how happy I am that we have always faced our troubles together. Although in the past we have taken rather a different view about the legal and practical considerations concerning the off-shore islands, my over-riding concern is that our countries should not be divided or appear to be divided. Of course, the Chinese may be bluffing over the islands, just as their revived propaganda about Hong Kong may be mere talk. All the same, I feel that I may have to try to steer public opinion here at very short notice and, if the worst should happen, in critical circumstances. I should therefore very much value a private message from you or Foster giving me some indication of the way your minds are working.

Meanwhile Dulles, who was about to give the most brilliant exposition of the art of 'brinkmanship' in his career, made a public statement to the effect that the President would not hesitate to act if necessary under the terms of the Congressional Joint Resolution of January 1955, which authorised the United States to go to the aid of the Nationalists in the off-shore islands should the President consider this necessary in order to ensure the defence of Formosa. Thus began a game of threats and bluffs on both sides which were to last throughout the months of September and October much to the detriment of any chance of my enjoying the Parliamentary recess. From a purely technical point of view it may be worth studying this episode as a miniature exercise in the dangerous game of militant diplomacy. Although there were moments of deep anxiety, I felt somehow in my heart that the President would never allow nuclear war to develop over this issue.

On the same day that Dulles spoke, the Chinese Government unilaterally proclaimed an extension to twelve miles of their territorial waters. In this they were only in the fashion; for other countries were starting on this mode of increasing their authority, although usually for more respectable reasons, their purpose being to protect their fisheries rather than to threaten their neighbours. We and the United States immediately rejected this claim, which, apart from Quemoy and Matsu, would have made Hong Kong untenable.

On 5 September I received a reply from Dulles. He told me that he had seen the President at Newport, and that he had dictated his message while *en route* to Washington after full discussions with his chief. Lord Hood, our Minister, on receiving the text was able to have some talk with Dulles. Hood observed that these off-shore islands were really hostages to fortune, and enquired why the Chinese Nationalists attached so much importance to them. Dulles answered that the Nationalists valued the islands as the only part of the mainland under their control. After the last trouble in 1955 Admiral Arthur W. Radford, Chairman of the Joint Chiefs of Staff, and Walter Robertson of the State Department had tried in vain to persuade Chiang Kai-shek to abandon these islands, but he had firmly refused. Dulles wondered whether they could be demilitarised, but admitted that there was little hope of either side accepting this situation.

> Foster Dulles has sent (at request of President and in his name, more or less) a most important message. It makes it clear that the President and the Administration hope, by a tough line on Formosa and the islands, to *stop* the threatened invasion. But it may turn into a blockade, and this is the purpose of the twelve-mile territorial waters claim announced today by Peking. If the Nationalist Chinese cannot deal with the blockade themselves, U.S. will help. This may or may not lead to direct Chinese–American attacks on each other. But the 'Red' Chinese may attack Quemoy, etc., by air. In this case (they have *not* so far done any air bombing–only gunfire) the Americans can only reply by attacks on the 'Red' Chinese airfields and the mainland. To be effective this will probably have to be with nuclear weapons (kiloton capacity). This may lead Russia to join in. We shall thus be on the brink of World War Three. All this is very clearly set out by the message in . . . simple, and restrained language.[1]

Although I was impressed, I was also somewhat depressed.

[1] 5 September 1958.

My colleagues have gone away—a few more leave this morning. The Foreign Secretary (on whose judgement I have great reliance) is on a well-deserved holiday. Sir Norman Brook is also away.[1]

Dulles's message, roughly summarised above, contained some passages especially interesting in the light of later developments. He stated that his advisers were unanimous in thinking that

if Quemoy were lost either through assault or surrender, this would have a serious impact upon the authority and military capacity of the present Government on Formosa; that it would be exposed to subversive and military action which would probably bring about a Government which would eventually advocate union with Communist China; that if this occurred it would seriously jeopardise the anti-Communist barrier, including Japan, the Republic of Korea, the Republic of China, the Republic of the Philippines, Thailand and Vietnam; that other Governments in South-East Asia such as those of Indonesia, Malaya, Cambodia, Laos and Burma would probably come fully under Communist influence; that Japan with its great industrial potential would probably fall within the Sino-Soviet orbit, and Australia and New Zealand would become strategically isolated.

This, in a somewhat exaggerated form, was the first statement that I had seen of the famous 'domino' theory. I also learnt, which I had not realised, that there were as many as 80,000 Nationalist troops in Quemoy, the best of their forces, and that the United States were helping them logistically

with equipment and with convoying on the high seas, i.e. up to within three miles of Quemoy. They and their artillery are well dug in and to take them would be quite an operation, particularly if there were no aerial bombardments. So far the Communists have refrained from using their air bases to bombard the off-shore islands, perhaps desiring to avoid retaliatory action against these bases.

Dulles expressed his doubts whether any intervention, if it became necessary, could be effective

[1] 5 September 1958.

without at least some use of atomic weapons; I hope no more than small air bursts without fallout. That is of course an unpleasant prospect, but one I think we must face up to.

He ended by saying that, serious as the position seemed, it was a case 'where while acting strongly involves serious risks, these risks seemed less serious than the risks of inaction.'

This message put me in some difficulty.

I composed and sent off last night without consultation with my colleagues (there were none to consult) a long reply to Foster and the President. I tried to set out, as objectively as possible, the point of view of the public in U.K. and in each of the Commonwealth countries. None of them will support, wholeheartedly, the U.S. position. How can we get into (*a*) a better posture; (*b*) a posture likely to cause the Russo-Chinese to halt? (*a*) is—on the surface—contrary to (*b*). If the Communists really believe that America will go to war about the off-shore islands—and if they believe that U.K. and others will back them up—there *will* be no war. For the Russians, anyway, don't want World War Three—not now. But if our public opinions and Parliaments (thank goodness ours is *not* sitting) show hesitation or weakness, then Communists may feel that U.S. will not really have the nerve to 'go it alone' (I think they will be wrong). So there may well be an invasion of the islands. If U.S. goes on, there may be World War. If U.S. gives in, there will be a collapse of the anti-Communist front (SEATO, etc.) all through the Far East. This will affect Middle East and eventually Europe. It will be a Munich.

This is the dilemma. I put to the Americans the only idea I have. But whether it's a 'runner' I do not know. It is suggested by some words of Dulles to Lord Hood.

It is this. Could we not get all the friends of U.S. to

(1) Denounce any attempt to alter *status quo* by armed force.

(2) Support U.S.—and anyone else—who will take this line, pending at least action in U.N. or outside.

(3) Suggest 'demilitarisation' of islands—and perhaps a zone on mainland, for a period.

Something on these lines would

(*a*) continue to [put] pressure on the Communists because of its insistence on 'no use of force'. This is best chance of avoiding war.

(*b*) give us a good 'public' position, in our different countries and in U.N. which would help us in achieving (*a*).[1]

As regards British public opinion I repeated to Dulles my difficulty, as simply and clearly as possible:

As for this country, as I warned you in my first message, public opinion will not be easy to steer. We are on record in 1955 as having said that Formosa and the off-shore islands were in different juridical categories, and Churchill took the line that 'a war to keep the coastal islands for Chiang would not be defensible here'. This, of course, was in a private letter to the President but represented fairly the instinctive reaction of the man in the street.

On the next day, 6 September, Chou En-lai came into action and declared that *all* Chinese territory would be liberated. However, he qualified this by asking for the resumption of direct talks between China and the United States. Informal talks had been held intermittently between 1955 and 1957. President Eisenhower in acknowledging my last message referred to this development and expressed the hope that as a result of Chou En-lai's proposal the immediate crisis would become less acute at least for the time being. He added, 'We have just issued a statement on our willingness to resume the Ambassadorial talks.' These were in fact resumed in Warsaw a week later.

This short message did not really do more than thank me for my suggestions to which he would give the most careful thought. But the President pointed out that one of his main difficulties was to be found in Chiang's temperament. Although depending upon American support, he was by no means easy to manage. Any idea of his abandoning a single foot of his defence perimeter would be automatically rejected.

Indeed, such rejection is so emphatic as to imply that if coercive efforts should be made to over-ride his objection, that would end his capacity to retain Formosa in friendly hands.

Fortunately, no doubt owing to the holiday spirit, the British public remained as yet comparatively undisturbed.

[1] 6 September 1958.

The British Press is fairly calm. The Foreign Office put out the formula which I had agreed with them yesterday.

'H.M.G. fully share the concern of the Government of the U.S. at any attempt to impose territorial changes by force.' This seems the best line for the present.[1]

Nehru now sent a long and friendly reply to a brief message of warning which I had sent him. In the course of it he observed that in his view not only should the off-shore islands be immediately surrendered to the People's Government of China, but in the long run Formosa should pass to them also. On the first issue he naturally reminded me of the attitude of my predecessors, Churchill and Eden. Although this did not add very much to the solution of my difficulties, I read it with delight because of its friendly and personal character. It was a message that bore the stamp of his own grace and elegance. One passage is worth recalling:

> I am always happy to hear from you and to have your views on current events which press upon us so much from day to day. It is true that I survive them and I am even a little embarrassed occasionally at my good health in spite of circumstances. About [the] . . . middle of this month, I am thinking of paying a visit to Bhutan which presumably is now one of very few remaining countries which are difficult of access. This will involve five days' hard trekking over the high mountains of our north-east borders and crossing three passes of over 14,000 feet altitude. Thus, the mere journey there and back will take me twelve days, apart from my stay there for about four or five days.

Sitting forlornly in London I felt consumed with jealousy. Even if I could not have reached the romantic scenery of the Himalaya mountains, I might have hoped at this time of the year to have set foot upon a Scottish golf course or grouse moor.

It was now Khrushchev's turn to take a hand, and on 7 September he sent a letter to President Eisenhower declaring that Russia would support China under the Treaty of 1950 and demanding the evacuation of Formosa and the neighbouring areas by American forces. It was difficult to assess the importance of this move.

[1] 6 September 1958.

Mr. K. has now issued a warning to the Americans—or else. I find this rather confusing. I doubt if he would threaten war if he really meant it.[1]

Two days later the Prime Minister of Canada not unnaturally got into the act. He expressed considerable alarm at the situation that was developing and felt that public opinion in Canada was becoming increasingly critical of American policy. Perhaps it might be possible without inflicting public humiliation on the United States to raise the matter in the Security Council. He was particularly anxious to hear my views and what action I was taking. I could only reply in general terms and inform him, as well as the Prime Ministers of other Commonwealth countries, as to our public position. On 11 September, President Eisenhower in a television address to the American people declared that the Communist bombardment of the islands was an act of aggression. His Government would not yield to force but was ready at any time for negotiations; and on 12 September he sent an answer to Khrushchev in similar terms.

While all this bluff and blustering was going on between the great powers of East and West, I had to face a minor explosion in Fleet Street. This arose from a visit from my old and dear friend Randolph Churchill who came to see me on 10 September. He was on his way to the South of France and called in for a chat. While he was with me we had a general talk about the Chinese trouble, and as a result he wrote an article in the *Evening Standard* which was published on the 11th. Unfortunately it

gave the appearance of an authorised interview with me, under the heading 'Mac backs Ike'. The rest of the Press have got tremendously excited and it was necessary to issue a statement from No. 10 making it clear that Randolph Churchill had no authority to give my views on the Far Eastern problem. The trouble was that his article gave the impression that we would give *military* support to United States. This is, of course, absurd. They do not want this. But they do need *moral* support, which (in spite of all the complications about the islands) I intend that we shall give.[2]

[1] 9 September 1958.   [2] 11 September 1958.

Randolph rightly pointed out in reply that he had made no direct quotation, and that his article was his own interpretation of the situation. I have always been devoted to Randolph, from his youth to his sad and untimely death. He sometimes caused me a little anxiety, but this never marred our deep and genuine friendship. At the time, however, I was annoyed:

> The Churchill article and the statement from No. 10 have made a terrible hullabaloo. It was really very tiresome of him. Actually, he came to see me on Wednesday afternoon, to get a message from me to Winston (for the golden wedding) and to show me the wonderful 'Book of Roses' which the Churchill family (and many leading artists) are giving to Winston and Clemmie. We got chatting about Far East and Cyprus. He went off and wrote a 'feature article'—making no reference to his talk with me—which would have been quite all right. Unfortunately, the Editor asked whether he had seen me. Randolph said yes— and the article appeared as an interview. The *Mirror* and the *Daily Herald* are very offensive—the rest of the Press make a lot of the story, but seemed quite 'understanding'. They all know their Randolph! However, I am *very* upset about it, for it's the first big 'gaffe' since I became Prime Minister and was quite unnecessary.[1]

Fortunately the Foreign Secretary had now returned from his holiday, and I had a more responsible ear for my confidences:

> Foreign Secretary came at 11.00 a.m., and we settled the Foreign Office statement in response to President Eisenhower's speech last night—which was pretty good. We are giving *moral* support, but making it clear that we have not been asked for or offered *military* support. (With Hong Kong in mind, even this must not be pressed too hard.)[1]

I knew well enough that we might ourselves be turning to America for active help.

More serious than our troubles at home was the position that was revealed by the last telegram from our Ambassador in Washington. It was clear

[1] 12 September 1958.

that the administration (including President and Foster Dulles) are in a dilemma. They don't know what they ought to do; nor do they know how far they can force their troublesome allies, the Chinese Nationalists, to conform to their wishes. Finally, I do not know the military position, or whether Chiang's armies *can* hold out under the punishing bombardment which is blockading the islands. Selwyn Lloyd leaves tomorrow evening for New York.[1]

Hearing that the Ambassadorial talks between the Chinese and the Americans which had been suspended in 1957 were to begin again in Warsaw, I thought I could take a few days' holiday and left on the night train for the North of Scotland. I was to stay with old friends in Caithness, and would find Dorothy already there. As usual we had all the arrangements for communications, with a Private Secretary and special telephone line. I now hoped for a short respite.

On the evening of my arrival at Berriedale Gaitskell sent a letter which reached No. 10 about 8 p.m. enquiring about Far Eastern policy and the British Government's relations with the United States: 'we ask you to make plain that, even if the United States becomes involved in a war to defend Quemoy, Britain would not join in.' He went on to say, 'Public opinion . . . is completely opposed to a war over Quemoy.' The letter ended somewhat peremptorily, 'I hope you will be prepared . . . to go to Washington and represent [these views] to the President.'

It was a 'governessy' sort of letter, written after a meeting of the Labour 'Shadow Cabinet'. Philip [de Zulueta] and John Wyndham were in charge at No. 10 and did very well. The text was telephoned to me just before dinner.[2]

Since I had heard of a probable meeting of Gaitskell with his colleagues and the likelihood of a letter being sent to me, I had prepared the draft of a reply before leaving London. This was now telephoned to me over the scrambler, and by 10 p.m. it had been approved for despatch after being slightly amended by the Lord Chancellor and Sir Frederick Hoyer Millar, Permanent Under-Secretary at the Foreign Office. The Foreign Secretary had already left for New York.

[1] 14 September 1958. [2] 16 September 1958.

It was rather mean of Gaitskell to insist on publishing his letter immediately. He actually sent it to the Press *before* it reached No. 10. But we got our reply to the Press in time for all except the first editions, and this apparently made a profound impression in Fleet Street. They thought it quick work to receive a letter practically at John O'Groats and get off the reply between 8.00 and 10.00 at night.

John Wyndham insisted on sending our reply to Hugh Gaitskell by hand to Hampstead, and kept him up pretty late. Then the Press mercilessly rang up Gaitskell all the rest of the night, asking if he would send a further reply.[1]

I certainly had a loyal and resourceful staff.

On 19 September Khrushchev sent a letter to the United States Government so harshly worded that it was rejected by Washington. The statement from the White House was firm and dignified:

> This communication is replete with false accusations; it is couched in language that is abusive and intemperate; it indulges in personalities; it contains inadmissible threats. All this renders the communication unacceptable under established international practice.[2]

The position therefore seemed to be one of complete stalemate. Nevertheless there was nothing like panic either in our Press or among the public.

On 21 September I got a full report from Selwyn Lloyd, who was now in New York for the meeting of the United Nations.

> The Foreign Secretary has had long talks with Dulles. . . . The Americans seem in a very reasonable mood, but do not see how to handle the next stages in the Far East. However, the supply position seems better—the islands can somehow be kept going, it appears, by use of tank-landing craft and amphibious tanks. So it may turn out a sort of Berlin situation—with the amphibious machines playing the role of the air-lift.[3]

But far the most important of his messages to me was contained in a note describing a private visit to Newport where he had seen the President alone.

[1] 16 September 1958.   [2] *Annual Register, 1958,* p. 201.   [3] 21 September 1958.

The President has told Selwyn Lloyd that he is against the use of even tactical atomic weapons in a limited operation.[1]

I was relieved, but not surprised.

Menzies now sent some useful suggestions, including a proposal that we should advocate the setting up of a special international commission to consider the problem of the off-shore islands, not as a purely legal question, but as a problem of international politics. If the decision went against Chiang the West could then withdraw their support in good order. Alas, this plan, whatever its merits, under-rated both the General's obstinacy and the impossibility of the Americans abandoning him without risking the collapse of the whole 'barrier' strategy.

On 30 September Dulles seemed to some observers to pull back a little from the brink. In the course of a Press conference he threw out the remark that he thought it foolish of the Chinese Nationalists to keep so large a contingent, composed of their best troops, in the off-shore islands. He also hinted that if there were a 'dependable cease-fire' the United States might urge the reduction of these garrisons. The President on 1 October followed this up with a some-what equivocal statement to the Press correspondents. To him, as a soldier, it seemed not a good thing to have all these troops on these islands. 'Anyone can see that the two islands as two pieces of territory are not greatly vital to Formosa', but he repeated that the basic issue was 'to avoid retreat in the face of force'.[2] I was back in London from my short holiday when I read these pronouncements. Even to me their meaning was obscure.

> Foster Dulles has made one or two statements suggesting a compromise over Matsu and Quemoy; but Chiang has reacted violently. It is clear that he can blackmail the Americans pretty thoroughly.[3]

In replying to Menzies I explained that the Foreign Secretary had suggested to Gromyko in New York that the Soviet Government should really try to bring influence to bear upon the Chinese Communists. It was difficult however to see how an international court—or even commission—could be set up with powers to make an

[1] 21 September 1958.   [2] *Annual Register, 1958*, p. 202.   [3] 4 October 1958.

effective judgement. Matsu and Quemoy were merely incidents in an extension of the Chinese civil war. Meanwhile the Chinese had hinted to the Indians (presumably for transmission) that if there were an agreement over the islands they would forget about Formosa for a while. This, coupled with the revival of the Warsaw talks, seemed to give some hope of a temporary solution without too much loss of face, oriental or occidental. This, in fact, was what happened. The dispute was never settled. It just began to fizzle out, like the last cracker in a fine display of fireworks.

On 6 October Marshal Peng Teh-huai blandly announced that the bombardment of Quemoy would be suspended for a week. The Nationalists would be able to bring in any supplies they wished provided these were not accompanied by American escort vessels. This strange truce actually continued unbroken for a fortnight. Then on 20 October the bombardment was resumed, the Marshal alleging that American escorts had come to the island. But five days later, since there seemed some uncertainty about the intervention of American ships, the Marshal reached a solution which even the British gift of compromise could hardly have bettered. He declared on 25 October that the bombardment (like parking on one side of the street) would only take place on the odd days of the month. This curious state of affairs continued to the end of the year. Then a conflagration which had burned so fiercely and so threateningly in the summer and autumn of 1958, after flickering on for six months, was finally extinguished. By the end of March 1959 all was quiet in the Formosa straits.

When I was visiting Washington about that time I made the following note.

Americans do not see any signs of the Chinese starting up anything very drastic against the off-shore islands. But they confessed that they had completely failed in persuading Chiang to evacuate them or even to reduce the garrisons substantially.[1]

So ended, at least so far as I was concerned, this strange episode. I am still wondering just what is the moral to be drawn.

[1] 22 March 1959.

CHAPTER XVIII

A Voyage of Discovery

I N spite of, or perhaps because of, my preoccupations with the
dangers which might arise from the tense situation both in the
Middle East and the Far East, my mind, in August 1958, began
to turn once more to the prospects of some relaxation between the
formidable groupings of powers now ranged round Russia and
America and facing each other, in every part of the world, with
growing antagonism.

I arrived back on 12 August from an apparently fruitless visit to
Athens, Ankara and Cyprus. I was consoled to find the situation at
home, in spite of all our difficulties, by no means discouraging. The
Press had been consistently friendly during my absence. A few
days later there was published

> a Gallup Poll which was very favourable to the Conservatives *and*
> to the Prime Minister. On this showing, we could win an election
> now. Therefore everyone is speculating about the likelihood of an
> Autumn election.

> These polls are encouraging when they are good, and we tend
> to regard them as of little value when they are bad. The truth is
> that the great British—and especially London and English—
> democracy is very fickle.[1]

A day or two after my return I read an illuminating despatch
from Sir Patrick Reilly, our Ambassador in Moscow, which led me
to pose a number of enquiries. The first was about Khrushchev's
own character. His sudden rise to supreme power was a fact of vast
significance. But how should it be interpreted? I wrote to Reilly on
13 August:

> You are, I am sure, right in putting your finger on the most
> dangerous feature about Mr. Khrushchev—megalomania. This

[1] 19 August 1958.

could not be said of the wicked men who began the revolution or guided it through its earlier years. Lenin, Stalin, etc., were pretty cold fish I should imagine; but megalomania frightens one because people who get it can do very stupid things and lead to great disasters. I wonder whether I am right in this; but I have an instinctive feeling that this is the most perilous point in the whole complex of confusion in which the world finds itself. Could Khrushchev do as foolish things as Hitler did?

The answer which history may well give to my question is that this tendency in Khrushchev's character grew with the exercise of power and found its final expression in the Cuba crisis four years later.

My second question concerned the 'emergency' Summit, which had been proposed in various forms, to deal with the problem of the Middle East:

> There is a point which interests me. Of course, your despatch was written while there was still a chance of a meeting between the Heads of Government either in New York or in Geneva. The Summit is now obscured with clouds, but I would be interested to know whether you think Khrushchev has gained or lost by his controversy with the President and me. Do they publish my replies in Russia? Am I right in trying to make my replies short and clear? Orientals are apt to think that unless you write at immense length you have nothing much to say. I would like your views on this for future use.

Turning to the immediate situation, I asked:

> Thirdly, what about the real Summit—I mean the old one we have been climbing slowly towards for so long? Ought we to take a new initiative from your point of view, and when?

My final paragraph referred to a project which I had long had in mind, and towards which I had made some hesitant and cautious advances. It was that of a personal visit to Russia. So far my colleagues had not been enthusiastic, nor were our allies likely to be any more understanding. Yet I felt unhappy at the steady deterioration and anxious to take some initiative.

It is difficult now, when visits to Moscow are almost *de rigueur* for any aspiring statesman, in or out of office, to recall the frigid atmosphere that prevailed some twelve years ago. A visit from a British Prime Minister at a period when Britain's power in the world was still formidable and her prestige following the Second War still undiminished would be no mere conventional courtesy, but rather a startling and almost sensational event. I therefore put frankly to the Ambassador, an old friend and colleague from Algiers days, the vital issue:

> The last and most important thing is the question of returning the Khrushchev–Bulganin visit. If the negotiations for the Summit fail altogether and nothing happens, I have it in mind to suggest a visit on my own in the course of the spring. What would you think about this? Would they regard it as just a climb-down or not?

To my first three questions the Ambassador, as I would have expected, sent replies admirably composed and argued. The fourth was not to become a matter for detailed discussion and decision until the beginning of the following year. Meanwhile there was at least some improvement in the commercial if not in the political sphere. On 14 August Britain, together with most other NATO countries, announced major relaxations of trade both with the Soviet bloc and with Communist China. The extensive list of prohibited raw materials and manufactured goods which had hitherto proved a serious obstacle to commerce was substantially modified. Only a few items remained, and those could really be defended on technical grounds as of vital military importance. The United States announced at the same time parallel reductions so far as the Soviet bloc countries were concerned. They maintained, however, a complete embargo on American trade with China, North Korea and North Vietnam. On 16 August:

> the Foreign Secretary has sent a telegram from New York to say that Foster Dulles now has in mind that we should abandon nuclear tests, pending a workable agreement on inspection. The question is now complicated by the French claims. I sent a holding reply and we will have to send something fuller tomorrow.[1]

A subsequent message, however, showed that Dulles, in the course of a private dinner with Selwyn Lloyd, was merely thinking

[1] 16 August 1958.

aloud and had not yet consulted anyone else in Washington. It seemed that he was contemplating a nine- or twelve-month suspension from a certain date, to include or exclude underground tests as might be agreed. The date would of course be settled with us to protect our next series. Writing to Lloyd I made it clear that I would have to get Cabinet approval, which during the holidays could not be done quickly. Moreover I pointed out that since the General Assembly was not due to meet until 16 September I did not see the urgency for an immediate statement. As regards the date, I would have to consult the experts as to when our next series of tests could be finished. Nor was I clear why underground tests should be excluded. Was it because the Americans wanted to go on with them? Or was it because they did no harm? Then there was the question of 'small' tests, which the Geneva talks had shown could not be detected by any existing system. We would also have to be fully satisfied as to the continuing information which we would receive from our American friends. Our experts were not due to begin until 27 August the vital talks in Washington which followed the amendment of the McMahon Act. We could not really have a firm policy until we saw how these conversations proceeded. I added as perhaps the most important consideration the need to protect the position of the French:

> Here we must be careful not to let them feel that we and the Americans have betrayed them. We must consider most carefully what to do, especially in relation to de Gaulle. There is much at stake there including the economic structure of Europe. The important point is for the Americans to decide what they are prepared to do to help the French and what stage the French must reach in their atomic programme to qualify for American help. Is it enough for them to have an explosion? One advantage of the formula in excluding small tests . . . is that it would allow the French to carry out a few small explosions without having to do so in moral isolation.

I now thought it best to announce our next test. This was done on 18 August. I hoped that my holding messages would give us at least a little respite; but, alas, I was mistaken.

I was looking forward to a quiet evening, and leaving tomorrow morning for Bolton Abbey. But tonight (about 10.30 p.m.) two telegrams arrived from Selwyn which raise the most serious questions. The Americans (led by the President, who seems determined to show his strength) want to announce abolition [or suspension] of nuclear tests as from 1 October. What will be the effect (*a*) on our programme, (*b*) on our relations with France, the Americans are too much in a hurry even to consider. I shall have to put off my journey and deal with this tomorrow. I made a first draft of a possible reply to the Americans.[1]

Accordingly, on the following day a conference of officials was arranged to discuss the draft reply. Sir Norman Brook, helpful and calm as usual, Sir Patrick Dean from the Foreign Office, wise and resolute, Sir Richard Powell, Ministry of Defence, full of resource, and Sir Edwin Plowden of the Atomic Energy Commission, skilful and determined, and one or two others met to discuss its terms. The Foreign Secretary was in Washington; other Ministers concerned were, very properly, on holiday.

Meanwhile, another message—personal from the President—promising (if we agreed to suspension of tests on the basis of their proposed declaration) full information 'so far as the law permits'. I told my advisers that I thought this message should be answered separately and that I should ask straight out the 64,000-dollar question. 'Does the law permit U.S. to give us full information on "vulnerability" of the Bomb and on making small bombs, but with megaton power.' The first is essential, for we believe that otherwise a bomb can be 'immunised'; the second is equally essential if we are to be able to make our own warheads for rockets, whether the rockets themselves are American (like Thor) or of our own design. Apart from my reply to President on this vital point—a satisfactory answer to which would of course make further tests unnecessary for us—there are all the general political arguments against precipitate action by the Americans. For one thing, the French will never forgive another act of what they will call 'betrayal'.[2]

[1] 19 August 1958.
[2] 20 August 1958.

After a full discussion, I sent two messages to the President. The first dealt only with the British position. If we were to abandon tests with a clear conscience we must be satisfied that we would receive full information on all the vital problems; above all on the two which I specified. On the larger issue I felt while some response must be made to the forthcoming report of the Geneva experts, we ought not to abandon tests until our long-held position requiring *practical* measures of inspection and control could be implemented at least partially. Moreover since the United States series of tests would not be finished until mid-October surely it would be wiser to link any Western initiative with the opening of the United Nations Assembly rather than with the experts' report. The Foreign Secretary when in New York had striven hard to point out to Dulles how we felt the cards should best be played. The President however in one of his messages seemed unusually excited—'We are up against one of those moments that we regard as psychologically correct.' Moreover Selwyn Lloyd reported that after discussing it with the French Ministers at the United Nations, they appeared to be altogether unconcerned, since the French had no intention of abandoning tests whatever anybody else might say or do. Naturally while all this was going on, there was no hope of starting any holiday. The grouse would be undisturbed by me at any rate for this season.

Great activity from London in the afternoon and evening. The President has sent a most categorical reply, pledging himself and his Government to give us *all* the information on nuclear weapons which we need and declaring that the law allows him to do so. Replies were drafted for me to send, which I approved. But again I cut our answer into two—sending one on the atomic pledge and another on the general question. I want the correspondence on the American nuclear promises to be short and self-contained. Since most of the other points seem to be met—the French do *not* object—I have agreed to associate U.K. with the U.S. action. The Americans have altogether changed their plan—at our suggestion—because they are not now offering to abandon tests *absolutely*, but only if Russians agree to negotiate on the control system. From our point of view, I think that we can rely on the American promise, which replaces the not altogether satisfactory 'bilateral' agreements [so far] made under the McMahon Amendment Act. This will save us both time and a great deal of money.[1]

Since Dulles redrafted his proposal to allow us to finish our proposed tests and assured me that the Americans would not feel prohibited from resuming tests if a control system was not agreed, I gave a cautious approval to the plan proposed. I made it clear, however, that my concern had not only been to protect the British nuclear programme; I was anxious to extract the maximum advantage from the experts' discussions at Geneva. I did not want the Russians to escape without paying at least some price for the suspension of tests or to throw away the prize which we all hoped to gain of making them accept some system of international control—the essential condition for any progress in general disarmament, whether in the unconventional or the conventional field.

In my final message to the President on 21 August I emphasised these political considerations.

Two factors, in particular, weighed heavily with me. First, I thought it would be a profound mistake to concede suspension without securing Russian acceptance of an international control system. Secondly, I was seriously apprehensive about de Gaulle's reaction.On both these points I have been reassured by your messages of today. On the first, I think that Foster's new draft is a great improvement. Though, even now, I am not sure whether the Russians will accept a truly international system of control. If they should take the line that each country should man the control posts within its own territory, we shall not have achieved our essential purpose. I hope we shall both keep a careful eye on this. On the second, I would feel happier if I knew what de Gaulle himself was thinking. But I am relieved to know that Couve [de Murville], at any rate, seems to be taking this quite quietly. I think that I must send the General a personal message about this just before the announcement is made. Perhaps you would consider whether you could do so too.

Early next morning I heard that the President and Dulles had accepted four out of five of our amendments and that both seemed

[1] 21 August 1958.

extremely pleased that we had reached agreement. Couve de Murville, the French Foreign Minister, had been seen both by the President and by Dulles, as well as by the Foreign Secretary, and had raised no objections. Messages were sent to all the NATO powers, and on 22 August a formal statement was issued by the American and British Governments in similar terms, welcoming the successful conclusion of the conference of experts on the detection of nuclear explosions, pointing out that the next task was to solve the practical and political problems relating to the organisation, installation, and functioning of a control organisation, and announcing their readiness to enter into negotiations on 31 October for an agreement on the suspension of nuclear tests under effective control, which would, it was hoped, also facilitate early negotiation on measures of disarmament. At the same time both Governments announced that from the date of the opening of negotiations they would be prepared to refrain from further testing for one year provided the Soviet Union and all Governments which had tested nuclear weapons did not resume testing in that period. This restraint would be continued on a reciprocity basis for successive periods of one year if satisfactory progress were made towards installing and working an inspection system and towards the adoption and execution of measures of disarmament. In addition it was stated that the British Government would complete their own short series of tests as soon as possible. The United States Atomic Energy Commission later announced that the current American programme of tests would be concluded by 31 October. On the next day I noted:

> Our announcement about nuclear tests has had quite a good press, including even *Manchester Guardian*. The first of our Christmas Island tests was done today—a small kiloton 'trigger' explosion. The megaton test is timed for 8 September or so. The question now arises about going on with it. In principle, we can rely on the latest American understanding. In practice, it might be as well to have the knowledge which we shall get from this test.[1]

I have described this episode in some detail because it emphasises the close and intimate relations between Washington and London

[1] 23 August 1958.

and the willingness of both the President and the Secretary to meet our points in detail as well as to treat us as full and equal partners on grave points of principle. It also shows our anxiety to meet French susceptibilities. In looking back over these years this relationship is my outstanding memory. If we sometimes felt a little impatient with the continual changes of policy and uncertainties of programme which emerged from Washington, it was gratifying to know that we were not merely informed about the projects or decisions of our partners; we were taken into full confidence at the early stages. This close co-operation and sense of comradeship was easy to sustain at our many meetings; but I was happy to feel that even if we could not speak in the same room we could, through our representatives and personal messages, maintain an equally full and fruitful dialogue.

This spirit was by no means confined to the White House or the State Department. The talks between the British and American nuclear scientists, which took place in the second half of August, proved to be of exceptional value. I was particularly glad to hear that, somewhat to the surprise of our friends, it was found that the specialist information was not all on one side. I had a talk with the leading members of our team on their return.

Meeting of atomic experts, just returned from U.S. The talks have gone off very well. Two important facts emerged: (*a*) Americans are doing ten more kiloton tests before end of October and would *not* wish us to stop before them; (*b*) in some respects we are as far, and even further, advanced in the art than our American friends. They thought interchange of information would be all *give*. They are keen that we should complete our series, especially the last megaton, the character of which is novel and of deep interest to them. This is important, because it makes this final series complementary rather than competitive—and therefore easy to defend in Parliament.[1]

It is indeed remarkable that our small team of British scientists and technicians had been able to achieve such notable advances with an expenditure of money and effort almost derisory compared to that

[1] 1 September 1958.

provided in America. I was so pleased with this that I thought it right to send a letter to Sir Edwin Plowden in the following terms.

I have had a very interesting talk with [Sir Frederick] Brundrett, [Sir William] Penney and [Sir William] Cook about their discussions in Washington last week, and I have been very impressed by the results which they achieved. It is clear that the Americans were amazed to learn how much we already know and that this was a major factor in convincing them that we could be trusted with more information than they probably intended originally to give us. I hope that these discussions will be only the first of a series, in which Anglo-American co-operation in this field will become progressively closer. But if we do succeed in gradually persuading the Americans to regard the enterprise as a joint project in which we are entitled to be regarded as equal partners in terms of basic knowledge, it will be because we have got off to a flying start under the bilateral agreement; and the credit for that must go to the team of scientists and technicians who have enabled us, single-handed, to keep virtually abreast of the United States in this complex and intricate business of nuclear weapons development. It is a tremendous achievement, of which they have every right to be very proud.

I tried to say this to them at our meeting; and I hope that there may be some opportunity for me to say it publicly in due course. But whether that opportunity occurs or not, I wanted you to know—and, if you can, to tell your staff—that the Government share the satisfaction which you yourself must feel at the outcome of the Washington talks and that we are very conscious how much the country owes to the devoted work of the men who, under your leadership, have kept us so well up in the running in this critical race.

The question of atomic tests continued to occupy much of our time and attention, but public opinion seemed satisfied with our action. Meanwhile the Anglo-American consultations continued to move on satisfactory lines. The only point at issue (and on this John A. McCone, the American negotiator, proved very reasonable) arose about the exchange of information on the civil side.

Although we believe in and practise full publication of *scientific* and *technological* information, we are not willing to exchange

*eplying to
hrushchev's
eech of welcome
Moscow
irport,
February 1959
he first time that
British Prime
inister had visited
e Soviet Union in
me of peace.'*

*ith Khrushchev
lso sported a
ite hat. . . . I had
realised that this
a form of head-
ss peculiar to
land, and to
ng it out now was
haps not the most
ful action.'*

At the gala performance of Romeo and Juliet *at the Bolshoi Theatre*

drawings of industrial designs, except (as agreed with the President) in the military field. Naturally, this is a very important matter for us, as we have a very good lead in this sphere.[1]

On 30 August the Soviet Government sent notes to the British and American Governments announcing their agreement that talks should open on 31 October. On the same day the Geneva Committee of experts published a report, the most important feature of which was that it was technically feasible to instigate 'a workable and effective control system'. Khrushchev made a statement published in *Pravda* expressing his full agreement with the conclusion of the experts. All this seemed hopeful; for it was clear, from the experts' report, that if the Russians really accepted an adequate system of control real progress was within our grasp.

In connection with the work at Geneva I thought the President would be interested in Penney's report to me and wrote to him accordingly.

> The recent expert conference at Geneva on suspending nuclear tests was clearly an outstanding success. This has been underlined by Khrushchev's willingness to open substantive talks with us on the subject on 31 October.
>
> I feel that a great deal of the credit for this success should go to your scientists led by Dr. James B. Fisk. Under his leadership the whole Western team worked in harmony and effectively. I think that Dr. Fisk is to be commended for the way he managed the Russians, who, I am told, were proficient and pertinacious on both technical and political matters. Sir William Penney described Dr. Fisk's performance as magnificent. If it is in order I would be glad if you would convey my personal thanks to him.

I also felt it appropriate to write to Churchill who still followed these affairs closely. He had deeply resented the exclusion of Britain under the McMahon Act and had continually urged its amendment. Accordingly on 13 September I wrote:

> You will be interested to hear that we have reached a most satisfactory arrangement both on the highest political level and on

[1] 6 November 1958.

T

the technical side with the Americans over the question of our co-operation. It has worked out much better than I could ever have hoped when the first suggestion of amending the McMahon Act was made a year ago at Washington. It is a great triumph for our scientists, and the Americans now realise how much we have done in a much shorter time and with fewer resources. We are by no means the junior partner so far as the genius of our scientists is concerned. All this amply justifies your decisions throughout and ending with the decision to make the hydrogen bomb.

On 30 September the Russians resumed their tests giving as a reason that they were entitled to continue until they had reached the number equal to the tests carried out by Britain and America since the last Russian test in March. All this, including the statement of the Russian delegate at the United Nations on 27 October that his Government would decline any proposal to suspend nuclear tests for one year, did not cause undue concern; for everything must depend upon the talks at Geneva. I was more worried by hearing of the line which the Americans now intended to take. It appeared that the American delegation were to be instructed not to be satisfied with a mutual suspension for a trial year; even the first year's suspension was to be conditional on the achievement of agreed measures not only of inspection but also of disarmament in general. I felt that while British public opinion would accept the first stipulation—an effective control system—they would regard the second demand as unreasonable.

On H-bomb tests, the Americans have suddenly and surprisingly turned round. Too weak in August, they are being too tough in October.[1]

To insist upon the second demand—progress in disarmament in the conventional field—seemed not only impolitic but unnecessary. This view was confirmed when the three-power conference on the discontinuance of nuclear weapon tests met on 31 October; for at the first session the Russian delegates announced that they had brought with them a draft treaty providing for the immediate and permanent

[1] 18 October 1958.

suspension of nuclear tests. If Britain and America would agree and sign such a treaty, then plans could be elaborated for the establishment of a control system on the lines proposed by the experts. This, of course, was quite unacceptable. The two must go together.

Nevertheless negotiations and discussions continued at Geneva, although somewhat confused by the opening of a ten-power conference on measures to be taken against 'surprise attacks'. The interchange of papers between the delegates of both sides continued without interruption, and by the end of the year when the conference had adjourned four articles in a proposed draft treaty had been agreed. But formidable and fundamental issues remained to be settled. The question of the link between disarmament in conventional weapons and forces and the abolition of nuclear tests had fortunately not arisen, and the doubts whether agreement could ever be reached upon the first seemed to make it still more inadvisable to introduce the second issue. Public opinion was so clearly on our side about inspection and control that it would be folly to allow it to become confused by extraneous and supplementary questions. There had been at least some concession by the Russians in that the conference, when it reconvened, would be able to discuss the problem of control. I therefore sent a message to the President on 1 January 1959 urging that we should drop our conditions directly linking the abolition of tests with general disarmament. Although we knew that the Americans attached great importance to the latter, to insist now seemed to me wrong. Since this was a matter which, as well as being of real substance, I knew would have great political importance at home, I elaborated my argument in a personal message:

After the first four weeks of stalemate at Geneva, there has been a move forward. The conference is now able to discuss controls and get down to drafting a treaty. But despite what they say, the Russians are still trying to get out of having an effective control system on their territory. They have cleverly disguised their position by making what they claim to be concessions, resulting in agreement on the first four articles in a draft treaty. We know that these articles are meaningless without a proper control organisation. But the Russians are now in a better position to fool the world into believing that it is we who are preventing agreement by insisting that discontinuance of tests should be conditional on satisfactory progress towards real disarmament.

How should we prevent this? I think the answer is that we should now drop our link with real disarmament all the more because the link is a vague formula, impossible to define precisely. We have a lot to gain by doing so, and in my opinion, nothing of any real value to lose. It would make it obvious to all the world that, if the Russians then refused an agreement on controlled discontinuance of tests, it would be because they would not accept a genuine control system on their own territory, despite their professed acceptance of the recommendations of the previous Geneva Experts' Conference.

And if, on the other hand, by dropping our conditions we oblige the Russians to make an agreement on the controlled suspension of tests, we should get an even more substantial gain. We should get a proper control system in the Soviet Union. I think all our advisers agree on the importance of this. It would certainly make it difficult for the Russians to refuse a control system later on for other forms of disarmament. In effect, it would safeguard what had been contained in our dropped condition.

There is another point. If, by insisting on this condition, we lose the chance of getting a controlled discontinuance of tests, there could eventually be an alarming increase in the number of nuclear powers. This would work to our disadvantage.

In conclusion, I think we have everything to gain and nothing to lose by adopting the course which I advocate. If our two Governments make this decision I think it would have a most favourable effect on world opinion and probably also on the negotiations at Geneva. We should need to consider how and when our decision should be made known. It might be best done at Geneva by our two delegates there, preferably at a stage in the conference when we might get a reciprocal concession from the Russians. This need not inhibit us from making clear to the world the size of the concession we are making in order to secure an agreement.

The President, while thinking it unwise that we should give this change in position any undue publicity, replied on 13 January in substance accepting my proposal. To use his own words:

Although, on the basis of the progress to date, it seems to me that the prospects are not bright that the Russians will accept an effective control organisation in the current negotiations, I agree that our public position would be much better if we remove as a point of contention the issue of the link to disarmament, which the Russians may use as a screen to evade accepting responsibility for failure in the negotiations or to evade facing up to the control problem.

So far, so good. But while the experts were carrying on their argument in Geneva, in a relaxed if somewhat academic atmosphere, Khrushchev suddenly introduced a note of harsh reality.

On 10 November he made a public demand for the withdrawal of the Allied troops from West Berlin. This declaration followed an interview a few days before in which he had compared the recent meeting of Adenauer and de Gaulle with that of Hitler and Mussolini in 1934. On 20 November the Russian Ambassador at Bonn called on the Chancellor and informed him brutally that his Government intended 'to liquidate the occupation statutes concerning Berlin'. The next day I received a personal message from Adenauer in which he expressed his deep concern. He had evidently been much shaken by his talk with Ambassador Andrei Smirnov which seemed to him 'to show that the Soviet Union is resolved to make the Berlin question a test for the policy of the free world.' He went on to make an urgent request:

> Please let me ask you to consider whether you could not with the whole of the influence of which the United Kingdom disposes in the world, make representations in Moscow with a view to drawing the attention of the Soviet Government to the fateful consequences of such a decision, and whether you could not attempt to prevent the Soviet Union from realising this intention.

After expressing his surprise that the Soviet Government should take this violent action at a time when discussions in Geneva were still being conducted on a friendly basis, his message ended with a moving appeal:

> This letter, dear Mr. Macmillan, is dictated by serious anxiety about a development the consequences of which we cannot foresee. I feel this responsibility not only towards the German

people; we all bear it towards all peoples in the world, and we should leave nothing untried which perhaps could prevent the Soviet Union at the last hour from setting in motion a stone which could become a destructive avalanche.

Although we had not yet received the formal Russian note, I found it difficult not to yield to the Chancellor's request. I therefore sent a message on 22 November direct to Khrushchev.

I am sending you this personal message to tell you of the anxiety which your recent statements on Berlin have caused me. I must tell you frankly that I find these statements difficult to reconcile with your many previous expressions of the desire to reduce tension in the world. The British Government have every intention of upholding their rights in Berlin which are soundly based. That also I believe to be the position of our allies as is well known to you. At the moment discussions are taking place in Geneva. I still profoundly hope that fruitful results will come both from the political conference on nuclear tests and from the technical conference on measures against surprise attack. I cannot imagine anything more calculated to increase tension at a moment of opportunity for an improvement in our relations than the kind of action which your statements appear to foreshadow. I hope therefore that you will seriously consider what I say before deciding to proceed to such action.

I also sent messages to the United States and French Governments explaining that I acted without formal consultation with my allies in order to try to get my message to Khrushchev before the Russians took any formal action.

On 27 November, however, an official Soviet note was delivered to all the Governments concerned. In this the Russian Government served notice upon the three Western powers that the Soviet Union regarded as null and void the existing arrangements about Berlin. At the same time it was prepared to negotiate with these Governments as to the establishment of West Berlin on the basis of a 'demilitarised free city'. The note went on to declare that the Soviet Government 'proposed to make no changes in the present procedure for military traffic from West Berlin to the Federal Republic of Germany for six months'.

When there is a prolonged state of tension between two nations or groups of nations, every move, formal or informal, great or small, is scrutinised and analysed by the experts on each side with microscopic care, to try to find the hidden and twisted motives which lie behind the simplest and most overt statements. This has always been so in the history of national conflict. But when, as in these years, the division lies not merely in the normal geographic, economic or political interests in the two sets of contendents but is based on a far more decisive opposition of the fundamental ideas of life and political organisation, this process becomes exaggerated. In the chancelleries of the free world, above all in Washington, there has grown up a race of 'Kremlinologists', trying to draw the most profound deductions from the most slender evidence. No doubt in the huge bureaucracy of Russia there are similar groups attempting to dissect the strange and uncertain motives which would seem to influence the Governments of the free world.

The immediate situation, although grave, gave us at least some interval for thought. Yet all these new threats were interlaced with existing difficulties and the latest was only a new turn in this wheel of complexity and danger.

After the receipt of the Russian note I sent a minute to the Foreign Secretary on 28 November:

> *The Berlin issue* is, in fact, an ultimatum with six months to run. We shall not be able to avoid negotiation. How is it to be carried out? Will it necessarily lead to discussion of the future of a united Germany and possible 'Disengagement Plans'?
>
> *Tests and Surprise Attack*
> These negotiations at Geneva seem likely to drag on more or less indefinitely. If we can get American consent to abandon the link altogether, we may make some advance from the propaganda point of view, but I doubt whether we shall reach any nearer agreement.
>
> *European Free Trade*
> You will have no doubt read an excellent article in the *Financial Times* this morning. If not, pray do so. It is clear that the Germans have really sold out to the French on every count.
>
> I do not think we can deal with these problems separately. The groups of powers in this strange quadrille keep changing. In the

first, it is Russia and the three occupying powers, with Germany the most interested and with most to gain. In the second, France is out and Germany is out. In the third, the United States seem uninterested and the Germans and French have made an unholy alliance against the British. We must think of all these problems together, for that is what the British people will do. . . .

As regards Russia, it may be that Khrushchev is really working for a Summit Conference without the Chinese. In that case, it would certainly not be bad politics for me to take the lead in suggesting it.

The visit of Vice-President Nixon to London at this time proved useful. Although I was never sure of the extent of his influence either with the President or with the Secretary of State, both Selwyn Lloyd and I took much trouble to hear his views, which seemed sensible and restrained.

In the Foreign Affairs Debate on 4 December there was no difficulty. The whole House, with very few exceptions, resented the Russian move, although there was a strong feeling in favour of trying to find some solution by negotiation.

The Foreign Affairs debate went off well. Foreign Secretary made an *excellent* speech in his new style—firm, clear and short. Bevan was rhetorical and quite effective until the end, when he started up again the controversy about arming Germany, over which the Labour Party had been split so deeply.[1]

Khrushchev sent me a long personal reply formally delivered by the Soviet Ambassador in London. He justified his action on the grounds that it was right for one Government to give warning of a dangerous situation.

The Soviet Government's main aim in proposing the abolition of the last vestiges of the occupation régime in Berlin, as was clearly stated in its note, is to eliminate a dangerous, indeed I would frankly say, an extremely dangerous, source of friction and tension which complicates the relations between our countries and creates an abnormal atmosphere in Europe as a whole. In taking appropriate steps in relation to West Berlin and in submitting its proposals in this matter, the Soviet Government has

[1] 4 December 1958.

been prompted by the consideration that in certain circumstances the situation existing in West Berlin, where the occupation régime is being artificially and illegally maintained, could lead to the gravest consequences for the cause of peace in Europe, and perhaps not only in Europe.

He went on to question our rights in Berlin, which we maintained were derived not from the Potsdam agreement, but from the unconditional surrender of Germany in 1945. Khrushchev devoted a long and ingenious argument to proving that the breakdown of the Potsdam agreement had in fact removed these rights. He went on to an interesting passage on the military value of Berlin to either side.

If one looks at things realistically, as statesmen are obliged always to do, one must admit that neither the security interests nor any other vital interests to Great Britain will suffer as a result of the liquidation of the quadripartite status of Berlin. And if those who now adopt a critical attitude towards the proposals of the Soviet Government on this question sometimes point to the military and strategic importance of the Western part of Berlin, this can only make anyone smile who knows more or less to what extent modern military techniques have changed the conception of war and the nature of military action when weapons of mass destruction are used. We think it unlikely that you, Mr. Prime Minister, will dispute this.

From this he drew the deduction that

even if Great Britain and the other Western powers were to relinquish something as a result of the abrogation of the quadripartite status of Berlin, this would only be the doubtful advantages which they enjoy from the use of Western Berlin for continuing the 'cold war' and for conducting subversive activities against the G.D.R.,[1] the Soviet Union and the other socialist countries.

There then followed a definite statement which could be regarded as a warning or a threat:

To make the proposals of the Soviet Union on Berlin completely clear I feel it necessary to stress that if the period of six

[1] German Democratic Republic, or Deutsche Demokratische Republik (D.D.R.), the official name for East Germany.

T2

months which was mentioned in the Note of the Soviet Government is not used to reach an appropriate agreement it goes without saying that the Soviet Union will carry out the proposed measures by means of an agreement with the German Democratic Republic and no one will be able to prevent the Soviet Union from abrogating its functions deriving from the maintenance of the occupation status in Berlin.

In the last two pages of this six-page document, Khrushchev returned to blandishment, if not blarney:

> In this connection we cannot help remembering our meetings with you, Mr. Prime Minister, and your predecessor, Sir Anthony Eden, in London in the spring of 1956 and that frank and, it seemed to us, useful exchange of opinions on the problems of relations between the U.S.S.R. and Great Britain as well as on many international problems. We expected that the visit of the Soviet Government delegation to Great Britain would lay a good basis for a rapprochement between our two nations and would contribute to the relaxation of international tension and to the cessation of the 'cold war'.

Next he deplored the present state of Anglo-Russian trade. Moreover Great Britain was almost the only major state with which the Soviet Union had so far no cultural, scientific or technical co-operation. Finally he declared:

> We sincerely wish that all the prejudices which clearly influence the attitude of the British Government towards the Soviet Union would yield to a more favourable approach to the problem of establishing mutual understanding and co-operation between the U.S.S.R. and Great Britain. The Soviet Government is convinced that a rapprochement of the two countries would not only bring material advantages to our peoples and enrich them spiritually but would also favourably influence the solution of important international issues, thus promoting the cause of peace.

I was still pondering on the recondite implications of this message, when the Soviet Government sent on 13 December a somewhat curious declaration to all NATO powers in connection with the forthcoming NATO conference. In the course of a restatement of their views in now familiar terms they renewed the call for a Summit Conference. Was this to be treated as propaganda or a serious proposal? Once again the experts on Russian psychology expressed their varying, but admirably presented, views.

The rest of December was taken up in the various preliminaries which are necessary for consultation within an alliance, such as that which held the Western powers together. These delays do not affect a monolithic power whose allies are satellite or even subject states. Nevertheless the task was rapidly performed. There were meetings of the Foreign Ministers, meetings of the NATO Council, meetings of the Western European Assembly, and by 31 December the replies of the British, French and American Governments were delivered in Moscow. They were in similar terms. They made it clear that the proposals for Berlin were unacceptable; that the three Western powers, in addition to their rights, had responsibilities towards two million West Berliners to remain in the city; accordingly they looked to the Soviet Government to adhere to its obligations and in particular to the agreement of 20 June 1949, to afford free and unhindered access from West Germany to Berlin. At the same time the notes stated that the Western Governments were prepared to discuss Berlin in the wider framework of negotiation for a solution to the German problem as well as that of European security.

Selwyn Lloyd had admirably set out our position in the House of Commons.

> The fact, however, that we intend to uphold our rights in Berlin, and find the Soviet proposals unacceptable, does not mean that we should fail to seek discussion with the Soviet Union on the German position as a whole. . . . We are ready to discuss the matter with the Russians in all its aspects.[1]

On this note, dangerous but by no means yet disastrous, the year ended.

During the Christmas holidays Selwyn Lloyd underwent a slight operation. This meant that I had to take control of the Foreign Office as well as my own work. Although the negotiations in Cyprus were about to reach a critical stage I was not unhopeful of their

[1] *Hansard*, 4 December 1958.

success. My main anxiety, therefore, was concentrated upon the
Russian declaration or ultimatum. I felt that, while the Western
allies must uphold their right of access to Berlin, we must avoid
giving Russia no choice but humiliation or war. Moreover a warning
with six months to run was scarcely an ultimatum in the ordinary
sense of the word. We had no right in law or equity to prevent the
Russians from giving the same recognition to East Germany as we
had given to the Federal Republic. Everything turned upon Berlin.
How would our position be affected if the Russians handed over
their rights to the Government of East Germany, the D.D.R.?

> The Berlin 'crisis' is approaching, and we have (as yet) no
> agreed policy with our allies. The Paris declaration only
> papered over the cracks. Are we really prepared to face war over
> Berlin? If so, just in what way are we to play the hand, so as to
> get the Russians sure that we are serious and be ready to come to
> a serious conference. I feel sure (although the Americans so far
> are *not* quite agreed) that we must not *over* play our hand. If we
> do, the Russians will see through and call our bluff.
>
> I doubt therefore whether we can make the question of
> whether Russians or East Germans approve the bills of lading
> or punch the railway tickets into a *casus belli*. What matters is
> whether civil and military supplies actually reach Berlin.[1]

At the same time we had to consider the more dangerous position.
If access by road or rail was interfered with either by the Russians
or by the D.D.R. after the Russians had unilaterally transferred
their functions, we should be back in the circumstances of the
blockade of 1948. In that event we should either have to repeat the
air operation, so successfully carried out ten years before, or take
steps to force our way through upon the ground.

Before Christmas I had received a long appeal from Adenauer.

> The unequivocal 'no' of the British Government to the Soviet
> demands has filled the German people and myself with deep
> gratitude. I believe that the important thing now is that the
> communiqué should eliminate all doubt for the Russians, too,
> about the firm attitude of the three Western powers on the
> question of Berlin. Should the Soviet Government or the people

[1] 5 January 1959.

of Berlin be able to detect any signs at all of a yielding attitude in that communiqué it is my opinion that such a mistake could seriously endanger the peace of the world. We know from experience, after all, that the Soviets have retreated each time they have met with energetic resistance, and I am convinced that in the case of Berlin, too, the Russians will undertake nothing that could jeopardise peace if the powers responsible for the freedom of the city maintain a clear-cut and unequivocal attitude. On the other hand, I believe we also know from experience that the slightest appearance of a yielding attitude when the legal position was clear has caused the Soviets to advance still further.

He rightly pointed out a significant and somewhat sinister change in the situation over the decade.

The situation of West Berlin is fundamentally different from what it was at the time of the 1948 blockade. The economy of the city has blossomed out remarkably, thanks to the help of the United States and the continual support of the Federal Republic, and, whereas in 1948 the citizens of Berlin were all more or less equally poor, and there was no appreciable difference between the standard of living in West and in East Berlin, there are sections of the population in Berlin today who again have something to lose and who must fear that they will lose their laboriously acquired possessions as well as their personal freedom.

For these reasons he declared that

it is clear to every thinking person that an air-lift would not manage to maintain even approximately the standard of living of West Berlin. Finally—and this is very important—during that blockade no one could leave Berlin, whereas at present everyone is free to do so.

Adenauer readily agreed that there must be negotiations at some point with the Soviet Government, not merely on Berlin but upon the whole German problem. Such negotiations would be necessary at the right time and after thorough preparation.

But I believe it would be unwise and also very dangerous to begin such negotiations under the pressure of a demand with a time limit. The point of departure of the West would in such an event be the worst imaginable. Any mixing of such demands made in the manner of an ultimatum with the all-German question would lead the West along a path ending either in a restriction of Berlin's freedom or in a more or less disguised capitulation in the all-German question, for it is inconceivable that even a basic outline of an acceptable solution could be found for the German problem in six months.

Nevertheless it seemed to me that the Russians' strategy was to force us either to recognise the East German Government or by refusing to deal with them to impose, as it were, a blockade upon ourselves.

In a reply to a message from Dulles, giving an account of a talk with Anastas Mikoyan, in which he seemed to be slightly drawing back, I said :

All the same I do not think that it has been the Russian intention to impose a blockade at the end of the six months. Their intention has been to make us choose between imposing a blockade on ourselves or dealing with the East Germans, whether as their successors or their agents. But they now seem to be a little alarmed that their note should appear to the Western world as having directly threatened a blockade.

I still felt that while making every possible plan for the emergency which might follow the Russians making a separate treaty with East Germany, we should stand upon the reality and not upon the form. I pointed out to Dulles that the Russians had already threatened that they would support the D.D.R. if we attacked them. The corollary was surely that the Russians must see to it that the D.D.R. carried out all their obligations including those that the Russians might purport to have transferred.

While this friendly interchange was going on between Washington and London, ably assisted by our Ambassador, Harold Caccia, who seemed to have won the complete confidence of the Secretary of State, our Ambassador in Bonn arrived in London.

Kit Steel . . . came for a talk . . . Chancellor Adenauer is in a bad way and ageing rapidly. The rest of them (Brentano, etc.) are unable or unwilling to think out anything new in these circumstances. At one moment Adenauer is violently pro-French and pro-de Gaulle, at another, highly critical. He is still, it appears, fond of me!

About Berlin, etc., he stands (officially) for absolute rigidity and a solid front against Soviet Russia. Behind the scenes, he wrings his hands and says that Russia and the West are like two express trains rushing to a head-on collision.[1]

Meanwhile, on 10 January the Soviet Government made a new move. In a note addressed to the three Western powers they proposed a peace conference to include a discussion on the Berlin question. No mention of a time limit was given in this note. This appeared to confirm the hints given by Mikoyan while in the United States. From this it would seem that the Soviet Government was, after all, keeping the door open for negotiations. Nevertheless the note insisted once more that

> no one can hinder the Soviet Government from relinquishing the functions which it performs in respect of Berlin and its communications with Western Germany and from regulating the questions which arise in this connexion by means of an agreement with the German Democratic Republic.[2]

With this communication the Soviet Government included the draft of a peace treaty. This in effect provided for the partition of Germany into the two existing states. It would consequently allow all the Allied powers to sign a treaty with those states without waiting for an all-German Government to be formed. The Allied powers would do their best to promote agreement between the two German states, which for their part were to renounce the use of force as a means of achieving unity. Pending reunification, the two German states were to abandon their membership of the Warsaw and the NATO alliances; military forces would be allowed so far as was necessary to keep order and the local defence. All this had a certain specious attraction. Yet since foreign troops were to be withdrawn from both Germanies, then in the absence of any real disarmament or security system, the U.S.S.R. would have an enormous military advantage. They could pour in their troops at a few hours'

---

[1] 16 January 1959.   [2] *Annual Register*, 1959, p. 136.

notice; whereas if Western Germany were once demilitarised and neutralised the strength of NATO would be, in fact, weakened almost to the point of inanition.

The Russian note was skilfully devised and would clearly need a careful and if possible a positive reply. To agree the terms of such a reply would necessarily be a matter of some weeks. Indeed it was not until 16 February that the answer could be sent. It was, for once, simple and constructive. While stating that the Soviet proposals were unacceptable, the Allied note called for a Conference of the Foreign Ministers of the four powers with German advisers in attendance to deal with the problem of Germany in all its aspects and implications.

Meanwhile I began to ponder over some method of dealing with the situation which might so easily drift from month to month with interchanges of diplomatic notes and *démarches* until a final disaster.

> I have decided to send telegrams to Washington expressing my anxiety and my desire to make some progress. I would like, above all, to go to Washington for talks with Dulles and the President. This method has worked very well during the last two years. But with French jealousy and German suspicion, it may be too dangerous. It seems therefore that I had better make a more complicated plan.
>
> For a long time there has been a sort of outstanding invitation to go to Moscow. Of course, the invitation might not be renewed. But it is worth trying. In that case, I would go to Moscow (with Foreign Secretary)—then to Bonn and Paris, and finally to Washington.[1]

On 20 January after full discussion at the Foreign Office the necessary telegram to Dulles was drafted and approved.

> Caccia will see Dulles tomorrow, and we should have our reply by Thursday morning. Some think the Americans will be incensed and go off the deep end; others think they will acquiesce.[2]

The House of Commons had now returned, and Parliamentary questions about Berlin and Russia were pouring in. Gaitskell and Bevan were naturally both pressing me hard, being apparently

[1] 18 January 1959.   [2] 20 January 1959.

converts to the idea of 'disengagement' and German neutrality. In view of the approaching end of the Parliament and the possibility of a Labour Government taking office, I did my best to discourage them, for I feared that any weakness could only serve to encourage Russian intransigence.

Meanwhile the reply arrived from Washington. The President and Dulles naturally pointed out that there were certain risks in my going to Moscow before any agreed Western position had been reached, but their attitude was not unsympathetic and afforded me great encouragement.

> The American reply has come and in most friendly terms. They say, in effect, that they have complete confidence in me and I must do whatever I think best.[1]

On the same day I had a meeting with the Foreign Secretary, the Chancellor of the Exchequer and a number of other leading Ministers, in which I told them about my plan. The Foreign Secretary had, of course, been fully in my confidence all through. After this conference, and with the approval of my colleagues, I telegraphed urgently to Sir Patrick Reilly asking for his views as to whether, if I were to take up the invitation extended at the time of the visit of Bulganin and Khrushchev in 1956, my proposal would be welcomed. A rebuff would be disconcerting. The Ambassador in reply felt bound to point out the dangers. The Russians would be sure to look at the visit against the background of what they considered to be the state of public opinion in Britain in a pre-election period and try to get all they could out of it. He doubted whether they could hope for any success in driving a wedge between Washington and London since my close relations and friendship with the President were well known. They would more probably try to use the opportunity to isolate Adenauer and the West German Government and to represent them as the chief obstacle to a settlement of the German problem. He felt, therefore, that not only the Americans but also the French and especially the Germans should publicly approve the visit and also that the visits to Bonn, Paris and Washington should be announced simultaneously with that to Moscow. He added that

[1] 22 January 1959.

it was no use trying to fish for an invitation; the request must be put forward simply and straightforwardly. In a further message Reilly expressed the hope that the visit would not be hurried. It should be of the same character as that which the Russian statesmen had made in Britain. Although it should be essentially a working visit, it should also provide the opportunity for me and my party to see some other Russian cities and something of the Russian countryside and people.

On receipt of this advice, and after much thought and discussion with the Foreign Secretary and other leading colleagues, I decided to take the risk. Instructions were sent to the Ambassador according-ly. Reilly saw Andrei Gromyko on 24 January and put forward my proposal of a visit of a week or ten days, starting if possible about 20 February. For some days there was no reply. On the 29 January the Ambassador sent me a message to say that the proposal had probably surprised the Soviet Government and might have upset their own plans. He thought an actual rebuff unlikely, but they were probably considering whether the visit would be to their advantage or not. Would I wish him to press for an answer? To which I immediately answered, 'No, let things take their course, we must not seem to be too anxious.'

However, by 31 January I was becoming rather concerned:

> Dulles comes Tuesday and leaves Wednesday lunch time. We must prepare for this, which will be a very important discussion. We can bluff the Russians—if we can—but we must not bluff ourselves.
>
> The French Prime Minister [Michel Debré] is to come early in March. I agreed a telegram to Reilly (in Moscow) asking his advice on what now to do with the Russians, who (no doubt occupied with their great Congress and all their visitors) have not answered my proposal. We must not run after them; but we must not let them insult us by too long a delay.[1]

On 2 February the reply came.

> I heard after luncheon that the Russian Minister had called at Foreign Office and given the Russian reply. All my anxieties are

[1] 31 January 1959.

removed. They have accepted the date, the length of visit, and the terms of the announcement. This will be 3.30 p.m. on Thursday. This is an immense relief, for we rather 'stuck our necks out' in making the proposal, and a rebuff (which would have leaked) would have been damaging as well as embarrassing.[1]

Now that the matter was settled I began to have some qualms. What would the Amercians really feel? What would the French say or do? How would Adenauer react? Would the visit prove a success and help at least to break the ice and gradually lead to more relaxed relations between East and West? Would it above all contribute to a solution of the urgent problem caused by Khrushchev's ultimatum? Or would it prove disastrous? It was certainly a perilous undertaking. I must avoid negotiation on the immediate subject of Berlin, for I had no authority to speak for my allies, nor had they any agreed plan. The visit would certainly be a great adventure; it might also be great fun. But before I could set out there was much still to be done.

I immediately sent messages to Adenauer, to Debré, now Prime Minister of France, as well as to the Prime Ministers of the Commonwealth. In my message of 2 February to Adenauer, who I knew would view my decision with dismay and even alarm, I referred to the long-standing invitation to Sir Anthony Eden, which I had not up to now thought it opportune to revive. It now seemed to me that something useful might come from a personal contact in Moscow. It would certainly help if we could know something of their real intentions, about which we were still in the dark.

The primary purpose of my visit to Moscow will therefore be to try to discover something of what is in the minds of the Soviet leaders. I shall make it clear that I am not coming to negotiate. It would not enter into my mind to try to negotiate on my own, nor indeed would I be in a position to do so because it will still be some time before the Western allies will be able to decide on the line which they are to take with the Russians at any conference. If I can bring anything useful back with me in the shape of some insight into their motives this might in fact be of some help to all of us in settling our line.

[1] 2 February 1959.

I also felt that my visit might serve a useful purpose with Western opinion. A firm policy required full and understanding support

> If our public opinion is to be kept resolute, as of course it can be, and if it is to accept the measures of military preparedness which it may before long be necessary for us to take and impossible for us to conceal, then we must demonstrate our readiness to talk to the Russians and the reasonableness of our approach to them. People in the United Kingdom are very ready to make sacrifices and run risks if they are really convinced that this is necessary. But they do not like to be put into these positions unless they are certain that their leaders have made every effort to reach understanding and agreement.

I added that, since my visit would be of an exploratory character, I hoped I would be able to discuss its results with him as soon as possible after my return from Moscow. I also proposed to visit Paris and Washington.

Since the Foreign Secretary was in Paris he was able to have a personal talk with Couve de Murville and pass my message direct to Debré, who sent a friendly if non-committal reply. My reason for sending a message to Debré asking him to inform de Gaulle was that my new plans involved postponing Debré's visit to London. On 3 February our Ambassador in Paris, Sir Gladwyn Jebb, reported that the French took the matter very calmly and Couve de Murville's only comment was that if my visit succeeded in persuading the Russians to withdraw their ultimatum it would be a very good thing. The Commonwealth Prime Ministers sent messages of approval and encouragement.

The news from Bonn was not so satisfactory. The Chancellor was at first inclined to regard my visit as purely an election manœuvre. When the Ambassador indignantly denied this, he observed that this was the only useful point in it that he could see. However, at the end of the interview, which the Ambassador described as far from happy, it was clear that Adenauer's attitude would be much affected by what line the French took, but above all by the American reaction. In his reply to my message, however, Adenauer only stressed one point, the importance of giving no official recognition to East Germany. This question was, of course, the one upon which he held throughout his life the strongest and most unshakable views.

On 4 February Dulles arrived in London. He came to Downing Street at 9 p.m., and I was shocked at his appearance. I had not seen him for some months, and it was clear to me now that he was a very sick man. Indeed ten days later it was announced in Washington that an operation for hernia had revealed that he was suffering from a recurrence of cancer. Although he showed remarkable courage and was determined not to abandon his high position, it was a tragic thing to see this once massive figure struck down by so terrible a disease.

He is not able to dine out. He has to eat some strange foods and rest to digest them. But Janet came to a dinner at No. 10 which Dorothy gave (wives only), and Foreign Secretary and I had a sandwich together, awaiting his arrival at No. 10.[1]

I had a few words alone with Dulles before the conference began. Dulles was accompanied by Livie Merchant (Under-Secretary) and the American Ambassador, Jock Whitney. With me were Hoyer Millar, Rumbold and Bishop. After discussing some other points we soon came to Berlin.

Here Foster had 'thoughts aloud'. The impression he gave was that he had *completely abandoned* the Pentagon plan and the idea of a large convoy of tanks, with perhaps a division or more of troops and artillery, to force and hold the road and rail approach. He put forward a much more modest and much less spectacular form of 'probe', to be followed by political pressure – in U.N. and by other means.[1]

Although the Secretary of State had told me this in our short preliminary talk I was very anxious

that he should restate this view to me, in the hearing of his American colleagues. For he *must* speak on the same lines in Bonn. This does *not* mean that we should abandon our position in Berlin or desist from a 'tough' point of view. But it means that while we must present a firm and united front to the Russians,

[1] 4 February 1959.

we must not deceive ourselves. Above all, we must not slip into the 1914 position—mobilisation sliding into war. I thought this exposition of the case very ably done. Foster Dulles knows that it is the opposite of what Murphy and the Pentagon have been saying for weeks, almost accusing us of being weak and defeatist—perhaps traitors—because we did not swallow the military plan without thought. I suspect that it is the President who has over-ruled the soldiers. Indeed, when we were alone, Dulles as good as told me this.[1]

The Berlin problem naturally led on to the wider question of Germany and European security.

I threw out various ideas—really to try out the Americans. We might propose 'thinning out'—without national discrimination. We might even prepare something much more ambitious—Russian troops to leave Poland, Hungary and Czechoslovakia—at a price....

To my surprise Foster Dulles was not unduly shocked. He seemed to be ready to discuss new ideas. This may be partly the result of having lost control of Congress and therefore having to accommodate the views of the Administration and the Senate.[1]

On the next day Dulles and the Americans came again at noon. We soon reached agreement on the timing of our plans, though we had not yet any precise draft of what we proposed to say when the Conference of Foreign Ministers took place. Much to my surprise, the main business being over, Dulles then began to talk in more general terms. One interesting thing he said

in a sort of parenthetical way, but nevertheless quite firmly—'a Summit Conference, to which the President would come, ought not to be *excluded* in May next'. Foster Dulles thinks the Conference with the Russians must last four to five weeks. I think his idea is that, if some progress could be made, *one* week of this could be a meeting of *Heads*. He also seemed to like my idea of a more or less continuous or permanent Conference—adjourning for long periods and reassembling for new work, with Ministers attending from time to time, and officials (Ambassadors, etc.) working on committees and reporting to

[1] 4 February 1959.

Ministers. Such a Conference, or Congress, would in itself 'relieve tensions'.[1]

When Dulles left I felt very sad. In spite of all the troubles and difficulties we had had with this strange man, I had grown to have an affection and respect for him. I was to see him again before his death, but already I felt that he was a doomed man.

On the same afternoon I made a statement after Questions in the House of Commons. After referring to the Soviet invitation extended to Eden in 1956 I continued:

Recent international developments have made me feel that a visit at the present time would be of value. On my instructions, therefore, Her Majesty's Ambassador in Moscow suggested to the Soviet Government some days ago that I should go to the Soviet Union on 21 February for a visit of a week or ten days accompanied by my right hon. and learned Friend the Foreign Secretary. I am glad to tell the House that on 2 February—that is, last Monday, the Soviet Chargé d'Affaires in London informed us that his Government welcomed this proposal. Our friends and Allies have been informed.

We are, of course, in close consultation with our Allies about how best to handle the serious issues which at present face us in Europe. On all these we act together. My right hon. and learned Friend and I will not be going to Moscow to conduct a negotiation on behalf of the West. Nevertheless, we hope that our conversations with the Soviet leaders will give them a better knowledge of our point of view and make it easier for us to understand what is in their minds. Thus, we and our Allies may be better able to judge what our policies and actions should be. Personal contacts do not in themselves solve international problems, but there are times when they may make a contribution to their solution.

There are, of course, other important aspects of this visit. There are many matters such as trade, information and cultural relations which we should hope to discuss. I shall also look forward to seeing something of the Soviet Union and the Soviet people. But my principal purpose will be to try to dispel misconceptions and to establish some basis for better understanding.

[1] 5 February 1959.

An agreed communiqué announcing the visit is being issued this afternoon in London and Moscow.[1]

The supplementaries were short. Although something had leaked out, the House seemed rather astonished.

Gaitskell and his party were rather put out, I thought. They were uncertain whether to praise or damn our initiative.[2]

The final question was from Mrs. Jean Mann, the Labour Member for Coatbridge and Airdrie. She said:

May I, as a back bencher, thank the Prime Minister, wish him god-speed, and ask him the date of the General Election?
The Prime Minister: The first two the hon. Lady may certainly do, but not the third.[1]

That evening I had a call from Jean Chauvel, the French Ambassador.

He brought a friendly message from French Prime Minister. It looks as if I had better go to Paris on 10 March. This would give an opportunity to see President de Gaulle as well and it seems that de Gaulle would welcome this.[2]

The next day, 6 February:

The Press is good about my visit to Russia. The Left-Wing Press tries to conceal its chagrin—and does not find the exercise too easy. The Press has followed very well the lead I gave in Parliament and in the Lobby: 'A reconnaissance not a negotiation'. This avoids the danger of rousing hopes which will afterwards be disappointed.[3]

Unfortunately I heard later that my word 'reconnaissance' when translated into Russian had some sinister connotations suggesting espionage. Patrick Reilly, however, had quickly used in his own statement 'a voyage of discovery'. This was calculated not to shock any susceptibilities. Although the next few days were almost entirely taken up with the concluding stages of the Cyprus negotiation, there was much to be done and many papers to be prepared and a vast dossier about individuals to be got ready and digested. One of

[1] *Hansard*, 5 February 1959.   [2] 5 February 1959.   [3] 6 February 1959.

the troublesome points was that of security. So highly developed at this time were the methods of 'intelligence' that even in our own Embassy the greatest precautions were necessary. When I got to Moscow I was to suffer the full implications of life under these strange conditions.

During the few days before our journey began the Press, both in Britain and America, and indeed throughout the world, showed an extraordinary interest in our enterprise. No Prime Minister in office or Head of Government of any of the Western countries had visited Russia since the end of the war. In spite of some doubts, there was general approval, although there was clearly, especially among our allies, some nervousness lest I should attempt to achieve more than I had undertaken to do. Nevertheless the intensity of the cold war and the shadow of the nuclear bomb oppressed the whole world, and any attempt to break through the clouds of suspicion was generally welcomed.

Much interest was taken by the gossip writers in the clothes with which our party were to be provided. Fortunately I was still able to obtain my father-in-law's fur coat which I had used in the winter war in Finland in 1940. I also sported a white hat which I had purchased at that time.[1] I had not realised that this was a form of headdress peculiar to Finland, and to bring it out now was perhaps not the most tactful action. However, when I was told this later I comforted myself that the Russians had doubtless a good dossier of my life which included this episode.

My party consisted of my two private secretaries, Freddie Bishop and Philip de Zulueta, as well as my Parliamentary Private Secretary Tony Barber. Norman Brook, the Secretary of the Cabinet, came with me, as well as Harold Evans, our incomparable public relations officer. Selwyn Lloyd, as Foreign Secretary, had a similar staff; besides two private secretaries, there were Sir Patrick Dean, F. R. H. Murray, who was a good Russian scholar, Con O'Neill, Sir Anthony Rumbold and representatives of other departments including the Board of Trade. We set off from London Airport on 21 February and arrived home on the evening of 3 March.

Before leaving, my wife and I received a vast correspondence

[1] See *The Blast of War*, p. 29.

and messages sending good wishes, including many from unknown friends. In looking through her papers I recently found one which was amusing and rather touching.

Please, don't allow our Prime Minister to go out shooting bears in Russia, it may be *very* dangerous—and what would we in Britain and America do if he had [an] accident.

I took this lady's advice, and when at one moment Mr. Khrushchev suggested a party to hunt the bear or the elk, I excused myself, chiefly because I thought such an expedition might be regarded at home as a somewhat frivolous way of spending my time. This, however, did not prevent Khrushchev sending me some weeks later a large stuffed head of an elk with magnificent horns, which somewhat overpowers the gun-room at home.

Before leaving I sent a message to President Eisenhower expressing the hope that the conference in Geneva on nuclear tests might still end in agreement. The main question in dispute was that of inspection and control.

Perfect control is in any case almost impossible in theory and quite impossible in practice. It seems to me that if we can create a control system which involves a sufficient degree of risk to a potential violator that he cannot get away undetected with a violation of the agreement, then we shall have done enough to justify our accepting the disadvantages and risks involved.

I already had the impression, which I hoped to confirm in Moscow, that the Russians still wanted an agreement, chiefly because they were concerned about the spread of nuclear weapons to other countries as well as worried about the mounting cost of the nuclear programme. Of course their demand for a veto over the crucial operations of the control system must be resisted, particularly in regard to despatch of any inspection team. Yet I hoped that wherever possible we might make concessions. At any rate I promised to press Khrushchev hard about the veto.

We arrived at Moscow at 3 p.m. (local time) and were greeted by Khrushchev, Mikoyan and other members of the Soviet Government. There was the usual guard of honour and speeches. Khrushchev certainly struck a friendly note, including such encouraging sentiments as

The Soviet Union is a peaceable country. The Soviet people, engaged as they are in carrying out a great programme for building a new life–Communism–are vitally concerned that never again should war interrupt their peaceful creative labour. The foreign policy of our state is based on the principle of the peaceful co-existence of states with different social systems, on the striving to safeguard and consolidate peace and international security. We shall follow this line without fail.

We are happy to meet the guests from abroad who have arrived in our country. We are prepared for useful talks with them for the benefit of our two countries and the cause of world peace.

Both the Government of the Soviet Union and the Soviet people will receive them with hospitality and friendliness. Welcome, gentlemen!

In my reply, after remarking that this was the first time that a British Prime Minister had visited the Soviet Union in time of peace, I continued:

My visit has three purposes. In the first place, the Foreign Secretary and I wished to repay the courtesy which you, Mr. Prime Minister, paid to our country by your visit in 1956. We regret that the course of events has prevented an earlier return call; we are glad that a moment has now come when we can accept your hospitality.

Secondly, we hope to see something of the people, industry and agriculture of the Soviet Union. This is not my first visit; I was last here, as an ordinary tourist, some thirty years ago. I fully expect to find that conditions in the Soviet Union today are almost as different from what they were then as England today is from the picture painted by Dickens. We in Britain are glad that such great developments in your production and standard of life have taken place; and I am anxious to see them for myself. For this reason, we particularly appreciate the care which has been shown in the preparation of the programme for our visit and I am happy that we shall see the heroic city of Leningrad and the great work which has been done in reconstructing Kiev.

Thirdly, we should like our visit to contribute to a wider realisation in the Soviet Union of conditions of life in Britain today and of where our country stands in the major world problems. In pursuit of this last aim we hope to have some serious discussion with you, Mr. Prime Minister, and with members of the Soviet Government. I do not come to negotiate on particular subjects. I do hope, however, that in our talks together we shall at least reach a better understanding of our points of view. Perhaps in this way our visit may help to alleviate some of the cares that at present bring anxiety to the world. That at least is my objective. Let us see if we can achieve it, together.

After a formal call on Khrushchev and his colleagues in the afternoon of our arrival—my first visit to the Kremlin, with all its historic memories and mysterious and sombre recollections—we attended a large dinner in the magnificent hall of that unique palace. After the usual Russian dinner, of which to our British tastes the most attractive parts were the preparatory dishes with the accompanying glasses of vodka, Khrushchev rose and delivered a speech apparently without preparation, certainly without notes. After referring to the thirty years which had passed since my last visit to Russia and the terrible events of the Second World War when we were allies against the common enemy, he continued:

> Unfortunately, relations between our two countries were strained after the war ended. Now is not the time to argue about how and why this happened. It is best for us to put our heads together and decide what should be done to melt the resulting 'cold war' ice.
>
> If we succeed, many obstacles to the improvement of the whole of the international climate, to the settlement of important international problems, will disappear—obstacles giving rise to disputes between States, including our two countries.
>
> The peoples expect the Governments to exert fresh efforts and overcome the obstacles preventing men and women from devoting all their energies to peaceful labour without fear of war.
>
> In our view there is every prerequisite for achieving this end. Needless to say, mankind has now approached a stage in its history when it is able to avert war. The solution of this problem is a vitally important matter for all countries and nations without exception.

He went on to recall with pleasure his visit to Britain three years before.

It cannot be said that they have been years of unmarred relations between our countries, and there have been some clouds, even storm clouds. There have been some frosty spells in our relations, if I may say so. The general cold climate in international relations accounted for this to a great extent. Now there is much talk of a 'thaw', indicated by livelier contacts and a desire for negotiations. We regard your visit as a result of this 'thaw', and today—on the day of your arrival—there has been a real thaw in nature.

He added that the Soviet Government had always been in favour of meetings and contacts between statesmen: such was their position now. For this reason he welcomed our visit.

We also welcome your intention to tour our country. To put it mildly, many people write about the Soviet Union in the West in a way that is not objective. We are glad to give you and your colleagues an extensive opportunity to see our country and meet our people. As the old saying goes: 'Better to see once than hear a hundred times.'

This was my first experience of Khrushchev's love for proverbs, some of which, as I got to know him better, I felt he must have invented off the cuff. In my reply, after thanking him for his hospitality and making a reference to the great changes in Russia and the vast progress made in the last generation, I ventured to try to dispel another Russian illusion. I had mentioned Dickens at the airport, hoping to challenge the illusion popular in Russia that the conditions which were represented in books like *Oliver Twist* still continued unchanged in our country. I now tried to deal frankly with the misuse of the word 'imperialism'.

In the international field too we have seen great changes. Imperialism is an episode in history. It is no longer a present reality. We inherited an empire which our fathers had built up, but because of the way they had worked we have been able to transform Empire in Commonwealth. Of course, there are still some people in Britain who think that what is red on a map is beautiful [which is a sort of pun in Russian: red and beautiful are basically the same words], but from the very beginning of the British Empire the prevailing concept was of trusteeship. Quite early in the nineteenth century the great British reformer and historian, Macaulay, was laying the foundations of that system of education in India which produced men to whom we were in time able to hand over power. This concept of trusteeship is now reaching its full development. I believe that the Commonwealth idea is of general interest. Indeed, I see that in the Declaration of the Communist Parties assembled in Moscow in October 1957, you yourselves have used the Russian word which translates our word 'Commonwealth'. So I hope you will forgive me if I say something about this idea tonight.

The constitutional ties which bind the Commonwealth countries together may seem tenuous to an outsider. Certainly the formal bonds are very slender. But Mr. Prime Minister, we in Britain are practical people. We believe that an association of friends will stick together if they wish to without formal agreements and that no amount of treaties will bind an alliance which is not founded in the hearts of the allies. The fragile formal ties of the Commonwealth do symbolise a real sense of community. The nations of the Commonwealth stick together and work together because they have a common belief in the rights of the individual; a common belief in the rule of law. This finds its expression in a belief in freedom of association, freedom of speech, freedom to differ within the framework of the law. The member States of the Commonwealth are very different; different in their colour, in their religion, in their histories, and in their geographical positions. Nevertheless, they maintain their association because they know that in the Commonwealth each country believes basically in the same ideals and that there is no domination of one country by another. This Commonwealth association has developed relatively quickly, but it is growing fast. Already since the war India, Pakistan, Ceylon, Malaya and Ghana have voluntarily joined this international family of nations. The door remains open. We hope in the coming years to welcome new members. The first of these may well be Nigeria which is due to reach independence in 1961. The Federation of the West Indies and other territories will not be long behind.

I added:

just as you regard the methods by which the Czarist Government extended the principality of Moscow into the Russian Empire as fortunate in their results, so we do not feel that our dependent territories need regret the British connection. These are territories which cannot yet stand on their own feet in the modern world: our policy is to help them to do so. That is the essential fact: we are determined to fulfil the responsibility towards the peoples of these territories which we acquired together with our sovereignty over them. We shall continue to grant independence as soon as the inhabitants of these territories are ready to exercise it; to grant independence earlier only promotes anarchy.

I ended with a reference to disarmament:

> In the state of tension in the so-called cold war which has existed now for over ten years with only intermittent and short thaws, the two blocs have been confronting each other with ever more terrible weapons of destruction. I wish with all my heart that this competition could cease. It is not that we fear acts of calculated aggression—and I hope that you do not. In modern conditions such aggression between the Great Powers at least would be suicidal folly. At the same time it is impossible to hide from ourselves the dangers of a war by miscalculation or by muddle. That indeed would be a calamity for us all. In such circumstances it is the duty of statesmen to see if it is possible to establish some basis of confidence or treaty or in some other way to reduce this danger.

All these speeches were reported in the world Press as well as in Russia in some detail. The general view was that there had been already a distinct thaw in the cold war. There had arrived in Moscow a host of foreign correspondents, and the Russian Press had clearly been given directions to encourage the view that the visit was proving a success. It was now being freely said that differences in social systems should not be an obstacle to the establishment of friendly relations. Even my decision not to go on an elk hunt was taken to indicate the need to concentrate on serious discussions.

It was not until the next day, Sunday 22 February, that the real business began. After the Kremlin dinner we drove down to the Soviet Government *dacha* at Semenovskoye, where we spent the night. Part of Sunday morning was spent in a variety of diversions, such as driving in a troika, shooting at clay pigeons, and coasting down an ice mound in wicker baskets. I was informed that the sight of Khrushchev and me huddled together in a round basket and sliding down the hill, the basket rotating all the time, was regarded by some with amusement and others with astonishment. It marked in the opinion of experts a high degree of intimacy. After a luncheon at which Mrs. Khrushchev and Mrs. Gromyko as well as Lady Reilly were present, there followed a concert.

Both in the morning and after dinner there was an opportunity for real discussions. Almost the whole of this time was taken up by a discourse by Khrushchev on the subject of East Germany and Berlin. He repeated all the arguments with great earnestness, and I did not feel that we were making much progress. Nevertheless it was no doubt an advantage to have him speak so frankly. It was clear, however, that the Russian Government were determined to proceed with their scheme and he argued that he stood by the plan of setting up West Berlin as a free city. I replied that there seemed to me to be three possibilities. First Germany could be reunited with Berlin as its capital. Secondly if the division of Germany was to include Berlin, should not East Berlin go to East Germany and West Berlin to West Germany? Thirdly, as a temporary expedient the establishment of a free city for the whole of Berlin might be considered. What logic was there in proposing a free city for West Berlin alone? All these three solutions must be provisional pending Germany's reunification, but all of them seemed to me at least as reasonable as that put forward by the Russian Government. In a reply to an argument that our rights in West Berlin flowed from the German surrender, Khrushchev maintained that a peace treaty with East Germany would extinguish these rights. Why did the Western powers, he asked, insist on prolonging the state of war? This discussion was at least helpful in that it was quiet and without emotion, and in the full record we were able to bring back a much more complete picture of what was in Khrushchev's mind.

All this took place at the first meeting in the morning. In the evening the talk was entirely devoted to disarmament, and really was extremely detailed and long. It seemed to me quite hopeful. It ended with the following exchanges, of which I preserved a note.

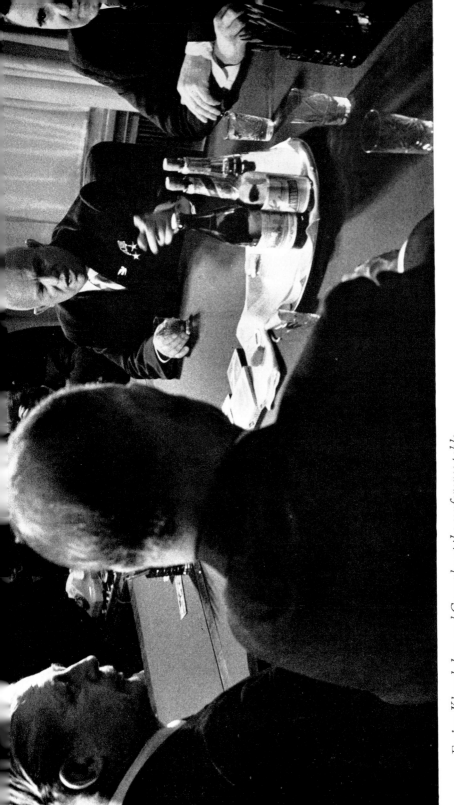

Facing Khrushchev and Gromyko at the conference table

'Mr. Khrushchev is a curious study. Impulsive; sensitive to his own dignity and insensitive to anyone else's feelings . . . never missing a point . . . he is the boss.'

Visit to a collective farm near Kiev
'We had a splendid welcome from the people, and appropriate photographs were taken of me in country clothes linking arms with two milkmaids.'

The Foreign Secretary said disarmament must be a gradual process.

Mr. Khrushchev said yes, and we must try to reach agreement.

The Foreign Secretary suggested the programme should be first an end of tests; then control over the use of fissile material for weapons purposes; then confidence would begin to grow.

Mr. Khrushchev said he liked that approach.

The Foreign Secretary said there was another idea. There might be certain areas in which one could have a controlled limitation of armaments of all kinds.

Mr. Khrushchev said the Soviet Union would be prepared to go quite a long way on that. He thought that was the main point. We should try to disengage our forces. The further apart we went, the greater the area we disengaged from, and the more thorough the inspection of that area, the better it would be.

The Prime Minister said he thought the technique, or art, of inspection needed study. If we started in a small way we would begin to learn how to do it. Then we could apply it in a wider field.

Mr. Khrushchev said that he thought that if the Prime Minister and he could lock themselves up in a room and seek agreement, they would achieve a result.

Then followed some talk about a possible Summit meeting.

After this strange but agreeable Sunday with its wide diversity of occupations ranging from serious although informal discussions to the various amusements prepared for our benefit, the first formal meeting took place in the Kremlin on Monday 23 February. We met in a long and narrow room, apparently at the very centre of the Kremlin complex. Khrushchev took the head of the table, which, like the rest of the furniture, was of simple polished wood; I sat upon his right with my colleagues next to me. Gromyko, Mikoyan and the others were upon his left. The talks covered much the same ground but in a rather less relaxed mood. Since the German question had been discussed on the previous day in some detail, Khrushchev began by saying that he had only one point to add. The draft peace treaty which the Soviet Government had circulated to the United Kingdom Government and other Governments proceeded from the basis of the Potsdam Agreement. But perhaps some

u

of the articles of the draft could be amended in negotiation. For instance, the draft had suggested that the two parts of Germany should leave NATO and the Warsaw Pact. Perhaps another way out could be found; and the Soviet Union for its part would have no objection to Western Germany remaining in NATO and Eastern Germany in the Warsaw Pact, for a period. After this introduction Selwyn Lloyd suggested that we might take note of what had been said and now proceed to discuss disarmament. There then followed a long, inconclusive, but by no means discouraging, discussion. After a detailed account of the history of disarmament over the years in the course of which Khrushchev claimed that the Soviet Union had been the first to produce the hydrogen bomb and inter-continental ballistic missile, he added that the only sensible thing to do was to accept our differences on other issues and at least achieve common agreement in a disarmament policy. For this he thought that the best thing would be to have a meeting of Heads of Government to work out principles, to give directions to the Foreign Ministers and then 'lock them up with a limited supply of bread and water and tell them to reach agreement'. In replying I said that I found Khrushchev's remarks of great interest, especially the last suggestion. Gromyko observed that it left open one practical question—how much bread and water? Khrushchev at once declared that he and I would settle that matter without difficulty. In the more serious part of my answer I observed that both of us had seen two wars. If the first had happened almost by mistake, the second had been planned and plotted by wicked men. We all agreed that some-thing must be done to avoid a third tragedy. There had been two possible methods of approach up to the present. The long and laborious verbal contests in the United Nations had not led to very much progress. A Summit meeting of Heads of Governments was now suggested. But great as was my natural respect for Prime Ministers, and both Khrushchev and I belonged to that trade union, I did not see how we could deal with this kind of problem in the five or six days of a meeting. Could we not tackle the matter by another method? There were already the scientists working at Geneva. Could we not get a quick agreement on the stopping of tests with some reasonable compromise on inspection? It was quite true that this would not bring about disarmament; but it would be a start. Could we not then put the scientists on to study further questions from the control of nuclear tests to a system of the limitation and inspection and control of armaments, whether conventional or unconventional, in some area of Europe big or small? Khrushchev did not quite agree, for he felt that the scientists were often as prejudiced as the politicians. Indeed at the Surprise Attack Conference at Geneva a representative of the West had started to ask technical details about Soviet rockets. There then followed a somewhat desultory discussion, in which I suspected Khrushchev of trying to drive a wedge between us and the Americans. Nevertheless the session ended on a very friendly note, and indeed before we parted we were able to move on to some quite practical talks about trade and so-called 'cultural relations'.

We lunched alone at the Embassy, and I was able to get off some telegrams to my colleagues in London, as well as to our principal allies, Eisenhower, de Gaulle and Adenauer. I thought it wise to give them my first impressions. I had meanwhile received from the President a not altogether discouraging reply to my proposal for a compromise on the question of control, if an agreement on nuclear tests could be reached. On the immediate question of Germany, I had to report to all my friends that Khrushchev had not liked the proposal for a Foreign Ministers' Conference which we had put forward in our notes of 16 February. They seemed to him an attempt to involve the Soviet Government in interminable negotiations since we had confused issues which were open for early settlement with others which were more remote. My general impressions which I sent at some length to the President were as follows:

From the way in which Khrushchev talked to me throughout yesterday when we were out in the country it was borne in on me that, in spite of their great new power and wealth, the Russians are still obsessed by a sense of insecurity. The old bogey of encirclement has not yet been laid. Like a poor man who has suddenly made a fortune, they feel uneasy in their new situation and they are resentful and nervous of their neighbours. Whenever Khrushchev mentioned the Germans it was possible to sense his hatred and distrust of them.

I believe that these feelings of apprehension are just as real as are their misconceptions about Western policy. Khrushchev treated me to a diatribe about mistakes which the West had made in the past and about the evil intentions which it had nurtured towards Russia. He said that we had made a wrong assessment of the situation after Stalin's death. We had counted on internal difficulties to enable us to extract concessions. We had even thought 'liberalism' might appear in Russia. We had tried to impose conditions and had followed slogans of containment, roll-back and liberation. Such concessions could not be wrung out of the Soviet Union. He did not accuse us of actually wanting war, but said that we had created an atmosphere of war.

In the afternoon Selwyn Lloyd and I paid a visit to Moscow University. The University building was a vast skyscraper, lavishly adorned with towers, pinnacles, turrets and arches, together with gigantic statues. If not classically beautiful, it was certainly impressive. We were received by the Rector, Ivan G. Petrovsky, and, in replying to an address of welcome, I said that I trusted that we would be able to arrange exchange visits from students, since we had much to learn from each other. I also expressed the hope that there would be a far greater number of English books circulated in Russia: 'There are other authors besides Dickens, just as there are other authors besides Tolstoy'. I was presented with a two-volume history of Moscow University and a small plaque. In return I gave the library a four-volume edition of Shakespeare's works and an illustrated book about the city of Oxford. When the students were gathered to meet me in the hall there was a dense crowd including lecturers, Press correspondents and officials. The students gave me a warm and even enthusiastic welcome, especially when I referred to some of the great sons of the University such as Lermontov, Chekhov, Turgenev and others whose writings were well known to us in England. At the same time I spoke of the newer Russian authors who were now becoming known among us. Both of us came away from this visit much encouraged. Moreover we were beginning to become known in Moscow and the crowds were friendly.

So far the visit was certainly an outstanding success. The Press of the world, in spite of the absence of any official communiqué, had rightly formed the impression that the talks, although still in general terms, had been conducted in a most favourable atmosphere. Moreover those journalists who knew the practice of the Russian Government were astounded by the special compliments which Khrushchev had decided to show his British visitors. His flamboyant nature had led him to almost extravagant demonstrations of friendship on every public occasion. He repeated his declaration that East and West could and should work together. This demonstration of goodwill was especially marked at a dinner for Khrushchev and his colleagues at the British Embassy on the night of 23 February. In proposing the toast of Khrushchev and his colleagues, after referring to the great war-leaders Stalin and Churchill, I recalled

the brilliant role which you played in the organisation to support the efforts of the armies, particularly at Stalingrad. The battle to which that city has given its name was indeed one of the most decisive turning-points of the war. You must be proud indeed to have played so large a part in that victory.

This compliment to Khrushchev, who was particularly proud of his war efforts, was received with beaming, almost pickwickian smiles. I continued on the same note:

When we think of those days of close comradeship between us, I, for one, am sad. It is no use pretending that since the war ended our relations have been anything like what they were in the face of the common danger. In those days, of course, we had a common interest; we were indeed both mortally threatened. No wonder we combined against a common enemy.

But when I reflect upon the present situation in the world, I wonder whether we have not at least as great a common interest today. That common interest is Peace. Let us combine for Peace.

In his reply, after he had paid me a number of compliments, Khrushchev added:

What we like in our discussions with you is your frankness and understanding of the interests not only of your country and your side, but also of our country and our side. This is pleasing to us because such an approach makes it easier to find reasonable solutions that could satisfy both countries, both sides.

There followed a passage which was considered very significant.

We greatly regret, just as you do, that it was not possible to maintain after the war that spirit of co-operation and friendship which arose in the battles against the common enemy.

We understand that the original cause of this lies in the difference between our social systems. But by now, it seems, enough time has passed and the situation has sufficiently changed for us to recognise that the difference between our systems must not create obstacles to the establishment of friendly relations between our peoples, between our countries.

The social conditions in one country or another depend on the will of the people of the given country. We must recognise this fact, just as we recognise that the sun rises every morning, and must proceed from the fact that we live under different systems, but on one planet; that we breathe the same air, enjoy the blessings of nature and the warmth of the same sun.

It was at this dinner that Khrushchev proposed the health of the Queen and the Royal Family. In the course of the evening I presented Khrushchev, on behalf of the British Government, with a beautiful George I walnut bookcase and some silver candlesticks. In addition, there was a silver tea-service and china dinner-service for Mrs. Khrushchev. At the end of the tour he gave me in return some noble gifts including a Russian-made shotgun and a fine gold and malachite box. In addition, experienced journalists observed some other equally significant signs of goodwill. Khrushchev and his colleagues had come to an unprecedented number of entertainments, and come in force. They had stayed late and seemed to enjoy themselves. They had given a great deal of time to the visit and it was already known that Khrushchev himself, together with Gromyko and Mikoyan and other leading ministers, would go with me to Kiev and Leningrad. This was an almost unprecedented favour. In addition, my public speeches were issued immediately by the Russian agencies and were highlighted in the Russian Press. The first three days, therefore, had more than satisfied our expectations.

The next day, 24 February, the Foreign Secretary and I left early in the morning for the Nuclear Research Station at Dubna. Gromyko and Frol Kozlov came with us. The Director explained to us the work on which the three hundred scientists employed in this institute were chiefly engaged. Naturally I understood little of what was shown to me, but this would have been equally true in visiting a similar institute at home. The Press again were admitted, and full reports appeared both in the Russian Press and all over the world. One of the points which the Director impressed upon me was that nearly half of these scientists had come from other Socialist countries, stretching from Albania to China.

On our return we found that while we were thus engaged a hundred and twenty miles from Moscow, Khrushchev had delivered an important and at first sight wholly unexpected speech in public. In the course of the afternoon our officials were able to obtain a copy, the text of which was being circulated by the Tass agency all over the world. It was apparently a public speech made as part of his election campaign—for it seemed that a General Election was at the time proceeding. But in a country where these contests are purely formal, the character of the speech could hardly be regarded as a sudden outburst intended only for local consumption. Although the references to our visit were cordial, and there were several passages underlining the desire for friendly relations between Russia and Britain, the whole effect of this sudden and unexpected oration—or declaration—of which we had been given no warning was in the circumstances deplorable. Khrushchev began by blaming Western powers for having proposed a Foreign Ministers' Conference on Germany, while excluding the foreign ministers of Czechoslovakia and Poland, Germany's neighbours and the victims of German aggression. He added

> the West wants to inveigle us in diplomatic talk, in the labyrinth of which the Soviet Union has had many years of experience—a bog without an exit. . . . It would be better if the Great Powers had a meeting of Heads of Government with full powers. . . .

He criticised in harsh terms Eisenhower and Dulles. About Adenauer he was brutally offensive. One of the greatest opponents of Soviet plans was Dr. Adenauer. To him he would say, 'Your policy contradicts the Christian interpretation, and you should reflect about it.' After some friendly words about Egypt and Iraq—'Russia will always stand by those who are fighting for liberation and against oppression'–he turned to a violent attack upon the Shah of Iran. The Shah had promised to work for good relations with Russia 'but then we found out about his backstage activities. We know about these secrets . . . literally everything.' The Shah had signed, or was about to sign, a pact with the United States. 'The text is already drawn up. We have this text.' The speech ended with an attack upon the 'so-called people's capitalism' in Britain, United States, France and elsewhere. This was a sham; capitalism remained a system dominated by poverty and mass unemployment. The only surprise was the offer of an immediate non-aggression pact with Britain.

The full report of this unexpected and offensive attack, particularly directed against our allies, was brought to us at the Embassy, where Selwyn Lloyd and I were resting. The Press representatives, British and foreign, were buzzing with excitement. Nevertheless, whatever our feelings, the programme had to be fulfilled without interruption.

At 7.30 p.m. there was a reception at the British Embassy, at which the Ambassador was the host and to which a vast number of people had been invited. Khrushchev and all the leading members of his Government again attended–a great compliment. They stayed a long time and were in apparently rollicking form, indulging in a good deal of schoolboy bandying of the usual quips and somewhat heavy jokes. There was a long and bantering exchange with Selwyn Lloyd about the relative merits of Scotch whisky and Californian wine. More serious argument came between Mikoyan and Selwyn Lloyd on the question of 'parity'. This was conducted in public and with good humour, but Khrushchev himself intervened and seemed to enjoy the public raillery, talking freely to the crowd of journalists of all countries. Some of these, including Emrys Hughes, were Labour Members of Parliament, acting as correspondents. The evening was long, the rooms intolerably hot, and at one moment I was overcome with faintness. However, after twenty minutes' rest I came back into the turmoil. At one stage I had a few minutes' talk with Khrushchev in a private room, but neither he nor I referred to the speech, which I knew would by tomorrow fill the Press and command the interest of the Western world.

After the reception Selwyn Lloyd and I drove out to a *dacha* some miles from Moscow which had been put at our disposal by the Soviet Government. It was a charming house of the usual Russian style, built of birchwood—much polished wood, polished floors, and simple but very comfortable chairs. I was tired and had not yet altogether thrown off the cold which I had when I left England. The night was for sleeping, the morning for reflection.

But reflection involves deliberation—if possible discussion, even debate. In the circumstances in which we found ourselves on the morning of Wednesday 25 February, the Foreign Secretary and I were faced with many difficulties. We had yet no reaction from the British or foreign Press as to the effect of Khrushchev's speech. Harold Evans, assisted by Peter Hope, the Head of the News Department of the Foreign Office, was able to provide us with a clear picture of the messages which the correspondents had filed; and although we had not seen, we could imagine, the headlines. Nor had we any official message from any of the capitals. We must therefore act upon our own initiative and follow our own instincts. Discussion was of course impossible in the guest house, or *dacha*, otherwise so attractive. It is said that walls have ears; certainly these wooden walls and the charming furniture with which we were surrounded would not be lacking in those essential aids to modern diplomacy. We must therefore deliberate outside in the snow, keeping as far as possible, so we had been warned, from the trees in the park; for in these too there were believed to lurk hidden dangers. Khrushchev was coming with his colleagues to lunch with us at 12.30, after which there would be a discussion—this time a vital discussion. So after a lavish breakfast, where caviare usurped the role of marmalade, Selwyn Lloyd and I sallied forth into the grounds of our little estate. You must imagine two middle-aged, not to say elderly, politicians, clothed in fur coats, fur hats and above all the inevitable but essential galoshes, tramping up and down with their advisers and engaged in long and earnest discussion—*sotto voce*—about a situation which if not immediately dangerous, threatened to become ludicrous. Since there was little material on which to base a judgement, it was clear that we must 'play it by ear'. Having come to this prudent, if somewhat vague, decision, we returned as quickly as possible to the well-warmed rooms with their agreeable surroundings.

One of Khrushchev's charms was his inability to hide his feelings. Many of the Russians in high places appeared to be almost wooden in their correctness. These orthodox bureaucrats permitted themselves scarcely any relaxation and, in the presence of the chief, little emotion. But Khrushchev, expansive, irrepressible, eloquent, seemed almost cast from a different mould. All the rest, with a few exceptions, were office-men, and as far as one could see, yes-men. Mikoyan, the sole survivor through many troubled days, in turn Menshevik, Bolshevik, follower of Lenin, of Stalin, of the short Cabinet Government that followed Stalin's death, and now apparently in high favour with Khrushchev, was a subtle oriental of a type who would make his way equally well in London, New York or Moscow. But Khrushchev with all his faults and crudities still gave one an impression of an excitable, petulant, occasionally impossible, but not unlovable extrovert. I wondered what would be his mood when he and his friends came to lunch with us today. I had not long to wait. While he was enjoying all the delicacies which we as nominal hosts provided for our guests, I could see in his face a sly, but rather engaging, expression of a schoolboy who has been caught doing something wrong, is conscious of his culpability, but certainly intends to brazen it out. As we sat down after luncheon, not at the conference table, but in armchairs drawn round the fire, it seemed to me that through the haze of cigar smoke and the fumes of alcohol, he gave me a wink. Oh yes, the speech to his constituents had been very naughty, but it had been great fun.

With Khrushchev came as before Gromyko, Mikoyan and Malik, the Ambassador in London. The Foreign Secretary and I had with us Sir Norman Brook and Sir Patrick Dean. The interpretation was as usual provided by the marvellous Russian interpreter, Mr. Troyanovski. In addition we had Murray, an admirable Russian scholar. We trusted to the Russian interpreter, but we had our own man to check any mistranslation or mistake. This had not been so important at the earlier meetings, but I was determined that now or at any other subsequent talks there should be no excuse for misunderstanding.

I began by thanking him for having devoted so much time to our talks. This had been of great assistance to me and my colleagues. I had long been unhappy at the failure of each side to understand the other's point of view and to find the reality that lay below the surface of official documents. In the last few days we at least had been able to see things through each other's eyes. As an example we had been able to discuss freely the problem of detecting atomic tests. I quite understood the Russian fear that any control mechanism which involved visits to each other's territory might be made use of for the purpose of intelligence. I had some new plans on this which I could put forward at the formal meeting on the following day. But the most urgent questions which faced us were those of Berlin, Germany, and European security. These were the matters which Mr. Khrushchev in his speech yesterday had declared that a meeting of Heads of Governments could profitably discuss. Indeed he had dealt with them at some length. Naturally this speech was an important event, both as regards its timing and its content. I did not yet know what effect it would have in the United Kingdom or among our allies or in the Press of the world. I would now like to discuss the situation in the same spirit of frankness as had animated both of us up to now. About the possibility of a conference, I could only speak for myself. The details of time and place and level must be arranged with all the Governments concerned. I was not now going to discuss whether such a conference should be of Heads of Governments or Foreign Ministers, or a combination of both; but I felt strongly that in the period of the next few weeks or months the two sides must get down to a practical discussion of the kind which we had been having in the last few days. Matters must not be allowed to drift into what he had himself called 'a dangerous situation'. At such a conference a settlement must be reached, at least on the main principles, and a determined effort be made to negotiate on all these problems, which, as Khrushchev had rightly said, were linked together. Naturally I did not agree with a good deal that was in his speech, but I did agree that it was necessary to negotiate and to take the poison out of the international situation. So much for the method of our work. As for the substance we could not disguise from ourselves that as a result of the initiative that the Soviet Government had taken about Berlin recently, a very dangerous situation was in prospect.

After this preliminary I now spoke with much deliberation and seriousness, using words which I had agreed with my colleagues and advisers. It was my duty to make it clear that the British Government would stand by and co-operate with their Western allies. Because of my anxiety as to the direction in which events were now moving I felt it right to leave the Soviet Government in no doubt. Nor could Britain be separated from her allies by attacks upon their leaders. I recognised that Khrushchev felt strongly about the Soviet position. The British Government and their allies felt equally strongly about theirs. I would be no use in the promotion of peace unless I acted in a sincere and true manner, behaving loyally towards the United Kingdom's friends and allies. Khrushchev would not respect me if I behaved in any other way.

I thought it necessary to make this rather formal declaration because so much of Khrushchev's speech, the pleasant as well as the harsh things—the offer of a pact of non-aggression to Britain as well as the threats—were all clearly intended, if somewhat clumsily phrased, to separate Britain from her allies. I knew that whatever might be the outcome, I must make this position clear. I went on to say that all the large questions which Khrushchev had referred to in his speech, although of vital importance, were nevertheless negotiable. These included the withdrawal of forces from foreign territories, the disposal of armed forces on each side, disarmament, the limitation of armaments, the banning of atomic and hydrogen weapons and the control of nuclear tests. All these were important, indeed supremely important questions. I felt that all of them could be discussed and in time all of them resolved. They could not be solved in two or three days even with the Heads of Governments meeting together. We had both some experience of that. But by an agreed process of negotiation it should be possible to solve some of these problems and to make progress on others. 'Meanwhile', and here I used words which I had carefully memorised after discussion in the frozen park of our *dacha* with my colleagues,

it is my duty to emphasise two points. I hope Mr. Khrushchev will take careful note of them. The first is that the German situation is full of danger and could develop into something tragic for us all. The second is that it must surely be possible to avoid this by sensible and co-operative work.

There followed a pause—during which Gromyko and Mikoyan looked at each other and then at their boss. Then the discussion was continued and lasted till after 5 o'clock.

Khrushchev was obviously put out, but in the early stages of his reply he kept his temper. He began by saying that I had no need to apologise for the length of my opening statement; he himself owed me an apology for the great length of his own speech the previous day, of which I had thought it necessary to take note and to which I had replied. He would speak with equal sincerity. But conscious of the logical weakness of his position he then began to show a certain petulance. He pretended not to be able to understand what the West wanted of the Soviet Government. He had advanced certain proposals about Germany. We had advanced none. Our last note of 16 February was not a reply to his note—it had no connection except a reference to the date. He simply could not understand why the West wished to keep a state of war with Germany. Nor did he understand why we wished to preserve the dangerous character of the Berlin situation. Was it because we wanted to maintain the possibility of moving from the state of armed truce which now existed to a state of real war? Were we arming the West Germans to make use of them in a future war? It seemed to him that this must be so for we produced no argument other than the statement that the situation was dangerous. That was not an argument at all. The Soviet Government had always been in favour of negotiations, he had said so over and over again. The truth was that the West were threatening the Soviet Government and trying to preserve a state of war under cover of threats. At this point Khrushchev began to show, or perhaps simulate, real anger. I was never sure at this or at other meetings with him how far this ebullition of temper was genuine. At any rate he now began to accuse us straight out of wanting war, preparing for war and choosing our own time for war. The Soviet Government would gain nothing by the proposal for a 'free city'. We said this was unacceptable; we seemed to think that the Soviet Government should make concessions. But what concessions— territorial, political or economic? He wanted to get the position stabilised by the signature of a peace treaty. He was sorry if his position was misunderstood; it was not his fault. After a good deal of talk on these lines he ended by a statement parallel to mine.

The Russian Government intend to conclude a peace treaty with the D.D.R. and with any other country which is prepared to join in. They will follow out this plan whether the Western Governments agree or not. If the West wish to maintain a state of war the responsibility lies on them. History will condemn them. The burden and blame will lie upon them.

After saying this in a solemn way, he added that the Soviet Government were prepared for negotiation at any time. This repeated accusation of the allied desire to 'preserve the state of war' was, as he well knew, the common jargon which it suited the Russians to use in the complicated situation which followed the occupation and division of Berlin. By a curious paradox the freedom of West Berlin was and is still maintained by a nominal state of war, or at any rate the absence of a peace treaty with the whole of Germany. The Russian plan would involve the surrender of the people of West Berlin and their ultimate absorption into a Communist society.

In the course of a long discussion in which Selwyn Lloyd and Gromyko now took a leading part, one or two interesting points emerged. The Foreign Secretary pointed out that it was of no military advantage to us to maintain our garrisons in West Berlin. On the contrary they were somewhat of a liability. He had asked Mr. Gromyko why the Berlin situation worried the Soviet Government so much, and Mr. Gromyko had referred to our espionage organisations in West Berlin which he said numbered more than one hundred. Khrushchev intervened in an excited way and said that West Berlin was a Western base on the territory of a Soviet ally. It was of no advantage to the Soviet Union to maintain Russian troops in East Berlin. Espionage was important but it was not a vital issue. The Foreign Secretary next referred to the fact that Mr. Khrushchev had himself admitted a greater flexibility in the Western position. Why then produce a plan with what amounted to an ultimatum, a threat that if it was not accepted war would result? Khrushchev intervened angrily saying that he had never uttered any threat of war. Selwyn Lloyd then referred to his own speech in which he had declared that any infringement of the territorial integrity of East Germany would be followed by war. To this Khrushchev rather sulkily replied that that would certainly be the case *after* a peace treaty had been concluded. This interchange continued not very satisfactorily until at last Khrushchev asked me a direct question. If it were true that West Berlin was of no importance from the military point of view, why did we wish to maintain our troops in occupation? I answered by saying that there were two reasons. It was the Soviet Government's position that the effect of their signing a peace treaty with East Germany would be to extinguish Western rights. This the Western Governments strongly disputed. The Soviet Government could not take away our rights. Secondly we had a duty towards the population of Berlin. This was accepted by both political parties in the United Kingdom. My concern was to find a solution which would preserve our rights and enable us to continue to carry out our duties. If the Soviet Government said that there was no ultimatum this would help. All possibilities could be discussed. But nothing was to be gained by either side trying to put pressure on the other. This fact must be recognised and a settlement must be found which was honourable to both.

After this the argument began to degenerate. Khrushchev somewhat angrily declared that we neglected altogether his proposal for a 'free city'. Anyway nothing would deflect his Government from signing a peace treaty with one side of Germany alone if they could not do it with both. After all the Western powers had signed a peace treaty with Japan disregarding the rights of the Soviet Government. It was obvious that the West wanted to help Adenauer to liquidate the D.D.R. He must add that if there was any violation of the D.D.R. after the signing of a peace treaty the consequences would be very grave and it would be the fault of the West. The West went on saying 'give us access', and for this reason were trying to maintain a state of occupation, that is to say of war. If a peace treaty were signed it was clear that all agreements which were a consequence of the capitulation and occupation would come to an end. It was a strange situation to join with the defeated enemy and to welcome that enemy as an ally when the question of a peace treaty with him was being considered. Dr. Adenauer was a negative influence and served only the purpose of blocking agreement.

After this outburst Khrushchev referred to the Shah of Iran. It was quite clear how disappointed he was at the failure of his own intrigue. 'We know all about Mr. Sandys's talk with the Shah. I could supply you with a full record.' He then asked me whether I had read a recent statement by the United States Secretary of the Navy about the number of minutes it would take to destroy the Soviet Union. All this seemed to be leading to very little good, and I did my best to bring the discussion to an end. It only remained for me to summarise our position. We were all for negotiation, but not for negotiation under pressure. We were ranged loyally with our allies but I felt certain from my personal knowledge both of General de Gaulle and of President Eisenhower that our allies would be as ready to negotiate on reasonable terms as we ourselves. It was the spirit of such negotiations that mattered.

Now Khrushchev was clearly disturbed and angry, and did not respond to the attempts of Mikoyan and Gromyko to restrain him. His final sentence was significant. The Soviet Government had proposed a free city of West Berlin in which the population would be free of all danger and they were ready to surround this arrangement with all necessary guarantees. In their replies, the West talked about rights of access and occupation status which merely meant a continuation of the state of war. The West talked about defending three million people who did not need to be defended. But, when they talked about war, what was really involved were the deaths of hundreds of millions of people.

The end of the conference was a signal for a return to geniality and common sense. Tea and vodka and other drinks were freely consumed and Khrushchev observed to me jovially how much he looked forward to seeing me and my friends at the Bolshoi Theatre that night. I would certainly enjoy the ballet.

The gala performance of the ballet *Romeo and Juliet* at the Bolshoi Theatre was indeed a remarkable occasion. The theatre was packed with what we were told was the 'cultural élite' of Moscow. As I walked into the State Box in the centre of the first balcony, the cheering was loud and enthusiastic. Khrushchev made a gesture towards me and then joined in the applause himself. We then shook hands. After the interval during which we were entertained at a most sumptuous dinner and again at the close of the performance Khrushchev repeated his friendly gestures and the applause was thunderous and prolonged. In the last act we moved from the State Box to the Government Box by the stage, only used by Khrushchev and other leading ministers. I was told afterwards that never before had a state guest been invited to use it. No doubt all this had been arranged before the coolness which followed Khrushchev's speech and our afternoon meeting. Nevertheless my host was assiduous in his attentions, and it was clear that he had not yet made up his mind as to the next step.

After the performance the Foreign Secretary and I and our staffs returned to the Embassy where we were able to consult together in the comparative secrecy provided by the special precautions. Although we had as yet little information as to the effect of Khrushchev's speech at home or in the world in general, I felt comforted by his attitude in the evening. He had apparently taken in good part what I had said in the afternoon and seemed as buoyant and demonstrative as ever. We were soon to be disillusioned.

Another formal meeting had been arranged for the morning of 26 February and this duly took place in the same room as that in which we had met before. I had with me Murray and de Zulueta, both Russian-speaking, as well as the Foreign Secretary and the Ambassador. The Russians fielded their usual team, Khrushchev, Mikoyan, Gromyko, Malik and an interpreter. I began the meeting by referring to a number of subjects which had been mentioned at earlier meetings and which I thought might now be further discussed. The first was 'cultural relations' on which I asked the Foreign Secretary to report on his talks with Gromyko. This item was dealt with satisfactorily, Khrushchev observing that he thought the proposals acceptable. It would make a beginning to co-operation in this field. There was then a useful discussion on trade conducted in a very sensible and business-like way. There was a general agreement that we wished on both sides to increase trade and make better arrangements for credits. We would propose to send a British mission, headed by a Minister, to study the whole problem in detail.

This was warmly welcomed by Khrushchev. After some discussion of a reciprocal air service between Moscow and London, which again was handled in a pleasant atmosphere, Khrushchev began upon the international situation. In the course of this he worked himself up into a state of considerable emotion; whether genuine or assumed, it was hard to tell. He began with a tirade about British policy in the Middle East combined with an attack upon Sir Anthony Eden. The British Government had started the war in Suez which had ended shamefully. Now the Soviet Government was being threatened with regard to Berlin. He must tell me in all seriousness that the Soviet Government intended to carry this thing through. It would of course be better to conclude a peace treaty with both German states, but Adenauer would doubtless refuse and the British Government would have to follow him. If we did not wish to sign the treaty the Soviet Government would conclude an agreement with the D.D.R. 'with all the results that will follow from this liquidation of the state of war'. He went on to say with growing emotion that if the NATO allies rejected the peace treaty his Government would use all their power to 'rebuff the aggressor'. He asked whether there was not a parallel between the present meeting and that when the British and French delegation came to Russia in 1939 to talk about stopping aggression by Hitler. The deputation stayed a month, but nothing was done and war broke out. If that should happen again the responsibility would lie with us. He wanted peace and friendship; he would sign a treaty of non-aggression immediately. This he felt sure would be welcomed by the British people. He was sorry to differ and to part in a worse spirit than the one in which we had met. I had created this situation by what I had said yesterday. At the end of this tirade he thumped the table and said, 'That is all !'

I thanked Mr. Khrushchev for having spoken so frankly. I would not say anything about Suez or the beginning of the Second World War which seemed to me quite irrelevant to our purpose today. What I had said yesterday I thought it my duty to say. There was a certain contradiction in Khrushchev's remarks to which he himself called attention. He wished to conclude a German peace treaty as a contribution to peace yet admitted that it led to a dangerous situation. If a situation of the kind envisaged by Khrushchev existed surely we had to try to deal with it by negotiation. My purpose was to bring about the opening of negotiations and ensure their success. That must be the object of all statesmen who saw the danger ahead. I could only add that I hoped that my visit had strengthened this purpose. I would certainly go home better able to contribute in concert with my allies to the peaceful solutions of the problems we had discussed.

Khrushchev then accused the British Government of 'planning the liquidation of the Socialist achievements in Eastern Europe'. He wanted peace; we and our allies seemed to want war. What I had said today was 'not in keeping with the threats which were uttered yesterday'. Those who uttered threats against the Soviet Government took a heavy responsibility. He had nothing more to say. Khrushchev seemed at this point uncertain whether to work himself up into a new outburst of indignation or to let the matter rest. I merely thanked him for what he said and added that we were due to meet again in formal session on 2 March, chiefly for the purpose of preparing a communiqué. Perhaps it would be better for the Foreign Ministers to discuss the draft. Khrushchev cynically observed that they would have a narrow basis on which to provide an interesting communiqué, to which I replied that our colleagues had wide and imaginative minds. By this time Khrushchev seemed to have made up his mind and in a short but offensive intervention went back to Suez, to the sale of arms, to Russia's enemies, and to a general attack on Selwyn Lloyd, as a man whose 'imagination' was dangerous. I tried to keep my temper and merely said that I was sufficiently friendly with Mr. Khrushchev not to answer his remarks but that did not mean that I could accept them. I thought it better to leave things on a joking tone in which Khrushchev had spoken. 'When guns fire,' declared Khrushchev in reply, 'it is not a joke, and guns fired at Suez.' However, there was little more to be said. He had made his protest. There was a short interval during which nobody spoke and then Khrushchev stood up and began to say goodbye in his normal manner. I thought the interview was over, when suddenly he said that he understood that I and my friend were leaving for Kiev. He had hoped to accompany me, but he had to have a tooth filled, and he thought it better to attend to it at once, since at his age new teeth would not grow, and without teeth a Prime Minister was no use. He would be sorry to disappoint his daughter, who lived in Kiev, and his other friends in that city. I said that I was very sorry indeed that I would not have the pleasure of enjoying his company on this journey. I hoped his tooth would soon be put right. I could hardly imagine him without teeth. On this Khruschev said that for the time being his teeth were good; he wished them to remain strong and sharp. He would seek the aid of science and technology. On this somewhat bizarre note the meeting ended, and the Foreign Secretary and I withdrew.

Thus began one of the most whimsical diplomatic episodes in history—the famous story of the tooth. When we got back to the Embassy there was much discussion as to what line we should take. That Khrushchev, Mikoyan, Gromyko—the three leading members of the Soviet Government—should have planned to come with us on our trip both to Kiev and to Leningrad was, of course, a marked honour. It had been announced as such and had been widely welcomed as an exceptional act of courtesy. The Press on 26 February was already aware of the coolness caused by Khrushchev's election speech. So far as we knew, little had leaked about our afternoon meeting, although the French commentators had already referred with unconcealed pleasure to my humiliation. When the story of the tooth and the change in plans for our tour became known the situation was bound to become tense. Moreover, the President had also made a statement which was, as far as we could obtain reports, rather tough. He declared that he could see no hope for a successful Summit meeting. What course then should we follow? One plan was to order our Comet and go home in a mood of affronted dignity. This did not attract me very much. A gesture of this kind can seem at first sight impressive and even command sympathy and support. But as my whole purpose was to bring about better relations and to lay foundations for a Summit meeting, it seemed a foolish and shortsighted reaction. Both the Foreign Secretary and I thought it better to continue in the calm spirit in which I had ended the last interview. Let us go to Kiev and Leningrad, enjoy ourselves, see the sights and wait upon events. We would have to face an immediate criticism among our allies when the story of the tooth became known; but in the long run we should be acting with greater dignity and in conformity with our overriding purpose. We therefore left by air after lunch, attended, not by the leading figures in the Soviet Government, but by pleasant Mr. Malik and a couple of under-secretaries in the Ministry of Foreign Affairs. So far as public criticism was concerned the first reactions were as I had expected: 'Mr. K. snubs the Premier and wrecks the talks', 'The talks have for practical purposes ended', 'The toothache insult', and similar headlines filled the front pages of almost every newspaper. The *News Chronicle* called my journey a 'monumental flop'. Khrushchev's discourtesy appeared all the more marked when it was known that, whether he had visited his dentist or not, he had spent the afternoon, when he should have been on his journey with us, in receiving a deputation from Iraq.

Harder to bear than the criticisms of our opponents were the condolences of our friends. I continued to send frequent telegrams to the heads of the three great Western allies, and received in return telegrams of genuine or affected astonishment at Khruschev's discourtesy. Eisenhower regarded 'this latest instance of deliberate bad deportment as an affront to the whole free world'. To Adenauer in particular I made it clear that I expressed my resentment at what had been said about him and my determination to stand loyally by my friends. We also had to give as much information as possible and our best appreciation of the situation to our Cabinet colleagues at home. The general view was that the reason for Khrushchev's sudden change of position may well have been twofold. First he perhaps realised that he had made a serious mistake in going so far in his speech of 24 February. He therefore in typical Russian fashion was trying to put the blame on me. He may also have been genuinely disappointed at my determination to stand by my friends and to refuse any detailed negotiation on Germany. In the circumstances it seemed best to leave Pat Dean and Peter Hope behind in Moscow in order to do their best to give guidance to the Press. Harold Evans was to come with me to Kiev where he could talk to those correspondents who chose to come on the tour.

Telegrams continued to arrive both from London and from Paris.

Butler, who presided over the Cabinet in my absence, sent, in the name of my colleagues, the warmest message of support:

> Public opinion has registered the difficulties created by your host's public speech and has not missed the stiff tone of the President's Press Conference. There remains, however, a strong desire that you should probe further despite what may appear to be rebuffs—and indeed the belief that you are the only person who can do so.

He also reported that the Press and Parliament were, with few exceptions, steady and sympathetic.

From Paris Gladwyn Jebb sent an account of a conversation with General de Gaulle, in which the General had observed that Khrushchev's speech in the middle of the present conversations was outrageous. Although he regarded the position as serious, he still did not think that Khrushchev was prepared to push things to the point of war. In thanking the General for his message I said I still believed that as a result of what we had learned by our visit we were all 'better enlightened as to the attitude which, as allies, we must adopt in common in face of today's and tomorrow's difficulties.'

At Kiev we had the usual reception with a guard of honour and appropriate ceremonies. Vasili Kuznetsov, Deputy Foreign Minister, proved a most interesting companion and pleasant host. It was clear, in spite of his attempt to conceal his feelings, that he was anxious and disappointed by the rift which had taken place. After a formal call upon the Chairman of the Presidium of the Ukrainian Supreme Soviet we attended the performance of *The Song of the Forest* at the Shevchenko Theatre. The next day was long but interesting. We first drove to a farm, where we had a splendid welcome from the people, and appropriate photographs were taken of me in country clothes linking arms with two attractive milkmaids. What struck me most about the agricultural system was the enormous number of people employed in relation to the acreage of the farm. This was partly because the mechanisation, of which they were very proud, was still in a somewhat primitive condition, and partly due to the need to make some use of the teeming population. The weather was now milder, almost springlike. Although the atmosphere when I left Moscow was freezing, in every sense, here, as the correspondents noted, it was very different. Large crowds were gathered and seemed interested.

On our return from the farm we spent the rest of the morning at an exhibition of the economic achievements of the Ukraine. This, like many exhibitions, was fatiguing as well as tendentious. We had to submit to long explanations and great masses of statistics poured out by the eager exponents of Communist success. Malik, the Ambassador in London, a man of considerable charm and culture, did his best to protect us from too much propaganda. However, all this gave us some fascinating sidelights on Russian life. In the afternoon we were taken on a sightseeing tour of Kiev, which, in spite of the terrible destruction suffered in the war, was still a city of outstanding interest and beauty. We were allowed to see St. Sophia's Cathedral and some other noble buildings.

In the evening we attended a dinner at which both N. T. Kalchenko, the Chairman of the Council of Ministers of the Ukraine, and I made speeches. We had now received a report of Mikoyan's election speech to his constituents of Rostov. Although he paid tribute to my initiative in beginning negotiations and in submitting proposals for trade and culture he went on with severe criticisms which clearly reflected Khrushchev's mood of indignation:

> In the course of talks about a peace treaty with Germany and the Berlin question, the British Prime Minister—possibly under the influence of the burden of his connections with the allies of Britain—chose a tough line.[1]

At the dinner I naturally made no reference to the painful incident in Moscow, but tried to strike a constructive and even confident note. Somewhat unexpectedly Khrushchev's daughter appeared at the dinner together with her husband. Whether this was on instructions from her redoubtable father or whether it was due to irrepressible curiosity on her part was obscure. Incidentally, except for a woman Minister, she was the only woman present. I rapidly adapted my speech to make a reference to her presence.

The next day, just before leaving for Leningrad, a message came from the Kremlin. It was from Khrushchev himself. After expressing

---

[1] Mikoyan, quoted in *Manchester Guardian*, 28 February 1959.

the hope that we had enjoyed our time at Kiev, he said he felt
sure that I would be glad to know that his tooth was better. The
dentist had used an excellent and newly designed British drill! The
next day, 28 February, we left for Leningrad, after a farewell speech
and a guard of honour. We reached Leningrad at 1 p.m., where we
were greeted both by Mikoyan and Gromyko, who seemed determined to remove all memories of the disagreement and showed
us the greatest possible courtesy. This action, on behalf of these
two leading Ministers, was, of course, regarded throughout by the
Press of the world as a peace offering, and the unexpected change
of atmosphere was equally reflected in the Russian Press. This
dramatic transformation was naturally emphasised when the story
of the tooth became generally known:

> It is hard to see why the Russians behaved in this way. It
> helped me enormously. In order to keep straight with the
> Western allies, I *had*—at some point—to take a '*tough*' line on
> Berlin and the consequences of unilateral action by the Soviet
> Government. This was *not* easy to do, although necessary.
> Khrushchev's public speech (especially its rather 'Limehouse'
> character) enabled me to do this, but in *reply*. He took offence, or
> pretended to take offence, and then realised his mistake.

> Probably (as so often) the simplest explanation is the right
> one. He had this party speech fixed long ago—a sort of 'Black-
> pool' speech. He did not realise how it could be taken as an insult
> to me. He tried to cover his mistake by taking offence at my
> protest. He saw that he had acted foolishly and impulsively, and
> then made amends.[1]

At Leningrad we spent the afternoon inspecting the atomic ice-
breaker *Lenin*, and in the evening enjoyed a fine performance of the
ballet, *The Stone Flower*, at the Kirov Theatre. The next day,
1 March, Selwyn Lloyd and I drove round Leningrad accompanied
by Mikoyan and were able to see the main features of this marvellous
city—the Venice of the North. We were taken, in addition, both to
a department store and to a polling-booth. There was a lot of
boisterous fun over the latter when Mikoyan cast his vote and
jokingly suggested that I should do the same. I said that I should,

[1] 4 March 1959.

of course, vote for the Government candidate and I was given a ballot paper for a keepsake. In the afternoon Mikoyan took us to the Hermitage, where we had all too little time to see this marvellous collection.

Apart from all the courtesies, some of which seemed to have been improvised in order to fill the cup of reconciliation to overflowing, there were useful opportunities in these two days for long conversations between the Foreign Secretary and Gromyko. Selwyn Lloyd made it clear that I personally was in favour of a Summit meeting, and I believed that it would be, in proper conditions, acceptable to the Americans and the French. But the principal point of issue still remained the Russian concept of such a meeting. They still seemed to expect that practical work could be done in two or three days' discussion between Khrushchev, Eisenhower, de Gaulle and myself. This seemed to be quite unrealistic, and we were determined upon preparation through diplomatic channels or better still a meeting of the four Foreign Ministers. In addition to this question of method, Selwyn Lloyd in his calm and efficient way was able to put forward to Gromyko a clear but moderate statement of how we saw the difficulties. Gromyko, as always cautious but now friendly, observed among other things 'the British cannot shelter behind the Americans. Your word carries weight when you want it to do so.'

Before we left Leningrad we were given an advance copy of a note which the Soviet Government intended to deliver to the French and the Americans as well as to ourselves. This was formally presented on 2 March, being the reply to our last note of 16 February. After a long preamble it proposed that a Summit Conference be called. This should discuss European security, disarmament, the mutual withdrawal of troops and the establishment of a nuclear-free zone in Europe, the reduction of forces of the four powers and the prohibition of nuclear weapons and the cessation of nuclear tests. In addition to the four great powers, Poland, Czechoslovakia and other interested countries should be invited and the D.D.R. and the Federal Republic should be represented during the discussion on German problems. All this was familiar enough. But the important change was the admission that if the Western powers were not yet ready for a Summit Conference, there should be a conference of Foreign Ministers. I, of course, pointed out both to President Eisenhower and de Gaulle as well as to Dr. Adenauer that this represented a real concession. Not only did it meet our request but in effect it superseded the ultimatum due to expire on 27 May. I therefore appealed to them that we should consider these proposals sympathetically and, although some of the details might prove unacceptable, answer positively and not negatively. Above all I begged President Eisenhower to make sure that the State Department and any official spokesman 'refrained from any hasty or too hostile reaction'.

After a formal dinner with Nikolai Smirnov, Chairman of Leningrad City Soviet, with more toasts, in which I made an appeal for quiet and steady negotiations, we left by the night train for Moscow. At the station there was another speech and another guard of honour. We reached Moscow at 9.40 a.m. on Monday 2 March, and after a quiet morning at the Embassy, chiefly occupied with reading telegrams and summaries of the world Press, the Foreign Secretary and I went to the Kremlin in the afternoon for a further meeting with Khrushchev and his colleagues. Once again Khrushchev was accompanied by Mikoyan and Gromyko, as well as Malik. Patrick Reilly and Norman Brook came with us. This was our first meeting since the famous quarrel. Khrushchev began, somewhat naïvely, by assuring me that a stopping really had come out of his tooth and this had prevented him from coming with me to Kiev. He also repeated his tribute to the English drill. I replied that I had been much touched with the message that Khrushchev had sent to me in Kiev in which he had said that if Britain could reach an understanding with the Soviet Union, they could not have better or more trusted friends. I hoped that our discussions had done something to lay the foundations of such a friendship.

We then turned to the business in hand. The whole discussion was carried on in the most amicable terms in spite of the underlying difficulties of the problems.

On Germany, Khrushchev made it quite clear that what the Russians really wanted was for us to accept the existence of Eastern Germany with its existing frontiers. He said that he was not interested in *de jure* recognition. If we preferred not to sign a peace treaty with the German Democratic Republic, some formula could perhaps be found whereby we would recognise the frontiers *de facto*. He also said that there would be no need for West Germany to recognise East Germany *de jure*. On Berlin, he said that the date of 27 May had no particular significance. It could be 27 June or 27 August or any date we liked to name. He repeated the assurance about working out with us and our allies the fullest guarantees for access if West Berlin became a free city.

I suggested that the main theme of our discussions had been that problems should be settled by negotiation. I thought we had identified during the talks a number of points on which progress could now be made. If we could get a settlement on some of these, it would become easier to deal with other issues. Khrushchev agreed with this approach.

Khrushchev himself raised the question of a non-aggression treaty. I did not discuss the Soviet draft in detail, but said that a non-aggression treaty, perhaps between NATO and the Warsaw Pact, might well come as the culmination of the negotiations on the immediate problems. Meanwhile, we might consider a joint declaration on the following lines—to agree that in all matters of dispute both sides should act according to the spirit and the letter of the United Nations Charter; to agree that neither side should seek unilaterally to prejudice the rights, obligations or vital interests of the other; on the basis of these principles to agree that disputes should be settled by negotiation and not by force. Khrushchev said that he thought the principles suggested were attractive, but that there should be something about the use of foreign bases in the United Kingdom. I made it quite clear that we could not contemplate anything which would destroy the Western alliances just as I would not expect Khrushchev to accept anything which would destroy the Warsaw Alliance.

As regards the next step I pointed out the difficulties of reaching agreement on major issues at a Summit meeting which must be limited to four or five days. I suggested that we might combine a Summit meeting with meetings of Foreign Ministers or other negotiators so as to get a procedure which was most likely to give results. Khrushchev said that he entirely agreed. He was not out for a Summit meeting at all costs. If a Summit meeting failed it would be worse than no meeting. He also liked the idea that there should be Summit meetings from time to time and that they should not be regarded as a fire-brigade to be called out only in times of crisis.

At the end of the conference Khrushchev again reverted to the peace treaty with Germany and Berlin. He said that he was not trying to put pressure on anyone, but that the question was ripe for settlement, and he was only asking for the position which had now arisen to be fixed and accepted.

We left the meeting feeling that the thaw was now complete. Indeed at the ceremony which followed Khrushchev and his colleagues went out of their way to emphasise the change. At a vast assembly to which all the notabilities of Moscow were invited, including the Diplomatic Corps and the Press representatives of all nations, held in the famous pillared hall of the Kremlin, unchanged from Tsarist days, with the white walls glittering with the light of vast chandeliers, Khrushchev seemed in a gay and bubbling mood. He followed his usual plan of making a series of little speeches to all and sundry. He declared that I had prepared the way for agreements which would ease the cold war. 'Of course the peoples look forward to something more; to solutions which will enable flowers to bloom for the happiness of both our peoples.' What with the crowds and the drink and the imposing military band, the music varying from classical items to a rendering of *Tipperary*, and after the strain of a two-hour conference, the day proved exhausting. But it was not yet over. Before it ended formal speeches had to be made and replied to, in the course of which I ventured to refer in detail to the suggested joint declaration which I would like to see result from our meetings.

When at last we got back to rest I could not help feeling satisfied that, whatever might be the final result of all our efforts, at least the Russians had accepted the idea of a Foreign Ministers' meeting and the ultimatum on Berlin was in effect withdrawn.

But there was one more task awaiting me before the day was over. This was the television broadcast which I was allowed, somewhat surprisingly, to make from an uncensored text. This privilege was indeed unique and represented a very substantial concession which

I was determined not in any way to abuse. We had prepared the speech with studious care, and I was fortunate in having a wonderful translator in John Morgan, third secretary at the British Embassy in Moscow, who was a brilliant Russian scholar. We had decided that the translations should take place paragraph by paragraph rather than sentence by sentence. This certainly added to its effect. It is not usually worth while recalling old speeches or broadcasts, but perhaps it is worth reproducing this address delivered in such unusual conditions at the end of so exciting a visit, with all its ups and downs and changing moods.

Let me say first how pleased I am to be in Moscow and to have this opportunity of speaking to you in your homes. I wish that I could speak to you in Russian, but I fear that I cannot do so. So I must have the help of an interpreter.

I should like also to express my thanks to the Chairman of the Council of Ministers of the U.S.S.R. for having invited the British Foreign Secretary and me to visit Moscow. As you know a Soviet Government delegation including Mr. Khrushchev visited Britain in 1956. We were very glad to have them and to show them something of our country. I am sorry that it has been so long before we could repay this visit. We too have a proverb which says 'better late than never' and I hope that you will feel that this applies to our visit now.

This is not my first visit to the Soviet Union. I came here as an ordinary private citizen in 1929 and spent some weeks travelling in your country. At that time you were going through great difficulties and your people did not find life easy. It is wonderful to see what changes there have been since then. You are beginning to see the fruits of all the efforts which you have made to develop your country. The Soviet Union is now the second industrial power in the world in total production. It is true that we in Britain still produce twice as much as you per head, but with us the period of the rapid expansion of our basic industries is a thing of the past. We can still increase our total production and shall do so; but our population is already as highly industrialised for its size as we can expect. Our small island is only five times larger than the Moscow oblast, but fifty-two million people live there. We have few natural resources except coal and some iron ore. That means that we have to live by the skill of our hands, the sweat of our brow and the inventiveness of our minds. We must somehow earn enough to pay for the food and raw materials which we need—and which we must bring from overseas.

It's not surprising, therefore, that some of the world's great basic inventions have had their beginnings in our little island. We needed them. In our own time those inventions have included radar, the jet engine and penicillin, and the first television pictures ever to be transmitted were seen in Britain more than thirty years ago. Today in this atomic age our scientists have pioneered in harnessing atomic power to man's needs. In 1956 we had the privilege of showing Mr. Khrushchev the work of our atomic energy research scientists at Harwell. It was in 1956 also that we opened our first atomic energy power station at Calder Hall. Our giant radio telescope at Jodrell Bank has provided valuable information about the progress of your wonderful Russian sputniks. British industry is tremendously active. We export more textile machinery, agricultural tractors, bicycles and motor bicycles than any other country in the world. Our exports of motor cars are running at an annual rate of more than 500,000 and the annual production is over one million each year. Our aircraft engineers built the first turbo-prop airliner and 400 are being operated by airlines throughout the world. Our agriculture is probably the most highly mechanised in the world—about one tractor to every nine hectares of arable land. And Britain holds the world's land and water speed records.

Besides these we have also many successes in consumption. For example, since the end of the war we have built over three million new permanent houses. Most of these outside the centres of towns are separate houses, one for each family, and have a garden. About a third of all households have a car. In addition there are one and a half million motor-cycles. The number of students at our universities has doubled since 1939. We provide free full-time education for all children for ten years from the ages of five to fifteen. In fact the British standard of living is the highest in Europe. All these are achievements of which we are proud—and I think rightly—but I cite them not so much because of that but because they illustrate the way our national life has been shaped by the physical environment in which we live.

We are a nation which lives by trade. There you have a key to understanding our approach to affairs. A nation living by trade needs peace. It also needs other people to be prosperous. Peace it needs because only then can trade flow freely backward and forward. And other people's prosperity it needs because only in that way can there be good markets for its products.

That is why we welcome competition in economic matters. We believe that this is good for all of us. It is very important to raise the standard of living and to wage war against poverty. But the Gospel says man cannot live by bread alone. We believe that man has a spiritual destiny also. Every individual should have freedom to develop his personality. On this foundation our whole political system is built. We hold that the State exists for Man. In our small island we have thought a lot about political philosophy and we have worked out our system gradually over a period of a thousand years. Of course the result is not perfect, but we think it represents a good compromise between the rights of the individual and the demands of the State. For the problem of the organised Society is really how to combine Order and Freedom.

You may think it a curious system which allowed our great war leader, Sir Winston Churchill, to be turned out of office as soon as he had achieved victory. As a politician I myself have been a candidate in ten Parliamentary elections; sometimes I have won; sometimes I have lost. When I won I thought to myself that the system was excellent; when I lost perhaps I had my doubts. All the same our system works well and suits our needs.

The British system is essentially flexible. Its fundamentals are free and secret elections, freedom to discuss and argue, compromise and toleration in public affairs, and the absolute separation of the executive and the judiciary. With various local changes this system has spread through many parts of the world. What used to be called the British Empire is now the Commonwealth. This is a free association of 600 million people of every race and creed which stretches right round the world. This is not a military alliance. It has no written rules of membership. It is an association of people who found that they shared the same ideas about the organisation of human affairs. This Commonwealth association is still growing in numbers. Since the war five nations have joined it and we expect that others will follow. We do not seek to impose our system on anyone. At the same time we hold it very dear ourselves. We believe that it makes a real contribution in the world.

You may well ask—if British policy is so pacific and so reasonable, why then are the relations between our two countries not better. Well, the reasons are complicated, and go back to all sorts of misunderstandings and perhaps mistakes. But I suppose the real reason is this—that we each see the world differently. We take a different view of life and politics. All the same, we are all men and women, and I am sure we have much more in common than many people would admit. So we must somehow establish confidence between our countries and Governments. How are we to do this? I would suggest three ways.

First we should each avoid acts which disturb the existing position anywhere in the world to the other's disadvantage; for such acts must, to use your Prime Minister's words, produce dangerous situations. Secondly, let us recognise that each side needs concrete reassurances. Words are not enough. Deeds count. Thirdly, let us see if we can make a start and go forward step by step. Agreement on one thing leads to agreement on another. It's the first step that counts. That's why I'm here.

There is one other practical step that I would also advocate. Visits by delegations such as mine are all very well in their way. But what we really need is thousands of visits to each other's countries by ordinary people. Nothing would do more to help understanding. Tourism between us is increasing: let it grow much more. We have never refused a visa to a Soviet tourist, so come to see us. Our people will certainly come to visit you. In the present state of the world military conflict between Great Powers can bring victory to no one but must mean disaster for all. Similarly, in the political field; an attempt to gain total victory may well produce disaster. So let us work together with patience and understanding.

It was difficult to know how many Russians had listened or what effect it may have had. But it was reproduced in the Russian Press, and in most of the British and many foreign newspapers.

The next morning Selwyn Lloyd and Gromyko met to settle the communiqué, which was, at any rate, more substantial and even

Signing the Joint Communiqué in Moscow, 3 March 1959
'It was, at any rate, more substantial and even frank than such documents often are.'

With John Morgan (translator) on Russian television
'I was allowed, somewhat surprisingly, to make it from an uncensored text.'

With de Gaulle soon after his return to power, 29 June 1958
'Outwardly everything seemed friendly and the omens hopeful.'

frank than such documents often are. After referring to the free interchange of views and ideas and the many discussions which we had held together, Khrushchev and I declared that our common objective remained the ultimate prohibition of nuclear weapons and the application of nuclear energy for solely peaceful purposes. Meanwhile we stressed the importance of an agreement to stop nuclear tests 'under an effective system of international inspection and control'. We considered that such an agreement 'would reduce tension, would eliminate the possible danger to health and life'. On Berlin we did not conceal the difficulty:

The Prime Ministers exchanged full explanations of the views held by their respective Governments on questions relating to Germany, including a peace treaty with Germany and the question of Berlin. They were unable to agree about the juridical and political aspects of the problems involved. At the same time they recognised that it was of great importance for the maintenance and consolidation of peace and security in Europe and throughout the world that these problems should be urgently settled.

The communiqué also referred to the purely Anglo-Soviet questions which we had discussed. While noting with satisfaction the improvement of trade which had already taken place, we recognised the need for further expansion. We agreed upon a mission, led by a United Kingdom Minister, to investigate the possibilities of further trade development. We also announced our agreement about increasing the scale of exchanges in the cultural field, books, newspapers, films and the like. The British Council would come to Moscow to discuss a programme for the cultural, educational, technical and scientific exchanges between the two countries.

Naturally the main interests and indeed the chief practical result was the postponement, if not the solution, of the Berlin crisis and the agreement upon arrangements to be made through the Foreign Ministers for an ultimate meeting of the Heads of Government.

At last the visit came to a close. After Selwyn Lloyd and I had given a Press conference in the House of Journalists we left for the airport. Here again Khrushchev laid himself out to show every

x

outward mark of attention. There were bands, guards of honour, speeches and all the rest. In the beginning of his speech he made a veiled reference to the earlier difficulties:

> I should like to draw the attention of our esteemed guests and of all those present here, especially Press correspondents and photographers who can record the fact, that a bright sun is again shining today. It has accompanied us throughout our talks and is now trying, as it were, to help us thaw the ice that has formed in recent years in the relations between our countries.

After some reference to our talks and the published account of their results he ended with these words:

> A great responsibility devolves on us, as persons placed at the head of Governments. We must do everything within our power to prevent war, to provide normal and peaceful conditions and justify thereby the trust and the hopes of the peoples.

After expressing my thanks for the generous hospitality which the Foreign Secretary and I had received and my appreciation of the many striking ceremonies and entertainments with which we had been provided, I thanked him for the frankness of our talks: 'We shall return to Great Britain the better able to tackle those issues on which the future of mankind depends.'

It had indeed been a gruelling eleven days. I had now to set about the task of explanation, particularly to our allies, and to seek their help. Meanwhile I spent my first evening at home, while these events were fresh in my mind, in recording my impressions:

> In the first place, the ten days of our visit were absolutely filled from morning to night. Three large dinners—at the Kremlin in Moscow, in Kiev, in Leningrad. Two large receptions—at the British Embassy in Moscow and at the Kremlin. Three ballets— Moscow, Kiev, Leningrad—all admirable in their different ways. Hours and hours of unofficial and fairly relaxed talks with Khrushchev, Mikoyan and Gromyko. Hours of 'official' conferences, with more officials present on each side. Luncheons; tourist visits to special places in the three cities; visits to universities, collective farms, shipyards, factories and so on.

The second impression—dominating everything else—was the strange experience of being surrounded by friends and advisers—(Foreign Secretary, Sir Norman Brook; Sir Patrick Dean; Sir Anthony Rumbold; Bishop; de Zulueta; Sir Patrick Reilly (Ambassador) and all his staff) and yet being unable [except with great precaution] to communicate with them. This is because you cannot speak in the residences, town or country, put at our disposal. Every room is 'wired'. You cannot speak in a car, or train, or even outside the house, if it be a small compound or garden. There is [always the] danger of the apparatus picking up what you say. In the British Embassy, in spite of constant searches, the modern methods are so good and the modern mechanisms so unobtrusive, that (with so many foreign servants, etc.) [security is almost impossible]. This makes everyone rather jumpy and is a very unpleasant feeling. Those who stay long here either disregard it or get very irritable and nervy. (I do not myself think that an Ambassador should stay more than two to three years.)

The third impression is more banal. The consumption of food and drink is tremendous. The food (except for caviar, smoked salmon and similar *pre*-dinner delicacies) is *not* good. The drink (other than vodka—which is *very* good) is bad—with the exception of some quite nice white wine from the Caucasus. Soviet brandy is just poison.

The fourth impression was how nice and how friendly all the people are. I spoke to many—crowds in the street, in the factories, outside the places where we dined and outside the 'residences' put at our disposal. These gatherings—which grew in size as the visit proceeded and my speaking to them in this way got known—were uniformly good-mannered and attractive.

Some of the crowds were clearly anxious about Peace and War. The propaganda was terrifying. Everyone in Russia seems genuinely persuaded that the Americans, and probably the British, have decided on a 'surprise attack'—a 'bolt from the blue'. Everyone asks anxiously whether we are going to keep the Peace. They are kept absolutely ignorant of all the provocations of Soviet policy all over the world.

The fifth—and clearest—impression of all is that Mr. Khrushchev is *absolute* ruler of Russia and completely controls the situation. The uneasy period after the death of Stalin is now over. The attempt at a 'directory' has not lasted. The First Consul is in authority.

Mr. Khrushchev is a curious study. Impulsive; sensitive of his own dignity and insensitive to anyone else's feelings; quick in argument, never missing or overlooking a point; with an extra-ordinary memory and encyclopaedic information at his command; vulgar, and yet capable of a certain dignity when he is simple and forgets to 'show off'; ruthless, but sentimental–Khrushchev is a kind of mixture between Peter the Great and Lord Beaverbrook. Anyway, he is the boss, and no meeting will ever do business except a Summit meeting. Neither Mikoyan (a clever Armenian, who cringes to Khrushchev) nor Gromyko (Foreign Secretary), who is afraid of him, will ever do any real negotiation on any essential points. . . .

We had expected to find difficulties about telegrams from England and conducting affairs while away (as one can do in most capitals, at any rate). But we had not reckoned on the difficulties of de-cyphering and cyphering telegrams, or of consultation, etc., owing to the tremendous espionage system.

We were very well treated–apart from this–and all the different residences and *dachas* put at our disposal were made as comfortable as possible. Food and drink were lavish.[1]

Perhaps the only change I would wish now to make in this apprecia-tion regards the undisputed supremacy of Khrushchev. He had not the strength of Stalin, for he had eschewed, or could not rely on, Stalin's chief weapon–the Terror.

At the meeting of the Cabinet on 4 March the

Foreign Secretary and I gave an account of what we had learned in Russia and of what we proposed to do. We are to visit Paris, Bonn, Ottawa and Washington. We want a negotiated settlement, because we do *not* believe that (in spite of all the brave talk) the allies will face war over not the right to supply Berlin but the insistence that U.S.S.R. and not D.D.R. police or customs officials shall issue the necessary permits. However, we (Britain) must not get into the position we got into at Munich (1938). I will be no Mr. Chamberlain. . . . What would be the worst thing of all for the West would be a humiliating climb-down *after* talking big.

[1] 4 March 1959.

I fear this may be the result, unless Western leaders consult together *en toute franchise* and not with the idea of shuffling off their responsibilities.[1]

After the Cabinet I went to luncheon with the Queen to tell her the story of our strange experience. In the afternoon I made a short statement in the House of Commons, in the course of which I welcomed the latest Soviet note to the Western Governments. It was vital that these grave questions should be settled by negotiation and not under duress. Gaitskell, who followed, showed great generosity and even cordiality. He would not wish 'to put anything in the way of an initiative towards peace on the part of the British Government'. All this was encouraging and showed the Opposition in a sympathetic mood. I had already had a splendid reception from my own supporters: 'All the Conservative Party rose and cheered when I came in, led by Winston Churchill.'[1]

Since the most important result of our visit to Russia was the proposal of the Soviet Government, contained in their note of 1 March (delivered 2 March) replying to the allied proposals of 16 February, it was vital not to let this opportunity slip. The Russians had again proposed a meeting of Heads of Governments. But they had declared themselves willing, if the West were not ready for a Summit Conference, to start with a meeting of Foreign Ministers. It was, naturally, easy and tempting to grasp at the second proposal while ignoring the first. Caccia had already warned me that opinion was hardening in America. Knowing that I could not be in Washington for some weeks, the Ambassador thought it would be wise to send a message at some length to the President since 'the drift in American thinking seemed to be towards tougher attitudes'. The French and German Ambassadors in Washington were talking in a similar vein. I had already sent a telegram thanking Khrushchev for my hospitable entertainment, full reports to all the Commonwealth Prime Ministers, and a suitable reply to a friendly personal message which I had received from President Eisenhower. I now had to send a longer explanation to Washington to try to hold the position.

[1] 4 March 1959.

636 RIDING THE STORM

The next days were spent in Belfast—a long-standing engagement
—where Dorothy and I had a tremendous programme on 6 March,
followed by a great meeting on the next day. At the Harland and
Wolff shipbuilding yard 'I had the most enthusiastic reception from
the workmen, such as I have never experienced in England or
Scotland.'[1]

It was not until we got to Chequers on Sunday 8 March that I
could get to grips with our task. A message arrived from Washington with the draft of a reply from the American Government to the
Russian note. This proposed a Four-Power Conference of Foreign
Ministers to open at Geneva on 11 May. The date was all very well,
but the tone of the note did not suit me at all. The Summit meeting
was simply ignored.

A large party had assembled at Chequers, including the Foreign
Secretary and his chief advisers.

We had a tremendous discussion, ending by drafting telegrams
to Washington, Paris and Bonn. I am trying to get the Allies to
send a really forthcoming reply to the last Soviet note, instead of
the usual quibbling answer. I am quite convinced that we can
have no effective negotiation with anyone but Khrushchev. We
ought therefore to propose, right away, a Summit meeting. I
would like this as early as possible, but would accept end of July
or early August. This would probably have the effect of getting
Mr. Khrushchev to take no dangerous or provocative action till
then. It would force the Allies to concentrate their minds on the
real problem—an acceptable compromise on Germany and
Berlin.[2]

Accordingly we made it clear in our reply to the Washington draft
that we believed the issues involved in the German situation were so
grave that only the Heads of Governments would be able to take the
vital and final decisions. A Summit meeting was therefore essential.
Meanwhile we would be willing to agree to a meeting of Foreign
Ministers provided that it was clearly regarded as a preliminary and
not a substitute.

The next day the Foreign Secretary and I left for Paris, and here,
after a noble luncheon given by the Prime Minister, Debré, at the

[1] 6 March 1959.   [2] 8 March 1959.

Matignon, we had a full talk lasting until six in the evening. This was followed by dinner at the British Embassy.

The French really agree with us entirely over the German problem. But they are trying to pretend that we are weak and defeatist, and that they are for 'being tough'. The purpose of this is to impress Chancellor Adenauer, and keep his support in their protectionist attitude towards European economic problems. I concentrated therefore a good deal of my talk, especially after dinner, on the practical measures which ought now to be taken . . . calling up reservists, organisation of Civil Defence, more troops to Germany, evacuation of children from Berlin, etc. This surprised and alarmed them very much.[1]

On the next day, 10 March, we called at the Elysée at 11.30 a.m. After I had had a short talk alone with the General, he invited Debré and Couve de Murville, who were chatting with Selwyn Lloyd, to join us. As usual, the conference proved something of a monologue.

De Gaulle rather put out of countenance his team, by admitting right away that one could not have a nuclear war in Europe on the question of who signed the pass to go along the autobahn or the railway to West Berlin—a U.S.S.R. sergeant or a D.D.R. sergeant. In his view the only question which would justify war would be an actual physical blockade. I asked, 'Did he say this to Adenauer?' He admitted that he had not. It would depress him. He also thought the Russians should be kept guessing.

On the two Germanies, de Gaulle also said that reunion was impossible without war, and that France and Britain could not fight such a war. But the 'idea' of reunification should be kept alive in order to give some comfort to the German people. This is 'the light at the end of the tunnel' idea, about which much has already been said. La chose allemande, that must be kept alive. Meanwhile there should be practical co-operation on economic, supply and cultural matters between the two Germanies. What Dulles had called 'confederation' should be pressed. Again, I asked, had he said this to Adenauer? He said, 'No.' It was clear that the French . . . expect Britain or America to put this forward.[2]

[1] 9 March 1959.   [2] 10 March 1959.

I next asked about NATO. General Lauris Norstad had been to see me to express his distress at the open flouting by the French of their NATO obligations, including the withdrawal of their fleet from NATO command. He had begged me to take up this matter with the General. But I got little satisfaction. My halting questions were swept aside with a splendid gesture. We turned then to the danger of war. 'War,' he said. 'Do not speak of it.' '*Je ne peux pas faire la guerre—on ne me donne pas les bombes atomiques!*'[1]

When we passed to the more immediate question of our reply to the Russians and the possibility of a Summit meeting,

> Debré and Couve de Murville more or less agreed with us. De Gaulle was rather uncertain as to fixing a precise date.[1]

After returning from Paris, and before leaving for Bonn, I held a full Cabinet. As I was going into the Cabinet Room I was handed a characteristic message from Bob Menzies, the Prime Minister of Australia:

> Harold. I think you did a great piece of work. I am old-fashioned enough to think that you gave back to Great Britain her proper intellectual and spiritual leadership in the Western world. R. G. Menzies.

Too generous, but very encouraging.

I was equally pleased with a letter which reached me a little later from my old friend. It was dated 1 April; but I still think it was genuine, and not a hoax:

> My dear Harold,
> I have had a letter from Mr. Ewen Waterman, who represents the Commonwealth Government on the Australian Wool Bureau, about the gift of British cloths to your Russian hosts on your recent expedition to that country.
> This gesture has filled with pleasure Mr. Waterman and his colleagues on the Wool Bureau, who have described your gift as 'one of the best pieces of promotional work to date this year'.
> I am sure that the many wool producers of this country have

[1] 10 March 1959.

also been gratified that, of the many gifts which you might have taken produced in Great Britain, a wool product was chosen.

Kind regards,

Yours sincerely,
Bob.

I had little difficulty in persuading my colleagues to accept my views as to the somewhat grudging nature of the American draft reply. They were equally glad to know that although the French might wish to put some of the odium on to us, they shared our view of the realities of the Berlin situation. 'Firmness without bluff' should be the motto for the Western Allies. Before leaving, I sent a long message to President Eisenhower giving my impressions of the visit to Paris.

On 12 March the Foreign Secretary and I left early in the morning for Bonn. We were met at the airport by the Chancellor and his Foreign Minister, von Brentano. The conference began at 3.30 p.m. and lasted for three hours:

> The first half of our conversation was a full account, given in detail by [the] Foreign Secretary, of what happened in Russia. . . . We then had an account of the Chancellor's six days in Russia, a year or two ago. Also, a very long speech giving his views on Russia generally, and the future of Western Europe. This was all rather pessimistic. The Germans then launched quite an attack upon us about 'disengagement', which they seemed to think we had agreed in principle with the Russians. We argued that 'limitation and inspection in an agreed area' was the only way to avoid 'disengagement', which we too thought very dangerous. It took an hour or more of quite heated discussion to get these suspicions out of their heads. The Chancellor was slow to understand and seemed to cherish some resentment. I was pretty sharp with him, and this had some effect. Von Brentano and his colleagues told Selwyn Lloyd afterwards that they were themselves perfectly satisfied. The Chancellor had got hold of the wrong end of the stick, but this talk would do a lot of good.[1]

The next morning I had a private talk with Adenauer from 10.15 to 12.30.

[1] 12 March 1959.

X2

This was very useful although very diffuse. I think I got him round to my view of a Summit Conference. Meanwhile, telegrams came in showing (*a*) that the Americans are against us, (*b*) that the French have ratted—and gone back on what de Gaulle and the others had more or less agreed.[1]

While the Chancellor and I were talking rather at large, the others held a much more businesslike discussion. At the full conference in the afternoon we persuaded the Germans to agree with our view of procedure; that is, that a date for the Summit should be fixed as well as one for the Foreign Ministers. They also agreed to try to persuade the French.

We left Bonn at 5.45 p.m. (German time), arriving in London just after 6 p.m. (London time). We at once decided to send a firm telegram to Washington maintaining our view. There was already an allied working group in Paris, drafting a joint reply to the Russian note. We therefore instructed our delegate

> *not* to accept any draft reply to the Russian note except on our lines. This means, for the moment, complete deadlock. But it is a great thing to have got such complete agreement with the Germans. For (if they do not switch back, like the French) they have a good deal of influence with the Americans.[1]

I noted in my diary:

> Dr. Adenauer seems to have said some very nice things about me and our visit to the radio and the journalists *after* we had left. This is encouraging.[2]

Although the Germans, like the French, seemed to be yielding a little, so also were the Americans. At any rate no answer could be sent on behalf of the three Western Governments until I had seen the President. Meanwhile, I had to turn my mind to another subject. So many are the preoccupations and so manifold the duties of modern Ministers—especially Prime Ministers—that the greater part of the day before I left for America was spent in listening to and answering an animated debate in the House of Commons on the Suez operations of three years before. It arose in this way. It was

[1] 13 March 1959.   [2] 14 March 1959.

necessary to obtain Parliamentary approval of the financial agreement which we had finally reached with the Egyptian Government.

Chancellor of Exchequer opened—with a dull but sufficient speech, explaining the provisions. Gaitskell followed with an admirable speech, attacking the whole Suez episode, and ending with a call for my impeachment. (This was the only mistake. It was a bit too melodramatic.) It was one of the best speeches I have heard him make.[1]

After this the discussion rather dragged itself along in a very thin House.

We got—very strangely—a majority of seventy[2] although both sides had Three-line Whips and it was a Vote of Censure.[1]

At 2 a.m. on the morning of 18 March Selwyn Lloyd and I, with our usual staffs, left London Airport in a Comet, arriving at Ottawa at 7.30 a.m., Canadian time. We were met by the Prime Minister, John Diefenbaker, and drove with him to Government House.

The Canadians have suffered a grievous loss by the sudden death of Sidney Smith, Minister for External Affairs. This happened yesterday afternoon. He died of a heart attack. He was an agreeable and talented man—a university professor brought suddenly into politics by Diefenbaker. . . . He had just begun to find his feet.

We asked the Canadians yesterday afternoon (when we heard this news) about cancelling or postponing our visit. But they were strongly opposed to this.

I naturally made a reference to this sad event in my little speech at the airport.[3]

It was pleasant to be once more at Rideau Hall. My bedroom was in the old oval room which Dorothy and her sisters had used as a sitting-room more than forty years before. Vincent Massey, the Governor-General, received me with his usual hospitality. He

has aged a lot since I last saw him. He is, however, as elegant, cultivated, and charming as ever.[3]

[1] 16 March 1959.
[2] At this time our normal majority in the House of Commons was only about fifty.
[3] 18 March 1959.

I was glad that this time we had reversed the usual process by going to Ottawa before going to Washington. The Canadians certainly appreciated the gesture.

From 10 a.m. until noon we had a talk with the Prime Minister. He had with him only Howard Green, the Conservative Leader in the House of Commons.

I made the Foreign Secretary do most of the talking. The Prime Minister asked intelligent questions. He and his Ministers are *very* sympathetic with our point of view and agree completely with us about how to handle the Berlin and German problem. This is partly due to confidence in us (Diefenbaker has always been very friendly with me personally, dating from the Commonwealth Prime Ministers' Conference) and perhaps even more results from their deep suspicion – amounting now to active dislike of the Eisenhower Administration.[1]

At noon we both attended a full meeting of the Canadian Cabinet.

I gave an exposé of the European situation, etc., and of our Russian impressions. They seemed to be quite happy about this.[1]

After luncheon with Diefenbaker we were taken to the gallery in the House of Commons where a curious little scene occurred.

The Prime Minister referred to our presence in the gallery. This was received with great applause. We got up and bowed.

We heard the Prime Minister's speech on Sidney Smith. Mike Pearson followed (as Leader of Opposition) and then a Socialist. It was all very well done, in the best Parliamentary tradition.[1]

The rest of the day was taken up with further talks with ministers and between officials on both sides on a number of Anglo-Canadian questions. This was followed by a party given by the High Commissioner and dinner at Government House. Considering our early start I was glad that the last event was small and informal.

The next day, 19 March, we arrived at Washington at noon where we were met by Vice-President Nixon, Chris Herter, Under-Secretary of State, and two old friends from Algiers days – Robert Murphy and Frederick Reinhardt. The British Ambassador was

[1] 18 March 1959.

also there, and when we got to the Embassy was able to give us the latest news.

Since Foster's last visit to Europe, Caccia has not seen him at all. He went straight into hospital, where he still is. (The President, incidentally, rang up before luncheon to welcome me and suggested that we should call at the hospital to see him tomorrow.)

Senator Fulbright (Democrat; Chairman of Foreign Affairs Committee) and Senator Aiken (Republican) came at 5 p.m. and stayed an hour. They both seemed to have moderate and sensible views.[1]

There was dinner at the White House where I was glad to meet again Mrs. Foster Dulles.

Janet was as delightful as ever—but she looked, not unnaturally, pretty tired and worn.

The position about Foster seems to be still obscure. He has had a new and very fatiguing treatment which may or may not succeed in 'retarding' the spread of the cancer. Nobody sees him, except the President—who goes every other day. He reads papers and summaries of telegrams and rings the State Department. He is still Secretary of State. . . . This has now been the position for several weeks and is causing a good deal of confusion at such a critical moment.

Janet Dulles wants [Foster] to resign. She told me that she wanted to take him away from Washington—to the South—for a bit. She clearly feels that he cannot live very long, and would like to make his remaining time as happy as possible. But I fear that to keep working is *his* idea of happiness, and that he clings to the job. The President, out of loyalty to his friend—whom he trusts and reveres—will *not* ask for his resignation.[1]

The next morning we went to the White House, where the President gave me his usual friendly welcome. Then followed a rather tragic scene which is best described from my diary:

Foreign Secretary and I went to White House. President met us, and we motored with him to the Walter Reed Hospital. Foster Dulles was sitting up, in dressing-gown, and although

[1] 19 March 1959.

very thin and even emaciated, talked with conviction and vigour. But it was even more of a monologue than ordinarily, and his views much more inflexible than they had seemed at our last talk. It was a strange scene. The President sat on a sofa, the Foreign Secretary and I sat in low armchairs in the sitting-room of this 'hospital suite' . . . while Foster—in another chair, higher and harder, discoursed on Communism, Germany, Berlin, etc. He was *against* almost everything. He was strongly against the idea of a *Summit*; he did not much like the Foreign Ministers' Meeting. He thought we could 'stick it out' in Berlin, and that the Russians would not dare to interfere with us. There would be no war—unless the Russians challenged it.

The President did not say anything. I said a few words, which I afterwards regretted, because I felt I ought not to have argued at all with this dying man. Foster could *not* have been nicer or more genuinely glad to see us. He had particularly asked to see me and took my hand and held it clasped in his two hands for quite a few moments when we said goodbye. It was a splendid exhibition of courage and devotion. But I felt that his illness had made his mind more rigid and reverting to very fixed concepts. I felt also sorry for the President.[1]

When we left the hospital at 12.30 p.m. we drove to a naval installation where the helicopters were waiting.

We had about thirty-five to forty minutes in the air and got . . . to Camp David (F.D.R.'s 'Shangri-La') about 1.30 p.m. The President has to rest *before* a meal—so luncheon was not till about 2.15 p.m.[1]

The President was in capital form, clearly very glad to escape from the White House.

This is a delightful spot, 1800 feet up, surrounded by woodland, overlooking a wide valley with the mountains beyond. There is a main hut or bungalow—a large 'sun-parlour'—with also room for ten or twelve to eat. My bedroom, the President's, Herter's and Selwyn Lloyd's are in this main building—very simple but very comfortable. The rest of the party live in huts—some with one and some with two bedrooms—which are scattered

[1] 20 March 1959.

about the camp. We have brought with us Brook, Caccia, Hoyer Millar and Bishop as *permanent* members of the Camp party. Others are flown in, as wanted, and return to Washington – by helicopter.[1]

We began talks at 3 p.m. which lasted on and off until dinner.

The whole of today was taken up with the draft reply to the last Soviet note and how to phrase our references to the Foreign Ministers' and the Summit meeting. At times, we got quite heated – indeed I made an outburst just before dinner, and said I would have to send a separate note, and we must 'agree to differ'. President got quite animated. Eventually, I said that each side had better produce their own drafts, going as far as they could to meet the other's point of view – then we could 'sleep on it' and reach a final conclusion the next day. This was agreed.

The fact is that the President – left to himself – is *very* reasonable and wants to help. He especially wants to help me. He took me out for a drive alone in his car to his Gettysburg Farm in the course of the afternoon – as a break between the discussions – and was most friendly and intimate. He spoke freely about Foster – a few weeks must decide whether the disease could be 'retarded' or not. He thought it unlikely that he could go on. But whom could he appoint? Herter was good – but after his own and Foster's illness, was it wise to have a man who could only walk with crutches? Foster has been ringing up from the hospital to find out what is happening, and of course Murphy and Libby Merchant take the rigid State Department view. Herter is himself much more flexible. He is also a really charming man. As he has been a long time (twenty years or more) in politics, he is much more aware of public feeling than the State Department officials.[1]

Throughout our talks the American Ambassador in London, Jock Whitney, was particularly helpful. He seemed to have a considerable influence with the President. After dinner the great problem of the draft reply was left aside.

We had a film, called *The Great Country* or some such name. It was a 'Western'. It lasted three hours! It was inconceivably banal.[1]

[1] 20 March 1959.

Telegrams from home began to arrive, sometimes a source of more trouble and sometimes comforting. On this occasion the news proved good.

The unemployment debate was obviously a triumph for Macleod. Bevan made a fool of himself in the Cyprus debate. Both the Harrow and Belfast by-elections have gone well. There is much talk of an early election in all the papers.[1]

The next morning, after nearly half-an-hour's discussion between the President and myself, we agreed a draft reply which was in the nature of a compromise.

Both 'sides' were up early and exchanging drafts and counter-drafts. The whole spirit was excellent and really co-operative. Merchant was helpful, and I felt that the President had told his people to go as far as they possibly could to meet us. So I thought it wise to accept, among many phrases and paragraphs that I liked, some words that I did not like so much.[2]

In effect Eisenhower accepted our definition of the purpose of the Foreign Ministers' meeting:

to reach positive agreements over as wide a field as possible, and in any case to narrow the differences between the respective points of view and to prepare constructive proposals for consideration by a conference of Heads of Government later in the summer.

We had to agree to the somewhat ambivalent formula proposed by the President to the effect that 'as soon as developments in the Foreign Ministers' meeting warrant holding a Summit Conference' the Heads of Government would be glad to participate. We got off the necessary telegrams both to the French and the Germans as well as to the NATO Powers. In spite of my apprehensions, none of these raised any objections, and the joint note from the United States, the United Kingdom and France was presented in Moscow on 25 March in the terms which had been settled at Camp David. The note in effect proposed that the Foreign Ministers should start their conference on 11 May in Geneva, and that arrangements for

[1] 20 March 1959.   [2] 21 March 1959.

a Summit meeting should be referred to it. On 30 March the Soviet agreement was received. This therefore brought to a conclusion the first stage of the results of the Moscow visit. We must now wait and see what the conference would bring.

After our discussions about the Summit at Camp David we went on to a useful discussion on Germany and Berlin. This is summarised in my diary.

> Emergency planning for Berlin in the event of a blockade. The American Defence people seemed much more realistic than they had been some months and weeks ago. I do not now fear that they will take (unless some generals get out of hand) any dangerous action. . . . There was a long argument about exactly what would be done in different circumstances, ranging from a D.D.R. NCO stamping a pass in place of a U.S.S.R. one, to something amounting to a refusal of passage of our military stores. They seem at last to be realising that civilian traffic, by which the two and a quarter million people of Western Berlin live and have their being, is much more important than anything else. Since there has not been, at present, any word about stopping this, we must be careful not to take—in relation to our military traffic—action which would lead to a general blockade. Then it would be really *we* who would have blockaded Berlin.
>
> We then passed to our ideas as to 'limitation and inspection of forces in an agreed area'. The President (in spite of almost universal disapproval of his military advisers) rather liked the idea. He quite saw that we *must* have something constructive if we are to resist the dangerous Rapacki plan and what is called 'disengagement'. The President felt that we should work out big and imaginative proposals and not always be driven to a purely negative position. General [Nathan] Twining winced at this.[1]

The next and most complex problem to be discussed was that of the abolition or restriction of atomic tests. Before leaving for Moscow I had taken up with the President the possibility of reaching some agreement by a compromise on the control system. But progress had been very slow, and on 10 March, since the Soviet representatives were still maintaining the right of veto over inspection teams, the President had told me that he thought the time had

[1] 21 March 1959.

come for the conference in Geneva to go into recess, if only to demonstrate that the West did not intend to make any further concessions. I accepted this in a message on 13 March; but I considered that a date for reconvening the Geneva conference ought to be made public at the same time. To this the President agreed. Accordingly, when we were at Camp David, we had a long discussion about the future of the conference.

Although no final conclusion was reached, we agreed that we could not let the conference fail. If it broke down, it would be best to do so on Russian intransigence about controls. Even then, it would perhaps be possible to get an agreed statement of differences on outstanding points and try to get them settled at the Summit.

I asked what would happen if the Russians were not unyielding about control. President said that we should take the agreement [about atmospheric tests]—at least for three or four years—and let underground testing go hang. He knew his advisers would be shocked, both he and Foster thought the political gain would outweigh any technical disadvantage. I was very glad to hear this.[1]

On Sunday 22 March, while the President and I went to church in a neighbouring village where he read the lesson, our advisers discussed in general the problems of the Middle and the Far East.

On returning, we started on Middle East and reached a good measure of agreement on what we could or could not do together and the dangers against which we must plan. The Americans did not try to push us too much into Nasser's arms, although (like us) they are very worried about Iraq.[1]

We also had in the course of the day an excellent discussion on economic questions. On our side

we deployed, with some vigour, our grievances—on tariffs, quotas, and cancelled contracts. The situation is getting worse not better. There is a threat that all 'electrical' contracts are to be forbidden.

President and Herter both proclaimed their own belief in 'liberalising' trade. But they were very eloquent about their difficulties. Congress is hostile; lobbying and log-rolling are rife;

[1] 22 March 1959.

the Republican Party is just as uncontrollable as the Democrats, and the Democrats (for all their talk) just as Protectionist as the Republicans. It was rather a pathetic reply to our protests. For the first time in our talks, President was really embarrassed. However, we stuck to our point, and I hope the discussion may prove useful.[1]

We continued our pressure on Washington with varying success in the months that followed. The only real satisfaction we achieved was the removal of the ban, often capriciously applied on grounds of national security after considerable expense had been incurred in winning a contract, on certain classes of heavy electrical supplies.

We left Camp David by road at 4 p.m. In the course of the drive the President

talked at large about the future of the world. He is certainly a strange mixture. With all his crudity and lack of elegance of expression, he has some very remarkable ideas.[1]

His chief theme was the need to 'institutionalise' the nations of the free world. Somehow or other Britain and the Commonwealth, Europe and the United States ought to be able to develop more precise methods of resisting Communism all over the world.

He developed this theme at some length—monetary, tariff and all other policy could be unified, and our power *together* would be much more—three or four times more—than our power separately, however closely we work together. For our present co-operation depends too much on personal factors, like our own friendship.[1]

On the way back

we called to see poor Foster Dulles at his house (he has left the hospital for a day or two, but returns for further observation). He seemed much better than on Friday—altogether a different man. He talked much more sensibly, and seemed to bear no resentment against the decisions taken at Camp David. No doubt his intransigence on Friday was the result of his weakness and the terrible time he has been through.[1]

[1] 22 March 1959.

This was the last time I saw Dulles. He resigned on 15 April and died on 24 May. With all his faults, he had an element of greatness – a strange and essentially lonely man.

The following afternoon, after the usual Press conference, we had a talk with Douglas Dillon and Robert Anderson, which although frank never ceased to be friendly.

> We had a good 'go' with Dillon and Co. about American Protectionism, particularly the wool quota and the disgraceful way our electrical machinery contracts are being treated. The trouble is that they agree with us, but seem to be helpless in face of the [vested interests] which dominate American politics on these issues.[1]

The final meeting at the White House served to initial an agreed record of our discussions and decisions and make our farewells. At 5 p.m. I saw the Commonwealth Ambassadors for an hour and gave them an account of our journeying since 20 February. At 6 p.m. a party was given by the Vice-President, Nixon, with a number of leading Senators and Congress leaders, Republican and Democrat.

> They gave us quite a 'gruelling' for an hour or more – this was a most useful exercise, as these are the men who really control Congress.[1]

We reached home the following morning. The long odyssey arising from my decision to visit Moscow was now concluded. We could only wait hopefully for the development of events. Meanwhile there were some skirmishes with the Russians before the meeting of the Foreign Secretaries, which seemed to me unpromising.

I sent as usual accounts of what had taken place at Washington to the Commonwealth Prime Ministers, de Gaulle and Adenauer. In the course of his reply the Chancellor once again expressed his fears lest the Western powers showed insufficient firmness. One paragraph is revealing:

> I do indeed hope that in the conferences to come the free peoples of the West will make a firmly united stand in their discussions with Khrushchev. I know from my experiences of the

[1] 23 March 1959.

National-Socialist era in Germany how strong a position the dictator holds in the conduct of negotiations, free as he is to disregard any possible effect on public opinion and the views of his own Parliament. During the years of National-Socialist rule I realised how difficult was the task of inspiring a spirit of unity amongst the free peoples *vis-à-vis* the dictator Hitler. I do most earnestly hope that we can all learn from history, thrusting differences of opinion into the background so that the common cause which unites us can come the more prominently to the fore.

I also made my usual report to the House of Commons, which went well enough. The NATO Council met in Washington from 2 April to 4 April, celebrating the tenth anniversary of its foundation.

The telegrams from Washington about the NATO meeting are not very good. The Germans are behaving in a very crude and silly way, and the French are joining them in attacking Britain for 'defeatism'. This is quite contrary to the real views of the German Ministers and officials, von Brentano; Scherpenberg, etc., as well as Couve de Murville and M. Joxe. But the Germans are frightened of Adenauer. . . . The French are equally afraid of de Gaulle, whom it suits to support Adenauer politically in return for German help financially and in economic policy—particularly French 'protectionism'. The Americans are leaderless (both Eisenhower and Dulles have left Washington for the South—the former for a 'golfing holiday', the latter (I fear) to die.[1]

The Geneva conference was about to reassemble after its recess. Unfortunately scientific opinion had changed since the report of the experts a year before. It was now believed possible to conceal much larger underground tests than had previously been estimated. But the President, and I agreed with him, was anxious to make some move before the conference reassembled. After an interchange of a number of messages a policy was settled. The United States repeated their wish to make a comprehensive agreement covering all forms of testing, if Russia would give up her insistence upon a veto on all inspections and become less intransigent in the application of control. However, if Russia would or could not co-operate on that basis,

[1] 4 April 1959.

then we would be prepared to accept a limited agreement prohibiting atmospheric tests up to a distance of fifty kilometres above
the earth. This agreement could be enforced without elaborate
controls and these after all were the tests which were the most
injurious to human health. At the same time, research into the
possibility of effective control either above fifty kilometres or underground might continue.

Unfortunately the Russians' first reactions were unfavourable.
Indeed Khrushchev now began a somewhat crude attempt to break
up the solidarity of the Western powers. He sent me a long letter,
dated 14 April, of nine closely typed foolscap pages. Much of it
was devoted to somewhat effusive praise of my efforts, both in going
to Russia and in my visits to Paris, Bonn and Washington and
expressing the hope that a Summit could soon be arranged. But the
most important part of the letter was an attack upon the aggressive-
ness of the United States and the 'stupid inflammatory statements
being made by their military leaders'. It was skilfully drafted and
being purely personal in character put me in some difficulty. In
acknowledging it briefly I reminded Khrushchev that we were still
awaiting his reply to the proposal for at least a limited ban on tests,
which had been sent to him a few days before. I also told the Russian
Ambassador that although I would treat the letter as a private letter,
I would make known to my French, American and German
colleagues that part of it which contained suggestions for the
Foreign Ministers' meeting and the points bearing on a possible
Summit Conference. In doing so I made it clear to our allies that
while it was obvious that Khrushchev was trying to drive a wedge
between Britain and her friends, he was genuinely afraid of the power
of the United States and was anxious for a Summit meeting.
Khrushchev followed up his letter by a protest to the United States
and Germany about missile bases in Europe. When he finally
replied to our suggestion for the ban of atmospheric tests he
declined the limited prohibition which we proposed, on the grounds
that it 'left the problem of the arms race unsolved'. At the same time
he took up a suggestion, which I had put forward in conversation
in Moscow, that the number of on-the-spot investigations of suspicious phenomena might be limited to three or four a year on each

side. This, on consideration, was unacceptable to our allies. Both Eisenhower and de Gaulle rightly felt that Khrushchev was merely trying to cause trouble between us before the Foreign Ministers' conference met.

In an audience with the Queen I had referred to Khrushchev's personal letter in some detail. After a visit to Windsor on 21 April I wrote to her in the following terms:

> Since Your Majesty showed such interest in the private letter which Mr. Khrushchev sent me I am arranging for a copy to be sent. What seems to me so important in this letter is not so much the proposals that it makes but the tone and character and style of the communication. It is quite unlike the normal and polemic epistle which he sends from time to time and publishes almost before the recipient has had time to get it. This seems to me to have certain elements of sincerity. At any rate it is worth studying from the psychological point of view if we are to make progress in negotiating with the Soviet Government—which in fact means Prime Minister Khrushchev.

Accordingly, in replying to Khrushchev, I thought it wise to adopt the same tone and to send as long a reply as I could devise, for it seemed bad manners to make a short answer to so prolix an epistle. I therefore began by reassuring Khrushchev that whatever might be the occasional foolish statements made by military men in all countries, from my personal knowledge the American leadership was working anxiously for peace:

> I can assure you of this: I have now known President Eisenhower intimately for some seventeen years. I know most of his leading advisers and friends. I am absolutely convinced that the American Government has no such intention as you fear, and this for two reasons: First, they are men of high moral standing to whom the idea of loosing all this horror upon the world would be utterly repugnant. They would think it wrong. Secondly, they know quite enough about the military strength of the Soviet Union not to underestimate it. Such a policy, therefore, in addition to being wrong, would be foolish; for nobody can make a nice calculation of the precise degree of damage which each country would have to face at the end of a nuclear war. I do hope

that you will put out of your mind the suspicion that the Americans have any such intention. I believe that if you recall even the short meeting that you had with President Eisenhower, at Geneva, you will be convinced of what I have said.

After referring to the Anglo-Soviet agreements which we had reached in March and the forthcoming visit of the President of the Board of Trade to Moscow, I argued that the best method of reducing world tension was to plod on steadily, even if slowly, with discussing the issues which might cause trouble and trying to deal with them one by one. In Khrushchev's long letter he had revived the idea of a non-aggression pact between Britain and Russia. On this I observed,

the re-creation of international confidence will be a gradual process. There are no short-cuts to this goal. We must work towards it by steady and patient discussion of the issues which still divide us—in the hope that the resolution of some of our differences will bring confidence to seek wider agreements.

The conclusion of a formal pact of non-aggression is no sub-stitute for this process of removing misunderstandings and resolving differences. It could not in itself give the international confidence which we need. All the members of the United Nations have, after all, bound themselves to renounce aggression by adhering to the provisions of the Charter: but this has not prevented the fears and suspicions which have grown up between the nations of the world since the end of the war. In my view, therefore, a pact of non-aggression cannot be our starting point: it must rather be the culmination of the efforts on which we are now engaged to reach a better stage of international understanding. But it is my earnest hope that, if those efforts succeed, they may be crowned by a formal multilateral pact of non-aggression to which all the principal countries of the world could adhere. Meanwhile I would be willing, as I told you in Moscow, to make a general declaration on the lines which I suggested in Moscow if you thought that this would be useful.

The Opposition, during this anxious time, were considerate in not pressing for too much information. There was a Foreign Affairs debate on 27 April, but I did not think it necessary to take part.

Greatly to the confusion of some of his Party, Bevan made an unequivocal declaration that if the Labour Party returned to power, they would at once stop all atom and hydrogen bomb tests. The debate 'passed off very quietly – Foreign Secretary made an excellent speech, pitched in a low and business-like tone'.[1]

This private correspondence with Khrushchev was something of an anxiety. De Gaulle took it very calmly as a mere piece of manœuvring. Adenauer was more concerned, and wrote on 30 April:

> An exchange of letters with Khrushchev at this moment seems to me a bad idea. Most probably it would give the Soviet dictator the impression that he will in actual fact succeed in driving a wedge in the Western front.

Eisenhower, who was now sending frequent and confidential messages about many of his own problems, had complete confidence in my good faith. Nevertheless I thought it right, in view of my long friendship and close relations with the President, to send him, through the British Ambassador, a package containing the text of the private correspondence between Khrushchev and myself. I asked him to read it and return it. No one else had seen this correspondence except the Foreign Secretary. As I told Caccia, I had not even mentioned it to the Cabinet. I thought it a good thing to keep this private, 'because, although it may be rather a long shot, I think it might be useful to keep this line open – it might be useful in ar emergency'.

On 7 May the American Ambassador in London handed me the following reply from the President:

> Thank you very much for your Top Secret and Personal letter of May fifth. I am handling it exactly as you suggested; I have made no copy of any kind and I am sending back the two attachments through the British Embassy in a sealed envelope.
>
> Your recent summarisation of the Khrushchev message had already given me a quite clear understanding of the entire document; but of course I do appreciate your anxiety to make sure that you and I personally remain as close on these matters as we possibly can.

[1] 27 April 1959.

I should like to say also that I am in complete agreement with your answer. It is courteous but firm.

Thus ended, on a note of uncertainty and even anxiety, this phase in the long struggle between the Communist powers and the free world. Much would depend upon the meeting of Foreign Ministers about to be opened. It was clear to me that the Russians would avoid any real negotiation, but try to treat it as a mere preliminary to fix the procedure and date of the Summit meeting which they wanted. It was equally likely that the President would not agree to a Summit meeting unless some reasonable progress had been made by the Foreign Ministers. It would be on the horns of this dilemma that I felt sure I should soon be impaled. Meanwhile we must wait upon events. The path to the Summit was indeed to prove both tortuous and perilous.

CHAPTER XIX

The Cyprus Tangle

THE problem of Cyprus, to which I had devoted so much fruitless endeavour during my short period as Foreign Secretary,[1] returned in a most painful form at the very beginning of my Premiership, when the decision to release Archbishop Makarios from detention in the Seychelles resulted in the resignation of my colleague and old friend Lord Salisbury.[2] Although the Government survived the shock of Lord Salisbury's resignation, we entered, in the spring of 1957, upon a painful and sometimes dangerous journey in relation to Cyprus, which was not destined to reach a conclusion for another two years.

The conference with the Greeks and Turks held in London in the summer of 1955[3] had at least demonstrated to the world that Cyprus was not a mere 'colonial' question but a great international issue. The Turkish Government's position was relatively simple. While they were rightly anxious to protect the interests of the Turkish inhabitants of the island they recognised that these represented a minority of the population. Any scheme of self-government must therefore include provisions for their protection. If these could be secured they might be induced to agree to self-government as an alternative to partition. What they could not stomach was a solution which allowed Cyprus to become a threat to their own security. It was true that Turkey was now allied with Greece through the NATO structure. Nevertheless in view of its geographical situation, lying off the Turkish coast and commanding, perhaps threatening, her main harbours, the island could not be allowed to pass into the hands of a nation which might become politically hostile. The Turks had watched ever since 1944 various Communist attempts to seize

---

[1] See *Tides of Fortune*, p. 660 ff.   [2] See above, pp. 228–30.
[3] See *Tides of Fortune*, p. 660.

power in Greece. They were fearful of their renewal. Consequently they were violently opposed to the incorporation of Cyprus in the Hellenic union.

The position of the Greek Government was more complicated. No loyal Greek could regard Cyprus as anything but the last of the unredeemed territories of the Greek world. Nevertheless successive Greek Governments were genuinely concerned about their relations with Turkey, and anxious not to undermine the work of reconciliation, which had been slowly if painfully achieved by the efforts of a whole generation. They therefore genuinely wished for a peaceful solution. Yet it was difficult, if not impossible, for any Greek Government, except in periods of dictatorship, to ignore, even if they might try to control, the emotions aroused by the irredentist movement both in Greece and in Cyprus itself, with its demand for 'Enosis'—Union of Cyprus with Greece. Their position was further complicated by the activities of Archbishop Makarios and by the outbreaks of terrorism conducted under the leadership of General Grivas, who commanded the admiration of many patriotic Greeks. Both the prelate and the guerrilla leader were a constant cause of concern and irritation. With all these conflicting pressures the power of negotiation of any Greek Government was limited to a narrow compass.

The position of Archbishop Makarios, apparently the protagonist of the 'Enosis' movement, was also complicated by his own interests and that of the Church. As Archbishop he succeeded to a long tradition of episcopal defenders of Hellenic rights and interests through the centuries of Turkish occupation. Nevertheless the immediate incorporation of Cyprus would have involved him in many embarrassments. For the Church in Cyprus had both spiritual and material interests. The latter might well be put in jeopardy by incorporation with Greece, where the Church had been moulded under Governments both of the right and the left into an Erastian tradition both as regards status and property. At the same time the increasing power of left-wing and Communist elements in the EOKA organisation was causing him anxiety. Although as a churchman the Archbishop was forced to deplore acts of terrorism, as a politician he was unable or unwilling to restrain them effectively.

Makarios was a proclaimed supporter of 'self-determination' to be followed by union with Greece; yet there were circumstances in which he might be induced to accept 'self-government' in one form or another, combined with 'independence'.

As for the people themselves, in whose name statesmen and agitators so confidently put forward their respective claims, it was difficult to know the truth. The standard of living in Cyprus was certainly higher than in any of the Greek islands. It was significant that out of the considerable number of Greek Cypriots who emigrated only a tiny trickle were inspired by patriotic reasons to go to Greece. Almost the whole preferred to join the large Cypriot community already flourishing in the United Kingdom and especially in London.[1]

In these circumstances, my mind turned in the spring of 1957 to another expedient, for which there was respectable, even biblical, authority. Could the solution devised by Solomon in a similar predicament now be proposed as an acceptable escape for our difficulties? Or could its threat perhaps bring the contenders to a sense of reality? If partition became a practical answer we need only be concerned about the future of the military base and installations, so necessary both for the protection of our interests in the Middle East and for the support of the right flank of NATO. Accordingly, after discussion with the Minister of Defence, I arranged for a committee of officials, under the chairmanship of Sir Norman Brook, to make a new enquiry into the whole problem of the base, whether the island was partitioned between Greeks and Turks or whether it became truly independent subject only to the retention of effective British control over the military area.

The Archbishop returned to Athens on 17 April, but was not allowed into Cyprus. Whether he was more troublesome in Athens or in Nicosia, it was difficult to say. Meanwhile in Athens and in Ankara the pressure was mounting. The Turkish Government itself now proposed partition. Debates in Parliament would soon be necessary, but we still had no clear or positive plan. Although for my part I disliked the idea of dividing so small an area into two separate nations with the usual frontier troubles and with the obvious

[1] In 1956, 3,387 Greek Cypriots emigrated to the U.K. and Commonwealth; 67 to Greece (*Hansard*, written answers, col. 128, 10 April 1957).

economic disadvantages, I began, however reluctantly, to feel in my own mind that 'perhaps partition will be the only way out'.[1]

However, at a series of meetings of Ministers and others in the first week of July, a new scheme was hammered out:

> Cyprus conference at 4 p.m. Butler, Selwyn Lloyd, Lennox-Boyd, Sandys–with Marshal of Air Force Dickson; Norman Brook, Hoyer Millar (F.O.), F.-M. Sir John Harding (the Governor). We talked till eight and then dined. At 10 p.m. I delivered a broadcast and television piece about the Commonwealth Conference. Then we resumed the Cyprus talk. It really is one of the most baffling problems which I can ever remember. There are objections to almost every possible course. Although for the moment the terrorist movement is quiescent, Harding thinks that Archbishop Makarios will start it up again after the next U.N. session. In any case, it will take us more troops than we can afford to hold the island through the next few years. (The Socialists will give it away anyhow, if they get in.) If we give it to Greece, there will be a war between Greece and Turkey. If we 'partition', it is a confession of failure–means [perhaps] civil war in the island [followed by] full war between Greece and Turkey. We really want only air-bases for ourselves, for Baghdad pact and general M.E. and Persian Gulf defence. We hammered out a new plan–which seemed quite good late at night, but will probably not look so good in the morning.[2]

This new plan provided for the delineation of British military enclaves, where full British sovereignty would remain, while the rest of the island would be ruled by a condominium of the United Kingdom, Greece and Turkey with sovereignty held in partnership. These three countries would be jointly responsible, through the appointed Governor, for external affairs and for certain reserved subjects. If the three powers could not agree upon selecting a Governor, his appointment in default would fall to the NATO Council. So far as internal affairs were concerned responsible government would be created upon the general lines of that proposed in Lord Radcliffe's report,[3] adapted to the concept of a triple sovereignty or tri-dominium. There would be two assemblies, Greek

[1] 31 May 1957.   [2] 7 July 1957.   [3] See above, p. 224.

and Turk, for communal affairs. Matters of joint interest would be under the Governor, assisted by a council of six, four Greek and two Turkish, chosen from their respective assemblies.

The broad outline was worked out during the next few days and on 10 July I noted

the chief event of the day was a long—and on the whole useful—meeting of the Defence Committee on Cyprus. The Chiefs of Staff seem quite happy about the new plan, from a purely military view.[1]

The next day there was a long Cabinet meeting upon the paper which I submitted in close consultation with the Colonial Office and the Ministry of Defence.

I (or rather Sir Norman Brook) submitted [it]. (He composed it; I only corrected it.) I made no attempt to get a decision. We had an admirable discussion under the two headings which I suggested: (1) Is this a good plan? (2) If so, when and how should it be launched?[2]

We were now approaching

the last—often the most dangerous weeks—of the [Parliamentary] Session. I have tried the Party pretty hard over Suez. I don't now want a panic about 'selling out in Cyprus'. Then there is 'disarmament'—where the Russians have refused our proposals, and are obviously going to concentrate on 'suspension of Tests' (a popular cry) with no relation to conventional arms, or to further stages in nuclear disarmament. Then there is a new flutter about 'the economic situation'—a heavy fall of 'gilts' and a good deal of popular alarm at the recent price increases of coal, gas, electricity, transport etc. . . . In addition, we have telephone-tapping, M.P.'s salaries, and so on, as well as compensation to British refugees from Egypt (an awkward one). For all these reasons, I am not too keen on starting a new policy on Cyprus until *after* the House has risen.[2]

On 16 July there was

A further talk on Cyprus in the Cabinet, and a wide agreement reached on the policy which we should pursue (the tri-dominium

[1] 10 July 1957. [2] 11 July 1957.

concept). But it will be most difficult (*a*) to work out, (*b*) to present, (*c*) to achieve.¹

Following the Cabinet meeting I was able, on 26 July with the help of my own staff, to work out and circulate a detailed scheme for implementing these decisions. In the first instance we must organise a conference of the powers concerned. In order to achieve this we must get the support both of the United States Government and of M. Spaak, in his capacity as Secretary-General of NATO. I would make it clear that although we were not tied to any particular solution and would consider alternatives, any acceptable plan must allow the United Kingdom Government to retain its minimum essential military facilities under British sovereignty; must protect the island from Communist infiltration; and must ensure peace and tranquillity.

At first the prospects seemed hopeful. Foster Dulles, during his visit to England at this time, was ready to give full support, and Spaak was, as always, helpful. But on 9 August

> The Greeks have refused our soundings (or informal invitation) to the conference. We decided *not* to take no for an answer and renew the invitation; also to ask for further American pressure on them. It is important that we should, at every step, have something which will put us in a good posture as the story is revealed. Our real difficulty will be to get the Greeks to any kind of meeting where our plan can be deployed. I have suggested to the Foreign Secretary that we might use NATO. Then, I suppose, the Turks will object.²

As I feared, our Ambassador in Ankara, Sir James Bowker, was soon to report that there was little hope of the Turks agreeing to anything which the Greeks might accept.

Indeed at the end of a trying summer it was difficult to take a calm and detached view. It seemed intolerable that the affairs of this little island should throw into disorder many important countries, put at risk the great alliance of NATO, and cause an embittered argument at the United Nations. The situation was still like one of those children's puzzles where the effort to get three or more balls

¹ 16 July 1957.　　²9 August 1957.

Touring the North-East, 13 January 1959
'Everywhere the people were very friendly.'

Meeting the people
'We had a most touching reception.... Dorothy was in great form and thoroughly enjoyed it.'

into their right position is continually frustrated; two would perhaps fall into place but then the third would immediately escape. To whatever Turkey might agree Greece would object. To whatever Greece might demand Turkey would be obstructive. What Makarios might be inclined to accept, EOKA, under General Grivas, would refuse. Britain had no interest except peace both in Cyprus and between Greece and Turkey, together with the preservation of the bases which were so essential to the defence of the Eastern Mediterranean and the resistance to Communist aggression. Yet in our own Parliament, in the lobbies of the United Nations and among what was called 'progressive' thought in the world, Britain was being pilloried for pursuing an obsolete colonialism backed by her military power and using as its instrument a high-ranking military governor.

Indeed on 2 August, after a Defence Committee lasting the whole morning, I found, either through my own fault or from mere fatigue, the afternoon Cabinet at 2.30 very difficult to handle:

> Everyone is so exhausted at the end of a really terrible year (July 1956–August 1957) that the Cabinet began to wrangle and almost to quarrel. So I sent them away.[1]

At the same time,

> The Press is terrible—it gets worse every day. There is a kind of masochism which has seized them, which is infuriating. Nothing is right; everyone is wrong.[2]

I suppose this entry reflects my own physical and mental weariness. It had certainly been a rough twelve months. Nasser seized the Canal at the end of July 1956. Now in August 1957, for those who had been through and survived the hazards of these strenuous and perilous months, perhaps it was excusable to feel a little irritation. Nevertheless I comforted myself at the time with a further thought. As regards the attacks of the Press,

> I think this reflects the tremendously high standard of comfort and well-being of the people. When things are really difficult, even the Press does not complain very much.[2]

[1] 2 August 1957.   [2] 9 August 1957.

Y

If the remaining period of the year brought at least the satisfaction that with American help we were able to prevent the Greeks from mustering sufficient votes at the United Nations for a resolution demanding self-determination, I had to face in the autumn an even more serious question. In 1955 Field-Marshal Sir John Harding, at the urgent request of the Prime Minister, Eden, and strongly urged by the Colonial Secretary, Alan Lennox-Boyd, had yielded to his high sense of duty and agreed to postpone his retirement from a long and distinguished public service. During his term as Governor he had enormously improved the security organisation. Although it had not been possible by the methods tolerable either to the British public or to British troops altogether to overcome the terrorist movement, nevertheless things were under much better control than before. Sir John had been able to secure deep personal loyalty to himself from all who served him. He had in addition shown both skill and sympathy in negotiation and had impressed all concerned, even the most intractable, with his integrity and sincerity. It was well known that the Archbishop admired him. Nevertheless he felt, and I could not but share this view, that in the new phase and in the light of the new policy which we were trying to put forward, in whatever form our plan might finally emerge, his immediate task was accomplished. His retirement was announced in the middle of October, and he returned early in the following month. I sent him a letter on 17 October to express my feelings of gratitude.

I cannot allow the announcement of your impending departure from Cyprus to pass without letting you know personally of my feelings. Your tenure of office as Governor of Cyprus has been an extraordinary example of public service and devotion. When my predecessor asked you in 1955 to undertake this task we all admired the way in which you so readily put aside what would have been a very understandable desire to enjoy a well-earned retirement. I cannot imagine a tougher assignment being given to any man, nor can I think of any man who could have discharged it with greater distinction.

During the whole of your tenure of office Cyprus has been the centre of bitter political and international controversies. This has made your task doubly hard, but you have steered your course with such courage, fairness and skill that I feel no doubt that your Governorship will long be remembered with pride even by those who have not agreed with our policies.

We have all been filled with admiration at the way in which Lady Harding has so nobly shared in your arduous task. I do hope that you will both now enjoy to the full your delayed retirement. In sending you my good wishes I hope I have been able to express to you something of the great debt which the country owes you for what you have done.

After full discussion with the Colonial Secretary and others, I decided to offer this exacting and unrewarding post to a member of the Colonial Service who had won much distinction and was generally regarded as a leading figure in the Service—Sir Hugh Foot. He had proved a most successful administrator and negotiator in many posts. In all my dealings with him from the first time I met him until the end of the story I was to find him not merely resourceful but loyal. I was aware, of course, of the radical opinions which, like other members of his family, he had inherited from his Cromwellian father. But I was persuaded that this reputation might assist rather than retard the search for some solution in Cyprus. His wife was charming and talented. As one of my staff observed, 'Surely these Feet will prove "beautiful upon the mountains" of that lovely isle and "bring good tidings and publish peace".'

On 6 January 1958, Sir Hugh attended a full meeting of the Cabinet. It was not a very auspicious moment, since as already described this session coincided with the resignation of the Chancellor of the Exchequer and what was to prove, in political parlance, 'a first-class ministerial crisis'.[1] Indeed before Sir Hugh was introduced I had had to read to my colleagues Mr. Thorneycroft's letter. However, having despatched this part of the business, I arranged for Sir Hugh to join us, and we proceeded to discuss the whole situation, including

the new plan for Cyprus . . . I am not very hopeful about it, for I don't think either the Greeks or the Turks will play, whether locally or nationally. However, it will help us to have Sir Hugh Foot's [ideas].[2]

[1] See above, pp. 366 ff.   [2] 7 January 1958.

During the early months of 1958 informal negotiations through the Ambassadors revealed that neither the Greeks nor the Turks were likely to be attracted by our new scheme. The objections raised revealed a firm determination of both Governments to hold by their own solutions. The Greeks would not agree to any abandonment of 'Enosis'; the Turks with equal fervour would not drop the demand for partition. Tentative suggestions were put forward that the granting of military bases in the island, both to the Turks and the Greeks, might be helpful, although it was difficult to see how the introduction of still more elements of discord were likely to maintain peace.

Meanwhile there were many serious clashes between the Greek and the Turkish communities as well as acts of terrorism against the British. The Foreign Secretary, after a visit to Athens early in February, reported that the Greeks might be prepared to accept the idea of a Turkish base if partition were thereby permanently excluded; but they equally demanded that the principle of 'Enosis' as a final solution should be accepted.

After much thought we agreed to regard our plan as an interim proposal, to be accepted for a seven-year period during which no change in the international status of the island should be made. We hoped by altering our scheme from a final to a provisional solution to meet some of the rooted objections of the rival parties.

At the same time the Americans certainly did their best to support us both with diplomatic pressure and argument. At a NATO Foreign Ministers' meeting held in Copenhagen on 6 May, the Foreign Secretary made a further but fruitless effort with both the Greeks and the Turks. Dulles was also to be present at Copenhagen, and in order to secure every help from him, I addressed the following minute to the Foreign Secretary before he left:

> If we are to go on with this Tri-Dominium Plan, we must do it with full enthusiasm. It must not be a tactical manœuvre. We must be able to say that it is the right thing for everybody and really believe it. I hope, therefore, when you talk to Dulles about it you will not fail to let him know that I, personally, am prepared to risk a great deal and put all the effort that I can command into persuading both our countrymen and the rest of the world that

this is a good and even a noble plan—an example of how Western countries should be able to sink their old differences in the light of much greater dangers. If the Americans are convinced of this, they might put a lot of weight behind it in persuading the Greeks and the Turks. But I do not think Dulles will do so unless he is sure that we really mean to run this as our plan seriously. I think also it might well appeal to the President. It would be very much in the spirit of what he has preached and practised—co-operation between allies.

My colleagues were resolute that we should continue our efforts. So far our proposals had merely been a matter for secret discussion. The point must soon come when, if we could make no further progress by such methods, we must publish them to the world in the hope of bringing the contestant parties to a more reasonable attitude.

In spite of the rival attractions of the Lebanon crisis and the railway strike, I called a meeting at Chequers for Sunday 11 May to agree on details. There were present Selwyn Lloyd, Lennox-Boyd (Colonial Secretary), Sir Hugh Foot (who had come home especially for this conference), Sir Norman Brook and a number of officials. The conference lasted all day. I had to leave Chequers at 6 p.m. to go to a meeting in London with Ministers concerned in the railway dispute, but in the course of the day we made real progress:

> The Governor was very helpful and I was impressed by his fervour. After several hours' discussion, a new draft was prepared, which embodies (*a*) Governor Foot's plans for *internal* self-government; (*b*) our original plans for the external solution of 'Tri-dominium'.[1]

Parliament had been very patient in not pressing us over Cyprus. Indeed nearly a year had passed since the last debate. This was, no doubt, partly due to so many other troubles engaging their attention. When, therefore, the Colonial Secretary made a holding statement on 19 May explaining that the details of the Government's new proposals could not yet be announced since they were being privately discussed with the interested Governments, the House of Commons accepted the explanation without protest.

[1] 11 May 1958.

Finally, on 5 June, instructions were given to our Ambassadors in Ankara and Athens to communicate the full text of our proposed plan to the Greek and the Turkish Governments on 10 June. On 7 June I left for Washington, and while I was there, since inter-communal rioting in Cyprus was increasing, I received a message suggesting that I should ask the Americans to use their influence with the Turkish Government to restrain their supporters. But the clashes between the two communities continued to grow. However, the Governor was firm and in complete command of the situation.

The first reaction to our official communication came from Ahnan Menderes, the Prime Minister of Turkey. It was disappointing. He declared that nothing short of partition, itself a great sacrifice on the part of Turkey, could assuage Turkish fears. Regardless of the fact that in previous discussion he had objected to our original plan on the ground that it was not provisional, he now said that it was unacceptable because 'unless the final international status of Cyprus were to be determined, no plan . . . could successfully be given effect in Cyprus'.

When the Greeks made their reply on 21 June they took a new and unexpected position. They now objected to Turkey playing any part in the controversy on the grounds that by the Treaty of Lausanne Turkey had surrendered all her rights. This seemed a strange argument since under the same Treaty Greece had equally accepted the British annexation.

On 16 June the NATO Council welcomed our efforts and, except for the Greek and Turkish representatives who naturally reserved their position, were unanimous in their praise. Accordingly soon after my return from Washington and after a talk with Gaitskell and some of his colleagues, on 19 June I formally set out, by a statement in Parliament, the British Government's proposals. Although the final agreement was made on a more comprehensive and, happily, more permanent basis, the impetus given by our plan and above all by our determination to implement our scheme, unless any other more satisfactory one could be agreed upon, was one of the main causes of the settlement reached nine months later. It is therefore of some interest to recall the terms of what was generally welcomed as a constructive and imaginative policy.

After declaring the main purpose of our policy to be the achievement of a settlement acceptable both to the two communities in
Cyprus and the Greek and Turkish Governments, subject to the
safeguarding of the British bases and installations, I said that we
felt it our duty to give a lead out of the present deadlock. I continued:

The following is an outline of the partnership plan:
Cyprus should enjoy the advantages of association not only
with the United Kingdom, and, therefore, with the British
Commonwealth, but also with Greece and Turkey.
Since the three Governments of the United Kingdom, Greece
and Turkey all have an interest in Cyprus, Her Majesty's
Government will welcome the co-operation and participation of
the two other Governments in a joint effort to achieve the peace,
progress and prosperity of the island.
The Greek and Turkish Governments will each be invited to
appoint a representative to co-operate with the Governor in
carrying out this policy.
The island will have a system of representative Government with
each community exercising autonomy in its own communal
affairs.
In order to satisfy the desire of the Greek and Turkish Cypriots
to be recognised as Greeks and Turks, Her Majesty's Government will welcome an arrangement which gives them Greek or
Turkish nationality, while enabling them to retain British
nationality.
To allow time for the new principle of partnership to be fully
worked out and brought into operation under this plan in the
necessary atmosphere of stability, the international status of the
island will remain unchanged for seven years.
A system of representative government and communal autonomy will be worked out by consultation with representatives of
the two communities and with the representatives of the Greek
and Turkish Governments.
The essential provisions of the new constitution will be:
(a) There will be a separate House of Representatives for each
of the two communities, and these Houses will have final legislative authority in communal affairs.
(b) Authority for internal administration, other than communal
affairs and internal security, will be undertaken by a Council

presided over by the Governor and including the representatives of the Greek and Turkish Governments and six elected Ministers drawn from the Houses of Representatives, four being Greek Cypriots and two Turkish Cypriots.

(c) The Governor, acting after consultation with the representatives of the Greek and Turkish Governments, will have reserve powers to ensure that the interests of both communities are protected.

(d) External affairs, defence and internal security will be matters specifically reserved to the Governor acting after consultation with the representatives of the Greek and Turkish Governments.

(e) The representatives of the Greek and Turkish Governments will have the right to require any legislation which they consider to be discriminatory to be reserved for consideration by an impartial tribunal.[1]

I concluded with these words:

If the full benefits of this policy are to be realised, it is evident that violence must cease. Subject to this, Her Majesty's Government intend to take progressive steps to relax the Emergency Regulations and eventually to end the state of emergency. This process would include the return of those Cypriots at present excluded from the island under the Emergency Regulations.

A policy based on these principles and proposals will give the people of the island a specially favoured and protected status. Through representative institutions they will exercise authority in the management of the island's internal affairs, and each community will control its own communal affairs. While the people of the island enjoy these advantages, friendly relations and practical co-operation between the United Kingdom, Greece and Turkey will be maintained and strengthened as Cyprus becomes a symbol of co-operation instead of a cause of conflict between the three Allied Governments.[1]

On 26 June a full debate took place. Since quite a lot of other matters were attracting the attention of Members as well as Ministers—the long bus strike had just ended, the railway strike was in the balance, and the Middle East crisis was in full swing— the House of Commons, which finds it difficult to think of more

[1] *Hansard*, 19 June 1958.

than one thing at a time, was in no mood for any violent dispute. The Colonial Secretary made an admirable speech, perfect in tone and manner, and went out of his way to pay a deserved tribute to Gaitskell and his colleagues for their forbearance.

Cyprus debate. This went off very well, partly due to the efforts of Sir Hugh Foot and the Opposition leaders. After much dispute amongst themselves, the Socialist 'Shadow Cabinet' decided not to have a division. But when this was put to the Party this morning, there was much argument. In the end, the majority agreed not to vote.

Callaghan, who spoke after Alan Lennox-Boyd, performed his task with great skill. Bevan, who wound up before me, with such obvious dislike of being sensible and moderate that it amused everybody including himself. Actually, the decision of the Opposition has great importance. For it must have persuaded the Greeks that, even if the Socialists win the next General Election here, they will be no nearer to 'Enosis'. Bevan in particular made it clear that by 'self-determination' they did *not* mean the imposition of majority rule on the minority.[1]

More often than not a debate in Parliament has little effect upon the development of any crisis overseas. But on this occasion it could be said that the firm and patriotic line which Gaitskell impressed upon his Party was of real value. The knowledge that none of the contestants could hope to gain more from the Opposition than from the Government had in the course of the next few months a sobering and fruitful effect.

Although the response of both the Greek and Turkish Prime Ministers was disappointing, this was not altogether unexpected. In writing to Diefenbaker, the Prime Minister of Canada, on 1 July, I said:

On the whole I think that our Cyprus plan has got off to a better start than I thought likely. I am relieved that both the Greeks and the Turks objected in the first instance. It would have been fatal if one had accepted and the other refused. I hope gradually to wear them down to a kind of acquiescence, if not acceptance, and then perhaps peace may come in the island.

[1] 26 June 1958.

Y2

Unhappily, fighting between the two communities was about to reach its peak. In order to prevent something like civil war, the Governor, with great courage, ordered the arrest of more than a thousand Greek and Turkish suspects. At the same time I asked the Greek and Turkish Premiers to make an appeal to their communities to end violence; to this in due course both agreed. There followed much diplomatic discussion, from which I concluded that both Athens and Ankara were becoming increasingly anxious and more ready to consider some accommodation. The Turks were now moving towards acceptance, and even the Greeks were chiefly concerned about the proposal that each Government should appoint its representative to the Governor's council. That a Turkish representative should act officially in this capacity seemed to the Greeks an admission of the Turkish interest, contrary to the legal and constitutional basis on which they had rested for so long.

The Baghdad Pact meeting, at the end of July, gave us an opportunity for a private discussion with Menderes and Fatin Zorlu, the Foreign Minister. They came to see me on 29 July accompanied by Nuri Birgi, the highly intelligent Turkish Ambassador in London. Our visitors

came through the garden door, from which also they left some three hours later. It was a curious talk. What it amounted to was this: Turkey now *accepts*, in full, the British plan for Cyprus. The Turkish Government (which a few weeks ago was inciting riots against it, both in Cyprus and in Turkey) now regards it as fair, honourable, statesmanlike, well-balanced! But—and here is the point—it must be 'the plan, the whole plan, and nothing but the plan'. It is so beautifully constructed—say the Turks—that the slightest alteration or amendment will destroy its equilibrium and mar its symmetry. (The object, of course, is to make it quite certain that the Greeks—who want some important amendments—will reject the plan.) If we, the British, will undertake to carry out the plan without amendment, the Turks will co-operate—will call off violence—and will abandon all their other claims—partition, a military base, etc.

I had the Foreign Secretary and the Colonial Secretary with me. We were rather surprised at this, which needed quite long speeches from them all to explain. I said that we were very gratified to feel that the Turks now thought our plan a good one. We meant to go on with it and would rely on their help.[1]

I had already made known my willingness to go to Athens and Ankara if it would help to obtain an agreement. As Menderes knew, I was anxiously awaiting a formal invitation both from him and the Greek Prime Minister.

While I understood that the Turkish acceptance was conditional on the plan remaining substantially unchanged, I must retain the right to discuss and perhaps accept Greek amendments. I would then put these to the Turks.[1]

A long and confused discussion followed.

The Turks tried to tie us down to proceeding with the plan forthwith, with no real negotiation with Athens. Eventually, a short note was prepared, summarising the discussion—to be looked at more carefully the next day.[1]

The next day there followed a curious sequel.

Apparently the Turks produced this morning a *bout de papier* which the Foreign Office found quite unacceptable. It tried to tie us down, in definite times and stages, to 'implementing the plan' and, in a word, to turn a 'gentleman's agreement' into an attorney's document. We put up a simpler counter-proposal. The Turks, who had intended to leave at 2.30 p.m., stayed on and asked to see me again. To this I agreed, and they came at 9.30 p.m. But this time I made them come through the front door. As they didn't want to be known to be doing more than saying 'goodbye' this ensured a reasonably short meeting. Having thought over how to treat them, it seemed the best thing was to express amazement— and some resentment—at their behaviour. Actually Menderes, who is a nice chap, was rather ashamed of himself. Zorlu . . . had gone. It ended up by my re-stating what I thought our agreement was. I made it clear that I should not hold them to their acceptance of the British plan *if* (as was indeed probable) I had to ask them to consider amendments later (to meet the Greeks). They would be absolutely and honourably free to accept or reject them. Finally, I said I thought all these attempts to put into

[1] 29 July 1958.

a sort of legal form what we had agreed as gentlemen, had better be torn up—which they were. The Turks had really no alternative [but] to accept this—which they did as gracefully as possible.[1]

Meanwhile the news from the island remained depressing. Two more British soldiers, one a colonel in the R.A.S.C., were murdered on 3 August. On the next day

> I got the news of EOKA's decision to declare a truce, till 10 August. Then—if *provoked*—terrorism would be resumed. It seems difficult to interpret this. We must await the Governor's views.[2]

The Governor was clear in his recommendation.

> A very large operation is going on—2,000 or more troops employed—following on the arrests made some days ago. It is hoped that a number of the worst terrorists are in the circle. No doubt Grivas and the inner circle will continue to escape—as they have before. But if to continue this operation constitutes 'provocation' we must take this risk. To stop it would be to abdicate all authority. The Governor, and all his advisers, take this view. (Foreign Secretary and Lord Perth—who is in charge of C.O. in Alan Lennox-Boyd's absence—agreed.)[3]

It was difficult to be sure of the reason for Grivas's gesture. This

> is thought to be either that the trap is really closing on them, or (more likely) that [they feel] that the latest outrages have really begun to alienate world opinion—especially after appeals by the ... Prime Ministers.[3]

On the evening of 6 August I heard that both the Greek and Turkish Prime Ministers had agreed to my proposed visit. Accordingly I left London the next day. We took off in the afternoon in an R.A.F. Transport Command Comet, and arrived at Athens about 6 p.m., where we were met by the Greek Prime Minister, Constantine Karamanlis, and the Ambassador, Sir Roger Allen. Archie Ross and Eugene Melville of the Foreign Office came with me, as well as Freddie Bishop. I also had with me Sir Hugh Foot who was of great assistance throughout this strange odyssey. We drove to the British Embassy.

[1] 30 July 1958.   [2] 4 August 1958.   [3] 5 August 1958.

It has been repainted and the marks of the bullet holes—
which were many—removed. Otherwise, it had not changed much
since the days of the siege in 1944–45.[1] How well I remember
those extraordinary scenes! The evacuation of the front rooms;
the snipers' shots if one ventured into the garden; the midnight
communion on Christmas Eve 1944; the telegram (given to us
immediately after the service) announcing the arrival of Churchill
and Eden on Christmas Day; the abortive conference in candle-
light with the Communists; the Field-Marshal's serenity (Lord
Alexander); the Ambassador's scholarly charm (Sir Rex Leeper);
and all the tragi-comedies of those months.[2]

My friend Spaak had warned me on 31 July that the Turkish
membership of the Governor's Council would be a stumbling block
with the Greeks. He had already had several meetings with the
NATO representatives of the two countries and was convinced that
this would be the point, indeed the only point, to which the Greeks
could really take exception. So it was to prove.

The first meeting was at 10.30 a.m. on 8 August. The Prime
Minister and Evangelos Averoff, the Foreign Minister, had one or
two officials with them, as well as the Greek Ambassador in London,
who had come in my party.

The morning was taken up with generalities. I began with a
big appeal for peace and the seven-year period. I claimed that this
was all the more necessary because of [the] state of world politics,
especially in Middle East. Partnership was a fine ideal, and a
noble one. Greek Prime Minister replied at considerable length,
with a frank objection to partnership with Turks, who were
essentially barbarians (he did not actually say this but implied it).
I suggested 'co-operation', pending 'partnership'. The discussion
(which with translations was rather slow) continued till 1 p.m.
At the end, I had got them to agree to two principles as desirable:
(1) End of violence; (2) Seven-year period, with provisional
solutions but without prejudice to final solution. We agreed to
meet at 6 p.m. to start a detailed discussion of British plan. This
seemed to me some advance. For if one wholly rejects a plan, it does
not seem logical to examine the different points.[3]

[1] See *The Blast of War*, chap. xxii.   [2] 7 August 1958.   [3] 8 August 1958.

When we met again the atmosphere seemed definitely improved.

The Greek Prime Minister seemed calmer and responded to the treatment which I had tried–a mixture of firmness and friendliness. It seemed that the Greeks–apart from their dislike of partnership as a principle, since this was equivalent to admitting *de jure* a Turkish 'presence' in the island, had four points: (1) Four to two on the Council was unfair. Population would entitle them to four to one. (2) There was no *joint* assembly. (3) They disliked the proposals for dual nationality. (4) They hated the two Governmental representatives on the Council. It was not clear whether it was their presence on the island in any capacity to which they object. We did not press for clarification.

Although the Greeks affected to attach equal weight to these *four* objections, it soon became apparent that they really feel far more keenly about the Governmental representatives than about the other points. Of course, for the same reason, the Turks regard this–I am sure–as vital. It is for this that they are abandoning the [demand for a Turkish] base and territorial partition. We adjourned about 8 p.m., after a full discussion.[1]

On the next morning it was clear that the Greek position had hardened. Accordingly I expressed my disappointment that they had not accepted or at least acquiesced in our scheme. I reminded them that

They had rejected [the] Radcliffe plan two years ago; now they wished devoutly that they had not done so. For the Turks had accepted Lord Radcliffe's constitution, which could by now have been in force–with a *single* legislative assembly. If they rejected this new plan, or made it unworkable by violence and terrorism, the end would certainly be partition in its worst form– territorial partition, with Turkish bases, etc. I felt that the Greek Government were not rising to the level of world events, as well as acting contrary to their real interests. I could not understand this, which was unworthy of them. Nor did I feel that an intransigent attitude would gain them world sympathy. All this was very sad for me. As a Minister in Churchill's Government I had seen something of Greek heroism in war, and helped them to the best of my ability in their struggle against Communism, which

[1] 8 August 1958.

(without our aid) would have overwhelmed them in 1944–5. The affection of the British people for the Greek people was as strong as ever. But we had made great sacrifices since the war–we had seen the old Empire fade away with a new concept. Independence was over; interdependence must take its place. Modern Greece should set an example and not lag behind.[1]

At this point, as I had rather hoped and expected, Karamanlis became very emotional.

They hated the Turks; they had fought them for 500 years; they would fight them for Greek liberty wherever and whenever they could. They could not be humiliated by the Turks. A Turkish veto on Greek aspirations was humiliating.[1]

It soon became clear that, having got all this off his chest, Karamanlis felt much better and we calmly discussed the four points until lunch-time. I was encouraged to feel that it was only really the point about government representatives that they deeply distrusted; the other matters could easily be settled.

After the conference 'we all went off to luncheon (Greeks included) at the British Embassy, where the atmosphere was very friendly.'[1] I liked both Karamanlis and Averoff, especially the former, who was a true and sincere man.

We had now completed all that we could do and got a much clearer picture of what we would have to achieve in Ankara. Since we did not leave until 4.30 p.m., I could not resist a little sightseeing.

I went first to the Acropolis (which I may never see again) and then to the National Museum. Here there are the new finds at Mycenae–gold ornaments, etc., of all kinds, which are very fine. There are also two bronzes–each perfect of its kind–a magnificent Zeus, (or perhaps Poseidon) about to throw a thunderbolt or trident–a splendid bearded figure, perfectly poised. This is of the best period. There is also a very attractive bronze of a boy jockey (of the second or third century) very naturalistic and very charming. He seems to fly through the air.[1]

When we left, both Karamanlis and Averoff were personally charming and friendly. In the aeroplane I recorded my impressions:

[1] 9 August 1958.

It is difficult to form a very precise impression, except that the Government is frightened of Makarios, frightened of Parliament, and frightened of the rise in the Communist vote at the last (May) elections–this partly due to Russian propaganda about 'British imperialism in Cyprus'. So the Government clearly cannot 'accept' the plan. But I have not come to sign a treaty or even an agreement. Can the Greek Government 'acquiesce' in the plan and co-operate at least to the extent that is inherent in the plan itself? Makarios will probably persist in violent opposition to the plan – unless, perhaps, he is attracted by the prospect of returning to the island. The big stumbling-block is, of course, the Government representatives. But the Turks cannot abandon this, which is of cardinal importance for them.[1]

In Athens the people, although not actually hostile, seemed silent and aloof, although I felt convinced that the old Anglo-Greek friendship, so often renewed to our common advantage, had deep roots. When we arrived at the Turkish airport it was clear that our hosts

had . . . decided to make my welcome a marked contrast to that in Athens. A band, a guard of honour, a great attendance of notabilities, a large and applauding crowd.[1]

The airport was twenty miles from the capital. The Prime Minister, Menderes, and I drove in the same car.

In Ankara, the population was all in the street, and applauding –occasionally by subdued cheers, more often by clapping. . . . Our Ambassador, Jim Bowker, thought that . . . the Government's wishes for a friendly welcome had obviously gone out. A hostile demonstration could, however, be got up more easily. He thought that in this large turnout–which included middle-class shopkeepers and traders–there was probably an element of genuine friendliness.[1]

The British Embassy at Ankara was well situated on a hill above the city, some 3,000 feet above sea-level. It was a fine building. Unfortunately the Ambassador, an old friend who had served with me in Algiers, had closed the Embassy, since he was about to leave

[1] 9 August 1958.

after four years' tenure. So we stayed at the Governmental guest-house, which was comfortable but, of course, without any security. I therefore spent any of my free time in the library of the Embassy, only a few hundred yards away.

There was a working dinner at the guest-house consisting of

our London party, plus [the] Ambassador and Michael Stewart—Counsellor—with Menderes, Zorlu and four or five of their officials. Birgi was *not* brought from London for this visit.

After dinner

I explained to Prime Minister what had happened in Athens. The Greek Government clearly accepted the two main principles —no more terrorism and a seven-year provisional settlement. This was satisfactory. But they had raised points upon certain aspects of the plan, which I explained. The Turks took a very rigid position and affected to be surprised, after our secret talks in London, that we should even discuss any amendments. As they had told us in London, the plan was well-conceived, well-designed, with a perfect balance and equilibrium. Not a word could be altered without disaster. This moved me to enquire why in that case the Turkish Government had stimulated spontaneous riots against it of hundreds of thousands of people through the length and breadth of Turkey. The Turks . . . were not at all put out by this retort. A long wrangle started about what we had said in London. I said that I had told them that we intended to pursue the policy outlined in the House of Commons debate and in the White Paper. But this was not to be absolutely inflexible. It was for these reasons, as doubtless he remembered, that I refused to initial a record of the meeting (produced by his officials) which had introduced the concept of 'no amendment'. The Turks . . . still maintained their admiration of the perfect harmony of our plan. In a word, they wanted 'the Bill, the whole Bill, and nothing but the Bill'. After some further argument, we adjourned till the next morning.[1]

This attitude, although not altogether unexpected, was rather rougher than I had allowed for; but the only thing to do was to persevere. Consequently we met the next morning, Sunday

[1] 9 August 1958.

10 August. But we made no progress. The Turks continued to praise the perfect symmetry and beauty of the plan as it stood and refused even to consider amendments. At noon on my suggestion we adjourned.

Luncheon with the President—all the same people. A rather heavy affair. Caviar and vodka and rather a Russian atmosphere.[1]

In the afternoon we reassembled at 4.30. I had spent the interval in discussion with my advisers.

I told the Turks that we intended to implement our policy, and we hoped that it would be in a form with which—as each stage developed—they would be able to co-operate. There was really nothing more to be said.[1]

The Turks agreed to terminate the discussion, which scarcely lasted an hour. We then proceeded to discuss the Middle East and other problems in a friendly fashion. Although Zorlu continued to be somewhat difficult, Menderes was courteous throughout. I was to meet these men again and work closely with them in the following year. Meanwhile I felt that, although we had failed to obtain any concession, we had made some impression upon our hosts. Turks, like Englishmen, do not easily reveal their feelings.

The dinner at the British Embassy consisted of the same party and the atmosphere seemed more relaxed.

We left Ankara airport at 12 noon. Once more, a very friendly drive through the city, and a band and guard of honour on the airfield. Before I left I saw the Commonwealth Ambassadors or Chargés and also had a Press conference. Menderes and Zorlu were at the airport to see me off. Everything was most friendly— but again I felt it all rather Russian. You do not get much sense of heart or feeling behind these smiling faces and pleasant gestures. Menderes is certainly more civilised than Zorlu. It may be that I am wrong, and that all this merely reflects the rather primitive way of thinking which they still follow. Everything is black or white—there is no such colour as grey. You are friend or enemy; if you are friend, you must want to destroy the enemies of your friend. If you don't do this, whenever you can, you are no friend.[2]

[1] 10 August 1958. [2] 11 August 1958.

We flew direct to Nicosia Airport in Cyprus, arriving about 1 p.m., and drove to Government House.

Very few people had been told—for security reasons—of my plan to come to Cyprus, although I had determined to do so before we left London. I told the Governor as soon as I saw him in Athens. A very large luncheon party—all the leading officials, civil and military, and their wives were assembled—about 40–50 in all. Neither had they been told that I was coming. They assumed that the luncheon was to welcome the Governor on his return. There was great surprise—and I think gratification—when I joined the party assembled before luncheon. I was glad to see that there seemed to be a high state of morale.[1]

After luncheon I said a few words to the company expressing the gratitude of the British Government and everyone at home to those serving in Cyprus and their wives and families. I also expressed our complete confidence in the Governor.

In the afternoon we took off in two helicopters—the Governor and I in one, Freddie Bishop and Philip de Zulueta in the other. We flew over the hills which lie south of Nicosia, over Episkopi, to Akrotiri, the site of the main base. The Air Marshal, General and Admiral who, together with a representative of the Foreign Office, formed the Middle East Council had been warned, and we held an informal meeting, the Air Marshal (Sir Hubert Patch) presiding. After some discussion of possible developments in Jordan, it was decided to send signals to the Chiefs of Staff to enable me to deal with the problem the next morning in London.

After this talk, I went round the . . . air base, and talked to a number of officers and went into various messes. We also drove (in a jeep) round the married quarters. I was quickly recognised, and everyone seemed very pleased to see me. Morale was clearly high.[1]

We went off again by helicopter

to a village called Lyssa, in the Limassol area. Here we landed in the square outside the church. An operation was going on. A cordon of troops (Third Battalion Grenadier Guards and a

[1] 11 August 1958.

company Royal Scots Fusiliers) had been put round the village some days ago and was still maintained. The population were confined to their houses, and only allowed out at stated times for stated purposes. A search of every house and of the church had revealed a lot of arms, including twenty–thirty bombs. One haystack (which was a cache) for some reason blew up, much to the delight of the troops. Six very dangerous men were arrested.[1]

The Battalion was commanded by Colonel P.C. Britten–son of Brigadier Charles Britten, who was in the Fourth Battalion with me at Loos in 1915.

The officers, N.C.O.s and men were scrupulously clean, and looked in splendid shape. One company was paraded in the schoolroom for my benefit (they being in reserve and not actually in the cordon), and I spoke a few words to them. I found all this very moving, and I almost broke down in speaking, for it all recalled so many memories.[1]

We returned by helicopter to Nicosia and spent an hour at the headquarters of the anti-terrorist organisation and were given a briefing by the General and the Chief Constable.

General [Sir Douglas] Kendrew (a fine officer with a wonderful war record–V.C., D.S.O. with three bars, etc.) is about to leave after nearly three years on this thankless job.[1]

After this we met two Mayors. Dervis, Mayor of Nicosia, rather an attractive character, talked for forty minutes without drawing breath.

He gave the history since the British occupation and made rather a good case against our chaps and changes of policy. The rest was a diatribe against the Turks, the Police, and the man Foot (who was proving nothing but a fraud).[1]

The Mayor of Kyrenia, Demetriades, remained unaccountably silent.

Then we had the leaders of the Turkish Community–Dr. [Fazil] Kutchuk (the very opposite to Dervis–for he could scarcely speak, and then only in Turkish and in a hoarse whisper) and Mr. [Rauf] Denktash–his deputy, a very able and voluble

[1] 11 August 1958.

lawyer. They said almost all that the Greeks had said, but the other way round. The most interesting thing was that they attacked the new British plan—so clearly the word to support it has not yet come from Ankara.[1]

At 9.30 p.m. we dined in the garden—a quiet dinner with Sir Hugh and Lady Foot, the family and staff. It was a great comfort to have the counsel of this wise and loyal public servant.

At 11 p.m. Press conference and T.V. From 11.30 p.m. we worked on telegrams. (1) Draft British Statement; (2) Draft telegrams to Athens; (3) to Ankara. These were on the assumption that we decided to carry out the plan, with some amendments to please the Greeks and *one* to please the Turks. But this is really the part to settle in London. Our object in working at all this tonight was to get these telegrams immediately to both Athens and Ankara, and get the Ambassadors' advice. Since this took longer than we had allowed for, we put the aeroplane back half-an-hour. Ultimately, we left at about 2 a.m. local time.[1]

The next day, 12 August, was the glorious twelfth! At noon the Defence Committee met to deal with the situation in Jordan. I had asked such Members of the Cabinet as were in London to come at 3 o'clock.

About eight members present, including Lord Chancellor, Chancellor of Exchequer, President of Board of Trade, Dr. Hill, Minister of Transport, Lord Home—otherwise various Under-Secretaries, including [David] Ormsby Gore (F.O.) and Lord Perth (C.O.).[2]

There was a long and varied agenda. When this was completed I gave a report about my visits, and there seemed general approval for the course which I proposed—that is, to go on with the plan undeterred. There would be one important modification—it would please the Greeks but displease the Turks. The two national representatives who were to be appointed under the plan, Greek and Turkish, would not actually be members of the Governor's Council. Otherwise their functions would remain unchanged. In other words, they would be representatives without direct responsibility for Acts

[1] 11 August 1958. [2] 12 August 1958.

of Government. This being agreed, the necessary telegrams were despatched. It was true that this and indeed any other course, except unconditional surrender by the British Government, would be likely to bring about a renewal of violence and terrorist acts. Nevertheless it was important not to exaggerate. In five years the British forces in Cyprus had suffered ninety fatal casualties, a sad but not a shattering result of what was, in effect, a military campaign. The changes we agreed were conveniently set out in the following letter which I now thought it wise to send to Gaitskell as Leader of the Opposition:

Had you been in London I would have asked you to be good enough to come and see me today, but I am glad for your sake to learn that you are on holiday in Italy.

My visits to Athens and Ankara enabled me to have full discussions with the two Governments about our plans for Cyprus. I did not aim at anything like a tripartite agreement, still less a treaty; the most I can hope for is acquiescence, and perhaps in practice some support. In spite of all the difficulties I think there is some chance of this. In my visits I certainly found an atmosphere of friendliness and greater understanding than I had expected. At any rate I have done my best.

I believe that further extended talks, either with the Governments concerned, or in NATO, will lead to a deterioration rather than improvement in the position we have now reached, and that our duty is now to act in the way we think best and fairest. I therefore propose to issue a statement tomorrow afternoon in time for the 6 o'clock news and for Saturday's newspapers. We have made certain modifications and extensions in the general policy announced in June, as a result of what we have since learned. On the whole these are definite improvements from the Greek point of view and I think that the Turks may in the end accept them, however unwillingly. You will observe that some of the changes, particularly the statement about the possibility of a joint elected body in the future, are drawn largely from points made from your side in the Debate. We have also decided to regard the representatives of Greece and Turkey in the nature of ambassadors and they will therefore not be members of the Governor's Council. We are dropping for the moment the proposals for dual nationality, as it raises very complicated questions of international law and would, I suppose, require legislation here.

What the immediate future will bring I cannot tell, but I am not without hope for an improvement after the inevitable first reactions. Naturally a wide degree of general support in this country would increase the prospects of success.

The Governor, for whom my admiration grows the more I see him, accompanied me to Athens and Ankara, and I spent a day with him in Cyprus. I think I can say that he is in full agreement with the course we have decided to pursue.

I do not expect that this will reach you before the announcement tomorrow, and I am therefore sending copies of my letter to Bevan and Griffiths, as I think this is what you would want.

At the same time I sent a telegram to Spaak informing him of the changes. Selwyn Lloyd, being in Washington, was able to explain the situation in detail to Dulles. A statement was accordingly released to the Press on 15 August. The British Press had received the plan with favour, and, even after its rejection by the Greek Government became known, supported the bold and statesmanlike decision to implement it at all costs.

Meanwhile Archbishop Makarios issued from Athens a somewhat ambivalent statement: 'The people of Cyprus will not accept any arbitrary and unilateral decision and are now more than ever intent on asserting their right to self-determination and achieving their freedom.' This could be interpreted to mean either independence or Enosis.

For the Governor's information I summed up the situation on 18 August as follows:

We have, at present, a very good moral position in the world and with our allies. The Press in England, including the left-wing Press, is sympathetic. The general view is that we have taken a justified course.

I am not myself surprised that Makarios has made a hostile statement and I shall not be unduly depressed if the Greeks' is a bad one, too. What we must do is to continue quietly on our course and bring in other influences which we can use. I am sure the Americans will be very helpful and I think the NATO powers are getting very tired of the Greek intransigence, just as, at one time, they were critical of the Turkish position. I do not believe that the Greeks will make much of a showing in the United Nations. So let us appear calm. I know it is easy living in London to say this and I fully appreciate all your difficulties, all the more so from the [limited] understanding [of them] which I got by travelling round with you last week. Nevertheless, I am sure this is the right attitude.

Although the two Governments had not yet pronounced themselves formally, I felt sure what would happen, at least at this stage.

The Turks are going to support the plan, in spite of the important changes introduced to help the Greeks (Cyprus). But the Greeks will oppose the Cyprus plan, chiefly out of weakness and internal dissension. They must know in their hearts that we have gone a long way to meet them. Whether terrorism will now start again on a large scale, no one knows. Some feel that the Archbishop and even Grivas are sensitive to world opinion and are worried as to what this will be in the new circumstances.[1]

On 19 August the Greek Ambassador called to see me.

He was very charming and rather sad. For he clearly feels that his Government are behaving weakly and foolishly. I went over the four points—the only points—which the Prime Minister had made in Athens in criticism of the plan. The first—the four—two majority in the Council—was obviously unimportant. On the other three—the comprehensive popular assembly in the future; the joint nationality; and the presence of the Governmental representatives on the Governor's Council, I had met the Greek Government's wishes either in whole or in part. The Ambassador brightened a little and wrote this down. But really he had little to say. He did however add that perhaps the return of Makarios to Cyprus would be now the only way out. He said, quite frankly, that his presence in Athens made the Government's position impossible.

[Then] the Turkish Ambassador—who said little, but that his Government was 'studying my communication' (it is clear that they will wait for the Greeks).[2]

[1] 16 August 1958.   [2] 19 August 1958.

The Foreign Secretary was now in New York dealing with the complications in the United Nations of the Lebanon–Jordan situation, but he was kept fully informed of every development. My expectations were confirmed. The Greek Government rejected the plan on the evening of 19 August, and a week later the Turks accepted:

> The Greek Government are in great difficulties, and there are gloomy telegrams from our Ambassador in Athens. The Greeks, he says, will threaten–and perhaps be compelled–to leave NATO. Or the present Government will fall and be succeeded by one of a 'neutralist' character. I rather doubt this. Meanwhile, EOKA have issued a rather strange threat–which seems to be more urging a political boycott of the British plan than a resumption of terrorism. Makarios is to go to U.N.–for the regular assembly. But I doubt if he will make much headway.[1]

All through September messages and advice arrived from many quarters. Spaak now proposed that our plan be suspended while a conference was called under his presidency at NATO. At the end of the month the Turks and Greeks agreed in principle to this suggestion. My colleagues rightly felt, however, that, while accepting the conference, we could not postpone the initiation of our plan. The Turks had already agreed on their representative under the scheme:

> Cyprus goes on; this time the Turks have behaved with great moderation and good sense. Instead of sending an Ambassador from outside as their representative they have appointed the Consul-General who is already in the island. This has had a good effect in NATO, and Spaak is still trying to find some compromise. However, it was quite impossible for us to have 'postponed' the operation of the plan. If we had done so, we should have lost the Turks for good, and civil war would have begun. Meanwhile, violence is increasing. Two women, soldiers' wives, were shot yesterday, one fatally. This will, of course, enrage the troops.[2]

Although acts of terrorism continued from time to time, nevertheless a great round-up of suspects was carried out successfully, nearly a thousand being arrested. Finally

[1] 23 August 1958.   [2] 4 October 1958.

The Greeks have refused the proposed Cyprus conference. After all these weeks, in spite of—or perhaps because of—the British and Turks having agreed on every point, they have run out. It's Makarios who has bullied poor Karamanlis, Averoff and Co. into their absurd position. But I have not given up hope.[1]

When Parliament met there was naturally some criticism and disappointment at the lack of progress, but it was chiefly confined to the failure to arrange the NATO conference despite all the concessions to which we had agreed.

It is clear that the Greeks are upset—perhaps even ashamed—at their behaviour over the Conference. Our White Paper has come out, which is really conclusive. The Greeks are . . . [behaving] rather desperately, because they know that *all* the NATO countries know the truth from their delegates in the NATO Council.[2]

On 10 November, owing to intensified terrorist activities, we decided that all Greek Cypriots employed at the air bases and in the NAAFIs must be dismissed. In response to an appeal, nearly 8,000 British volunteers immediately came forward to fill the vacancies. At the same time the military operations against the terrorists continued to meet with considerable success.

At the United Nations, with the help of our friends, we achieved a considerable success. For the Assembly unanimously expressed its confidence 'that continuous efforts would be made by all the parties concerned to reach a solution in accordance with the United Nations Charter'. Until the end of the year the situation underwent no change.

Allegations were made about the conduct of British troops after the murder of Mrs. Cutliffe, the wife of a British soldier, and on 7 December some of the Opposition asked for an enquiry.

I made a long statement on Cyprus after questions in the House of Commons today. It dealt with the allegation of undue force against our troops and also with the political situation. It was well received in all parts of the House, and the Opposition had little to say.[3]

[1] 25 October 1958.   [2] 2 November 1958.   [3] 10 December 1958.

In the course of a long and sympathetic message, Eisenhower added some comforting words on this issue.

I admire your refusal to be disheartened by recent Cyprus developments and your determination to continue to work toward a settlement of this vastly difficult problem. For our part, we always shall be ready to help whenever and however we appropriately can.

With warm regard, As ever,

Ike

The Governor, with whom I was also in frequent correspondence, seemed content with the support he was receiving:

Those who work closely with me here join in deep gratitude for your message and I add my own personal message of most respectful devotion.

But just before Christmas a sudden and unexpected development took place in which were to be found the seeds of a final settlement. During a meeting of the NATO Ministerial Council in December, the Foreign Secretary was asked by the Greek and Turkish Foreign Ministers whether the British Government would see advantage in their pursuing an agreement on Cyprus, under which the United Kingdom would hold the bases in full sovereignty and the two communities would enjoy a measure of autonomy in an independent Cyprus; and whether we were agreeable to the two Foreign Ministers continuing their private discussions. The general plan was that they should discuss between themselves the internal aspects of a settlement in Cyprus, and that when they considered they had made sufficient progress there should be a round of tripartite discussions, both to consider the results of their discussions on the internal aspects and to discuss the external questions such as treaties and guarantees.

Although friendly messages had passed between me and both the Prime Ministers after the NATO Conference, such a development was as encouraging as it was unexpected. All attempts to find a solution to the Cyprus problem had come up against the inescapable fact of Greek–Turkish disagreement, and, although it seemed clear that so far no details had been settled and there had merely been an exchange of very general ideas, nevertheless if they could work out together an agreed basis for a settlement, very different and more hopeful prospects would open up for us. Accordingly, Selwyn Lloyd and I decided, after much consideration, to let the matter develop without interference from us, and the two Foreign Ministers were told that Her Majesty's Government welcomed their new initiative and wished them every success.

We were now faced with a dilemma as to what to do about the implementation of our own plan. As I explained to Dulles at the time:

> In advance of any new agreement, the internal arrangements for Cyprus which we announced last June and August have to go steadily forward. It is not possible to stand still in Cyprus. If we do not go forward, there is the risk of slipping back and losing the ground gained since last summer. The steady advance of our progressive plan seems indeed to have been an important factor in bringing about the improved attitude of both Greeks and Turks. Certain further measures fall due to be taken at this stage. . . . There is also the question of enabling legislation for the preparation of electoral rolls and constituencies for the Turkish House of Representatives. If the current talks come to nothing, we must be ready to fulfil our undertaking to the Turks to hold elections this year; and there is inevitably a time-lag between publication of the electoral legislation and the elections themselves. We had therefore decided that the electoral legislation should be published on 15 January. However, when we heard that the two Foreign Ministers were to meet again in Paris this weekend, we decided that it would be right to defer publication of the legislation to enable the talks in Paris to take place in the best possible atmosphere. Unless the talks show some real signs of progress, we should not be justified in delaying more than a week or so. It must be remembered that in certain towns separate Turkish councils have actually been functioning for some months and the situation requires to be regularised. As to the electoral lists, it is hardly conceivable that any agreement between Greeks and Turks could be other than on the basis of communal autonomy.

About the same time a proposal was received from EOKA for a cease-fire, provided all operations against them were suspended. I immediately minuted to the Colonial Secretary my views:

In spite of EOKA's assurance to the contrary, I believe that offer now is a sign of their weakness and, in any case, it seems to me that the offer is not one that we could possibly accept.

Lennox-Boyd came to see me on 31 December.

I had prepared a directive to the Governor, which Colonial Secretary accepted. He is told *not* repeat *not* to relax the pressure on EOKA and above all not to enter into any kind of discussion or negotiation with the terrorists. Even if the present talks really led to a 'solution' (as between Governments) it is more than likely that EOKA would continue—rather like the I.R.A. in Ireland. *Executions* are another thing. I think the Governor has done right to commute in the cases now before him.[1]

The New Year opened quietly.

Cyprus is relatively calm, but there seems little news of any further Turko-Greek talks. Zorlu is under a good deal of pressure in Turkey. He is now accused of abandoning the sacred cause of 'partition'. In the same way, Averoff is accused of abandoning 'Enosis'. So—by a curious logic—both approach, necessarily, to a compromise.[2]

The future of Archbishop Makarios now became exceedingly urgent. All through the autumn the question had been argued backwards and forwards without any conclusion being reached. It was urged upon the one hand that he was less troublesome in Cyprus than in Athens. Moreover if he returned he might be subject to the growing pressure of the Greeks in Cyprus who were anxious, for economic and political reasons, to see the state of emergency brought to an end. Equally he was the only spokesman acceptable to the Greek Cypriot community. On the other hand he opposed our proposals, and we had made it abundantly clear that, short of any other agreement, we proposed to implement them. On the afternoon of 4 February I had a talk with the Foreign and Colonial Secretaries:

Shall we let Makarios back into Cyprus? I would rather like to do so now; but agreed to await the result of the next Turko–Greek meeting. We believe that this will be next week at Zürich,

[1] 31 December 1958.   [2] 5 January 1959.

with both Foreign Ministers and Prime Ministers of the two countries.[1]

We also discussed the question as to whether and at what stage we should intervene in the private discussions either ourselves or with Spaak's assistance. The Governor was now naturally anxious and to comfort him I sent a message

You and I are naturally watching Zürich with crossed fingers. Much will depend on these talks. But we can at least take comfort from the fact that they are taking place in a vastly improved atmosphere.

I shall always admire your strength of purpose and loyal support of our dual policy—the Bible in one hand and the sword in the other.

We must take counsel together when we know what comes out of Zürich. Meanwhile, I feel impelled to send you this little message.

All good wishes.

Harold Macmillan

To this he sent a characteristically generous reply.

Thank you, Sir, for as kind a message as ever was sent from a Cavalier to a Roundhead.

On 10 February,

Late in the evening, Foreign Secretary rang up to say that he expected M. Zorlu and M. Averoff to propose a visit to London tomorrow (11th). This is getting very interesting. What one fears is that they may join in asking us more than we can concede. But we only need our 'Gibraltars'.[2]

Then, beyond all our hopes, on 11 February a joint Turkish–Greek communiqué was issued stating that the two governments had reached a compromise solution subject to agreement with Great Britain. My colleagues, after hearing an exposition of the new developments,

authorised the Foreign Secretary to continue the talks on certain understandings:

[1] 4 February 1959.   [2] 10 February 1959.

(1) Our 'bases' to be under British sovereignty.
(2) Other points, e.g. Radar stations, to be ours in perpetuity.
(3) Full facilities—harbours, roads, etc.
(4) Special arrangement for Nicosia Airfield.
Many other questions will have to be settled—but this is a start. Foreign Secretary made a short statement [to the House] *after* Questions, which was well received.[1]

The general feeling in Britain was one of relief. Splendidly as our troops had behaved, nothing is more poignant than the sufferings of families bereaved through operations of this kind. War, with all its tragedy, has its own dignity and honour; but for British soldiers and their wives to be shot in a street or murdered in a shop brings intolerable grief without its corresponding sense of glory.

All the Press is good—except the Beaverbrook Press which calls it a 'sell-out' and makes a most violent series of attacks—headlines, leaders, and cartoons, against me and Foreign Secretary.[1]

The next few days seemed more like a film than real life.

13 February. Cabinet at 11 a.m. Two hours on Cyprus. All Ministers agreed to main lines. Foreign Secretary thinks we shall have no difficulty in getting what we want militarily. If it really comes about, it is like a miracle. Menderes (Turkish Prime Minister) has written me a nice letter. He attributes Greek flexibility to *my* firmness!

Cyprus going on all right. We are working on our document which the three powers could perhaps initial on Monday. We shall then have Makarios and Kutchuk—representing Greek and Turkish Cypriots. If all goes well, Greek and Turkish Prime Ministers will arrive on Tuesday, and we shall sign again on Wednesday. Zorlu and particularly Averoff are anxious to associate their Prime Ministers. . . .

There is some doubt about the tenure of the 'bases', and I still fear that Makarios may [be difficult] about this. We shall see.

15 February. . . . Alan Lennox-Boyd and Sir Hugh Foot . . . arrived. We had a good talk and worked on various papers. The position is this—the Greeks and the Turks have agreed the Zürich concordat. This deals with the government of the island,

[1] 12 February 1959.

the various constitutional arrangements, etc.–including the 'built-in' Turkish veto through the mechanism of the 'Vice-President'. But it left us to make our demands. These we are now putting into writing. The Greek and Turkish Ministers say that we can 'have what we like'. The Greek [Minister] says . . . that Archbishop Makarios has 'agreed to everything'. . . .

16 February. In the morning, while Foreign Secretary saw Zorlu and Averoff, I tried to get agreement on our paper. Minister of Defence was (quite properly) rather stiff. . . .

17 February. Cyprus in the balance. The Governments seem pretty firm. The Archbishop is 'making reservations'. Meetings all the morning and afternoon. I expect the Greek and Turkish Prime Ministers today.[1]

In the evening of 17 February I had an audience with the Queen and was able to give her a full account of how the affair was proceeding to which she listened with her usual sympathy and knowledge. Since I was largely employed in the preparations of my visit to Russia, a settlement could not come at a more timely moment. The Foreign Secretary and I could hardly have left the country with this new development still unsettled.

Just as I was leaving for the Palace I heard the terrible news that Mr. Menderes and his party had crashed in an aeroplane outside Gatwick. Ten or twelve were believed to have been killed; but the Turkish Prime Minister himself was said to be safe, though very much shaken.

Menderes was coming to the Cyprus Conference, and was to have dined with me at No. 10. After a great deal of discussion and consultation, it was arranged that our dinner should be put off till 9 p.m. and only the Greeks to come. The Turks (including Zorlu) went to the London Clinic (where Menderes was taken) and to other hospitals.

The dinner was naturally rather sombre, owing to this tragic affair. But I had very good talks with both Karamanlis and Averoff. Although they had got the Archbishop's consent to the Zürich agreement and had warned him that we should have to retain sovereignty in our bases, the Greeks [were] obviously [anxious]. . . . Mr. Karamanlis talked very boldly about the

[1] 13–17 February 1959.

pressure that he would bring on him, and I felt that he meant it. Karamanlis seemed to me much more confident than when I had seen him in Athens last summer. Averoff, I thought, was less certain and more mercurial.

At about 10.30 p.m. Mr. Karamanlis and I went to the London Clinic, to ask about Menderes and to pay our respects. We did not, of course, see him, but we saw M. Zorlu and others and I think our visit was appreciated.[1]

On the next day, 18 February, although there were no formal meetings of the conference, the three Foreign Ministers met and made a good deal of progress.

At the same time, the Archbishop seemed to be quite intransigent. At 5 p.m. I heard that the Greek and Turkish Governments were 'fed up' and wanted to go home!

However, Selwyn Lloyd—who has managed all this with consummate skill—got a *full* meeting called at 7 p.m. (but without Prime Ministers). Once more, the U.K., Greek and Turkish Governments expressed their agreement with the Cyprus plan. M. Kutchuk (Turkish Cypriot) also agreed. The Archbishop (who, so Selwyn reported, seemed nervous and not sure of himself) stated his objections, which were *all* concentrated on the *Zürich* agreement—that is, on the Greek–Turkish constitution for Cyprus, etc. He made no reference to the *London* declaration—that is, the British requirements.

Since the newspapers have widely reported that the Archbishop objected to our retaining *sovereignty* of the bases, and since this is vital to us both militarily and politically, I was very glad to hear that he had *not* in fact taken this line.

In a struggle about this, we shall have been very hard pressed here—by the Socialists, by the Liberals, by all the wet-fish Press. . . . If we stood firm on sovereignty as against leases, we would have been accused of being the wreckers. If we had given in, we should have had a Parliamentary crisis with the Party.

Selwyn Lloyd—seeing the way things were going, and seeing how firm Averoff and Zorlu continued—adjourned the meeting at 9.15 p.m. He told the Archbishop that the Zürich–London agreements stood as a whole. What the conference—indeed what

[1] 17 February 1959.

z

the world would want to know was whether the Archbishop–as leader of the Greek Cypriots–would say 'Yes' or 'No'–would open the road to peace or bar it. Let him think about it–and give his answer in the morning. So this was agreed.

I went to Foreign Secretary's flat at 10 p.m. and heard all the story from him. Colonial Secretary and Foot were there.

We discussed our plans–if Archbishop said *no*; if he said *yes*. If *no* we would have a full meeting of the national representation (U.K., Greek, Turkish) . . . reaffirm our plan and our belief that it would be acceptable when understood. (Averoff had said–'if he says "no" now, he will say "yes" in a week.') We must then set up the machinery to take the necessary steps, just as if he were to say 'yes'.

Rather a late sitting, and a large miscellaneous 'box' on return.

19 February. An extraordinary day. Colonial Secretary rang at 9 a.m. (followed quickly by Foreign Secretary). The answer is 'yes'. The Cyprus agreement is therefore made![1]

The main terms of the agreement provided that Cyprus should be an independent republic subject to the retention of British sovereignty over the base areas, together with such rights as were necessary to ensure that they could be used effectively as military bases, these to be guaranteed by Greece and Turkey as well as the new Republic. The President was to be Greek and the Vice-President Turkish. The official languages were to be Greek and Turkish. The republic would have its own flag, but the two communities would have the right to fly the Greek or Turkish flag on holidays, together with the new Cyprus emblem. The President and Vice-President would be assisted by a Council of Ministers, consisting of seven Greek and three Turkish representatives. Legislative authority would be vested in a House of Representatives elected for a period of five years by universal suffrage. In this assembly there would be seventy per cent Greeks and thirty per cent Turks. In addition each community would have its own Communal Chamber which would provide for matters within their authority, such as religion, education, cultural questions, as well as matters of personal status. For this purpose each of the Communal Chambers could raise taxation from members of its own community. The

[1] 18–19 February 1959.

Civil Service would be seventy per cent Greek and thirty per cent Turkish. Other arrangements were included, regarding civil disputes between members of the same or different communities.

A full meeting of the conference was called for 3.30 at Lancaster House:

> We worked out our plan—signing first, speeches after. (We must make sure that the Prelate does not raise any point or wriggle any further.) I took the chair. The British delegation on *one* side of a rectangle of tables; the Greek and Turkish Government delegation opposite; on my right the Archbishop (with two supporters), on my left, Dr. Kutchuk (with two supporters also).
>
> I called the meeting to order and asked Foreign Secretary (on my right) to make a statement. He did this very shortly, ending by the message from Archbishop this morning, expressing his acceptance. Everyone, therefore, he was able to report, was now agreed.[1]

There was only one formality needed—the signing of the various agreements and declarations, to which I called the attention of the conference.

> 'When this is over,' I said, 'I propose to say a few words—no doubt the heads of delegations will wish to do the same. There is,' I added, 'one document to be signed by the three Prime Ministers. I would suggest that M. Karamanlis and I might go after this meeting to the Hospital (if the Turkish Prime Minister is well enough to receive us) and *all* sign the document together in his room.' After all signing was safely over, I made a little speech; the others followed.[1]

After this we went down to the gallery for refreshments and conversation.

> I had quite an interesting talk with Archbishop Makarios, whom I saw for the first time. He was not at all as I had pictured him. I had thought of him as a big man—like Archbishop Damaskinos. Not at all; 5 foot 8 inches or so, at the most. . . . Good hands, flexible and artistic. I would have said agreeable, subtle, intelligent, but *not* strong. This explains, perhaps his hesitations.[1]

[1] 19 February 1959.

The eating and drinking over, Karamanlis and I drove together to the London Clinic.

We were taken up to the room, into which a mass of people forced themselves, including a Foreign Office messenger with a fine silver ink-pot! We all signed and after some little talk with Prime Minister Menderes, withdrew. Menderes seemed all right and *very* happy—as well he might be.

The Greeks are delighted—although they realise that they have *not* had the best of the bargain. They could have done better by accepting the Radcliffe plan *or* the Macmillan plan. But all our friends—and they are legion—like the Ambassador and others, are delighted that the long Anglo-Greek dispute is over and that our old friendship can be renewed.[1]

Later in the evening I went to the House of Commons, where a debate on Foreign Policy was proceeding, and made a short statement on the successful termination of our negotiations. After explaining the details to the House, I added:

I regard this Agreement as a victory for reason and co-operation. No party to it has suffered defeat. It is a victory for all. By removing a source of bitterness and division it will enable us and our allies and the people of Cyprus to concentrate on working together for peace and freedom.[2]

Gaitskell, in replying for the Opposition, could not resist a few sarcasms to which I replied with some vigour. This little interchange was helpful, because there were naturally some Conservative doubts about surrendering our treaty rights over the island.

Gaitskell made the mistake of a sneering (instead of a generous) reply—and I *went for* him. This was very pleasant for our Party, and they cheered rapturously.[1]

In answer to further questions, both from the Conservative and Labour benches, I tried to summarise the true effect of the agreement.

In any settlement, if it is to be a satisfactory one, sacrifices are made by all sides. The claim to Enosis has been abandoned. That

[1] 19 February 1959. [2] *Hansard*, 19 February 1959.

is a big sacrifice. The claim to partition has been abandoned. That is a big sacrifice. We have abandoned our sovereignty except over those bases which are necessary for our military needs, with the rights and facilities which are necessary to make them effective. Therefore, if we call it sacrifice, it is a sacrifice all round.[1]

The question had already been raised as to whether Cyprus would be a member of the Commonwealth. I pointed out that this would depend partly upon the new Republic and partly upon the other members of the Commonwealth. All this must still take a little time. However, I was glad, in due course, to be able to preside over a Conference of Commonwealth Prime Ministers which elected Cyprus and welcomed the Archbishop as a member of our body.

There were sincere congratulatory telegrams from President Eisenhower and other friends to be attended to, as well as the despatch of formal notification to all the Commonwealth Governments. I was particularly touched by a personal letter from Alan Lennox-Boyd.

Thank you very much for the generous words you used yesterday on my efforts over Cyprus. No settlement could ever have been achieved without your own patience and skill. From my talks with all of them, nothing is more clear than that you have contrived to give to the Greek and Turkish Ministers that confidence in us and that confidence in themselves which has enabled them to make these agreements together. You have re-established the Concert of Europe.

There were, as was only to be expected, a number of difficulties still to be overcome; but troublesome as these might prove to be, I felt that neither the Greek nor the Turkish statesmen would go back on their word. Karamanlis, who served his country well in a firm and steady Government for many years, was a man of real integrity, and Averoff could equally be relied upon to honour the agreement both in the letter and the spirit. This was also true of the Turkish statesmen. These were, indeed, strangely dissimilar in character. Zorlu, rough, tough, sometimes rude, but with an occasional gleam of humour, occasionally seemed to put the chances

[1] *Hansard*, 19 February 1959.

of success at risk by the brusqueness as well as the obstinacy with which he presented his arguments. Nevertheless he was a considerable man. Menderes, who must, I think, have had in his ancestry some Greek blood, was very different. Flexible in discussion and with considerable charm of manner, he would often come to the rescue when the situation seemed hopeless. Less than three years later I heard with horror the news of the brutal murder of Zorlu and Menderes in a period of national emergency. They were both hanged like convicts. This dreadful act came as a blow to all friends of Turkey. To me it came with special poignancy, for I had got to know them intimately. Moreover I have an interest in preserving the tradition that former Prime Ministers should be pensioned, not executed.

Before the end of February arrangements were made for the release of prisoners from the Cyprus detention camps, as well as for an amnesty for the EOKA terrorists. A safe conduct to Greece was given to General Grivas and the order exiling Archbishop Makarios was revoked. By the end of March the Parliaments of Greece, Turkey and the United Kingdom had formally ratified the Agreement, although during the remainder of the summer and early autumn many minor difficulties arose between all the parties concerned which needed both patience and resolution for their final settlement. Yet by the time of the end of my first Premiership and the General Election in October 1959 the problem of Cyprus was rightly regarded as settled. It may, however, be convenient briefly to complete the story.

It had been proposed that the final transfer of power would take place within a year of the agreement. Nothing much remained to be agreed with the Greek and Turkish Governments; but a long and wearisome negotiation with Archbishop Makarios continued throughout the first half of 1960. The date of independence had therefore to be postponed from month to month as these tedious and almost Byzantine arguments were pursued, first at a round-table conference in London in January 1960, and then throughout the spring and early summer in Cyprus. The main dispute was about the size of the base areas and about the undertakings for the protection of their essential requirements. But since I was convinced that the bases could only be truly effective if we had the goodwill of the Cypriot Government and people, I was ready to face prolonged negotiations. There were other, almost equally obscure issues. At one point in this immensely drawn-out debate, experts in the Foreign Office discovered two minority groups in the island whose plight should command our sympathy. This seemed to me to go far beyond our duty, and I accordingly sent a minute to the Foreign Secretary. 'What is all this about Maronites and Armenians? Don't let us spoil the ship for a ha'p'orth of heretics.'

Early in February 1960 I sent out Julian Amery, at that time Under-Secretary at the Colonial Office. I had already had experience of his negotiating skill and exceptional combination of patience and determination in his dealings with the Sultan of Muscat. I told him that he would be up against an adroit negotiator, determined to reduce the size of the sovereign bases to the minimum. Nevertheless he had this advantage that the Archbishop wanted independence as soon as possible. If the Archbishop stalled, our reply was to postpone the date from month to month. Amery proved to have as robust an endurance as his episcopal opponent. In the end a full agreement was reached on 1 July 1960, and the transfer of power took place formally on 16 August, when Archbishop Makarios was invested as President of the Republic of Cyprus.

CHAPTER XX

Boom or Slump?

THE absorbing claims of foreign, Commonwealth and
Colonial affairs, together with the need for frequent journeys
abroad, demanded a high proportion of my time and attention. This was only made possible by the forbearance of all concerned. It is, perhaps, not generally known that a Prime Minister
cannot leave the island without the specific permission of the
Monarch. In addition he needs the patient and generous co-
operation of his colleagues. In the conduct of external affairs, I had
the able assistance of three devoted Ministers in Selwyn Lloyd
(Foreign Secretary), Alan Lennox-Boyd (Colonial Secretary), and
Alec Douglas-Home (Commonwealth Secretary). The last-named,
then sitting in the House of Lords as Lord Home, added his great
weight to the presentation of the Government's case on many
aspects of their policy. Contrary to the general opinion, the House
of Lords, except in the first confident morning of a Party victory,
can be more troublesome to a Government of the Right than to one
of the Left. As exhausted or discarded Ministers and retired
Members of the House of Commons begin to congregate in the
Upper House, the combination of experience with disappointment
can sometimes become formidable. Since it is a law of our imperfect
nature that men must either command or obey, it requires more skill
to soothe the ruffled waters caused by a sudden Conservative squall
or storm than to meet day by day the more constant tides of Liberal
and Labour criticism. In the peculiar situation following Lord
Salisbury's resignation, the position of Alec Home was one of
special importance. He was ably assisted by Lord Hailsham.

The domestic front, however, was one of constant anxiety. I was
only able to overcome the difficulties by the assistance, not only of
my leading colleagues, but of all the members of the Cabinet. On

external affairs this Cabinet, like others in which I have sat, was ready to follow the advice of the Prime Minister and the Ministers immediately responsible. But on internal affairs all Ministers felt both the right and the duty to express their opinions sometimes at considerable length. Moreover all were of equal weight, because all were equally ignorant or informed.

I must, in addition, record my obligation to the second member of the Government, 'Rab' Butler. He held, in his single command, the three important posts of Lord Privy Seal, Home Secretary and Leader of the House of Commons. He was universally accepted as my deputy. He presided over Cabinets in my absence. To him I sent my messages from abroad for communication, as he might think fit, to our colleagues. Although younger than me by eight years, he had a longer administrative experience, having held office in the pre-war administration. He had been chosen by Churchill himself to rescue our financial affairs from the disastrous trough into which they were thrown and abandoned by Attlee's last Government. He sat always next to me in Cabinet, and to him I used to turn, after other colleagues had made their contribution, for final words of advice. If these were sometimes Delphic in formulation they were none the less profound.

Together with the Chief Whip, Edward Heath, Butler managed the House of Commons in my many absences. His long experience was of equal value in the political machine, especially with reference to the Research Department, over which he had long presided.

Next to him I depended, after Thorneycroft's resignation, on Derry Heathcoat Amory, the Chancellor of the Exchequer, who, succeeding at a difficult moment, soon established an almost unique position in the House of Commons, by his combination of wit and good humour with common sense. He commanded the affection of the Labour Members, whom he always treated with a courtesy which they felt to be the genuine product of his sweet and Christian nature. We had feared that the controversial circumstances surrounding Thorneycroft's resignation might prove fatal to a Government whose position was in any case insecure. I fully expected that in all the usual troubles that were bound to follow, we would be faced with the opposition of a formidable trio—Thorneycroft, Enoch Powell and Nigel Birch. But the first assault proved to be the last;

z2

these somewhat ill-assorted musketeers carried out the unusual plan of *sauter pour mieux reculer* !

David Eccles, as President of the Board of Trade, with his quick and brilliant mind gave excellent support to Amory on economic matters, and our councils were fortified by Reggie Maudling, Iain Macleod and John Hare, who had succeeded Amory as Minister of Agriculture. Henry Brooke, Minister of Housing, could be relied upon for sound administration and good advice. Duncan Sandys, at Defence, was always reliable and sometimes brilliant. I had readily available the advice of my old friend Lord Mills. These, together with Lord Kilmuir, the Lord Chancellor, then in the most active and efficient period of his life, made a powerful team. I was especially happy to have brought back into the administration my old friend from Housing days, Ernest Marples.

Even the casual reader will have observed that the greater part of this volume is concerned with world and Commonwealth affairs. The struggle between the Communist and the free world; the special problems of Europe and NATO; the strengthening of the Anglo-American alliance; the recurring dangers of the Middle and the Far East; the enigma of Russia; the divisions of Western Europe—all these occupy the greater part of my record, because they attracted the greater part of my thoughts and actions. On looking back, I realise the reason for this concentration on external affairs. At this period Britain, in spite of all her wounds and her weaknesses, was still a great and dominating nation, held in deep respect by her partners and her allies, feared by her enemies, deploying powerful and well-organised forces in the vital strategic points throughout the world. The decision to grant to the emerging colonial countries the same independence which had been given to India and Pakistan did not seem necessarily to involve a weakening of British prestige or even power. Whether the changes that were soon to follow were inevitable or culpable, it is not for me to judge. I have recorded only what I saw and experienced.

'Home affairs' in this century of progress mean, largely, economic affairs. Gone are the happy days when our Victorian forebears could conduct their gladiatorial performances in Parliament on great political issues without much concern for those perplexing and degrading difficulties. During the long domination of the Manchester school, which had established Free Trade and Free Enterprise, with the minimum of Government interference in social or economic questions, the nation's thoughts could be concentrated on two major issues. First, the role of Britain in the world. Secondly, the expected effect of science on religion. The second of these was regarded as the special field of Mr. Gladstone's activities.

Economics has now usurped the place held one hundred years ago by theology. The *odium economicum* has taken the place of the *odium theologicum*. The vast output of economists from every university, old and new, is provided for by the same kind of machinery as once supported the clergy with benefices or employment. The more accomplished devotees of the conflicting sects, who might be called the regular clergy of the economic church, are supported by academic endowments. Others who might be compared to the secular priests are to be found in the daily, weekly, monthly Press; in the journals published by banks and other industrial bodies; on the radio and television and all the other means of communication 'declaiming with no little heat their various opinions'. For it is not to be supposed that in the field of economics there is today any more agreement than in the field of theology throughout the ages. Indeed, so bitter are the feelings that inside the various schools a sectary is often more odious than an unbeliever. Nevertheless, while Ministers, as well as the public, are apt to be confused by this proliferation of pundits, it cannot be denied that their authority is now generally respected. I have enjoyed many intimate friendships with both professionals and amateurs. I have always particularly enjoyed the most fervent exponents of their particular creed. For, after all, if an enthusiast is sometimes absurd, he is never languid. The practical statesman must however endeavour to steer a middle course between extremes.

During 1956 and 1957 I was prepared to accept the diagnosis and follow the advice given by our most experienced advisers. These included not merely the Bank of England and the clearing banks, but the professional economic advisers to the Treasury and the great majority of the economic commentators through all the various media of public information. These all seemed to agree that the economy was, to use the jargon of the day, 'overheated and needed cooling', or 'overextended and needed relaxing'. In other words a measure, moderate but significant, of deflation, or disinflation, ought to be introduced. The symptoms at any rate were easy to see, and were the traditional guides which had been followed by successive Governments. These were the fall in the value of the pound relative to the dollar; a weakness which might even amount to something like a run on the exchange; an undue rise in wholesale and retail prices with a fall of exports and a corresponding deficit in the balance of payments; over-full employment, where the 'unfilled' vacancies—that is, the demand for labour—far exceeded the supply. (In this last indicator there was a complication, since even a very low rate of national unemployment might be accompanied by disagreeably high rates in certain localities or areas.) If these symptoms were generally recognised and accepted, so was the nature of the appropriate remedies. These included a reduction of Government expenditure both on current and on capital account; an increase in Bank Rate and various measures such as hire-purchase restrictions calculated to reduce demand; open market operations by the monetary authorities to mop up purchasing power; stern taxation and finally a determined effort to resist pressure on what became known as the 'wages front'.

Of course, in the times about which I am writing, both the malady and the recommended cures were of a very modest nature compared to the immense dimensions of later troubles. Equally the remedies, instead of being on the heroic scale of later years, were restrained. Bank Rate of 7 per cent seemed an appalling sign of disinflation, and could not be tolerated for more than a few months. As for the recourse to international borrowing on a vast scale, overt and covert, such a concept went far beyond our modest and pedestrian ambitions. To touch the brake or to lift the foot off the accelerator was not intended to be more than an attempt, however amateurish, to drive safely along a crowded road, amid many pitfalls and dangers.

In this exercise it was then considered of great importance to prevent an undue rise in wages in the producing or servicing industries beyond what could be justified by increased productivity. It was for this purpose that the council on prices, productivity and incomes, the 'Three Wise Men', had been set up in the summer of 1957.

This may be taken as perhaps a forerunner of an organisation called the National Board for Prices and Incomes set up many years later by a Socialist Prime Minister. In each case the Government tried to rely upon the authority of these supposedly impartial men to sustain their policy. In each case the Opposition were inclined to minimise their influence or question their findings. Gaitskell went so far as to attack the report of the 'Three Wise Men' in derisory terms. 'They produced' he said, 'not a scientific report but a political tract. We did not need' he continued, 'a judge, an accountant and an ex-economist to tell us what to do.'[1] 'Ex-economist' was perhaps a little hard, from one professional to another. The Cohen report did give general support to the measures taken by the Government and was likely to have an influence upon the wage-claims now pending. Indeed it was argued as a reason against arbitration that the arbitrators might be unduly influenced by the views of Lord Cohen and his colleagues.

The next effort after the 'Three Wise Men' was the policy of the 'guiding light'. Based upon the view that, if the rate of increase in wages could be kept broadly in step with the rate of increase in the volume of output, we might be reasonably secure, our expert advisers calculated in present conditions a rise of 2 per cent in wages and salaries, and not more, should be considered compatible with price stability. Therefore, it was argued: let there be a 'guiding light' 2 per cent or perhaps, in certain circumstances, 3 per cent, to be applied to basic wages as a whole, with, of course, flexibility for special groups, and above all for incentive bonuses. This theme too has somehow become familiar, but perhaps more honoured in the breach than in the observance.

In my own mind I had demanded in 1956, and accepted loyally in 1957, the need for a prudent and even a disinflationary course. But one of the reasons why I was not unduly concerned by the resignation of Thorneycroft was that I sensed, more by instinct than by reason, that the situation was about to change. After all, at the beginning of 1958, sterling stood at its highest point for over eighteen months. The gold and dollar reserves in January rose by $131 million, and although the proportion of unemployed was only 1·8 per cent, there had been a rise of 60,000 in total numbers.

[1] *Annual Register, 1958*, pp. 10–11.

Surely this was satisfactory to the most rabid exponents of deflation. The Exchequer returns for the first nine months were equally reassuring. Government spending had been very fractionally over the expenditure of the previous year, while the revenue was coming in at a faster rate. The balance of payments seemed likely to improve, and although outwardly it was still important to press the general principles of restraint in every sphere, it was equally prudent to be alert for a change.

Early in 1958 I began to hear accounts of an American 'recession', following the determination of the Republican Government, under the powerful impulse of George Humphrey, to return to orthodox finance after years of what they called reckless Democratic expenditure. The effects might be to us painful and even fatal.

We had a long meeting—Chancellor of Exchequer, Lord Privy Seal, Maudling, with Treasury officials, including Leslie Rowan and Professor [Robert] Hall, who are just back from Washington. It was a pretty depressing meeting, because it is clear that the Americans have no idea what to do about their own 'depression' and still less about the approaching 'world slump'. I wish I could persuade the American administration that the free world cannot be defended by H-bombs if it is allowed to fall into trade collapse and large-scale unemployment.[1]

I now began to press the new Chancellor of the Exchequer on the need to have plans ready in case the tide turned. We might need both major and minor public works at short notice to pump more money into the economy rather than to squeeze it out. Nevertheless we must still be cautious. There were some unpalatable facts to be faced. The maximum we could expect from Germany for support costs was £47 million not the £63 million we had hoped for. The emerging deficit on the National Insurance fund in the current year would be £23 million, not £14 million. (The latter we had met boldly by an increase of 8d. in the stamp.)

I began now to bombard my unhappy colleagues at the Treasury with arguments about the inadequate liquidity of the free world. On 28 February I wrote:

[1] 27 February 1958.

Of course it is right that we should come down to earth and be told the hard reality of our own position and the American scene. But it is also sad, because one feels that a plan for steady economic expansion in the free world could be made—and could be made to work—if only we could agree internationally on proper financial machinery.

After all, gold is only a symbol, and currencies are only a convenience. The fact is that all the resources are there, in raw materials and labour and knowhow, and the demand is there. The free world ought to be able to work, and at full pressure too, for the material benefit of all. Our failure is really a failure to organise.

At the same time an old friend, Roy Harrod, a stalwart expansionist, was warning me that the danger ahead was a slump not a boom. I have seldom found him wrong in his prophecies, although often doomed to the unhappy position of an economic Cassandra. Nevertheless I had to remind him that it was possible that while it was internationally true that recession or slump was the main danger it was still important not to yield too quickly at home, and especially to make no concessions on the wages issue. If reinflation were needed, it might be better to do it by monetary methods than by a wholesale relaxation of the limitations on Government capital expenditure. In this mood there was general agreement to the more or less standstill Budget which Amory proposed to introduce. In the intimate discussions on the Budget I noted on 14 March:

> 7 p.m. I had Chancellor of the Exchequer and Lord Privy Seal (Butler) to talk and supper. We argued for some hours about the state of the economy and what should now be done. The Treasury think that the 'boom' or the 'inflation' is still on. Butler and I have our doubts.[1]

Nevertheless, we had no disagreement as to the immediate need.

> We all agree about trying to win the wages battle now upon us —bus and railway. But, if and when these are over, we need an expansionist policy again.[1]

Some advance was made a few days later when the Bank Rate was reduced from 7 per cent to 6 per cent. Two months later, on 22 May,

[1] 14 March 1958.

it fell to $5\frac{1}{2}$ per cent. Nevertheless, while new ideas, including even that of reverting to a floating rate of the pound, were being, at my insistence, widely discussed within the Treasury and with leading bankers, the main decision remained unchanged. We must first hold the wages front. After some signal success, a change might safely be made by a halt or a reversal of the restrictive measures which had been in operation for so long.

The test was to come in the transport world. On 25 March the London busmen rejected a report of the industrial court to which, with their agreement, their claim was submitted at the beginning of February. About the same time there was a negative award of the Railway Tribunal, the constitutional procedure to which the competent railway unions had agreed at the time of nationalisation.

> To all our other difficulties, the almost certainty of a railway, bus, dock and general road transport strike is now added. The Railway Tribunal will give its award a week today. Whatever it is–3 per cent or nothing–the unions will not accept.[1]

The award was issued by Sir John Forster on 10 April. He recommended no wage-increase at all for the railway workers on the ground that there was 'no money available'. The trade union representative on the committee (not, of course, a railwayman) not unreasonably proposed a modest increase–say 3 per cent–to meet the rise of the cost of living since the previous year.

> Sir John Forster has, however, 'passed the buck' firmly to H.M.G. saying (*a*) that railway wages are on the *low* side, compared with other nationalised and some private industries; (*b*) that since the Transport Commission is bankrupt and H.M.G. (the bankers) have in effect refused to lend any more money, he has no alternative to a 'nil' award.[2]

When I met my principal colleagues the chief points appeared to be :

> (*a*) The large difference between wage-rates and average earnings: e.g. Porter. Basic rate £7. 7. 0.–average earning £9. 9. 6. (*b*) That H.M.G. are giving railways £50 and £60 m. to meet deficit (current) as well as £150 m. or more for capital.

[1] 3 April 1958.   [2] 10 April 1958.

(*c*) That it is *not* just railway wages that are at stake. It is whether or not we have another wage-spiral throughout industry.[1]

At the same time I was anxious that the Government, while firm, should not seem to be obstinate.

Above all, we must not 'challenge' the Trade Unions as some . . . would like. We must appeal to the Unions, and try to take ourselves some constructive initiative.[1]

There were so many difficult questions to be resolved at this time that I was anxious to avoid a railway strike which

if it comes, will be terribly damaging. For, as it goes on, the present good feeling will change and bitterness begin. The middle classes are so angry, anyway, that the spirit of Liberalism (now the same as poujadism) will encourage the class war.[2]

Accordingly I circulated a paper

On the 'initiative' which H.M.G. might take at the right moment. (It is really based on the idea that we might *accelerate* the capital programme, and the management and men might agree on 'economy through efficiency'—no restrictive practices; shutting up branch lines and *accepting* redundancy.[2]

To add to our troubles a strike of the meat-lorry drivers at Smithfield began on 21 April and soon spread to the whole market and later to the docks. We had therefore three disputes, the threatened bus strike, the threatened railway strike and the beginning of a dock strike. It seemed to me that it was of vital importance to keep the railways going. Moreover I shared with the public the general feeling of sympathy with the railway workers. Nationalisation had brought them no benefit, and all their dreams had vanished into thin air. General Sir Brian Robertson, Chairman of the British Transport Commission, struggled nobly with his task, but it was beyond the strength of any man at that time. In agreement with Robertson and with Iain Macleod, the Minister of Labour, I issued an invitation for joint discussion to all concerned.

In response to my invitation, issued last Friday, Sir Brian Robertson accompanied by some of his principal officers, Mr.

[1] 10 April 1958.   [2] 11 April 1958.

[Sidney] Greene (N.U.R.), Mr. [Albert] Hallworth (ASLEF) and Mr. [William] Webber (Railway Clerks) and their supporters came to No. 10 at 3.45. The meeting lasted just over two hours. Sir Brian introduced the deputation shortly; then each of the three Union secretaries spoke; then Sir Brian, in his capacity as Chairman of the Transport Commission.

The Unions asked for an increase of wages and argued that the Arbitration Tribunal would have granted this if it had not been for the financial difficulties of the Railways and the Government's refusal to lend more than the £250 m. for current needs. The Chairman of the Commission said that he could not pay any more wages *at present*, and therefore accepted the Tribunal's findings. However, he felt that if the Government would reconsider their attitude to the Modernisation Plan and help in one or two other ways, things would improve. I then put forward the Government's position (speaking generally from a brief which had been agreed at a meeting of Ministers chiefly concerned last night). I said that what was needed was a concerted effort. The Commission should attack the problem of making fresh economies with greater urgency, and work out detailed plans; these would no doubt involve closing some lines and stations and other fairly drastic measures. Manpower must be saved. The Unions should agree on accepting redundancy and in getting rid of any remaining restrictive practices, etc. Provided this was done, the Government would (as a matter of urgency) consider any scheme for increasing the tempo of modernisation.

The Unions asked a lot of questions after this, but in a very amicable and reasonable tone. A good deal of whisky was consumed.

Finally, they agreed to have a meeting with Robertson tomorrow afternoon to discuss the various statements made and especially to consider the Government's proposal.

A communiqué was then agreed—its terms had been prepared by officials before the meeting, and very few alterations were required. So far, so good.[1]

On 28 April a new proposal was made by the London Transport Executive to the leaders of the bus drivers which was immediately rejected.

[1] 22 April 1958.

I had a talk with Iain Macleod. We agreed on the terms of his reply to Cousins about the London bus dispute. The strike now seems inevitable. It may be salutary.[1]

On 5 May the bus strike started, and it looked as if the railway talks, which Sir Brian was conducting with the unions, would break down. The Parliamentary side was not without its difficulties: 'The Conservatives are waiting anxiously to see what we do. [Some] . . . are ready to pounce.'[2] On the other hand I was more anxious about the industrial and practical side:

It is not going to be easy to keep the people fed and in good heart unless they are absolutely with us. This means that the railway unions must have rejected an offer which everyone would regard as fair and reasonable.[2]

The general economic situation was improving, with the reserves rising steadily. But as might be expected, this argument was used both ways. Some said a strike would injure our credit; others declared that to give in to an 'inflationary demand' would do more harm in the long run. Fortunately at this moment the Opposition chose to move a vote of censure on the Government, and particularly on the Minister of Labour, for not intervening on the bus dispute.

[Alfred] Robens opened, with a well argued speech, well delivered. Macleod replied. He spoke without a note—which much increases the effectiveness of a speaker in the House. I did not myself think his speech out of the ordinary, until the end. He finished with a short passage, expressing his scorn and contempt for Gaitskell, which was a fine bit of invective. Gaitskell spoke at 9 p.m., and I followed him. We had a very good majority—67. Our party seemed quite cheerful, though everyone is anxious.[3]

The busmen had not so good a case as the railwaymen. They had agreed to arbitration and had at least been offered some increase. Moreover, while they could inflict inconvenience on the public, they could do no serious injury to the economy. Indeed, if one was to take a cynical view, nothing could suit us better than to satisfy the desire for calling a halt over an issue where no vital national

[1] 29 April 1958. [2] 6 May 1958. [3] 8 May 1958.

interests were at stake. While I was ready to accept the bus strike in London and even in the provinces, I was determined to find some concession which would bring a settlement on the railways. On Sunday, 6 May, I came up from Chequers in the afternoon and had a long meeting with the Ministers chiefly concerned. So-far Robertson had offered 'some increase of wages' in October and a 'review' in July. This certainly would not avoid a strike.

Of course, some Ministers and a lot of the Party want a 'showdown'. But I don't think they realise how it may end. Even if we win (which is doubtful) it will be at a heavy cost.[1]

The orthodox doctrine, to which the Treasury now seemed especially wedded and some Ministers revered with almost brahminical devotion, was that there should be no advance of wages unless it could be got out of economies. As this doctrine seemed to command general support I thought it best to use it as a basis for a settlement. The economies already agreed amounted to some £10 million a year.

If we could get the total to a rate of £12½ m. p.a., this would justify paying out some. (£10 m. = 3 per cent on wages.) In other words, it would be legitimate to anticipate for three months, if the *total* of the savings were increased by a quarter. I finally got the Ministers to accept this view (Butler supported well—also Macleod) and we must now await tomorrow's Cabinet.[1]

To such almost Byzantine subtleties can the practice of industrial negotiation be reduced or elevated, but it was the language to which the pundits, especially in the economic Press, seemed much attached. In any case, if one cannot block the flow of a stream one can, at least, seek to divert it. Some Ministers were very reluctant to agree to my proposal and did so only out of loyalty.

But I am sure I am right. Public sympathy is (on the whole) with the railwaymen. The cost of living figure (owing to potatoes and tomatoes) will go up by TWO points on 23 May, and who knows what Lord Justice Morris may give the coal miners? If we are to face a strike, which we can only break by *volunteers* and full public sympathy, we must get into a better posture.[2]

[1] 11 May 1958.   [2] 12 May 1958.

In these disputes the position of the Minister of Labour is extremely difficult. He acts nominally as an impartial conciliator to bring the parties together. This is something of a farce when one of the parties is a nationalised industry in which the Government is both equity holder and banker. It is indeed one of the underlying problems arising from nationalisation which cannot be resolved. During a Cabinet nominally confined to the future of Cyprus,

> General Robertson rang up to say that he had offered 3% in July (or rather from 30 June) together with the enquiry into railway wages, but he did not think they would accept anything by 1 June or even earlier. They might also ask for 4%. After some discussion, we agreed to stand by our offer (or rather General Robertson's offer) whatever the consequences.[1]

The next day the Chief Whip warned me that trouble was being stirred up in the Parliamentary Party, but I was not unduly alarmed. More exciting was the news from the trade union front.

> We have heard that the railway unions have decided to consider what to do. This at least is a good sign. Later in the day we heard that the clerks union will probably accept—so will ASLEF (Engine Drivers). N.U.R. carried a resolution *against* accepting by seventeen to five. . . . The Communists then moved a resolution in favour of a strike, and the voting was eleven–eleven.[2]

This information was brought to me at a Defence Committee discussing military plans for Jordan and Lebanon. Finally, after Robertson had refused any further concessions the N.U.R. as well as ASLEF and the Transport Salaried Staffs' Association decided to accept the 3 per cent offer, the original terms to which the Cabinet had agreed. This was an immense relief. I was now prepared to face the bus strike and the partial dislocation in the London docks.

Although there was naturally some criticism expressed on the back benches, this did not cause me great concern.

> The Party is grumbling about the railway settlement. But when they get to their constituencies, they will find a good deal of sympathy for the railwaymen.[3]

[1] 13 May 1958.   [2] 14 May 1958.   [3] 15 May 1958.

The Times, of course, returned to the attack with a very critical leading article. I could not help feeling that in view of their own record on the wages front this was rather disingenuous.

The employers have offered 5% (cost of living) *plus* 6½% (betterment) and since the London Typographical Association have asked for still more, *The Times* is likely (with the other proprietors) to give in. Yet the Editor has the impertinence to write an article about the railway settlement entitled 'The Price'. *The Economist* has been rather more ashamed and has made its strictures milder.[1]

A few days later agreement on a 3 per cent basis was reached for the Underground staff. The bus strike continued, but the public seemed more angry with the strikers than with the Government. At any rate I felt comforted by the Treasury and the Bank deciding to lower Bank Rate at this particular moment. It showed confidence that the railway settlement would be regarded abroad as reasonable and firm.

At this point it became clear that since the Transport Workers Union had failed to get the railways into their dispute they must now take some further action. There was accordingly a threat

to withdraw 6,000 men who drive the oil delivery vans, and [thus] paralyse all road transport. . . . [There is also a threat] to stop the electric power stations.[2]

At this juncture a T.U.C. deputation called to see me at their own request. They were accompanied by the two secretaries, Vincent Tewson and George Woodcock.

The discussion was very friendly, but rather ineffective. It was clear that (*a*) T.U.C. want to avoid a General Strike—or even *any* spreading of the strike; (*b*) that they have been and are still frightened of Cousins—partly because of his size (1¼ m. members) and partly because of his character; (*c*) they are desperately anxious that Cousins should be helped out of the position into which he has got, if H.M.G. or Transport Board can do so. . . .

I made it clear to them (*a*) that we were going to maintain essential services—petrol, light, etc., (*b*) we did not want a show-down. We wanted a fair settlement.

[1] 16 May 1958.   [2] 28 May 1958.

I took them all through the bus dispute; the industrial court agreement; the moves which Sir John Elliot had made, improving on the award in some respects. What had Cousins done to match all this?

I took them all through the way I had personally handled the railway problem; the way the trade union leaders had helped me had led to a settlement which was generally approved by all moderate people.[1]

We ended the discussion with an agreed Press report and an agreed statement of what they had asked and what I had replied. I had suggested that Frank Cousins and Sir John Elliot should meet immediately and seek a basis on which a fair settlement could be made. The T.U.C. members put a good deal of pressure on Cousins, but, as I had expected, the talks broke down because no immediate pay increase was offered to workers not covered by the arbitration award.

All kinds of proposals were now made; but both Harold Watkinson (Minister of Transport) and Macleod (Minister of Labour) thought that Cousins would now call a delegate conference in order to share the burden either of retreat or of a further widening of the strike.

I feel that, somehow or other, there will be a settlement in a few days. But we must *not* make a false step. No troops, till absolutely necessary.[2]

On 3 June the delegates decided to continue the strike. How far it could be spread it was not yet clear.

Meanwhile a bad position is building up in London docks, where half the men are out—unofficially—in support of the Smithfield meat porters.[3]

The next day,

I saw the T.U.C. at 10, and urged them strongly *not* to widen the strike and to give no support to Cousins. I made it clear that I could not and would not urge Sir John Elliot to go beyond my Friday formula, which still seemed to me the basis for negotiating a fair settlement.[4]

[1] 30 May 1958. [2] 1 June 1958. [3] 3 June 1958. [4] 4 June 1958.

It was now clearly a contest of will. Although I had treated the
T.U.C. delegates with courtesy and understanding in private, in
public we had taken firm action. To Cousins's threat to withdraw
the petrol distribution workers and to the T.U.C. appeal to intervene, our only overt reply was to cancel the weekend leave for the
selected troops and the announcement that we would take immediate
action if vital services to the community were threatened.

4 June was the vital date. The T.U.C. were flatly against any
extension of the strike and, after a long and sometimes stormy discussion, passed a resolution urging further negotiation on my
formula. I had to leave for Washington on 7 June, but before I
went it was clear to me that if we remained calm the strike would
slowly peter out, greatly to the advantage of further industrial peace.

In my absence the Cabinet discussed the use of troops in the docks
in view of a reported remark by Cousins that neither the dock nor
the Smithfield disputes would end while the bus strike remained
unsettled. But later news showed that the Smithfield strike and hence
the sympathetic dock strike might soon fade out.

I returned to London on 14 June, and, although the majority of
the bus garages on whom the responsibility had now been definitely
put by their leaders voted for continuing the strike, yet gradually
this fresh 'illustration of the fact that the Englishman did not know
when he was beaten'[1] made me feel a genuine, if somewhat reluctant, admiration for their doggedness. On 19 June the bus strike was
clearly about to end, and the news seemed to have spread to the
Treasury and the Bank of England, for a further reduction of Bank
Rate to 5 per cent was now made. This second fall within a month
and in a period of considerable industrial disorder, made me feel
more and more certain that the time had come for a cautious reversal
of policy. Events now began to move quickly. On 20 June the bus
strike was definitely over. A salutary lesson had been learnt that
even in the state monopolies pressure could be exerted too far, for
one of the first results was the reduction of nearly 10 per cent in the
services which could be offered to the public. In the first ten days
of June the strike in the docks and at Smithfield also began to peter
out, and at the end of the month a useful, if comparatively painless,

[1] *Annual Register, 1958*, p. 28.

victory had been won against the arrogant policy which had been adopted by the leaders of the Transport Union. In spite of some captious criticism, public opinion, both at home and abroad, believed that broadly the wages front had been firmly held.

Certainly from the political aspect the bus strike seemed to be a turning-point. Up to then, although I felt no doubt that the Government had succeeded in maintaining itself and even imposing a moral ascendancy in the House of Commons, there had been no similar advance in the country. My fears were confirmed by the Rochdale by-election in February 1958, at which the Conservative vote showed a shattering decline. Although the art of psephology was comparatively new, it did not require any very advanced mathematical calculation to observe that in this curious election, although the Labour vote had suffered a slight reduction, a large block of the Conservative vote, 16,000 or 17,000, had been transferred to the Liberals. It was true that the Liberal candidate had the advantage of representing the new and coming power in British public life. The staid author of the *Annual Register* described this as follows:

> There was no doubt that the Liberal was the most personable of the three candidates; he was in fact a television star, Mr. Ludovic Kennedy ('Ludo' to his fans); and his wife was perhaps an even greater draw, the ballet dancer and film actress Miss Moira Shearer.[1]

The same writer pointed out that Rochdale had always followed the fashion of the day. In the century before it had found in John Bright the most satisfactory exponent of the ruling philosophy of Manchester. It had later been the birthplace of no less an artist than Miss Gracie Fields. Although this new combination could hardly be said to have reached so high a plane, it had certainly excelled anything that the other parties could show. But the revival of Liberalism was not to be confined to Rochdale.

In the spring of 1958 I felt little doubt that in spite of our bold attempt to ride the storm after the events of 1956 we were still slipping backwards. After a Conservative rally on 4 April I made this note in my diary:

[1] *Annual Register, 1958*, p. 5.

A good audience and a good reception. But, in spite of their courage, they seem to feel the tide going against us. Will it gain in impetus, or turn in the next two years? It will soon be necessary to consider whether we would do a more patriotic thing if we went to the country now—riding for a fall but not too severe a one. I do not myself think that is yet necessary or desirable.[1]

As usual there were no lack of suggestions from a mass of correspondents. At Cabinet meetings, in my experience, the political situation is seldom discussed as such. Ministers are far too busy dealing with the immense burden of current issues. But I had previously set up a party 'steering committee' of selected Ministers, based upon the Research Department of the Conservative party, and under the management of Michael Fraser. This proved a most useful instrument in preparing policies and plans for the Election, as well as for obtaining advice on current issues.

The Torrington by-election on 27 March showed some slight improvement:

We *lost* the Torrington by-election by 200 votes. Actually, this is 2,000–3,000 *better* than we expected, and it is certain that in the last few days our candidate has been gaining ground. But it is irritating to lose by so little, and I'm afraid the triumph of the Asquiths (Violet Bonham Carter and her son) will encourage the Liberals elsewhere.[2]

Undoubtedly the Liberal revival was based upon a certain disillusionment with both the larger parties. Moreover every short-term trouble, such as a mounting agitation against the decontrol provisions of the last Rent Act, which affected particularly the more well-to-do classes, as well as genuine apprehensions about the power of any Government to withstand the demands of the trade unions, led to the Liberals becoming the natural refuge of all those who were discontented. Incidentally the partial decontrol of rents, so persistently urged in principle by all detached commentators, but so difficult to carry out in practice, was the cause of the loss of the Kelvingrove by-election—Walter Elliot's seat in Glasgow. Dame

[1] 4 March 1958.   [2] 28 March 1958.

Katharine, his widow, had made a splendid fight, but she was over-whelmed by the temporary abstention of many normal Conservative voters. I was glad when the day came to recommend this remarkable public figure for a life peerage.

On 14 June I arrived back from my journey to America and Canada to hear the results of five vital by-elections all held on the same day. The three Conservative seats were held with good majorities, and the Liberals were less successful than either at Rochdale or at Torrington.

> These have turned out *very well indeed* for us—a great change in the last few months.[1]

At the beginning of July it was clear to me that the political as well as the economic tide had turned.

Some commentators were kind enough to regard the improve-ment in our political fortunes as partly due to a television broadcast arranged with Ed Murrow and Charles Collingwood and made on 24 May. At that time the appearance of political leaders, which has now become an almost daily feature of the television programmes, was rare and perhaps correspondingly important. At any rate this discussion, which owed much to the sympathetic handling of the two American interviewers, seemed to have a considerable effect on the public, and my stout defence of the greatness of our country and its role in the world was perhaps received with all the greater satis-faction by my many listeners, because it was in tune with their deepest feelings. Others, perhaps more correctly, dated the change from the defeat of the bus strike and the collapse of the sympathetic strikes which were threatened in its support.

The Gallup Poll in the middle of August, followed by a *Daily Express* poll a few days later, certainly seemed to show a marked change. As a result all the newspapers began to discuss the likeli-hood of an early General Election.

> While this course has its attractions, my instinct is against it. I feel that the people would regard it as rather unfair and slick. Such revival as we have had has been based on a certain con-fidence in our character.[2]

---

[1] 14 June 1958.　　　　　[2] 23 August 1958.

Indeed the widespread speculation became embarrassing and perhaps damaging to industry and trade. Accordingly on 12 September
I took the unusual course of making a public statement that there
would be no General Election during the coming winter. I added that
this public statement 'would put the Opposition out of their agony'.

Further by-elections in November revealed the same tendencies;
but, as I rather expected, by January 1959 the position was not so
favourable. However, in March our fortunes seemed once again to
be on the mend and the Press now began to expect an early appeal
to the people.

Meanwhile the Chancellor of the Exchequer was able to recommend the removal of restrictions on the total level of bank lending
and the easing of control over the raising of capital and credit. The
so-called credit squeeze initiated in 1955 was thus brought to an
end. Discussions soon turned on the rate at which Government
expenditure should now be allowed to increase. Heathcoat Amory
proposed a 5 per cent increase per annum—roughly £75 million.
He argued that a surplus of £450 million on the balance of payments
was necessary to cope with the various demands made upon us,
which included not merely repayment of loans but a demand for
Commonwealth development. By the end of July agreement was
reached on certain reflationary measures to be concentrated on the
areas where unemployment was threatening. Indeed, so encouraged
was the Governor of the Bank by the improved conditions of our
affairs, that he suggested urgent consideration of bringing together,
at an early date, the two rates of sterling, the official and the transferable rate,

> thus concentrating the whole sterling market in London, instead
> of letting the transferable market be more or less permanently
> transferred to Amsterdam. Of course, this is really 'convertibility'
> with all that is implied.[1]

Although the final decision was postponed, this was, in fact, to be
achieved before the end of the year. The 'Three Wise Men'
published a second report on 25 August, which showed that wages
had not gone up as much as they had in a comparable period of the

[1] 6 August 1958.

previous year, and that prices had remained more stable. By October the general view in the Cabinet was moving rapidly towards greater Government investment in face of the shadow of rising unemployment which might well reach 3 per cent in the winter. As so often, before and since, the problem was how to stimulate the economy without risking a fresh inflation.

The rise in the unemployment figures from $1 \cdot 9\%$ to $2 \cdot 2\%$ has given the Socialists a good chance for criticism. The 'shadow' of unemployment is our real danger. Of course, even 3% (which the figure will go to during the winter) is still within the famous Gaitskell definition of 'full employment'. But it is something to be watched. I am awaiting the return of the Chancellor of the Exchequer and the meetings of the Cabinet next week to discuss the present state of the 'economy' and what steps to further stimulation (if any) we ought to take. We must be careful not to plunge into another inflation. But we must equally try to stop too great a deflation. (I have had a good memorandum from Roy Harrod on all this.)[1]

All through the autumn the Cabinet discussed these questions, and in order to be ready to act rapidly I had already arranged for the departments concerned to prepare their forward programmes, in order to see how far they could provide immediate opportunities for further investment should conditions allow or call for such measures. Before Parliament met a full discussion in the Cabinet took place on 24 October.

It was left for me to make proposals as to action to the Chancellor for some 'reflationary' measures. Chancellor accepted this, and it gives me just what I wanted. It is a heavy responsibility, for the whole future of the Party depends on whether
(*a*) we ought to reflate
(*b*) we can reflate in time . . .
(*a*) Means can we risk *another* inflation if we go too far. (*b*) Means how long does it take to stop a slump, if it takes two years to halt a boom ? It will be a 'close-run thing'–like Waterloo.[2]

With all the immense refinements and improvements that have been made in the nice calculation of economic movements, this approach

[1] 9 October 1958.   [2] 24 October 1958.

must today seem somewhat primitive. In addition, in spite of the President's assurances, I was alarmed by the fear of an American recession casting its dark shadow over our smiling land.

In order to allow room for further productive expenditure, there had been a continuous effort to make savings in Government expenditure. These were broadly successful due to the co-operation of all Ministers concerned. At the same time, in the course of a short tour of the West Midlands, a so-called 'Meet the People' tour, during the recess, I had found my personal position in the country definitely improved. But I was not to be misled; everything would depend upon our being able, when the time came, to present a balanced picture of steady improvement in our affairs at home and of our national reputation abroad.

The opening of Parliament on 28 October was as usual impressive; in addition, for the first time in history, the ceremony, from the time of the Queen leaving the Palace, was televised.

> The various ceremonies (the arrival of the Crown, etc.) which nobody ever sees, were included—everything, indeed, except the Robing. I am sure that the effect has been good. The whole history of Parliament is enshrined in these ceremonies. Nor can it do the people any harm to be reminded of the antiquity and continuity of the realm. (All sorts of new pieces of information— new, at least, to most of us—were given—e.g. that the emerald in the cross above the Crown belonged to Edward the Confessor and the ruby was worn by Henry V at Agincourt.)[1]

Although this session of Parliament was likely to be the last before the dissolution, the mood of Members was strangely restrained. Even the traditional Conferences, held in the previous weeks, had failed to rouse much enthusiasm either inside or outside the Parties. Gaitskell was chiefly occupied in defending, with skill and courage, his middle-of-the-road position. Bevan seemed to have lost his fire. Cousins, in spite of his eloquence and the control of more than a million votes, could not take his place. The Labour Party Conference had been, in the words of the *Annual Register*, 'a decorous affair'. The Conservative Party Conference had been more

[1] 28 October 1958.

militant, largely owing to the activities of an organisation known as the League of Empire Loyalists. The mood, apart from this disturbance, was quietly confident. Similarly the debates on the Address were pedestrian. The Offshore Islands crisis had passed away, and the problem of nuclear tests awaited another Conference at Geneva. The Government programme included a number of measures, of which the most important was the Bill to implement the new pension scheme. Other proposals were practical but not particularly controversial. The question chosen by the Opposition for their amendment to the Address was 'unemployment' and the fear of a substantial rise in the autumn.

We have a good programme, which will be lively and (in parts) popular. The only shadow remains—'unemployment'.[1]

I began now to bring increasing pressure upon the Chancellor of the Exchequer and the Treasury. As a result Bank Rate was reduced to 4 per cent on 20 November; indeed it was to remain unchanged at that figure during the whole of the following year. Just before Christmas, Amory and Butler had come for a general talk about the Budget. We hoped to achieve without danger a reduction of £200 million in taxation. We now prepared for the bold step from which we had hitherto shrunk—the amalgamation of official and transferable sterling, thus bringing about the convertibility in the modern and technical sense—that is of sterling (other than capital transfers) held by non-residents.

At a meeting of Ministers on 12 December

it was agreed to go ahead in principle, but the timing to be left with Chancellor of the Exchequer and Foreign Secretary together while in Paris next week. We believe that the Bank of France is trying to persuade the French Government to *devalue* and to go convertible. In other words, what we propose to do from strength, they want to do from weakness. But I suspect a French plot to put the blame on us and thus create another grievance.[2]

On their return we agreed to take the plunge. On 27 December the decision was officially announced. I had always felt that this operation

[1] 28 October 1958.   [2] 12 December 1958.

should be regarded as a great move towards the unity of Europe and happily this had been arranged

> with all other European countries (including France) and is accompanied (in the case of all) by 'convertibility' and in the case of France by 'devaluation' of the franc. It will be in the Press tomorrow (Sunday) and of course Monday—when we shall get the views of *The Times* and *Financial* Press, as well as of the popular papers. The French are, at least in official quarters, in full agreement. Indeed, the timing has been arranged for their benefit.[1]

Somewhat unexpectedly the Press was all favourable.

> Even *Daily Herald* merely printed Gaitskell's criticism without comment. At any rate the 'European' character of the decisions reached is fully understood at home and by most of the French Press.[2]

One of the incidental results was the description of the reserves as 'consisting of gold and convertible currencies' instead of 'gold and dollars'. Our decision was fortified by the fact that the balance of payments for the year showed a surplus of £455 million.

Until now I had been content with delivering a series of Minutes to the Chancellor of the Exchequer under which bombardment he remained, as one might have expected, calm and cool. After a few days of reflection at Christmas, I began to feel that something more was needed.

> Meeting of Ministers on the Economic situation. Some progress towards 'Reflation'—but the Chancellor of the Exchequer (urged on by the Treasury) rather stiff. He still fears another inflationary boom. For six months or more I have had the opposite fear—the approaching slump. Fortunately, we have done something—by reduction of Bank Rate, end of credit squeeze, abolition of hire purchase restrictions and (by immense pressure from me) by injecting another £50 m. into the public investment programme. But I am still not sure that this is enough.[3]

On the same day Dorothy and I set out on a tour throughout the North-East, with which we had been so long familiar.

[1] 27 December 1958.   [2] 29 December 1958.   [3] 12 January 1959.

It was very cold–snow everywhere–but fine. We had a most touching reception in Stockton, and everywhere the people were very friendly. It was really extraordinary. Of course, all this means very little when it comes to voting. All the same, there is no bitterness–on the contrary, great friendliness. Dorothy was in great form and thoroughly enjoyed it. We were 'on' for ten to twelve hours a day, and completely exhausted at the end. But the exhilaration of it all enabled us to get through this immense programme–visits, works inspections, luncheons, dinners, receptions, visits to Mayors, and all the rest. At Newcastle I gave a big speech–forty minutes–more for the Press than for the audience! I was, however, concerned about the future–the immediate future–of heavy industry in this area. Order books are thin; and I feel sure we must do more 'reflation' if we are to avoid a serious increase in unemployment.[1]

My anxieties were confirmed by the Minister of Labour, Macleod, on my return.

The January count (taken on Monday) will show an increase of 86,000–2·8% in all. This will cause a great Parliamentary outcry and some real alarm. Of course, the bad weather will have had some effect–especially on building workers, etc.–but I do not like it.[2]

I now began to work on a short paper setting out my thoughts. I

dined with Lord Mills and went through the Economic paper. Broadly, I disagree with the official Treasury view that the danger is a boom. I think (and Lord Mills agrees) that the danger is a serious slump. My plan is: (*a*) To inject another £50 m. capital expenditure on Public account into the economy at once. It can only begin to have some effect in five or six months' time. This would be *in addition* to the £50 m. we have already done. (*b*) To bring the Budget date forward from 7 April to 17 March and so get the stimulus which we hope the Budget will provide as soon as we can. This will be a difficult battle–but I must make an effort to get one or other (if not *both*) of these.[3]

On 22 January a little progress was made.

6.15 p.m.–8.15 p.m. Foreign Secretary, Chancellor of the Exchequer, Lord Privy Seal, Minister of Labour, Minister of

---

[1] 16 January 1959.   [2] 16 January 1959.   [3] 19 January 1959,

2A

Power, Chief Whip. My economic plan fully discussed, but no conclusions reached. I told them, before we began, about my Russian and American plans. They approved initiative in the Foreign field; I hoped they would sympathise with my desire to show equal initiative on the Home Front. Lord Privy Seal supported me fully; also Lord Mills. Chancellor of the Exchequer reserved his decision—or his final decision, but gave an analysis which rather depressed me. He (with Treasury) believes in the doctrine of automatic recovery. I do not.[1]

Five days later I noted:

After the division (Pension Bill) we had a meeting of our (adjourned) employment committee. Nearly all Ministers supported me in asking for more 'reflation'. But the Chancellor was very guarded. I think the Treasury is giving him as bad advice as it has to every Chancellor in turn. Certainly the Bank of England is very timid and 'orthodox'. I have a greater belief in Roy Harrod.[2]

However, on 3 February a meeting of the same Ministers was held.

We definitely decided *against* an early Budget, but *for* another £30 m. or so of reflationary Government expenditure on capital account. I am very pleased about this.[3]

So varied are the burdens of a Prime Minister that I feel tempted to quote the note on the next page of my diary:

Our operations in Muscat seem to have been very successful. The mountain has been occupied by a small and highly trained force (Life guards etc.) and there is now some chance of a temporary period of quiet there.[4]

But the commanding heights of Whitehall are not so easily stormed.
On 11 February the news of the addition of 60,000 to the unemployed was published. Had we yet done enough?

Roy Harrod came in the evening. He is still very critical (and I think rightly so) of the Treasury and the Bank of England. By their obsession with the problem of 'funding' they are continuing

[1] 22 January 1959. [2] 27 January 1959.
[3] 3 February 1959. [4] 4 February 1959.

to narrow the credit base at a time when it should be expanded. They should be using 'open market' operations to create *more* money—by buying securities, not selling. I am trying to compose a paper on all this, and his help will be useful.[1]

On 17 February, while the future of Cyprus was in the balance,

I worked on my paper on 'Money', in which I am trying to demolish the Treasury and the Bank of England! Roy Harrod has sent me a paper about 'open market operations'. Just as [the Bank used to be] obsessed by the gold standard, so [now it] is obsessed by 'funding'. So [it] is selling securities when [it] ought to be buying—at least this is what I feel (supported by Roy Harrod and others, including Lord Monckton, Midland Bank).[2]

On the evening of my return from Russia, a few weeks later, I had

a long talk with Heathcoat Amory about (*a*) monetary policy (*b*) Budget. Treasury and Bank of England are rather sticky about (*a*). However, although they are not yet buying securities in the open market (as they *should* be doing), they have stopped selling and have lately even bought a little. On (*b*) the prospects for a stimulating Budget are distinctly good.[3]

Indeed when we came to his final Budget plans the Chancellor of the Exchequer proved himself in a definitely expansionist mood. Knowing his great integrity, unshakeable by any argument that could not convince him, I was satisfied that in his decision to make reductions in taxation amounting to some £360 million in a full year he felt certain of the strength of our position.

The Budget was simple and attractive. Income tax, which had stood for some years at 8*s*. 6*d*., was reduced by 9*d*., with 6*d*. off each of the lower rates. The three higher rates of purchase tax were cut by one-sixth. 2*d*. off a pint of beer. Improved acceleration for the repayment of post-war credits with $2\frac{1}{2}$ per cent interest accruing to the sum unpaid. The restoration of investment allowances at 20 per cent for new plant and machinery, plus 10 per cent initial allowance. There was also a general reconstruction of the system of investment and initial allowances. The Budget was well received in the country

---

[1] 11 February 1959. [2] 17 February 1959. [3] 4 March 1959.

and by the Press. The only cry against it was—why nothing for the old age pensioners?

"Actually, we have done this class in the community exception-ally well—as a leading article in *The Times* showed very forcibly today.[1]

Later, in the middle of June,

John Boyd-Carpenter made a statement about another £32 m. for the impoverished old people by raising National Assistance. The Opposition were much taken aback.[2]

With unemployment rising—but not too much; with a moderate Bank Rate, low, but not too low; with the pound steady, was it possible that we were neither suffering the cruel hardships of a slump nor exposed to the debilitating ease of a boom, but enjoying that happy state of felicity which the older economists used to seek, with all the ardour in which earlier illuminati pursued the philo-sopher's stone? Could it be that we were in equilibrium? In any case, we seemed now safely poised to consider and decide how and when to face the 'appeal unto Caesar'.

[1] 9 April 1959.   [2] 15 June 1959.

CHAPTER XXI

The Last Lap

IT must not be supposed that during these last two years the activities of Ministers were solely concentrated upon these financial and economic issues. The two sessions of 1957–8 and 1958–9 were marked by important legislative as well as administrative measures. Perhaps the most dramatic of these was the introduction in February 1958 of the Bill for the appointment of life peers. I owed a great deal to Butler and Kilmuir for their help over this measure. It was, of course, not at all acceptable to those members of the Opposition who disliked a second chamber in principle and who feared in a reformed House of Lords a more effective barrier to their hopes. Nor was it altogether to the taste of some of my Conservative friends who believed that any infraction of the hereditary system was dangerous. The third reading passed the House of Commons on 2 April, 1958. I immediately saw Gaitskell and asked him whether he would send me any suggested names for the first list to be submitted for Her Majesty's approval.

> I asked about life peers. He is a little embarrassed—his party is again divided about all this.[1]

However, after the Bill had successfully passed the House of Lords and received Royal Assent, I made a new approach to him.

> After all the Socialist protestations regarding life peers—they would never touch it, etc., etc.—he . . . produced five or six nominations !²

The first list of creations was published on 24 July, and it included ten men and four women, for the Act was based on the concept of equality of the sexes. Among the latter stood the name

[1] 2 April 1958.   [2] 1 July 1958.

of Lady Ravensdale, a peeress in her own right, one of a class whose claims to sit had hitherto been rejected. This modest constitutional reform has had important results. Undoubtedly the powers and prestige of the House of Lords have been buttressed by the extension of its membership. Whatever the future may bring, it seems clear that the country is now persuaded of the advantages of a second chamber, even though the House of Commons may continue to be jealous of its powers and authority.

In these years other Bills were introduced and carried through Parliament. They depended, for their success, on the skilful management of their authors. Useful reforms were introduced dealing with local government reorganisation, compensation for property compulsorily acquired, loans for small farmers, opportunities for house ownership and the future management of the New Towns. Another curious by-product of the affluent society was a Bill to repeal those clauses of the Act of 1948 which had limited the use of motor-cars in elections; for by now the car, which had been regarded as the privilege of the few, was the instrument by which as many Labour as Conservative voters might expect to reach the polling stations.

Nor did my colleagues shrink from tackling more delicate questions which they approached under the prudent guidance of the Home Secretary, who trod along this dangerous path with the delicacy of Agag. Feeling that I belonged to an older generation, I frankly left decisions on these matters to my younger colleagues, only trying to steer them away from the major pitfalls. I remember one whole Cabinet session being devoted to a discussion of these somewhat distasteful matters. I allowed it to take its own course without any attempt to intervene. In the end Butler reproved me for lack of interest in the long debate. It is true that my mind was, at the time, filled with the difficult and dangerous issues already described in the earlier pages of this book. However, I denied the charge of inattention. 'No, no,' I replied. 'I quite understand what it is you want to do. You want to popularise abortion, legalise homosexuality and start a betting shop in every street. All I can say is if you can't win the Liberal nonconformist vote on these cries you never will.' Happily, only the last of these 'progressive' reforms was attempted in my time.

In the 1958–9 session, the last of this Parliament, the most important measure was that giving effect to the new pensions proposals. This was admirably conducted by Boyd-Carpenter with the help of the Treasury Ministers.

In addition, the Government had to face a number of critical situations, sometimes unexpected and unpredictable, sometimes arising from deep-rooted causes.

Among the former was a tragic incident following the suppression of the Mau Mau rebellion in Kenya. By the end of 1956 this terrible tale of barbarity was brought to a final conclusion, and the military were able to restore full responsibility for law and order to the civil authorities. In the course of the 'emergency', which caused dreadful loss of life to Europeans, Asians and Africans alike, 88,000 members of the Kikuyu tribe had been detained in custody. But by the beginning of 1959 all had been released except 4,000, who were serving prison sentences, and 1,000 'hard-core' incorrigibles held in special camps.

In one of these, named Hola, eleven prisoners died on 3 March. The inquest revealed that death was due to 'multiple bruising'. This story was widely reported in the British Press, and the Opposition immediately threatened a vote of censure. I felt particular concern for Alan Lennox-Boyd, the Colonial Secretary, whose deep sympathy for all African peoples had won him not only their respect, but their affection. A full enquiry into this regrettable event was held by W. H. Goudie, the Senior Resident Magistrate. There seemed to be no doubt that the fact that responsibility for the detention camps was shared between two Ministers in the Governor's Council had resulted in a failure to provide efficient control by either. My colleagues were at first somewhat divided as to whether to accede to an Opposition's demand for a public enquiry, but the publication of the White Paper[1] on 10 June brought a good reaction.

This morning's Press, following publication of the White Paper, has been pretty good. *The Times* (perhaps an *amende honorable*) wrote a very sensible leader.[2]

[1] *Documents relating to the deaths of eleven Mau Mau detainees at Hola Camp in Kenya*, Cmnd. 778 (H.M.S.O., June 1959).

[2] 11 June 1959.

The enquiry had been full and explicit. It was clear that only the most nominal responsibility could be attributed to the Colonial Secretary and little to the Governor, Sir Evelyn Baring.

On 16 June the matter was fully debated in the House of Commons.

The debate has gone off 'as well as could be expected', but it has been an anxious day. Soskice (ex-Attorney-General) opened for the Opposition with a clever and well constructed speech, based largely on the Coroner's report. He ended with a bitter, but not ineffective, personal attack on Sir Evelyn Baring and the Colonial Secretary. Perhaps this was rather too highly coloured— for everyone on both sides of the House respects Lennox-Boyd and knows how much sympathy and devotion he has brought to his task. Colonial Secretary followed. His speech was very long, but in the main succeeded in its purpose. He frankly admitted the mistakes and muddles of the Hola tragedy. But by giving the whole story of Mau Mau, and particularly by a vivid story of how the original 80,000 detainees had been brought down to under 1,000 by the 'rehabilitation' work, he did succeed in putting this unhappy incident in its proper perspective.[1]

Nevertheless the Colonial Secretary thought it his duty to offer his resignation, which he pressed on me both in conversation and by letter. Although I respected his honourable sentiments, I went into great detail in my reply both as to the precedents in other departments and the special relationship between the Secretary of State and the Governor in the Colonial Office. More directly,

I kept telling him that it would be a fatal mistake and quite uncalled-for. But (with all his extraordinary charm and real ability) he is a highly-strung, sensitive, and rather quixotic character. I tell him that to resign now over this affair would (*a*) be a great blow to Her Majesty's Government at the most critical period before the General Election, when all is going well otherwise; (*b*) would be a very sad end to his splendid career as Colonial Secretary; (*c*) would upset the whole Colonial Service, whose loyalty and devotion he can command; (*d*) would have very bad—even dangerous—effects in Kenya and Africa . . . (*e*) that it would involve Sir Evelyn Baring's resignation. This would really be a tragic end to a fine career of voluntary service in Africa.[2]

[1] 16 June 1959.　　　　[2] 22 June 1959.

On 23 June I had a meeting with the Colonial Secretary and the Governor, who had returned to London for consultation.

We discussed Hola and a plan of action. I proposed that Colonial Secretary should write a despatch to the Governor (he returns [to Kenya] in a few days) giving his reflections on the affair, now that the debate is over, and laying down certain principles, etc., and asking what Governor is going to do. (This may be shutting the stable after the horse, etc., etc. But there are other horses!) Then (when the present disciplinary trials are over) Governor can reply and set out the organisational changes he proposes. In the course of these structural changes in the Government, the most notorious figures can pass on or be transferred to other jobs or colonies. All this was accepted.[1]

These despatches were formally published in July.[2] Nevertheless, a further debate was called for and took place on 27 July.

The Hola debate began about 10 p.m. and lasted till 3 a.m. It was not an easy affair, because the Kenya Government had really muddled it. But the Colonial Secretary put up a good case for the action we had taken and the administrative reforms we had made. The Opposition muddled the attack—in two ways. By taking it on the Appropriation Bill there could be no vote. By taking it late at night (which since they control the business on this day they could have avoided) they got no Press. Yet, on a vote, there might well have been quite a number of Conservatives voting against the Government or abstaining.[3]

I was indeed glad when this affair was concluded. It had been an anxious, if minor, incident exaggerated by the hysterical attitude of some critics and the not unnatural desire of others to gain political advantage. Nevertheless it revealed some weaknesses which could not be denied. On 3 August, in writing to the Queen, I summarised my conclusions:

Although I have always thought that the Hola incident was by no means satisfactorily explained, or excused, by the Government

[1] 23 June 1959.
[2] *Further documents relating to the deaths of eleven Mau Mau detainees at Hola Camp in Kenya*, Cmnd. 816 (H.M.S.O., July 1959).
[3] 27 July 1959.

AA2

of Kenya, yet I felt it would be quite wrong to have allowed it to result in the resignation either of the Governor, Sir Evelyn Baring, or of the Secretary of State for the Colonies. The former is nearing the end of his term after a remarkable and successful tenure of various posts in Your Majesty's service. His record is a fine one. The latter can hardly be held responsible for the faults of commission or omission of quite minor officials.

By a singular piece of ill-fortune the Colonial Secretary was involved in another African difficulty, this time in Nyasaland. In January 1959 a meeting of the African National Congress in Nyasaland decided to embark on a policy of defiance and sabotage, including violence. Mounting disorder culminated in the declaration of a State of Emergency on 3 March 1959, and one hundred and sixty-six members of Congress were arrested. By the time order was restored, fifty-two Africans in all had been killed by the security forces since the start of the disorders. The Cabinet immediately decided on a formal enquiry into this grave affair, and Mr. Justice Devlin undertook this task. An advance copy of the report reached me on 13 July. Although the troubles in Nyasaland were un-doubtedly bound up with the whole problem of the Federation of Rhodesia and Nyasaland, by general agreement the debate would be confined to the question on which the distinguished Judge had been asked to report. A problem now arose about the Governor's position. In accordance with normal practice Sir Robert Armitage should be allowed at least four weeks to prepare his reply, and the report and the reply published together. But this would mean holding up the whole matter until after the holidays—an intolerable situation. The Governor only arrived in London on 18 July, and it did not seem practicable to get his detailed comments in time for the debate.

> The fact that the Governor has hardly had as many days as the Devlin Commissioners have had months will, perhaps, get him some sympathy.[1]

A long session was drawing to an end. Members of Parliament and Ministers were in a restless mood. The Governor was assisted

[1] 18 July 1959.

by many hands and was able to produce, in a remarkably short time, a good document which fortunately we were able to publish on 24 July at the same time as the Devlin Report. 20 July was certainly an interesting day:

I asked the Lord Privy Seal (Butler) to come at 10.30 a.m. and the Colonial Secretary at 11 a.m. I talked over with the former the tactics which I proposed to pursue in the Cabinet. This met at 11.30 a.m. Every member of the Cabinet had received the Devlin Report last Saturday morning. This morning (11.15 a.m. to 11.30 a.m.) they were asked to read the *Governor's* reply–which is to be published at the same time. This is a pretty good document. It has been written at Chequers in two days (Devlin and Co. had several months) largely by Lord Chancellor, Attorney-General, and Julian Amery. Before the formal meeting began Ministers sat in the Cabinet room, reading these documents; Rab and I and Alan Lennox-Boyd sat in the garden. Alan Lennox-Boyd once more pressed on me his readiness to resign and thought this the best way out. Rab agreed with me that such a decision would be (*a*) *wrong*–colonial administration in the dependent Colonies would break down if Her Majesty's Government were to betray them; (*b*) *impolitic*. A rather difficult debate in the House of Commons with perhaps a few Tory abstentions is one thing; hardly a ripple over the constituencies. But the resignation of the three Colonial Ministers–Lennox-Boyd, Perth and Amery, together with the dismissal of the Governor, would be a major event at a most critical time. But in order to satisfy Colonial Secretary, I told him that I would *not* give the Cabinet much of a lead. I would let each express his view before I expressed mine. Then we should know the unbiased view of each Minister–not a view tinged with loyalty to me as Prime Minister.[1]

I called on all Ministers in turn starting with the lawyers, the Lord Chancellor and the Attorney-General.

Every single one said, with absolute conviction, that we must stand by the Nyasaland Government and the Colonial Secretary. (I told them that the Colonial Secretary had placed his resignation in my hands–this was part of my short preliminary remarks.)

[1] 20 July 1959.

This was a fine performance and most impressive. Mr. Gladstone used to call his last Cabinet the 'Blubbering Cabinet'. This is a 'Manly Cabinet'. I told them, *after* the decision had been taken, that had it gone otherwise, I should have *not* continued as Prime Minister. But I had thought it unfair, *before* the decision, to offer such a temptation to such a brilliant and properly ambitious set of men as composed the Cabinet. This broke the tension—and after a short discussion on tactics, Press, debates, etc., the Cabinet dispersed.[1]

As so often happens, difficulties firmly faced soon began to melt away.

The Devlin Report is published today . . . *The Times* has a good news story and a robust and sensible leading article. *Daily Telegraph* equally good. *Manchester Guardian* bad headlines but a *very* good and *very* fair leader. *Daily Mail, Daily Express*, good. *News Chronicle* very hostile. *Daily Mirror* 'goes to town' in a big, hysterical way. The party seem pretty steady. The 'frondeurs', who make the mistake of opposing on everything, are quite active.[2]

When the debate came all our anxieties were quickly dispersed.

The Attorney-General opened with a massive speech, which greatly pleased our Party. He was given a great ovation when he finished. Callaghan answered—some parts good and imaginative . . . Bevan wound up with an agreeable, whimsical speech, and the Colonial Secretary ended with a fine defence of his administration. We had a *very* good division—sixty-three majority (with the Liberals against us).[3]

I was certainly relieved, partly for the sake of the Government, but above all for the sake of my friend and colleague, Alan Lennox-Boyd, who had already told me that for family reasons he would not be able to serve in the next Government, even if we were to win the election. Indeed he had decided not to stand for the House of Commons. I deeply regretted this for many reasons; but it would have been an intolerable hardship had his fine career been tarnished in the public mind at its close.

[1] 20 July 1959.   [2] 24 July 1959.   [3] 28 July 1959.

These were temporary, if dangerous squalls, violent but soon forgotten. Another storm which gave us infinite trouble over these years was less easily weathered.

By a strange irony the most devastating effects of the policy of free trade, or, to be more accurate, free imports, had fallen upon the county of its birth. The cotton textile industry and the cotton towns of Lancashire found themselves one hundred years after the triumph of Cobden and Bright in a situation of increasing difficulty due to the competition, both in semi-finished and finished products, from India, Pakistan and, above all, Hong Kong. The problem was simple enough. Free entry was not merely in accordance with the general principle of 'free trade' but was specifically guaranteed in the case of Commonwealth products by the Ottawa agreement made nearly thirty years before and reasserted, in spirit at any rate, at Montreal in September 1958. In earlier years the danger had been thought to come largely from Japan and her admission to GATT in 1955 had been strongly opposed in Lancashire for that reason. In order to help the cotton industry at that time purchase tax was reduced in whole or in part. Yet now the Commonwealth imports kept flowing in, and there was a wide demand that some ceiling should be set. Nevertheless even on this issue, as so often, the cotton trade was itself divided. The manufacturers of all the processes in the industry wanted a quota on all imported products and exclusion of all imports beyond its limit. But many of the finishers were only too anxious to import cheap semi-finished material in order to make their final products more competitive, both at home and in the export market.

The Chairman of the British Cotton Board was Lord Rochdale, a man of infinite patience and skill, combined with absolute integrity. Without Rochdale we could have achieved nothing. I never ceased to admire his devotion to a task which he had undertaken purely from a sense of public duty.

In the course of my Commonwealth Tour at the beginning of 1958, I had talks both in India and Pakistan urging some form of voluntary limitation, at least for a period of years. On my return in the spring of 1958, there were long ministerial discussions on this question. So far as India and Pakistan were concerned, it was, of course, a matter for their own decision as self-governing countries. But Hong Kong was under the Colonial Office and Alan Lennox-Boyd fought for his ward with commendable loyalty. After one of these discussions I summed up the situation.

11.30. A long meeting about Lancashire and cotton imports from India, Pakistan and Hong Kong. The Colonial Secretary is very intransigent about this. If we *force* Hong Kong to conform to an agreement which India and Pakistan seem ready to make, he will resign. If we accept his view, we shall lose a lot of Lancashire trade . . . (perhaps inevitable) and nine [or even] fourteen Lancashire seats ! This dilemma was *not* resolved by lunch time.[1]

However, a few days later I was able to record,

I think we have persuaded the Colonial Secretary to let us have one more try at 'voluntary' limitation by Hong Kong. If this could be done, we have a good chance of getting the same from the Indian and Pakistani industries.[2]

Four days later,

Colonial Secretary has agreed my plan for cotton, and Sir Frank Lee is off to Hong Kong quite soon. If anyone can bring it off, he will.[3]

Meanwhile, attempts were being made to get some voluntary limitation agreed with India and Pakistan in advance of any satisfactory conclusion of the Hong Kong talks. These negotiations were slow but not unhopeful. On 9 July I wrote to Lord Rochdale to say that we would continue to press Hong Kong for an agreement, but I must make it clear that if we could achieve this as well as an agreement with India and Pakistan, the industry must use the opportunity to undertake an extensive and orderly reconstruction. They could not hope for perpetual protection against Commonwealth industries. The next day I heard from Lord Rochdale that he and the Board had reached an agreement with India and Pakistan subject to similar limitations being accepted by Hong Kong. So we were faced with the familiar triangle, each agreement being contingent on some other agreement which was not in fact forthcoming. Feelings began to run quite high.

[1] 4 March 1958.   [2] 14 March 1958.   [3] 18 March 1958.

The President of the Board (Eccles) and the Colonial Secretary (Lennox-Boyd) have ceased to be on speaking terms—they are only on bawling terms. Indian and Pakistan cotton industries *have* made a voluntary limitation agreement, subject to Hong Kong. But Hong Kong is shy; and Secretary of State, quite rightly, takes the line that, as trustee for Colonial interests, he cannot *press* Hong Kong unduly. He cannot order. Yes, but can he suggest? On this, another metaphysical argument has been carried on with violence between the two ministers. I did not take this to Cabinet, because all of them are *against* the Colonial Secretary, and he might easily resign. I cannot lose him, for he is a fine man, with noble qualities. Finally, they agreed to my settling the matter—which I did. I hope that on the basis which I settled, Lord Rochdale and his colleagues will go to Hong Kong and get at least a temporary agreement.[1]

On 20 October, with some temerity, I agreed to attend a conference of the industry at Harrogate.

All Lancashire is in a ferment about the textile industry. On Saturday I had a long meeting with the consultative committee. This was followed by a vast cocktail party; then a dinner. On Sunday, I spoke to the 1,200 delegates and had another meeting with the committee. The 64,000-dollar question is how to get a 'voluntary' agreement with India, Pakistan and Hong Kong to limit imports into the United Kingdom of grey cloth and (latterly) 'made-up' goods. The feeling about this is intense.[2]

Nevertheless, apart from the letter and spirit of the Ottawa and Montreal agreements, I knew well that

the newly emerging countries *must* be allowed some exports of manufactured goods if they are to achieve the progress on which their hearts are set.[2]

But with the declining exports of cotton textiles and increasing imports the industry was certainly in a perilous state. I often wondered what the answer of Cobden and Bright would have been. To them free imports meant free food, low wages and good profits for the manufacturers. How would they have faced the reversal of the situation? Would doctrine have been strong enough to overcome interest? Indeed there was a great deal to be said for the view that

[1] 13 July 1958.   [2] 20 October 1958.

this famous industry could not continue to play its old role. Our broad task was to facilitate the change of employment and production from textiles to engineering and the most modern form of sophisticated products in every field. In this Lancashire has, in fact, been signally successful. Nevertheless the transition was painful, especially from the human point of view, and the suffering was great in the towns where cotton textiles were the main, if not the only, source of employment. I was anxious to get at least three or four years' interval and to use the breathing-space to bring about a reconstruction and modernisation of the industry. Our plan therefore was limitation on the one side and reconstruction on the other.

In the event Lord Rochdale and his team set out for Hong Kong with the full authority of the industry to make whatever might seem to them the best arrangement. The negotiations did not go well, and the Colonial Office were very unwilling to exert any effective pressure. Lord Rochdale and his team returned at the beginning of December and came to see me. India and Pakistan were now more or less 'in the bag'. But Lennox-Boyd still felt under a deep obligation to protect the colony at all costs. However, we made a little progress.

> I think I have now persuaded him that in default of a 'voluntary agreement', the Government will have [to threaten] to *impose* one. I still believe, that under this sanction, we may be able to get a 'voluntary' agreement.[1]

I sent urgent messages to the Governor, Sir Robert Black, asking him to bring all his influence to bear to persuade the Hong Kong traders to accept one of the latest Lancashire offers on a ceiling. I told him on 19 December that

> if . . . there is no voluntary arrangement, the pressure for a quota on cotton textile imports becomes irresistible. Nor would delay be to the advantage of Hong Kong, for it might lead to a situation in which a solution less generous . . . would prevail.

Finally, by the end of the year an agreement was reached, and the Hong Kong textile producers announced their willingness for a limitation to last for three years. But now, in January 1959, India

[1] 14 December 1958.

and Pakistan, who were due to confirm their agreements as soon as the Hong Kong settlement had been reached, began to run out. India claimed that the Hong Kong ceiling was too high; although I sent urgent messages to Nehru to use his influence with the industry to accept the settlement the talks dragged on all through the first half of 1959.

Warnings began to reach me from Lord Hailsham, the Chairman of the Party, about the political situation in Lancashire. His paper was brilliantly composed, balanced, well-argued and written in his usual limpid prose. It was given to me the day after my return from Russia. I cannot resist quoting the two opening sentences.

When Alexander the Great was interviewing the ancestors of Mr. Khrushchev somewhere in the middle of Kazbegistan it is related that his Agent from the Peloponnese handed him an account of a battle between Sparta and Argos, and that Alexander contemptuously dismissed it, saying that it was a battle between mice and frogs.

It is somewhat in the same spirit that on your return from Moscow I feel bound to recount to you the modest products of my recent visit to Lancashire constituencies.

It would be tedious to recount all the further stages of this dreary auction, the only hero of which was Lord Rochdale himself. At last an agreement was reached between all the four parties and announced on 30 September 1959. The limitation would last for three years from the beginning of 1960. One could not help feeling a deep sympathy for the industry. The home market was invaded by products from low-wage countries. Lancashire's products were excluded by outrageous tariffs from advanced countries where they might have hoped to compete by their greater skill. Thus they were equally the victims of Free Trade and Protection—as indeed the most brilliant of Cobden's critics had prophesied.

But the limitation agreement was only a shield to assist the industry during a period of reorganisation. Our constructive plans were contained in the Cotton Industry Bill published on 13 May 1959. It was the result of tireless work by David Eccles at the Board of Trade, and its purpose was to facilitate the reconstruction of the industry and the reduction of excess capacity which was reckoned at between 25 and 40 per cent. A redundancy agreement to assist employees was announced at the same time. The estimated cost of modernisation was put by the industry itself as between £78 and £93 million. Without arguing the accuracy of this estimate, the Government undertook to contribute £30 million to this end. The Bill had what is called a mixed reception. The Mayor of Oldham, a town of which it used to be said that half of it was engaged in putting the other half of Oldham out of business—they were the largest manufacturers of cotton-spinning and weaving machinery exported to other countries—said that the Government were prepared 'to pay the funeral expenses of part of the industry'. Nevertheless the limitation of imports and the Reorganisation Bill were undoubtedly as much as any Government could have done. They were not achieved without a vast expenditure of time and effort.

On 3 April, a few days before the introduction of the Budget, I decided to discuss the electoral prospects with a few intimate friends and colleagues.

> At luncheon at No. 10 were Butler, Hailsham, Poole, Macleod, Ted Heath, and Derry Heathcoat Amory. We discussed the next General Election for three hours.[1]

A most careful analysis of every constituency in the country had been made and

> in the light of (a) the agents' report, (b) the Liberal intervention, (c) the state of the various [opinion] polls, Central Office say that a dissolution *now* would give us a majority of thirteen in House of Commons.[1]

The questions which had now to be answered were—what would be the effect of the Budget; how should we stand on 11 June, the proposed polling day for a summer election, and finally would we be any better off in October?

> All this must be considered chiefly in connection with the European crisis. If this gets worse, or if there is a Summit in a critical situation in August, what authority will British Ministers have, as they approach the *end* of their power. (We could [in practice] *not* go on later than October.) Would it be better for the

[1] 3 April 1959.

British Ministers, be it us or the Socialists, to have a recently acquired or renewed tenure of power? But suppose the Socialists win? What will be the effect on the allies?

Suppose nobody wins—a sort of stalemate and a constitutional and political crisis in June or July? What *ought* I to do, not as Party leader but as the Queen's First Minister? All these are terribly difficult questions.[1]

During the next few days I pondered on these matters and by 18 April I had made up my mind. After much thought the over-riding consideration seemed to me that October was the normal, almost conventional, date for a Parliament which had been elected more than four years before. To spring an election in the summer because unexpected might seem almost sharp practice. There is nothing which an electorate more dislikes than this.

The big decision has been taken—not to have an early election, but to go on with our job, both at home and abroad.[2]

On 22 April I was entertained at the Savoy to luncheon by the 1922 Committee. This gathering included practically the whole Parliamentary Party.

After discussion with Chief Whip I decided to use this 'private' meeting to let it be known that there *will* be no spring Election this year, perhaps in 1960 ![3]

As I expected, this announcement was fully reported in the Press. The next night I repeated it at a great meeting in Preston. I was now engaged in a four-day visit to Lancashire,

a long tour, with . . . an even better [reception] . . . than the other two 'meet the people' tours. Six or seven speeches—impromptu. We covered many Lancashire towns, including Oldham, Roch-dale, Bury, Stockport, Manchester. Dorothy was with me. It was really a most heartening experience. With the masses of people whom we saw—they waited in large numbers in the streets—there was scarcely a 'boo'.[4]

This was an encouraging experience and confirmed that we had done right in going ahead with the Cotton Bill, and finishing in a

[1] 3 April 1959.   [2] 18 April 1959.   [3] 22 April 1959.   [4] 24 April 1959.

proper and orderly way the legislative task that we had announced at the beginning of the session. I was now in a buoyant mood.

The more I think of the visit to Lancashire the more pleased I am. Of course, I don't mean that the people who were so polite and friendly will all vote Tory. But I cannot believe that such courtesy and so little bitterness are not good signs. It is very different to the mood of 1945 or even 1950.[1]

We had now to deal with both the preparation for the General Election, for which by the end of June the first draft of the election manifesto had been prepared by the 'steering committee', and the ordinary course of Cabinet meetings with all the variety of topics, ranging from the Obscene Publications Bill to Dollar Liberalisation.

With the exception of the African troubles, the situation on the home front was calm. The cost of living was steady; the opinion polls showed a continued improvement, and even the printing strike with all its tiresome implications did not cause the public undue concern. The unemployment figure went down to 1·9 per cent, and although there were pockets of unemployment in Wales, Scotland and Lancashire, it was clear that these could not be solved by general reflation with the risk of

a renewed inflation, with all that this means to our balance of payments and to sterling. We must therefore treat this disease differently. I think we can work out quite a good policy to present at an election and to pursue afterwards, if we are elected . . . I am amazed and delighted by the vitality of my colleagues. We are now reaching a point when nothing can be *done*—as opposed to being *planned*—until the election is over.[2]

At the end of July the printers' strike was settled—a long and irritating dispute, damaging to all concerned.

Among other arguments that had weighed with me against the June election was care for the Queen's comfort. She had undertaken a long and strenuous tour in Canada, starting towards the end of June with the official opening of the St. Lawrence Seaway. A June election would have been very inconvenient from every point of view. I was equally concerned about the strenuous character of the

[1] 25 April 1959.   [2] 9 July 1959.

Queen's tour, and when the announcement of her pregnancy was made public on 7 August, while I shared the public pleasure, I was glad indeed to feel that she was safely home.

On 22 August I wrote to the Queen warning her of the probability of my soon asking her to approve a dissolution. Apart from the publication of the Radcliffe Committee Report on the monetary and credit system, which by a happy arrangement had been timed to appear in the middle of August to provide light reading for politicians, economists, bankers and stockbrokers on holiday, only one other event held the public attention. This was the visit of President Eisenhower. His journey was part of a diplomatic adventure into which he had launched himself by inviting Khrushchev to be his guest at the White House. In preparation for this he was anxious to see both Adenauer and de Gaulle. Although, since our personal contacts were so close, a visit to the United Kingdom was not necessary, nevertheless I felt, and he agreed, that it would be regarded as a slight if he seemed to neglect the country which had entrusted him with the command of its armies in two great campaigns. It was accordingly arranged that he should pay a five-day visit to Britain, some of which would be spent in a happy holiday at Balmoral with the Queen and the Royal Family. He arrived at London Airport punctually at 6.45 p.m. on 27 August. We drove together in an open car to the American Embassy.

The distance is seventeen miles. It took us nearly two hours. There was a wonderful turn-out all along the route, and great enthusiasm.[1]

It was a remarkable demonstration of confidence and goodwill. It was also impressive from another point of view. The car moved at a snail's pace. All the roads and streets were crowded, and there was no security control of any kind. Most of the time the President stood up and waved to the people, and some of the time I stood up also and waved by his side. After two days at Balmoral he came to Chequers.

Left at 11 a.m. for Benson Airfield (R.A.F.). President arrived at 12 noon. We drove (in open car) to Chequers. Another lovely summer day. Good crowds at airport and all along the roads and villages. Again a most enthusiastic and personal reception.[2]

[1] 27 August 1959.   [2] 29 August 1959.

In the afternoon there was a certain amount of serious discussion during which the President got somewhat restless. But there were good intervals for making golfing strokes between the house and the drive. Unhappily, since the grass was long, a large quantity of balls were struck in proportion to those ultimately recovered. On Sunday morning there was an hour's serious talk. But it was broken off for church at 11 a.m.

President and I went together. The church was packed. Since the service was relayed outside, there were large crowds in the churchyard.

After luncheon, we allowed the 'experts' to come in on a 'nuclear tests' talk—chiefly not to disappoint them. But the argument was not [much] advanced, and the President soon became pretty restless. So I suggested a drive. We drove to Oxford together—had a walk round Magdalen and Christ Church—and then drove home. President enjoyed this, and since our visit was unannounced, there were no crowds. I found once more these drives much the most useful part of our meetings. We had a shut car and could talk freely. He told me a great deal about U.S.; about U.S. politics; about the hopes and fears that he has concerning NATO; about how he means to handle Mr. Khrushchev; about de Gaulle. It was clear that he was not looking forward to meeting de Gaulle. I did my best to plead for de Gaulle. Without him, France might collapse into anarchy or Communism. Algeria (not his silly gestures in NATO and in Europe) is the key to the whole problem. We have our Algerias coming to us—Kenya and Central Africa. De Gaulle is the only man who could 'put over' a 'liberal' policy. Even he is taking great risks with the army. He is not Napoleon I. He is the Prince-President. I begged the President to be sympathetic over Algeria. The 'anti-colonialism' of America was out-of-date and could be very dangerous.[1]

The next day

President and I motored to St. Paul's from Chequers. The crowds were so great that we changed into an open car. The East End of St. Paul's and the American Chapel are now really magnificent and an immense improvement over the old reredos.[2]

[1] 30 August 1959.   [2] 31 August 1959.

It had been arranged that there should be a short discussion between the President and me on world affairs which would be televised. I was nervous about this, because it would be almost impossible to steer between dangerous indiscretions and mere trivialities.

> I spent most of the afternoon pondering over the T.V. discussion with the President, which was due for 7.20 p.m. to 7.40 p.m., in the pillared room at No. 10. The whole house has been filled with technicians and workmen of all kinds. After the television, I have a dinner party of some forty. The guests are invited for 7.15, and there are T.V. sets in the various rooms for the viewers.
> *Midnight.* It is all over. The discussion wasn't bad, although we were both very nervous. The first account from viewers seems to be . . . enthusiastic. The dinner was a great success. The President proposed 'The Queen'. I proposed 'The President of the United States'. Then, after a short interval, I made a little speech proposing the health of General Eisenhower. He responded admirably. Churchill, Attlee and Eden spoke–all with great distinction.[1]

The Press, usually pretty critical about such television performances, were on the whole favourable. Naturally I was accused of arranging this visit for my own electoral purposes. But although the coincidence may have been happy, it was certainly not by my design. On the next day there was a nostalgic party:

> The President gave a dinner at the Embassy to his old comrades–Field-Marshals (like Alanbrooke, Alexander, Montgomery)–Admirals (like Royer Dick–A. B. Cunningham was unfortunately laid up after a motor-car accident); Marshals of the R.A.F. (like Lord Tedder, 'Bomber' Harris, etc.); Generals Morgan, Humfrey Gale and many others.
> The civilians asked were myself (as ex-Minister Resident *not* as P.M.) and my old staff (Makins and Caccia).
> I asked the President *not* to put me next to him, but to rank me only as 'Political Adviser AFHQ'. This was a good idea, and enabled him to put Alanbrooke and Alexander next to him. Churchill came and was put next to the American Ambassador.

[1] 31 August 1959.

It was a very enjoyable evening, with lots of stories and plenty of jokes . . . My remark that even when I was a publisher I had never seen so many authors in one room was well received.[1]

The decision had now been taken, and accordingly on 7 September, after first stopping at Aboyne where I had a talk with James Stuart,

I went on to Balmoral, arriving about 6.15. Audience before dinner. The Queen was very gracious. I ventured to impress on her that a P.M. had no right to 'advise' a dissolution. 'Advice', in the long run, the Crown must today accept. The P.M. 'asks' for a dissolution, which the Crown can agree to or not. This, the last great prerogative of the Crown, must be preserved. It might be of vital importance at a time of national crisis.[2]

The Queen formally agreed to my request. The date seemed to her well chosen.

The next day the Cabinet met at 3 o'clock, and the announcement that Parliament would be dissolved on 18 September with polling to take place on 8 October was made an hour later. So after much speculation and anxious deliberation the die was now finally cast. We had ridden the storm. Could we now hope to be entrusted with a fresh command?

[1] 1 September 1959.   [2] 7 September 1959.

Appendixes

Appendix One

Plan G: 29 September 1956

1. The United Kingdom would enter a partial Free Trade Area with the Customs Union of the Messina Six (Benelux, France, Germany, Italy) and all other O.E.E.C. countries that wished to join (probably Norway, Sweden, Denmark, Switzerland, Austria).

2. We would not expect the Free Trade Area to include dependent territories of any of the members, but this would remain uncertain until we found European reactions to our main proposals, and their views on this question; in the meantime, we are consulting our own Colonial territories on their possible interest.

3. The Free Trade Area would cover all commodities without exception except foodstuffs (defined broadly to include not only raw food but also manufactured foods, feeding stuffs, drink and tobacco). The exclusion of foodstuffs is an essential condition on which we should insist without qualification both in the interests of home agriculture policy and in the interests of the Commonwealth.

4. Within the Free Trade Area, tariffs (except revenue tariffs in the strict sense), protective quotas and other protective devices (e.g. export taxes and controls, export subsidies) would be reduced and ultimately abolished in defined stages over a period of about a decade.

5. We should retain our existing freedom of action in our tariffs on imports from the rest of the world, subject to our commitments in the General Agreement on Tariffs and Trade (GATT) and elsewhere; this is the essential difference between a Free Trade Area and a Customs Union. We should remain free to continue to give free entry to Commonwealth goods. The preferences provided by our tariff against imports from foreign countries outside Europe would be unaffected.

6. We should insist that there should be no discrimination by the Messina Six in each other's favour and against us. This implies the same time-table for tariff reduction throughout the whole Free Trade Area.

7. We should retain the right under existing rules to impose quantitive restrictions for balance of payments reasons to protect sterling. The area would be working under the present GATT and O.E.E.C. rules unless it were decided that stricter rules should be applied by members.

8. The proposals would be entirely consistent with the collective approach to freer trade and payments, and to convertibility; they would represent one step forward towards the world-wide reduction of trade barriers. The size of the Free Trade Area and the extent of its extra-European interest would ensure that it did not develop into an inward-looking regional bloc. We should aim to continue the progress which we have made in recent years in reducing and removing quota restrictions on imports from Canada and the United States.

9. The international management of the Free Trade Area might be conducted in O.E.E.C. by a 'Managing Board' (at Ministerial and official level), consisting only of the members of the area, operating under Article 14 of the O.E.E.C. constitution. This Article enables a group to proceed without the positive assent of non-members of the group (provided they agree to this course).

Appendix Two

Members of the Cabinet: January 1957

PRIME MINISTER AND FIRST LORD OF THE TREASURY — Rt. Hon. Harold Macmillan, M.P.

LORD PRESIDENT OF THE COUNCIL — Most Hon. Marquess of Salisbury, K.G.

SECRETARY OF STATE FOR THE HOME DEPARTMENT AND LORD PRIVY SEAL — Rt. Hon. R. A. Butler, C.H., M.P.

LORD CHANCELLOR — Rt. Hon. Viscount Kilmuir, G.C.V.O.

SECRETARY OF STATE FOR FOREIGN AFFAIRS — Rt. Hon. Selwyn Lloyd, C.B.E., T.D., Q.C., M.P.

CHANCELLOR OF THE EXCHEQUER — Rt. Hon. Peter Thorneycroft, M.P.

SECRETARY OF STATE FOR COMMONWEALTH RELATIONS — Rt. Hon. Earl of Home

SECRETARY OF STATE FOR THE COLONIES — Rt. Hon. Alan Lennox-Boyd, M.P.

SECRETARY OF STATE FOR SCOTLAND — Rt. Hon. John Maclay, C.M.G., M.P.

MINISTER OF DEFENCE — Rt. Hon. Duncan Sandys, M.P.

PRESIDENT OF THE BOARD OF TRADE — Rt. Hon. Sir David Eccles, K.C.V.O., M.P.

MINISTER OF AGRICULTURE, FISHERIES AND FOOD — Rt. Hon. Derick Heathcoat Amory, M.P.

MINISTER OF LABOUR AND NATIONAL SERVICE — Rt. Hon. Iain Macleod, M.P.

MINISTER OF HOUSING AND LOCAL GOVERNMENT AND MINISTER FOR WELSH AFFAIRS — Rt. Hon. Henry Brooke, M.P.

MINISTER OF EDUCATION — Rt. Hon. Viscount Hailsham, Q.C.

MINISTER OF POWER — Rt. Hon. Lord Mills

MINISTER OF TRANSPORT AND CIVIL AVIATION — Rt. Hon. Harold Watkinson, M.P.

CHANCELLOR OF THE DUCHY OF LANCASTER — Dr. Rt. Hon. Charles Hill, M.P.

Appendix Three

Declaration of Common Purpose

The President of the United States and the Prime Minister of the United Kingdom, at the end of three days of meetings at which they were assisted by the Secretary of State and the Foreign Secretary and other advisers, issued the following statement—

I

We have met together as trusted friends of many years who have come to head the Governments of our respective countries. These two countries have close and historic ties, just as each has intimate and unbreakable ties with other free countries.

Recognising that only in the establishment of a just peace can the deepest aspirations of free peoples be realised, the guiding purpose of our deliberations has been the determination of how best to utilise the moral, intellectual and material strength of our two nations in the performance of our full share of those tasks that will more surely and promptly bring about conditions in which peace can prosper. One of these tasks is to provide adequate security for the free world.

The free nations possess vast assets, both material and moral. These in the aggregate are far greater than those of the Communist world. We do not ignore the fact that the Soviet rulers can achieve formidable material accomplishments by concentrating upon selected developments and scientific applications, and by yoking their people to this effort. Despotisms have often been able to produce spectacular monuments. But the price has been heavy. For all peoples yearn for intellectual and economic freedom, the more so if from their bondage they see others manifest the glory of freedom. Even despots are forced to permit freedom to grow by an evolutionary process, or in time there will be violent revolution. This principle is inexorable in its operation. Already it has begun to be noticeable even within the Soviet orbit. If the free nations are steadfast, and if they utilise their resources in harmonious co-operation, the totalitarian menace that now confronts them will in good time recede.

In order, however, that freedom may be secure and show its good fruits, it is necessary first that the collective military strength of the free nations should be adequate to meet the threat against them. At the same time the aggregate of the free world's military expenditure must be kept within limits compatible with individual freedom. Otherwise we risk losing the very liberties which we seek to defend.

These ideas have been the central theme of our conversations which, in part, were participated in by M. Spaak, the Secretary-General of NATO.

In application of these ideas, and as an example which we believe can and should spread among the nations of the free world, we reached the following understanding—

II

1. The arrangements which the nations of the free world have made for collective defence and mutual help are based on the recognition that the concept of national self-sufficiency is now out of date. The countries of the free world are inter-dependent and only in genuine partnership, by combining their resources and sharing tasks in many fields, can progress and safety be found. For our part, we have agreed that our two countries will henceforth act in accordance with this principle.

2. Our representatives to the North Atlantic Council will urge an enlarged Atlantic effort in scientific research and development in support of greater collective security and the expansion of current activities of the Task Force working in this field in accordance with the Council's decision of last December.

3. The President of the United States will request the Congress to amend the Atomic Energy Act as may be necessary and desirable to permit of close and fruitful collaboration of scientists and engineers of Great Britain, the United States, and other friendly countries.

4. The disarmament proposals made by the Western representatives on the Disarmament Sub-Committee in London and approved by all members of NATO are a sound and fair basis for an agreement which would reduce the threat of war and the burden of armaments. The indefinite accumulation of nuclear weapons and the indiscriminate spreading of the capacity to produce them should be prevented. Effective and reliable inspection must be an integral part of initial steps in the control and reduction of armaments.

5. In the absence of such disarmament as we are seeking, international security now depends, not merely on local defensive shields, but upon reinforcing them with the deterrent and retaliatory power of nuclear weapons. So long as the threat of International Communism persists, the free nations must be prepared to provide for their own security. Because the free-world measures are purely defensive and for security against outside threat, the period for which they must be maintained cannot be foreseen. It is not within the capacity of

each nation acting alone to make itself fully secure. Only collective measures will suffice. These should preferably be found by implementing the provisions of the United Nations Charter for forces at the disposal of the Security Council. But if the Soviet Union persists in nullifying these provisions by veto, there must otherwise be developed a greater sense of community security. The framework for this exists in collective defence arrangements now participated in by nearly fifty free nations, as authorised by the Charter. All members of this community, and other free nations which so desire, should possess more knowledge of the total capabilities of security that are in being and in prospect. There should also be provided greater opportunity to assure that this power will in fact be available in case of need for their common security, and that it will not be misused by any nation for purposes other than individual and collective self-defence, as authorised by the Charter of the United Nations.

For our part we regard our possession of nuclear weapons power as a trust for the defence of the free world.

6. Our two countries plan to discuss these ideas with all of their security partners. So far as the North Atlantic Alliance is concerned the December meeting may perhaps be given a special character in this respect. This has been discussed with the Secretary-General of NATO, M. Spaak.

7. In addition to the North Atlantic Treaty, the South East Asia Collective Defence Treaty, the Baghdad Pact and other security arrangements constitute a strong bulwark against aggression in the various treaty areas. There are also vitally important relationships of a somewhat different character. There is the Commonwealth; and in the Western hemisphere the Organisation of American States. There are individual mutual defence agreements and arrangements to which the United States is a party.

8. We recognise that our collective security efforts must be supported and reinforced by co-operative economic action. The present offers a challenging opportunity for improvement of trading conditions and the expansion of trade throughout the free world. It is encouraging that plans are developing for a European Free Trade Area in association with the European Common Market. We recognise that especially in the less developed countries there should be a steady and significant increase in standards of living and economic development.

9. We took note of specific factors in the ideological struggle in which we are engaged. In particular, we were in full agreement that—

Soviet threats directed against Turkey give solemn significance to the obligation, under Article 5 of the North Atlantic Treaty, to consider an armed attack against any member of the Alliance as an attack against all.

The reunification of Germany, by free elections, is essential. At the Geneva Conference of 1955 Messrs. Khrushchev and Bulganin agreed to this with us and our French allies. Continued repudiation of that agreement and continued suppression of freedom in Eastern Europe undermine international confidence and perpetuate an injustice, a folly and a danger.

III

The President and the Prime Minister believe that the understandings they have reached will be increasingly effective as they become more widespread between the free nations. By co-ordinating the strength of all free peoples, safety can be assured, the danger of Communist despotism will in due course be dissipated, and a just and lasting peace will be achieved.

25 October 1957

Appendix Four

Correspondence with Selwyn Lloyd on Resignation

24 February 1958

My dear Prime Minister,

I have thought again about our conversation last night, but nevertheless feel that I must ask you to accept my resignation. I believe that the Government will be stronger without me.

You will remember that I wished to resign at the end of November 1956 and that there was a subsequent occasion when for private reasons I asked you to consider my resignation. Now I feel that I must press it again.

I cannot express too warmly my thanks to you for your personal friendship and encouragement. The last 12 months have been for me an exceedingly happy period of strenuous endeavour and hard work.

The fact remains that I believe that you will now do better to have someone else in my place.

I can more effectively support you from outside the Government, and that I will do to the utmost of my capacity.

Yours ever,
Selwyn

25 February 1958

SECRET AND PERSONAL

Dear Selwyn,

I have received your characteristically generous letter, but my answer must be that your duty is to carry on. First, you have all the threads in your hands of a lot of difficult negotiations, which I know you can conduct better than anybody else. Some of them are not without hope of success. Secondly, although I sympathise with your feelings in view of the attacks made upon you, I think this is something which you have just got to carry; for we really cannot allow a combination of the Opposition and the popular press to drive a Minister from office. Thirdly, if I were to accept your resignation the Government would be very much shaken. I would be regarded as bending to a storm, and the same treatment would be applied successively to one Minister after another. I know this is asking a great deal of you, and I do appreciate your feelings. But I believe the Party is already beginning to resent the personal nature of the attack upon you. Of course, if ever we got into calmer waters and you wished to exchange for a less onerous office, that is another thing. But this is not the time, either from your point of view or from mine.

Do not forget that in the old days politics were just as rough as now – rather rougher. All the same I do appreciate your offer, which I know comes from the most honourable motives.

Yours ever,
Harold

27 February 1958

Dear Harold,

Thank you for your letter of 25 February, and for what you say in it. In the circumstances, I bow to your judgement, and will battle on! I repeat how grateful I am to you for your understanding and encouragement.

Yours ever,
Selwyn

Index

Aboyne, 750

Abyssinia, 111, 156

Adeane, Sir Michael, 184

Aden, 504–5, 525, 536

Adenauer, Dr. Konrad, 54, 66, 70, 246, 291, 296, 306, 330, 492, 498, 601, 637, 655; and Common Market, 69; hostile to European army reduction, 248; and British defence plans, 291–5; pessimism, 317, 334–5, 639; and European Free Trade Area, 435, 451–452, 454–5; London visit (1958), 442, 485; and de Gaulle's defence idea, 453–4; on Russian disarmament offer, 485; and Summit talks, 490, 624, 640; and Middle East crisis, 526, 527–8; concern over Russian demands on Berlin, 571, 578–80, 581; and author's visit to Moscow, 585–6; Khrushchev's criticism of, 605, 616, 619; author's visit to (March 1959), 639–40; urges firm Allied stand against Russia, 650–1

Aiken, Senator, 643

Akrotiri, 681

Albert Hall, author's speech to Primrose League in (April 1958), 486–8

Aldermaston marches, 297

Aldrich, Winthrop, 104, 118, 123

Alexander, Field-Marshal Lord, 104, 105, 273, 675, 749

Algeria, 148, 330, 331, 334, 748; insurrection in, 443–4, 446, 448, 455

Allan, Robert, 192

Allen, Sir Roger, 674

Amery, Julian, 125, 173, 187, 737; negotiation with Sultan of Muscat, 275–6, and with Makarios, 701

Amman, 90–1, 517, 519, 524, 525

Anderson, Sir Colin, 346

Anderson, Robert B., 496, 650

Anglo-Egyptian Treaty (1954), 101

Ankara, 678–80

Aqaba, Gulf of, 170, 206, 212, 215, 216–19, 259, 524, 525

'Arab Federation': formed by Jordan and Iraq, 502–3, 504; Anglo–American financial aid to, 508

Arab League, 276

Arab Legion, 90, 92

Arab States: conflict with Israel, 89, 95 ff, 206; Nasser's intrigues in, 89–91, 93, 97, 100, 102, 110, 146; and Pan-Arabism, 93, 100, 102, 146, 149; fresh troubles in, 269–87, 502–37; Russian infiltration, 277–87

Armitage, Sir Robert, 736–7

ASLEF, 712, 715

Aswan Dam, 90, 93–4, 97–100, 102

Athens, 674–8

Attlee, Clement: agrees to American bombers in Britain, 462, 494, 749; recognises Communist China, 541

Auckland, 397

Australia, 77, 78, 151, 380, 412; and Suez, 375; author visits (1958), 402–9, 413

Austria, 80

Averoff, Evangelos, 675, 677, 688, 691, 692, 693, 694–6, 699

Baghdad, *coup* in, 510–11, 514, 515

Baghdad Pact, 220, 269–70, 283, 467; American reluctance over, 91, 94; American support on Military Committee, 260, 269; American economic aid, 502; discussion on future of, 528–529; and Iraq, 528–9, 530; Iraq withdraws from, 535

Bahrain, 523

Balmoral, 747, 750

Baltimore, 494–5

Bandaranaike, S. W. R. D., 393, 394–6, 542–3

Bank of Egypt, 233, 234

Bank of England, 9–10, 13, 117, 234, 705, 718, 728–9

Bank Rate, 3, 8, 11, 40: increase (1955) 4, (1956) 14, 28–32, 35–7, 38–44, (1957) 356–7, 361, 706; reduction (1957) 344, (1958) 709–10, 716, 725 'leak', 415–30

Banyak Suka, 405

Barber, Anthony, 192, 591

Baring, Sir Evelyn, 734–6

Basra, 510

Beaverbrook, Lord, 194, 236, 350, 377, 433

Bech, Joseph, 336

Beddington-Behrens, Sir Edward, 434

Bedford, 'never had it so good' speech at (July 1957), 350–2

Beirut, 512, 513, 514

Belfast, 636; by-election (1959), 646

Belgium, 72, 151

Bell, Dr. G. K. A., 223, 224

Belles, Dr. Joshua (grandfather), 129, 133

Ben Gurion, David, 520, 523, 524

Benelux, 67, 78, 475

Berlin, West, Russian demand for 'demilitarisation', 571–81, 585, 598, 611–13, 614, 616, 625, 626, 631, 639, 647

Bermuda Conference (March 1957), 222, 227, 241, 242, 245, 249–62, 290, 304, 317

Bevan, Aneurin, 221, 340, 359, 582, 646, 671, 685, 724, 738; and Suez, 172, 173, 237–8; and Khrushchev's letter on Syria, 284–5; and nuclear tests, 298–9, 308, 313, 484, 487, 488, 655; 'conversion', 313, 329, 487; attack on Washington talks (Nov. 1957), 329; evasive speech (Feb. 1958), 471–2, 487; and Lebanon crisis, 509, 515, 520, 521, 526

Beveridge, Lord, 16

Beyen, Dr. Johan, 68, 72

Birch, Nigel, 368, 369, 372, 703

Birgi, Nuri, 672

Bishop, Frederick, 192, 250, 280, 281, 373, 418, 492, 493, 494, 516, 520, 587, 591, 645, 674, 681

Black, Sir Cyril, 38

Black, Eugene, 135, 239

Black, Sir Robert, 742

Blank, Theodor, 54

Blankenhorn, Herbert, 248

Bligh, Timothy, 192

Bloomington (Indiana), 129

Bolte, Henry, 407

Bonham Carter, Lady Violet, 720

Bonham Carter, Mark, 720

Bonn, 291–6, 435, 452–5, 639–40

Bowker, Sir James, 662, 678

Boyd-Carpenter, John, 345, 730, 733

Boyle, Sir Edward, 2, 9, 54, 153, 191

Brand, Thomas, 9

Brentano, Heinrich von, 330, 452, 580, 639, 651

Bretherton, R. F., 69

Bridges, Sir Edward, 2, 9, 14, 28, 46, 73

Bridle, Mr. and Mrs., 405

Brighton: Conservative Party Conference (1957), 359, 419–21; Labour Party Conference (1957), 472

Brisbane, 405

British Council, 631

British Motor Corporation, 57

British Petroleum, 44–5

Brittain, Sir Herbert, 2, 10

Britten, Brigadier Charles, 682

Britten, Colonel P. C., 682

Brook, Sir Norman, 188, 192, 193, 250, 321, 322, 323, 337, 357, 373, 384, 387, 397, 418, 492, 494, 497, 518, 519, 520, 547, 561, 591, 608, 624, 645, 659, 660, 661, 667

Brooke, Henry, 2, 189, 704

Brooks, Sir Dallas and Lady, 407

Brown, George, 268, 340, 521

Bruce, Lord, 404

Brundrett, Sir Frederick, 566

Budgets: (1955) 4, 6, 9; (1956) 11; (1957) 348; (1958) 709; (1959) 727–730, 744

Bulganin, Nikolai, 32, 283, 332; visit to Britain, 95–7, 288; and Suez crisis, 165, 237; and need for improved relations, 288–9, 291, 310–11, 387–8; urges nuclear disarmament, 289–91, 296–7, 304–6, 308, 464, 465; and Summit

meeting, 387–8, 398, 402, 408–9, 465–70, 479; resigns, 479

Burns, General Eedson, 167

Burrows, Sir Bernard, 273

Butler, Brigadier Mervyn, 161

Butler, R. A., 13, 31, 137, 202, 304, 337, 368, 373, 411, 660, 709, 714, 731, 732; as Chancellor of Exchequer, 4, 6, 21, 30, 40, 68, 70; and Suez crisis, 125, 170, 172, 173, 174; deputises for Eden, 170, 174, 185; and Eden's resignation, 180, 182, 185–7, 201; Home Secretary, 186; as author's deputy, 227, 249, 346, 374, 398, 620, 703; in Bank Rate 'leak' debate, 430; and Free Trade Area, 428; and Middle East crisis, 517, 518, 520; and Devlin Report, 737

Caccia, Sir Harold, 169, 178, 319, 322, 485, 492, 494, 496, 507, 580, 582, 643, 645, 655, 749

Cahill, John Joseph, 405

Cairncross, Neil, 192, 384

Callaghan, James, 671, 738

Camp David, 644–9

Canada, 75, 258–9; and Suez crisis, 113, 160, 162–3, 375; author visits, 326–7, 497, 641–2; Queen Elizabeth tours, 746–7

Canberra, 402–5, 408, 409

Capital Issues Committee, 15, 52, 59

Carrington, Lord, 402, 407, 409, 413

Casey, R. G., 168

Ceylon, 393–6

Chamoun, Camille, 505, 506, 507, 508–509, 511, 512, 514

Chataway, Miss, 427–8

Chauvel, Jean, 447, 590

Chehab, General Fuad, 508–9, 533

Chequers, 207, 376, 636, 747–8
Cherwell, Lord, 22
Chester by-election (1956), 156
Chiang Kai-shek, 540, 542; and Formosa, 538, 541, 543; and offshore islands, 546, 555, 556
China, Communist, 98, 111, 386, 394; trade with, 317–18, 483, 542, 559; agreement with Yemen, 502; aim to 'liberate' Formosa, 538, 546; bombardment of Quemoy and Matsu, 539, 543–7, 551, 556; American attitude to, 541; Russian support for, 550–1
China, Nationalist: and offshore islands, 538–9, 541, 543–9, 555–6; American support of, 541–3, 545, 553; in United Nations, 542–3
Chou En-lai, 394, 538, 543
Christ, George, 197
Christchurch (New Zealand), 400–2
Christmas Island, atomic tests on, 262, 296, 326, 327, 332, 564
Churchill, Lord Randolph, 368
Churchill, Randolph, 93, 551–2
Churchill, Sir Winston S., 1, 18, 21, 112, 184, 189, 192, 250, 257, 266, 317, 332, 376, 382, 552, 635, 749; and European unity, 61, 65; relations with Eisenhower, 94, 134; supports Eden's Suez policy, 153–4; letter to Eisenhower on Anglo-American relations, 175–6; his note on Suez, 206; on Thorneycroft resignation, 367–8; and offshore islands, 544, 550; and Anglo-American nuclear research, 567–8
Clifford, Dr. John, 152
Cobbold, C. F. (Governor of Bank of England), 9, 13, 14, 18, 52
Cobham, Lord, 400, 412
Cobham, Lady, 400

Cohen, Lord, 352, 707
Collingwood, Charles, 721
Common Market – see European Economic Community
Commonwealth Finance Ministers' Conference (1957), 377–8, 404
Commonwealth Prime Ministers' Conference: (1956) 77; (1957) 338, 377–380
Compton, Sir Edmund, 28, 36
Cook, Sir William, 566
Cosgrove, Robert, 408
Cotton Industry Bill (1959), 743, 745
Cousins, Frank, 313, 352, 355, 713, 717–718, 724
Couve de Murville, Maurice, 447, 450, 455, 456, 563, 564, 586, 637, 638, 651
Covent Garden strike, 352
Cripps, Sir Stafford, 35, 42
Crookshank, Harry, 70
Cunningham, Knox, 192
Cutliffe, Mrs., 688
Cyprus, 91, 199, 212, 525; Anglo-French attack on Egypt from, 152, 160; terrorism in, 223, 225, 227, 658, 666, 668, 674, 687, 688; negotiations on future of, 223–30, 577, 590, 657–701; Radcliffe plan for, 224, 660, 676, 698; Salisbury resigns over, 227, 228–9, 231, 657; partition proposal, 659–60, 666, 668, 691, 699; problem of military bases, 659, 662, 663, 666, 689, 693, 694, 700–1; tri-dominium plan, 660–2, 666, 667; Sir Hugh Foot appointed Governor, 665; his plans for internal self-government, 667; intercommunal rioting, 668, 670; proposed Constitution, 669–70, 675, 676, 683–684, 686, 690, 693–4, 696–7; partner-

ship plan, 669–70, 671, 673, 675–6, 679–80, 683, 686; author visits, 681–683; Turco-Greek compromise, 689–696; full British sovereignty in bases, 689, 694, 695, 696; Zürich conference on, 691–3, 695; London conference on, 694–8; independent republic, 696–701; elected to Commonwealth, 699; Makarios as President, 701

Czechoslovakia, 90, 113, 132, 213, 291, 462

Daily Express, 236, 341, 422, 470, 721; on Trinidad oil take-over, 46, 48–9; personal attack on author, 349, 433

Daily Herald, 46, 48, 60, 341, 421, 552, 726; and *l'affaire Sandys*, 476

Daily Mail, 738

Daily Mirror, 357, 552, 738

Daily Telegraph, 236, 313, 357, 473, 738

Daily Worker, 46, 48

Dalton, Hugh, 21, 25, 28, 221, 222

Darwin, 397

Davies, Clement, 124

de Freitas, Geoffrey, 475

de Gaulle, General Charles, 148, 331, 492, 496, 571, 586, 601, 620, 624, 655, 748; return to power, 443–6; author visits (June 1958), 446–9, 498, 509; unhelpful towards European Free Trade Area, 448–51, 452, 455–9; critical of NATO, 453, 638; his idea of Anglo-American–French defence organisation, 453–5; and Middle East crisis, 526, 527–8; his ambitions for France, 527, 528; and suspension of nuclear tests, 563; author visits (March 1959), 590, 637–8; on German reunification, 637; and idea of Summit, 638, 640; French attitude to him, 651

DePauw University, Greencastle (Indiana), author given honorary degree by, 490, 493

De Silva, M. W. H., 380

Dean, Sir Patrick, 250, 322, 494, 561, 591, 608, 619

Debré, Michel, 584, 586, 636, 637, 638

Declaration of Common Purpose, 323–4, 328, 756–9

Defence: economies in, 51; reorganisation of, 50, 244–6, 263–6; White Paper on (1957), 263–8, 292, 365

Defence Estimates (1956), 10

Demetriades (Mayor of Kyrenia), 682

Denktash, Rauf, 682

Denmark, 80, 439

Dervis (Mayor of Nicosia), 682

Desai, Morarji, 387

Devlin Report on Nyasaland disturbances (1959), 736–8

Devonshire, Mary, Duchess of, 185

Dickson, Marshal of the R.A.F Sir William, 244, 245, 515, 660

Diefenbaker, John G., 283, 327, 377, 497, 641–2, 671

Dillon, Douglas, 322, 496, 650

Dixon, Sir Pierson, 151, 159, 162, 168, 257

Dubna, 604–5

Dulles, Allen, 322, 496

Dulles, Janet, 587, 643

Dulles, John Foster, 74, 105, 137, 142, 157, 177, 210, 211, 258, 272, 287, 304, 402, 442, 496, 580, 582, 662; and Baghdad Pact, 91, 94, 528; 'brinkmanship', 91, 545–9, 555; and Egypt–Israel dispute, 94–5; and Aswan Dam, 98–9, 100; and Suez crisis, 103, 104, 106, 107–8, 113, 118–23, 125, 127–9, 135–6, 143–5, 148, 157–8,

159, 240; proposes international Suez Canal Board, 108; resists recourse to United Nations, 118–19, 121, 122, 129, 135–6; his SCUA scheme, 119–120, 122, 125, 128, 129, 136, 138–40, 145; declares that SCUA has 'no teeth', 138–9; supports Britain and France at United Nations, 143–4; attacks British and French action, 158, 159; hurt by criticisms and 'lack of confidence', 178–9; and Eisenhower Doctrine, 213, 214, 277, 282; and Gaza dispute, 216, 218, 219; Sandys's firm line with, 241–2; anxiety over Afro-Asian lobby in United Nations Assembly, 243; at Bermuda talks, 250, 251, 257; and Syria, 278, 279, 280–2, 284, 285; and disarmament, 309, 313–314; and McMahon Act repeal, 316, 323, 324; at Washington talks (Oct. 1957), 320–6; at NATO meeting (Dec. 1957), 334, 336–7; and idea of Summit, 467, 470, 477–8, 479, 481, 485, 586; change in policy, 492; and Middle East crisis, 507–8, 513, 514, 517, 519, 526, 527–9, 533, 536; and offshore islands, 545–9, 553, 555; 'domino' theory, 547; and suspension of nuclear tests, 559–60, 562, 563; visits Britain (Feb. 1959), 584, 587–9; increasing ill-health, 587, 643–4, 645, 651; on German problem, 587–8, 637; author's last visits to, 643–4, 649–50; death, 650; and Cyprus, 666–7, 685, 690

Dunedin (New Zealand), 400

Eccles, Sir David, 187, 374, 433, 704; and 'Budget leak', 220–2; and cotton industry, 741, 743

Economic Implications of Full Employment (White Paper), 29

Economist, 7, 345, 716

Eden, Sir Anthony, 4, 12, 13, 31, 70, 76, 229, 263, 288, 289, 464, 576, 585, 749; and European Army, 64; and Plan G, 85; visit to Washington (Feb. 1956), 74, 91; anxiety over American wavering, 93; relations with Eisenhower, 94; and Russian leaders' visit, 95–6; and Aswan Dam, 99; urges strong action against Nasser, 100–1, 103, 123, 128; and Suez crisis, 106, 112, 121, 123–7, 128, 141, 147, 148–149, 150–1, 153–5, 162, 163, 170, 236; speech in debate on, 123–6; issues ultimatum, 150; agrees to cease-fire, 163, 166–7; reply to Bulganin's threats, 165–6; his last Commons speech, 173; ill-health, 174–5, 180–1, 183; resignation, 180–4, 198, 200–1, 204; and Cyprus, 223–4; and offshore islands, 544, 550; Khrushchev's attack on, 616

Eden, Lady (Clarissa), 204

Edgar Bonnet (tug), 212

Edinburgh, Prince Philip, Duke of, 319

Egypt: intrigue and pressure on Arab States, 89, 91, 93–4; support from Russia, 90, 166; and Aswan Dam, 90, 93, 97–100; threat to Israel, 89–90, 93, 111, 146–7, 149; 'nationalises' Suez Canal, 100–1; Anglo-French action against, 105–6, 126, 140–2; refuses to attend conference, 107, 109; American attitude to, 109, 110–11, 118–22, 125–8, 139–40, 148; and Users' Club scheme, 122, 123; joint command with Syria and Jordan, 149; invaded by Israel, 150–2, 206; Anglo-French

military action against, 152, 160–2,
166; defeat, 166, 238, 269; obstacles to
Canal clearance, 168, 209, 210, 212,
214–15, 230–4; British forces leave,
169; dispute over Gaza and Aqaba,
215–19; financial negotiations and
renewed diplomatic relations, 239, 641;
supports Oman revolt, 271, 273;
unites with Syria in U.A.R., 502; and
pressure on Lebanon, 506, 508–9, 534
Eilat, 149, 170, 215
Eisenhower, President Dwight D., 94–5,
264, 287, 291, 296, 341, 494–5, 498,
601, 635, 689; Dulles's influence on,
94, 99, 178, 477, 481; and Suez crisis,
103, 105, 107, 116–17, 134, 148,
150–1, 157, 159, 167; disclaims use of
force, 116–17; author's visit to (Sept.
1956), 133–5; disquiet over Anglo-
French action, 151, 157; resentment
and hostility, 157, 159, 167, 168;
Churchill's letter to, 175–6; congratu-
lates author on becoming Prime
Minister, 194–5; illness, 211; and Gaza
dispute, 216–18; at Bermuda Conference, 240–3, 249–58; faith in United
Nations, 243, 257; concern over
proposed European army cuts, 247;
on perpetual criticism of America,
257–8; and British action in Oman,
271–2, 276; and Stassen's nuclear disarmament indiscretion, 301–4, 307;
and Anglo-American defence efforts,
314–16, 322; on British trade with
China, 317–18; Washington talks (Oct.
1957), 319–25; and Declaration of
Common Purpose, 323–4, 328, 756–9;
sudden illness, 333, 335; at NATO
meeting (Dec. 1957), 334, 335–6, 363
and idea of Summit meeting, 464–5,

467, 470, 477, 481, 624, 646–7; and
Russian offer to abolish nuclear tests,
485; and author's thoughts on economic
policy, 491–2; and Atomic Bilateral
Agreement, 500; and Lebanon crisis,
512–15, 528, 530, 533–4, 536; and
offshore islands, 543, 545, 546, 550–3,
554–5; and suspension of nuclear tests,
561–5, 569–71, 592, 647–8; and
author's visit (March 1959), 643–50;
on Berlin issue, 647; agrees with author's
correspondence with Khrushchev, 655–
656; visits Britain (Aug. 1959),
747–9
Eisenhower, Dr. Milton, 495
Eisenhower Doctrine, 119, 213–14, 237,
238, 243, 259, 277, 282, 511
Elizabeth the Queen Mother, Queen, 442
Elizabeth II, Queen, 180, 184, 185, 189,
191, 344, 372, 373, 376, 442, 635,
653, 694; visit to America, 319;
Canadian tour, 746–7; grants dis-
solution, 750
Elliot, Sir John, 717
Elliot, Dame Katharine, 721
Elliot, Walter, 200–1
Engineering Union, 362
'Enosis', 658, 671, 691, 698
EOKA, 224, 225–8, 658, 663, 674, 687,
690–1, 700
Erhard, Dr. Ludwig, 54, 69
Errington, Sir Eric, 201
Erskine, Sir John, 36
Euratom, 78, 87
Europe, Council of, 61, 65, 66, 67, 76
European Coal and Steel Community, 64,
65, 67
European Defence Community (E.D.C.),
64, 74, 76, 336; failure in France, 66
European   Economic   Community

(E.E.C.), 65; origin of, 67–8; development of, 69–88, 434, 440; Spaak's scepticism, 76–7; and Plan G, 77–88; and Free Trade Area, 80–88, 295, 434–59

European Free Trade Area, 295; Plan G for, 77, 79–88; negotiations, 431–59; Maudling appointed Minister for, 437–8, 440; policy on foodstuffs, 438–440; French opposition, 441–2, 448–452, 455–9

European League for Economic Co-operation, 436

Evans, Harold, 193, 384, 476, 591, 607, 619

Evans, Sir Horace, 173–4, 180, 183

Evatt, Dr. Herbert, 405

Evening Standard, 551–2

Exchange Control, 44, 46

Exchange Equalisation Account, 4

Family Allowances, 31

Farm Price Review, 22–3; (1956) 23–5; (1957) 210, 345

Fawzi, Mahmoud, 141–2, 143

Feisal II of Iraq, 101, 146, 147; and Iraq-Jordan union, 502; murder, 510, 528

Festing, General Sir Francis, 397

Fighter Command, 11, 264

Financial Times, 7, 573

Fisher, Geoffrey, Archbishop of Canterbury, 36, 49–50, 124, 224, 344

Fisk, Dr. James B., 567

Foot, Sir Hugh, Governor of Cyprus, 665, 667, 671, 674, 681, 683, 689, 692, 693, 696

Foreign Press Association, 53

Formosa, Nationalist China and, 538, 541–2, 543, 545, 546–7, 550

Forster, Sir John, 710

Fort Assarir, 504

Foster, Andrew, 104

France: distrust of Germany, 62, 66, 72, 74; rejects E.D.C., 64, 66; and Saar, 66, 70, 72; and Common Market, 67, 69, 73, 76, 87, 432–3, 457–9; protests over revival of German army, 72; disregards O.E.E.C. obligations, 75, 76; and Aswan Dam, 90; and Suez crisis, 103, 105, 107, 115, 120–1, 129, 135, 139–40, 145, 147–52; and SCUA, 120–1, 123–4; fears for North African territories, 148; ultimatum to Egypt and Israel, 150–1; military action against Egypt, 152, 160–2, 166; censured in U.N. Assembly, 158–9, 160; withdraws troops, 167, 169; and re-opening of Canal, 234; objects to reduction of British troops in Europe, 246, 247, 248; government changes and growing weakness, 303, 330–1, 332, 442, 443–4; collapse of franc, 354; and European Free Trade Area, 432, 435–6, 439, 441–2, 448–52, 455–9; return of de Gaulle, 443–6; author's visit (June 1958), 446–450; growing reconciliation with Germany, 453, 454, 651; and Summit talks, 475, 476–7, 486, 501, 638; in 'Standing Committee' in Washington, 498; accepts Russian idea of Summit of five, 526, 527, 529; atomic programme, 560, 561, 563, 565; flouting of NATO, 638; and Berlin problem, 637, 639; changed attitude to Summit, 640; devaluation, 725–6

Franks, Sir Oliver, 9

Fraser, Michael, 720

Fulbright, Senator William, 495, 643

Gaillard, Félix, 330, 331, 334, 442, 447

Gaitskell, Hugh, 183, 204, 221, 284, 285, 329, 358, 398, 471, 582, 590, 635, 707, 713, 724, 726; on fully planned economy, 59; denounces Nasser, 102, 118, 131; suggests appeal to United Nations, 118, 126, 155; opposes Suez action, 124–7, 150, 153, 154, 155, 156, 173, 236, 237–8, 516, 641; and nuclear tests, 261, 262–3, 266, 298–9, 419, 482, 487, 488; and Bank Rate 'leak', 415, 419, 425, 426, 427, 428; and Russian offer to abandon tests, 482, 484; and Lebanon, 509, 511, 514, 515–16, 519, 520, 521, 526, 529; and Quemoy, 553–4; and Cyprus, 671, 684–5, 698; and appointment of life peers, 731

Garner, Sir Saville, 497

Gaza Strip, 147, 170, 211, 212, 214, 215, 216–19, 259

General Agreement on Tariffs and Trade (GATT), 80, 83, 84

Geneva: Conference (1955), 95, 291, 310, 312, 470–1; conference of nuclear experts (1958), 498, 499, 564, 567, 600, 651–2; proposed Summit meeting of five, 526–7, 529; Foreign Ministers' Conference (1959), 646, 648, 653

Germany: reunification of, 293, 300, 306, 335, 479, 581, 637; lessons of Nazi era, 651

Germany, Eastern, 293, 578; Russian anxiety for recognition of, 580, 624–5; Russian proposals for peace treaty, 581–2, 599–600, 601, 611, 612–13, 616, 626, 631

Germany, Federal Republic: 'support' costs, 53–4, 210, 246, 247, 334, 501; French distrust of, 62, 66, 72, 74; and entry into NATO, 64, 335; and Saar, 66, 70; integration into Western Europe, 67, 335; and Common Market, 67, 69, 73, 87, 295; revival of army, 72, 574; and Aswan Dam, 90; reduction of British forces in, 210, 246–7, 248, 262, 265, 291, 501; concern over new defence plans, 291–295; and Free Trade Area, 435; growing reconciliation with France, 453, 454; Russian peace treaty proposals, 581–2, 599–601, 611–13, 626; suspicion of 'disengagement', 639

Ghalib bin Ali (Imam of Muscat and Oman), 270–2

Ghana, 200, 375, 378–9, 380, 413

Gilbert, Sir Bernard, 2

Gladstone, W. E., 20–1, 187, 365, 738

Glubb, Sir John, 90, 92

Godber, Lord, 45

Godfrey, William, R.C. Archbishop of Liverpool, 36

Goode, Sir William, 397

Goodman, L., 428–9

Goonetilleke, Sir Oliver, 393

Goudie, W. H., 733

Greece, 107, 154; and Cyprus, 224–5, 226, 230, 657–8, 660, 662–79, 683–689, 691–700; and Free Trade Area, 439

Green, Howard, 642

Green, Senator T. F., 495

Greencastle (Indiana), 490, 492–3

Greene, Sidney, 712

Grenfell, David, 204

Griffiths, James, 173, 183, 418, 509, 520, 685

Grimond, Jo, 204

Grivas, General, 658, 663, 686, 700

Gromyko, Andrei, 308, 481, 485, 555,

584, 599, 600, 604, 608, 611, 612,
614, 615, 618, 622, 623, 624, 630,
634
Gromyko, Mrs., 598
Gwadar, 276

Habbaniyah, 510, 535
Hagerty, James, 255, 335
Hague, The, Congress of Europe at
(1948), 61
Hailsham, Lord, 359, 702, 743; as
Minister of Education, 187, 188–9,
191; Deputy Leader in Lords, 229; as
Party Chairman, 415–16, 419–21
Haley, Sir William, 349
Hall, Sir Robert, 3, 9, 10, 708
Hallworth, Albert, 712
Hallstein, Dr. Walter, 248, 292, 330
Halsinger, General, 292
Hammarskjöld, Dag, 144, 163, 168, 179,
211, 230, 467; on Russian power, 483;
Middle East tour, 509, 533
Harding, Field-Marshal Sir John, 223,
227, 228, 660, 664–5
Hare, John, 372, 704
Hare, Raymond A., 230, 232, 508
Harland and Wolff, 636
Harper, Arthur, 397, 398–9
Harrod, Sir Roy, 355, 709, 723, 728–9
Harrow by-election (1959), 646
Head, Antony, 173, 188
Heald, Sir Lionel, 125
Heath, Edward, as Chief Whip, 192, 195,
201, 368, 373, 476, 520, 703
Heathcoat Amory, Derick, 13, 23, 24; as
Chancellor of Exchequer, 372, 703,
704, 708, 709, 722, 725, 726; his 1959
Budget, 729–30
Henderson, Arthur, 526
Henderson, Loy, 109, 269, 279, 284

Herter, Christian, 251, 642, 644, 645,
648
Herzen, Alexander, 311
Heuss, President Theodor, 452
Hill, Dr. Charles, 189, 197, 298, 358, 683
Hinchingbrooke, Lord, 340
Hobart, 408
Hoffmann, Johannes, 70
Hola incident, 733–6
Holland, 72, 113
Holland, Edward Milner, 425
Holland, Sir Sidney, 310, 375
Holmes, Julius, 309
Holyoake, Keith, 283, 326, 375
Home, Lord, 229, 304, 411, 683, 702
Hong Kong, 545, 546, 552; textile
industry, 739–43
Hood, Lord, 546
Hope, Peter, 607, 619
Hornsey by-election (1957), 349
Howitt, Sir Harold, 352
Hughes, Emrys, 606
Humbert, Dr. Russell J., 493
Humphrey, George, 98–9, 136, 137–8,
496, 708; and American loan, 137,
177–8; and Middle East, 177–8, 179
Hungary, 1956 revolution in, 161, 166,
213, 288, 289, 291, 297, 311, 378
Hussein of Jordan, 90, 146, 534–5; dis-
misses Glubb Pasha, 92; conflicting
pressures on, 146, 147, 150; and Iraq–
Jordan union, 502; seeks Anglo-
American aid, 513–14, 516–18, 522
Hussein, Ahmed, 98

India, 382; and Suez crisis, 108, 200, 375;
tension with Pakistan, 210, 380–1,
386, 392; and Kashmir, 210, 257, 381,
386, 392; and Indus waters, 381,
392; author's visit (1958), 384–9;

economic Five-Year Plan, 386–7; textile industry, 439–43
Indianapolis, 493; author's speech at (Sept. 1956), 130–2
Indonesia, 394, 399
Indus waters, 381, 392
Institute of Directors, 362
International Monetary Fund, 127, 128, 137, 164–5, 167
Iran, 535
Iraq, 91, 92, 94, 102, 278; firmness under Egyptian pressure, 146, 147; and Gaza crisis, 215, 216; danger from Russian infiltration, 280, 282, 285, 286; union with Jordan in Arab Federation, 502–503, 504; danger from Syria, 503; *coup* in, 510–11, 514, 522; new government recognised, 528, 530; 'Nasserite' revolt in, 535; withdrawal from Baghdad Pact and drift to Communism, 535–6
Ismailia, 150, 161
Ismay, Lord, 226
Israel: dispute with Egypt, 89–90, 93–5, 111, 146–7, 149, 150–2, 166, 206; and Suez crisis, 111, 146ff, invades Sinai peninsula, 150, 206; censured in Security Council, 151; accepts Anglo-French note, 152; partial withdrawal, 170; retains Gaza strip, 170, 209, 212, 214; dispute over Gaza and Aqaba, 215–19; sanctions demanded against, 215; allows British aid to Jordan to fly over, 519–20; orders airlift to cease, 524–5
Italy, 432, 439, 475, 481

Jackson, Basil, 45
James, Morrice, 384
Jebb, Sir Gladwyn, 447, 586, 620
Jifri brothers, 504–5

Jinnah, Mohammed Ali, 391
Johns Hopkins University, 494–5
Johnston, Sir Alexander, 2
Johnston, Charles, 220
Jones, Aubrey, 188
Jordan, 90–1, 102, 280, 534–5; Russian offer of arms, 92; Israeli threat to, 111, 146–7; Egyptian pressure on, 146; British treaty obligations to, 146–7, 148; joint command with Egypt and Syria, 149; new agreement with Britain, 220; American arms to, 282; union with Iraq in Arab Federation, 502–3, 504; Anglo-American financial aid, 508; seeks aid after Iraq *coup*, 513–514, 516–18, 522; British troops sent to, 519–22, 524–5, 526; troops withdrawn from, 532–3
Joxe, Louis, 447, 651

Kaganovich, L. M., 307, 308
Kalchenko, N. T., 621
Kandy, 396
Karachi, 390–3
Karamanlis, Constantine, 674, 675–7, 688, 694–5, 697, 698, 699
Kashmir, 210, 257, 381, 386, 392
Kassem, General Abdul Karim, 528, 530
Keightley, General Sir Charles, 161, 167
Kelvingrove by-election (1958), 720
Kendrew, General Sir Douglas, 682
Kennedy, Ludovic, 719
Kenya, 734–6
Khan, Mohammed Ayub, 391
Khrushchev, Nikita, 32, 308, 329, 387, 467, 567; visit to Britain, 95–7, 288, 583, 594–5; and Syria, 284–5; and Summit talks, 477, 480, 483, 485–6, 490, 499, 525, 526, 529, 558, 636, 652; becomes Prime Minister, 479–80;

offer to abandon nuclear tests, 483–5, 488, 489, 498–9; and Middle East crisis, 523, 525–6, 527, 529–32; calls for emergency meeting of General Assembly, 530–2, 538, 543; visit to Peking, 544; and Formosa, 550–1, 554; megalomania, 557–8; demands withdrawal of troops from West Berlin, 571–6, 585, 598, 613, 614, 625; and author's Moscow visit (Feb. 1959), 592–6, 598ff, on German question, 598, 599–600, 601, 611–14, 624–5, 626; on disarmament, 598–9, 600–1; expressions of goodwill, 603–4, 631–2; attack on Western powers, 605–6, 607, 610, 616–17, 618, 620; 'toothache', 618–19, 620, 624; suggests non-aggression treaty, 625, 654; as absolute ruler, 633–4; attempt to break Anglo-American solidarity, 652–655

Khrushchev, Mrs., 598, 604
Khyber Pass, 392
Kiev, 617, 620–2
Kilmuir, David Maxwell Fyfe, Viscount, 125, 182–3, 704, 731; investigates Bank Rate 'leak', 418, 421
Kirkbride, Sir Alec, 92
Kirkpatrick, Sir Ivone, 95
Kirkuk, 510
Korean War, 118, 158, 541
Kozlov, Frol, 604
Kutchuk, Dr. Fazil, 682, 693, 695, 697
Kuwait, 503, 504, 523, 536
Kuznetsov, Vasili, 620

Lahej, 504–5
Lancashire, 744, 745–6
League of Empire Loyalists, 725
Lebanon, 280, 285; unrest in, 505–10, 511–15; U.A.R. threat to, 505–6,

508–10; Anglo-American promise of help, 506–8, 511; tension after Iraq revolution, 511–13; American military intervention, 512, 513–16, 526–7, 532, 534
Leeper, Sir Reginald, 675
Leicester, 248–9
Lenin (atomic ice-breaker), 622
Leningrad, 622–4
Lennox-Boyd, Alan (Colonial Secretary), 49, 505, 674, 702; and Cyprus, 225, 227, 228, 660, 664, 667, 671, 672, 690–1, 693, 699; and Hola incident, 733–6; and Nyasaland disorder, 736–8; and limitation of Hong Kong cotton imports, 740–1, 742
Leslie, S. C., 3
Lewisham North, by-election (1957), 345
Liaqat Ali Khan, 391
Libya, 93, 94
Life Peerages Act (1958), 731
Lim Yew Hock, 396, 409
Llandudno, Conservative Party Conference (1956), 86
Lloyd, Selwyn (Foreign Secretary), 54, 76, 92, 186, 208, 215, 247, 248, 269, 304, 306, 308, 334, 339, 402, 447, 559, 560, 702; visit to Washington (Feb. 1956), 74, 91; and Suez crisis, 113, 119, 124–5, 138–9, 141, 144, 153, 167, 168, 170, 172, 173, 237; and SCUA, 138, 139; at United Nations, 138–9, 141, 144, 145; and Cyprus, 228, 660, 666, 672, 674, 685, 689–90, 692–4; at Bermuda talks, 250, 251, 254, 256; and Syrian problem, 282, 283–4, 286–7; at Bonn meeting (May 1957), 291–2; and disarmament talks with Dulles, 313–14, 316; at

Washington talks (Oct. 1957), 320–3; and Free Trade Area negotiations, 431, 441; and Summit talks, 466, 467, 478, 623; talks with Dulles in Ankara and Manila, 467, 477–8; failure in debate (Feb. 1958), 472–3; offers resignation, 473–4, 760–1; and Nuri's plan for Kuwait, 504; and Lebanon crisis, 507–508, 514–15, 526, 532, 536, 687; and offshore islands, 552, 553, 554–5; and Berlin issue, 573, 574, 577, 583, 612–613; in Russia (Feb. 1959), 591, 599, 600, 602, 606, 607, 612–13, 615, 617, 622–3, 630–1; Khrushchev's abuse of, 617; in Paris and Bonn, 636–40; in Canada and America, 641–5; at London Conference on Cyprus, 695–6

Lloyd George, David, 28

Lloyd George, Gwilym, 186–7

Lodge, Henry Cabot, 151–2, 162, 215, 219, 233, 243, 257, 344

Luce, Sir William, 505

Luns, Dr. Joseph, 113

Lyssa, 681–2

Macaulay, Lord, 19, 41

McBride, Sir Philip, 407

McCone, John A., 566

MacDonald, Malcolm, 389, 412

McEwen, John, 78

McIntosh, Mr., 428–9

Mackintosh, Lord, 8, 33, 35–6, 37

Maclay, John Scott, 189, 243

Macleod, Iain, 368, 704; as Minister of Labour, 249, 265, 345, 347, 646, 711, 713, 714, 717, 727

McMahon Act, 200, 464; repeal of, 315, 316, 321, 323–4, 327, 332, 476, 479, 483, 489, 492, 494, 500, 560, 563, 568

Macmillan, Lady Dorothy, 18, 20, 21, 22, 127, 184, 200, 204, 207, 297, 326, 368, 373, 376, 442, 516, 553, 636, 641; author's tribute to, 194, 201–2, 410–11; created D.B.E., 194; influence on No. 10, 206, 208; dislike of Chequers, 207; on Commonwealth tour (1957), 384, 385, 393, 401, 406, 410–11; on visit to Washington and Ottawa, 492, 497; on North-East tour (Jan. 1959), 726–7; on Lancashire tour (April 1959), 745

Macmillan, Harold: takes over as Chancellor of Exchequer, 1; expansionist views, 6, 9, 39–40, 351, 709; his proposals, 9–13; and abolition of bread and milk subsidies, 12, 14, 15; prepared to resign, 13–14; measures to combat inflation, 14–19, 342–3, 351–2; and Farm Price Review, 22–5; his April 1956 Budget, 28–44; his 'Savings' theme, 28–9, 31, 42–3; plan for Premium Bonds, 32–8; economies in Defence, 50–1; and German 'support' costs, 53–4, 247, 501; pleads for wage and price stability, 55–60; plans for European integration, 64–88; and Common Market, 68, 72–88; and Plan G for Free Trade Area, 77–88, 431; announces intention to open negotiations, 87–8; scepticism over Aswan Dam, 93–4, 97; supports policy of force over Suez, 104–5, 106–8, 127, 136, 171–2; views on military operation, 111–12; on Suez political aims, 112; and SCUA, 119–21, 124, 127, 128, 136, 138–9; disillusion over Dulles, 121; and pressure on reserves, 127–8, 163–5, 171; visits America (Sept. 1956), 128–38; honorary law degree from Indiana University, 129–133; visits mother's old home, 129, 133; talks with Eisenhower and Dulles, 133–136; attends I.M.F. meeting, 135; supports cease-fire and withdrawal in Egypt, 163, 169; negotiates for revision of American loan, 177–8; and Eden's resignation, 180–2; becomes Prime Minister, 184–205; forms Administration, 185–91; his staff, 192–3; radio and television broadcast, 196–7; his 'dual nature', 197–8; difficulties and dangers facing, 198–200, 209–10; elected Party leader, 201–3; first visit to Chequers, 207; discouraging by-elections, 210–11, 298, 345, 349, 411, 719; and strikes, 211, 249, 255, 343, 345, 346–7, 352–3, 507; and aftermath of Suez, 214–23, 230–39; and Eccles incident, 220–2; and Cyprus negotiations, 223–30; first big Parliamentary test as Prime Minister, 235–8; restoration of Anglo-American relationship, 240–2, 249, 250, 258, 317; Bermuda talks, 240–1, 249–59; reviews defence policy, 244–7, 263–8, 291–2; debate on conference, 259–63; and continuation of nuclear tests, 261–3, 267–8, 296–9, 310, 314; and Muscat rebellion, 271–9; and Communist infiltration into Syria, 277–87; delays visit to Moscow, 288; talks with Adenauer, 291–6; determines to seek *détente* with Russia, 298, 305, 311–12; concern at Stassen's nuclear disarmament plan, 300–6; replies to Bulganin's proposals, 305–6, 408–9; proposes limitation of tests, 314; and Anglo-American co-operation against Russian challenge, 315–17, 321, 328–9, 341; visits Washington

(Oct. 1957), 319–29; seeks repeal of McMahon Act, 321, 323, 324, 332; agrees Declaration of Common Purpose, 323–4, 328; in Ottawa, 326–7; and 'inter-dependence', 328, 330, 338; at NATO meeting (Dec. 1957), 334–339, 363; alarm at economic situation, 349–58; warns of dangers of inflation, 350–2; uses phrase 'never had it so good', 350–1; resists idea of deflation, 355; agrees to increase in Bank Rate, 356; and defence of sterling, 357–62; search for economy in Civil Estimates, 363–5; disagreement with Thorneycroft over Estimates, 365–72; leaves for Commonwealth tour, 373, 381; and Commonwealth Prime Ministers' Conference (1957), 375–81; thoughts on Commonwealth, 378–80, 382–4, 412–413; talks with Nehru in New Delhi, 384–5; in Pakistan, 390–3; in Ceylon, 393–6; in New Zealand and Australia, 397–409; return home, 411; and Bank Rate 'leak', 415–30; and negotiations for Common Market and Free Trade Area, 433–59; visits de Gaulle (June 1958), 446–50; and Adenauer, 452–5; broadcast on foreign policy, 461–4; replies to Bulganin on nuclear tests, 464–6; and idea of Summit, 465, 467–470, 475–82, 486, 488, 495, 499, 525–7, 558, 623, 625–6, 636, 638, 640; supports Lloyd after Press attacks, 473–4, 760–1; and suspension of nuclear tests, 482–90, 499, 559–70; exposes Labour ambivalence over defence, 486–8; visits America (June 1958), 490, 492–6; ideas on economic struggle against Communism, 491–2; honorary degree at DePauw University,

493; in Canada, 497; and Lebanon crisis, 507–9, 511–15, 533–4; discusses support for Jordan, 516–22, 524–5; and Iraq, 528–9, 533, 535–6; correspondence with Khrushchev, 530–2; and 'offshore islands' crisis, 544–52, 555–6; misunderstanding over moral not military support for America, 551–2; considers visit to Russia, 558–559, 583–90; and Berlin crisis, 571–583, 612–13, 647; Russian visit (Feb. 1958), 592–635; tries to dispel illusion over 'imperialism', 595–7; talks on Berlin and disarmament, 598–601; and Khrushchev's attack on Western powers, 605–12; plain speaking, 610–618, 622; emphasises Allied solidarity, 610, 625; warns of dangerous German situation, 610–11, 616–17; and 'toothache insult', 618–19; visits Kiev and Leningrad, 620–4; more cordial talks with Khrushchev, 625–6; television broadcast, 626–30; his impressions of Russia, 632–4; visits Paris and Bonn, 636–40; in Canada and America, 641–651; talks at Camp David, 644–9; and Khrushchev's attempt to split Western powers, 652–6; on idea of non-aggression pact, 654; and Cyprus negotiations, 660–701; Press attacks on, 663; outlines partnership plan, 669–70; visits Greece and Turkey, 674–80; in Cyprus, 681–3; and signing of agreement, 697–9; concern over accounts of American 'recession', 708–9, 724; determination to hold wages front, 709–10; and transport strikes, 708–19; urges 'appeal' rather than 'challenge' to trade unions, 711; turning of political tide, 721–2; improved personal position,

724; urges 'reflation', 723, 725–30; concern over unemployment, 727, 728; creates life peers, 731–2; and Hola incident, 734–6; supports Lennox-Boyd over Nyasaland, 737–8; discussions on textile industry, 739–44; and electoral prospects, 744–5; decides on Oct. 1959 election, 745, 746–7; tours Lancashire, 745–6; and Eisenhower's visit, 747–50; asks for dissolution, 750

LETTERS: to Adenauer (on de Gaulle's attitude to Free Trade Area), 452; (on Moscow visit), 585–6
to Beddington-Behrens (on Common Market and Free Trade Area), 434
to Bulganin (on visit to Moscow), 288; (on European security), 310–311; (on meeting of Heads of Governments), 467–9
to Butler (on European Customs Union), 70–1
to de Gaulle (on coming to power and possible meeting), 445–6; (on Free Trade Area), 449–50, 451, 456–9
to Dulles (on Washington visit), 325–6; (on offshore islands), 549; (on Berlin), 580; (on Cyprus), 690
to Eden (on abolition of bread and milk subsidies), 12–13
to Eisenhower (on Bermuda meeting), 242; (on Stassen's nuclear disarmament plan), 301–2; (on trade with China), 317–18; (on Washington visit), 325; (on Summit), 477–8; (on Atomic Agreement), 500; (on offshore islands), 545; (on suspension of nuclear

tests), 563, 567, 569–70, 592; (on Moscow visit), 601–2

to Foot (on Cyprus), 685–6, 692

to Gaitskell (on Cyprus), 684–5

to Harding (on departure from Cyprus), 664–5

to Hill (on defence of sterling), 358–9

to Khrushchev (on experts' talks), 485–6; (on nuclear tests), 486; (on Summit), 499, 532; (on Middle East), 531–2; (on Berlin), 572; (on attempt to split Western powers), 653–4

to Lloyd (on proffered resignation), 760–1

to Mackintosh (on Premium Bonds), 35, 37

to Plowden (on Anglo-American nuclear co-operation), 566

to Reilly (on situation in Russia and visit there), 557–9

to Salisbury (on his resignation), 228–9

to Spaak (on Plan G), 85–6

to Thorneycroft (on resignation), 370–2; (on European integration), 436–8

SPEECHES quoted: on economic measures, 15–17, 55–7, 59, 78–9, 359

on 1956 Budget, 39–44

on Trinidad oil take-over, 48–9

on Plan G, 86–8

on Suez crisis, 130–2, 171–2, 217

on election as Party leader, 201–3

on Gaza strip, 217

on Bermuda meeting, 249, 259–62

on Defence, 264–8, 293–5, 305, 383, 486–8

on nuclear weapons, 266–8, 305, 461, 463, 487–8

on 'inter-dependence', 328

on NATO, 340

on dangers of inflation, 350–2

on relations with Australia, 403–4

on East-West relations, 406

on Bank Rate 'leak', 423–4

on problems of peace, 461–4

on disarmament, 463–4, 597

on Summit meetings, 470–1, 495

on suspension of nuclear tests, 487

on Moscow visit, 589

in Moscow, 593–4, 595–7, 603–4, 627–30

on Cyprus, 669–70, 698–9

WRITINGS: *Dizzy with Success*, 5
First Thoughts from a Treasury Window, 7–8

Macmillan, Maurice (son), 88

Macmillan, Mrs. Maurice Crawford (mother), 129, 133, 185, 494, 496

Makarios, Archbishop, 212, 235, 663, 678, 687, 688; and terrorist activities, 223, 226–7, 658, 660; deported to Seychelles, 223–4; bargaining with, 227–8, 230; decision to release, 227, 657; and Enosis, 658–9; return to Athens, 659, 686; insists on self-determination, 685; his return to Cyprus considered, 686, 691–2; and London Conference, 694–7; arguments over independence, 700–1; President of republic, 701

Makins, Sir Roger, 2–3, 178, 749

Malaya, 200, 397, 399

Malenkov, Georgi, 307, 308

Malik, Charles Habib, 505

Malik, Jakob, 608, 615, 619, 621, 624

Mallaby, George, 412

Malta, 210

Manchester Guardian, 24, 236, 469, 564, 738

Mann, Mrs. Jean, 590

Manningham-Buller, Sir Reginald, 517

Mansfield, Sir Alan and Lady, 405

Mao Tse-tung, 530, 540

Marples, Ernest, 189, 704

Marshall Plan, 63

Massey, Vincent, 497, 641

Massigli, René, 332, 433

Matsu, bombardment of, 538, 539, 543–547, 551, 556

Mau Mau, 733–4

Maude, Evan, 32

Maudling, Reginald, 189, 372, 704, 708; and Free Trade Area negotiations, 437–8, 439, 440–2, 443, 450, 451, 455, 459

Maxwell, William D., 493

Maxwell Fyfe, Sir David (later Lord Kilmuir, q.v.), 65

Melbourne, 383, 407–8

Melbourne, Lord, 19, 204–5, 407

Melville, Eugene, 674

Menderes, Adnan, 668, 672–3, 678–80, 693, 694–5, 698, 700

Mendès-France, Pierre, 70, 248

Menzies, Sir Robert, 77, 108, 109, 117, 142, 283, 310, 326, 327, 377, 638; his mission to Nasser, 114–16, 118, 375; recommends recourse to U.N. 232; concern over U.N. Assembly, 243; and author's Commonwealth tour, 402, 403–5, 409; and offshore islands, 555

Merchant, Livingston T., 323, 587, 645, 646

Messina Conference (1955), and E.E.C., 67–8, 69–70, 72, 73–4, 78, 79–80, 82, 83–4, 431, 432, 434

Mikoyan, Anastas, 580, 581, 592, 599, 604, 606, 608, 611, 614, 615, 618, 621, 622–3, 624, 634

Millar, Sir Frederick Hoyer, 286, 397, 476, 553, 587, 645, 660

Mills, Lord, 9, 188, 189, 355, 535, 704, 727, 728

Minto, Miss S. A., 192

Mintoff, Dominic, 210

Mirza, Iskander, 390, 393

Moch, Jules, 301, 302

Mohammed Reza Shah Pahlevi, Shah of Iran, 606, 614

Mollet, Guy, 69, 74, 103, 120–1, 167, 219, 246, 291, 303, 448; Washington visit, 241, 247; hostile to European army reduction, 248, 434; and Free Trade Area, 433, 434

Molotov, V. M., 307, 308

Monckton, Lord, 10, 50, 187, 729

Montgomery, Lord, 492, 749; on Defence reorganisation, 245

Montreal, Commonwealth Economic Conference at (1958), 451, 452

Morgan, John, 627

Morrison, John, 183, 282

Moscow: author's visit to (Feb. 1959), 592–634; University, 602; Bolshoi Theatre, 614–15

Mountbatten, Lord, 161

Mouvement Républicain Populaire, 74

Muhammad al Badr, Yemeni Crown Prince, 502

Murphy, Robert, 104–5, 106, 138, 257, 588, 642

Murray, F. R. H., 591, 608, 615

Murrow, Ed, 721

Muscat and Oman, revolt in, 270–7, 728

Nash, Walter, 397, 542

Nasser, Gamal Abdel, 209–10, 211, 253; propaganda and intrigues, 89–90, 92, 102, 145–8, 506, 509, 534; support from Russia, 90, 98, 100, 102, 148, 166, 171; and Aswan Dam, 90, 97, 98–100, 101; dispute with Israel, 91, 147, 148, 149–50; aim at Arab leadership, 91, 102–3, 145–8, 171; elected President, 98; nationalises Suez Canal, 100–2, 107, 130–2; Gaitskell's comparison with Hitler and Mussolini, 102, 131, 148; condemnation of and pressure against, 107–8, 109–10, 113, 114–18, 136ff; Menzies' interview with, 115–16, 375; military defeat, 160–1, 166, 269; obstacles to Canal clearance, 168, 212; intransigence over use of Canal, 214–15, 217, 230–4; joined by Sultan of Lahej, 504–5; threat to Lebanon, 506, 509, 534; and Kuwait, 523; failure of Iraq 'revolt', 535

National Assistance Board, 13

National Board for Prices and Incomes, 707

National Debt, 26, 40–1

National Health Service, 344, 366

National Insurance Fund, 343, 708

National Production Advisory Council, 12, 58

National Savings, 8, 33–4, 43

National Service, 265

National Union of Railwaymen, 712, 715

NATO – see North Atlantic Treaty Organisation

Nehru, Jawaharlal, 99, 257, 375, 465, 743; appeal to abolish nuclear tests, 337–8; at 1957 Commonwealth Conference, 376, 380–1; author visits, 384–9, 390, 391; and Five-Year Plan, 387; and Middle East crisis, 522

New Delhi, 384–9

New York Times, 241

New Zealand, 78, 375, 412; author visits, 397–402, 413

Newcastle-on-Tyne, 727; speech on prices and wages, 55–7

News Chronicle, 341, 619, 738

Ngaruawahia, 400

Nicklin, Francis, 405

Nicosia, 681, 682, 693

Nixon, Richard, 256, 574, 642, 650

Nkrumah, Dr. Kwame, 379, 380

Noel-Baker, Philip, 172, 173

Noon, Sir Malik Firoz Khan, 390, 391–2

Norstad, General Lauris, 247, 638

North Atlantic Treaty Organisation (NATO), 63, 64, 65, 66, 131, 157, 260, 291–2, 310, 383, 479; and Suez, 113; rearming of, 134, 137, 340; and reduction of British forces in Germany, 210, 246–7, 264, 265, 501; and Cyprus, 226–7; meeting (March 1957), 247–8; Bulganin on, 290, 305; meeting (Dec. 1957), 330, 331, 334–41, 363, 468; proposes Foreign Ministers' meeting, 468, 475, 478; and reply to Moscow, 481, 529; Russian proposal for both Germanies to leave, 581–2, 600; tenth anniversary meeting (April 1959), 651; Turco-Greek alliance in, 657; importance of Cyprus bases to, 659; and Cyprus negotiations, 662 666, 668, 675, 684, 687–8, 689

North-West Frontier, 392

Northern Conservative Club, 55

Norway, 80

Nuri es-Said, 101, 146, 215, 216, 270, 280, 281; plans for Kuwait and Iraq-Jordan union, 502–4; murdered, 510, 514, 528

Nutting, Anthony, 153
Nyasaland, 736–8

O'Neill, Con, 494, 591
Observer, 526
Oldham, 744, 745
Oman, revolt in, 270–7
Opinion polls, 156, 557, 721
Organisation for European Economic Co-operation (O.E.E.C.), 53, 63, 66, 68, 72; French disregard of, 75, 76; and plan for common market or customs union, 78–80; and Free Trade Area, 80, 81–2, 87, 432, 440, 457, 459
Ormsby Gore, David, 683
Ottawa, 326–7, 377, 404, 497, 641–2
Oxford, 748

Padmore, Sir Thomas, 2
Pakistan, 276; tension with India, 210, 380–1, 386, 392; and Kashmir, 210, 381, 392; and Suez, 375; and Indus waters, 381, 392; author visits, 388–393; political instability, 386, 390–1, 393; American defence agreement with, 535; textile industry, 439–43
Palmerston, Lord, 530
Panama Canal, 118, 140
Paris: NATO meetings, 334–9, 341, 363; author visits, 446–50, 636–8
Parker, Lord Justice, 425
Patch, Sir Hubert, 681
Pearson, Lester, 113, 160, 162–3, 258, 375, 642
Peng Teh-huai, Marshal, 556
Penney, Sir William, 566, 567
Perth, Lord, 674, 683, 737
Pescadores, 538, 543
Peshawar, 392
Petch, Louis, 32

Petrovsky, Ivan G., 602
Pflimlin, Pierre, 443–4
Phelps, Antony, 192
Pinay, Antoine, 66, 448, 450
Pineau, Christian, 103, 105, 139, 141, 219; hostile to European army reduction, 248, 434; and Common Market, 434; and Summit, 477
Plowden, Sir Edwin, 304, 322, 492, 494, 561, 566
Plummer, Sir Leslie, 422
Poole, Oliver, 182, 415–16; and Bank Rate 'leak', 422–4
Port Said, 98, 150, 160, 161, 167, 168, 174, 232
Potsdam agreement, 575, 599
Powell, Enoch, 368, 369, 372, 374, 417, 418, 703
Powell, Sir Richard, 292, 322, 561
Premium Bonds, 8, 32–8, 50
Preston, 745
Primrose League, 486
Pulliam, Eugene C., 493, 494
Pumphrey, J. L., 427–8

Quemoy, bombardment of, 538–9, 543–547, 551, 556

Radcliffe, Lord, plan for Cyprus, 224, 660, 676
Radcliffe Committee Report (1959), 747
Radford, Admiral Arthur W., 546
Railway Tribunal, 710
Ramadier, Paul, 75
Rapacki Plan, 464, 465
Rashid Ali, 533
Rashid Karami, 533
Ravensdale, Lady, 732
Regent Oil Company, 45
Reilly, Sir Patrick, 557–9, 583–4, 590, 624

Reilly, Lady, 598
Reinhardt, Frederick, 642
Rent Act (1957), 345, 349, 720
Reynolds News, 428, 429
Rhineland, 111, 113, 131, 155–6
Robens, Alfred, 713
Robertson, Sir Brian, 346, 507, 711–13, 714, 715
Robertson, Sir Dennis, 352
Robertson, Walter, 546
Rochdale by-election (1958), 411, 473, 719
Rochdale, Lord, 739, 740, 741, 742
Rome, Treaty of (1957), 434, 435, 439, 449, 455, 456
Roosevelt, Franklin D., 540
Ross, Archibald, 674
Rowan, Sir Leslie, 2, 46, 73, 708
Royal Air Force, 11, 264, 265; in Oman operation, 271, 272, 274; leaves Iraq, 535
Royal Navy, 265
Rumbold, Sir Anthony, 454, 587, 591
Russia: support for Egypt and Arab cause, 90, 92, 100, 108, 147, 148, 166, 176; offers arms to Jordan, 92; and Aswan Dam, 93–4, 98; and Suez crisis, 142–3, 145, 147, 148–9, 154, 161, 165–6, 288; uses veto in Security Council (Oct. 1956), 145, 158; aims in Middle East, 171, 176, 177, 277–87; infiltration into Syria, 277–87; and disarmament and abolition of nuclear tests, 289–91, 296–8, 299–308, 310–12, 339, 460, 464–70, 479, 481–6, 599, 600–1; government changes, 307–8; first I.C.B.M. test, 310; rejects 'package' proposals, 309–10, 313; launches Sputniks, 314, 320; Western co-operation against, 315–17, 321; trade with China, 317–318, 483; and Summit meeting, 387–8, 398, 402, 408–9, 465–70, 479, 480, 483, 485–6, 499, 525, 526, 529, 558, 636; enigma of policy, 461–2; unilateral decision to abandon nuclear tests, 481–2, 484–5 488; and Middle East crisis, 523, 524–8, 430–2, 535–6; and offshore islands, 550–1, 554–5; author proposes to visit, 558–9, 582–5, 589–90; trade with, 559, 576, 615, 631; and suspension of nuclear tests, 562–3, 631, 651–2, 661; and control system, 562, 563, 567, 569–71, 592, 600–1, 631, 647–8, 651–2; resumption of tests, 568; demands withdrawal of troops from West Berlin, 571–81, 585, 598, 613, 614, 625, 626; renews call for Summit, 577, 600, 623–4, 635; proposes German peace treaty, 581–2, 599–600, 601, 611, 612–13, 616, 626; author's visit to (Feb. 1959), 591–634; sense of insecurity, 601–2; agriculture, 620; seeks recognition of East Germany, 624–5; proposes non-aggression pact, 625, 654; agrees to Foreign Ministers' meeting, 625–6, 635, 636, 646; author's impressions of, 632–4; veto over inspection teams, 647, 651

Saar territory, 66, 70
Said bin Taimur (Sultan of Muscat and Oman), 270–7
St. Laurent, Louis, 247, 258, 497
St. Lawrence Seaway, 746
Salisbury, 5th Marquess of, 118, 174; and Suez, 125, 127, 232, 235, 236; and Eden's resignation, 180, 181–3, 184, 185, 200, 201; resignation, 212, 222, 227, 228–9, 231, 235, 262, 473, 656, 702; and Cyprus, 224, 227, 231, 235, 656

Sami es-Solh, 505

Sandys, Duncan, 65, 241–2, 304, 308, 334, 614, 660, 704; appointed Minister of Defence, 188, 244; and defence reorganisation, 244–6, 266; reduces Estimates, 368; storm over Moscow invitation, 476

Saud II of Arabia, 271, 284, 285, 535

Saudi Arabia, 94, 102, 146, 285; supports Oman revolt, 270–1, 273; alarm over Iraq, 535

Schäffer, Fritz, 54

Schuman Plan, 64, 68

Scott, Sir Robert, 396

Security Council: Dulles's reluctance to refer Suez to, 122–3; British intention to go to, 123–4, 125, 126, 128–9; presentation of case, 139–45; impotence of, 145, 146; resolution censuring Israel, 151; and future use of Canal, 231–4; and Oman action, 276; and Middle East, 514, 518, 257, 531–2

Selkirk, Lord, 187, 235

Semenovskoye, 597

Sharett, Moshe, 89

Sharm-el-Sheikh Heights, 170, 212, 214, 260

Sheffield, 264, 305

Shell Petroleum, 44–5, 239

Shepilov, D. T., 98, 142, 143, 162, 308

Shinwell, Emanuel, 217, 340, 482

Simon, John, 372

Sinai peninsula, 150, 170, 206, 212, 214

Sinclair, Sir Laurence, 273

Singapore, 396–7, 409–10

Six Principles, 140–1, 145, 158, 170, 230, 232, 233

Slattery, Sir Matthew, 235

Slim, Field-Marshal Sir William, 402, 412

Slim, Lady, 402

Smirnov, Andrei, 571

Smirnov, Nikolai, 624

Smith, Sidney, 641, 642

Smith, General Walter Bedell, 138

Smithfield strike, 717, 718

Snyder, General Howard, 255

Soames, Christopher, 372

Soskice, Sir Frank, 734

Soustelle, Jacques, 458, 459

South Africa, 375

Spaak, Paul-Henri, 67, 69, 324–5, 336, 454, 757; and Messina 'Common Market' plan, 67, 69, 72, 75–6, 77, 81; and Suez crisis, 113, 167; and idea of Summit, 475; and Cyprus, 662, 675, 685, 687, 792

Spencer (Indiana), 129, 133

Stassen, Harold, 299, 309; indiscretion over nuclear disarmament proposals, 300–4, 306

Steel, Sir Christopher, 452, 580–1

Steel, Lady, 452

Stewart, Michael, 679

Stockton-on-Tees, 727

Strasbourg, 69; Council of Europe inaugurated (1949), 61

Strauss, Franz-Josef, 292

Strauss, Admiral Lewis, 304, 314, 315, 322, 327

Stuart, James, 23, 97, 186–7, 189, 750

Sudan, 522

Suez Canal: British evacuation of, 89, 93, 97, 98; Nasser's seizure of, 99, 100–101, 130, 131, 146; crisis over, 101 ff; first London Conference on (Aug. 1956), 107–8, 115, 116, 118, 120, 143, 146, 158; second London Conference (Sept. 1956), 127, 129, 145;

payment of dues, 120, 123, 136, 141, 145, 209, 210, 230, 233–4; Anglo-French military action, 152, 160–2, 166, 171, 175–6; controversy and debates on, 153–75, 236–9, 640–1; clearance and reopening of, 168–9, 179, 199, 210, 212, 214, 216, 219, 229–34; aftermath of, 199, 206–39; Nasser's intransigence over use of, 214–15, 217, 230–4

Suez Canal Company, 101, 105–6, 107, 144

Suez Canal Users' Association (SCUA), 119–23, 124, 125, 127, 128, 129, 136, 138–40, 145, 158, 231, 233

Suhrawardy, Shahid, 375, 381

Sukarno, Achmed, 384, 394–5

Sulzberger, Arthur Hays, 241

Sunday Times, 349

Sweden, 66, 80

Switzerland, 66, 80

Sydney, 383, 405–6

Syria: pressure from Egypt, 91, 146, 149; Russian arms in, 147; raids on Israel from, 146, 147; joint command with Egypt and Jordan, 149; and opening of oil pipeline, 209, 210, 212, 214, 215, 219, 278; Russian infiltration into, 277–287; union with Egypt in U.A.R., 502, 503; danger to Iraqi oil, 503

Tachen, 438, 539

Talib bin Ali, 270, 275

Tewson, Sir Vincent, 58, 716

Texas Oil Company, 44–50

Thompson, Llewellyn, 490

Thorneycroft, Peter, 13, 65, 374, 703; and European unity, 65, 69, 71, 77, 79, 83, 85, 431, 433, 435; and Suez, 171; as Chancellor of Exchequer, 187, 343,

344–5, 347–9, 352, 353, 356, 358, 359–61, 363–72; and economies, 344, 363–72; reliefs in first Budget (1957), 347–8; and increase in Bank Rate, 356–7, 417, 421–2, 423, 426–7; defence of pound, 358, 359–61; resignation, 367, 368, 369–72, 400, 665, 707; and European Free Trade Area, 433, 435, 436–8

'Three Wise Men', 352, 706–7, 722

Times, The, 24, 357, 425, 438, 469, 473, 730, 733, 738; on Suez, 112–13, 236; on higher wages, 350; on Commonwealth Conference (1957), 378; on railway settlement (1958), 716

Tiran Straits, 170, 218

Tito, Marshal, 99

Torrington by-election (1958), 720

Trades Union Council, 58–9, 347, 355, 716–18

Transport Command, 274

Transport Commission, 360, 710, 711–12

Transport Salaried Staffs' Association, 715

Transport and General Workers Union, 362, 716, 719

Trend, Sir Burke, 193

Trinidad Oil Company, 44–50

Troyanovski, Mr., 608

Trucial Oman Scouts, 271

Truman, President Harry S., 159

Tunisia, 331, 332, 442

Turf Club, 195

Turkey: and Cyprus, 223, 224–6, 657–8, 659–63, 666–80, 682–4, 686–7, 690–700; and Russian infiltration into Syria, 281, 282–3, 284–5; and Free Trade Area, 439; and Iraq, 522, 530; American defence agreement with, 535

Turner, Sir James, 24

Twining, General Nathan, 647

United Arab Republic: formed by Egypt and Syria, 502; suspected campaign against Lebanon, 505–6, 508–10; danger to Jordan, 517, 518, 520, 522; organises revolt in Iraq, 535

United Nations Emergency Force (UNEF): in Gaza and Aqaba, 219, 259; in Lebanon, 513

United Nations Organisation: and Suez, 118–19, 124–5, 128–9, 139–45, 151, 154, 158–60, 162–3, 166–70; Dulles resists recourse to, over Suez, 118–19, 121, 122, 129, 135–6; Eisenhower's faith in, 134, 243, 257; Dulles supports Britain and France at, 143–4; emergency meeting of Assembly calls for Suez cease-fire, 158–9; and clearance of Canal, 168–9, 212; confusion over Gaza strip, 170, 211, 214–19, 259; question of Canal dues, 230–4; and British action in Oman, 276; and 'Turkish threat' to Syria, 284, 285; and disarmament, 299, 313–14, 315, 463; and Middle East crisis, 513–14, 530–3; de Gaulle's dislike of, 527; Nationalist China's seat in, 540, 541. See also Security Council

United States of America: and Messina plan for common market, 74; schism with, 89–179; and Arab–Israeli problem, 89–90, 93, 94–5, 103–8, 110–11, 116–17; and Aswan Dam, 90, 97–9; reluctance to join Baghdad Pact, 91, 94; withdraws support from Aswan Dam scheme, 98–100; ambivalence over Suez, 103–9, 118–22, 125–8, 139–140, 144, 148, 150–1, 320; excludes use of force, 116–17; resists recourse to U.N., 118–19, 129, 135–6; plans for SCUA, 119–22, 124, 127–8; Presidential election, 127, 136, 167; author's visit (Sept. 1956), 129–38; attacks Anglo-French action in Egypt, 157–60, 162–3, 269; blocks drawings from International Monetary Fund, 164–5, 167; hardening attitude, 166–7, 168–9; demands immediate evacuation of Egypt, 167; revision of loan in favour of Britain, 177; and Eisenhower Doctrine, 213–14, 217, 237–8, 243, 259, 277, 282, 511; and Gaza dispute, 216–19; and Cyprus, 230; and re-opening of Canal, 230–1, 232, 233; renewal of Anglo-American relations, 240–68, 317–41; and I.R.B.M.s in Western Europe, 245, 260–1, 267, 290, 336–7, 474, 652; and reliance on United Nations, 257, 259; joins Military Committee of Baghdad Pact, 260, 269; and continuation of nuclear tests, 261–262; and British action in Oman, 276 277; and Russian infiltration into Syria, 277–87; schemes for nuclear disarmament, 300–4, 309, 330; and full nuclear co-operation, 315–17, 321, 329, 332, 462–5, 565–8; author's visit to (Oct. 1957), 319–26; and Declaration of Common Purpose, 323–4, 328, 756–9; and Summit talks, 470, 475–8, 481, 485, 495, 501, 586, 624, 646–7, 648; and suspension of nuclear tests, 488, 561–71, 647–8, 651–2; author's visit to (June 1958), 490–6; move to greater interdependence, 496, 498; and Atomic Bilateral Agreement, 500; economic aid to Baghdad Pact, 502; and Middle East crisis, 503–35; promise to help Lebanon, 506–8, 509,

511; financial aid to Jordan and Iraq, 508; military intervention in Lebanon, 512, 513–16, 526–7, 532, 534; withdrawal from, 533; and offshore islands crisis, 538–43; attitude to China, 539–543; and Berlin crisis, 587–8, 647; proposes Foreign Ministers' Conference, 636, 639, 646, 648; author's visit to (March 1959), 642–50; and control system, 647–8, 651; trade Protectionism, 648–9, 650; Khrushchev's attempt to break solidarity with Britain, 652–5; and Cyprus, 666–7

Veale, Geoffrey, 425
Vos, Simon, 46, 47

Wairakei Geyser Valley, 400
Washington: author's visits to (1956) 133–138, (1957) 319–26, 328–9, (1958) 490, 492–6, (1959) 642–50; NATO meeting (April 1959), 651
Waterhouse, Charles, 125, 173
Waterman, Ewen, 638
Watkinson, Harold, 189, 717
Webber, William, 712
Wednesbury by-election (1957), 345
Welensky, Sir Roy, 379
Wellington (New Zealand), 400
Western European Union (W.E.U.), 65, 66, 67, 69, 72; doubts on limited Common Market, 73; and reduction in forces in Germany, 210, 246–7, 248, 264

Wheeler, General Raymond, 168, 212, 216
Whitney, John Hay, 322, 587, 645
Wiley, Senator Alexander, 495
Williams, Lady Rhys, 71, 436
Wilson, Charles, 322
Wilson, Harold, 17, 51, 221; attacks Premium Bonds, 36–7; attacks Trinidad Oil deal, 48, 49; attacks surtax concessions, 348; supports rise in Bank Rate, 357; and Bank Rate 'leak', 415, 417–30
Windsor, 376
Woodall, Lieut.–General Sir John, 250
Woodcock, George, 716
Woodfield, Philip, 192
World Bank, 90, 99–100
Wright, Sir Michael, 503
Wyndham, John (Lord Egremont), 192–193, 384, 407, 553, 554

Yemen, 502, 505, 536
Yorkshire Post, 357
Younger, Kenneth, 237

Zhukov, Marshal G. K., 308
Zinc, Colonel, 474
Zorin, Valentin, 299, 306, 308
Zorlu, Fatin, 672, 673, 679, 680, 691 692, 693, 694, 695, 699–700
Zulueta, Philip de, 192, 250, 492, 493, 553, 591, 615, 681
Zürich conference on Cyprus (1959), 691–3, 695

1958

HOME AND COMMONWEALTH AFFAIRS	FOREIGN AFFAIRS
Jan. 6 — Resignation of Thorneycroft. Heathcoat Amory becomes Chancellor	
Jan. 7–Feb. 14 — Commonwealth Tour	
	Feb. 1 — Egypt and Syria form 'United Arab Republic'
	Feb. 14 — Iraq and Jordan form 'Arab Federation'
	Feb. 22 — Agreement published on stationing American I.R.B.M.s in Britain
	March 27 — Khrushchev becomes premier of U.S.S.R.
April 30 — Life Peerage Act receives Royal assent	
	May — Crisis in Lebanon
May 2 — State of Emergency in Aden	
May 5–June 20 — Bus strike	
	June 1 — De Gaulle becomes premier of France
	July 2 — Atomic Energy (McMahon) Act amended in U.S.A. to permit sharing of nuclear information
	July 14 — King Feisal of Iraq assassinated
	July 15 — U.S. troops land in Lebanon (withdrawal by 25 October)
	July 17 — British troops land in Jordan (withdrawal by 2 November)
July 24 — First creations made under Life Peerages Act	
	July 28–9 — Baghdad Pact meeting. U.S.A. accepts same responsibilities as members.
	Aug. 4 — Anglo–American Atomic Bilateral Agreement comes into force
Aug. 23 — Race disturbances in Nottingham	Aug. 23 — Chinese begin bombardment of Quemoy
Aug. 31 — And Notting Hill	
Sept. 15–26 — Commonwealth Economic Conference in Montreal	
	Sept. 28 — Referendum in France approves constitution for Fifth Republic